REPRINTS OF ECONOMIC CLASSICS

THE THEORY OF
SOCIAL ECONOMY

Also publshed in

REPRINTS OF ECONOMIC CLASSICS

BY GUSTAV CASSEL

THE DOWNFALL OF THE GOLD STANDARD [1936]
THE NATURE & NECESSITY OF INTEREST [1903]
ECONOMIC ESSAYS IN HONOR OF GUSTAV CASSEL [1933]

THE THEORY OF
SOCIAL ECONOMY

By GUSTAV CASSEL

Professor at the University of Stockholm

Translated by S. L. BARRON, B.Sc. (Econ.).

NEW REVISED EDITION

REPRINTS OF ECONOMIC CLASSICS

AUGUSTUS M. KELLEY · PUBLISHERS
NEW YORK · 1967

oe 5/70

Revised translation of fifth German edition first published 1932

(New York: Harcourt, Brace & Company, 1932)

Reprinted 1967 by

AUGUSTUS M. KELLEY PUBLISHERS

By arrangement with HARCOURT, BRACE & WORLD, INC.

LIBRARY OF CONGRESS CATALOGUE CARD NUMBER

67 - 19584

PRINTED IN THE UNITED STATES OF AMERICA
by SENTRY PRESS, NEW YORK, N. Y. 10019

PREFACE

THE first edition of my *Theory of Social Economy* having been sold out, a new edition has become necessary. In the meantime, I have gone through the whole work several times, made many additions, and brought it up-to-date. I have also omitted several parts, and shortened the text as far as possible in order to prevent the work from growing to unwieldy dimensions.

Under such circumstances it was thought advisable to make an entirely new translation from the manuscript of the fifth German edition, which is in preparation. This work has been taken over by Mr. S. L. Barron, B.Sc. (Econ.), of the London School of Economics, and I am much obliged to him for the great interest and care he has taken in his work.

The present edition includes all the additions and improvements which post-war development has induced me to make in my exposition of the theory of money. It contains in particular a summary of my theory of Purchasing Power Parity. I have also added a fifth book, containing a short exposition of the theory of international trade as this theory presents itself in the light of the Purchasing Power Parity theory.

The fourth book, which contains a theory of trade cycles, I have left essentially in the form I had already given it before the war. The post-war economic difficulties are governed to such an extent by political causes and by shortcomings in the administration of the world's monetary system that this period must be studied as a problem in itself. The attempts which are continually being made to bring the analysis of the economic history of this period under the old scheme of regular trade cycles are, in my view, a grave mistake, preventing us from seeing clearly the essential features of the great economic revolutions taking place in our own time. A clear understanding of these events, which go far beyond all previous experience, is only possible on the basis of a consistent and clear economic theory. It has been the aim of the author that the present work should prove to be of some use in this respect.

GUSTAV CASSEL.

DJURSHOLM,
September, 1931.

EXTRACT FROM THE PREFACE TO THE FIRST EDITION

A PROGRESSIVE science will always find it necessary, in order to make room for new investigations, to leave out such old matters and old discussions as are no longer of essential importance, and to find ways for introducing the student as directly as possible to the questions of actual interest. This need certainly exists also for the science of economics. From the first beginnings of my study of this science I have felt that it ought to be possible to do away with the whole of the old theory of value as an independent chapter of economics and build up a science from the beginning on the theory of prices, and that we would be able to rid ourselves in this manner of a lot of unnecessary discussions, mostly of rather scholastic nature, which had burdened earlier treatises on economics. I made a first attempt to draw up the outlines of such a presentation of economics in the paper *Outlines of an Elementary Theory of Prices* (published in German, 1899). Since that time, I have worked further on the programme laid down. In *The Nature and Necessity of Interest* (London : Macmillan, 1903), the treatment of interest as a price was carried through. The abolition of a separate theory of value, and the direct construction of economic theory on the basis of a theory of prices, naturally required a theory of money adapted to the new system of economics. In the general economic theory we must reckon all values in a unit of money. The value of this unit cannot be determined here. To do this is the separate function of the theory of money. The central point of this theory is that the value of money is determined by the scarcity of the means of payment valid in the given monetary system. This conception of the theory of money is first outlined in *The Nature and Necessity of Interest* (Chapter V.).

I call this work *The Theory of Social Economy*. The meaning of this is that I intend to treat the economic relations of a whole social body as far as possible irrespective of its extension, its organisation, its laws of property, etc. The ultimate aim of economic science must be to discover those necessities which are of a purely economic nature and which cannot be arbitrarily mastered by the will of men. An intimate knowledge of these necessities is the first condition for Social Reformers being ever able to produce something more than cheap speculations on the economic organisation of the future or costly disturbances of the very delicate machinery of present economic life.

GUSTAV CASSEL.

DJURSHOLM,
SWEDEN,
January, 1923.

CONTENTS

BOOK I

GENERAL SURVEY OF ECONOMICS

CHAPTER   PAGE

I. THE ECONOMIC SYSTEM IN GENERAL . . 3

§ 1. The Characteristics of an Economic System   3

§ 2. The Means for Satisfying Wants . . 11

§ 3. Production 16

§ 4. The Continuous Process of Production . 22

§ 5. The Stationary State 27

§ 6. The Uniformly Progressing State . . 32

II. THE EXCHANGE ECONOMY 42

§ 7. Exchange Economy and Money Economy . 42

§ 8. Capital and Income in the Money Economy 51

III. THE ECONOMIC PRINCIPLE IN THE EXCHANGE
ECONOMY 64

§ 9. The Scope of the Problem . . . 64

§ 10. The Restriction of Wants. The Case of
Collective Wants 66

§ 11. The Restriction of Wants. General Case 72

§ 12. The Regulation of Production. The
Principle of Scarcity 88

§ 13. Supplementary Principles of Pricing . 99

§ 14. The Organisation of the Modern Exchange
Economy 115

§ 15 The Socialist State 131

CHAPTER   PAGE

IV. The Mechanism of Pricing . . . 137

§ 16. Arithmetical Treatment of the Problem of Equilibrium 137

§ 17. The Pricing Factors 155

BOOK II

THE PRICING OF THE FACTORS OF PRODUCTION

V. Introduction 167

§ 18. The Factors of Production and the Functions of Entrepreneur . . . 167

§ 19. The Problem of Imputation and the Social Problem of Distribution . . . 177

VI. Interest 185

§ 20. The Development of the Theory of Interest 185

§ 21. Capital-Disposal as a Factor of Production 197

§ 22. Interest as a Price 207

§ 23. The Demand for Capital-Disposal . . 216

§ 24. The Supply of Capital-Disposal . . 232

§ 25. The Determination of the Rate of Interest 246

§ 26. Interest in the Socialist State . . . 256

VII. Rent and the Prices of Raw Materials . 260

§ 27. The Development of the Theory of Rent 260

§ 28. The Nature of Rent . . . ⁚ 268

§ 29. The Pricing of Land 275

§ 30. The Pricing of Natural Materials . . 289

VIII. Wages 298

§ 31. Ricardo's Theory of Price and the Socialist Theory of Value . . . 298

§ 32. Pessimistic Theories of Wages . . 304

§ 33. Optimistic Theories of Wages . . 310

§ 34. The Place of Labour in the Pricing Process 321

§ 35. The Demand for Labour . . . 330

CHAPTER   PAGE

§ 36. The Supply of Labour as Determined by the Number of Workers . . . 343

§ 37. The Supply of Labour as Determined by the Supply of Work per Worker . . 355

§ 38. Wages in the Socialist State . . . 362

BOOK III

MONEY

IX. ANALYSIS OF THE MONETARY SYSTEM ON THE BASIS OF ITS EVOLUTION . . . 371

§ 39. The Origins of Money . . 371

§ 40. The Minting of Money and its Significance 383

§ 41. The Problems of the Coinage Circulation 389

§ 42. Free Standards . . . 402

X. BANK MONEY 409

§ 43. The Concentration of Cash Balances in Banks 409

§ 44. The Limitation of Deposits . . 416

§ 45. Bank-notes 421

§ 46. The Cover of Bank Money and its Reflux 428

§ 47. The Limitation of the Supply of Money through the Rate of Interest . 435

§ 48. The Significance of the Means of Payment in regard to the Utilisation of Income . 440

XI. THE VALUE OF MONEY . . . 446

§ 49. Introduction 446

§ 50. The Quantity Theory of Money . . 449

§ 51. The Significance of Changes in the Quantity of Money 459

§ 52. The Measurement of the Price-level by Index Numbers . . . 462

§ 53. The Price-level and the Relative Stock of Gold 467

CHAPTER   PAGE

§ 54. The Price-level and the Cost of Pro-
       duction of Gold 478
§ 55. The Price-level and Bank Money . 481
§ 56. The Price-level and the Demand for
       Gold 489
§ 57. The Regulation of the Price-level by
       the Bank-rate 494
§ 58. The Stability of the Value of Money . 502

XII. INTERNATIONAL PAYMENTS . . . 512
§ 59. The Adjustment of the Balance of
       Payments – First Case: Free Indepen-
       dent Standards 512
§ 60. Second Case: Metallic Standards . 519
§ 61. The Significance of Banking Policy
       with regard to International Payments 524

BOOK IV

THE THEORY OF TRADE CYCLES

XIII. INTRODUCTION 533
§ 62. The Nature of the Problem . . 533

XIV. THE INFLUENCE OF TRADE CYCLES ON PRO-
       DUCTION 542
§ 63. The Chief Branches of Production
       during Trade Cycles . . 542

XV. THE INFLUENCE OF TRADE CYCLES ON LABOUR 558
§ 64. Changes in the Numbers of Workers in
       the two Chief Branches of Production . 558
§ 65. The Agricultural Population as a
       Source of Additional Labour to Industry 566
§ 66. Unemployment 575
§ 67. Changes in Working-time . . 580

XVI. INFLUENCE OF TRADE CYCLES ON THE DURABLE
       MATERIAL MEANS OF PRODUCTION . 583
§ 68. Changes in the Quantity and Efficiency
       of the Factors of Production . . 583

CHAPTER   PAGE

    § 69. Variations in the Use of Factors of
          Production   588

XVII. THE INFLUENCE OF TRADE CYCLES ON THE
    DETERMINATION OF PRICES AND INCOME,
    AND ON CAPITAL CREATION.   .   .   599

    § 70. The Prices of Commodities   .   .   599

    § 71. Wages   606

    § 72. Income   610

    § 73. Consumption   .   .   .   617

    § 74. Capital from Savings   .   .   619

XVIII. THE INFLUENCE OF TRADE CYCLES ON THE
    CAPITAL MARKET   .   .   .   622

    § 75. Supply and Demand   .   .   622

    § 76. The Rate of Interest   .   .   626

    § 77. The Changes in the Value of Stocks
          and Shares   .   .   .   630

    § 78. The Scarcity of Capital during the
          Trade Boom   .   .   .   635

XIX. THE DETERMINING FACTORS OF TRADE CYCLES   639

    § 79. The Principle of Action and Reaction .   639

    § 80. Further Explanation of Trade Cycles .   642

    § 81. Crises   648

BOOK V

INTERNATIONAL TRADE

XX. THEORY OF INTERNATIONAL TRADE   .   .   655

    § 82 International Trade as a Problem of
          Currency   655

    § 83. Pricing under International Trade   .   665

    § 84. The Significance of International
          Movements of Capital   .   .   673

    § 85. Practical Conclusions   .   .   680

APPENDIX   691

INDEX   703

BOOK I

GENERAL SURVEY OF ECONOMICS

CHAPTER I

THE ECONOMIC SYSTEM IN GENERAL

§ 1 *The Characteristics of an Economic System*

THE object of all economic activity is to satisfy human wants. The satisfaction of these wants is impossible without activity of some sort, but the actual satisfaction itself is not included within the concept of economic activity. The actual satisfaction of a want generally involves some kind of action on the part of the person satisfying his wants; if he wishes to appease his hunger, he has to eat; if he desires to take a walk, he must step out; if he likes to provide his own music, he must play some instrument or sing, and so on. Actions of this nature are outside the scope of economics.

Certain wants can be completely satisfied by actions of this kind, as, for example, when we drink out of a stream, or eat wild berries on a walk, or bask in the sun, or satisfy our need of air by breathing. Usually, however, the satisfaction of wants involves some preparatory activity to supply the necessary means, or, where this is not the case, the labour of third persons to enable the satisfaction of one's own wants. The erection of water-works or preservation of fruit for the winter are instances of preparatory activity to supply the means for the satisfaction of wants, while to satisfy one's desire for music by going to a concert is an example of the immediate satisfaction of wants through the exertions of others. The economic system is nothing more or less than the sum of actions making the satisfaction of wants possible. It excludes the actual processes of satisfaction.

The greater part of all economic activity is of a preparatory nature; it aims at creating the means for satisfying future wants, thus implying the pursuit of some distant aim. Thus purposive action, having a certain amount of regard for the future, is the very

3

essence of economic activity. Crusoe-economics, the economics of isolated man, is conceivable, but is bound to be a poor system, and is very exceptional in actual life. As a rule, an economic system presupposes the co-operation of several individuals for the mutual satisfaction of their wants. Such co-operation naturally implies some degree of conscious organisation. As soon as an economic system includes more than one person, it implies, therefore, organised economic activity. These two factors – namely, activity directed to the satisfaction of future wants and organisation – become more prominent as economic development proceeds, and the higher the stage reached, the greater their importance. Civilisation, as judged from the economic point of view, can be regarded as the progressive development of these two factors and their ever-increasing significance for the economic system as a whole.

Agriculture has undoubtedly been fundamentally important in stimulating this increasing regard for the future. The fact that he who would reap must sow has become symbolic of economic activity as such. But agriculture also presupposes continuous care of the soil, and consequently forces the cultivator to look even further ahead. The house has had a similar significance; the desire to occupy a substantial dwelling could only be satisfied within an economic system in which people had become accustomed to consider the wants of a far distant future. Future aims must determine economic activity to an even greater extent in an economic system using the durable and very costly machinery of modern industry and transport. Circumstances such as these, then, have necessitated an ever-increasing regard for the future. The desire to take account of aims directed to an increasingly distant future has slowly been cultivated by the strict discipline of modern science, and has been stimulated most of all by the development of private property. The laws of inheritance included, within the realm of economic motives, aims beyond the lifetime of individuals. But the greatest regard for the future is possible for permanent organisations with extensive economic resources, such as the vast limited companies, so typical of modern times, and, above all, the State.

Although the sphere of human activities which are to be regarded as economic must be as comprehensive as it has been sketched in the preceding paragraphs, these actions can, nevertheless, be considered as economic only if seen from a certain point of view. They all have other aspects as well, such as technical, moral, or æsthetic. Water-works, cooking, music, all have their peculiar technique, important and interesting for those concerned; they can also be discussed from the view-point of their hygienic or æsthetic significance, and so forth.

Economic action as a whole, however, is the outcome of an underlying unity of endeavour, a unity of which every one of these activities, seen from a particular point of view, forms a minute part. This common element, which determines the specifically economic character of all economic activity, is the final condition of such activity – that is, the fact that there exists a definite limit to the satisfaction of wants as a whole. Some wants, it is true, can be satisfied to an unlimited extent; this, for example, is normally the case with the desire for breathing. But the satisfaction of such wants must be excluded from the sphere of economic activity. Only those actions which are carried out on the condition of a limited possibility of the satisfaction of wants can be regarded as economic. Since, generally, only a limited quantity of means for the satisfaction of wants is available, and since the wants of civilised humanity as a whole are insatiable, the means for satisfying wants are generally *scarce* relatively to the wants themselves. Only means of this kind are considered in economic theory. Only scarce means are economic means. Every economic system thus labours under the condition of a scarcity of means for the satisfaction of wants; in this sense, economics is governed by the *"Principle of Scarcity."* Hence the special task of economy is to equate wants with the available means for their satisfaction in the way which is most advantageous. In so far as this task is completed successfully, the economic activity may be regarded as truly economic.

The solution of this problem can be achieved in three different ways; first, by proportionately limiting wants and eliminating the less important ones; secondly, by using the available means for the defined ends in the best possible way; thirdly, by increasing, if possible, the productive power of the individual.

The way in which wants are limited depends on the varying conditions engendering such limitation. If a store of means for satisfying wants must be made to last for a certain period of time, it is the task of economic organisation so to distribute these means that the necessary uniformity in the satisfaction of wants is assured throughout the time in question. There may be a great temptation to draw largely upon the available means in order to attain a relatively high degree of satisfaction at once; but then the means available for the satisfaction of wants at a later period are so much the less. Economic control aims at limiting wants from the very beginning in such a way that the available means will last for the whole period. Such control may be called "economising of means." Thus the harvest of a self-contained agricultural community, after a certain amount has been put aside for sowing, must suffice for the whole year's consumption, and must therefore, if scarce, be divided more or less uniformly over the whole year. This need for economising may, under certain circumstances, severely test the character of those who are confronted by it. The modern workman or official receiving wages for a certain period of work is faced by a similar exigency; the wage must suffice for the whole period, his expenditure must be distributed over the period and his wants correspondingly adjusted.

If we consider any economic system as a whole, we shall find that, in all cases, means for the satisfaction of wants, which can be used for very different purposes, are available. It follows that, with the available means, different wants can be satisfied to a varying extent, and choice of wants, for satisfying which the available means shall be applied, therefore becomes a necessity. In other words, it will be the aim to achieve that use of means which can be regarded as the most economical. Economic endeavour will thus tend to a certain degree of uniformity in the satisfaction of different wants, and this necessitates a correspondingly uniform limitation of these different wants.

A less important want may not be satisfied in preference to a more important one, nor may a want, in itself very necessary, be considered to such an extent on its own merits alone that other wants will be neglected altogether. Something approaching a classification of wants according to their importance, though it be unconscious and by no means rigid, is consequently indispensable in any economic system. In this classification, different degrees of satisfaction of the same want will be considered as if they were different wants, and will be assigned different rank in the established scale of wants. In a self-contained agricultural community, it may, for instance, be the most urgent object of economy, at a certain moment, to obtain a larger supply of foodstuffs. After this has been accomplished, however, other requirements, such as the repair of the dwelling or the supply of new clothes, may appear the most important for the time being. When these wants have also been attended to, economic activity may perhaps be again directed at improving the means of food production, but here also the necessity of keeping other wants in mind will determine the degree of satisfaction which can be aimed at. This relatively uniform limitation of wants, then, is a part of the general principle of economising the available means. The necessity for a uniform restriction in the satisfaction of wants in respect to both the sequence of wants in time and multiplicity of wants may be called the "Principle of the Uniform Satisfaction of Human Wants."

The second method of approximating to the ideal of economy is that of attaining a certain end with the least possible expenditure of means. This principle, which may be called the "Principle of Minimum Means," leads to a careful choice of technical means, and is the criterion for efficient economic organisation. The whole technical equipment of modern industry and the entire organisation of modern business arose from the necessity of satisfying the need for economy in this sense. Wherever a want can be satisfied equally well in various ways, economic activity is applied to find out the way incurring the least possible expenditure of means for the achievement of that end, even if slight modifications in the actual degree of satisfaction are implied. The need for food, for instance, can be satisfied by various different kinds of food, and to select the cheapest of these is, in general, to act in accordance with the principle of minimum means, even if that implies the suppression of some less important preferences of taste. In such cases it is impossible to draw a sharp dividing-line between the principle of the uniform satisfaction of wants and the principle of minimum means.

These two principles are the essence of the general demand for "economy" in human action.

Once these two conditions are satisfied, an increased satisfaction of wants will only be possible if greater efforts or sacrifices are made, or, in other words, if the productive capacity of the individual is increased. If, and to the extent to which these increased efforts are regarded as disadvantageous, this sacrifice must be balanced with the gains to be achieved thereby, it must, figuratively speaking, be deducted from the gain; that economic scheme must be used which affords the greatest gain, taking all factors in consideration. This widens our conception of economy. For the purposes of a preliminary survey of the economic system, it is legitimate to assume that human productive capacity is fixed at a definite rate, and this is the assumption which underlies the discussions of the first part of this work. At a later stage it will be necessary to investigate the conditions under which men may be induced of their own free will to increase their productive capacity.

We have now described the requirements of the general principle of economy as far as that is possible at this preliminary stage. Their meaning and implication will be the subject of the following pages. The general principle itself, that under given conditions the highest possible degree of satisfaction of wants shall be achieved, we will call the "General Economic Principle."

In real life the principle of economy is, of course, not strictly followed. Frequently, people even act highly uneconomically. A uniform distribution of means for satisfying wants over a period of time or over different classes of wants is an ideal which is presumably never completely realised, and which is often in very marked opposition to the realities of life. The young student or artist not infrequently spends in a few days what should have sufficed for a month or more, and enforced parsimony for the remaining period is the result. Custom demands for whole classes of women so great an expenditure on clothes that they cannot afford a really good meal. Moreover, experience shows that the principle of minimum means is very imperfectly applied in daily life, and is really only carried out to approximately its full degree in a few model businesses. Similarly, scarcely anyone really economises his own resources of energy. On the one hand, we see the man who works himself to death in order to make money which affords him personally very little pleasure, and, on the other hand, the sluggard who, though badly enough off, cannot summon sufficient energy for a serious and continuous effort to improve his position in life. In such cases what is lacking is the correct balance between effort and the satisfaction of wants.

Thus what distinguishes economic action from other human activities, or rather what characterises it as a peculiar aspect of human activity, is not the fact that, in the economic sphere, people act in accordance with the economic principle, but rather that action can be judged from the point of view of this principle, and that, moreover, however people may act, the whole economic system is dominated by the principle of scarcity, or is, in other words, subjected to the necessity of adjusting wants to the means available for satisfying them. The sole purpose of action in accordance with the economic principle is to help to find the most advantageous way of attaining this equilibrium. But whether the equilibrium reached is the most advantageous or not, in some form or other it must always result.

A science which takes the actual economic life as its subject must consider this life in its entirety, must describe its realities and attempt to explain them. If we agreed to consider only "rational economic action," it would be difficult to define the border-line. Such a programme strictly carried through would at best yield an abstraction bearing little resemblance to the realities of economic life. We cannot, th refore, select as the subject of economic science only those human actions which are in accordance with the economic principle, and leave out those which are not. On the other hand, to judge whether particular actions are economically sound is part of the task of economics. Economics must judge human action from this point of view, but only from this point of view. Economics as such must strictly avoid judging human activity from the ethical or any other non-economic point of view. In particular, it is essential that wants in the different degrees of intensity in which they are found in actual life must be once and for all taken as given quantities.

As we have said, human co-operation for the satisfaction of mutual wants presupposes a certain amount of organisation. The nature of this organisation has a very great influence on a large number of economic phenomena. Certain economic processes are entirely conditioned by the particular organisation of the economic system; others are, in their essence, common to all possible forms of organisation, even if their outward form is influenced by the particular organisation in which they are found. It is important for economic science to distinguish those economic processes which will be found in any economic system from those which are more or less conditioned by the kind of organisation existing, and also to show the relative degree of independence of these latter processes. If this is not done, a tendency may easily arise to believe that economic phenomena are wholly conditioned by the accidental organisation of any particular economic system, and would be superfluous in an ideal State. That one must, with such an attitude, lose sight of the most important essentials of economic life, is obvious, and has been abundantly proved in the past. In contrast to the appalling levity so characteristic of popular and, unfortunately, even political discussions of economic problems, it is the central task of economic science to discover the *final necessities of economic life*, and to insist upon the dependence of man on these economic necessities.

In this chapter the discussion will be confined to those processes which are found in any economic system, and which are thus true of economic life in general. For this reason no assumptions are made regarding the organisation of the economic system. Our discussion will be valid for any economic system.

But, as in any gen eral ecn omic inquiry, we have to assume that the system discussed is complete, that all processes take place from beginning to end within that system, or, in other words, that it is a self-contained and completely isolated system. Only on this assumption can scientific analysis discover economic relationships in their entirety. The popular attitude to economic problems is invariably characterised by an arbitrary isolation of a small field of economic reality, and only those processes which are active within this field are observed. Such an attitude inevitably leads to a neglect of essential and, perhaps, highly relevant relationships. On the other hand, it must be a first principle of the science to aim at understanding economic relations as a whole. This is only possible if attention is confined to a self-contained economy.

§ 2 *The Means for Satisfying Wants*

The means for satisfying wants are partly *material goods* and partly *services*.

Goods are divided into *consumption goods* and *durable goods*. Consumption goods are those material goods which are destroyed in a single act of consumption, i.e. cease to exist as goods of the same kind. Durable goods are those which can be used several times in succession or continuously throughout a certain period of time, i.e. which are perhaps more or less worn out in use, but which, at any rate, continue to exist as essentially the same goods for a certain period of time. This division of material goods into consumption goods and durable goods is one of the most important classifications of economics, as will be apparent from the following discussion. It is, at the same time, one of the most clearly marked distinctions. But it must be remembered that economic classifications can never attain mathematical precision; even where the categories are selected quite naturally, and where the dividing-line has been drawn with the greatest possible logical precision, it will always be possible to discover cases which must be regarded as being on the border-line between them. But the boundary between the two categories now defined is far more precise than is usual in the realm of economics. For example, the food I eat is destroyed in the process of eating. Final consumption is the very essence of the use of food; only by being consumed can food fulfil its useful purpose. The plate from which I eat is of a very different nature in this respect. Of course, it can easily be broken by careless hands, but this destruction is not an essential element of the use of a china plate; normally, it is expected to serve for daily use during a period of years. The distinction between consumption goods and durable goods is in this case as precise as it is natural. Certain durable goods have a very short period of duration, but that does not prevent them from being clearly distinguishable from consumption goods. Gloves, for instance, are comparatively quickly worn out. But the fact that they are thus worn out by no means constitutes their specific use. They would be just as serviceable if, by some chance, they could preserve their new appearance. Coal, burnt in a stove, is, on the other hand, useful precisely because it is so burnt. It may take hours before the coal I have placed in the stove has been completely burnt; but each calory of heat which is gained implies the destruction of a precisely corresponding quantity of coal. But there are also goods which can be put to several different uses: used in one way, they may be consumption goods; in another, durable goods. Cows are perhaps the best example; as cattle for slaughter they are consumption goods, but as milch cows they are durable goods.

As is well known, consumption in the sense of annihilation is non-existent in the physical world; consumption is a purely economic conception. But we must not regard only eating and burning as consumption in the economic sense; we must include every use of a commodity which involves its destruction. Thus any raw material used in the manufacture of durable goods is consumed by that use and ceases to be available as material, at any rate during the life-time of the product in which it is incorporated. The iron used for the construction of a railway engine has been consumed as material, although in the physical sense it still exists in the shape of the engine, and, once the engine has served its time, can again be used as scrap-iron. All raw materials of this kind must obviously be classified as consumption goods. The same is, of course, true of raw materials used for the manufacture of consumption goods; for example, of the flour used in baking bread, because as flour it has thereby been consumed. If desired, it is possible to distinguish raw materials which, when used, are embodied in another commodity as a special group of consumption goods. The other consumption goods would then be regarded as consumption goods in a more specific sense. Their substance is lost by their use either wholly or in part, not, of course, in the physical sense, but for economic purposes. Our food, drink, coal, or motor-oil, are examples of such consumption goods.

From what has been said, it is clear that the distinction between consumption goods and durable goods is necessarily derived from the kind of use to which they are put, and usually, though not necessarily, also from the physical nature of the goods themselves.

Services are rendered by persons and also by durable goods. We must thus distinguish between *personal services* and the *services of durable goods*.

Labour is the most important of personal services. But, as will be seen in Book II., there are also other kinds of personal services which are of great importance in economic life, namely, saving and, from a certain point of view, the services of the entrepreneur. It is customary to distinguish between mental and physical labour. This division, however, is of little significance in economics; moreover, it is impossible to draw the dividing-line between these two categories with even approximate precision. True, the difference between the work of a scientific thinker and that of a navvy employed on the road is considerable, but every kind of "physical" activity necessitates a certain amount of mental work. The mental activity involved in certain classes of "physical" labour is sometimes of a fairly high quality, such as that involved in looking after complicated machinery, or in setting the type for scientific works, especially if written in a foreign language, etc. On the other hand, certain classes of office work entail very little mental activity.

The services of durable material goods are of very great importance among the means for satisfying wants. The use of land is the most important item in this group; other instances are the use of the house, of factory buildings, of machinery, and of all other produced durable goods which are used so extensively in modern industry and transport. The services of durable goods are, as such, means of satisfying wants. The durable goods themselves can only be regarded as means for the satisfaction of wants in so far as they render the succession of services of which they are capable during a certain period of time.

As pointed out, certain durable goods last for a short period only, and can thus render only a small number of services. Others last a very long time, if not for ever, and, in the course of time, render a very large, even an infinite, number of services. The essential difference between the durable goods on the one hand and their services on the other is obvious in cases of goods of very great durability, but it is always present even in the less durable goods. At a later stage of the discussion the fundamental importance in economic science of this distinction between the use of a commodity and the commodity itself will be easily appreciated. At this stage, it is sufficient to point out that this distinction is peculiar to durable goods, and separates them sharply from consumption goods, for a consumption good and its use are identical as far as the satisfaction of wants is concerned.

Material goods and services can be grouped under the common name of goods. Only goods which are scarce are considered by economic science as economic goods. For, as was shown in § 1, it is the fundamental assumption of the concept of economy that there is a certain limitation to the means available for the satisfaction of wants, that, in other words, the problem of economising means arises. Those goods which, though serving for the satisfaction of wants, are not scarce, are not objects to the use of which economic activity is directed, and thus must be excluded from the realm of economic science. But there are very few goods of this kind. The air we breathe is an obvious example. The water used for the production of steam on a steamer is similarly available in abundance, so that there is no need for economising it. In certain, though now relatively rare, cases the same is true of drinking-water.

Goods are, as a rule, scarce. This scarcity is, as has already been emphasised, the fundamental cause of economy. The scarcity of a commodity is conditioned by two circumstances: there must be some limit to the quantity in which the commodity is available, and the quantity of the commodity which could be used for satisfying human wants must exceed the quantity which is available. Economic scarcity is thus an entirely relative conception, relative solely to the wants of mankind.

The means for the satisfaction of human wants can also be classified as direct and indirect means. Direct means are those which serve immediately to satisfy wants. They can be material goods as well as services. If material goods, they are consumption goods, such as bread; if services, they may be personal services, such as those of a masseur, or the services of durable goods, such as clothes or houses or the transport services of the 'bus. Indirect means for the satisfaction of wants are those whose co-operation is required in order to obtain the direct means. They may be raw materials, such as cotton; consumption goods proper, such as coal; services for durable goods, such as those of agricultural soil or of machines; or the transport of goods by the railways; or, finally, they may be personal services, labour, etc. Durable goods must be classed as indirect means for the satisfaction of wants, because, not they themselves, but only their services, satisfy wants. The distinction between direct and indirect means is based primarily on the use which is made of them, and not necessarily on their physical nature. Some goods can be used for the direct as well as for the indirect satisfaction of wants; this, for example, is the case with coal and most human labour.

The nature of the scarcity of a commodity is chiefly determined by the way in which its supply is limited. Although in certain cases the supply is fixed for the time being, it may be possible to increase it by a better direction of economic activity. In such cases, the scarcity of the commodity is determined, not independently, but by the limit to which this method of increasing the supply can be carried. As we shall see in the next section, this limit is determined by the scarcity of those indirect means for the satisfaction of wants the supply of which cannot in this way be increased.

If we disregard these cases, goods are either available in definitely fixed quantities, or augmentable by increased efforts on the part of man. The conditions under which such an increase is possible determine the scarcity of this latter class of goods. But, as already mentioned, this possibility is disregarded in Book I.

§ 3 *Production*

The scarcity of some classes of goods is absolute in the sense that the available supply cannot be increased, and that, when consumed, the goods are irreplaceable. But in most cases it is possible to create new goods of the same class, and thus to increase the supply and replace those which have been consumed. Since it is obviously impossible to create a commodity that is absolutely identical with another that is still available or that has been consumed, scarcity can only be overcome if individual goods of the same type can replace one another; that is to say, when not one definite individual commodity is demanded, but *any* one of a certain class. It is quite possible to copy an old painting, but if the original is demanded the painting in question is irreplaceable. In some cases, an object, which to most people would seem easily replaceable, has a purely sentimental value for its owner, who is only interested in that particular specimen, and will never acknowledge another one as a substitute, however closely it may resemble it.

If we disregard such cases, the supply of any material commodity is solely determined by the technical conditions of creating a similar article. This possibility is either wholly absent, or exists only under certain limiting conditions, in the case of land and of raw materials found in nature. The majority of the other material goods can be "reproduced." The activity by which new goods are made for the satisfaction of human wants is called *production*.

New material goods are obviously not created out of nothing, but are produced through the transformation of natural resources. Materials which cannot be produced by men, or which, at any rate, are not usually produced, since it is easier to obtain them from nature, are called raw materials in the specific sense. The process of acquiring raw materials from nature usually implies economic activity to a greater or less degree, which must be regarded as a part of the productive process. Raw materials which can be obtained in unlimited quantities without any such activity have no economic scarcity, and thus cannot be regarded as economic goods. If those raw materials the acquisition of which involves some kind of effort are more closely scrutinised, it will be found that the natural supply of some of them is very limited indeed, and that, in consequence, man is forced to observe strict economy in their use. Although some, in fact the vast majority, will be found to be abundantly present in nature, the technical and local difficulties to be overcome in acquiring them are so great that their supply must be regarded as scarce for the purposes of economic production. Thus the coal deposits of the world, if added together, would yield a quantity which, relatively to present consumption, could be regarded as very plentiful. But the distribution of coalfields is very irregular, and some of them are so remote that at present they cannot supply our demand at economic rates, and the same is true of others in which the technical difficulties of mining are too great. However, even in those coalmines which are actually worked, coal can only be obtained at a cost, and not the whole deposit at once. Causes such as these always limit our supply of raw materials. This limitation conditions our ability to produce material goods.

In addition to raw materials for the purposes of production, we require the use of those durable goods which nature places at our disposal. These durable goods are traditionally grouped together as "land," although they include such things as water-falls and rivers used for transport purposes, etc. The most important form of land, i.e. that which is used, or can be used, for agricultural purposes, covers an area which, for the present needs of mankind, may be regarded as more than sufficient. If, in spite of this fact, such land is scarce, then this is due to the technical difficulties and the disadvantages of location which prohibit the use of all the available land by man. Since, however, such difficulties can be overcome, to a certain extent, by technical improvements, etc., the scarcity of land is not absolute. If this is true for agricultural land, how much the more so is it for urban sites, which are almost entirely the result of the productive activity of man. The scarcity of land is thus primarily due to the difficulties of using land given by nature for productive purposes. This scarcity puts a further limit to the possible production of material goods.

Furthermore, the production of material goods requires, as a rule, the use of machines, factory buildings, means of transport, etc., and also of prepared materials, semi-finished goods, etc., or, in other words, of material goods which are themselves the result of production. The scarcity of the supply of such goods at any moment of time is a further limitation upon the possible production of goods. It may be objected that, since these instruments of production have themselves been produced, theirs is not a fixed or independent scarcity. But the supply of new material means of production takes time. The supply of them available at any one moment imposes beyond doubt, therefore, a definite limit to the scale of production.

Moreover, it must be remembered that the desire to use means of production for the production of material goods which in turn will serve productive purposes, and not for the immediate satisfaction of wants, must obviously be limited. This implies a permanent limit to the production of material means of production, and therefore to possible productive capacity in general. At a later stage we shall find that this limit is based on the scarcity of the personal service known as saving.

Finally, the limited supply of human energy imposes an independent and very general limit on the possibilities of production.

Thus we see that the scarcity of the various factors of production definitely limits the possibility of producing new material goods. Production does not, therefore, dispose of the scarcity of means for the satisfaction of human wants, but merely traces it back to the scarcity of the primary factors of production.

Factors of production, especially human labour, can normally be applied to very different branches of production. This manifold applicability of factors of production is of great significance for economic life as a whole. Thanks to this fact, the scarcity of any particular class of goods is usually not determined by the absolute scarcity of the factors used for their production, but by the proportion of all factors that is set aside for this particular branch of production, which implies that scarcity is mainly relative. The relative scarcity of different classes of goods, therefore, results from the distribution of the available factors among different branches of production. This distribution in turn must be determined by the scarcity of the different factors of production on the one hand and by the importance of different wants on the other. Under such conditions, economy essentially means an economising of factors of production, and largely consists of a due distribution of these factors among different uses. Just because the factors of production can be applied to so many different uses, the different relative combinations of wants which can be satisfied are exceedingly numerous. The scarcity of factors of production, however, always remains an important restriction on the totality of wants that can be satisfied.

In our analysis of the economic activity which we have called production, we have so far, for the sake of simplicity, considered only the production of material goods, i.e. the process of transforming, and adapting to human uses, raw materials, and it is possible to conceive of production in the narrow sense of the word merely as a manipulation of materials. There is no reason, however, from the economic point of view, why the concept of production should be thus limited. Economically, there is nothing to distinguish the transport of raw materials and manufactured articles from their actual production. This is most easily realised if it is remembered that the process of manufacture itself includes many transport services; think, for example, of the work in a blast furnace, of agriculture, or of forestry. If we regard the entire preparation of material goods for the satisfaction of human wants as a single process, the numerous transport services involved in that process cannot be excluded from it. But if that is admitted, there is no reason whatever to exclude the final transport service which carries the finished article to the consumer. It is possible to distinguish those economic activities whose function, in any economic system, is to regulate the movement of goods between different parts of the system, and which, under modern conditions, are collectively called commerce, from production in the narrow technical sense; but, since it is difficult to determine the dividing-line, it is far better to regard them as part of that wider process of production supplying man with the means for satisfying his wants. Thus production, in this wider sense, can be regarded as a particular part of the economic system, namely, the part furnishing the supply of goods. The economic system is still, however, the wider conception, for, besides production, it includes, on the one hand, the limitation of consumption and, on the other, the regulation of the supply of personal services; the economic system represents the entire activity of adjusting human wants to the means available for their satisfaction. Moreover, production, in this wider sense, is not limited to the manufacture of material goods. All personal services immediately satisfying human wants, in so far as they fall within our previous definition (§ 1) of economic services, must be regarded as productive, and therefore as integral parts of the whole process of production. Thus, not merely the work of the farmer or the manufacturer or his workmen must be regarded as productive, but also that of domestic servants, school-teachers, doctors, etc. All contribute their part to the great economic process of satisfying human wants. This process is in actual life so much of an entity, its constituent parts are so closely interlocked, that an exclusion of services immediately satisfying wants would seem to falsify the picture of reality.

This definition of the conception of production is much disputed. The classical economists considered as productive labour only that which was embodied in the production of material goods. All services which were intended for the immediate satisfaction of wants, and served the consumer without the intervention of material goods, were regarded as unproductive. We must abandon this classification, because it so easily gives rise to vague notions of the superior economic importance of "productive" labour. In fact, this terminology is derived from the conception which sees the sole purpose of economic activity in the production of material goods, and thus regards services not embodied in material goods as, at best, "indirectly productive," or as productive only in the degree to which they indirectly further the production of material goods. Whether a service assists in the production of material goods or not is, according to our view, entirely irrelevant to the question whether it is to be regarded as an economic or productive service; the important question is, whether it helps directly or indirectly to satisfy a human want. If this is the case, the service must, subject to the limitation mentioned in § 1, be regarded as economic and productive.

Only in this way is it possible to find a satisfactory definition, not merely of the conception of an economic system, but also of economic science itself. The argument that this definition of an economic system would include all sorts of vocations, such as medicine, teaching, art, etc., within the sphere of economics, is fallacious. No economist considering only the production of material goods would attempt to master the vast subject of modern technology. In the same way the economist can direct his attention to the whole complex of human activities directed to the satisfaction of wants, without entering further than is necessary for his purpose into the details of what may generally be called the technology of the satisfaction of wants. Every human action directed to the satisfaction of some wants has an economic aspect, and, as such, falls within the sphere of economic science. Economists need never fear overstepping the natural limits of their science, as long as they confine their attention strictly to the economic side of human activities.

To distinguish between productive and unproductive economic services would, furthermore, lead to some very strange classifications. All personal services connected with the manufacture, transport, and distribution of material goods would, of course, in any case have to be regarded as productive. But, in that case, it would be difficult to see the reason why domestic service should be excluded, since one of its most important functions, cooking, is surely nothing but the final stage in the preparation of goods for human consumption. One has only to try to imagine how it would look to divide the work of our domestic servants into "productive" and "unproductive" services according to whether it concerned material goods or not! It would scarcely be possible to maintain the assumption that the relation between services and material goods must be a direct one. Much labour and many arrangements in a large factory, though connected only very indirectly with the actual process of production, are of the highest importance for the efficiency of the worker; for example, the cleaning of the rooms, dust collection, the provision of baths, etc. It would be difficult not to include such services among productive services. In that case, the services of the factory inspector or doctor would also have to be regarded as "productive." Where, then, is the dividing-line? The great transport services undertake, as is well known, both the transport of persons and of goods. Should the transport of persons be regarded as "unproductive," and that of goods as "productive"? How is the labour of the engine-driver or sailor to be classified? The workers employed in municipal water-works would have to be regarded as engaged in "productive" labour, since they supply the inhabitants with the material good, water. The same is true of the employees in gas-works. But what is the position in regard to the electricity supply? No material commodity is supplied, only the immaterial one of lighting; thus the supply of electricity would have to be regarded as "unproductive"! The fact that this distinction between productive and unproductive services according to their relation to material goods is so difficult to draw suggests strongly that this distinction does not correspond to any economically significant difference between these classes of services, and is therefore artificial and barren. Further, if the logical conclusions are drawn and the "unproductive" services are completely excluded from economic activities, and thus from the realm of economic science, obvious absurdities must ensue.

§ 4 The Continuous Process of Production

It has been customary for economists to approach the subject of production from the technological point of view. To trace the origin of material goods, then to follow the various stages of transformation throughout the productive process, and, finally, to follow the details of their consumption, was taken as the task of economics. This method of approach was, no doubt, largely responsible for the view which regards the services not embodied in material goods as unproductive, or outside the realm of economics, and which thus leads its adherents to unnecessary difficulties. In addition, it has frequently determined the entire arrangement of economic textbooks, by inducing their writers to consider the consecutive technical stages of production in the same sequence in economic theory, and thus to start with the acquisition of raw materials and to end with a discussion of consumption. It is responsible, above all, for the completely distorted picture of the process of production, its conditions and factors, which, even to-day, still largely predominates in economic science.

Since economists attempted to describe the processes of production by giving a historical account of the manufacture of separate goods, they were forced to investigate the technical origin of each material commodity used in production, and, on final analysis, could thus reduce every product to the primary factors of labour and raw materials freely offered by nature. This result was accepted as the basis of a theory according to which labour is the sole factor of production, and all wealth is produced by labour. At a later stage we shall have to consider this theory, which has been just as important for economic science as for political propaganda, in greater detail. At this point, it is sufficient to point out the strong support which this theory was bound to receive from the method of approach which we are discussing.

The fact that all production takes time is, naturally, highly significant in any economic system, and thus also for economic theory. It has led economists to the conception of the "period of production" which occupies so large a space in the work of writers on the theory of interest. But if we adhere to the conception of production which has been described, the significance of the time factor in production must always remain very vague and indefinite, for it is impossible to fix a point in time at which the production, in this sense, of a material good can be said to commence. At every stage of production, the co-operation of already available material goods is necessary, and if the production of these goods is to be included in the process of production of the final product, the starting point of the entire process will never be reached. These difficulties show very clearly how completely hopeless is the attempt to retrace the productive process to its technical starting point.

An economic discussion of production must start with the fundamental fact that the satisfaction of the wants of mankind, or of an isolated group of human beings, must be continuous, and that, therefore, production must also be a continuous process. This process in its entirety must be made the subject-matter of a scientific discussion of production; its full extent, at any one moment in time, must be described and the conditions for its continuance as it was at that moment must be stated. For these conditions are the necessary implications of a continued satisfaction of wants, unaltered in quantity or quality, and are thus fundamental factors in the social economy. If necessary, the conditions of a progressive development of the whole economic system must also be studied, for they must be regarded as fundamental factors in any economic system which is in process of development.

This method of approach leaves no room for a discussion of the circumstances which gave rise to the production of the material goods that are available to-day, or of agencies which co-operated in that production. These are all historical problems, and, though they may be of interest to the economic historian, they are economically of no importance at all, or, at any rate, have no direct importance for the conduct of economic affairs. Naturally, this does not exclude the possibility that the history of some old building or the origin of some painting may greatly influence the valuation of these goods by contemporaries, and may thus also influence economic action. But such monuments of the past act exclusively through the medium of the sentiments of living people, and are quite irrelevant to a discussion of the possibilities of satisfying wants through production.

We are faced here by the general principle, fundamental in every economic discussion, which is implied in our definition of an economic system – the principle that economic activity is essentially directed to the future and is logically regardless of the past. The significance of this principle will be apparent at many later stages of our discussion. Thus our general conception of the nature of an economic system in itself renders of no account the way in which a particular material commodity, now in existence, was produced. This reasoning shows how completely futile the traditional approach to problems of production, with its analysis of the technical history of the production of goods, must be in economic theory.

In actual life, production is always a continuous process, whose partial processes are continually being concluded and commenced again, and which, after a certain lapse of time, will show the same features as at present, provided its scale has not increased and methods of production have remained unchanged. In other words, the productive process as a whole does not share the characteristic movement of the material it transforms, which, in production, ascends to higher and higher stages of transformation, until it emerges from the process as a finished article. The productive process has no beginning or end in the sense in which the production of some material object has a beginning and an end; it remains unchanged as a continuous flow of production. In the full stream of that flow, there will be found, at any one moment, articles in all their different stages of production. Raw materials, semi-finished goods, and finished articles, are all present at the same time, and in quantities, moreover, which suffice to continue the flow of production, even though there may be slight variations in the quantities produced. The comparative amounts of these goods are changed in production only if the productive process as a whole is changed.

It must be admitted that in actual life there are irregularities in the continuous process of production. But for industry – for example, the iron and steel industry – the picture as sketched above is substantially correct. New iron ore and new coal are daily and hourly being mined, a steady flow of pig-iron is simultaneously being produced and transformed into steel, while, at the same time, the different products in which iron and steel are used will be found in all stages of manufacture. Under stable conditions, the flow of production in this industry can continue in so uniform a way that changes in its character, if a large industrial area is looked at as a whole, are practically negligible. This, however, is not true of agriculture. In that industry, production is so much dependent on seasonal change that, in most cases, it commences once every year. The amount of goods in process of production thus changes its composition in the course of the year. But if a period of years is taken as the basis of the survey, it is possible to disregard the changing phases of the productive process, and therefore the changes in the comparative quantities of goods in process of production, and to regard production as a continuous process which may be invariable but which may also show some variations in the quantities involved and the methods applied. The different phases of agricultural production disappear to an even greater extent if the entire world production of, say, wheat is considered. Wheat is, at present, grown in such different climates in both the northern and southern hemispheres that the irregular distribution of harvest throughout the year is almost, if not entirely, counteracted. This levelling influence is increased in the further stages of the preparation of wheat for human consumption. The European demand for wheat is almost uniformly satisfied throughout the year through a practically continuous stream of wheat shipped from countries oversea. The supply of wheaten bread to consumers is entirely continuous. Naturally, the varying phases of the agricultural productive process which are produced by seasonal changes must be taken into account, and their effects examined by economic science as soon as it proceeds to a more detailed analysis. But if, in order to obtain an understanding of the essential forces of economic life, one wants to base one's study on an economic system which has been sufficiently simplified by an abstraction and which nevertheless reflects the essential features of economic processes, then there can be little doubt that the continuous flow of production which has been sketched is the right abstraction to make. None the less, the actual general productive process is still highly complicated. For the purposes of economic theory, it is legitimate to concentrate attention, for the beginning, on two simplified hypothetical cases which are particularly important if we are to understand essential facts and processes. These are, first, the hypothesis of a stationary flow of production, and, secondly, the hypothesis of a uniformly expanding flow of production. The study of the first hypothesis will show the conditions of economic equilibrium in so far as they are determined by production, and will enable us to define in the clearest possible way some phenomena which are of fundamental importance in any economic system. The study of the second hypothesis will throw some light upon the possibilities of quantitative economic progress under the simplest conditions, and will thus enable us to distinguish in a clear way some phenomena specifically connected with economic progress.

§ 5 *The Stationary State*

Let us begin, then, with the extremely simplifying assumption that the flow of production remains entirely unchanged through time. Let us also assume that the number of people in our system and their individual wants – in other words, the sum of all wants in that society – remain constant. We have, then, the stationary state of economic life. The satisfaction of wants in that state proceeds entirely unaltered both in formal composition and quantity; all economic phenomena are therefore constant. It is obvious that this state affords the best opportunities of studying the most general and fundamental economic phenomena.

In the stationary process of production there will be, at a given moment, a definite number of durable material goods co-operating in production and of raw materials and consumption goods at different stages of manufacture; this number is constant, and the proportions of its constituent elements never vary. The presence of this quantity of goods is the necessary condition for the continuously uniform flow of production. It is thus, in the stationary state, a necessary task always to maintain this fixed flow of goods. It follows that production in the stationary state is a process which, first, always maintains the total quantity of goods being worked upon, and, secondly, supplies the wants of man with a continuous flow of goods and services.

We must now discover how these problems of production are solved. Regarding the first of these problems, our separation of durable and consumption goods is highly significant. The first question to be investigated is, then, how it is possible to maintain at a constant rate the number of durable goods in the productive process.

According to our definition (§ 1), the productive process ends where the actual satisfaction of wants begins. Thus it is necessary to determine which durable goods are to be regarded as a part of the productive process. This category comprises primarily all tools, machines, and buildings used in production; also ships and other means of transport, lighting, and telephone plant, etc.; also durable goods co-operating in production irrespective of whether they serve for the manufacture of material goods or whether they supply services for the immediate satisfaction of wants; but not personal property such as clothes, etc. (see § 7).

This definition of "durable goods in the productive process" is sufficiently precise for our purposes. If we exclude land, the rest represent the produced durable goods in the productive process. These goods may be called *fixed real capital.*

The problem now to be discussed may thus be formulated as follows: how is the quantity of the fixed real capital in the productive process of the stationary state maintained at a constant rate? The majority of durable goods which are fixed real capital are subject to more or less rapid depreciation. The rate of depreciation can be slowed down somewhat if the goods are properly cared for, but in most cases it is impossible to prevent their becoming completely worn out and rendered useless for the economic purposes they were made to fulfil. When that stage is reached, they are excluded from the supply of available durable goods; if they are old houses, they are demolished; if useless machines, scrapped. But if the supply of such goods is to remain constant, it is obviously necessary that new goods of the same kind shall be produced continuously, and, in the stationary state, at the same rate at which the old ones are scrapped. Let us, for example, assume that in a self-contained economic system all houses are of the same type, that each of them lasts for a hundred years, and that the supply of houses is constantly being maintained at the same level by the construction of new ones. We can thus select in this stationary economic system, at any given moment, a group of a hundred houses of which the oldest is a hundred years and therefore ready for demolition, the most recent was built during the preceding year, and in which each intermediate year is represented by one house. This group of houses is kept constant by the production of one house and the demolition of another during each year. All remaining houses increase their age by one year in the course of each year, and, owing to the fact of regular rebuilding, the proportionate scale of depreciation of the whole group will be exactly the same at the end of the year as at its beginning. If we consider the stationary economic system as a whole, it is obviously conceivable that the total supply of durable goods is maintained in practically the same composition by this process of maintenance and reconstruction, or, in other words, by the continuous process of production. This process of maintaining at the same level the supply of fixed real capital in a stationary economic system may be called the *process of reproduction of fixed real capital.* It is obvious that, in a stationary state, a constant quantity of labour and other factors of production must be applied in this process of reproduction.

Turning to consumption goods, it is necessary, in the first place, to settle which of these can be regarded as being in process of production. First, there are all raw materials entering the productive process as they are acquired from nature; these materials undergo a series of transformations, until they finally leave the productive process as integral parts of durable goods or consumption goods proper. The latter leave the productive process when they are consumed, that is, when they are either used for the purposes of production, such as lubricating oil or coal, or, like bread, for the immediate satisfaction of wants. If production continues and is constantly repeated in the same way, the total supply of material goods in the stationary state will also remain constant. A definite quantity of iron, for example, is used daily for different purposes, but a constant quantity of iron ore is mined daily to replace it, and material in intermediate stages of production is regularly carried to the next stage, so that the total quantity of materials in this branch of production, and its relative composition, are kept at a constant level. Consumption goods finished daily are supplied to final consumers or are used in production, but, at the same time, the whole quantity of raw materials and semi-finished articles is taken one step forward in the process of production and new raw materials are introduced, with the result that the quantity of goods in process of production is maintained at a constant level, and that, from day to day, the same quantities of consumption goods are supplied to producers and consumers.

The final result, then, is that the total quantity of raw materials, semi-finished articles, and goods at all stages of production, as well as the total quantity of consumption goods required in production, remains constant in the stationary state. This quantity of goods may be called the *circulating real capital* of the economic system. The process by which it is maintained at a constant level is the *process of reproduction of circulating real capital*. This process also requires a constant quantity of factors of production in the stationary state, and this quantity serves, at the same time, to supply the consumer with finished products, a function which is evidently closely related to the process of reproducing the circulating real capital. Those services which are rendered immediately to consumers require an additional and similarly constant quantity of factors of production.

The sum of the fixed and circulating real capital, or, in other words, the total quantity of material goods in the productive process with the exception of land, is the *real capital* of the economic system, and the process of maintaining this real capital at the same level is the *reproductive or turnover process of real capital*.

The total quantity of material goods in an economic system is its *real wealth*. This real wealth thus includes land and all durable goods in the hands of consumers in addition to the real capital.

Production in the stationary state, then, maintains itself by keeping constant the material factors required for its continuance, and, at the same time, supplies a steady and unvarying flow of services and material goods for the satisfaction of human wants. This flow of services and material goods which the human beings in an economic system receive from production for the satisfaction of their wants is called the *real income* of that economic system.

The real income thus consists partly of direct services rendered by others for the immediate satisfaction of wants, such as the services of doctors or domestic servants, partly of the services of durable goods which are still part of the productive process, such as the services of dwelling-houses, the transport of persons, etc., partly of consumption goods for final consumers, such as foodstuffs, and partly of durable goods which, when produced, are handed to consumers and are then no longer part of the productive process, such as our clothes.

It is of considerable importance for economists to state in a clear manner the meaning of all their ideas in respect to time. Much confusion and innumerable irrelevant discussions can be traced back to neglect of this essential. First and foremost, it is necessary to state whether a particular economic concept refers to a point or a period in time. The former is the case with the concepts of real capital and real wealth. If one wishes to find out the total quantity of material goods in an economic system, it is necessary to select a certain moment in time for the inventory. Such a calculation will record a certain amount of material goods present in the economic system, but no services. For a material commodity is present at such a given moment; a service, on the other hand, is rendered during a certain period of time. At any moment, there are physically present only human beings and goods, not the services they render. This is the reason why services are not counted as a part of real wealth, though they form a part of real income. Those services satisfying immediate wants of consumers do not create anything that could ever be taken into account in an inventory. It will scarcely be an error to connect this fact with the theory, criticised at an earlier stage, which regards such services as unproductive.

The concept of real income, on the other hand, refers to a

certain period of time. The number of services and of those material goods which are supplied to consumers can only be stated relatively to some period of time. Thus one can refer income to the period of one year and speak of one year's income.

Real income per annum, for example, can only be maintained in the stationary state if the flow of production continues unaltered. But the unaltered continuation of the flow of production and the maintenance of its real capital by no means follows from mechanical necessity, since production must be consciously directed to the achievement of this end. From this point of view, the whole stationary state is the result of the human will. Thus the conditions for a continued flow of a definite and constant real income can be summarised as follows :

(1) The presence of a certain amount of land and of natural raw materials.

(2) The presence of a certain amount of real capital.

(3) A certain annual amount of labour services.

(4) The direction of the productive process in such a way that both the fixed and circulating real capital are maintained at a constant level.

The available factors of production, in the stationary state, are applied in fixed proportions to the following task:

(*a*) the maintenance of the fixed real capital;

(*b*) the maintenance of the circulating real capital and the resulting supply of consumers with material goods;

(*c*) direct services to consumers.

§ 6 *The Uniformly Progressing State*

The stationary state is a first hypothesis, the study of which is important for the clear recognition of processes which are fundamental in any economic system. But there are some other phenomena of general economic importance which are not conspicuous in the stationary state, since they are essentially connected with economic progress and can, therefore, only be observed in a progressing economic system. It will still be necessary to assume the simplest possible conditions in the discussion of the progressive state which is our next task.

To begin with, we must state what we mean by "progress." This conception, like any other economic term, contains no qualitative element, but is purely quantitative. The problem whether quantitative growth of an economic system can be regarded as real progress from a deeper ethical or æsthetic point of view is interesting in itself and of great practical importance, but it is outside the sphere of pure economic theory and can thus be disregarded in this treatise. It is advisable to accept this principle which limits our task from the start. Progress in this connection, then, means no more than the purely quantitative conception of increasing production.

A general cause of progress in this sense is the growth of population. If the same number of wants of each individual must continue to be satisfied in a society with a growing population, it is obviously necessary that production must be increased to a corresponding extent. It is conceivable that production should be continued in the same way, with the same methods, and that progress thus merely consists of an expansion of production proportionate to the growth of population. If the population remains constant, economic progress must manifest itself through an increase in production per head of population; in other words, in a satisfaction of more individual wants. Up to a certain limit, such an increase can be achieved through a quantitative increase of labour per head of the population, but, quite obviously, the limit up to which such measures are possible will soon be reached. Steady progress in a society with a constant population is, therefore, only possible if there is a continuous improvement in the methods of production. But in such a state the whole productive process and, in most cases also, the relative wants which are satisfied are themselves constantly changing. Progress in such cases is a very complicated phenomenon, and the simplifying assumption of uniform progress is faced with

certain difficulties, at any rate at the present stage of our inquiry. [1]
If we wish to study the simplest possible form of economic progress,
we must select the case in which progress continues in the same way
and with a constant amount of individual labour, and is thus merely
increased in the same proportion as the population grows. If, in
addition, we assume a uniform growth of population, we have the
simplest case of a uniformly progressing economic system. If the
annual percentage increase of the population is given, then we
know the rate at which the economic system as a whole is progressing, and we can speak of the definite rate of progress which is
characteristic of that particular economic system.

In order that production may expand at the annual rate of
progress thus obtained, it is necessary that the real capital of the
system shall grow in the same ratio. Since the relative composition
of this real capital remains constant, this increase will simply mean
that every component part of the real capital is increased at the
same rate. Only by so growing can the real capital keep pace with
the continuous increase of labour units and with the expanding
wants of the growing population. Such an increase in real capital
can only be achieved if production is directed towards that end.
Thus, in the uniformly progressive state, production has three
main tasks to fulfil:

(1) The continuous supply of goods and services to consumers,
      and the resulting necessity of maintaining the circulating
      real capital at the same level.

(2) The maintenance of the fixed real capital.

(3) The steady increase of the total real capital.

Since the annual net increase of the real capital, as a constant
percentage of the real capital in existence as any moment, necessarily itself grows in the same proportion as the real capital, each
of these three tasks requires a uniformly increased production,
and fixed proportions of productive resources are directed towards
these aims. As it is impossible to reduce the different factors of

---

[1] The possibilities of dealing with this difficulty by applying a suitable index of production are discussed in the *Federal Reserve Bulletin*, March, 1927, Washington.

production to a numerically comparable standard, this result can only be expressed by saying that the quantity of factors of production applied to each of the three main tasks of production grows according to the common rate of progress.

In our progressive economic system, therefore, there will be, at any moment of time, more factors of production than would be required to satisfy all wants at that moment. One can thus assume that the factors used at any moment could make possible a more ample satisfaction of wants at that particular moment, or, if that satisfaction is kept at the old level, could bring about shorter hours of work, that is, a decreased demand for personal labour services. The application of a certain proportion of the available factors of production to a steady increase of the real capital thus involves *sacrifice*, namely, a voluntary restriction of wants that could be satisfied, or a larger amount of labour than would be necessary for the present satisfaction of wants. This restriction in the satisfaction of wants to enable the production of real capital to increase its present supply is called *saving*. The increase of real capital made possible through saving may be called the *material creation of capital*.

The necessity of saving and of producing capital is, like all other facts and processes described in this chapter, entirely independent of the way in which an economic system is organised; it is present in any progressive economic system. In a closed peasant economy, progress is only possible if labour and other factors of production, such as horses, are diverted from the immediate satisfaction of wants and are used to increase real capital by building new houses or clearing new land, for instance. The condition of progress is thus restriction of the possible satisfaction of wants, or effort beyond the needs of the present satisfaction of wants; in other words, the condition of progress is saving and the utilisation of the productive resources thus liberated in the production of real capital, that is, the material creation of capital. These processes are precisely the same as the corresponding processes in the modern economic system of one country or of the world.

It may be argued that even the stationary state requires a certain amount of sacrifice, in order to apply a sufficient quantity of factors of production to the constant maintenance of the real capital. If this were unnecessary, it would no doubt be possible to acquire productive resources to make the satisfaction of more wants for the present moment possible. This, for instance, is the way in which the peasant who is too busily engaged in the production of the current necessities of life to find the time to repair his house, acts. This was also the way in which the belligerents acted in the Great War; it was only by neglecting to maintain the fixed real capital (buildings, railways, rolling stock, ships, etc.), and to replace the consumed circulating real capital, that productive resources could be liberated for war purposes. But, in the long run, a society following such principles must suffer, since it must reduce the wants it is able to satisfy. Such a use of factors of production used ordinarily to maintain the real capital, and thus just preventing the impoverishment of society, scarcely corresponds to the customary connotation of the term saving, though it is undoubtedly a service of the same quality as saving which leads to a net increase of capital. Such economising may require a great deal of self-control and regard for the future. But, for our definition of saving, and for the purposes of economic theory, it is necessary to keep to the boundary just indicated; saving proper commences when the real capital is increased.

Saving, as here interpreted, consists in a particular method of applying factors of production. This conception of saving is necessarily connected with the idea of the continuous economy which is at the base of all our discussions. But many writers hold a different view. Saving, according to them, is a certain degree of abstinence from the consumption of the available supply of finished goods. These goods are usually thought of as consumption goods, and saving thus would mean the disposal of a certain quantity of consumption goods, in such a way that some of them are consumed, others "saved," or reserved for future consumption. Saving of this type is, of course, necessary in all those cases in which a store of existing consumption goods must be made to last for a certain period of time; the consumption of these goods must be distributed fairly evenly throughout the period. This is particularly true of the harvest. Those writers who, as we have seen at the beginning of § 4, discuss production by following the technical process of the manufacture of a commodity from beginning to end, naturally direct their attention to the store of goods accumulated by the productive process and to its gradual consumption, and thus come to be primarily interested in the disposal of existing stores of finished goods. But if we regard production in our way as a permanent process, essentially stable as regards both form and content, this discussion of existing stores of finished goods loses its primary significance. For the results of production in the continuous process of economic life do not issue forth as a store of goods created at one moment which will then gradually be consumed in the course of time, but as a continuous flow of finished goods which are immediately taken into consumption. The significance of small stores of finished goods that may be found at various points of the system is, in the continuous state, entirely negligible as compared with the steady stream of finished goods the continuance of which is ensured by the continuous process of production. This is particularly true under conditions of modern productive and transport facilities. But under such conditions, any form of direction of consumption must essentially mean the disposal of available factors of production. From this point of view, there is no concrete saving such as the idea of saving as a deferred consumption of an accumulated store of finished goods presupposes. Those finished goods which, in a state of continuous economic equilibrium, are not consumed because the extent to which wants may be satisfied has voluntarily been limited, are never actually produced. There is, therefore, no concrete object which is saved in the sense that its consumption is deferred.

The view which regards saving as deferred consumption of a store of finished goods must offer a supplementary explanation for the formation of concrete capital, for it is obviously impossible to increase the existing stock of real capital by deferring consumption. The formation of concrete capital is regarded by writers taking this view as the previous accumulation of a store of material goods which later will be used in production for the maintenance of those co-operating, in particular of the labourers, and used too, perhaps, as raw materials and tools. [1] But this view is entirely out of harmony with the essential features of the continuous process of economic life. In the continuous state of economic equilibrium there is, in general, no accumulation of a store of finished goods, nor, further-more, of materials and tools for future use, in the sense of the theory criticised, nor are there, as a rule, stores of goods which at any moment are inactive because they have been stored in prepara-tion for future purposes of production. A continuous economic system, as we have seen above, possesses real capital which, under normal conditions, is always in use. In the progressive state this capital is steadily increased by production, but the goods which are thus gradually added to the real capital are normally not stored for future productive purposes, but are consumed or transformed, or, if durable, used. The view which regards the concrete formation of capital as the storing of goods reserved for future purposes therefore distorts the picture of the fundamental processes of the continuous state of economic equilibrium.

In the uniformly progressive state, the direction of production in general, and also the distribution of factors of production among the three main tasks of production, always remains constant. Thus the same relative quantity of productive factors (and an absolute quantity which steadily grows in the ratio of progress) is always set aside for increasing the real capital. Saving is therefore a continuous activity growing proportionately to the progress of the economic system as a whole, and is thus always of the same significance for the system. It was difficult to understand this relationship accord-ing to the older view of saving. Once a stock of goods had been accumulated, it necessarily had to be used up at some later date. The conception of saving as continuously expanding at a constant rate, without a limit in time, was quite impossible according to that

---

[1] "A stock of goods of different kinds must be stored up somewhere sufficient to maintain him [the labourer], and to supply him with the materials and tools of his work" (Adam Smith, *Wealth of Nations*, Book II., Introduction). Jevons regards the goods required for the maintenance of the labourers as the sole form of capital: "Capital consists merely in the aggregate of those commodities which are required for sustaining labourers of any kind or class engaged in work" (*Theory of Political Economy*, p. 242).

view. And thus one meets the statement over and over again, both in scientific and in popular discussion, that continuous saving (*read* "storing of goods") by humanity as a whole is an impossibility. It is undeniable that such views have had the greatest influence on the discussion of the phenomenon of saving and on economic theory as a whole. It is therefore of the greatest importance to discover the real nature of saving and to recognise its function in a progressive economic system. Saving which is not merely continuous, but which, moreover, keeps pace with the increase in production, is not only possible, but is, in fact, an indispensable condition of uniform progress in any economic system. Only through such saving is the steady formation of new real capital at the same rate as the general economic progress made possible, and, with it, the uniform increase of the total available real capital and the proportionate expansion of production and the satisfaction of wants.

It is necessary to widen the conception of real income for the purposes of the progressive state. *Real income* must, in this context, be defined, in harmony with the common use of phrase, as the *total real income serving for purposes of consumption plus the increase of real capital during the income period selected.* The first quantity of this sum must, in a progressive economic system, be regarded as the total mass of services and material goods placed by production at the disposal of society for the satisfaction of wants. The second quantity is the sum which correlates the formation of concrete capital in the system. In the uniformly progressive state, real income grows, as do also its constituent elements, consumption and the formation of capital, at the general rate of progress characteristic of the economic system as a whole.

It follows that if income is to grow in this way, the formation of capital must also grow in the same way; in other words, that the available factors of production must be allotted to the various tasks of production in such a way that this rate of growth in the formation of capital is made possible. This distribution of productive resources is the continuous activity which, together with labour, is necessary for the maintenance of uniform economic progress. In addition, the existence of a certain amount of real capital at the initial point

– and any given moment can be regarded as the initial point – is a necessary condition of the progressive state.

Saving always means, as we have seen, some sacrifice for the cause of progress. In that particular type of progressive state which has been selected for discussion, and in which progress merely consists of an expansion of economic processes in proportion to the growth of population, the sacrifice of saving is undergone purely for the benefit of the increasing population. This observation is of interest, because it shows that the costs of an increase in population are somewhat greater than the mere bearing and rearing of an increasing number of children. If individual wants are to be satisfied to an unaltered extent, real capital must be increased in the same ratio as the population, and a certain proportion of the available factors of production must always be reserved for this task. First and foremost, new houses must be built for the new population, but under modern conditions the economic system must also be equipped with additional transport facilities, factories, machines, etc., in proportion to the growth in population. The productive resources used for this increase of real capital cannot be used for the satisfaction of daily wants, so that, at any moment, less wants will be satisfied than could have been without the increase in population.

The concepts introduced in this chapter have not been arbitrarily selected, but are definitely necessary. We have regarded the economic system as a continued social activity, without any limiting assumptions regarding, for instance, the technical or legal organisation of that system. Our results have therefore general significance for any economic system. In examining this general economic system some phenomena necessarily become apparent which represent definite logical conceptions, and which we must name. The names of these phenomena have been selected as being in the closest possible conformity with the ordinary meaning of the words. It is in this way that our definitions of real capital, real income, etc., have been arrived at. These conceptions are indispensable for a real understanding of the most elementary and, at the same time, most general economic phenomena. Similarly, in drawing the limits of our conceptions, we have avoided, as far as possible, arbitrary departures from the usual; the economic nature of the subject has always been the final criterion. Our definitions, therefore, have the intrinsic necessity that is required to make them the natural basis for all further economic analysis. In our later studies of more complicated economic relationships, it will be necessary constantly to introduce new conceptions. The validity of these will be more restricted according to the degree in which further concrete assumptions are introduced; nor can they be limited in all cases with the same degree of objective necessity. But as we proceed in our definitions, the firm ground we have gained through our fixing of the most elementary economic conceptions will become abundantly clear.

CHAPTER II

THE EXCHANGE ECONOMY

§ 7 *Exchange Economy and Money Economy*

As already remarked, it is always assumed in our inquiries that the economy is complete – that is, that all economic processes take place inside it, or, in other words, that it is self-contained and closed to the outside world. This is true in the main of the old type of family economy or "self-supporting community," which in general survived on country estates, even in Europe, until the nineteenth century. In proportion, however, as these various households associated with each other to exchange surplus products, and so gained a wider and more complete satisfaction of wants, and still more as the individual members of these households devoted themselves to particular occupations and placed their services and products at the disposal of the family economies in order to have themselves command over the products of the latter, the self-contained aspect of the household disappeared. The earlier type of rural household became increasingly specialised in agricultural production, was transformed into an economy which could no longer satisfy its wants entirely by its own production, and so became part of a larger economic unit. This larger unit consists, where the development is complete, of a definite circle of individual economies linked to each other by their economic relations, and satisfying their needs only by co-operation and mutual exchange. Such a community is termed an exchange economy, and it is self-contained and complete when it has no relations with economies outside itself. If we wish to make the processes of an exchange economy the subject of a theoretical study, we must clearly concern ourselves with a complete economy of this type, and to it applies all that was said in the previous chapter about the complete or self-contained economy as a whole.

The mutual dependence of the various separate economies may be more or less marked. Historical development has only gradually brought them into a general system. The different branches of production which belonged to the old households were gradually removed from them and transformed into specialised and professional production. Parallel with this development occurred a shrinkage of the individual household, in the sense that those labour-forces which were rendered superfluous by professional industry were removed from the economy and drafted into organised production. The result of this development up to now has been a separate and distinct economy existing only in the family circle in its modern, narrower sense, its mission confined to the final preparation of things for the satisfaction of wants, but, on the other hand, obtaining the means for satisfying those wants only by taking part in organised production. From this point of view the modern family may be called a "consumption economy." The older type of household has generally become a farming undertaking, increasingly specialised and increasingly occupied with the problem of using its surplus agricultural products to obtain in exchange a more complete satisfaction of its wants. In this agriculture production always remains closely related to consumption, though at least in the larger undertakings the division between the two is clearly recognisable.

In an exchange economy conducted on these lines, production is organised mainly in independent undertakings separated from the private consumption economies. Labour is for the greater part concentrated in these trades. But production is still carried on directly for consumption by domestic servants and by the members of the free professions (doctors, lawyers, etc.). Between the different trades, each of which is engaged in only a part of the whole production, there is a co-operation of such a kind that the production is carried right through to the ultimate satisfaction of wants. From production so organised there flows a steady stream of goods and services to the consumers. The latter obtain these goods in exchange for their participation in the productive process or for services which they render by virtue of their possessions. Production organised in this way is called "social," because it only becomes self-contained and complete through the organised co-operation of a society. No individual economy can be completely self-sufficient in such an organisation. Every man is either mainly or completely dependent upon the general production for the satisfaction of his wants; but he receives the fruits of this production only in return for a definite contribution to the productive process.

The development has therefore tended to make the individual household more and more dependent upon the general economy, and has consequently made the latter increasingly important. But with this development, which has fundamentally altered the problems and aims of the individual economies, the economic interest of such units has, in the main, been left untouched. The economic activity of such a unit consists, as is the case with every economy, partly in so regulating consumption as to obtain the maximum possible satisfaction of wants with the available resources, and partly in efforts to increase these resources. In this respect the separate households pursue their own ends, and therefore form independent units in the larger general organisation.

By the continuous and organised exchange of goods and services, a certain, if more or less limited, satisfaction of the wants of all the members of the community is made possible. The whole community may from this point of view be called a social economy, or, if we want to stress the underlying importance of exchange, an *exchange economy*. The organisation of modern nations is essentially of such a type, based on the principle of exchange. If we wish to designate such an economy a unit, we call it a "national economy."

This organised exchange economy necessarily presupposes a more or less widespread system of private property. We must at least include in private property one's own work and what one obtains for it. It is of the very essence of exchange that it shall be a free act. As the exchange is primarily one of work for goods for consumption, it is essential that in the exchange economy there should be a free choice of one's occupation, or of the extent and nature of one's work, and of the particular kind of consumption one prefers. The closer study of the significance and consequences of these two kinds of freedom and of the circumstances in which they are practicable forms the nucleus of the theory of the exchange economy.

Freedom to choose one's own kind of consumption is, from this point of view, the fundamental assumption of the following chapters of this Book. The meaning of the freedom to choose one's occupation is discussed in Book II., especially in the last chapter, and will be more closely considered there.

In the exchange economy it is found that production is almost entirely effected by the mechanism of exchange. The residue of the productive activity which the individual performs for himself is relatively so unimportant that it may be ignored here, and productive activity considered only in so far as it falls within the processes of the exchange economy. This means that we regard production as completed at the point at which the products pass into the sphere of consumption. From this there follows a corresponding limitation of the concept of real capital, and in what follows the term real capital will be applied only to those produced material goods which are included in the productive process defined in this way.

In regard to those durable goods which yield direct utilities for the satisfaction of wants, it may at times be doubtful whether they ought to be included among the goods in the productive process. To answer this question we must find out whether the durable commodity yields its utilities with the co-operation of other factors or not. Our clothes, for example, are durable, but they satisfy our wants directly, without the co-operation of other factors of production. But, although trams satisfy personal wants, they need, in so doing, the co-operation of the power station, the tramway employees, and so on. We therefore regard trams as goods belonging to the productive process, but not clothes. In the case of houses the decision is not so easy. It is evident that large tenements, in which the individual only rents a flat, must be regarded as belonging to the productive process. The landlord provides certain services; he places the use of a dwelling for a certain time at the disposal of the person who rents it. Only the use of the house comes within the category of direct satisfaction. Between the construction of the house and its use there is a not inconsiderable period of activity, the nature of which will be discussed later (§ 21); but we may notice here that it includes supervision and maintenance, perhaps also stair-lighting and heating. If the owner of a private house undertakes these things himself, they are in any case best conceived as productive activities outside the consumption economy. We must therefore decide to include houses in general among the durable goods in the productive process.

As soon as exchange takes place, there arises the need to decide how much of each of the goods shall be given in the exchange; that is, there must be a valuation of both of the commodities. This valuation will, clearly, be much simplified if it is customary to calculate the value of all goods in terms of one particular good. It is found, as a matter of fact, that this custom arises contemporaneously with that of exchange itself. As soon as exchange has become so general that we may speak of an exchange economy, the custom of valuing all commodities in terms of one general commodity becomes predominant.

An article that has the function of common measure for the valuation of other goods is called *money*. The primary and fundamental function of money is to serve as the basis of a scale of reckoning by which the values of exchangeable commodities can be determined. Once this use of money is established, all economic goods are valued in terms of this scale, and thus in money. The exchange may still be direct, but the valuation of the groups of commodities to be exchanged for each other is effected by the use of money as a medium. But a developed exchange economy requires, as a practical necessity, an indirect exchange with the use of a generally recognised medium of exchange. The functions of a medium of exchange and of a scale of reckoning are evidently necessarily different, and they may be discharged by different commodities. But both are commonly described as the functions of money.

In the following theoretical inquiries into the exchange economy in general, we shall regard money merely in its use as a common scale of reckoning in all economic valuations. This does not mean that the eventual actual use of a material commodity as a medium of exchange has no special economic significance. Such a significance there is, but the study of it belongs to the special theory of money, and must be deferred to Book III. There we shall examine more closely the development of money, as well as its functions and nature.

As soon as money is used as the basis for calculation, the acts of exchange are replaced by those of buying and selling. The seller hands over the commodity, and the buyer undertakes to pay a certain sum of money for it. By what means he discharges this obligation will be shown in the theory of money. The sum of money paid for an article is called its *price*. The more developed the exchange economy is, the more frequent do buying and selling become, and the larger is the group of economic goods included in this trade. As, consequently, prices are fixed for most economic goods, those who are concerned will know approximately what price must be paid for a particular article at a particular time, and thus, as the exchange economy develops, there is established gradually the general custom of valuing goods in money. This custom simplifies and facilitates the exchange of goods. The valuation of goods in money is therefore an aspect of the exchange economy, which becomes more marked as that economy develops. If we wish to emphasise this aspect, we call the exchange economy a *money economy*.

The course of economic development is often represented as if an exchange economy, with direct exchange but without money, preceded the money economy, which is then represented as if it were essentially different, and on an independent, higher plane of development. This view, as we shall see in Book III., receives no support from historical fact. On the contrary, a more careful inquiry shows that the development of money has always been parallel to that of the exchange economy; that the exchange of goods and the use of money have mutually aided each other at every stage; and that the development of a co-ordinated monetary system of the modern type is approximately coincident with the effective establishment of the general exchange economy. Furthermore, there has never been an exchange economy of any degree of development – one with an organised exchange of products between independent economic units – without money. The term "money economy' must not, therefore, be taken to mean something different from the exchange economy, but as something essentially the same, though with special emphasis on the importance of money in it.

In economic science, the presentation of a pure exchange economy as an earlier and simpler form of economic organisation has been fatal. It can scarcely be doubted that this notion is responsible for the fact that economic theory has felt bound to deal with an imaginary exchange economy without money, and to make the study of this the basis of the whole theoretical structure. This method of approach has involved the science in immeasurable difficulties, and has led to numerous useless discussions. As it was considered necessary to study the factors regulating the exchange of goods in the absence of money, prices, or valuations of goods in terms of money on the part of the members of the community, could not be made the subject of inquiry, and thus the possibility of precise arithmetical expression of the valuations of goods was excluded. The very indefinite and varying idea of "value" was used instead. Value was supposed to show the relative economic importance of the goods, but just because it lacked arithmetical precision the idea of value was bound to remain obscure, and could not have the precision of an arithmetically expressed idea of magnitude. It is true that there have been attempts to remedy this recently by trying to measure the economic significance of goods by the intensity of human desire for them. On such fictions was it desired to construct the whole of economic theory, and this " subjective theory of value" was held to be a great advance in economic science. But the complete absence of arithmetical basis in this theory, though it was so often expressed in arithmetical forms and mathematical formulæ, prevented it from having that internal solidity which is necessary in a scientific theory, and showed at the same time where the essential fault of the theory lay. It was the rejection of the standard of valuation actually used in economic life, the exclusion of money from the whole study of the economics of exchange. Human valuations are by their very nature relative, and man has always found it necessary in practice to reduce them to a common denominator – that is, expressed them in money. In practical economic life the intensity of desire, as we shall see later, enters into consideration only in so far as it affects money valuations. This fact ought to define the limits of the science of economics; it can consider subjective economic factors only as they are manifested in pricing.

Consequently, it follows that a special theory of value is, to say the least, quite unnecessary in economics. Every attempt to frame such a theory without using a common measure to express estimates of value must encounter great difficulties. But as soon as such a common measure is introduced, money in its essence is postulated. Values are then replaced by prices, valuation by pricing, and we have a theory of prices instead of a theory of value. From this we must conclude that the whole of the so-called theory of value ought to be discarded in economics. The theoretical exposition of the exchange economy must, from the start, take money into consideration, and thus be essentially a theory of pricing.

This will show itself to be a great simplification. We shall be able to avoid completely a great number of contentious questions on which much useless trouble is now expended. We shall be in the position to free the science from discussions which only too often degrade it into scholasticism of the worst kind. Such a radical purging is absolutely necessary if we wish to concentrate as far as possible on the real and undoubtedly very important problems of economic theory.

We lose nothing by such a procedure that we might have gained by a study of the framework of the so-called theory of value. Indeed, the study of the psychological foundations of "valuation" can derive nothing but benefit from the fact that, from the beginning, there is placed at its command a definite measure for estimates of value, and that man in his actual life is observed to express all his economic valuations directly in money.

The attempt to present the foundations of economic theory

without introducing the concept of money was influenced by the pedagogical belief that so difficult a subject as the nature of money should be postponed, if possible, and not treated at once in connection with the general principles of economics. This idea will be taken into account now Money shall, as we said, be introduced only as a scale of reckoning. That economic theory has sought to avoid this method is due partly to the fact that the relativity and variability of every money scale were noticed and it was attempted to place the theoretical expositions of economic life in a form free from this variability But this attempt was fruitless. The most that could be done was to base economic valuations on an ideal imaginary scale. But this leaves unanswered the question of how the money scale is stabilised in actual life, and postpones it to a later stage. That is precisely what we intend to do here. We simply postulate a scale of reckoning on which all valuations are made. But, in order to have a concrete idea of the money economy at this stage, we may assume money calculations to be merely bookkeeping, and payments in money as so many book entries. For the moment we will ignore the existence of a material commodity used as money. The question of how the scale of reckoning is itself decided upon – how prices are fixed in concrete figures – must be left open until we consider it in the special theory of money.

Such a procedure is not really an artificial expedient, but comes within the nature of economic science In actual economic life all the various phenomena are so welded together that it is impossible to isolate any one of them. Economic science must be guided by these circumstances. It must, of course, examine the various aspects of the economy in successive chapters, but it must not maintain that each separate inquiry is complete in itself. A division of economic science in this sense is impossible. On the contrary, from the very nature of the case each inquiry leaves many things unexplained, and the explanation of them must be sought in another chapter. One cannot have a perfect comprehension of any special economic phenomenon until one knows the science as a whole. Thence follows an important hint for the study of any scientific exposition of economic life; the student must always read such a work twice.

Not until he has gained from the first reading a survey of the whole field will he be able to understand completely the several parts.

On the other hand, it is plainly the duty of economic science to construct its various chapters so that they appear part of a whole. It must be particularly remarked that a general economic theory is impossible without an organically related theory of money, and, conversely, that a theory of money which is not an organic part of a general economic theory can have little value.

Thus, in turning to the study of the exchange economy, we will from the start regard it as a money economy. So the first thing we must do is to describe the facts and processes which we found in the first chapter to be characteristic of the economy in general in the form in which they appear in the money economy. This will be the task of the next section. Only after that will we proceed to the study of the particular phenomena of a money economy.

§ 8 *Capital and Income in the Money Economy*

As soon as the custom of valuing economic goods in terms of money is established, the goods we have called real capital are regarded mainly from the point of view of the sum of money for which they can be bought or sold. They are thus conceived as the temporary representative of this sum of money, while the abstract sum of money itself seems, to the business world, the essential thing. Popular use of words calls this sum of money simply " capital." In this abstract sense capital is thus a sum of money which, for the time being, is embodied in a certain concrete real capital, but which may, by selling this and buying something else, assume at any time any other concrete form we choose.

This conception of capital, however, is enlarged for obvious reasons and in two different ways. First, it is clear that a piece of land may be bought for a sum of money as well as a piece of concrete capital. So, from the point of view of the money economy from which capital is envisaged here, there is no difference whether the "capital" is represented by real capital or by land, and in each case the "capital" is substantially the same. Secondly, the sum of money need not be used to purchase a material object; it may be lent and put at the disposal of other persons on certain conditions, as, for instance, a loan to or shares in a company. The "capital" is still substantially unchanged; the owner still possesses the same capital, though it is now embodied temporarily in a claim, a share, or something similar. One consequence of this extension of the idea of capital is that these obligations which are correlative with the claims must be regarded as negative capital and taken into account when estimating the total capital of an individual economy. The total capital of such an economy may therefore be negative – that is, when the liabilities, reckoned in money, are greater than the positive capital. Further, it follows that if the total capital of a self-contained exchange economy be calculated, all these claims and liabilities must be set against each other and omitted from the total So the total capital is only represented by the real capital and land, or, in other words, by the material commodities in the productive process.

Again, capital may be used to purchase business rights, patent rights, etc., without causing any essential change in it. These rights differ from those already mentioned in so far as they represent a positive result of human enterprise, not arising, as claims and similar rights do, because other people have undertaken corresponding liabilities. Hence, in calculating the total capital of a self-contained exchange economy, they do not disappear, but form part of this capital. In order not to complicate the following discussion too much, we will ignore these rights. We may then again state that the total capital of a self-contained economy is represented entirely by its real capital and land.

The ownership of goods and rights in a money economy yields a certain regular return to the owner. This is really the one point of view from which capital is regarded in that economy. From this point of view it is customary to call the capital "remunerative capital." The word "wealth" has generally a rather wider meaning in the phraseology current in a money economy. It, like "capital," means a sum of money, but it includes the monetary value of such material goods as furniture and works of art which are already in the hands of the consumer, and thus, from our point of view, may be called real wealth, but not real capital. So in this sense capital may be defined as profit-bearing wealth.

Capital in this monetary sense – in the sense of a sum of money which is for the time embodied in some material commodity or right – will be called, in accordance with general usage, simply "capital" in the following pages. As a contrast to real capital, capital in this sense might be termed "formal" or "abstract." To continue with such a terminology might, however, prove rather difficult, and it also diverges unnecessarily from common phraseology. There is no doubt that ordinary speech, adapted as it is to the money economy, does use the word capital in the sense of an abstract value expressed in money, no matter what objects it refers to. For instance, the word is used in this sense when it is said: "This railway requires a capital of £500,000," or "He has invested his entire capital in foreign Government securities," or "This unfortunate business has swallowed up a capital of £5,000." The word capital has the same meaning in book-keeping, as, for instance, in the balance-sheet of a limited company, where the company's capital is entered among its liabilities and covered by its assets, but is also regarded as a quantity independent of the quantity, and perhaps variable items, of the assets. Both the concepts of capital and real capital are best illustrated from the debit and credit sides of such a balance-sheet. In agreement with ordinary usage, we may thus use the simple word capital in the sense described here without any risk of mis-understanding, on condition, of course, that the scientifically defined, and, for the science, indispensable idea of real capital is always connoted by the term.

Real capital is an absolute category in every economic order, and has been so in older as well as in modern kinds of economies. But capital in the sense given here may be correctly asserted to be a special feature of the money economy. Thus, when it is stated in historical accounts of economic development that at the end of the Middle Ages capital established itself as a new factor in economic life, accumulated in the great trading towns, and gave the subsequent economic and political development its special character, this only means that the money economy at that time had reached a higher development in some places than in others; that in these places there was a regular market, with a fairly active exchange of goods, which were the important constituents of the real capital; that, therefore, these goods flowed in a steady stream through these places, and were bought and sold for money there; and that, in consequence, the merchants of these places were able to dispose relatively quickly of their real capital (goods) in the form of money for any purpose they chose, and so gained an economic and political power which had an important influence on subsequent development. The "rise of capital" should thus not be taken to mean the creation of a new class of material goods. It means, really, a great intensification of economic activity, whereby goods of the type already in existence for a considerable time were introduced in larger quantities into the money economy; though the simultaneous great development of production must obviously not be overlooked.

For a business-man who in such circumstances is always able to dispose of his capital in the form of money, and meanwhile can embody it in any form he chooses, it is but natural that the amount of value, expressed in money, should form the permanent, the essential, conception of capital, while the changing, concrete forms of the capital should, on the other hand, only be thought of as accidental and secondary. In this sense the capital retains its identity even if the material goods which represent it are sold and exchanged for others. Hence the use of such common expressions as that capital is "realised," or "converted" into money. The easier and more frequently does this process of conversion occur, the more "mobile" or "fluid" does the capital seem to be. So the term "circulating" is applied to capital that frequently undergoes this conversion, and "fixed" if it is so invested that such a realisation is avoided for a long time. But this distinction is very relative and does not coincide with the distinction we drew between fixed and circulating real capital. It is very probable, however, that circulating real capital has a special position in the exchange economy in so far as in the normal course of production it passes from one enterprise to another until it is used up in production, or converted into fixed capital, or finally passes into the sphere of consumption as a finished product. With the organisation of production in an exchange economy it is natural that there should be a frequent exchange of circulating real capital. But this is not the case with fixed real capital. In the normal course of events it remains in the enterprise where it is used, and often it cannot, or, at least, not without great difficulty and loss, be transferred to another branch of production. Fixed real capital is, therefore, from the point of view of the money economy, something more or less definitely intransferable. But trade in the money economy has to a great extent overcome this intransferability, in that shares and mortgages which represent the capital are regularly dealt in on the Stock Exchange, and can thus always easily be sold. Therein lies, so to speak, an artificial mobilisation of capital, which introduces an element of mobility into capital invested in real capital, land, or even long period or perpetual loans. This shows very clearly the relativity of the distinction in a money economy between circulating and fixed capital.

The conception of a sum of money as the money value of a certain quantity of goods is characteristic of the money economy, and has very important consequences for our treatment of the theory of social economy. Only by valuing goods in money is it possible quantitatively to form an idea of a mass of different goods and to treat it as an arithmetically measurable sum. In a money economy, this possibility is an imperative practical necessity, which, as we have just seen, forms the basis of the money conception of capital. The possibility also plays a correspondingly important rôle for theoretical investigations. Economic science is striving in vain as long as it is trying by other constructions to make a quantitative conception of a mass of goods possible. Our whole conception of several theoretical questions is getting a far more clear definition as soon as we express the quantities of goods in sums of money. In practical economic life as well as in theory it is necessary that a sum of money can be conceived as a quantity remaining unaltered during a certain period. Every loan is made on the tacit assumption that the sum to be refunded is identical with that once lent. As we shall see in Chapter VI., this reservation is indispensable for the theory of interest. In fact, the sum of money has a definite meaning only when prices are given. The continual existence in time of a sum of money as a quantity identical with itself presupposes, strictly speaking, that all prices remain constant. The owner of the money has then, later on, identically the same freedom of choice in using it as earlier. For the elementary treatment of questions of economic theory the assumption of constant prices is generally necessary. If we want to adapt our considerations closer to a constantly changing reality we may in certain cases substitute the assumption of a constant average level of prices for that of fixed prices, and in this way give a certain real meaning to the conception of a sum of money as a quantity identical with itself. As we shall find in Book III., this method is of great importance for the whole theory of money. Here we must be content with the statement that the conception of a sum of money as a quantity continuing to exist in time must be entirely indefinite and inconceivable as long as no assumption is made with regard to the invariability of prices.

Originally, we defined real income as the mass of consumable goods that, within a certain period, flows from the productive process to the consumers. When an increase of capital has to be taken into account, the conception of real income has in so far to be widened as the real capital produced in the period has to be included in the real income. In all circumstances the real income is a quantity of goods flowing into an economy during a certain period. This quantity of goods will now be conceived as the sum of money that represents the total value of the goods calculated on the basis of existing prices. This sum of money may be regarded as the money income of the economy. According to what we have said above, this money income can have a definite meaning only when prices remain constant.

In the way now explained it is possible to define the total money income of a closed exchange economy as well as of a private person. In the latter case it is necessary to widen the conception of money income in accordance with the widening of the conception of capital accomplished above. An increase in capital may, for the private individual, take the form of claims instead of a possession of real goods. A growth of such claims must be regarded as an income, and thus the total income of the private individual may be larger than the quantity of goods actually flowing into his possession. On the other hand, the money value of the consumption of a private individual may also exceed his money income – that is, if he consumes a part of his capital by exchanging it for consumption goods.

These considerations lead up to the following definition of money income: money income is the total value expressed in money of the goods consumed in an economy during a certain period, with the addition of the increase of capital or with the deduction of the decrease of capital during the same period. As the increase or decrease of capital must be equal to the difference between the capital at the beginning and at the end of the period, this definition can also be formulated as follows: the income in a certain period is equal to the value of the consumption, with the addition of the newly created capital and with the deduction of the initial capital. This definition is wide enough to include the case where the decrease of capital exceeds the value of the consumption and where the income is therefore negative. Our definition also includes cases when the capital is negative; for instance, in the case where a part of the income is used to pay off debts. The individual incomes defined in this way may be aggregated into a total income of the exchange economy defined in the same way.

So far, the conception of money income is built on the conception of real income, and represents the money value of a certain quantity of goods. In the money economy, however, the income is most generally looked at from another point of view, namely, from that of its acquisition. The co-operation of the individual in the productive process is paid for in money, and with this money he buys a certain quantity of goods. Neither this quantity of goods nor its money value, but the acquired sum of money, is regarded as income. The economic efforts to acquire means for the satisfaction of wants take the form, in the most part, of efforts to acquire money, and the money which the individual receives for his co-operation in the process of production is regarded as his true income. The goods and services which comprise the real income are considered as particular forms of the use of the sum of money acquired, while this sum is looked upon as the essential comprehension of the income. Even industrial products, not yet sold, are valued in money, and in this form regarded as income. The same is the case with food produced and consumed on the farm.

In the money economy the co-operation of the individual is paid for in money, maybe directly by the buyers of the products, or more generally by an entrepreneur acting as a middleman. Such payment represents cost of production expressed in money. From the point of view of its origin, money income is therefore *the payment, reckoned in terms of money, which the individual receives for his participation in the process of production.* If the entrepreneur himself succeeds in making a profit, this may be regarded as remuneration for his co-operation in the productive process and is therefore included in our definition of money income.

This definition at once clears up the old controversy as to how far income should be regarded as "original" or "derived." The money that anybody receives as a gift is, in accordance with our definition, not income, since it is not a payment for co-operation in the productive process. Again, the wages of domestic servants and the fee of the doctor are to be regarded as original income as they are payments for a productive activity (§ 3).

An immediate consequence of our definition is that the total money income of the community corresponds exactly in any period to the total price of the results of the production in the same period. For this total price must obviously be equal to the sum of all remunerations paid for co-operation in the productive process. If the price of the products of an undertaking exceeds the price paid for the co-operating factors of production, the difference represents a money income for the undertaking. In the case where the price of the products is lower than the cost of production the income of the undertaking is negative, and represents a loss which correspondingly diminishes the total income of the community. Thus we arrive at the conclusion that for any period the total money income of the community is exactly sufficient to buy the total outcome of the process of production. In this sense the conceptions of money income and real income are synonymous, and do not represent different quantities. The money income can never be too small in the sense that it would be insufficient to purchase the total product. The very widespread idea that a productive process may be driven so far that it will exceed the total buying power of the community, and that it is therefore necessary to put a brake to the speed of progress in order to leave the buying power time to grow, is false, and must be rejected as belonging to the sphere of economic superstition.

The money income arises at the moment of production. True, the co-operation of the individual may sometimes be paid for somewhat later; but the co-operation itself creates a right to a payment in money which already represents an income. In such cases the money income has from its very origin the character of a claim. For instance, the income of labour arises in the moment when the work is done. A correct book-keeping system must continually credit the labourer for the work he does. We may assume that the factory acquires a certain amount of products as an asset corresponding to the claims of the labourers. The income of the labourers is then for the moment lent to the factory and invested in its floating capital. Thus, already from its origin, the income has a definite use. In the cases where the work is paid before it is done the workers receive money in advance as a loan, but the true income arises even in such cases at the moment when the work is done. What is said here about labour income holds good for any income which represents a remuneration for productive co-operation of any type. The income of an entrepreneur that is represented by the money value of his products obviously arises at the moment of production. In this way any money income is already invested from its origin in real capital. In the present Book, where money is postulated only as a unit of account, we exclude the possibility that the income is received in money or other means of payment, and until further notice is kept in such form – that is to say, invested in cash. This case can only be discussed in our theory of money (§ 49).

As the money income is invested from the time of its origin, a later conscious choice of the definite investment only means the exchange of one investment for another; for instance, the exchange of a money claim for the possession of real capital. The income therefore continues to be invested until it is consumed. The consumption consists in buying goods to be consumed, and thus means that a claim is exchanged for definite consumption goods. From the time of its origin to the time of its consumption there is, therefore, no moment when the income is not used.

A part of the income may not be consumed during the income period but may remain invested at the end of the period. The income of the individual is therefore divided into two parts, the first of which serves for buying goods for consumption, the second for buying fixed or floating real capital or land or claims or other rights representing capital, or, in a word, for accumulation of capital. We speak of the first part as "consumed," and of the second part as " saved."

Very vague ideas prevail with regard to the meaning of this process. It is often said that there is a certain danger in connection with saving, if saving becomes general, and people refuse to a great extent to consume their income, this must make it impossible for the producers to find buyers for their products, thus a stagnation in the movements of goods must ensue; this would at any rate be the result if such a general saving were to continue for any length of time. In reply to such ideas we need only point out here that in the *total economy*, if we take an income period with unchanged prices, both the saved and the consumed income are used entirely for the purchase of what is produced. The difference is simply that the saved income purchases goods which represent real capital, while the consumed income purchases goods for consumption. The only effect of this difference is to cause an adjustment of the total production in a definite ratio between both classes of goods. So saving as such cannot restrict the demand for production. It would be just as incorrect to state that in a saving community production is directed, in too great a degree, to the creation of capital goods. For, clearly, production must be in accordance with the wishes of purchasers. Even the idea that general saving could not be continued indefinitely is incorrect. Saving, in the sense in which we understand it here – a withdrawal of money income from consumption – is, from the concrete point of view, a restriction of the satisfaction of wants to facilitate the formation of capital in the material sense. But we have proved in the preceding chapter (§ 6) that the continuous formation of capital is not only possible, but is an indispensable condition of the progressive economy. If, during the income period, there were a rise in prices, the results would still be the same. For this rise in prices would, on the one hand, cause a rise in the total value of real capital and land, and, on the other hand, an addition to the total income corresponding to this increase in value.

The meaning of the continuous formation of capital is most clearly shown in the uniformly progressive economy. This may now be defined in more general terms than in the previous chapter. In the money economy, economic progress, assuming constant prices, may be measured by the increase in the abstract total capital and regarded as an unaltered percentage. Let this capital be called C and suppose that it increases annually by p per cent., p being constant. This increase in capital is, as is known, only possible on condition that a certain amount of saving s is done. Let the annual income be called I, and suppose that annually the proportion $1/s$ – in absolute amount I/s – is saved. Call this quotient, which represents the community's thrift, the "degree of saving." Clearly $\dfrac{I}{s} = \dfrac{p}{100} C$. So the annual formation of capital grows by the same percentage as the total capital. A continuously increasing capital formation of this kind is thus a necessary condition of a uniform progress. Further, $I = \dfrac{sp}{100} C$.

The degree of saving $1/s$, the relative "thriftiness" of the people, may be assumed to be constant. As saving is the chief element in progress, this assumption is evidently necessary for a uniformly progressive economy. The total income I thus stands in an invariable ratio to the total capital C. The practical necessity of our assumption is made clear if we bear in mind that in the opposite case an abnormally slow increase of income would have to be balanced by an abnormally high degree of saving, in order that a normal increase of capital might take place. But such an assumption is hardly compatible with experience.

We therefore come to the conclusion that, in the uniformly progressive exchange economy, *the total income as well as both its parts – consumption and capital accumulation – increases in the same percentage as the capital.*

This principle is approximately correct in normal circumstances for every economy. Only during transition periods will there be a material difference between the rate of increase of capital and of income. This conclusion is important in that it furnishes ground for a critical examination of data concerning the rate of increase of income and capital. We also find it is possible to estimate the income of a uniformly progressive economy by multiplying the capital by the product of the percentage of increase and reciprocal value of the degree of saving. This should be borne in mind in statistical calculations and estimates. In every social and political consideration of the problem of progress it is, of course, of fundamental importance to know that consumption cannot generally increase more rapidly than capital. If this were recognised, many wrong judgments and unnecessary controversies could be avoided, and, in particular, the basis of the widespread enmity to the accumulation of capital would collapse.

If we assume, for example, that the rate of progress is equal to 3 per cent., and that therefore the capital C increases annually by $0.03C$, and if we further assume that one-fifth of the annual income is saved, then, according to what we have said, the income equals 15 per cent. of the capital. These figures must be approximately correct for Sweden, where the national capital and income in 1908 were estimated at 14,000,000,000 and 2,100,000,000 kronor respectively. An official commission for national defence, in fact, estimated the annual percentage of increase of the nation's capital during the period 1885–1908 at 3.18 per cent. [1]

Such a figure, of course, can never be accurate, but the figure given must be a fairly correct estimate. It doubtless also shows the increase of the total income approximately correctly. Contradictory and generally higher estimates of this increase must be based on statistical errors.

For the countries of Western Europe we may assume that in pre-war days an increase of about 3 per cent. was normal. Although the figure is clearly only approximately true, it is good to have some ground for comparison, and we need to be reminded that in general the increase of capital and of income, and thus also the annual capital accumulation, must be indicated by the same figure. The figures given in the *Denkschrift Zur Reichsfinanzreform* (Berlin, 1908) show that such a percentage increase was probably true under German conditions at the time. [2]

[1] These estimates are based mainly on tax and insurance valuations of real capital. If we wish to consider alterations in the value of money, it may on that account be correct to take the average price-level for a five-year period before and up to the year when the estimate was made. According to Dr. Amark's price index, the average index number for the period 1881–5 was 100, and that for 1904–8 was 102. The alteration is unimportant.

[2] During the period 1850–1907, the world's production of pig-iron rose annually by about 4.2 per cent. (Sundbärg, *Aperçus Statistiques*, xi.). If we take, on the basis of the figures of pig-iron production of the world (Table 5, Appendix), the average increase of the output of pig-iron during the period 1866–70 and the period 1906–10, we find during this whole period of forty years an increase of 4.33 per cent. The development of the iron output may, as we shall see in Book IV., be regarded as typical of the whole industrial development. If we assume that the production of foodstuffs rose by 1.2 per cent. annually, which, taking into account the increase in population and the raising of the standard of living, is not improbable, and if we further suppose that foodstuffs represent one-third of the national income, and that the remaining part of this income grew at the same rate as pig-iron production, 4.2 per cent., we get an average percentage of progress of 3.2. If we take both percentages to have the same importance, we obtain an average percentage of progress of 2.7. This figure can serve as the lower limit for our valuation of the average progress. As we must obviously assign greater importance to industrial production, we would be fairly safe in stating that in the Western World during the fifty years before the Great War, an average progress of approximately 3 per cent. was normal. Of course, a difference of one or two units per thousand is not excluded.

CHAPTER III

THE ECONOMIC PRINCIPLE IN THE EXCHANGE ECONOMY

§9 *The Scope of the Problem*

AN essential characteristic of the exchange economy is the existence of a number of individual households within the total economy which, in virtue of their productive work or of their possessions during a given period, have control of certain sums of money, to use as they please in purchasing goods, produced in the society as a whole, for the immediate satisfaction of their wants. However, as these goods are to be had only in limited quantities, it is clear that individual wants must be similarly limited; and, naturally, in accordance with the general economic principle, the more important wants will have to be given preference over the less important. But as the available factors of production, particularly labour, can be applied within very wide limits, to various branches of production, and as, therefore, the provision of commodities depends on the direction given to social production, the general economic principle further requires that the factors of production shall be used to the best possible advantage. This can only mean that they shall be used in those branches of production in which they satisfy the more important wants. Thus the application of the economic principle in the exchange economy always depends on the question as to which are the "more important" wants. There must obviously be, in the whole exchange economy, a uniform restriction of wants to ensure that a less urgent want shall not be satisfied before a more urgent one. Hence the central problem of the exchange economy is the classification of wants.

In the self-contained individual household, this problem is simply solved by the will of the head of the household. By assigning different degrees of importance to different wants he is in a position to draw a certain limiting line as regards the satisfaction of wants and at the same time to give a certain direction to production. In the exchange economy there is no such single will; it is, on the contrary, a feature of the exchange economy that each household shall, as far as its means permit, choose its own way of satisfying its wants. At the same time, the wants of all the individual economies must be classified according to their relative importance, at least in so far as a line must be drawn between those wants that are to be met and other wants. The whole of production must be directed in this way. How this is actually done, and what sort of organisation in the exchange economy is required for this purpose, are questions that we have to answer in the present chapter.

The first task of economic science is to describe the economic facts as they are found in real life and to explain them and their inner connections. Actual economic life, however, presents such a mass of detail that a view of it can only be obtained by taking what is typical or normal and omitting details and variations of minor importance. It is therefore appropriate here to show how, in essentials, and yet in broad outline, the economic principle is realised in the exchange economy. Economic science has, however, yet another task to perform – that of examining the institutions of actual economic life with regard to the degree of the necessity for them. We shall first consider an exchange economy, in respect of which we assume only that it fulfils the requirements of the economic principle – the uniform restriction of wants and the economic direction of production. It is naturally always advantageous to study the exchange economy first of all on these general lines. It brings out the essential features of actual economic processes and puts them in the clearest possible light. We must, above all, avoid making any special assumptions in advance as to the organisation of the economy, such as would not have even an approximate general validity for actual economic life and are not essential for the realisation of the economic principle.

The problem in hand can profitably be treated in two different stages. That is to say, we can first devote our attention to the question of how a uniform restriction of wants is secured in the exchange economy and to the nature of this uniformity. We must then inquire how the available factors of production are distributed ar ᴐng the various branches of production, and how a social production corresponding with the demand is ensured. These two questions do not, of course, form two distinct problems; they are merely different aspects of one and the same problem – namely, the most economical use of the factors of production with reference to the given wants. If we confine ourselves at first to the question of how wants are regulated, it means that we are studying the regulation of wants first on the simplifying assumption of a given, invariable production – that is to say, on the assumption that the quantities of finished goods available in any given period for the satisfaction of wants are fixed in advance. When, subsequently, we drop this assumption, we shall have before us the whole problem of the realisation of the economic principle in the exchange economy.

It is by this method and in this order that we shall now approach the problem.

§ 10 *The Restriction of Wants. The Case of Collective Wants*

With the money which individual households are prepared to spend on the satisfaction of their wants, they make certain demands on the supply of goods in the society. As these goods are always limited in quantity, the demands on them must be restricted in some way, i.e. certain wants cannot be satisfied. This restriction is effected by fixing prices. In view of the limitation of the amount of money which may be spent on goods, the necessity of paying certain prices for various commodities means a restriction of the demands made for different commodities by the individual households. *The fixing of prices thus has the social economic task of so restricting the demands for goods that they can be met with the available means.*

One finds, however, on a closer examination of this task, that commodities behave very differently as regards the possibility of restricting the demand for them by fixing prices. Frequently, the demands upon the supply of commodities can be diminished by the exclusion of certain individual demands. This is the case, for instance, with all consumption goods which are used for the immediate satisfaction of wants, and especially, as can easily be seen, with all goods which are demanded exclusively by the individual consumer. If, for example, an individual reduces his consumption of potatoes, then the demand which the community as a whole makes upon its supply of potatoes is reduced correspondingly. But there are large classes of commodities to which this does not apply.

Chief among these are durable goods which can be used simultaneously by several persons. If, for example, certain persons are forbidden to use a bridge, the demands upon the community's supply of goods are not in the least reduced; at least, not if we suppose that the wear of the bridge resulting from their use of it is so slight as to be negligible. If the demand for a bridge is to be met, the bridge must be built. Once it is built, it can within certain limits be used to any extent within a given period of time. A diminution in the extent to which it is used is of no consequence to the remaining supply of goods, for it releases no goods or productive powers for other uses. A real restriction of demands upon the stock of goods can, in this case, only take place when the question arises whether, and how, a new bridge is to be built. The price which must be paid for a new bridge, and the price of the annual use of it, which depends upon the former price, but is also influenced by other factors, impose a definite limit upon the demand. The money must be raised in some way or other from among those interested. This may be done by levying a toll, or else by contributions, which will in general have to be compulsory upon the interested parties. The former method has the practical disadvantage that it may easily keep the use of the bridge below what is possible, thus restricting the satisfaction of wants without effecting a corresponding restriction of the demands upon the stock of goods, and, furthermore, that it often leads to an excessive cost of collecting the toll. For these reasons, it has been the growing practice in recent times to abandon the ancient tolls on bridges and roads in favour of a system whereby costs are covered by levying compulsory contributions in one form or another.

What we have shown in this particular instance is generally applicable to those durable goods which can be used any number of times, within certain limits, of course, and is also true in some measure of certain personal services (orchestral music in the open air, for instance) which, once they are rendered, can just as well be enjoyed by a great number of people.

In the cases we have considered so far, the exaction of a payment as a condition of the use of a particular good is possible, although not, perhaps, convenient. There is, however, a very considerable class of cases where this is not possible, consisting of services which benefit all the individuals of a particular class without any action on their part.

In dealing with the satisfaction of wants, we must distinguish between an *active* and a *passive* satisfaction. In the former case the satisfaction of wants involves some activity on the part of the person concerned. This is the case, for instance, when a man eats, goes to the theatre, or crosses over a bridge. In such cases the payment of a certain price as a condition of the use of the particular economic good can be fixed, for it is possible to exclude those individuals who will not pay the price from the use of that good. But in the latter case the satisfaction of wants involves no active exertion, nor even an expression of will. The satisfaction of these wants is purely passive. To take a simple and clear example, this is the case when a country takes measures to protect itself against a threatened epidemic of cholera. Once an effective protection has been provided, all the inhabitants of the country benefit by it, whether they want to or not, even if they know nothing at all about the matter. In such circumstances, it is not possible to make the payment of a certain price a condition of using the particular service, for the individual cannot be excluded from the benefit of it.

These wants which are satisfied while the individual remains purely passive must obviously be attended to collectively, being in their very nature social. We shall call them pure or absolute *collective wants*, and the goods which serve directly to satisfy them *collective goods*. To meet these wants, it is generally necessary to exact compulsory contributions from those interested. The restriction of collective wants is effected by the price which has to be paid by the community for satisfying these wants. The authority who acts for the community in this matter must carefully consider how much importance shall be attached to the collective want, and must compare this with the importance of the individual wants of the various households.

In the cases mentioned above, where it is possible to make each individual pay a price for having his wants satisfied but where the demands upon the stock of goods are not regulated by this means, and where, therefore, the community undertakes to pay the total price, we may speak in a relative sense of collective wants and collective goods. The antithesis of these collective wants is provided by the individual wants, the satisfaction of which presumes a definite individual claim to goods, and which are restricted by fixing prices which the individual must pay for those goods.

In modern civilised society, collective wants constitute a very large group. The need which we instanced previously for protection against infectious diseases may serve as typical of a whole series of collective wants. We may mention, among other things, a nation's need for personal and legal security at home, for protection against foreign enemies, etc. To satisfy these wide collective needs, a great authoritative economic organisation, the State, is required. This is not, of course, intended for an exhaustive description of the nature of the State. From the view-point of economic science, however, the State is to be conceived of in this way as a great organisation possessing authority for satisfying the general collective needs of the people, and the essential function of the State is to be seen in the economic activity required for that purpose. It is only from this standpoint that we clearly perceive the necessity for the State, about which so much that is obscure has been written, on the strength of purely economic considerations. This necessity, based on the nature of the purely collective needs, should be made the starting-point of the science of public finance. It is only in this way that this science acquires a firm foundation, that its essential sphere is laid down from the start with rigorous logic, and that it is organically connected with the whole of economic science.

There are also collective needs of a more local character, which are met by smaller local organisations with compulsory powers. Constructing dykes against the sea is a typical instance. When dykes of sufficient strength and extent have been erected, they serve to protect a certain area. All landowners in this area benefit by the construction; and they do so purely passively, so that it is not possible to make a charge as a condition of sharing in that benefit. Here too, therefore, we have a purely collective need. To meet this need, there is obviously required a compulsory organisation of the landowners affected, a local organisation. The need in question is, in fact, one of those collective needs which led to the formation of the earliest communal organisations. Another example is the need for street lighting. If streets are illuminated, the benefit of this is enjoyed by all users of the streets without the need for any special activity on their part, and it is impossible to prevent people who have a right to use the street from benefiting by the light, or to make a charge in each case for the privilege. In these circumstances street-lighting is a purely collective need, to meet which compulsory contributions must be exacted. These examples should suffice to illustrate the economic character and necessity of the municipality as a local organisation with compulsory powers for satisfying local collective needs.

The compulsory contributions which are levied by these organisations are known as taxes, in the broadest sense of the word. Financial policy has, however, often emphasised that, to meet collective wants which affect only a limited number of people, the burden should as far as possible be confined to those people only. Compulsory contributions restricted in this way are known as "special assessments" or "rates," and are distinguished from general taxes. As we have already observed, the authority determining the expenditure of the particular organisation must carefully consider the importance of individual wants, and must restrict the burden of taxation accordingly.

It is a common occurrence for the machinery for satisfying collective wants to extend its operations to wants which can only be called collective in a relative sense, or which are in themselves purely individual, although the satisfaction of them has also a certain collective interest. We have already given instances of the satisfaction of collective wants of the first kind in bridge and road construction, which to-day is undertaken by local authorities or various kinds or by the State as a collective work to be met out of taxation. An instance of the satisfaction of collective wants of the second kind is furnished by public education, when such education is provided free or below cost, as is usually the case. It is true that the individual is primarily interested in being trained for his future work, and to this extent the need for education and instruction is primarily an individual need, the satisfaction of which can be made dependent upon the willingness of the particular person, or his family, to pay. However, the community as a whole has a very considerable interest in seeing that the general education of the people is carried to the highest possible standard, in so far as social productivity – to consider the matter from a purely economic point of view – upon which every individual is, economically, absolutely dependent in any highly developed exchange economy, is increased by education. From this point of view education may be regarded as a collective interest. Modern social policy has in this way given a certain collective character to a large number of wants. We have only to think of the numerous measures in the interests of social hygiene, such as free or cheap public baths. Every extension of this kind of the collective satisfaction of wants clearly means an encroachment of public authority upon the sphere of individual choice, for certain individual needs are held to be particularly important, and individuals in the aggregate are compelled to use their means more liberally in meeting these needs than they would if they were not compelled. In this way the freedom of the individual to regulate his own demand for goods and services is restricted.

The State and the municipality are not the only compulsory organisations in modern society for satisfying collective wants. There are also organisations, even though they may not be publicly authorised, for certain special economic purposes, such as trade unions and employers' associations. The interest of the workers in raising wages is, under modern industrial conditions, essentially a collective interest; thus, once an increase in wages has been secured, the benefit of the increase usually accrues to all the workers in a trade, irrespective of whether they are members of the trade union or not, and, consequently, even to those workers who have not contributed to the cost of the struggle. The only way of making all who benefit contribute to the cost is, as in the case of every collective need, by means of a compulsory organisation; and the same is true in the case of employers. The observation may help to bring out the nature of the satisfaction of collective wants by compulsory organisations.

The representatives of these organisations appear in the community, side by side with other individuals, as consumers who make demands upon the stock of goods. By treating these collective organisations, therefore, as individuals, we simplify the problem of the limitation of wants in the exchange economy. The demands upon the stock of goods then become a single quantity, and our next step is to examine how it is possible so to reduce these demands by fixing prices that they can be met with the available supply of goods. We now turn to this question.

§ 11 *The Restriction of Wants. General Case*

It is possible to conceive of a society in which the collective whole has authority to regulate the satisfaction of all the wants of all its members; in which not only the collective, but also individual, wants are left to be satisfied by an authoritative organisation, and no scope is left for the individual to regulate his own consumption. This is the *communistic* society. In the present economic order the family is, in a sense, a communistic economy; but we must reserve the name, communistic society or economic system, for a somewhat larger society which, in the main at least, is a self-contained economy with unified control of all consumption. Examples of such communistic societies are to be found in the communistic colonies, usually religious in character, which have been founded from time to time and in some cases have lasted quite a long time, though as a rule they have broken up very quickly.

The antithesis of this communistic system is provided by the exchange economy, which, as was shown in § 7, is characterised by the existence of independent private economies with a free choice as regards the satisfaction of their wants within the means at their disposal. There can be no doubt that civilised people attach much importance to this free choice on the part of the individual or of the family. It is true that there is an encroachment by the collective economy upon the sphere of the individual satisfaction of wants, as we have seen, in the shape of the provision to certain classes of certain services, such as baths or libraries, either free or at a reduced price. These, however, are exceptional cases, and are not regarded as a material restriction of free individual consumption. The free regulation of consumption by the individual must certainly be regarded as one of the elements most essential to our economic system, which is, in its very nature, the very reverse of communism.

Our task is now to see how the problem of restricting the satisfaction of wants is solved in the exchange economy. We shall deal in this section first with the simplified theoretical case in which the goods which serve for the direct satisfaction of wants are available in given quantities; or, rather, since the provision of goods to society is effected by a constant flow, and not out of a given stock, these goods are available in definite quantities within a given period. We shall call each of these quantities the *supply* of the commodity in question. The assumption in this section is that the supply is a given quantity in the problem in the case of each of the commodities or services which directly satisfies needs. We are thus leaving aside for the moment the difficult questions relating to the regulation of the supply of goods; we shall have to deal with these questions in later sections. For purposes of simplification we further assume that the sum of money which each individual pays for the satisfaction of his wants in a particular period is given.

Under the present economic system the demands of individuals upon the supply of goods are regulated by the fact that prices are placed on all goods, and these prices must be paid if the individual wishes to acquire the goods. As the money resources of individuals are limited, the fixing of prices compels them to restrict their consumption in various directions, so that the sums of money they can spend will give as uniform a satisfaction of their wants as possible. If the prices are fixed high enough, therefore, the demands of consumers can be so far restricted in every direction that they can be met out of the available supplies of the various goods intended for consumption. This restriction of the demands of consumers is, in the case considered in this section, the object of pricing. The need for this lies in the fact that the competition of consumers for goods in the exchange economy can only be regulated by fixing prices at a suitable level. This method of restricting the demands of consumers is clearly the one which allows the greatest possible scope for free selection on the part of the individual of what he will consume.

As the restriction of consumption must be all the more vigorous, the greater the scarcity of goods in relation to the demands of consumers, and as, therefore, prices are largely determined by this scarcity, we see that the indicated purpose of pricing is an expression of the principle of scarcity which we outlined in the first section. *Thus, in the exchange economy, the principle of scarcity signifies the necessity, by the pressure of prices, to adjust consumption to a relatively scarce supply of goods.* In this principle, which brings out the social economic necessity of prices, is to be found also the general and necessary basis of the determination of prices. The principle of scarcity is, in fact, of fundamental importance to the theory of prices, and therefore to the whole of economic theory.

If there exists only one unit of a particular commodity, the price must clearly be fixed so high that all purchasers but one will be excluded. Where, in the same category, many commodities are available, which are, however, somewhat different in quality – houses in a residential suburb, let us say – the prices must again be so fixed that there will be only one purchaser for each house.

With regard to those commodities which are made so exactly alike by mass production methods that one product is as good as any other, the problem of pricing is rather different. As a rule, a uniform price is placed upon each such product, chiefly because it is difficult, if not impossible, to make a distinction between the various purchasers and to sell the product at a lower price to one and at a higher price to another. There are, however, exceptions to this rule, when vendors try to get a higher price from the wealthier customers, if possible. In medical practice, for instance, it is the custom to make wealthier patients pay more, and, in not a few cases, there is a scale of charges graduated according to the economic position of the patients. But, even in the case of absolutely identical mass-produced articles, attempts are made to graduate prices in this way. Thus, a tablet of a particular brand of soap is priced at sixpence, and is sold at this price in the shops in the West End of London; but the same brand of soap can be bought more cheaply in other parts of London, and at varying prices. It is well known that a similar discrimination in the price of clothes is the rule everywhere, but it may always be argued with regard to these that there are differences in quality, cut, etc., and that it is these differences which determine the difference in price. On the other hand, we sometimes find that the poorest people have to pay the highest price. This, however, is mainly due to the greater relative losses and expenses of small retail businesses.

In most cases, discrimination in the price for one and the same commodity presents insuperable difficulties, since, naturally, all buyers as a rule want to buy at the cheapest price. One uniform price for commodities of exactly the same quality for sale on the same terms in one and the same market is therefore the prevailing rule. The moment the object for sale shows any variation whatever, varying prices can, of course, be fixed. The extent to which these variations are based on objective conditions, or really involve differences in the price of a particular commodity, can only be determined in relation to a study of production. We shall leave such questions aside for the moment and take the case in which only absolutely identical goods or services are sold at identical prices.

If the prices of all commodities are given, we can assume that all the factors which influence the individual in determining his consumption are fixed; the quantity of each commodity which the individual wishes to buy for the satisfaction of his wants in the particular period is then fixed. This quantity is known as the "demand" of the individual for the particular commodity. If we aggregate the quantities of a particular commodity demanded by every individual, we obtain the "total demand" for it in the exchange economy in question. This total demand must, if there is to be equilibrium, be covered by the total supply in each given period, since, in accordance with the principle of scarcity, it is the task of prices so to restrict the demand for any particular commodity that the supply shall be sufficient to meet the demand. The same must be true of all other commodities. The series of conditions we get in this way generally suffices to settle the problem of prices, for, once these conditions are realised, any change in price must cause a change in the demand for the various commodities, and as a result the balance between supply and demand is disturbed. With this, the task which we set ourselves in this section is substantially accomplished, and in what follows we have only to consider more closely the nature of the restriction of the satisfaction of wants which is effected by the pricing process.

It should first be observed that, in considering the total demand for commodities by any one individual, the total value of this demand, reckoned on the basis of prevailing prices, must correspond to the amount of money which that individual is prepared to spend for consumption purposes. Similarly, the aggregate demand of the entire exchange economy for finished goods must cover the aggregate supply, and, like the latter, must represent a money value equivalent to the total sum of money set aside for consumption purposes.

The individual demand for a commodity is in general dependent upon the prices of all commodities, or, at least, of all those commodities which have any significance for that particular individual. For instance, the demand of a worker for newspapers or other relative luxuries, in certain cases even for clothing, is dependent upon food prices. A certain demand for these necessaries must be met even when prices are high, and there then remains only a small sum for less urgent needs. That this has so general an application is readily understood if we reflect that the demand for a particular commodity only represents a special result of the regulation which the individual exercises upon his total consumption on the basis of the existing price situation. Naturally, the price of the commodity is itself the most important factor determining the demand for it; and it is of theoretical as well as of practical interest to find what influence a small alteration in that price has on demand, assuming that all other prices remain unchanged.

Given a definite scheme of prices, the individual is generally compelled to restrict the satisfaction of his wants in various directions, although this restriction need not affect all his wants. As a rule, a number of wants can be satisfied to the point of satiety. This is, of course, mainly true of the rich, but is also, to a certain extent, true of the middle and poorer classes. Anybody who is not extremely poor can buy as much ink as he needs. Even if the price of ink were to go up a little, he would not feel obliged to curtail his use of it. Whatever the price, within the ordinary limits, he will satisfy his need for ink completely. The same is true of very large classes of people as regards common condiments, particularly salt, and is also true of the more well-to-do classes as regards beef, beer, etc. In such cases the individual's demand for the commodity is independent of its price, but only, of course, within certain limits – only as regards those price fluctuations which in fact are usual. When the normal supply of a commodity is cut off as a result of certain extraordinary events, and its price consequently rises to an unusual level, it is found that even those households which hitherto had never thought of restricting their demand for that patricular commodity must now diminish their consumption of it.

On the other hand, it is the rule for the great mass of consumers that, even when prices are at a normal level, they must restrict most of their wants, even urgent wants, and can by no means satisfy them completely. In these cases the demand of any individual for the particular commodity is, as to speak, compressed. When the pressure of price again relaxes a little – i.e. when the price falls – the compressed demand expands with some degree of force. This force, on the analogy of a physical force, is known as the *elasticity* of the demand. This elasticity can be measured by the alteration in demand brought about by a given small change in price. It varies greatly for different commodities and for different persons. If a want is satisfied to the point of satiety, the elasticity of demand is nil; a slight fall in price will then bring about no increase in consumption. The elasticity is again nil if the price is so high that it is in any case prohibitive for the particular individual; a small fall in price cannot in this case create a demand. If a want is partially satisfied, a small fall in price may produce either a proportionate increase in the demand, or a proportionately greater or smaller increase in the demand. In the first case the elasticity is equal to one; in the other cases it is greater or less than one. If the elasticity is equal to one, the total expenditure on the satisfaction of the particular want is clearly independent of small fluctuations in price. But if the elasticity is less than one, the total expenditure increases as the price rises, and is reduced as the price falls. If the satisfaction of the want approaches the point of satiety, the elasticity is generally less than one. The bread consumption of an average working-class family will not be reduced by the same percentage as that by which the price of bread rises in a year of scarcity, nor will it increase in the same proportion as that in which the price of bread falls. The need for bread, which is a prime necessity, is almost satiated when prices are normal, and must remain the same when there are only small fluctuations in the price of bread. The total expenditure of the family on bread will therefore show fluctuations approximately as great as those in the price of bread. The need for housing is much more elastic in the case of large classes of people in modern society. The elasticity should here at times approach unity, this being explained by the fact that a family spends just as much on house accommodation whether rents are high or low. Elasticity greater than unity is comparatively infrequent, and is only found in the case of those wants which are relatively unnecessary, where the total expenditure of a consumer upon the want in question rises when the price falls. A man may, for instance, be led by a reduction in railway fares to spend more on railway travel than he did before.

The elasticity of the demand of the several households for a commodity determines the elasticity of the aggregate demand of the community for that commodity. Here it need only be observed that a reduction in price can lead not only to a rise in demand, where such demand already existed, but can also create a new demand on the part of those households which were hitherto unable, by reason of the high price, to satisfy their want. A knowledge of the elasticity of the demand is of great practical importance in all cases where the price of a commodity or service has to be arbitrarily fixed or moved in a particular direction, as, for example, in fixing railway rates or in introducing or varying customs or excise duties. Theoretically, this knowledge of the elasticity of a particular demand is always of interest in calculating the effect upon consumption of some proposed change of price. Unfortunately, we have very inadequate means of obtaining statistical information as to the elasticity of particular demands from an observation of the actual working of society. The difficulty lies not only in the deficiencies of our statistics of consumption, but also in the nature of the problem. What we want to know is how the demand for a commodity changes when its price is slightly changed, all other prices remaining constant. The condition is never absolutely realised, and, as we shall see later, cannot be realised. In addition, there is the fact that customs, tastes, and, at times also, the real needs of consumers may change considerably in any given period. Hence our observation of the effects of a change in price within a given period is always obscured by various complicating factors. To obtain some idea of the elasticity of the demand, we can of course start with a comparison of a number of typical domestic budgets, over the same period, of families in various classes of society, and attempt to deduce from this material the various ways in which different needs are restricted when income is reduced and when prices, therefore, rise relatively to income. Such a study is of considerable interest in connection with our knowledge of the effect of prices on the aggregate demand of the community, and of the way in which the satisfaction of wants is restricted by prices. But it is clear that from such material we can only make general conclusions upon the elasticity of the demand for various commodities.

A knowledge of the elasticity of the demand for different commodities gives us some idea of the tendencies towards a change in demand resulting from a change in commodity prices. These tendencies are, on the whole, in the nature of a reaction against the change in prices, a rise in price causing a diminution in demand, and *vice versa*. This reaction against price changes is clearly a necessary condition of stability of prices once price equilibrium has been achieved.

It follows from this that it is sufficient for a solution of the problem of prices (to the extent to which we are here considering it) if we assume that the demand for each of the commodities in question is fixed once the prices of these commodities are given. No further analysis of demand is needed in connection with the problem of prices. The extent of the demand at a given price is a tangible fact which has a quantitative and purely arithmetical expression, and in this form can be used directly by economic science as part of its structure. The psychological processes under-lying this fact have, of course, a certain interest for the economist, inasmuch as a knowledge of them helps him to estimate correctly the influence of prices on demand; in so far as they can be elucid-ated, they are best studied from this standpoint. Such a study can only derive advantage from the fact that it is pursued in terms of a clear quantitative conception of the problem; the idea that the theory of prices discussed in this Book, in contradistinction to the so-called theory of value, would render more difficult, or even exclude, a psychologico-economic study, is therefore based on a complete misunderstanding. Such studies, however, lie outside the realm of economic theory proper.

These remarks are of special importance in relation to what is known as the *Marginal Utility Theory*. The first objection to this much-discussed theory is that it is superfluous in economic science. The marginal utility theory is an attempt to reduce the psychology of demand to an abstract mathematical form. The "utility" of the satisfaction of a want is regarded as arithmetically calculable. If a want is satisfied by successive equal doses, the corresponding total utility increases, but at a constantly diminishing rate, and the final addition to the total utility, the *marginal utility*, becomes smaller and smaller. The marginal utility must, in a state of equilibrium, correspond to the price to be paid for the last dose. This is the general formula which, according to the marginal utility theory, governs every economic action.

If, for the sake of simplicity, we assess utility in terms of money, then the utility of the final unit of a commodity used for satisfying a want, or the marginal utility, must be equal to the price of that unit. This coincidence of marginal utility and price in every branch of the satisfaction of wants is a sign that the total utility of the satisfaction of wants attainable by the particular community has reached its maximum. For an extension of the satisfaction of wants in one direction would now mean an increase in utility which would fall short of the price to be paid for it, while the money used for this purpose would be withdrawn from other branches of the satisfaction of wants and would thus cause a loss of utility greater than that amount of money. The whole theory of marginal utility can also be conceived of as a theoretical deduction as to economic behaviour from the assumption that the economic man aims at securing a maximum total utility.

This purely formal theory, which in no way extends our knowledge of actual processes, is in any case superfluous for the theory of prices.

It should further be noted that this deduction of the nature of demand from a single principle, in which so much childish pleasure has been taken, was only made possible by artificial constructions and a considerable distortion of reality.

In the first place, an abstract estimate, expressed in no matter what scale of reckoning, of the utility of the various degrees of satisfaction of wants in all its branches, is an impossibility for the economic man. In such estimates he requires at least the aid of the existing prices, and the most he can do is to calculate with some degree of probability what change would be caused in his demand by a change in *one* price. This whole scale of reckoning is thus necessarily bound up with existing prices. If we keep strictly to the bare facts, we can only say that the economic man decides what he shall buy as soon as all prices are given, or, in other words, draws a line between those wants he will satisfy and those he will not take into account.

Again, the proposition that marginal utility is equal to price has no general validity. Even when a want can be satisfied in successive doses, it is by no means certain that the last dose of utility is valued equally with the price. As far as those wants which are fully satisfied are concerned, it is, on the contrary, the rule that even the utility of the last dose has a value greater than its price, as is shown by the fact that these wants are satisfied to precisely the same extent even if the price is a little higher, or, in other words, that the elasticity of these wants is nil. Moreover, the various stages of the satisfaction of wants do not always run in the continuous series which the theory assumes. A tenant who rents a house at £100 will often, as experience shows, keep the house even if the rent rises to £105. Marginal utility in that case is higher than price. Yet the tenant will not take a larger or better house, because one which will suit him might not perhaps be obtainable at a rent below £115. Hence the solution of the problem of the uniform satisfaction of wants by the individual, as it is usually formulated in terms of the theory of marginal utility, is not a correct one. If we are to speak at all of an evaluation of wants, we must be content with some such proposition as the following: at the existing prices, every want that is considered of less value than the price of satisfying it is denied satisfaction, while the remaining wants, which are considered to be at least equal in value to the price, are satisfied.

If we consider all the different individuals within a large exchange economy, we can say with fair accuracy that a commodity, which can be sold in a number of small portions and is universally demanded, yields a marginal utility equal to its price. For there will probably be someone among the large number of purchasers who will think a unit quantity of the commodity just worth its price. This purchaser is usually called the marginal purchaser. Thus, in the case of this kind of commodity, it is approximately true that the ratio between marginal utility and price is the same in all branches of the satisfaction of wants, and this proposition can, subject to certain limitations, be accepted as a solution of the problem of the uniform satisfaction of the wants of the whole of the exchange economy. But it has neither the same general validity nor clearness as the proposition to which we must be led by a consideration of the necessarily restrictive influence of price on the satisfaction of wants — the proposition, namely, that those wants, for the satisfaction of which the particular individual is prepared to pay the price, are satisfied, and that other wants are not satisfied.

Thus the introduction of the conception of marginal utility is of no material advantage, though it may at times be convenient to apply the term. In seeking to make this conception the basis of a whole economic theory by declaring marginal utility to be the determinant of price or "value," a wholly untenable position has been taken up. The task of price, in accordance with the principle of scarcity, is so to restrict demand as to enable it to be satisfied out of the available stock of commodities. The demand for a commodity must thus be cut down somewhere by means of its price. Although the significance attached to the final satisfaction of the want is then equal to the price, this cannot possibly be construed to mean that this significance determines the price. On the contrary, the price determines the extent to which wants shall be satisfied, and, accordingly, which is the "final" or "marginal" want. The price, however, is itself fixed by the condition that demand must be so reduced that it can be met by the existing supply of goods. We must therefore reject absolutely any attempt to represent the theory of marginal utility as a solution of the problem of prices, or even of the problem of value.

The idea that the economic man can estimate in terms of money the importance of his wants *in abstracto*, independently of existing prices, has led to comparisons being made between the importance of a want measured in this way and the price actually paid for satisfying that want, and, if the importance attached to the want exceeds its price, the difference is regarded as a special gain to the consumer. This consumer's gain or "surplus" is supposed to be equal to the difference between the highest price which the consumer would pay for the commodity, if he could not get it more cheaply, and the actual price. [1] In reply to this, it must be asserted that the

[1] "Consumer's Surplus," Marshall, *Principles of Economics*, Book III., chap. vi.

evaluation of commodities is a matter essentially bound up with actual prices, and is, after all, merely the decision determining what will be consumed at a given set of prices. The money scale in terms of which the commodity is valued has no precise meaning except in relation to a definite series of prices. If we consider two widely differing sets of prices, the valuations placed upon a particular commodity are expressed in different money scales in the two cases and are therefore not directly comparable. It is true that the difference is so small that it may be ignored in the case of a slight alteration in the price of a commodity which is of little importance in the budget of the economy in question. It must nevertheless be insisted that it is impossible to give an exact definition of what is called the "consumer's surplus."

In the case of those commodities which can be consumed in successive doses, the consumer's surplus for each separate portion is calculated, and the sum of these surpluses is called the total surplus. Or else the utility which the consumer derives from each portion is aggregated, giving what is known as the total utility he derives from the consumption of the particular commodity. By subtracting the aggregate price from this total utility, we again get the total "consumer's surplus." If, for example, we assume that a person is prepared to pay a maximum of two shillings for one glass of beer, sixpence for a second, twopence for a third, a penny for a fourth, and still less for subsequent glasses of beer, we should calculate the total utility of consuming four glasses of beer at two shillings and ninepence. If the actual price of a glass of beer is a penny, that person would consume four glasses of beer and pay fourpence for them. He would thus have to his credit a consumer's surplus of two shillings and fivepence! It is, in effect, difficult to see what can be gained by such calculations. They reflect no psychological process which might be of importance from the view-point of prices. They are incapable of any exact formulation which could be used as a basis for a general application of this particular method of approach. This is admirably demonstrated when it is attempted to calculate by the same method the total utility which a consumer derives from the whole of his consumption, and the result arrived at is that the value of a consumption amounting to, let us say, £100, was in fact £150!

The conception of economy requires a certain restriction of wants, a selection determining which of an indefinite number of wants are to be satisfied. The economic principle postulates that every want which is satisfied is more important than each of the wants that are left unsatisfied. The way in which this is achieved is of great importance in any economic system. In the self-contained individual economy the necessary classification of wants is effected by a single will. In the exchange economy, every individual makes a corresponding classification of his own wants. But for the classification of the aggregate wants of the entire economy there is no such authority. How is it possible to compare the importance of one particular want with that of another, if the wants are those of different individuals? The community requires for this purpose a common measure of the importance of all the different wants. It finds this common standard by fixing uniform prices for identical commodities and making the payment of these prices a condition for the satisfaction of wants. What this amounts to is that a want for which the price demanded is paid is always regarded as being more important than a want for which that price is not paid. The exchange economy thus measures the importance of the various wants by the sums of money which are offered for satisfying them.

This is a fact of such general validity that it must necessarily be made the basis of an elementary analysis of the exchange economy. The selection of this standard gives the exchange economy, to a certain extent, the character of a centralised organisation, the administration of which can be tested by its usefulness. In this way, the conception of "economy," too, acquires a specific meaning, and it becomes possible to deduce, from the general economic principle, fundamental principles of price-determination in the exchange economy.

Any criticism of the standard selected is, in effect, a criticism of the exchange economy itself. The criticism may, for instance, proceed from the observation that a hungry man's need of bread is far more important than the need of a rich man for bread with which to feed his dogs, and that a society which satisfies the latter want before the former is not employing its available resources rationally. But this objection is directed either against the irrational use which the rich make of their money, and is to that extent not an objection in principle to uniform prices, or it is in the main a criticism of the actual distribution of income. It is this latter, and not the uniform price of bread, which is responsible if the poor cannot get sufficient bread. The matter is approached predominantly in this way in political discussion, too. The demand for a more just distribution of income is very frequently made, and plays a leading part in developing the opposition of interests of the different social classes. The system of uniform prices, on the other hand, is chiefly considered as in itself natural and normal. This conception is thus suitable as a starting-point for the theoretical treatment of a "normal" exchange economy.

It might be suggested that the evil referred to should be remedied by selling commodities to the poor at lower prices. If this proposal were completely carried out for all commodities, it would be absolutely equivalent to raising the incomes of the poorer classes. On what conditions this is possible, and how it can be reconciled with the fundamental principles and economic conduct of a society based on exchange, are questions which we will carefully consider in the last chapter of the next Book. If, however, the cheapening of commodities for the poorer classes were only partially carried out, for certain selected commodities, this would amount to an encroachment upon the free choice of consumption of the poorer classes. This is in conflict with the general principle of the exchange economy, by which the distribution of the available consumption goods in the various directions in which wants are satisfied is left to the individual. It is true that frequent attempts are made, particularly by public bodies, to provide certain commodities at reduced prices or even gratuitously to the poorer classes. These attempts, however, as was previously observed, proceed from ideas foreign to the nature of the exchange economy, and are essentially communistic in character. We see, at the same time, attempts made to raise the price of certain other commodities, such as brandy, by taxation, with the intention of diminishing the consumption of them. This is a sort of paternal authority exercised over the individual's free choice in regard to consumption, as to the practical value of which nothing need be said here, except that it is not an essential part of the exchange economy, and we may therefore ignore it in an introductory examination of the essential features of the economy.

In addition to charging prices, there is another method of effecting the necessary restriction of consumers' demands, namely, the method of rationing. This method came into widest use during the Great War, not only in the belligerent countries, but also in neutral lands. With the extraordinary shortage in commodity supplies, it was believed that in a free market the prices of necessary commodities could be forced up to such a level that the supply of them to the poorer classes might be seriously imperilled. For this reason, it was sought to restrict consumers' demands by means of a highly developed system of coupons, which fixed a definite ration for every person. However, this regulation, which makes such a deep and obvious encroachment upon free choice in the sphere of consumption, does not eliminate the restrictive effect of prices. For a price still has to be paid for the rationed commodity, and it is thus conceivable that some consumers are obliged by the pressure of that price to restrict their demands even more than the rationing system would require. In any case, paying for the rationed commodity makes a claim upon a certain amount of purchasing power, and correspondingly diminishes the purchasing power available for other commodities. The function of price as a restraint upon consumption is thus retained in a system of rationing.

The price of a rationed commodity can clearly be lower than it would be in the absence of rationing. For in the latter case price itself would be sufficient to compel the necessary restriction of demand, and rationing would be superfluous. If a rationing system, with all its attendant difficulties, is to justify its existence, it must permit of a considerably lower price than would otherwise be necessary.

Bread is a notable example of a commodity which, for these reasons, may be considered as appropriate for rationing in a period of extreme shortage, although not, as is often imagined, primarily for the purpose of restricting the consumption of the wealthier classes of society. For the gain by this restriction would only release a very small additional amount for the consumption of the rest of the population. The importance of the rationing of bread would lie rather in restricting the consumption of the upper working classes. Large numbers of workers earned high wages during the war, and very high bread prices would have been demanded if the demands of these workers for bread were to have been restricted to the necessary extent by prices alone. The rationing of bread thus meant, in the main, a more equal distribution of the available supplies between the different sections and individuals of the working class whose economic positions varied greatly.

After the war, rationing was for the most part quickly removed. It was found to be very undesirable on account of its inconvenience and cost, and it seems highly improbable that such a method of restricting consumption will ever again be employed under normal conditions. We are therefore justified in regarding the fixing of uniform prices as the normal method of effecting the necessary restriction of consumers' demands. The following development of economic theory must be based on the assumption of such a fixing of prices. If we take this method of price-fixing as normal, we can do it without fear of any misunderstanding, since we have now demonstrated the relative nature of this assumption.

Equally relative in character is the statement that a system of uniform prices determines the most "economic" use of available commodities. The theoretical treatment of the typical exchange economy must proceed from this conception of "most economic use." This conception should, however, be made to include nothing but what it really contains according to what has been discussed above.

§ 12 *The Regulation of Production. The Principle of Scarcity*

In the preceding section, the available supplies of the different commodities were regarded as given and fixed in advance. We shall now drop this assumption. It is not in accord with reality, for, as most goods can be produced, the quantities of the various finished goods which are offered to consumers depend, in general, on the direction given to production. As a rule, the existing factors of production can, of course, be used for widely differing purposes, and thus supplies to consumers can be greatly varied. We shall therefore now assume that the various *primary* means of production, i.e. those means of production which cannot themselves be increased by production and which we shall henceforth refer to as "factors of production," exist in definite quantities or, rather, are available in definite quantities within a given period. Calling these quantities the *supply of the factors of production*, we have now to consider this supply as one group of the given factors of the problem in hand.

The question then arises as to which goods shall be produced. The general economic principle requires that the available factors of production shall be used in the most economic way, that is, that production shall be directed into those channels in which the most important wants are satisfied. The realisation of the economic principle with regard to the direction given to production in society thus depends on the order of precedence attaching to wants. If, as regards the most economic regulation of consumption, the amount of money which is offered for the satisfaction of the different wants is now accepted as the criterion of the importance of those wants, the same criterion must be applicable to the regulation of production. We thus reach the conclusion that the factors of production should be applied in those directions where they must meet the demands with the greatest ability to pay. The solution of the problem therefore lies in placing uniform prices on the factors of production, calculating the prices of finished goods on the basis of these prices, and in so directing production that those wants are satisfied for which the price so fixed for their satisfaction is forthcoming, all other wants remaining unsatisfied. If correct prices are placed upon the factors of production, consumers' demands are so restricted that they can be met with the relatively scarce available factors of production, the latter at the same time being demanded to their full extent. This condition is sufficient for determining the prices of the factors of production, and, therefore, the prices of finished commodities, too. In this way both demand and the entire direction of production are determined. This solution of the problem, it can be seen, is merely an application of the *principle of scarcity* to the general case which we are considering.

The demand for commodities is indirectly a demand for factors of production. This demand seeks to attract the factors of production to one particular use or another; it represents a conflict between consumers for the factors of production, a conflict which can be adjusted only by placing on the factors of production prices high enough to effect a coincidence of demand with the available quantities of the factors of production. If the importance of any want is measured by the amount of money which is offered to secure its satisfaction, the prices of the factors of production must be uniform, i.e. the same price must be paid for identical factors of production, independently of the purpose for which they are used. This method of pricing ensures that every want which pays the price is satisfied, that all other wants are left unsatisfied, and that, therefore, each factor of production is attracted to the most "economic" use according to the standard adopted.

If, for example, copper is used both for domestic utensils and in the electrical industry, the most economic use of the available stock of copper requires that the coppersmith shall pay the same price for copper as the electrical industry. If copper were to be sold more cheaply to one branch of production than to the other, this would clearly mean that some copper would be used for less important purposes than it might be. The same applies in general to labour. The economic principle requires that labour shall be used where it gets the highest wage. This requirement is met when there is only one price for all labour of the same kind and quality – when, that is to say, this labour receives the same wage in all the different branches of production in which it is employed.

No price need be placed upon factors of production which are present in abundance, it being unnecessary to restrict the demand for them. But for all other factors of production prices must be calculated according to their relative scarcity, so that the effective demand for any one of them, i.e. that demand which is prepared to pay the price, becomes sufficiently small to enable it to be covered by the available quantity of the particular factor of production. Thus economic operation requires that the factors of production, too, shall be priced in accordance with the principle of scarcity.

The process of determining prices in the exchange economy thus extends both to the primary factors of production and to finished consumption goods, and also, of course, to all goods in the intermediate stages of the productive process. This general price-fixing process is determined by the conditions applicable to it, through which in turn all the prices are determined, and determined simultaneously. The social economic task of this general price-fixing process is, briefly, the realisation of the general economic principle in the exchange economy. The pricing process solves this problem by simultaneously securing the necessary regulation of demand by the elimination of the less important wants and the proper direction of production by the fullest and most economic use of all the available factors of production. This complete pricing process thus includes the fixing of prices for finished commodities, discussed in the previous section, the object of which is to bring demand into harmony with the available quantities of those commodities.

Once a scheme of prices has been fixed for the factors of production, there will be calculated for every finished product a price corresponding to the total price of all the factors of production used to produce it. We are assuming in this section that this quantity of factors of production is fixed, so that the total price referred to can be accurately calculated. This price we call the *cost* of the finished product. Cost in this sense is essentially an idea pertaining to an exchange economy, and is determined by the fixing of prices in that economy. The word "cost" is also used to mean real cost of production, the aggregate of the necessary quantities of factors of production. This conception is, however, incapable of arithmetical definition, and thus excludes the possibility of any quantitative comparison of different "costs."

It is necessary to point out the difference between the

conception of cost as we have defined it here and that as it is usually defined in economic theory, particularly in Marshall's exposition of it.[1] For Marshall, cost represents essentially a personal service, an exertion, a sacrifice, for which there must be a certain compensation if it is to be made. Here, on the other hand, cost is being viewed in a purely objective manner as a consequence of the pricing process. The only material assumption which this conception of cost involves is that of the scarcity of the particular factors of production. Price need only be based on this scarcity, and is by no means necessarily to be regarded as a condition of the supply of the particular factors of production. We shall find that this distinction is of far-reaching importance in dealing with the fixing of prices for the principal groups of factors of production, and therefore in economic theory in general (cf. § 18).

From the point of view of the individual or of some special branch of production, the cost of production of a commodity must naturally seem to be fixed. For the demands which are made from such a quarter on the factors of production are for the most part insignificant in comparison with society's total demand for those factors of production, the prices of which must therefore be substantially determined by external factors. This has led to cost of production being sometimes represented as the determinant of commodity prices. This conception is naturally untenable from a social economic standpoint, for cost of production has no independent existence, but is determined by the prices of the factors of production, and these prices, as well as the prices of the finished products, become established as means of regulating production and demand through the price-fixing process. Some support has been given, too, to the opposite theory, namely, that the prices of the factors of production are determined by the prices of the finished products, and ultimately by the valuation placed upon these latter by demand. The whole of the recent so-called subjective theory of value is in the main an expression of this theory. Against all such views, it must be asserted that in the general price-fixing process there is no order of precedence allotted to the various prices in the

[1] Marshall, *Principles*, Book V., chap. iii., § 2.

sense that some of these prices are the determinants of the others.

The pricing process which we have here described means that every finished commodity receives a price which corresponds to its cost of production, or, more generally, that every demand shall bear the whole of the cost of satisfying it. This may be called the *principle of cost*. By the very nature of cost, the principle must be regarded simply as following from the general economic principle; it is an expression of the economic principle in regulating production in society by means of prices. The principle of cost is thus just as necessary as the fixing of prices, and is an essential part of the exchange economy in the same sense as we may say this of the pricing process.

The absolute antithesis of the principle of cost is the "gratis principle," whereby economic goods are offered to consumers without any special payment being required. This clearly implies authoritative regulation of both consumption and production, and thus leads, in effect, to the form of social organisation which we have called Communism. However, slight deviations from the principle of cost are possible without giving effect to the gratis principle; thus, certain commodities may be sold at a price below their cost, or a demand may be satisfied without it bearing the full cost of its satisfaction. Such deviations are of quite frequent occurrence in the existing exchange economy, but they are in general regarded as departures from what is normal, if not as results of bad policy or defective organisation of our national economy, or as temporary measures brought about by necessity.

This suffices to give a preliminary view of the character of the price-fixing process. In reality, however, the matter is not quite so simple. The factors of production which exist and are demanded to-day serve for future rather than for present satisfaction of wants. Hence the connection between the prices of existing finished goods and the prices of existing factors of production is not a direct one, but one which is based on the condition required of our exchange economy that it shall be in equilibrium, that prices shall remain unchanged, therefore, as long as this equilibrium is maintained, and that, as a consequence, future prices, particularly those of finished goods, shall be the same as existing prices.

The analysis of our problem must throughout be conducted in terms of this state of equilibrium, for the general theory of prices cannot be anything but a determination of the conditions necessary for the prices prevailing at any given moment to remain unchanged. This state of equilibrium is conceivable in either a stationary or a uniformly progressing society. The former case is of course by far the simpler; but the latter, too, must be taken into consideration, if we wish to be clear with regard to price-fixing in a society in which wealth is increasing.

In a stationary society demand is constant, and is always restricted to the same extent by the constant prices of finished goods. We may then be justified, on a first survey of the pricing problem, in speaking of the demand for finished goods as an indirect demand for factors of production, without going into details as to the time of that demand. But if we wish to be accurate, we must regard the stationary society as a continuous process, and we must settle the conditions under which this process remains unchanged. We then find that a continuous stream of factors of production is drawn into production, and that by means of them production releases a continuous stream of finished goods for consumers, and that the whole process remains constant in extent. Uniform prices are placed upon the primary factors of production, and these prices remain unchanged. On the basis of these, the prices of finished goods are calculated. These latter prices, which also remain constant, determine the demand for finished goods, and this demand then remains unchanged, too. Continuous production of these goods requires a constant flow of primary factors of production in definite quantities, which must coincide with the quantities actually available. These conditions suffice to determine the prices both of the factors of production and of finished goods.

As the past is for the most part of no interest to economics, our analysis must really begin with the present. We have, then, to take a cross-section of society as it is to-day. This section reveals the existence of a certain quantity of real capital which, as its origin is not to be further analysed, must be placed on a level with the primary factors of production. If, however, this real capital is maintained, or if new real capital is produced to take its place, the prices of the existing real capital must, under conditions of equilibrium, be equal to the prices of the real capital created by the ensuing process of production. To this extent, therefore, the fixing of prices is traced back to the prices of the constantly renewing stream of factors of production. It is, therefore, only those forms of existing real capital which are permanent that are to be regarded from the point of view of prices as independent primary factors of production; they are to be placed in the same category as land.

In the uniformly progressive economy, both the inflow of primary factors of production and the outflow of finished goods are constantly increasing. In such a case, the future demand is different from the present demand, and this fact must not be overlooked in studying pricing. In order to solve the problem, we have to determine the conditions of equilibrium in the uniformly progressive economy with constant prices. In form these conditions are the same as those indicated in the case of the stationary society. Prices, therefore, are determined in it by the fact that the demand for finished goods must be so restricted that it can be met with the help of the available factors of production. But the supply of finished goods to meet demand is here increasing in volume at a uniform rate, and the supply of factors of production is increasing at the same rate. The factors of production available in the present unit period must be sufficient to cover the demands which are made on them by a continually increasing demand for finished goods. The demand in question belongs to whole series of unit periods extending from the present far into the future. The prices of the factors of production must be fixed at such a level that the prices of finished goods based upon them adequately restrict this steadily growing demand.

As the pricing process extends to the factors of production, and thus a price is paid for every factor of production which is scarce, this price will be passed on to the owner of that factor of production and will represent one element in the composition of his income. Who these owners are depends upon the organisation of society, particularly upon the relative extent of private and of collective ownership, but this question is not of fundamental importance as far as our conception of the nature of income is concerned. There is, however, one factor of production, as we have already seen (§ 7), which necessarily belongs to the individual member of society, namely, personal labour. It is only by the control of the individual over his own labour that the individual economy becomes an independent economic unit, the existence of which within society is a characteristic of the exchange economy. Thus within the exchange economy individual economies always have independent incomes, whether these are derived wholly from labour or from the ownership of other factors of production, too; and these incomes are fixed once the prices of the factors of production are fixed. If some of the factors of production are owned collectively, the particular collective organisation derives an income from them; but such organisations must, as we have seen (§ 10), be considered in the same way as individuals when we are dealing with society as a whole.

By looking at the matter in this way, we place the conception of income in its true place in the exchange economy. We originally conceived of income as the quantity of finished goods which accrues to an individual in any unit period, afterwards supplementing this by the increase of real capital; we then represented income in the money sense as the money value of this real income. Finally, we selected a definition of money income with reference to its source; "money income is the payment, reckoned in terms of money, which the individual receives for his participation in the process of production" (p. 58). This income is now traced back to its source, and is conceived of as that sum of money which the individual receives for the factors of production made available by him during the unit period. From this standpoint, income may be described as the sum of the prices of a number of factors of production. The existence of any entrepreneur profits is for the present left out of consideration. The aggregate of individual incomes, thus conceived, may be taken as the total income of the exchange economy. This income purchases the whole of the finished consumption goods resulting from the productive process in the particular period, together with the entire increase of real capital during that period, and it thus serves ultimately for full payment for the participation of the factors of production during the period. It follows from this that our conception of income is in fact one and the same, even though it may appear in a different light from different points of view. This entire process of the formation of income falls completely within the general pricing process, by which it is determined. Hence the fixing of prices also includes the process which is usually known as "distribution," and which may simply be described as the real formation of income. That this formation of income, however, contains other forces which lie outside the pricing process will be shown in § 19.

The income of the individual, as we have already said, is generally partly saved and partly spent. Sometimes the individual spends more than his income, this being made possible by the fact that the saved incomes of others are placed at his disposal by way of loan, for example. The income set aside for consumption in each individual case represents "the sum of money which each individual pays for the satisfaction of his wants in the particular period" (p. 73), and which we have so far assumed to be given. We now find that this sum of money depends, in practice, upon income, and thus upon the prices of the factors of production. Possibly the individual is influenced also with regard to the extent of his saving both by the amount of his income and by the prices of finished goods. The sum of money expended is, then, in any case determined once the prices of the factors of production are given. [1]

Our previous assumption, by which this sum of money was treated as a given factor in the problem, must now be dropped. This does not, however, alter the conditions indicated by which the pricing problem is governed, for these only assume that the demand for finished goods is fixed once the prices of the factors of production, and therefore the prices of finished goods, are given.

In a stationary society, in which there is on the whole no saving, the income determined by the prices of the factors of production is

[1] For the significance of the rate of interest in this connection see § 25.

used exclusively for buying the finished goods handed over for consumption during the particular income period. The aggregate value of the factors of production which are drafted into the productive process during the period is equal to the aggregate value of the goods produced in the same period. The sum of money used for the purchase of finished goods in each unit period is constant in the stationary economy.

In the uniformly progressive economy, on the other hand, only a part, a constant fraction, of the income determined by the prices of the factors of production is used for purchasing finished goods. This part is, however, equal to the value of the finished goods produced in the income period. It is obvious that the aggregate value of the factors of production must here be greater than the aggregate value of the finished goods, for the use of factors of production during the period is calculated on the basis of a production of finished goods extending from the present far into the future, and therefore necessarily greater than the present production in the progressive economy. This supply of factors of production will, therefore, given constant prices, represent a higher value than the quantity of goods produced in the same period. The remainder of the income determined by the prices of the factors of production is used, as we have said, to pay for the increase of real capital. The sum of money which is used in the unit period for purchasing finished goods increases steadily and at the same rate as that at which the exchange economy is progressing. This is, of course, also true of the sum of money which purchases the increase in real capital. When the conditions which govern saving are given, the rate of progress, too, and consequently the entire equilibrium of the uniformly progressive economy, are determined. But this aspect of the problem cannot be fully discussed until we come to § 25.

Up to now we have dealt with the fixing of prices in general, and the determination of income in particular, on the assumption that the total extent, expressed in terms of money, of each individual demand is given. There is no logical defect in this procedure, as one might be inclined to suppose. In actual economic life, all the unknown factors in the pricing process are interdependent, and are only determined, and then all determined together, when we solve the problem of pricing. The demand and the income of individuals are necessarily dependent upon the prices of the factors of production, and can therefore only be determined in connection therewith by the single process of pricing. This does not prevent us from taking for granted the prices of the factors of production, and consequently also the income and the total demand in terms of money of the individual, and asking what conditions must be fulfilled in order that, at those prices, the demand for finished goods shall be covered by production.

This method is prescribed by the nature of things for all our investigations of the general pricing process. The causal connection between the different variables in the pricing process is not a single-sided one, tending in one definite direction, in which one link always follows upon another and is determined by it, but it is rather in the nature of a closed chain of causes, in which every link depends upon the other links, and which can be followed equally well in any direction. Economic science has wasted a good deal of effort in controversies as to whether one group or another of unknowns in the pricing problem was to be regarded as cause or effect. It is time that such discussions were eliminated from our science.

We shall get a deeper and more complete insight into the nature of the causal connection to which we have referred by studying in the following chapter the general mechanism of the pricing process.

§ 13 *Supplementary Principles of Pricing*

In actual practice the pricing process is characterised by a series of complications which we have so far disregarded. We began with the assumption that the cost of production of a commodity is in every case known once the prices of factors of production are given. In practice, however, matters are different in various respects. There are, in fact, very frequent cases in which the cost of production is indefinite in one respect or another. In such cases the pricing problem, too, is obviously open to a certain extent, and can only be completely settled when certain new conditions for price-fixing are introduced. This means that the principle of scarcity is not by itself sufficient for determining prices, and must be supplemented by certain other principles which represent new conditions of pricing and which remove any indefiniteness in the problem. We shall find that these supplementary principles are themselves consequent upon the general economic principle, and in actual economic life, at least, obtain as normal rules of price-fixing.

In the first place, the same commodity may be produced in different undertakings under more or less favourable conditions of production. Then, for the satisfaction of demand, those enter-prises should naturally be chosen which have the best conditions of production. It is, however, possible that the demand can only be satisfied if production is carried on by a number of undertakings with varying conditions of production. In that event the same commodity will in fact be produced by different independent enter-prises at varying costs of production, while at the same time, being a uniform commodity, it must bear a uniform price. At what price shall the commodity then be sold? The general economic principle clearly requires that the commodity shall receive a price corres-ponding with the highest of the various costs of production; other-wise the enterprise with the highest cost of production would be using factors of production to satisfy a demand which was not paying the full price for those factors, and this, according to the method of classifying wants adopted in the exchange economy, clearly means that a less important want is being satisfied in pre-ference to a more important one. If the price of the commodity were not sufficient to cover the cost of production of the particular undertaking, that undertaking would best be cut out or closed down, and, as we are here concerned with independent under-takings, this could be accomplished independently of the other undertakings. Consequently, in virtue of the general economic principle, there must be calculated for every commodity a price which will cover the cost of production of that undertaking which has the highest cost of production of all the undertakings that have to be employed to meet the demand. This is the *first* supplementary principle of pricing, which we shall call the *differential principle*.

The explanation of this name is as follows. The other undertakings, which have a lower cost of production, receive for the commodity they produce a price which exceeds their respective cost of production by a greater or smaller amount. There thus arises in each of these undertakings a surplus over and above the cost of production, representing a *differential profit* on the part of that undertaking. To whom this profit accrues is another question, depending on the organisation of society, and one to which we shall return in the next two sections. But that such differential profits are necessarily of general occurrence in the exchange economy is beyond all doubt. We may regard the necessity of this as a special aspect of the principle of price-fixing which we have just formulated. The name "differential principle" represents this principle, so to speak, from the standpoint of fixing the prices of the factors of production.

The great practical importance of this principle will be made abundantly clear as we proceed. Divergences between the costs of production of different undertakings are primarily engendered by nature through the different conditions which it imposes upon production in different places. Chief among these are differences in the fertility of the soil. As the great demand for agricultural products necessitates the extensive cultivation of land of varying quality, the differential principle has a very general application in this sphere. The importance of this principle in determining the rent of land we shall see later (Chapter VII.). In the second place, different conditions of trade, particularly of transport, cause great variations in costs of production if, as we invariably do here, we extend our conception of the term to include the cost of transferring commodities to the consumer. The milk supply of a large town, for instance, employs a great number of agricultural concerns with different transport costs. In accordance with the differential principle, the town must pay for its milk a price corresponding to the highest cost involved in satisfying the demand, and therefore the better placed concerns will make a differential profit. We shall have to refer to such circumstances, too, when studying the rent of land. Thirdly, differences in costs of production are largely caused by personal differences in the management and organisation of undertakings. A fourth and very important cause of variations in costs of production consists in differences in the size of undertakings. Large-scale undertakings often have an advantage over those on a smaller scale in that they work at a lower cost relatively to output. The importance of such differences as those mentioned in the last two cases in determining entrepreneurs' profits we shall examine more closely in § 18.

Having now dealt with the particular indeterminateness of costs of production caused by the existence of undertakings operating simultaneously at different costs, we shall assume in what follows that costs of production are the same in all undertakings and shall consider the case of a single undertaking. The cost of production of this undertaking may, in the first place, be indeterminate for the reason that it varies with the scale on which the undertaking operates. If cost of production *rises* as the scale of operation is extended, then clearly the price of the product, on the analogy of the case previously discussed, must cover the cost of the ultimate extension of production. We shall now leave this case and consider the opposite case, in which cost of production *falls* as the scale of production is extended.

This is a common occurrence in actual economic life. The very general advantage of large-scale over small-scale enterprise is in the main due to the fact that production on a large scale tends to reduce the cost of production per unit of the product. What price, then, is to be placed upon commodities produced under such conditions? In a sense it may be said here, too, that production is carried on at varying costs, the first few commodities being produced at a high cost and the others at a progressively lower cost. The differential principle does not, however, apply, because production at the higher cost is inevitable, in that it lies, as it were, at the base and not at the peak of production. It might be thought that the price would be fixed by the extra cost entailed by the final extension of production by one unit. This is not possible, however, since the total cost of production would not be covered by the total price calculated on the basis of the price of that unit. The general economic principle requires that it should be so covered. This requirement is met when the price of the product is equal to the ratio of the total cost to the total product – when it is equal, that is to say, to the average cost of the production which is necessary to satisfy demand. The coincidence of price with average cost represents a new condition of pricing, and one that is necessary in the present case in order to remove any indeterminateness in the pricing problem.

There still remains the question of the extent to which production is to be carried on. Not until this question is answered can the price be fixed on the basis we have indicated. If we take the price of the product as known, we can calculate the demand at that price, and thus also, if the prices of all the factors of production involved are assumed to be given, the total cost of production. This total cost must be covered by the total price, obtained by multiplying the price per unit of the product by the demand. This condition, in general, determines the price per unit, i.e. it expresses it in the prices of the factors of production involved, and thus the cost of production is no longer indeterminate. At the same time the precise extent of the demand, and consequently that of production too, is determined.

We may therefore lay down the principle that, in the case of an indeterminate cost of production such as we have here considered, price must be equal to the ratio of total cost to demand at that particular price; that is to say, price is arrived at by a uniform distribution of total cost over demand, and must therefore correspond to the average cost calculated in this way. It often happens, however, that this condition is satisfied by two or more prices. This is quite natural, since a fall in price or in average cost corresponds to an increase in demand or in the scale of production, and thus price and average cost may coincide at several points. If we assume that price is equal to average cost at one point, and that the two are, within certain limits, inversely proportional to the demand (or to the scale of production), then clearly there must remain a correspondence between price and average cost within the given limits, and consequently our requirement that price shall be equal to average cost is realised, within certain limits, by all prices. Hence in all cases in which our requirement does not definitively determine the price, it must be supplemented by another requirement, which can only be that, of all those prices which satisfy the first requirement, the *lowest* shall be operative, for in that way wants are satisfied to the greatest possible extent.

We thus come to our *second* supplementary principle of pricing, the principle that, where a larger output means cheaper production – where, that is to say, the average cost of the commodity decreases as the scale of production increases – the price of the commodity must, under conditions of equilibrium, correspond to the average cost of production; in those cases where a number of prices fulfil this condition, the lowest of those prices is to be adopted. We shall refer to this principle as *the principle of pricing under conditions of decreasing average cost*.

The assumption made by this principle is that the total cost of production increases at a slower rate than does production itself. There is the special case in which the total cost is fixed within certain limits, and therefore does not increase as production increases. When a durable good is capable of different degrees of use without it being necessary to take into account any increased amount of depreciation, and therefore the amount of service it actually gives depends upon the demand for it, or when a personal service can be enjoyed by an indefinite number of people at the same time, and therefore represents a number of services which depend upon consumption, then the cost of the individual service which is actually utilised is indeterminate; that is, it is not determined by the prices of the factors of production called into use. If, as we always do here, we conceive of the productive process in a broad sense so as to include the actual rendering of services, we can then say that the cost of production of these particular services is indeterminate. The pricing of these services cannot then be carried out in conformity with the principle of scarcity, since there is no immediate need to restrict demand – not, at any rate, to the extent to which that restriction is actually brought about by price-fixing – on account of the scarcity of the available services.

In certain cases, as we have seen (§ 10), we can avoid fixing any special price for such services, and can cover their cost according to the rules relating to the collective satisfaction of wants. This, however, is not always possible, especially when the particular services are a constituent element of the process of production, and are used for further production, and consequently the pricing of them is a link in the general pricing process. In effect, the problem of fixing prices for services of this kind is one of considerable importance in actual economic life.

An accurate appreciation of the nature of the difficulties which are met with in this connection is best obtained by taking a concrete example. Let us suppose that a tramway company has to maintain the traffic on a particular system of lines in conformity with an officially determined plan. We take the cost of this for granted; but this does not mean that the cost of the actual conveyance of the individual passenger or the cost of the actual number of passenger-miles run is thereby determined. For these costs depend upon the density of traffic, and are calculated in the form of an average by dividing total cost by the number of passenger-miles run. An objective calculation – a calculation, that is to say, based exclusively on the prices of the co-operating factors of production – of cost of production per passenger-mile is thus impossible. If, as is often the case, it were now attempted to calculate the "real cost," and hence the "true price" per passenger-mile according to the average cost on a particular existing scale of charges, highly doubtful conclusions might be drawn. It might happen, for instance, that the cost per passenger-mile was greater than the actual price, and one might then be inclined to conclude from this fact that the price must be raised. Raising the price, however, would probably cause a considerable falling-off in traffic, and consequently an increase in cost per passenger-mile; and there might then be a further rise in price, with the same result.

The correct solution of the problem lies, as is shown by our discussion of the general case, in bringing about a coincidence of price and average cost of production. But for this purpose the average cost must not be taken as a given factor in the problem; it is always dependent upon demand, which is itself generally affected by price. If this coincidence can then be brought about – which is by no means always certain in actual practice – it determines the correct price as a function of the prices of the co-operating factors of production; that is to say, it enables us to calculate the price, which in the present case we have to assume to be the cost of production, from the prices of the factors of production, and thus the normal conditions of the pricing problem are established. To the requirement that the price shall agree with the average cost of production we must, as we have shown, add the further requirement that the lowest price which satisfies that requirement shall be adopted. In the special case we are considering, then, our second supplementary principle of pricing takes the following form: when the cost of an equipment is fixed, and that equipment can, within certain limits, be used to any extent without increasing the cost, the price of a single service must be calculated according to the smallest amount which will yield a total return corresponding to the total fixed cost. We shall call this principle, which is of course not an independent principle but merely a special aspect of our second supplementary principle, the *principle of pricing under fixed total cost*.

As we see, this principle contains two requirements, one general and one special. By the general requirement, the fixed total cost must be uniformly distributed over the services demanded; that is, the price of each individual service must be calculated as being the ratio of the total cost to the amount of services demanded. In those cases in which the amount of services can be regarded as given, the price of each individual service is determined by the general requirement. In effect, this is what not infrequently happens in productive undertakings. The daily cost of a rotary press in a big newspaper concern, for instance, must be spread over the number of papers printed each day. From our present standpoint this number may be taken for granted; in other words, it does not depend upon the printing cost per copy of the paper, for a change in this would hardly lead to an alteration in the price of the newspaper. If the circulation of the paper is a large one, then the proportion of the daily cost of the press borne by each paper will be correspondingly small.

This conclusion brings out one aspect of the economic superiority of large-scale enterprise. Large-scale undertakings are in a position to make greater use of those factors of production which represent fixed costs, and can therefore work on a lower price for each special service of those factors of production. It is also important to calculate the price of a single service, in that such a calculation shows whether the purchase of a particular factor of production capable of a great amount of use, such as a rotary press of a certain type, is profitable. If the number of papers to be printed is quite small, then the cost of printing borne by each copy on a large rotary press will be too great, and it will be cheaper to use a smaller press. The superiority of the large undertaking, in its ability to employ larger and, given proper use, cheaper machines, is clearly marked.

The costs of production of a commodity may also be indeterminate for the reason that different methods of production are technically possible, but give rise to differing costs of production. If at any of the relevant prices of the factors of production one method is clearly the cheapest, that method must naturally be preferred. For any other procedure would, in order to satisfy the particular want, make a demand upon factors of production which are valued more highly for the purpose of satisfying other wants, and this would be a negation of the economic principle. The cost of production is, then, no longer indeterminate. If, however, the position in any branch of production is such that the cheapest method of production cannot be determined in advance, but depends upon the prices of the factors of production, or, in other words, is affected by the actual variations of those prices, then the selection of the method of production is not independent of the prices of the factors of production, and there is thus a certain indeterminateness in the pricing problem. The requirement that the cheapest method of production is to be chosen then becomes of importance in fixing prices; it represents a new condition for pricing which removes the indeterminateness from the problem. We shall call this condition the *principle of substitution*, and shall establish it as a *third* supplementary principle of pricing. The principle of substitution demands that where one method of production can be substituted for another without any alteration in output, then that method shall be adopted which is the cheapest at the given prices of the factors of production.

The replacement of one method of production by another need not necessarily mean a complete transformation of production. It often consists merely in exchanging a certain quantity of one factor of production for a certain quantity of another. Where a quantity of a particular factor of production or of a particular group of factors can be exchanged in this way for some other factor or group of factors, we refer to these quantities as being mutually *substitutable* in the relevant process of production. The principle of substitution requires that there shall be chosen, from among substitutable quantities of the various factors or groups of factors of production, those quantities which are the cheapest at the given prices.

As an example of this substitution of one group of factors of production for another, we may mention the replacement of steam-driven machinery in a factory by a complete electrical plant; or, as an instance of a more restricted substitution, the introduction of a type-setting machine in a printing works in which setting of type by hand had hitherto been the rule.

If we are concerned only with a definite number of individually distinct methods of production, we can, once the prices of the factors of production are given, calculate the cost of each method and ascertain which is the cheapest, and therefore, according to the principle of substitution, the method to be adopted. But it is also conceivable that a particular method of production may be subject to continual variation as certain factors of production displace others by very small amounts without thereby affecting output. Where this is so, we must choose another way of applying the principle of substitution. Let us assume for purposes of simplicity that there are only two competing factors, or groups of factors, of production, and that the method of production is therefore altered only in so far as one factor of production gradually displaces another by a very small amount at a time. As simple illustrations of such substitution we may instance the wide margin for variation in the feeding of domestic animals or in fertilising the soil, or the gradual substitution of motor-vans for horses in the postal service. If we follow up some such process of substitution in a particular direction, we shall in general find that at every step a small final amount of one factor of production may be substituted for a definite final amount of the other, but that the ratio between these substitutable amounts constantly changes. The question now is: where is the point of lowest cost of production? To what extent is the one factor of production to displace the other? What is the best ratio between the quantities of the two factors of production? As long as one of the substitutable quantities is dearer than the other, this point is clearly not reached, for in that event a cheaper method of production can be had by replacing a further small amount of one of the factors of production by a substitutable amount of the other. The test of the cheapest methods is therefore whether the last mutually substitutable quantities of the two factors of production used in production have the same price. This coincidence of prices thus represents the principle of substitution in the present case. It clearly determines how much of the two factors of production shall be used at given prices, and therefore also determines which method of production is to be employed at any particular level of the prices of the factors of production. By this means the indeterminateness of the problem is eliminated.

How much of the two factors of production is to be used obviously depends upon the ratio between the prices of the two. If this ratio alters in favour of one of the factors of production, so that it becomes cheaper in terms of the other, it will displace the other still more until a new *point of substitution* is reached at which the final substitutable quantities have the same price, and substitution is therefore a matter of indifference. The position of the point of substitution is thus dependent upon the interrelation of the prices of the factors of production.

Let us now suppose that in an undertaking employing only two factors of production (or groups of factors of production) which can continually displace one another, one factor is kept unchanged in quantity, while the quantity of the other is steadily augmented. We assume that this increase proceeds in equal increments, and that all prices remain constant, in which case each such increment has the same price. We can then select the increment in such a way that its price will be equal to one. The addition to output corresponding to the final increment is called the *marginal productivity* of the variable factor of production. When the best combination of the two factors of production has been arrived at, then clearly an increase in the variable factor of production by one increment will result in an addition to output, the price of which is the same as that of the particular increment of the factor of production. In other words, every pound that is devoted to the particular factor of production will manifest itself in a rise of one pound in the value of the output. The principle is expressed thus: the price of the factor of production is equal to its marginal productivity.

Just as some theorists have tried to base the theory of prices, or "value," on the concept of marginal utility (§ 11), so too it has been stated that marginal productivity is the determinant of price. The fundamental error is in both cases the same. Marginal productivity is not a given factor in the pricing problem, for the relative quantities of the various factors of production to be employed according to the principle of substitution can only be determined when prices are taken into account. Marginal productivity and price are, in fact, two completely similar unknowns in the pricing problem, and it is consequently impossible to present the one as the determining factor of the other. We must, moreover, bear in mind that marginal productivity can only be strictly defined in cases of continuous substitution in the sense we have indicated.

If the undertaking employs the variable factor of production to a less extent than is required by the principle of substitution at the given prices, every additional pound applied to that factor of production will effect an improvement in the economical operation of the undertaking, and will thus raise the value of the output by more than a pound. If the undertaking already employs the variable factor of production to a greater extent than is warranted by the principle of substitution, the effect is the reverse. An increase of the particular factor of production will in that event prejudice the economical working of the undertaking; it will still perhaps increase the value of the output, but not by an amount equal to the extra cost of production. It is only at the substitution point that an increase in the factor of production will lead to an equivalent increase in the value of the product. If far too little of a factor of production is employed, then obviously an augmentation of that factor of production must generally bring about a more than proportionate increase in the value of the output. This increase, however, gradually diminishes with every additional increment of the factor of production until, at the substitution point, it is equal to the price of the factor of production.

Changes in the relative use of co-operating factors of production are, from both a practical and a theoretical point of view, of great importance, and the effects of such changes therefore merit comprehensive study. In contrast with the frequently obscure discussions of "increasing" or "diminishing" returns which figure so prominently in economic literature, a more penetrating analysis must first of all examine the underlying changes, the nature of which we have indicated here.

If, for example, appropriate factors of production are applied in increasing quantities to a given piece of land, the value of the output will increase at first by amounts greater than the cost of those factors of production. As the use of factors of production continues to be extended, however, these amounts will gradually diminish until a point is reached at which the increase in value of the output is equal to the increase in cost, after which every further increase in the use of the particular factors of production brings about an increase in the value of the output which is less than the increase in cost. The economic importance of this relationship will be studied later, in the chapter on rent.

The fact that the extension of an undertaking leads in many cases to a relative increase in returns depends largely, as we have seen, upon the possibility of a better use of certain items of equipment which have a fixed cost. The increasing return then clearly means that a larger quantity of other factors of production can be profitably combined with that equipment, and thus merely shows that the most profitable combination of the two groups of factors of production has not yet been reached.

Thus far, we have invariably assumed that in the productive process under consideration only one commodity is produced. Indeterminateness in the cost of production may, however, also come about when a number of diverse commodities are produced from one and the same productive process. We will call these *joint products*. Frequently, the proportions between quantities of these products may be changed to a certain extent by a suitable modification of the method of production. We shall, however, first consider the simple case in which the given process of production brings forth two or more different products in a *fixed* proportion as to quantity. There are numerous instances in practice of productive processes which approximately realise this condition. In the Thomas process, for example, pig-iron and Thomas phosphate are simultaneously produced in definite proportions determined by the quality of the materials used. Our municipal gas-works produce gas and coke simultaneously. Cattle-breeders in the Argentine produce meat, hides, and bones. Wheat-growers produce wheat and straw. In all these cases the total cost of the joint products is fixed, but how much of that cost is to be allotted to one or other of the products remains undetermined. Here again, then, we come to a point where prices are indeterminate, and a supplementary principle of pricing is required in order to eliminate this indeterminateness.

How much one or other of a number of such joint products "really costs" cannot easily be said, and any attempt to answer this question is a pure waste of time. All that we can do is to find a principle in accordance with which we can fix the prices of such products. This is not a difficult matter, and the solution is really already to be found in the principle of scarcity. We need only assume that the process of production begins with the joint products, which are to be regarded as primary factors of production available in definite quantities. Then, according to the principle of scarcity, prices must be placed upon them high enough to adjust the demand for them to the available supplies. In other words, the prices of the joint products must be so regulated as to secure the sale of the entire quantity of each of them. The quantities of the joint products are, we assume, in a fixed proportion to each other, and the total quantity may therefore be expressed as a single arithmetical magnitude. This total quantity, again, determines the quantities of all the joint products, and once it is known we can, by following the stipulation indicated above, calculate the total prices of the joint products and consequently the selling prices of the total product. There thus exists a definite relationship between the price of the total product and the quantity of it which can be sold at that price. Hence we can now regard the aggregate of the joint products as the final outcome of a process of production which begins with the actual primary factors of production. The demand for this final product is given as soon as a price is fixed for it. This product thus occupies the same position in the pricing process as any other product, and the fixing of the price is determined in the usual way by the principle of scarcity.

We may refer to this method of fixing the price of joint products as the *principle of the pricing of joint products*. As we see, this *fourth* supplementary principle of pricing is merely a direct application of the principle of scarcity, and it thus has the same general validity. It is best expressed by saying that there is attached to the prices of joint products the condition that they shall all be completely disposed of, i.e. that the demand for these products shall be proportional to their relative quantities. In this way, the level of the prices of the joint products, and hence, too, the absolute volume of production, is fixed according to general rules in connection with the general pricing process.

This principle has become of great importance under modern industrial conditions in a large number of branches of production. This is especially true with regard to the economic use of waste materials for making various by-products, in which such extraordinary progress has been made in recent years.

Let us now turn to the case where the quantities of the joint products can be altered by a modification in the method of production. The fixing of prices is then determined for every given method of production in accordance with the principle we have just established. Thus it only remains for us to ask which method of production is to be employed, or, in other words, which relative combination of the joint products is to be chosen. This question clearly must be answered in terms of the principle of substitution; the cheapest method of production must be adopted. As long as only one product is produced, we can immediately decide which is the cheapest method of production; it is that method under which a unit cost of production will yield the greatest volume of output. This criterion cannot, however, be applied here without some reservation, because it cannot be said which is the greater of two quantities, each of which is composed of a number of differing products. Thus we cannot decide whether 50 lbs. of meat + 8 lbs. of wool is greater or less than 55 lbs. of meat + 7 lbs. of wool. The method of production which gives the greatest return can clearly only be determined when the relative prices of the products are given.

In order to solve this particular problem of price-fixing we may make it a condition that the method selected shall, at prices at which the products are completely disposed of in accordance with our fourth principle, yield a product which is greater, or at any rate not smaller, than that yielded by any other method. If two products are produced, and the method employed can be continually varied in such a way that a small diminution in one of the products is accompanied by a certain increase in the other, and *vice versa*, without any incidental change in the cost of production, then one feature of the correct solution of the problem is that, at the prices determined in accordance with our fourth supplementary principle, these final mutually substitutable quantities are equal in price. For if either quantity were priced higher than the other, a small change in the method of production could at the existing prices bring about a greater value of output, and the method selected could not be the most economically advantageous method.

The principle which emerges from these conditions is, as we can see, in effect to be regarded merely as an extension of the principle of substitution. If we assume the prices both of the factors of production and of the products to be given, the general principle of substitution embodies the requirement that the method of production employed cannot be replaced by any other in which the total price of the product per unit of cost of production is greater.

The principle of substitution as we have here extended it, together with the principle of the pricing of joint products, determines the problem, now before us, of the pricing of joint products which are produced in quantities varying in proportion.

§ 14 *The Organisation of the Modern Exchange Economy*

In the preceding sections of this chapter we examined the conditions required of the exchange economy by the general economic principle. We found that these conditions emerge under a system of prices which is governed by the principle of scarcity and the supplementary principles of pricing. As the supplementary principles are only of use in determining the conception of cost with greater precision, we may briefly refer to this system of prices as the fixing of prices on the basis of the principle of cost (§ 12). We obtain thereby a conception of the exchange economy in the widest sense, as we have made only that assumption which is essential to the exchange economy, namely, that there are within it independent individual economies which receive a money income in return for their share in the process of production, and which regulate their own consumption within the limits of the money resources at their disposal and thus give a direction to production. Our conclusions, therefore, hold good of every exchange economy, independently of its particular type of organisation or legal order. The realisation of the general economic principle must obviously be of vital importance to every exchange economy, since the degree of perfection with which it is achieved measures the efficiency of the particular economic order. The study of a system of prices based upon the principles in question must therefore always play a very considerable part in economic theory, in that it elucidates the essential processes within an exchange economy which satisfies the ideal requirements of economic operation.

If we wish to look further into actual economic life and into the existing economic organisation, we must inquire how far the requirement of economic operation is satisfied by that exchange economy. If our inquiry shows that this is substantially the case – that, in other words, our exchange economy is substantially governed by price-fixing on the basis of the principle of cost – then the principle of cost provides the necessary starting-point for the study of that exchange economy. This means that in the elementary theoretical study of our existing exchange economy we ignore any deviations from the principle of cost. In this we do not, of course, overlook the possibility of such deviations, but merely reserve consideration of them and of their disturbing effect for a separate inquiry. In so doing we act in the same way as the astronomer, who first describes the movement of a planet as though it were not affected by the other planets, thus reaching the Keplerian system, and then takes into special consideration the disturbance caused by the other planets. In order to proceed along these lines we need only make sure that the first movement is the essential one.

The organisation of the modern exchange economy is therefore to be tested by the degree in which it satisfies the requirements of the principle of cost. This will enable us to learn the *means* which our exchange economy employs in realising this principle. We shall find that they vary widely in character, and are subject to considerable change in practice as well as in political opinion. Hence, while they may be features of the present condition of the exchange economy, they may not have the essential character which is required in the fundamentals of a general theory of the exchange economy.

When the exchange economy was still in its infancy, during the Mercantilist period, it was held as a matter of course that it needed central control, which could at that time be exercised only by the State or by the towns. The division of human labour among the different callings and localities was governed by the guild system, and in other cases by legislation. The distribution of the other productive forces, too, was planned and controlled from above. Thus, for example, the Swedish iron industry, which at that time was very considerable, was localised in different parts of the country in such a way as to provide for each centre of the industry sufficient fuel from the surrounding forests and sufficient quantities of iron-ore, or, in the case of finishing works, sufficient pig-iron; in other words, the available factors of production were distributed in the way that seemed necessary in view of the conditions of transport at the time. By thousands of different measures the Mercantilist State protected the sale of the commodities it produced, and, moreover, even undertook to see to it that consumers were properly supplied in the case of the most important of all commodities, wheat. Only by means of a highly developed system of such regulations, the Mercantilist believed, was it possible to direct production by private enterprise, based on division of labour, along the proper channels, and to co-ordinate all economic activity and mould it into an integral national economy. There was, of course, a good deal of talk about liberty in the Mercantilist period, but the conception of liberty was a very narrow one judged by modern ideas, and nobody seriously questioned the need for a single authoritative control of economic activity.

The idea that an exchange economy, in which the whole of production is undertaken by private entrepreneurs working for their own profit, and which is split up into isolated partial processes, can automatically govern itself and form a coherent and comprehensive economy, and is thus without need of any single conscious control, is in strong contrast to the older views. This idea, which was so completely to revolutionise practical economic policy, was reserved for Liberalism. It was clearly developed by Adam Smith, the aim of whose economic policy was a social order "where things were left to follow their natural course, where there was perfect liberty, and where every man was perfectly free both to choose what occupation he thought proper, and to change it as often as he thought proper." The interest of the individual would then impel him to seek the most profitable employment. The productive forces are correctly distributed by this means among the various branches of production, no central control being necessary for this purpose. On the contrary, any attempt by the State to encroach by means of regulation upon economic life would probably produce a deterioration in the economic effectiveness of the particular society. Adam Smith gives us his view of the automatic regulation of the free economy in the classical words: "Every individual is continually exerting himself to find out the most advantageous employment for whatever capital he can command. It is his own advantage, indeed, and not that of the society which he has in view. But the study of his own advantage naturally, or rather necessarily, leads him to prefer that employment which is most advantageous to the society." "Every individual necessarily labours to render the annual revenue of the society as great as he can. He generally, indeed, neither intends to promote the public interest, nor knows how much he is promoting it. He intends only his own gain, and he is in this, as in many other cases, led by an invisible hand to promote an end which was no part of his intention."

Free competition is thus the means whereby the exchange economy is automatically regulated. But free competition can only take place if the economic individuals are not bound together by any common organisation. Even the social intercourse of people of the same occupation is detrimental to free competition, in that it may easily lead to a "conspiracy against the public," an attempt to raise prices. The ideal society is one which we may call "atomistic," consisting of isolated individuals who come into contact with each other in the economic field alone and over whom there is only a State, whose sole business is to attend to the legal order of the society.

The theory of the regulation of the exchange economy by free competition is very simple. The whole of the economy is conceived as a single market, in which prices are determined by supply and demand. As all buyers wish to buy at the lowest price, then under conditions of equilibrium no vendor will be able to demand a higher price than the others. There can, therefore, be only one price for each commodity. As soon as demand inclines predominantly to a particular commodity, sellers of it will take the opportunity to raise the price. This will diminish the demand until it can be met by the supply. If the price continued to rise, the demand would be so greatly diminished that the supply would be excessive and the sellers would accept a lower price in order to get rid of their supplies of that commodity. The market can therefore only be in equilibrium when prices are such as to bring about a coincidence between supply and demand. The market also regulates production. If insufficient productive forces are devoted to a particular branch of production, as a result of which the demand for the particular product cannot be satisfied at the existing price, the consequent rise in price will not only diminish the demand, but will also attract new productive forces to this particularly remunerative branch of production, and thus lead to an increase in production which must persist until equilibrium between supply and demand is reached. This increased production will, perhaps, restrict the rise in price a little, but in general the equilibrium attained implies a somewhat higher price. If, on the other hand, at a particular price, there is over-production in a certain branch of production, the relevant producers are forced to sell their products at a lower price. Production thus becomes less remunerative, and productive forces are withdrawn from that particular branch, thereby reducing the supply. At the same time the demand is stimulated by reason of the lower price, and equilibrium is restored at a definite price.

According to this theory, therefore, the operation of supply and demand under free competition would result in prices conforming to our principle of scarcity. These prices would cover, not only commodities, but also services and factors of production of all kinds; and this process of pricing would thus, on the one hand, be a general regulator as regards the choice of occupations, and particularly the distribution of the productive forces of society among the various branches of production, and, on the other hand, it would act as a regulator of the entire satisfaction of wants.

It is thus quite understandable that under these circumstances free competition should have been made the starting-point of the whole body of economic theory, and that the task of our science should have been seen to lie in the study of an exchange economy in which free competition is the rule. This point of view, however, is only justified if free competition really does produce those effects which the theory assumes, that is, if, in a general way at least, it determines prices according to the principle of cost and, moreover, does in fact predominantly rule our exchange economy. Even then, strictly speaking, it is only justified if free competition is an essential element in the process of pricing and in the functioning of the exchange economy in general. To what extent these conditions are satisfied we have now to inquire.

The regulation of production by free competition which the classical theory, for the reasons given, felt justified in accepting as a universal law, depends upon two important assumptions, which were nearer the truth a hundred or a hundred and fifty years ago than they are to-day.

In the first place, the theory of free competition assumes perfect *mobility* of all the factors of production, in that it must assume that productive forces can be transferred without friction from one branch of production to another, according to the prices prevailing at any time. However, in actual practice, production now employs fixed real capital to a great extent, and this fixed capital, when it can no longer be employed for its original purpose, either cannot be utilised at all for other purposes, or can be so utilised or transferred elsewhere only at a more or less substantial loss. The capital which was used by a boot manufacturer to obtain stitching machines cannot, when the boot trade comes to a standstill on account of over-production, be withdrawn from that branch of production and employed in another. It is tied up once for all in the boot manufacturing industry. The same is true of most specialised machinery, and to a less extent of general machine tools, factory premises, etc.; and it is, above all, true of railways and similar fixed constructions, such as canals, gas-works, etc. If a railway is un-remunerative, it is unfortunate, for the shareholders at least, but there is no remedy. The capital is "locked up," to use the common expression, in that particular undertaking. Such locking-up of capital also exists, to a certain extent, in the case of specialised professional work.

In these circumstances, therefore, the regulation of production cannot be as complete as the theory supposes. If, on account of an excess of supply over demand, the price of a product falls, and no longer covers the cost of production in a particular undertaking, that undertaking would, on this theory, go out of business, and supply would thus be diminished, so that equilibrium would ultimately be restored. The theory has concluded from this that price must always cover the cost of production, or at any rate that it must cover it in the long run despite any casual temporary disturbances. Experience shows that this conclusion is hardly justified. Once capital is locked up in an undertaking in the manner described above, that undertaking need not be closed down simply because the price of the product does not cover the whole of the cost or production. As long as the price makes it possible to cover the current expenses of the business and to obtain a return, however small, on the capital tied up in it, it is better to continue producing than to abandon the undertaking. In the latter case the capital might be completely lost; in the former it does still yield a return. In these circumstances an undertaking which does not cover the whole of its cost of production can be maintained for long periods. In periods of industrial depression production below actual cost is of common occurrence.

All real capital must, however, as a rule, be used up in course of time. Most real capital, in effect, is used up comparatively quickly by the normal process of production. The effects of an economically unsound use of capital are therefore limited in duration. The exchange economy is thus over and over again faced with the task of creating new real capital, and is to that extent always in a position to direct its new production of capital in conformity with the requirements of the principle of cost. Under such conditions the principle of cost represents the normal pricing process of the exchange economy, about which the actual pricing process is always oscillating. Free competition, however, in consequence of the lack of mobility of fixed capital (and also of labour), is not capable of completely effecting this normal settlement of prices.

The theory which regards free competition as the means of realising a normal scale of prices further assumes the existence of a *market*. What is essentially required of this market is that there shall be a large number of small sellers together with a large number of small buyers. The term "small" here means that the individual's demand or supply is, in relation to the total demand or supply of the market, insignificant, or, as is sometimes said, a magnitude of the second order, and so has only a subordinate influence on the market. A stable equilibrium is possible in that case only, as both theory and recent experience have shown.

Such markets are present in different spheres in the exchange economy, but it would be an error to suppose that they arise spontaneously, as it were, or that they are a "natural" phenomenon. Free competition was, in the main, conceived by classical economics simply as non-interference on the part of public authority, an absence of conscious organisation and of regulated co-operation. But these purely negative assumptions do not create a market. The modern municipality, no less than the mediæval, organises a market for foodstuffs, builds market-halls and slaughter-houses, appoints brokers, and establishes some place where quotations may be made, and in this way ensures a regular supply of the necessaries of life at prices which correspond approximately to the actual scarcity of the factors of production. Regular quotation of prices, and an organisation which makes sales at those prices possible, are necessary conditions of any highly developed market. These conditions are best fulfilled by the great stock and produce exchanges, which likewise have their proper place in a system of prices corresponding to the actual state of supply and demand, but which are, as is well known, the results of a strict and highly developed organisation. In all these cases where a market is created, there prevails a situation which corresponds most closely to what is rather vaguely described as a state of "free competition." There is thus free competition, to a certain extent, in our modern exchange economy, but that free competition is not the inherent condition, as it were, of an entirely unorganised and unregulated exchange economy, but rather the result of deliberate efforts to create conditions for a rational fixing of prices in accordance with the principle of scarcity.

It is only when there is an organised market of this sort that sales are so secured that it is possible to produce "for the market"; and only then, too, are supplies so secured that consumers may expect to be supplied by the market. If that condition is not fulfilled, we have only a vague "market" – a hope of finding buyers – for which it is possible to produce only with great difficulty, if at all, particularly in view of the fact that, as there is no regular market, there are no general price quotations. It then often happens, too, that buyers cannot always rely upon finding a seller. In all such cases we can perceive strong tendencies to put an end to free competition and to bring about closer relationship between producer and consumer.

Under modern conditions the technical character of industrial enterprises and the superiority of large-scale industry make it necessary to have great industrial units over an increasingly large field. Railway enterprise is probably the most conspicuous instance of this, and next to it come other industries which direct communications, such as telegraph and telephone undertakings. But even in the sphere of production in the narrower sense, such as the iron, electrical, electro-chemical, sugar, and other industries, it is often necessary to have large industrial units.

If these industrial units are large even in proportion to the total demand, there can be no market, free competition being then incapable of bringing about equilibrium. We must here distinguish three different cases.

In the first place, we have to consider the case of a few large producers as against a large number of small consumers. In that case, if any branch of production were particularly profitable, new undertakings would be set up or existing ones enlarged, according to the theory of free competition, and thus the supply would be increased by just such an amount that profits would fall to the normal level, but would not go below it. But equilibrium cannot be brought about in this way if the addition of even a single under-taking means a relatively large increase in production, or if even a moderate extension of one undertaking materially prejudices selling prospects in the others. This is very often the case under modern conditions. In some industries – for example, in the manufacture of steel rails, in the weaving of curtains, and, to a less degree, in the sugar industry – the smaller business unit which is technically and economically practicable is already so large that one or a few under-takings are sufficient to supply the wants of a whole country of small or medium size. In such cases any increase of competition will seriously threaten the returns of the whole industry. If a new undertaking enters into competition with those already in existence, or if one of those undertakings is considerably extended, the result will in all probability be that all the undertakings will become un-remunerative. As, however, a considerable amount of capital is tied up in each of these undertakings, none of them will be aban-doned simply because the entire cost of production is not covered, but the competition can still be continued and intensified for a long time to come. In such circumstances those concerned are simply compelled to protect themselves against a free competition which cannot be reconciled with sound business activity, and thus in the modern business world we find a strong tendency to organise the satisfaction of wants in some other way which excludes free compe-tition. This tendency manifests itself in the creation of cartels and trusts, whereby the whole body of consumers is either divided among the different producers or is supplied by a single selling organisation of those producers. In either case a buyer will find only *one* seller, and there is no longer a market or free competition among sellers.

The difficulties of free competition are seen very clearly in the case of railway enterprise and other large transport undertakings, and also in undertakings for the supply of water, gas, and power. The fact that one railway is very profitable does not prove that an additional railway over the same stretch would be profitable. If a competing railway appears, possibly neither will yield any profit, and the capital tied up in them is to a greater or less extent lost.

Free competition in the real sense is, in effect, not possible in this sphere, because public concessions are required in order to get possession of the necessary land. As a rule, the public authority deliberately gives such a concession the character, more or less, of a monopoly, accompanying it, however, with detailed directions regarding the rates to be charged, relations with other railways, and so on. There is apparent in all these regulations an attempt to maintain the principle of cost in those cases in which it cannot be realised through free competition.

Secondly, we have to deal with the case of a large number of small producers as against a few large consumers, of which the relation between sugar-beet growers and the sugar industry may be taken as an example. The farmer cannot produce sugar-beet for an indefinite market. The cost of transport is too high to allow the beet to be sent any great distance, and the individual beet-farmer has, as a rule, only one buyer to produce for. As he is absolutely dependent upon this buyer, he must establish some definite relationship with him, and contract with him in advance as to deliveries. The sugar factory, for its part, must have a guarantee that it will be supplied with beet. The tendency then is for the sugar factory to deal collectively with the particular beet-growers, and for the conditions of supply to become uniform. By this means the price will, as a rule, cover the beet-growers' cost of production.

Thirdly, there may be a few large producers as against a few large consumers. Free competition and a market, in the real sense of those terms, are then impossible. The producers cannot produce in the mere hope that they will be able to sell. The consumers are equally unable to rely on being always able to satisfy their wants. It is absolutely necessary to establish closer relations between producer and consumer.

For the security of both producers and consumers it is necessary to conclude contracts for supplies, often over long periods. German iron-works provide for their need of Swedish ores by means of supply contracts which often stretch over a period of ten years or more. On the other hand, pig-iron producers wish to sell their output for long periods in advance. We find, too, that modern large-scale industry works to a great extent on commission in the same way as the older artisans used to do. It is only the standardised products of the "heavy" industries that are to some extent produced for the market. The consumption of pig-iron, for example, is so enormous that even the largest smelting-works may be regarded as a small producer relatively to the world market. There are, therefore, certain markets with regular quotations for this commodity (Glasgow, Cleveland, Pittsburg). On the other hand, locomotives, railway carriages, steamships, bridges, large iron constructions for the building industry, large power-machines, munitions of war, and great masses of semi-manufactured goods are manufactured to order in the particular industries. There is, of course, a tendency towards standardisation – rolling-mills aim at producing only certain "standard sections," and engineers must construct accordingly. In the engineering industry small machine tools, dynamos, engines, etc., are standardised. The aim is thus, wherever possible, to create the conditions necessary for production for the market. But in order to ensure the possibility of being able to buy and sell, modern large-scale industry often finds itself compelled to establish close relations in a backward as well as in a forward direction. The method chiefly used for this purpose is that of acquiring shares, so that a large industrial undertaking often comes to be "interested" in a number of undertakings of quite a different kind; for example, steel-works acquire interests in blast-furnaces and docks, the electrical industry acquires interests in the metallurgical industry, in tramways, and in lighting equipment, etc. In more recent times this method of shareholdings has come to be replaced by that of complete ownership, subsidiary companies being set up for the purpose of supplying the parent undertaking with materials or semi-manufactured goods or finding a market for its products. With the same object in view, existing enterprises engaged upon consecutive stages of production are brought together under a single control. This process is known as that of the *integration* of industry. Integration has made particularly great progress in the iron and steel industry, of which the American Steel Trust provides a typical instance, and in the electrical industry, in which the large undertakings control the whole process of production from the raw material right up to the many varied uses of their products in central power stations, electric railways, electric light undertakings, and so on, extending even to administration of these undertakings. In these cases we find the whole of production, from the raw material to the final satisfaction of wants, under the control of a single undertaking. In proportion as the integration of industry proceeds, so production for sale, for a market, disappears from the intermediate stages. At the final stage the work is very often done to order – as, for example, in the case of munitions of war, public lighting installation, railway material, and so on – or for directly supplying the wants of the consumer; but in all the preparatory stages production is carried on to the order of the succeeding stage. In these circumstances competition is of effect in regulating production to the extent only to which it affects the final stage, and here it is always important. When contracts are placed by public authorities or by large associations, keen competition frequently develops between large undertakings which are in a position to undertake the order, as a result of which the price is not infrequently forced below the actual cost-price. To prevent this, and, naturally too, to make an additional profit wherever possible, the undertakings concerned come to more or less secret agreements for the purpose of sharing orders and profits. In many cases a large undertaking also has various means of excluding certain customers from competition and keeping them for itself.

Even when competition between the different undertakings in a particular industry is completely eliminated, the fixing of prices is not entirely arbitrary. It may still be necessary to compete with other means of satisfying the same want. Thus electric light undertakings are in constant competition with undertakings for the supply of light by other means, such as oil and gas. This competition compels the particular industries concerned to keep prices as low as possible, and by this means the principle of cost is for the most part maintained. Even if there should be no competitive means of satisfying the same want, the producer must none the less still bear in mind that he is competing against all those producers who propose to satisfy other wants. For the distribution by consumers of their means among the various branches of the satisfaction of wants is dependent upon the prices of commodities, and there is therefore constant competition among all producers to attract the purchasing power of consumers.

According to the classical theory, wages, too, would be determined by free competition among the workers on the labour market. This competition was supposed to be realised by the removal of all obstacles to the individual worker's freedom of movement. The modern community, however, makes use of highly developed organisations, both of workers and of employers, for the purpose of wage regulation, and as a result so-called free competition is largely eliminated. The perfect trade union has a monopoly of labour within a particular trade, but is normally open to all skilled labour in that branch. The monopoly cannot, then, be used arbitrarily for forcing wages up, because, although the trade union has no competitor in its own trade, it has to face the competition of other trades that meet the same want, and has always to participate in the general competition for the purchasing power of consumers. Consequently, wages cannot be raised above a level that will maintain a demand corresponding to the supply of labour. In so far as the characteristic policy of trade unions brings about uniformity of wage-rates and of other conditions of labour for work of the same kind and quality, the regulation of wages under modern forms of organisation is substantially based on the principle of scarcity. There are, of course, exceptions to this rule: thus attempts are made to withhold the supply of labour by artificial means, and in this way to raise wages above the rate determined by the principle of scarcity. Such attempts, however, are always resisted and are regarded as excesses on the part of the labour movement.

This brief survey of the actual forms of modern economic life is sufficient for us to be able to draw the following conclusion. Free competition does not, as the theory claims, guarantee that prices will be fixed in accordance with the principle of cost, nor can it be said that our modern exchange economy is ruled by free competition, for the latter has been completely eliminated from large and important spheres of economic life by recent developments. Competition, it is true, still plays a very considerable part in modern economic life, but the forms which it takes differ essentially from the ideal of *free* competition. Even the conception of free competition is very vague. The negative definition of free competition as the absence of any regulation or organisation excludes the essential condition under which modern society succeeds, in certain spheres, in establishing competition which serves towards the realisation of the principle of cost. It would be very difficult to construct a satisfactory positive definition of free competition, the conception of which, in fact, is absolutely inconsistent with a matter which is of considerable importance under modern economic conditions, namely, the economic superiority of the large-scale business. In cases where this superiority is apparent, free competition is logically bound to bring into being its own antithesis – monopoly; for at what intermediate stage would the accepted superiority of the large-scale undertaking permit of a state of equilibrium under free competition? This result cannot be avoided without forms of organisation which interfere, by way of strict regulations, in economic life, and thus mean the elimination of free competition in the cases we have considered.

In these circumstances, it should be clear that, to take free competition as the starting-point for a general theory of prices is of very little use. If we impose on the basic assumption of our theory the stricter scientific condition that it shall not restrict the applicability of the theory unnecessarily, but shall be a necessary assumption, then it is still more obvious that free competition cannot be taken as the starting-point of our theory. For there is no doubt whatever that, even without free competition, prices can be fixed in the same way as they would be fixed, according to the theory, under free competition. We shall see in the next section that this method of pricing would have to be maintained in a society which rejected private enterprise and therefore excluded free competition. But even our own society at present, as we have seen, succeeds in many cases where free competition is not possible in fixing approximately normal prices in other ways.

The question as to the extent to which prices in our present exchange economy are governed by the principle of cost can now be answered by stating that the principle of cost in some degree rer esents a normal condition about which actual pricing oscillates. Any appreciable deviation of prices from the principle of cost gives rise, as a rule, to counteracting forces. Competition between a few relatively large undertakings, which might easily force prices down below costs, is avoided by industrial combinations of various kinds. The primary motive behind the whole movement towards concentration, which is characteristic of the present time, is undoubtedly a desire for protection against unprofitable and, in the long run, ruinous competition, and to ensure prices which will cover costs. It is true that some combines and single undertakings which have secured a monopoly try to make use of that monopoly for the purpose of fixing prices that will yield them an abnormally large profit. Such attempts, however, usually provoke a strong reaction, either in the form of competition in the same trade or in a trade that satisfies the same want in another way, or in the form of special protective measures on the part of society in the sphere of legislation, transport policy, particularly as regards railway rates, tariff policy, and so on. Reaction of this kind shows that pricing in accordance with the principle of cost is to be regarded as the normal procedure, and is in effect universally so regarded. In the same way, attempts at organisation on the part of the workers are largely due to the urgent need for protection against pressure on wages which is inconsistent with sound pricing principles, and attempts by labour organisations to raise wages above the level fixed by the normal pricing process are strongly resisted. By fixing maximum charges when granting concessions to railways, electricity undertakings, gas-works, etc., by encouraging competition by appropriate measures, as in the case of transport, by organising markets, and so on, public bodies endeavour to keep prices as far as possible in agreement with the principle of cost. Consumers' co-operation, too, which aims at securing the most direct relation possible between producer and consumer, serves towards the realisation of the principle of cost. The business world likewise recognises the operation of the principle of cost, as is clear, among other things, from the universal requirement that undertakings which are permanently incapable of covering their real cost of production shall put themselves in a position to do so by writing down their capital by a suitable amount – a requirement which is, moreover, simply a consequence of the general rule, which conforms with the principle of scarcity, according to which durable goods, once they have been produced, are valued purely in terms of the return which they yield (cf. § 22).

Consequently, although, in view of the high degree of flexibility of modern economic life, prices can never be completely fixed in exact conformity with the principle of cost, this method of pricing on the whole indicates the position of equilibrium round which actual prices fluctuate, and is generally regarded as the normal procedure in the exchange economy and as being desirable in principle. If we wish to obtain a preliminary comprehensive picture of our present exchange economy, showing its essential features, we should clearly be well advised in the circumstances to study the fixing of prices on the basis of the principle of cost, in conformity with the principle of scarcity and the supplementary principles of pricing. As these principles merely represent consequences of the general economic principle for the exchange economy, the study of such a process of pricing must be important for any exchange economy, and must *make manifest the essential functioning of the general exchange economy.*

There is no doubt that all economic theory has been directed towards the study of this process of pricing. But if we wish to make this normal pricing process the subject of our study, then, from what we have been saying, we are not justified in proceeding from the assumption of free competition. It is more accurate, and certainly more natural, to direct our inquiry immediately upon the normal pricing process.

§ 15 *The Socialist State*

The principles of pricing are, as we have shown (§§ 11–13), simply consequences of the general economic principle for the exchange economy. We have taken the exchange economy in the widest sense, stipulating only that it shall allow the individual freedom of occupation and freedom of consumption within the limits imposed by his means. It follows that the principles of pricing hold good for every exchange economy, and are independent of the particular organisation of production within the economy. With regard to the latter, our present economy is marked by a predominance of private enterprise and private ownership of the material factors of production. These characteristics, it is true, have a considerable effect on the distribution of income, and consequently on the demand for different goods and on the direction of consumption in the society, and have, therefore, in the long run, a certain significance in the actual fixing of prices, though they do not affect the validity of the principles of pricing. These principles would remain unchanged in an exchange economy in which the State had assumed control of production and reserved to itself the ownership of the material factors of production.

Such a society is known as "socialistic." The name is thus used to indicate a closed exchange economy in which the whole of production is directed solely by and for the society itself through some ultimate State authority appointed for the purpose, all the material factors of production being the property of the society, but in which there is still freedom of occupation and of consumption to the extent to which this is essential in the exchange economy. This definition, it is true, does not apply to every economic order which is described as "socialistic." But the socialistic economy as defined in this way is theoretically the simplest, and represents a true type, whereas the others are to be regarded as varying and, in part, rather vague intermediate forms between it and an economic system which, like our present economic system, leaves production to a number of different economic units which pursue their own interest.

The study of pricing under a typically socialistic system is from several points of view useful and profitable in economic theory. It shows absolutely clearly, in the first place, how untrue it is that free competition is a theoretically necessary condition for giving effect to the principle of cost, and of what universal importance the principle of cost is in the exchange economy. Secondly, the study of pricing under a socialist system is useful for the reason that the socialist economy may to a certain extent be regarded as the simplest in theory, and, therefore, many features of the exchange economy, which under the present system are rather complicated, can be more easily surveyed under a socialist system and viewed in their proper connection. Thirdly, a comparison of the present system with the socialist system enables us to test actual economic processes and institutions as to their necessity. Fourthly, the study of pricing in the socialist state is important in so far as it allows us to correct those misconceptions of the possible nature of a socialist system which have been so extravagantly fostered by unrestrained imagination and political rhetoric.

We do not intend to consider here the practical possibility, and still less, of course, the desirability, of giving effect to a socialist system. We are concerned solely with pricing, and the consequent distribution of productive forces among the various branches of production in what we conceive to be a typical socialist economy.

How, then, are we to conceive an economic system of this kind? Collective wants must of course be collectively met by the socialist society itself through specific organisations, in the same way as under the present system. There is, for the rest, no reason why the socialist society should extend the sphere of operation of the gratis principle; for this principle belongs to Communism, not to Socialism. If we wish to examine a typical socialist system, we must distinguish it as clearly as possible from the communist system, though this in effect is only rarely done in political discussion. Our socialist economy must thus essentially be based on the free exchange of personal services and means of satisfying personal wants. It is then, however, substantially an exchange economy, and if the general requirement of economic operation is fulfilled it is also an exchange economy governed by the principle of cost.

The socialist economy, like every highly developed exchange economy, is also a money economy. It is true that there has been much talk of the socialist system dispensing with money. Many of the early Socialists, such as Robert Owen, even made the exclusion of money one of the main points in the socialist programme. Ideas of this kind are, however, based on a misconception as to the nature of money, a failure to recognise the essence of the idea of money. As we have shown (§ 7), money is essentially a scale of reckoning in which the exchange economy expresses all prices. The socialist society, too, must use such a scale of reckoning if it recognises the fundamental principle of the exchange economy. Many even of the clearest socialist thinkers have thought that reckoning in money should be replaced by reckoning in "hours of work." But changing the name does not change the nature of the matter. Reckoning in hours of work, too, is reckoning in money. According to the usual proposals, the socialist state would, in return for the number of hours worked, give vouchers which would be used in buying goods at prices stated in terms of hours worked. But these vouchers, which are obviously a practical necessity in some form or other, are undoubtedly a means of payment, and in that respect perform the function of money. Consequently, the socialist economy is a completely developed money economy.

It is not, of course, necessary that the abstract unit of reckoning in the money-scale of the socialist economy should be a real work-hour. Since all work-hours cannot be valued equally, it would rather have to be an ideal or "normal" work-hour. Work must be measured in so many "normal work-hours" per hour's work actually performed, or according to the volume of output produced, or in a term of a unit of work calculated in some other way. All prices of goods and services placed at the disposal of its members by the socialist state must be calculated in terms of these normal work-hours. As the members of that society have no income from the ownership of material factors of production, wages constitute the individual's entire income. Within the limits of that income the individual has complete freedom to satisfy his wants according to the prices prevailing.

In these circumstances it follows, for precisely the same reasons as we gave above in connection with pricing in the general exchange economy, that the socialist state is obliged to calculate the prices of the goods to be supplied to consumers primarily in accordance with the principle of scarcity. That state has no method of keeping the demand for a commodity in adjustment with the available supplies of it other than that of placing upon the commodity a price high enough to effect this. This fixing of prices must clearly extend to the whole of the book-keeping of the society, and thus cover the whole of production. The prices of the factors of production, too, are thus determined through the principle of scarcity. The demand of consumers is indirectly a demand for factors of production, which demand can be adequately restricted only by placing suitable prices on the factors of production. The principle of scarcity thus has exactly the same application to the socialist economy as to the present economic system, except that in a socialist society subject to a single rational control it would, in fact, have to be maintained much more completely than is possible under the present system. From this it follows as a matter of course that the supplementary principles of pricing, too, have the same application to the socialist economy as to the present economic system.

What we have been saying about pricing in the socialist economy in general applies particularly to labour. The price of every kind of labour must be just high enough adequately to restrict the demand for that labour. As long as the society recognises the right of the individual worker to the value of the economic return on his work, his wage must correspond to that price. It is generally emphasised by Socialists that the socialist system would put an end to the wage-system, and this, they argue, would mean that the worker's wage would be determined on some objective basis or other and not by the state of the market for the time being. This, we can see, is wrong. Wages in a rationally governed socialist economy must always be in adjustment with the state of the labour market, which is equivalent to saying that wages are determined by pricing in accordance with the principle of scarcity and the supplementary principles. To what extent the socialist state would be able to control the state of the market itself by other measures, is another question. We shall see later (§ 38) that this is possible to a certain extent by appropriate regulation of the system of education under a

socialist system as well as under our present system. If the socialist
state were to attempt to go beyond this, and regulate the labour
market by restricting the free choice of occupation or the mobility
of labour, or by controlling births, etc., in order to create a market
situation which would permit a scale of wages regarded as suitable
on objective grounds irrespective of the state of the market, then
this would of course be possible to a certain extent, but only to a
certain extent – for even the socialist state could hardly overcome
the natural scarcity of certain natural gifts; but it would amount to
an infringement of the individual's right of disposal over his own
labour and particularly of his personal liberty, which would bring
the socialist state perilously near to the position of a slave state,
and would, at all events, deprive it of the essential features of an
exchange economy.

In what follows we shall have numerous opportunities of verify-
ing the necessity of economic processes by examining the conditions
of the socialist economy we have analysed, and in many cases we
shall reach conclusions which are opposed to generally accepted
ideas.

CHAPTER IV

THE MECHANISM OF PRICING

§ 16 *Arithmetical Treatment of the Problem of Equilibrium*

In the preceding chapter we ascertained that the principles governing pricing in any exchange economy are necessary consequences of the general economic principle. The reader who has grasped these principles is thus now able to form an accurate idea of the general nature of pricing and has a safe foundation for the treatment of most of the problems of theoretical economics. The science, however, also sets problems which require a profounder examination of the mechanism of pricing. These relate mainly, on the one hand, to the controversial nature of the causal sequence in the pricing process, and, on the other hand, to an important problem of monetary theory, with which we shall deal later – the degree of definiteness of the problem of pricing. In order to illustrate clearly the mechanism of pricing, it is necessary to present the relation between the various factors in the price-fixing process in mathematical form. This is not to be understood as meaning that it is necessary to represent the pricing process by difficult mathematical expressions which are beyond the grasp of persons of average education. The essentials of the mechanism can be grasped by anyone with a general acquaintance with equations with several unknown quantities. The mathematical presentations of facts in the first two sections of this chapter need therefore deter nobody from reading them.

The work is, however, so arranged that these paragraphs may be omitted without interrupting the general connection. The reader, in that case, will simply have to put aside any thought of a deeper study of the problems just mentioned.

In conformity with the conclusions drawn in the preceding chapter, we have to consider here a self-contained community based on exchange, in which the determination of prices is governed entirely by the principle of scarcity and the principles incidental to it. It is immaterial for the purposes of our present inquiry how such a state of affairs is brought about. We know that prices can be fixed in this way in economies which are very differently organised, and particularly that our existing economy approximately effects this by widely varying methods. In this section we shall first assume that, with regard to cost of production, there is no indefiniteness of the kind mentioned in § 13, and that the principle of scarcity is therefore sufficient for the complete determination of prices. [1]

Let us first consider the simple case, corresponding to § 11, where the influence of production does not affect the problem, and the quantities of goods available to consumers in a particular period are given; which is equivalent to assuming that production is invariable and fixed once for all. Let us call these quantities the supply of the particular commodities, and represent them by $S_1, S_2 \ldots S_n$, where n is the number of different commodities.

We shall assume that consumers and producers are different individuals. Where a producer consumes part of his own product, we shall consider him in his capacity of consumer as a separate individual. Thus any consumption on the part of producers is not to be deducted beforehand from the supply, but is to be compared with the total supply in the same way as consumption in any other form.

We first assume that the quantity of money which every consumer expends on the satisfaction of his wants in the period under consideration is fixed in advance. Given such conditions, it is obvious that the demand of each consumer for the different commodities during the period is fixed, once the prices of these commodities are fixed.

The relation between the demand for and the price of a commodity is most effectively shown where, as independent variable, the price of the commodity is chosen. If we then vary the price, we can determine how much of the particular commodity an individual will buy at any particular price, or, in other words, how individual demand varies with the price. The result of this inquiry can be expressed in tabular form; or else individual demand – the quantity

---

[1] See Cassel: "Grundriss einer elementaren Preislehre," *Zeitschrift für die gesamte Staatswissenschaft*, 1899.

of a commodity which an individual will buy at a given price – can be conceived of as a function of price, the form of this function expressing the personal valuation.

The advantage of this way of expressing individual demand is emphasised when one wishes to deal with the demand of several individuals together. We then have a common independent variable, the price, and we know the demand of any particular consumer at every value of this variable. These demands are each represented by a number which expresses how many units of the particular commodity the consumer in question wishes to buy. These quantities can therefore be added together; in this way we get the conception of the total demand for the particular commodity. This, too, can be shown in the form of a table giving the total quantity of the commodity which is demanded at any given price; or we can represent this aggregate demand as a function of the price.

If, however, we examine the demand-function rather more closely, we find that it also includes, as variables, the prices of all other commodities. The demand of the individual consumer for a certain commodity is, as we have seen (§ 11), not fixed until the prices of all commodities which can be the object of his demand are given. Not until this is done has he all the data which influence him in regulating his consumption within the limits imposed by his means; only then is he in a position to determine his demand for any particular commodity.

The demand of the individual consumer, and hence also the total demand of consumers in the aggregate, for any particular commodity is thus determined by the prices of the n commodities. If we represent the total demand for the n commodities in the given period by $D_1, D_2 \ldots D_n$, we can then express these magnitudes as functions of the n prices, thus:

$$(1) \quad D_1 = F_1 \,(p_1 \ldots p_n)$$
$$D_2 = F_2 \,(p_1 \ldots p_n)$$
$$\cdot \qquad \cdot \qquad \cdot \qquad \cdot \qquad \cdot \qquad \cdot \qquad \cdot \qquad \cdot$$
$$D_n = F_n \,(p_1 \ldots p_n)$$

where $p_1 \ldots p_n$ are the prices of the n commodities.

Now, the demand for any particular commodity, given a state of equilibrium, must coincide with the supply of it, since the fixing of prices, in accordance with the principle of scarcity, must be such as to restrict demand so as to satisfy it with the available supply of commodities. It follows therefore that:

$$D_1 = S_1, \; D_2 = S_2 \; \ldots \; D_n = S_n$$

and hence, according to (1):

$$
\begin{aligned}
(2) \quad & F_1 \, (p_1 \, \ldots \, p_n) = S_1 \\
& F_2 \, (p_1 \, \ldots \, p_n) = S_2 \\
& \quad \cdot \qquad \cdot \qquad \cdot \\
& F_n \, (p_1 \, \ldots \, p_n) = S_n
\end{aligned}
$$

To solve the pricing problem in the simple case considered here, we have therefore only to regard the n prices as the unknowns in the problem and to assume them according to the usual mathematical method to be given. We are then in a position to express the demand for the n goods at these prices in conformity with equations (1), whence equations (2) follow as a consequence of the principle of scarcity. This series of equations contains n equations for determining the n unknown prices; which is, in general, sufficient for determining the n unknown quantities. In the present case, where the money expenditure of consumers is given beforehand, prices, too, are obviously fixed at their absolute level. As soon as the prices are known, however, the demand of the individual consumer, and also the aggregate demand, for any particular commodity can be calculated. Since the demand is satisfied at the prices so calculated, the whole problem of the distribution of the commodities available for consumers is solved.

That the problem of pricing for each separate commodity cannot be dealt with in isolation is seen to be due to the fact that the demand for a commodity depends not upon the price of that particular commodity alone, but upon the prices of all commodities in general. It is this fact which necessitates the representation of the pricing process by a series of simultaneous equations, such as our series (2). The homogeneity of the pricing process cannot be adequately conveyed in any other way.

We have assumed here that the supply is fixed, i.e. that during the particular period commodities are available, or will be provided by production, in unvarying quantities, fixed in advance. Let us now abandon this assumption and introduce the whole question of production into the pricing problem. As we intend in this section to consider a pricing process based entirely on the principle of scarcity, we shall assume that the cost of production of any particular commodity is clearly determined by the prices of the factors of production.

In our discussion of the present problem we must consider a continuous process of production, and must present in arithmetical form the conditions, established in § 12, of equilibrium in a society with unvarying prices. We shall first deal with the simplest case – that of a stationary society.

The limits to the production of new commodities are imposed, as we saw in § 3, by the scarcity of the factors of production. The restriction upon the satisfaction of wants is simply referred back, through production, to the scarcity of the factors of production. The general nature of the factors of production, too, was indicated in the third section. Here, where we are particularly concerned with the mechanism of pricing, we must assume the quantities of the factors of production as given. To provide a concrete foundation for our inquiry, we may take as types of the factors of production, labour, the raw materials provided by nature, and the services of durable goods already in existence. The answer to the question as to how far these factors of production may be regarded as primary, or are themselves reproducible, must be reserved for the next Book, as must also the complete and final analysis of the factors of production. There we shall be able to deal with the question of how far the factors of production, although not reproducible, are nevertheless subject in another way, varying in degree according to the quantities available, to the influence of the pricing process. Here we must be content merely to assume a series of factors of production to be primary factors, and available in given quantities. Let r be the number of these factors of production, and R_1, R_2 ... R_r the quantities of them which are available in a given period. This period, which we may call the "income period," or, if we select a unit of time for the purpose, the "unit period," may, if the productive process is sufficiently uniform, be made as short as we choose; it may, according to the nature of the problem in hand, represent, for example, a day, a week, or a year.

With the help of these factors of production, commodities of n different kinds are produced. To produce the unit quantity of commodity 1, quantities a_{11} ... a_{1r} of the factors of production may be necessary; for the unit quantity of commodity 2, quantities a_{21} a_{2r} of the same factors of production may be necessary, and so on; finally, for the unit quantity of commodity n, the quantity a_{n1} ... a_{nr}. These quantities may be called "technical coefficients." They represent the technical conditions of production. As we have assumed these conditions to be fixed, the technical coefficients are to be regarded as given magnitudes in the problem. Obviously, several a may be equal to zero, since not all the factors of production are necessary for the production of any particular commodity.

With regard to the significance of these technical coefficients, the following observation may be made: the production of a unit quantity of a commodity requires in general the use of factors of production belonging to a whole series of different unit periods. Production is only completed, and the finished product made available for consumption, in the last of these periods. Our a designate primarily the total quantity of the factors of production of each particular kind which are required in this way for the production of the unit quantity of any commodity. As such, they are aggregates of quantities of factors of production of different unit periods. In the stationary state, however, production is maintained at a constant level. The manufacture of a commodity of a certain kind is therefore repeated in every unit period. In order that the unit quantity of a commodity shall result from this continuous productive process in each unit period, there must be available in each such period a definite quantity of factors of production. The demands which the continually repeated production of finished goods imposes on the factors of production in a given period are totalled and determine this quantity. It is, therefore, obviously the same as the quantity of factors of production of different unit periods which is necessary for the production of a definite unit quantity of the commodity. Our a thus designate the quantities of factors of production defined both in the first and in the second way.

The necessary limitation of demand, according to the principle of scarcity, must now be secured by uniform prices; that is to say, there must be one price for every single factor of production as well as for every finished article. We now take the prices of the different factors of production as the unknowns in the pricing problem. Let us for the moment assume these unknowns to be given, and let us represent them by $q_1 \ldots q_r$. The price of each of the n finished goods can now be calculated :

$$(3) \quad a_{11} q_1 + a_{12} q_2 + \ldots + a_{1r} q_r = p_1$$
$$a_{21} q_1 + a_{22} q_2 + \ldots + a_{2r} q_r = p_2$$
$$\bullet \qquad \bullet \qquad \bullet \qquad \bullet \qquad \bullet \qquad \bullet$$
$$a_{n1} q_1 + a_{n2} q_2 + \ldots + a_{nr} q_r = p_n$$

Once the prices of the finished goods are known, however, then, according to what has just been said, the aggregate demand for each commodity in each unit period is known and can be calculated by means of the following series of equations:

$$(4) \quad D_1 = F_1 \, (p_1 \ldots p_n)$$
$$D_2 = F_2 \, (p_1 \ldots p_n)$$
$$\bullet \qquad \bullet \qquad \bullet \qquad \bullet \qquad \bullet \qquad \bullet \qquad \bullet$$
$$D_n = F_n \, (p_1 \ldots p_n)$$

In accordance with the principle of scarcity, when prices are in equilibrium every demand must be satisfied by the supply, and we thus get

$$(5) \quad D_1 = S_1, \, D_2 = S_2 \ldots D_n = S_n,$$

where S_1, S_2, S_n are the quantities of each of the different commodities produced within a unit period.

Thus we now know the quantities of the particular commodities which are to be produced in each unit period. From this we can calculate the demands which are made upon the factors of production of a particular unit period, let us say the present, as follows. In order constantly to produce in each unit period a unit of commodity 1, we require quantities a_{11} . . . a_{1r} of these factors of production. For the quantity S_1 we therefore require quantities $a_{11} S_1$ . . . $a_{1r} S_1$. The same thing holds in the case of the remaining products. In all, therefore, for the continuous production of quantities S_1 . . . S_n, we require

(6) the quantity $a_{11}S_1 + a_{21}S_2 + \ldots + a_{n1}S_n$
of factor of production 1.

the quantity $a_{12}S_1 + a_{22}S_2 + \ldots + a_{n2}S_n$
of factor of production 2.

· · · · · · ·

the quantity $a_{1r}S_1 + a_{2r}S_2 + \ldots + a_{nr}S_n$
of factor of production r.

These quantities thus represent the indirect demand of consumers for the factors of production needed in each unit period in the continuous stationary society. In accordance with the principle of scarcity, this demand for each factor of production must be equal to the quantity of that factor available within the particular unit period, since it is the task of pricing to limit demand as far as is necessary for this purpose. Therefore

(7) $R_1 = a_{11} S_1 + a_{21} S_2 + \ldots + a_{n1} S_n$
$R_2 = a_{12} S_1 + a_{22} S_2 + \ldots + a_{n2} S_n$

· · · · · · ·

$R_r = a_{1r} S_1 + a_{2r} S_2 + \ldots + a_{nr} S_n$

The S, in conformity with the series of equations (5) and (4), are here functions of the p, and therefore, from equations (3), functions of the q. The series of equations (7) thus contains as unknowns the r prices of the factors of production. It also contains r equations, and the series is thus in general sufficient for determining the unknowns. Once the prices of the factors of production are known, the prices of the products can be calculated in accordance with the series of equations (3). Similarly, the demand for each of the finished commodities in each unit period is obtained from the series of equations (4). Consequently, we can calculate the demands which are made on production. Equations (5) show how much of each particular commodity must be produced in each unit period which determines the distribution of the factors of production among the various branches of production. The requirements which the continuous demand, regulated by these prices, makes of the different factors of production available in a particular unit period are to be calculated according to formulæ (6). The coincidence of these requirements with the available quantity of factors of production is guaranteed by equations (7). The pricing problem is thus completely solved for the case considered here.

Our equations reveal the true nature of pricing, and the pricing process cannot be accurately presented in any simpler form. The demand for a product represents an attempt to attract certain factors of production to a particular use. Conflicting with this attempt are similar attempts in the form of demands for the other products. There arises in this way a struggle for the relatively scarce factors of production, which is decided in the exchange economy by placing uniform prices on the factors, which prices in turn determine the prices of the products and thus form a means of effecting the necessary restriction of demand. The demand for a particular factor of production arising from the continuous demand for each particular product is totalled for each unit period, to form a total demand for that factor of production, which is represented by the right-hand side of equations (7), and which must, in a state of equilibrium, equal the given quantity of the factor of production. An equation of this kind must be applicable to each factor.

There has been a great deal of discussion as to what are the factors determining price. This question can now be answered. The determining factors of price are the different given coefficients of our equations. These coefficients may be classified in two main groups, which we may call the objective and the subjective factors determining price. The objective factors are partly the quantities of the factors of production (R), and partly the so-called technical coefficients (a). The subjective factors are the coefficients of equations (4), which show the dependence of demand upon prices. All these factors are essential in determining prices. An "objective" or "subjective" theory of value, in the sense of a theory that would attribute the settlement of prices to objective or subjective factors alone, is therefore absurd; and the whole of the controversy between these theories of value, which has occupied such a disproportionately large place in economic literature, is a pure waste of energy.

The system of equations (7) states that the indirect demand, made by continuous consumption, for the different factors of production in each period must be covered by the quantities of those factors of production available in that period, and that prices must be at such a level that demand is regulated in agreement with this condition. We can therefore say that prices are determined by the scarcity of the factors of production relatively to the indirect demand of consumers for them. The scarcity of the factors of production, in accordance with our assumptions, is a given factor in the problem. Demand, on the other hand, is itself a function of the prices of finished goods, and hence also, in conformity with equations (3), a function of the prices of the factors of production, and cannot therefore be regarded as a factor determining them. What is, on this side, a given factor determining prices is the way in which the functions of demand are dependent on the prices of the factors of production, i.e. the form of these functions or the aggregate of their coefficients which characterise the nature of the demand for the factors of production. If we thus give the scarcity of the factors of production and the nature of the demand for them as the two price-determining factors, it at once becomes clear that there can be no question at all of the priority of one or the other of these factors. They are both, in the full sense of the word, essential determining factors of price.

The solution of the pricing problem is general in so far as it also embraces the previously considered case where commodities, which are directly demanded, are not reproducible at will, but are available in given quantities. These commodities are on a level with the factors of production only in our general solution of the problem. That a commodity is reproducible only means, of course, that its scarcity can be ascribed to the absolute scarcity, from the viewpoint of production, of other commodities. These absolutely scarce commodities we call the primary factors of production. The solution of the pricing problem is accordingly uniform for all kinds of goods. The attempts that are sometimes made to construct different theories of prices for reproducible and non-reproducible goods are thus both superfluous and misleading.

We have reduced the pricing problem to factors which, for the moment at least, we may regard as given factors of the problem. We often find indicated, however, as factors determining prices, factors which, in effect, are themselves variables in the problem just as prices are, and which can only be determined by the given factors we have described. That demand represents such a variable has already been shown. How far each particular demand both for factors of production and for finished products can be satisfied, and therefore who the marginal purchaser is or which is the last need to be satisfied, and, consequently, also, how great the "marginal utility" is, are all questions which can be answered only in connection with the determination of prices through our series of equations. What we call "marginal utility" – if we now wish to introduce this conception – thus occupies exactly the same place as an unknown in the problem as does price, and it is therefore obviously absurd to cite "marginal utility" as a factor explaining price.

Much the same as we have said about demand may be said of the "cost of production" of a commodity, which likewise is usually given as an independent factor determining price. The cost of production of our commodities is given by equations (3), and is thus not known until the prices of the factors of production, which represent the unknowns of the problem, are known. If we wish to quote the "technical cost of production" as a co-determining factor of price, we must simply understand by this the "technical coefficients" *a*. Cost is, as has already been observed (§ 12), essentially an economic conception, chiefly originating from the fact that demand must be restricted through prices on account of the scarcity of the means for satisfying wants.

The cost of production of a commodity is not, as is sometimes supposed, an isolated phenomenon. The factors of production which are used for producing a commodity can generally also be used for producing other commodities, and are, as regards the consumption of those commodities, subject to a demand which emphasises their relative scarcity. The prices of these factors of production, and thus, too, the cost of production of the first commodity, are also dependent on this demand. For instance, as long as the waterfalls of Scandinavia were used only for the production of mechanical power, chiefly for the timber and iron industries, natural water horse-power was very cheap, if not valueless, in many districts, and the industries which used this power scarcely needed, as a rule, to reckon it, in its natural state, among the costs of production. Now that there has arisen a demand for water power for the production of electrical energy, however, this demand has in many cases raised the price of natural water power, and this must be taken into account in calculating costs of production in the timber and iron industries.

This dependence of the cost of production of a commodity upon the demand for other commodities is the counterpart of the dependence of the demand for a commodity upon the prices of other commodities, to which we referred previously. It is this general interdependence of the unknowns in the pricing problem, as was shown in the simple cases above where production does not enter into the question, that makes any isolated treatment of the pricing problem for a single commodity impossible; it is this that shows that the pricing problem is essentially a single problem extending over the whole of the exchange economy and gives the pricing process an intrinsic consistency which can only be expressed by a system of simultaneous equations.

To get this clearest possible presentation of the essential homogeneity of the pricing process, it was necessary to make a number of assumptions in order to simplify matters. Our main assumptions were that the sums of money to be spent by consumers are fixed beforehand, that the technical coefficients are of given fixed magnitudes, and that the primary factors of production are available in given quantities. If we wish to make a closer approximation to reality, we must forgo these assumptions at every stage. The magnitudes which we assumed to be given now appear as variables which are themselves dependent upon prices and must be conceived of as functions of the prices of the factors of production for the purposes of our present treatment of the pricing problem. It may here be objected – and misunderstanding in this direction has often arisen – that we are now arguing in a circle. Prices of the factors of production, together with all other prices, are first ascribed to certain constants, which must therefore be taken as the natural determinants of price. It is then said that these constants are, in fact, not constants at all, but are themselves dependent upon prices. Further consideration of the matter, however, shows that there is no contradiction here, but a gradual extension of the causal connection we are considering. If a series of factors which were previously treated as constants are now conceived of as functions of the prices of the primary factors of production, then the form of these functions, i.e. the nature of the dependence which we have now recognised, represents a new independent determinant of price. In place of the factors which, in our first treatment of the problem, we assumed to be given, there emerge new constants which mark this dependence. The whole of the pricing process is, in this way, traced back by degrees to more remote factors which, for the purpose of economic analysis, may be assumed to be given. We have in effect already been proceeding in this way. At the beginning of this section we assumed the quantity of finished goods available for consumers to be given, and on this assumption, which greatly simplified matters, we found a solution of the pricing problem which provides a very useful introduction to the essential nature of the pricing process. But we subsequently dropped this assumption. We recognised that the quantities of commodities themselves depend upon prices, and, in place of these constants, we took more remote factors as fixed determinants of prices. By this means our survey of the pricing process was materially extended. We must now continue in this way, by substituting certain dependent factors step by step for constants. We shall now do this with direct reference to the amounts of money to be spent by consumers. The substitution of certain dependent factors for the fixed technical coefficients is done in § 17. The corresponding extension of our treatment of the pricing process with reference to the quantities of factors of production, which we at first took as given, is a very extensive task, which will be one of the main objects of Book II.

We first assumed, as we said, that the sum of money which every consumer expends for the satisfaction of his wants in the unit period is fixed in advance. On this assumption, a knowledge of the prices of the finished goods is obviously adequate to determine the demand of each individual consumer for those goods. The aggregate demand for various goods can then be calculated by means of our series of equations (4). If, finally, prices are calculated by means of equations (7), they are fixed relatively to the aggregate money expenditure of consumers, which we assumed as given. We can therefore conclude that prices, by means of the series of equations (7), are fixed absolutely and not merely relatively to one another.

The assumption that the money expenditure of consumers on the purchase of finished goods for satisfying their wants is fixed in advance must now be dropped. The money payments of a consumer are clearly determined by his income. At least, this is generally the case if we consider payments and income over rather longer periods. Payments need not, therefore, be equal to income in every period. The consumer can, of course, save part of his income. In certain cases too, he may spend more than his income, by borrowing money to purchase commodities, and leaving his debts unpaid for a time. Both saving and consumption in excess of one's income may be influenced by the prices current at any moment. If, however, all prices are given, we must assume that the extent of the total payments of each individual consumer, and their distribution among the various classes of commodities, are determined by his income. These payments are constant in the case of the stationary state, and, as no saving takes place in that society on the whole, are also equal to the income. For the sake of simplicity, we may assume the same in the case of each individual.

The income of the individual is, however, determined by the prices of the factors of production which he sells in the course of the productive process. The various incomes of the members of the exchange economy are thus determined by the pricing process, and neither these incomes nor the payments made with them should therefore be regarded as magnitudes, fixed in advance, in the pricing problem. Not until we regard income, too, as one of the unknowns in the pricing problem are we in a position to deal with the pricing problem in a way which accurately reflects our exchange economy, shows that consumers are at the same time producers, and indicates how much of the final product the individual producer is in a position to acquire in exchange for his productive labour. The pricing problem, thus given a general application, contains in itself the problem of economic distribution. The problem of distribution is, therefore, not an independent problem of economic science, but is to be regarded essentially as a special aspect of the general problem of prices. Incidentally, the solution of the problem of distribution, viewed in this way, is included in our series of simultaneous equations. This, of course, does not mean that the practical problem of distribution cannot be regarded from other angles; indeed, it must be thus regarded (cf. § 19). The character of economic distribution always lies in the prices fixed by our system of equations for the factors of production co-operating in the social productive process, and the shares of the various members of society in the social product are thus necessarily determined by the relative scarcity of those factors of production which are at their disposal. Only a study of pricing conceived in these general terms can give us a complete and harmonious picture of the processes within the exchange economy.

Our new assumptions do not alter anything in the outward form of the series of equations which serve to determine prices. But the content of equations (4) is now changed. Previously, these equations stressed the dependence upon commodity prices, on the assumption that the aggregate payments of consumers were given. Now we have to start from the prices of the factors of production, provisionally assumed to be known, and by means of them to calculate the incomes of the individuals. In conformity with our assumption, these incomes, in conjunction with commodity prices, which, too, are calculated from the prices of the factors of production, determine the aggregate payments for consumption made by the individual; and, therefore, we can construct equations (4) in the same way as before. But these equations no longer include the total payments which we previously assumed to be given as constants. Now, however, the coefficients of the functions $F_1 \ldots F_n$ are functions of the prices of the factors of production. But the variables $p_1 \ldots p_n$ are themselves, in accordance with the system of equations (3), functions of the unknowns $q_1 \ldots q_r$. Thus the functions $F_1 \ldots F_n$ now include, besides the variables $q_1 \ldots q_r$, only constants which must be taken as given in the problem, and which represent the dependence of demand on the general price position and on the division of income fixed by that price position.

So far, we have conducted our analysis on the assumption of a stationary society. We must now take into consideration the society which is progressing at a uniform rate. In it, the quantities of the factors of production which are available in any period, that is our $R_1 \ldots R_r$, are subject to a uniform increase. We shall represent by c the fixed rate of this increase, and of the uniform progress of the society generally. If we assume the prices of the factors of production to be given, then the money incomes, which are received by selling those factors and which thus increase in the same percentage c, are fixed. Part of this income is saved; the rest is spent on the purchase of finished goods. In the uniformly progressive state, however, the degree of saving is constant, and the sums of money which are available in every period for consumption increase likewise in the percentage c. By means of technical coefficients a, the prices of the finished goods are determined in accordance with equations (3) in the same way as in the previous case. Since these prices remain constant, demand, with its continually growing purchasing power, can be satisfied to an increasing extent. In the uniformly progressing economy, we must therefore assume that our $D_1 \ldots D_n$ all increase together in the fixed percentage c. The same must then also be true of our $S_1 \ldots S_n$.

The continuous production of these steadily increasing quantities of goods, however, makes special demands upon the factors of production $R_1 \ldots R_r$ that are available in a given unit period. Outwardly, equations (7) remain unchanged; but the coefficients a must be replaced by others. As we have already seen, the a are sums of other constants, which show how much of them refers to each unit period; that is, how much of each factor of production in each unit period is taken into account for the production of a definite unit quantity of each finished commodity. As production is now assumed to increase uniformly, there must be substituted, for these unit quantities, other quantities which steadily increase in the percentage c. Therefore, the corresponding constants also increase in the same ratio. That is, if a series of successive unit periods are considered, they must be multiplied by ascending powers of a constant factor, which is clearly determined by c. The constants thus determined must be added again to sums which have to replace the a in equations (7).

The essential thing is, however, that these new coefficients contain, in addition to the elements of the old "technical coefficients," only the rate of progress c, and they are therefore to be regarded as given quantities in the pricing problem under discussion, if the prices of the factors of production are taken as known. Thus the equations (7) retain their character, and suffice, as in the previous case, to fix the prices of the factors of production, so that the whole pricing problem is solved.

The demands which a steadily increasing production makes upon the factors of production during a present unit period are naturally greater than those which a stationary production, corresponding to the present supply of finished goods, would make. The income of the present unit period, determined by the prices of the factors of production, also exceeds, in the same proportion, the total value of the available finished goods in that period. This income falls into two parts, one of which is used to buy finished goods, and the other to buy the increase of real capital during the period in question. The first part is used to pay for those factors of production which are needed for the production of finished goods, including the maintenance of the existing real capital. The second part is used to pay for the remaining factors of production, which are devoted to the increase of real capital. The ratio between the two parts determines the degree of saving and the rate of progress c. The special significance which the rate of interest has in this connection will be considered in a later section (§ 25).

It is clear that the functions F_1 . . . F_n must be of the same form, and that they will remain unchanged if all the q expressed in the money unit are multiplied by any multiplier whatever. For, in an exchange economy that is in a state of constant equilibrium, the demand can only be determined by the relative prices. The same equilibrium could be preserved just as well if, let us say, the prices were doubled, since the income would then be twice as great; and the distribution of the income among the various means for satisfying wants can only depend upon the ratio between the prices of goods and income, when there is a stable equilibrium, and not upon the absolute amounts themselves. That the result would be different if the equilibrium were altered, since regard must be had to a price position other than that of the moment, will have to be borne in mind when we consider the theory of money (§§ 49–51).

We can see, too, in other ways, that the functions F_1 . . . F_n must have this characteristic. It is well known that in modern physics the calculation of the dimensions of the different magnitudes discussed in the science plays an important part. Theoretical economics can make use of the same method. Price, reckoned in money, is one of the fundamental economic measuring-rods, and can be called the measure of value. Now, the demand for a particular commodity is expressed by the number of units of the commodity desired, and this can be expressed as a length (so many yards of cloth, for example), or as a weight (so many pounds of sugar), and so forth. It clearly does not include the value measurement; with regard to value, its dimension is nil. This is equivalent to saying that a multiplication of all the q expressed in the money unit, which now alone represent the measurement of value in the demand-functions F, by one and the same factor, does not influence these functions.

A multiplication of all the prices q by any factor whatever has, therefore, no influence upon the equations (5) and (7). As the latter, which fixes the prices q, has this attribute, it must also be realised by a system of prices q, in which all the q, expressed in the money unit, are multiplied by any factor we please to choose. Hence the system of equations is indeterminate, in that it determines the prices in question only up to a multiplicative factor; or, as it is popularly expressed, determines only the relative and not the absolute prices. In order to obtain the absolute prices, a new condition must be introduced; for example, the price of a commodity or of a group of commodities must be given. This condition was fulfilled so long as the total expenditure of the consumer, reckoned in money terms, was taken for granted. In the general pricing problem, a multiplicative factor of all prices remains undetermined. The determination of this factor, and, consequently, the final solution of the pricing problem, belongs to the theory of money.

§ 17 *The Pricing Factors*

By the study we have just made, we have answered in principle the question as to which are the determining factors of prices. The essential subjective factors in prices are inherent in the dependence of the demand for finished products upon prices. The objective factors, even if the principle of scarcity alone is taken into consideration, are the technical conditions of production on the one hand, and the supplies of the available factors of production on the other. In cases where the supplementary principles of pricing also apply, these pricing factors are modified in part and replaced by others. The differential principle, for example, introduces, as an objective factor of pricing, the nature of the dependence of the technical conditions of production upon the extent of production. The principle of substitution likewise takes into account the nature of the connection between the quantities of the factors of production, each of which may partly replace the other.

We call these three groups of factors the immediate price-determining factors. Up to the present in our treatment of the pricing problem, these factors have been regarded as given. But they themselves depend upon a variety of different elements of the economic and general social aspects of human life. If we want to study the influence of these elements on prices, we have first to study their influence on the immediate pricing factors. It is only through them that remoter factors can affect prices. Hence all such inquiries bring us back to our solution of the pricing problem. The causal link which connects prices and their direct determinants, the real nature of which we have now learned, remains always the clearest and most precise explanation of the problem.

Important factors which thus influence prices externally are, for example, changes in the size of the population or its composition regarding age, sex, civil status, classes and occupations, migration within the economic area in question, changes in economic organisation, in the legal order, in taxation, in the economic customs of the people (in regard to saving, or to the general conception of the requirements of one's social position, for instance), the destruction of things by war, the exhaustion of natural resources or discoveries of new sources and opening-up of new regions, and, finally, progress in technical processes – in a word, all the factors which give mobility and vitality to economic life. In so far as these movements affect prices, and are in turn affected by them, we have to deal with dynamic problems of pricing. These dynamic problems of pricing have, of course, a considerably larger content than the static problem of pricing, in which the immediate pricing factors are taken for granted, and in which all we have to do is to explain how they determine prices and what direction production takes in a state of equilibrium. It would be a mistake, however, to imagine that the solution of the static problem is without any significance for the dynamic problems. On the contrary, all questions relating to the dynamic problems of pricing are converted first into questions as to the effect of certain movements and changes upon the immediate pricing factors, and consequently as to the fixing of prices by those factors in accordance with the causal sequence already described. It is true that the conditions of our solution of the pricing problem are very often not realised, particularly when violent economic changes occur. In such a case there may be a period when, for example, goods which were produced at the old cost have to be sold at the new and lower prices, the principle of cost thus remaining unfulfilled. But as soon as the transitional stage is over, the fixing of prices in any system which fulfils, in some degree, the requirements of a sound progressive economic organisation will closely follow the principle of cost, and will therefore be elucidated substantially by our solution of the pricing problem. This solution is also very significant in connection with all the dynamic problems of theoretical economics. Nevertheless, we must always bear in mind that the conditions of a period of transition considerably influence the conditions of the normal settlement of prices which follow: they may, for instance, permanently alter the composition of the population, or the quality of the labour of certain groups of the population.

How remoter causes affect the direct pricing factors is a question which must naturally be answered separately for each particular case. However, it does not fall within the scope of a general economic theory. Here, we have only to show how variations in the direct pricing factors affect pricing, and also the problem which is bound up with this, namely, the determination of the direction of production. We have already made the formal side of the problem clear. It is, however, unnecessary for us to examine in what respect the influence of these particular changes, also, will actually be realised, or whether the actual changes in certain of the given factors have a greater significance in the pricing process, so that these problems need not be dealt with. In this case, a more or less substantial simplification of the whole theory of pricing, which various schools of economic thought have attempted to achieve, would perhaps be possible. We have essayed an answer to these questions in relation to each of the three principal groups of direct pricing factors.

In connection with the subjective factors, which show the dependence of the demand for finished goods upon the prices of them, we notice, above all, that a change in the demand only influences prices when it affects either the demand for the factors of production or the methods of production. Given these two groups of factors, the prices of finished goods are also determined according to our assumptions.

Consequently, it is appropriate to estimate the effect that a change in the demand for finished goods has on the demand for factors of production. A change in the direction of demand frequently simply means that the factors of production are applied in other ways, without thereby causing any alteration in the total demand for any particular factor. We need not go very far to see that this is theoretically possible, since a given supply of factors of production can quite easily be put to many different uses. If, for example, the taste of bread-consumers alters in such a way that wheaten-bread partially displaces rye-bread, all that this really means is that a little more arable land and agricultural labour will be devoted to wheat-growing, and a little less of each to rye. A change in the total demand for arable land or for agricultural labour need not take place on account of this. If the land can be used for wheat-growing just as well as for rye, then the price of this factor of production need not alter at all. All that happens in this case is that the change in the demand results in the factor of production being put to a partly different use. With regard to actual industrial products, such a condition is fairly general. Whether the demand for knives or for skates is relatively the greater is, in the long run, a matter of indifference to the prices of these articles, since the labour and particularly the material used in the production of knives can just as easily be used, as a whole, in the production of skates. In all such cases it depends only upon the quantities of the appropriate factors of production necessary to produce the one or the other article. As the changes in the demand for these articles do not affect the demand for the factors of production, the prices of these factors may be assumed to be fixed, and it can then be asserted that the prices of the articles vary in direct proportion to their costs of production. One would arrive, therefore, at a "cost of production theory" for a limited circle of commodity prices.

But under no circumstances may we conclude from this that the subjective factors, in such cases, have completely lost their significance in the pricing process, and that prices may finally be reduced to purely objective factors. It can well be a matter of indifference to pricing whether the demand changes in the direction of one or another of a specific group of goods, so long, that is, as the total demand for the different factors required to produce these goods remains unaltered. This total demand for a factor of production, arising as it does out of the whole group of goods, is, however, not without importance for the price of the factor. The existence of this total demand is, clearly, an essential condition of the maintenance of the price of the factor of production, and, through this, of the entire pricing process. As long as this total demand remains constant, it has naturally no tendency to alter the price of the factor of production. But it can change, however, and such a change must obviously affect pricing.

It is plainly undeniable that the supply of many of the most important materials in the generation preceding the Great War maintained an approximately equal pace with the growing demand for special finished products and that no very substantial changes in the relative scarcity of these materials have occurred since. It is undeniable, too, that, in so far as this is true, the great changes in demand have not had much influence on the pricing process, and that the control of prices through the technical costs of production has become of the first importance. This steadily uniform provision of materials is, however, in no way a usual phenomenon. It is, for instance, indisputable that the continually growing demand for new houses, and the building activity engendered by this, materially enhances the prices of the wood used for building purposes. The great strides made in general literacy during the last decade have led to a very marked demand for newspapers, which, in turn, has had a definitely increasing influence on the prices of wood-pulp, and consequently on those of forests. In such cases, the demand obviously exerts a powerful influence on the scarcity-values of the materials, and thus on the whole pricing process.

The steadily increased provision of certain types of raw materials, sufficient to meet growing requirements, was, moreover, only possible at a time when the progressive economic development of the world constantly provided new possibilities of catering for the increasing need for the most varied materials. We naturally cannot assume that the supply of materials will keep a steady pace with each growing demand in the future, too. Without indulging in pessimistic reflections as to the possibilities of providing for a growing world population, we can and must keep the truth constantly before us, that, in the case of certain materials, an acute shortage is to be expected in the future. This fact is now generally recognised. Since the war, world politics have been strongly influenced by a fear of an approaching scarcity of certain materials, such as fertilisers and, above all, petroleum. This, too, is well known. However, as soon as the limitation to our material resources becomes more marked, it will undoubtedly be proved that the development and growth of demand exercise a real and active influence on pricing.

A special case in which a change in the demand for a finished article exercises a direct and active effect on the pricing process is that of joint products. Our fourth supplementary principle shows that the prices of joint products must be fixed in such a way that a market is found for them all. If the demand for one of the products increases, then, as a rule, its price must also increase, because the increase in the total production that would be necessitated would unduly lower the prices of the remaining joint products (for which the possibility of a bigger market has not been realised). For example, since central-heating came into general use, municipal gas-works have obtained prices for their coke often much higher than would otherwise have been the case.

Furthermore, a change in the subjective factors of pricing can also influence the costs of production, and, in consequence, the pricing process. Theoretically, the nature of these effects has already been made clear by the construction of the first two supplementary principles. In certain cases, an increased demand may mean a rise in the prices of the products; in other cases, a fall. A rise in price occurs when, in order to satisfy the increased demand, new firms, with higher costs of production, enter the market, in which case the differential principle comes into force. An example of this is the increase which takes place in the price of milk or firewood in a growing city which, already large, must satisfy the need for those commodities out of supplies coming from increasingly distant sources. A fall in price occurs, on the other hand, when production is carried on under conditions of decreasing costs. The extraordinary increase in the demand for bicycles, for example, has made a very cheap mass production possible, resulting in substantially lower prices to buyers.

The foregoing account should be sufficient to show that those pricing factors which we have called subjective also have a real, and in no way a merely passive, influence on prices.

Most variations in prices, however, and usually the most substantial ones, are produced by changes in the technical conditions of production. At all events, this is the case in the period of progressive industrialism when revolutionary changes in the methods of production continually create new foundations for pricing. As usual, we must regard transport as a stage in the productive process. The transformation in the technical methods of production has been of particularly great importance for the whole pricing process. The facts with which we have to deal here are so well known as to make it unnecessary to quote examples. The reaction of the pricing process on the selection of the methods of production has already been illustrated during the construction of the supplementary principles of pricing.

Finally, when we come to the factors of production, there remains no doubt that their supply in the exchange economy, according as it is more or less ample, exercises a fundamental influence on pricing. This influence makes itself directly felt as soon as considerable changes occur in the supply of these factors.

The relevancy of such changes is plain, without further consideration, from a study of actual economic life, particularly with regard to the raw materials provided by nature. Changes in the quantities of the available factors of production affect pricing, partly directly through their influence on the relative scarcity of the factors, but also partly indirectly through that on the selection of the methods of production. When two factors of production compete with each other, and when, therefore, the principle of substitution comes into force, an intensified shortage of one factor can be more or less completely modified by an increased use of the second. The effect on pricing extends, in this case, too, to the second factor, but, in regard to the product, will become much attenuated, sometimes even absolutely reduced to zero. This latter, of course, can be particularly the case if the quantity of the second factor is increased simultaneously. A considerable number of changes can therefore take place in the exchange economy, having only a relatively small, or sometimes absolutely no, effect upon the pricing of finished goods. The possibility of satisfying one and the same need in several different ways exercises, on the whole, a stabilising effect upon prices. We can take as an example the satisfaction of the need for lighting; a growing scarcity of petroleum, let us say, will not necessarily influence the price of illumination, since so many substitutes are available to fill the gap. The price of petroleum cannot be increased excessively. Such cases where changes in the supply of the factors of production have only a slight effect upon prices should not, however, hide the fact that our supply of them, according as it is more or less plentiful, still constitutes a fundamental and, usually, very active pricing factor.

Thus we observe that the three groups of pricing factors discussed, to wit, the demand of the consumers, the technique of production, and the supply of factors of production, have collectively a fundamental significance in the pricing process in actual economic life. It is obvious, too, that none of them can be omitted by constructing an even more elementary and simplified theory of pricing. But if all three groups of factors must be taken into account, then the theory of pricing is in full accord with our solution. And besides this solution, there can be no other theory of pricing which is descriptive and explanatory of the actual conditions of an exchange economy.

In our analysis of the pricing process we have so far taken for granted the quantities of the primary factors of production available – that is, we have assumed them to be determined by external circumstances, and, consequently, to be objective factors independent of the pricing process. This assumption is only justified in a preliminary survey of the problem. In any case, it is really only a first approximation, and is only realised within certain limits of the fluctuation of prices. The prices of the factors of production have, in fact, an influence on the supply of them to the exchange economy. This influence may be latent in normal circumstances, but may be very active under other conditions. The analysis, therefore, must be carried further on this point.

Implicit in our conception of the primary factors of production is the fact that they cannot be produced, and therefore cannot be increased by production. Thus, on the one hand, we have to find to what extent what are usually called primary factors of production really satisfy this strict requirement, or are capable of being increased by some activity which must be looked upon as productive. On the other hand, the supply of a factor of production may conceivably depend upon the price, even when there is no possibility of producing it. Our task, therefore, will be to discover the nature of this dependence.

When we drop the assumption that the factors of production are available in fixed quantities, a certain change in our idea of scarcity takes place. The scarcity of a factor of production is then no longer determined by an invariable quantity of itself, but is due rather to the way in which the quantity of the factor offered depends upon the price. The scarcity makes itself felt in the slowness with which the increase of the factor of production follows a rise in the price. This makes the pricing problem somewhat complicated, but is of very little importance in the theoretical treatment of it. The fixing of prices on the more general assumption referred to above can be dealt with entirely within the limits of our analysis of the mechanism of pricing. The dependence of the supply of the factors of production upon their prices is really only the antithesis of the dependence of the demand for the finished products upon their prices, which we have already considered. It therefore offers no new obstacle to our survey of the general mechanism of pricing.

However, the way in which the supply of some of the principal factors of production depends upon the prices of them must be made the subject of a special study. As the same condition holds good for the demand, the task which now confronts us can be formulated as follows : we have to study the effect of the prices of the factors of production upon the supply of, and demand for, them.

The next Book will be devoted to this work, which is of the greatest importance in theoretical economics.

BOOK II

THE PRICING OF THE FACTORS OF PRODUCTION

CHAPTER V

INTRODUCTION

§ 18 *The Factors of Production and the Functions of the Entrepreneur*

IF we wish to make a detailed study of the pricing of the factors of production, we find it obviously necessary to classify them into a few large groups. The classification is determined according to the different places which the factors occupy in the pricing process. It has long been the custom to distinguish three principal groups, namely, *labour, land,* and *capital.* In recent times, it has often been said that this classification is based essentially on the particular social conditions obtaining in England at the height of the classical economics, and that it thus cannot lay claim to a general significance. Nevertheless, it must be emphasised that this classification is without doubt in complete accord with the requirements of the theory of pricing, and that its place in theoretical economics is fully justified. It only remains necessary, as is pointed out in Chapter VII., to join the independent category "natural materials" to the category "land." Each of these four broad groups has its special characteristics as a factor in the pricing problem, and must be analysed individually in order to fulfil the purposes of this Book.

These fundamental categories will be referred to in the following chapters simply as the "factors of production," and it will be our task to discover whether they may be justifiably called primary factors of production, or whether, and under what conditions, their supply can be augmented by an activity which we are bound to call productive. Yet even where production is impossible, the supply of a factor of production need not – as we assumed in Book I. – be a given magnitude of the pricing problem, and independent of its own price. Indeed, the supply, when it implies some exertion by the men engaged in economic activity, may vary with the price offered for this effort. We must carefully study, in a similar fashion, the nature of this dependence. The specific qualities of the various factors of production are made clear in the two aspects referred to above. It follows from this, too, that the traditional classification of the factors is satisfactory enough for the purpose of our inquiry.

As long as we take the available quantities of the factors of production for granted, all of them have the same position in the pricing process, as our inquiries in the preceding Book demonstrate. This assumption is particularly useful, on this account, in an elementary study of the pricing problem, because it makes the organic unity of the problem strikingly clear. Any distinction, then, between the different factors of production is unnecessary in the theory of pricing, until we have to know in greater detail the special circumstances regulating their supply and demand, and, in particular, the dependence of the supply upon the prices of the factors themselves.

Prices are paid for the factors of production in accordance with the general principle of scarcity, because it is necessary to restrict the demand for them in such wise that it can be met with the available supplies. The costs of production of a commodity are, from this standpoint, simply an expression of the scarcity of those factors of production required to make it. If we drop the general assumption – that the factors of production are given in specific quantities – and so take into account the possibility of a clear dependence of the supply of the primary factors of production upon their prices, the nature of the scarcity alters, as we noted earlier (§ 17). The scarcity now expresses itself in the form of a certain slowness in the response of the supply to a rise in prices. In addition to the primary duty of prices to check the demand, they perform the task of stimulating the supply in those cases where there is actually this dependence of the supply upon price. This change, however, does not imply any theoretical alteration in the mechanism of pricing, as we have already seen. Our general treatment of the pricing problem remains substantially unchanged. The pricing of the factors of production can be described on the same lines, in respect of all the different cases. In this treatment, the principle of scarcity retains the fundamental and universal significance that is its due.

In pursuing our study of pricing, we deviate almost entirely from the path which the customary method takes. Classical economics has reached its fullest expression, inclusive of the most modern ideas, in Marshall's writings, and it seems advisable to indicate briefly the chief differences between Marshall's method of treatment and that followed here. As we have already shown (§ 12), Marshall regards as costs, in the real sense, only the "efforts and sacrifices" that are necessary for production, and as money costs of production only the prices which must be paid to elicit the requisite supply of these efforts and sacrifices. [1]

Labour and capital, alone of the factors of production, represent the outcome of efforts and sacrifices, and thus only these factors can be taken into account in calculating the costs of production. The price for the use of land is excluded from costs simply by definition. From this basis, the theory of the pricing of the factors of production must necessarily assume, on the one hand, that the supply of labour and capital actually depends on the prices that are offered for the relevant efforts and sacrifices, and increases with these prices; it is also bound to assume, on the other hand, that "on the margin of production" no price need be paid for the use of land, and that, therefore, the price of the product at the margin actually equals the "costs" in the sense indicated – the cost of labour and capital. [2] This introduces, from the first, as is obvious, a pronounced dualism in the treatment of the theory of pricing.

The theory of pricing built upon these first principles cannot be attacked on the ground that its assumptions are not an accurate reflection of realities. A theory has always to start from certain simplified assumptions of only approximate accuracy. But any explanation of the general mechanism of pricing must not depend for its validity upon unnecessary assumptions in respect of pricing, and it must also find room for all the different forms of pricing which occur, or are likely to occur, in real life. This requirement is not fulfilled in the theoretical structure of Marshall's theory. Even if his assumptions are approximately correct, they are

[1] Marshall, *Principles*, Book III., chapter v., § 2.
[2] For further details, see Chapter VII.

unnecessary. A situation is readily conceivable in which they are not realised, in which the supply of labour and capital is, within certain limits, independent of the prices of the corresponding efforts and sacrifices, and in which the use of land has a scarcity-price which undoubtedly influences the prices of the products. Any explanation of the mechanism of pricing which cannot cover such a case cannot satisfy our demand for a deeper analysis of the basic processes of pricing. When we find that a theory depends for its validity upon entirely unnecessary assumptions, we naturally feel that something fundamental is lacking, and that the theory has not gone to the roots of the problem. In Marshall's theory of pricing, it is the principle of scarcity that is lost sight of – that is to say, the significance of the limitation of the available factors of production. The entire Marshallian theory of economics is an attempt to dispense with the principle of scarcity, to reject scarcity as a determining element in pricing. Unequivocally, the attempt has formally succeeded, after a fashion, in Marshall's masterly work. But this was only possible because, according to Marshall's particular assumptions, the pricing process is such that the principle of scarcity does not make its appearance in any objective manner, though, of course, it always lies at the root of all the processes of pricing as the ultimate regulating principle. But such a treatment of the pricing problem cannot be really satisfactory. The theory must give the principle of scarcity the fundamental place which really belongs to it.[1]

Our four factors of production are, of course, only types of factors of production – the most important ones, it is true; they must be taken in a wider sense if they are to represent all the factors of production. For instance, the terms labour and wages refer properly to wage-earners who perform manual work, but they must be extended to technical and commercial employees, etc., also. Thus the factors of production clearly need to be defined with greater precision and detail. This is especially the case with regard to "capital," whose meaning as a factor of production can only be made plain by an exhaustive analysis. Consequently, we will

[1] Cf. § 29.

begin our study with capital and deal with the other factors afterwards. It is necessary to follow this arrangement if we are to study the theoretical difficulties in a definite order.

In our economic system, the work of directing production in conformity with the requirements of consumers falls principally upon the entrepreneurs. This task is by no means so simple as Socialists imagine when they say that all that is necessary is to compile statistics of wants in advance and then officially to regulate production on the basis of these statistics. Regulating consumption in this manner would be equivalent, in a large degree, to suppressing the freedom of choice of consumption that is characteristic of the exchange economy. But the consumers wish most decidedly to retain this freedom of choice to the last moment.

The difficulty of the problem lies precisely in the fact that the constantly varying demands of consumers, which cannot be determined in advance with any degree of certainty, must be satisfied, despite incessant changes in the methods and conditions of production. This work is actually done – naturally not perfectly – by a number of independent entrepreneurs, each of whom, on the whole, looks merely to his own interest.

This solution of the problem is possible because, whenever a want that can be paid for is left unsatisfied, or is not completely satisfied, or satisfied only at an abnormally high price – every time, that is, the problem of the economic direction of social production is not satisfactorily solved – an entrepreneur is encouraged by the prospect of earning a special profit to make a better provision for the want in question, and the productive process is thus steadily improved. The entrepreneur intervenes, not only where something is to be done for the immediate satisfaction of consumers' wants, but everywhere where the productive process, somewhere among the thousands of its component processes, exhibits a gap which leaves room for his enterprise. In this way, all these partial processes are united into a single productive process, embracing the entire satisfaction of wants in the exchange economy.

The standard by which we can judge the use to be made of the various factors of production is, as has been shown, the pricing process. The factors of production, however, do not flow spontaneously in the direction marked out for them by prices. They must be directed by human activity, as is done when the entrepreneur buys factors of production, uses them in co-operation, and sells the products of his enterprise. Thus the pricing of the factors of production is, in general, in the hands of the entrepreneurs, and is effected by their work.

The part played by entrepreneurs can be best explained by saying that they bring together other factors of production than their own labour for productive purposes, and set them to work. The entrepreneur is, above all, a type for us. The director of a large business in which all the factors of production are used is a typical entrepreneur. This man can be regarded as essentially "the entrepreneur." It is true that he usually has capital of his own invested in the business. In this respect, however, he is a capitalist, not an entrepreneur. He also does work of one kind or other on behalf of the business. To that extent, he is a worker, in the wider sense of the word. Hence we must, as it were, distinguish the different aspects of his personality, in order that we may be able to grasp the nature of the work which he performs in his specialised capacity as an entrepreneur.

In actual economic life, the business of entrepreneur is largely exercised by individuals who can scarcely be called entrepreneurs in the proper sense. The manual worker or the peasant uses other factors of production besides his own labour in his productive process: the labour of others, capital, and land. Possibly he is himself mainly a worker. But we have to dissect his personality so that theoretically we can conceive of him as an entrepreneur in that aspect of his work. In this way we are able, when we speak of entrepreneurs, to include under that head all individuals who in one way or other perform the work of entrepreneurs.

The economic motive of this work is the desire to make a profit. The entrepreneur's profit is the surplus of gross proceeds above cost; that is, above the price which has to be paid for the co-operation of the factors of production. If the entrepreneur himself acts, to some extent, as a worker or official, or puts capital or land into the business, he must allow a certain sum, based on prevailing prices, as payment for the co-operation of these factors of production. It is only the remainder that represents the pure profit of enterprise.

This profit of enterprise is, at first sight, akin to a pure differential profit that is made merely as a result of the difference in costs in different undertakings. It includes, however, other elements which have an approximately definite price, and which must therefore be regularly taken into account in the calculations on which a business is based. These prices must, therefore, be put on the same footing as costs, and must normally be covered by the prices of the products.

To this class belongs, first of all, the personal work of the entrepreneur in his capacity of employer, in organising and directing the undertaking. This work may in part be replaced by the paid work of officials. The manager of a medium-sized business performs a number of functions which are only handed over to the heads of departments, etc., at a later stage, when it has grown to a large business. Work of this kind must clearly be reckoned among the costs of the undertaking. Even the general management of the business, however large, may be entrusted to a salaried official. This, indeed, is the customary thing in the case of limited companies. There is a price for each of these functions of enterprise in every economically advanced country. This price follows the ordinary rules of pricing: the relative scarcity of competent individuals in proportion to the demand for them is the primary determining factor of the price of the entrepreneur's work. Hence the determining factors of this price are substantially the same as those of wages, though the pricing of the work done by entrepreneurs naturally has its special features. The price of the entrepreneur's work must be included among the costs of the business. Every limited company does this, and every private entrepreneur who carries on his business sensibly must do the same. If an entrepreneur, making an annual profit of £1,500 in his own business, can earn £1,000 as a director of a limited company, he will reckon £500 only as the actual profit derived from his business. If the net proceeds are only £750, it will be clear to him that he is really working at a loss, since his managerial ability is worth £1,000.[1]

A second element of the profit of the entrepreneur, in the broad sense of the word indicated above, which must be reckoned as a cost, is the risk – in so far as it can be calculated with some degree of probability and so included in the estimate of cost. This, of course, is particularly the case with regard to any risk against which it is possible to insure, such as fire, or shipwreck, and so forth. Generally, insurance premiums are paid for these risks and included in the costs. They must be put on the same footing, among the costs, as depreciation of buildings, of machinery, etc. When we consider production as a whole, accidents of this kind occur with a certain regularity, and are therefore part of the normal wear and tear of the things used in production. The payment of insurance premiums is, substantially, merely a method of spreading evenly the amount to be written off for depreciation. This idea is put into practice in the case of the big shipping companies, which do not insure, in view of the large number of their ships, but form instead an insurance fund of their own and enter the sums assigned to it under the head of current costs.

As a rule, it is not possible to insure against the actual business risks of an undertaking. That these risks, within certain normal limits, are taken into account in business calculations is beyond question. It is seen, for example, in the fact that in planning a business the interest on the capital is reckoned at (say) 10 per cent., although the usual interest on the best securities is perhaps only 4 per cent. A sound trading account of a limited company also reckons among costs the sums that must be set aside to form a proper reserve, since this must serve to cover losses incurred in the normal course of business. In so far as the risk of a business consists in a faulty estimate of costs, it must clearly be included as a special item in the estimate. The same is also obviously true of the risk arising out of an unavoidable falling-off in sales or in selling price; normally, a price must be fixed which will cover occasional losses of this type, so that, on the average, taking long periods, the price

[1] The work of an entrepreneur can, if so desired, be regarded as a special factor of production, in addition to labour in the usual sense of the term. The peculiarity of the determining factors of the wages of management would account for such a distinction.

actually obtained for the product will suffice to cover the whole
of the actual cost. This incurring of risk may itself be regarded as a
special factor of production. Under economically advanced conditions this factor has a market of its own and a fairly definite price.
It may also be substituted for other factors of production, as always
happens when, in order to reduce costs, a lower grade of security is
tolerated.

If we separate these two elements from the profit of the entrepreneur, both of which can be calculated to some extent in advance
and must be considered a real cost of production, we may regard
whatever remains of the net proceeds of the business as the entrepreneur's profit in the strict sense of the word – as a pure profit of
enterprise. This corresponds accurately with our definition of such
profit as the surplus of gross proceeds over costs; for, now, all the
items that can be regarded as costs have been subtracted. There
can be no doubt that in real life there is an entrepreneur's profit of
this kind. It is particularly evident when limited companies, which
remunerate their directors and consulting experts very generously,
and also put aside large reserves for all sorts of objects, not only pay
normal interest on their capital, but also distribute additional
dividends. However, only in comparatively few cases is the pure
entrepreneur's profit very large. Most of them make a pure profit
only during a trade boom. Probably, on the average, the returns
are barely sufficient to cover all the costs, as we understand them
here. A relatively large number of entrepreneurs can never cover
these costs, but work at some loss. The pure profit of the entrepreneur is, in such cases, always negative. Experience shows that
some of these businesses are only maintained after adequate
writing-off of capital and "reconstructions." But the number of
businesses that fail completely and disappear from the public view
is very large. The public, which sees little of this, is dazzled by
the enormous profits of a few prosperous firms, and is always
disposed to exaggerate the amount of the total pure profit made
by entrepreneurs in the national economy.

There are, of course, no norms as to the extent of pure profit.
Pure profit is not a normal thing, but a specific element of the

individual business. It is often the outcome of sheer accident, as, for example, when some development of the market takes place that is particularly profitable for a certain firm, but over which the entrepreneur has exerted no influence whatever. It varies a good deal, as a rule, with the trade movements in the branch of business in question. It further depends upon a favoured position which the business has secured in one respect or other. Possibly, the business has long had an assured circle of customers, a patented trade mark, favourable long-term contracts with suppliers of raw materials, good conditions in the business world, etc. Perhaps, being fully developed and well-organised, it enjoys an advantage over smaller competitors; or it possibly has at its disposal so much capital that it can crush competition; or it may have a legal monopoly, or perhaps has secured a monopoly by forming a trust. The exceptional position may also be due to personal factors. The business may employ managers, officials and workers who do more and better work than similarly paid managers, officials and workers of rival firms. The whole organisation of the business, the training and the efficiency of the employees in their work, the interest of all in the prosperity of the business, are also factors which tend to consolidate the position of a firm. In many of these cases the position is the fruit of years of endeavour, and the pure profit of enterprise now made is in part the outcome of the position that has been won. It can, however, be easily lost in the continual changes of modern economic life, in which forces are always at work to displace old and favoured firms and give place to new ones. Its maintenance necessitates, as a rule, a ceaseless effort, an unrelaxing vigilance – in a word, exertions which must be paid for, and the price must be included in the costs.

In the cases where a favoured business position – whether won or whether due to external circumstances ("unearned") – secures a permanent pure profit, this profit must be regarded as being akin to a rent of position, and the position itself has a capital value which is realised when the business is sold. But these things cannot be fully understood until we come to the inquiries in the next chapter.

The question of the extent to which the profit of the entrepreneur enters into the price of the product can now be easily answered. Those elements of profit, in the broader sense of the word, which we have shown to be real costs must, of course, be regarded as normal constituents of the price of the product. Whether the pure profit of the entrepreneur is included in the price of the product depends upon the conditions of competition. If the business which makes such a profit is not in a position to supply the whole market, and other entrepreneurs must have a share in the work, it is possible that the final business thus required will yield no pure profit, and that, consequently, the price will only just cover the cost in this marginal firm. In this case the price, in accordance with the differential principle, is fixed by the marginal cost, and the pure profit made by the more favourably placed firms is entirely in the nature of a differential profit, and is irrelevant to the price of the product. If, on the other hand, the business in question is in a position of monopoly, and succeeds in using it to make a pure profit, this can only be done by raising the price of the product above the cost, and the entrepreneur's profit must, in that case, be regarded distinctly as a part of the price of the product. The question whether the price of the product is increased on account of the monopoly is not examined here. In many cases the monopoly profit is obtained only by means of an extensive and efficient organisation, which keeps the costs down to a minimum, perhaps to such an extent that the product, despite the monopoly profit, is sold more cheaply.

§ 19 *The Problem of Imputation and the Social Problem of Distribution*

When two individuals have co-operated in making a certain article, the question immediately arises as to how much each of them has contributed, or what is the share of each in the production of it. The primitive feeling of justice demands an objective standard for settling the division of the proceeds, and is disposed to find this in a causal link between work and product. We thus arrive at the so-called problem of imputation or attribution. Its importance increases when we pass from the simple case of sharing between two individuals to the more complex one of the general distribution of social production. It holds a fundamental position in an age of widespread division of labour and sharp stratification of classes in the community.

The idea that the proceeds of production can be shared according to the principle of causality, in proportion to the work done by each of the several factors, is very popular. It is confirmed when we consider cases where the activities necessary to make the product are homogeneous, and can therefore be reduced to a common measure. It is then possible to distribute arithmetically according to work done. But if the activities required to make the product are of very different kinds, it is impossible to reduce them to a common measure, and there can be no "correct" distribution in the objective sense.

This applies primarily to activities of the most heterogenous nature which we are accustomed to lump together as "work." There is no common measure for the work of the thinker, the artist, the manager of a business, and the manual worker. Their common product can never be shared according to the work done by each.

The impossibility of this kind of imputation is made still clearer when other factors of production of various kinds are added to "labour" – capital, natural materials, or land. It is, however, precisely in this case that the problem of imputation attracts the widespread interest which it has in modern economic life. It is just when the activities co-operating in production are quite different that the most bitter controversy as to who is to have the proceeds of production arises. Each party is naturally inclined to emphasise the importance of its own share of the work, to claim as large a portion as possible of the returns, and, consequently, to denounce the actual apportionment as unfair. As a rule, the so-called proof of this is to imagine one's own share of the work withdrawn and then ask what the other factors of production would do without it. Unfortunately, this argument suffers from the weakness that it can be used with the same striking effect with regard to each factor of production that is indispensable. Taking away that particular factor of production always reduces the result of the activity of the others to zero.

With the support of this argument, it has actually been claimed that the whole proceeds of the productive process belongs to labour; that is, "the right of the worker to the full product of his labour." We need not linger over the advocacy of this programme. The programme itself is interesting as a fundamental tenet of Socialism, representing the positive expression of the denial in principle of the justice of an income based upon private property. Theoretical economics is obliged to make it perfectly clear that, and why, an imputation along the lines of this programme is economically impossible; that, and why, it is an economic exigency for every exchange economy, independently of its legal order and particular organisation, to "impute" back definite shares in the total proceeds of production to the other primary factors of production.

Since the share of the total product to be assigned to one of the co-operating factors of production cannot be calculated by measuring the effect upon the total product of the withdrawal of that particular factor, an attempt has been made to calculate its real share by imagining the loss caused by withdrawing a small part of it. This method, however, manifestly breaks down when the factor of production is indivisible, or when one part of it cannot be withdrawn without throwing other factors of production out of work. This is generally the case. We cannot, moreover, judge the effect of the factor of production in question by comparing the increase in the product due to a small increase in the factor with the increased total product itself, or, in other words, estimate the so-called "marginal productivity" (§ 13). The latter is equal to nil as long as the addition to the factor of production, without any corresponding addition to the other factors of production, has no effect. If a pit has to be dug, the labour of one additional man will make very little difference to the day's output unless the man is provided with a spade.

Thus the concept of marginal productivity can be properly applied only when the factors of production can co-operate effectively, within certain limits, in any proportion we care to choose and when, therefore, the factor of production in question can be steadily substituted for the other factors without altering the final product. In that case, as we have seen, we can define the marginal productivity of this factor of production. Its price must clearly, in a state of equilibrium, be equal to this marginal productivity, otherwise it would be more economical to use more or less of the factor in question. The marginal productivity is, then, a measure of the share of that factor of production in the results of production.

The concept of marginal productivity applies properly to a productive process concerned with the manufacture of one single product. It cannot be extended forthwith to the distribution of the outcome of the entire social production among the factors of production. When we consider the production of the economy as a whole, it is quite possible effectively to employ all the factors of production even after slightly altering their proportions. This depends only partly upon a real substitution of one factor for another in the various intermediate industrial processes into which the total production is divided. Apart from this, the full use of the different factors of production in accordance with the principle of scarcity is secured mainly by fixing a uniform price for each factor and distributing the existing quantities of them among the different branches of production according to the demand for them as regulated by these prices. Thus, in the first place, room is provided for an increased quantity of a factor of production by reducing its price and so stimulating the demand for those products for the making of which it is chiefly used. The marginal productivity of a factor of production cannot, however, be defined in the social productive process as a whole as long as the prices of the products are indeterminate, and, consequently, a definite measure of the total product is lacking. In any case, the proposition that the price of a factor of production is equal to its marginal productivity in the productive process as a whole can have no other meaning than that its price is the same in every one of its uses in the different branches of production, and that the prices of the products can be determined in accordance with the principle of cost on the basis of this pricing of the factors of production. But this condition merely brings the pricing of the factor of production back to the general pricing process which is examined in the preceding Book.

The attempt to solve the problem of imputation along the lines of marginal productivity only proves that the problem cannot be solved as a question concerning the technical effectiveness of the several co-operating factors of production, but that it is fundamentally an economic problem, one that is really only one side of the general problem of pricing. But in the pricing process, as we have seen, the principle of scarcity is the paramount principle. The apportionment of the common proceeds of production is therefore mainly governed by this principle, and the shares of the various factors of production are, consequently, substantially determined by supply and demand, and in no wise exclusively by the objective features of production. That the principle of scarcity is modified in certain cases by the principle of substitution, and that this establishes a correspondence between the price and the marginal productivity of the factor of production, by no means signifies that the relative scarcity of the factor of production has lost its fundamental importance with regard to pricing, and therefore to "imputation." The problem of the distribution of the total outcome of social production among the factors of production is, then, primarily determined by the relative scarcity of these factors in proportion to the indirect demand of consumers for them.

The problem of imputation has its roots, as we have seen, in the endeavour to find an objective standard for a just distribution. This standard was sought in a kind of technical relation of cause and effect between activity and product. Since there is no such key to the problem, there can be no just distribution in this objective sense. The problem is essentially an economic one. All that has been written or said about justice regarding distribution among heterogeneous factors of production is consequently to be regarded as merely the expression of vague and sentimental ideas that ought to have no place in a scientific work. Instead of the ethical problem, concerned with how much of the total product ought justly to be imputed back to each co-operating factor, we must take the purely scientific problem – that is, how much, in the actual economic situation, goes, on economic grounds, to each of the different factors of production.

The solution of the problem lies in pricing. This is determined by the principle of scarcity in conjunction with the supplementary principles, and all of them are, in turn, merely consequences of the general economic principle. It follows that, for every economy which fulfils the fundamental economic requirements, the principles of pricing, and therefore of economic distribution, are established. We can hardly imagine an organisation of the exchange economy in which a faulty observance of economic rules would not be felt as a defect, and would fail to provoke efforts to attain a higher economic standard of efficiency. The economic organisation would not reach a state of equilibrium until the general economic principle and, consequently, our principles of pricings were realised. In this sense, a distribution in accordance with our principles of pricing can claim objective correctness from the economic point of view, and the shares which will fall to the various factors of production by virtue of this pricing may be described as their economically just shares.

These observations, however, are very far from closing the practical problem of distribution. No exchange economy can continue to maintain prices, and therefore a distribution, in express opposition to fundamental economic requirements. But the practical result of pricing in accordance with the principles of the exchange economy depends necessarily upon the relative scarcity of the various factors of production co-operating in the social productive process and upon the total product of the process. The problem of imputation presents itself from the start as a problem of abstract justice; but in the light of economic science it is reduced to a question of the actual nature of pricing in the economy. The social problem of distribution is something more. It includes the practical question as to how the given factors of the pricing process can be so influenced that the social economic distribution resulting from this pricing will also be socially satisfactory, and will promote the vitality of the nation and the effectiveness of its work. This, however, as we shall see later, opens out a wide field for the action of practical economic and social policy upon pricing, and therefore on the social distribution. Unfortunately, ignorant politicians and philanthropists try only too often to urge a social policy in opposition to the principles of pricing. The clearer we can make the hopelessness of these efforts to politicians, the more surely will they direct their power to objects in which their useful activity might be able to secure a better distribution or a fairer fixing of incomes from the point of view of social policy. Not only social policy, however, but economic policy generally, ought always to remember that it can only achieve permanently advantageous results for the community if it works in harmony with the general principles of the exchange economy.

In the present economic system, where private ownership extends to the material means of production, the shares which are assigned to land and capital in the pricing process go to the owners of those factors of production. Naturally, the distribution of income in such an economic system is strongly influenced by the existing distribution of property. The development of private property is, in turn, determined to a certain extent, by the distribution of income and by saving, in the widest sense of the word. In addition, the question of property is governed by the conditions regarding heredity, the customs and laws which regulate the transmission of property at death. These things exert an important influence on the distribution of income in the community.

Regarding labour, it must be borne in mind that its value depends to a great extent upon general education and upon the special technical training of the worker. In an exchange economy in which the cost of educating the young is borne for the most part by the family, the conditions of income and property play a very large part in determining the distribution of income in the next generation. To a certain extent the community can obviously neutralise this influence by its general educational work, and particularly by assuming the cost of education.

The practical problem of the distribution of the total proceeds of social production is, therefore, not wholly settled by pricing, but includes different elements apart from pricing, which open out possibilities of a deliberate regulation of the distribution. Thus any inference from the necessity of pricing as to the supposed necessity of the present distribution would be unsound, and any attempt to construct a "natural harmony" of the economic life would fail. General social and economic policy covers a much wider area than theoretical economics proper. The task of the latter is to elucidate pricing. A general theory of social policy is only possible on the basis of a strict economic theory, but it has other tasks in addition, with which theoretical economics cannot deal. These mean an enlargement of the problems of pricing and "imputation" into a general problem of social distribution. A general theory of social policy must naturally also work in part with different methods and definitions. For example, it might be correct for it to distinguish the forms of income primarily as the two broad categories "income from property" and "income from work," and direct its attention to the various possibilities of favourably affecting these incomes and their distribution. Theoretical economics has nothing to do with these matters. Its special object requires that it shall make it its chief business to explain the nature of the different kinds of income. It has thus to classify the types of income according to their different characteristics from the standpoint of pricing, and it must, therefore, return always to the old broad division into wages of labour, rent of land (to which has to be added the price of natural materials) and interest on capital. It must focus its attention principally upon the correct description of these forms of income and the corresponding factors of production, as well as upon the study of the factors determining the pricing of these factors of production. That is the task of the following chapters of this Book.

CHAPTER VI

INTEREST

§ 20 *The Development of the Theory of Interest*[1]

ALTHOUGH it is best to leave forgotten the greater part of what has been written on the subject of interest in previous centuries, it is, however, instructive to follow the main lines of the development of human thought on this subject, for in this way we can obtain a clear insight into the problem of interest, and by discussing the difficulties connected with it we may be helped in our attempt to attain the conclusive solution of the problem. In this connection we have only to understand the different tendencies which we find, in their relation to the general development of the theory, and so form a correct estimate of their value.

It is very difficult for a person in these times to understand the condemnation of interest by the mediæval Church. But even here impartial consideration allows us to see circumstances which throw light upon, and to a certain degree justify, this point of view. As loans were perhaps mainly made, in those days, to people who were economically badly off, there was an attempt to make such loans the source of profit, and this appeared to be an exploitation of hardship. This, undoubtedly, was generally the case. From this point of view, as Roscher shows, nations in early stages of economic development have generally shown a distaste for the taking of interest, and most religions, based on primitive economic conditions, have forbidden it.[2]

But while we appreciate the practical policy of the Church in this connection, we must at the same time point out that the Canonists, by their attitude towards the question of interest,

[1] For a more detailed treatment of the subject, as well as for a bibliography, see Cassel, *The Nature and Necessity of Interest.* (London, 1903).
[2] *Grundlagen der Nationalökonomie.*

increased very considerably the difficulty of understanding its nature. Since they had of necessity to permit the taking of interest in certain cases, they used all the weapons of their sophistry to distinguish these cases from the rest, and thus helped to obscure the essential unity of the phenomenon of interest. The right of the lender to compensation for the risk of making a loan was recognised and called "interest," a word now in general use. As this interest was thought justifiable in cases where the lender might have made a profit by using his money in other ways, people were bound to see that the interest on loans was the same as that which capital yields when employed in profitable business. This understanding was necessarily encouraged by the custom of buying fixed ground-rents, for in this form the landowner could always raise capital for improving his land by paying a rent, which was in reality a kind of interest. In Germany, where buying rents was general, customary usage gave the name *Zins* (= census, or "rent") to every payment for a loan which was recognised to be just. But the struggle between the indisputable needs of practical life and the hypercritical distinction of canonistic scholasticism necessarily lasted for centuries before the essential identity of the different forms of interest was generally realised, and the ground won on which a scientific theory of interest could gradually develop. This period, however, saw the rise of freedom of thought. The appeal to mediæval authority had, consequently, to give way first, in the Mercantilist period, to the discussion of the practical advantages and disadvantages of lowering the rate of interest, and secondly, under the influence of Liberalism, to real inquiries into the factors determining the rate of interest in a state of free competition.

The power of the State which, in modern times, succeeded the hegemony of the Church, sought to check exploitation in the taking of interest by establishing a definite maximum rate. This policy naturally led to perpetual discussion as to the correct maximum, and thus encouraged inquiries into the effects of high or low rates, so giving a certain insight into the significance of this rate in economic life. Reflection on the effect that this rate had on other factors in economic life was bound, gradually, to make clear the fact that these factors were important in affecting the rate of interest, and that this rate was a purely economic phenomenon which the State could not control as it pleased. In England, where this conception of interest was developed very clearly by the end of the seventeenth century, the treatment of interest as a market price determined by supply and demand was taken for granted.

But it still remained to determine more accurately the kind of service which was the object of supply and demand, and for which interest was consequently paid. In this respect the period of the rise of Liberalism led to important advances. First of all, the theory of interest had to be freed from the old confusion of money and capital. As loans are generally made in money, it is only too evident that money should be considered the essential object of loans, and that fluctuations in the rate of interest should be traced to the scarcity or superfluity of money. Even the modern business world has scarcely outgrown such beliefs, as may be seen in any leading article in the financial newspapers, especially in such commonly used phrases as "cheap" or "dear" money. In spite of all this, however, there has grown up the view that money only plays an intermediary part in a loan, and that the loan consists essentially of the transference, for a time, of the right to dispose of capital. This is a considerable advance.

Since that time the theory of interest has been based upon the assumption that money is only an accidental and quite unnecessary form of the transference of capital, and that this form must be disregarded if the dependence of the rate of interest upon the market for capital is to be explained. Undoubtedly, this assumption has been useful in that it has liberated the problem of interest from the theory of money, and thus made possible the separate treatment of the former. But it is equally certain that this assumption is only permissible as a temporary simplification of the problem. A theory of interest which ignores entirely the influence of the supply of money upon the rate of interest consciously or unconsciously assumes a static condition of money, and excludes any understanding of the link between the rate of interest and the value of money, and thus any deeper conception of the nature of money.

So if we half ignore, by this simplification, the monetary form of the loan in discussing the theory of interest, this only means that we reserve the reciprocal relations of money and interest for a later inquiry. This inquiry has its proper place in the theory of money, and is, in fact, the concluding part of it (cf. Chapter XI.).

The conception of a loan as the temporary transference of the right to dispose of a certain value – an abstract capital – was treated with great clarity by the French economists, Turgot and J.-B. Say. This conception of interest as the price of capital-disposal has been very useful, in that it shows the service for which interest is paid, and, besides that, emphasises the price aspect of interest, thus placing it on the same footing as other prices. It also makes clear, from the beginning, the organic position of the problem of interest as an integral part of the general problem of price-determination.

From another point of view, also, the idea of interest needed to be more precisely defined. It was the custom, especially in England, to designate as "profit" the total income of a business, including in this the interest on the personal capital of the owner of the business. For the development of the theory of interest, it was of particular importance to distinguish, in profit, between the interest on the employer's own capital invested in the business and his profit as an entrepreneur. Not until this was done was it possible to conceive accurately the factors which determine, through supply and demand, the rate of interest, and to take into account the whole supply of, and demand for, capital-disposal in studying the problem. A sharp distinction of this kind, between interest and profit, between the capitalist and the entrepreneur, was made by J.-B. Say. He regarded capital-disposal as a distinct and definite productive service. The determination of the rate of interest was thus for him only a part of the whole pricing process, by which the prices of all productive services are fixed. The real demand for the control of capital in this pricing process comes from the consumer of those finished goods for the production of which a command over capital is necessary.

These results provided the ground-work on which a complete theory of interest might have been developed. What was still necessary was, partly, a more solid general theory of pricing, within which interest could find its natural place as a price, and, partly, a thorough study of the circumstances which determine the supply of, and demand for, capital-disposal, and especially the influence of the rate of interest itself upon these factors. Unfortunately, the development of the theory of interest was interrupted, the serious study of the problem being set aside by two highly speculative theories, both very alien to actual economic life. One of these was the socialist theory of value, the other the so-called wage-fund theory. These theories can be more closely discussed only in connection with the theory of wages (Chapter VIII.). As to their importance in connection with the theory of interest, only a few remarks can be made here.

The thesis of the socialist theory of value is that the value of a commodity is equal to the amount of labour which is necessary under normal conditions to produce it. This assumption is quite arbitrary, and in contradiction to the actual facts. It not only excludes in advance interest as such, but also makes a sensible theory of interest impossible, for in it there is no place for an objective treatment of the problem of pricing, and interest cannot, consequently, be conceived as a price in this general process. A theory of interest based upon such an assumption is evidently nonsensical, and cannot claim to be regarded as a scientific exposition. A science which on this point makes concessions to Marxian scholasticism does not know what it owes itself. However, on the other hand, the study of interest in a socialist community has a definite significance in that it throws light upon the economic nature of interest. We shall return to it in § 25.

The wage-fund theory regarded capital as a definite fund for supporting the workers during the period of production. The average wage of the individual worker was determined by the ratio of this fund to the number of workers. With such a conception of the function of capital it is clear that any explanation of the significance both of the varying demand for finished goods and of the choice of methods of production must be excluded from discussion of the rate of interest. Concerning the supply of capital-disposal the wage-fund theory taught, as did Adam Smith and Ricardo, that a fall in the rate of interest must contract the amount of saving and thus reduce the supply of capital-disposal, but it impressed its sterile dogmatism upon this idea too, and obtained results which were incompatible with the real facts of economic life.

Both the last-named schools were a hindrance to the further development of a scientific theory of interest, because they continually carried the question into the sphere of ethics and politics. As a contrast to the socialist denial of the justness of interest, the opponents of Socialism made a strenuous attempt to find a moral justification for it; and also between the wage-fund theory and its opponents there took place a controversy which was based mainly upon moral and practical political grounds. The real duty of the science was thus neglected.

But in spite of this, the nineteenth century made positive contributions to the theory of interest. These consisted mainly of a more careful study of the conditions which determine the supply of, and demand for, capital-disposal. On the supply side the inquiries were encouraged by the desire to justify interest by the sacrifice which the accumulation of capital imposed upon those who saved. The English economist Senior [1] showed that such a sacrifice must be regarded as a necessary "factor of production," and as such must be placed on a level with labour and natural resources. This factor of production he called "abstinence," a word with rather a moral connotation, which at once evoked Lassalle's derision; he made this "abstinence" look ridiculous by presenting the spectacle of the great millionaires of Europe as ascetics for the good of the community. [2] Later writers have shown that the accumulation of capital in a modern community is carried on only to a small extent by those strata of society for whom saving really means "abstinence" and sacrifice; for the greater part it is the result of the reserves of large businesses, speculators, and big capitalists. [3] For an act that is performed under such very different conditions a term that was

---

[1] Senior, *Outlines of the Science of Political Economy*, 5th edition, pp. 58–60.

[2] Lassalle, *Herr Bastiat-Schulze von Delitzch, der ökonomische Julian, oder Kapital und Arbeit* (Berlin, 1864).

[3] Cf. Schmoller, *Grundriss der allgemeiner Volkswirtschaftslehre*, II., pp. 176–7.

ethically colourless had to be found – a term which would express only
the essential and consistent meaning of the act in an exchange
economy. As such were suggested the French word "*ajournement*,"
and the English words "postponement" and "waiting." The last
word seemed to be the most satisfactory. We must regard interest,
in relation to supply, as the price which must be paid for "waiting."
As with any other price, it must be high enough to attract a sufficient supply, and, on the other hand, to restrict demand sufficiently.
It is of no importance that some waiting would be done, and a
certain amount of capital-disposal available, if the rate of interest
were lower than it is now, and even if it were zero.

"Waiting" implies that a person foregoes for a time the disposal
of a certain amount of value. By doing so he frees, for a corresponding period, a certain amount of capital-disposal. "Waiting" is,
consequently, if considered arithmetically, of the same magnitude
as the control of capital, and, like the latter, is measured by the
product of the capital and the time. On that account it is not
necessary for the general theory to use both expressions. In the
following discussion we shall use the term "capital-disposal" to
designate the service which savers render to the capital market, as
well as the service which the borrowers buy and for which they pay
interest.

In defining "waiting" as the service for which interest is paid,
we define it at once as an arithmetical quantity. In comparison with
this distinct conception, it seems a definite retrogression when
Menger and Böhm-Bawerk try to construct the general theory of
interest upon an assumed general lower estimation of future
satisfaction compared with that of the present. For this formula
can only mean that in certain circumstances the "waiting" entails
a sacrifice which must be compensated by the payment of interest
if it is to take place. But such circumstances do not exclusively
prevail in reality, for a certain amount of saving would be done
even if there were no rate of interest. Also, the under-estimation of
future goods has a very varying force, and cannot be regarded as a
uniform quantity or as an average. The idea of a discounting of
future goods is not new, and certainly does not suffice to form the

basis of a real theory of interest. Such a theory must know how far and to what degree this under-estimation occurs in real life, and thus how far interest must be paid as a compensation for this "waiting." It is then not sufficient merely to state that "waiting" must be compensated by interest; we must ask how much "waiting" is offered at any particular rate of interest – that is, how far the supply of capital-disposal depends upon the rate of interest. So if we wish to regard the supply of capital-disposal as a function of the rate of interest, we must clearly have an arithmetical expression of this supply.

Let us now pass to the conditions which determine the demand for capital-disposal. It was impossible to obtain a deeper understanding of this as long as the significance of concrete capital was kept in the foreground, and the use which this has for directly satisfying wants as well as in production – that is, the direct applicability and productivity of real capital – was given as an explanation of the phenomenon of interest. Such a consideration, which suits only durable goods or fixed real capital, could only explain why the services of a durable good, as well as the good itself, must have a price. This, it is true, is certainly important in the theory of interest, but it tells us nothing about the core of the problem, for it gives no information on the question of how the relation between the price of the services of a durable good and that of the good itself is regulated. This question, as we shall see in what follows (§ 22), can only be completely explained if we regard capital-disposal as an independent factor of production, and the pricing of durable goods as well as of their services as one side of a universal economic pricing process.

The older national economists had in general depicted capital as a fund of the necessaries of life, with which the workers could be supported during the course of the productive process. Capital thus consisted essentially of food, clothes, etc., intended for the workers. The larger the amount of such capital in existence, the longer could one wait for the result of production and the more efficient could the production process be made by the use of tools and machinery, a better cultivation of the soil, and so on. The real significance of capital in this sense must therefore rest in the fact that it makes possible the lapse of time between the beginning and the end of production. This idea, which seems to have been generally accepted earlier, received its most accurate form from Jevons. He asserted that the only use of capital is that it allows us to lengthen the period between the moment when work is begun and that when its results are obtained. [1] This extension of the period of production increases the productivity of labour. Given the rate of interest, the extension of the period of production can and must continue until the increase of the product that is obtained by means of the final extension covers the special interest charges which this extension entails. The interest which is paid for the unit capital-disposal is thus equal to the marginal productivity of the extension of the period of production which is facilitated by this capital-disposal. That is Jevons's theory of interest.

This theory undoubtedly marks an important advance in our knowledge of the conditions which regulate the demand for capital-disposal, but it suffers from an evident one-sidedness from which we must free ourselves. First, Jevons's idea of capital is clearly artificial and unnecessarily limited; what enables the advanced exchange economy to leave a period of time between productive labour and the outcome of production is, as we know (§ 4), not an accumulated stock of staple commodities, but the whole existing and actively continuous process of production, including the total real capital employed in it. This defect in Jevons's theory, due to an imperfect analysis of the conditions of a uniformly progressive social process of production, can, however, be remedied, since, in place of his concept of capital, we can simply substitute our concept of capital-disposal.

But there is another one-sided feature of the theory, bound up with his idea of capital, namely, that he sees the significance of capital only in that it allows us to undertake production that requires time. The gradual using-up of a durable good also takes time, and by far the greater part of capital-disposal is, as we shall

---

[1] Jevons, *Theory of Political Economy* (London, 1879), p. 248. Compare also pp. 242–4, where capital is defined.

see (§ 23), required for waiting for the successive services of durable goods. We must not attempt, by artificial construction, to compress these essentially different sources of the need for capital-disposal ir) one type. Finally, it is a defect of Jevons's theory that it assumes the significance of the last instalment of capital-disposal to be only in the lengthening of the period of production. By the very nature of the idea of capital-disposal, capital and time have a symmetrical position ; a certain amount of capital-disposal used in the productive process may thus not only be used for lengthening the process, but also for increasing the size of the product without increasing the period necessary. The lengthening of the period of production, in Jevons's sense, really means a substitution of capital-disposal for labour, or, in general, for other factors of production. As Jevons wants to determine interest by the marginal productivity of the extension of the period of production, this means that the pricing of capital-disposal is traced back entirely to the principle of substitution, and completely omits the principle of scarcity. But this latter principle is, as we know, always the fundamental principle in pricing, in relation to which the supplementary principles may only be regarded as modifications. This conception of pricing must be applied to capital-disposal; interest, as the price of capital-disposal, must be primarily determined by the scarcity of this factor of production. This fundamental explanation must not be obscured by the condition that the scarcity of capital-disposal can be modified by the possibility of the substitution of other factors of production for it. Interest must still be determined on the basis of scarcity, even when such substitution is impossible. In a conservative agricultural community which is run on unchanging lines, an increase in the capital, for example, would lead to no alteration in the period of production, but would probably, given the opportunity, cause an increased area of land to be cultivated. Interest, in such a case, would be dependent upon the yield of the application of capital on new land; it would not, therefore, be determined by the productivity of a lengthened period of production, but would be due directly to the scarcity of capital-disposal.

But even where the quantities of the other factors of production are given, the interest must, given unaltered methods of production, be determined by the principle of scarcity. An increase of capital-disposal can always be used, on account of a relative increase in the demand for such finished goods as require much capital-disposal for their production. This case evidently does *not* come within the scheme of an "extension of the period of production," unless that extension is given another meaning than that of a change in the technical methods of production. Above all, it is quite unsatisfactory to construct the theory of interest in such a way as to lose sight of its essential nature, the dependence of the demand for finished goods upon the rate of interest.

In this connection it must also be noticed that the assumption of an "average period of production" is, strictly speaking, equivalent to assuming that only *one* process of production occurs with *one* unit production period. This assumption at once excludes a demand for goods whose production would have different claims upon capital-disposal. An unscientific use of the term "average" is, unfortunately, only too apt to introduce such significant assumptions unwittingly into the discussion.

Böhm-Bawerk's great book, *Kapital und Kapitalzins*,[1] held a prominent position for a long time in scientific discussion. In spite of the enormous and extraordinarily careful work put into this book, it seems faulty not only in its criticism of historical theory, but also in its positive part. The author has not been able to assimilate the new scientific conception of pricing as that of a single, general process determining simultaneously not only the prices of finished goods, but also those of factors of production. His ideas are still at least partly of the type characterised by the question: Is the value of the goods determined by that of the factors of production, or, *vice versa*, is the value of the factors of production determined by that of their products? From the very beginning, Böhm-Bawerk is unacquainted with the central idea of the theory of pricing, that these factors occupy a parallel position in the pricing process and determine each other, though both, in the last resort, are determined by factors which are based partly on the nature of things and partly

[1] Translated into English by W. Smart, in two parts: *Capital and Interest* (1890) and *Positive Theory of Capital* (1891).

on the peculiarities of man in his economic aspect. It is but natural that in such circumstances he has not been able either to portray, in his critical exposition, even a generally accurate picture of those theories which, for all their faults and incompleteness, were still definitely conscious of the further conception of the problem shown here, or, in his positive exposition, to formulate a theory of interest which was in general satisfactory or organically consistent with pricing as a whole. Böhm-Bawerk's treatment of the separate sides of the problem of interest is not very fruitful. His general formula – "the discounting of future goods" – fits in badly, as we have seen, with the foundation of a real study of the interdependence of the rate of interest and the supply of capital-disposal. If the formula is used for showing the actual condition of the capital market, it is an unnecessary and by no means clear description of the fact that interest is paid. In respect of the conditions which determine the demand for capital-disposal, Böhm-Bawerk has, in the main, taken over Jevons's theory, with all its faults. [1]

The essential stages of the development of the theory of interest have thus been made sufficiently clear to allow of a deeper under-standing of the problem, and of the claims which must be satisfied by a conclusive theory of interest. Here we need no longer follow the ever-growing literature on the problem of interest. A critical appreciation of that is, at all events, only possible from the point of view of a positive theory of interest which regards interest as a price similar to all other prices in the general pricing process and treats the factors on the side of supply and of demand as co-ordinated factors in the pricing of capital-disposal. We now pass on to the exposition of such a theory.

[1] The 3rd edition of the *Positive Theory of Capital* (1909 and 1912) has not been able to make me alter my general opinion of Böhm-Bawerk's work. Böhm-Bawerk's criticism of the theory of interest developed in my *Nature and Necessity of Interest* seems to assert that I have not proved the existence of a "capital-disposal" which may be regarded as the independent object of business transactions, and therefore that the conception of interest as a price, on which my whole exposition is based, is incorrect. For my part, I find it strange that anyone can doubt the existence of a capital-disposal which, in reality, is every day the object of hundreds of thousands of transactions involving millions of pounds. I hope also that this idea has been formulated with sufficient precision. I leave it to the reader to decide whether the theory of interest as a special theory of prices, organically consistent with the general pricing process, is not easier to understand and more complete in scope than a theory of interest based on the very artificial conception of an exchange between present and future goods.

§ 21 *Capital-Disposal as a Factor of Production*

If we wish to divide all factors of production into certain main categories, it is evident that we must reckon labour and land as such, even though the more accurate definition of these general classes may need a special analysis. Among the other factors of production our attention is drawn at once to the produced material commodities which are still in the process of production. We term these goods real capital. But is it possible to put this real capital on the same footing as the other two categories? This question is closely linked up with the old controversy as to whether "capital" may be regarded as an independent factor of production, a question which, as is so often the case, could be disputed chiefly because the object of the controversy was not clear. Real capital is obviously necessary for production, and from this point of view must be regarded as a factor of production. But it can be split up into other factors which have co-operated in producing it. So if we ask about the primary factors which are not themselves a result of the productive process, it might appear as if, apart from nature, no other factor but labour, including in that term the work performed by entrepreneurs, were necessary for production. This, in fact, is a view that has often been held, and it plays an important part in Socialism.

To make this point clear we must now consider more carefully the actual conditions of production, and recall our distinction between durable and consumption goods (§ 2).

A durable commodity is produced for the sake of the services it yields when used. These services form the direct object of the demand. The commodity itself is only an intermediary, necessary for the satisfaction of this demand, and cannot therefore be regarded as the ultimate stage in the process of production. From the economic point of view this process must be regarded as a continuous one, attaining the ultimate satisfaction of wants by a series of different productive services. The building of a house is therefore only the initial stage in the process, the object of which is to satisfy the desire for house accommodation. The process of production is not complete until this want has been satisfied, and this only occurs with the gradual using-up of the house. The second stage of the process implies supervision, maintenance, and so on – that is, further output of productive activity, if only to a less degree. The fundamental point is that it takes time, and, in the case we are considering, far more time than that needed by the first stage. After the house is completed, the owner-occupier must still wait for a long time before he can enjoy all the fruits of his sacrifices.

This circumstance is universal, based on the very nature of things, and is in no way conditioned by the form of the economy. The farmer who is self-sufficient must still wait many years after making the sacrifices necessary for building a house for the full fruition of them in the use of the house. In the exchange economy this inevitable waiting for the fruits of the sacrifices of the first stage of production may be taken over by another person. This waiting is thus clearly recognisable as an independent economic function. It is, of course, conceivable that a group of workers, having built a house together, will wait to receive their wages in the form of the rent that gradually comes in the future. But as a rule they either cannot, because they need the means to satisfy unavoidable wants, or will not, because they prefer to enjoy the fruit of their labour now rather than in the distant and uncertain future. Another person, however, comes along and buys the house in order to be able to receive the rents that are gradually paid in. The workers then receive their wages as soon as the house is completed, while the other man undertakes the special task of waiting.

What has been said regarding houses applies equally well to all other durable goods. Whether its services are used for the direct satisfaction of wants or in production does not matter. The manufacturer who buys a machine must wait for compensation for his sacrifice until the machine has given its full complement of productive service in his factory. In many cases even the producer transfers the work of waiting to another, and is content, like a tenant of a house, to rent the durable commodity; manufacturers rent factories, merchants rent their premises, and even large railways sometimes rent their trucks and coaches.

The function of waiting for the services which a durable commodity is able to yield during its life is therefore a condition necessary before the commodity will be produced. If neither the producers themselves nor any other person will undertake this waiting, then the production of this commodity must remain economically impossible. Who undertakes the function is of secondary importance. The main point is that it must be undertaken by somebody. But in order to do so a man must have at his disposal a certain amount of abstract capital (i.e. money), corresponding to the cost of production of the commodity. The man who buys a completed house must have the sum necessary at hand. He pays this sum to the builders, who do as they please with it. But he has tied up his capital in that house. So a certain command over capital, or "capital-disposal," is necessary if people have to wait for the services of a durable commodity, and this command over capital is a necessary condition of production. If the capital-disposal which is needed for this waiting cannot be found, the commodity cannot, economically, be made. If a man wishes to know in advance whether or not a certain durable article is going to be made, he must remember that this article is produced only in order to obtain the services it yields, and this production can only be carried out if he possesses sufficient command over capital to be able to wait for the whole succession of these services, or if there is a reasonable prospect that someone will put this capital at his disposal when the article is finished. Thus, for the purpose of production of durable goods, this command of capital is just as necessary as any other factor required in the actual production itself, and must consequently be put on the same footing as the other factors of production.

"Waiting" and "capital-disposal" are synonymous terms for this factor. "Waiting" emphasises the negative aspect of it, the foregoing, for a certain time, of the consumption of an existing capital. 'Capital-disposal' is the positive command of capital, during the same period, which is thus provided.

We have restricted the conception of real capital only to those material goods which are actually in the process of production. The conception of capital-disposal must evidently be restricted in the same way, and it must therefore not be applied to waiting for the services of those durable goods which have already definitely passed to the consumer.

Waiting for the services of durable goods is, of course, only a necessary factor of production in so far as there really is a question of production. As soon as it is intended to make a durable article, the capital-disposal that is necessary if the waiting for its services is to be done must be regarded in the same way as anything else required for its production, and for that very reason capital-disposal is a necessary factor of production. If, on the other hand, the durable article is finished, then one must wait, and the necessary capital-disposal may or may not be found. If no one is willing to pay more than half the cost of the article, there is a loss which must be borne by the producer. The buyer has then, of course, only half the capital-disposal to offer. But then the conditions necessary for the continuance of production are disturbed. We cannot deduce from this that the command of capital is more or less superfluous, or that any amount of it will be suitable. This would be almost the same as saying that there is no need to pay for a piece of work that has been done, if one has merely promised in advance to pay for it. If the production of durable goods is to continue unchanged, it is clearly necessary that the requisite capital-disposal shall always be available to take over the finished article.

Capital-disposal is therefore only a condition of a continued production. The use of non-reproducible goods, especially land, involves waiting for services, but as the prices of these goods are not determined by cost of production, this use does not require a definite capital-disposal.

The need for capital-disposal in the economic process of production, which we have now demonstrated, arises because *the use of durable goods take time*. But this, though the most important, is not the only reason. Capital-disposal is also needed for production in its narrower, technical sense, because *that production takes time*.

Certain kinds of work, such as cooking and massage, yield an immediate satisfaction of wants. The fruit of such work is enjoyed at the moment the work is done, or immediately afterwards. But most work has to be done in the earlier stages of production, and is not of use until the article is finished. To simplify the matter we may assume that raw materials and tools are not of appreciable importance, and that the article is made by a group of workers without any outside help. It is conceivable that the workers may wait for their wages until the article is finished, and so receive as wages the article, or the price of it. But they may transfer this waiting to someone else, so as to be able to draw the wages for their work at once. The other, who undertakes this waiting, must then pay the workers as production proceeds, and he receives in return the finished article, or the price of it. In order to undertake this waiting he must have at his disposal a capital corresponding to the price of the article at the time, and equal to the price of the finished product at the end. If the workers themselves undertake the waiting, they must have at their disposal exactly the same amount of capital. Of course, neither they nor anyone else need have the whole sum in advance. If they have sufficient capital to allow them to live during the period of production, they can collect the capital that is necessary for taking over their product gradually, by means of their productive but unpaid labour. This gradually increasing capital is, during the period in which the article is produced, tied up in that article. It is only when someone is prepared to furnish the necessary capital-disposal that production can be undertaken at all. The corresponding command of capital is thus in all circumstances a necessary condition of production, and must, consequently, be regarded in the same way as the other factors of production.

What has been said about labour applies equally well to the other factors which co-operate in the productive process. This co-operation must be done in the earlier stage of production, and its use only appears when the product is completed. So there must be some waiting for compensation for this co-operation. The fact that production takes time means that it requires a certain and generally increasing amount of capital to be placed at its disposal during the period of production. The capital required is at each moment equal to the value of the product.

In some cases the product can be used to satisfy wants even at earlier stages, but it is better and larger if its further development is permitted. That is especially so in the case of forests. A tree may be used now, or it may be allowed to grow for another ten years. For this, however, one must have at one's disposal a capital corresponding to the selling price of the tree at the time. This act of allowing things to mature – it applies in other cases, also, such as the maturing of wine – plays an important part, and must be regarded as one of the reasons for needing capital-disposal.

We could consume the whole, or at least the greater part, of the wheat harvest in autumn, but in that case we should not be able to satisfy the needs of the later part of the harvest year. We economise with the wheat, and spread our consumption of it more or less evenly over the whole year. For this we must have at our disposal at any moment a capital equal to the total price of the remaining stock of wheat at the time. This necessary economising of a stock that must last for a certain time is another source of the need for capital-disposal.

These last two sources need not, however, be regarded as separate, but as part of the general need that arises because production takes time; for by production we mean a process which continues until the products are handed over to the consumers.

Our division of capital-disposal into that which is required because the use of durable goods takes time, and that which is required because production in its technical sense also takes time, clearly corresponds to the division of real capital into fixed and circulating capital (§ 5)

In our study of the stationary state we found that a constant reproduction of capital was necessary to maintain it. This reproduction naturally presupposes that in the exchange economy the various commodities constituting real capital have prices corresponding to their cost of production, and that, therefore, the capital-disposal needed for acquiring them is always available. Since the two forms of real capital, fixed and circulating, are themselves kept unchanged, they each require, in conformity with the above-mentioned two chief reasons for the need for capital-disposal at constant prices, a constant command of capital. So there must be a fixed command of capital equal to the constant total price of the real capital. This means a definite demand upon the willingness of the community as a whole to "wait," or to "save," using the word in its general sense. In our actual exchange economy the individual capitalist generally finds it possible to consume part of his capital. He may, for instance, collect a debt and use the money for his current consumption. There are always some capitalists doing this, and thus a certain amount of capital-disposal is withdrawn from the general economy in each period. A corresponding amount of new savings must therefore be provided. Only if this is done can the economy remain in its stationary condition. The demands made on the members of the community for this purpose therefore have a real continuous importance. Waiting is a factor of production which, even in the stationary state, must always be available. This is a more careful explanation of that characteristic of man in his economic aspect which we stated, in § 5, to be a condition necessary for the maintenance of the stationary state. In this respect the progressive economy naturally makes greater demands, since in it real capital must not only be maintained, but continually increased. Consequently, a constantly increasing amount of capital-disposal must be available, and there must be continuous positive saving on the part of the community.

Capital-disposal – the command of a certain amount of capital for a time – is not only, for the two reasons given, a factor of production, but is also a *primary* factor. On the supply side it implies, as we have seen, a "waiting," a temporary abstention from the satisfaction of wants for which the means are available. This is evidently a personal service of a particular kind, which cannot be further split up into other services, but which must really be termed "primary." We must remember that in this inquiry we have as yet said nothing as to the extent to which this service must be paid for. So far we have merely proved that capital-disposal is an essential factor of production which must be placed in the same category as the other factors, labour and land.

This conclusion is further strengthened if we remember that capital-disposal may replace other factors. The mutual substitution of capital-disposal and labour is a phenomenon which is particularly important in the theory of interest as well as in that of wages, and one to which we must return. Here we need only show the general nature of this substitution to demonstrate the fact that capital-disposal must be regarded in the same way as labour. The restriction of handwork by machine-work is a universally recognised fact. The services of machines which are replacing labour to a certain extent must not, however, be regarded as a primary factor of production, but can, if we consider the essentials, be resolved into the labour necessary for the manufacture of the machine and the capital-disposal necessary for waiting for its successive services. If we assume that the machines last ten years, then every year a tenth part of this labour is consumed. Individual labour is thus partly replaced by this quantity of labour and partly by capital-disposal.

The source of the supply of capital-disposal is saving. The means which savers make available by undertaking the function of waiting are for the most part, though not completely, used for paying wages, and are then used by the workers for buying the necessaries of life, paying rent, and so on. It is for this reason that the classical school thought that the rôle of capital was the maintenance of the workers for the duration of production, and conceived capital as an accumulated stock of commodities needed by the workers. We know that this is fundamentally incorrect (§ 6). In the modern continuous economy there is no stock of such commodities. From the continuous process of production flows a steady stream of products, partly goods for the immediate satisfaction of wants, partly real capital. Because they have saved part of their income, the savers have a claim on a certain proportion of these products, and they make this claim effective by buying, either directly or through the medium of others, the newly produced real capital. At the same time the workers, by virtue of their wages, have claims to a certain part of the social production, but realise their claims chiefly in the form of a demand for finished goods for their consumption. In this way the whole of the unsaved income of the community is utilised. In a state of equilibrium, production is directed by these claims, and, in conformity with them, is divided between the increase of real capital and the immediate satisfaction of wants. The means which the savers make available are therefore really only their claims upon the results of the social production, and not concrete consnmption goods.

These means are not accumulated in advance. The savings are invested at the time they are made (see §48) by placing them at the disposal of entrepreneurs. So the new demand for capital-disposal is fed daily by new savings which are directly or indirectly used for the purchase of real capital.

The unsaved income of the exchange economy is used to pay for current consumption. This consumption consists partly of the consumption goods which flow in a steady stream from the production process and thus need not be accumulated in advance, but also partly of the services of durable goods, such as houses, streets, railways, and theatres. As was shown in §§ 5 and 6, the exchange economy must, to satisfy all these needs, possess a certain real capital, partly fixed and partly circulating, and in the progressive economy this capital must increase steadily. But a stock of finished goods is generally quite unnecessary.

Naturally, the workers may save, and, in so far as they do so, a part of the newly produced real capital belongs to them. If the savings-bank deposits of the labourers in the building industry are loaned on mortgage to the master-builder, then the workers really take over part of that capital-disposal which is needed in building the houses on which they themselves are working. A peasant who builds his own house does the same thing to an even greater extent, and he himself provides the greater part of the necessary capital disposal. He can do this partly because he draws an income from agriculture with which he can, if necessary, support himself while he is building, and partly by restricting the satisfaction of his wants, this being carried much further than would be necessary if such strenuous work were done for wages. So here again there is saving which sets free productive power for the production of real capital. The capital necessary for acquiring the house is created by the man himself, by his work, for which he demands no immediate satisfaction of wants in compensation.

The capital made available by the savers is, in the exchange economy, expressed by a sum of money. A sum of money – that is, an abstract sum expressed in the price unit – is an elementary arithmetical quantity which has its own dimensions, just as length, weight and time have in physics. We will call this purely economic quantity M, and the time dimension which is very important in economics T. The productive service we call capital-disposal is thus MT. This means that this particular service is measured by the product of a sum of money and a period of time. The unit of this product is the disposal of a unit of money for a unit period of time. If, for instance, we take £100 as the unit of money and one year as the unit of time, the unit of our capital-disposal is the use of £100 for a year. As this capital-disposal is only measured by the product of a quantity of goods and a period of time, it is in principle independent of alterations in the sum of money and in the time as long as they leave the product unchanged. Thus the disposal of £1,000 for one month is equivalent to that of £500 for two months. But we shall see in the next section that there is, in practice, a certain difference between the disposal of capital for short and long periods.

Now that we have made clear the significance of capital-disposal as a necessary and primary factor of production, we return to the question from which we started in this section – to what extent we must regard real capital as a separate factor of production. To answer this question we must refer to §§ 5 and 6. The use of fixed real capital resolves itself, on the one hand, into a using-up, which must be replaced by maintenance and renewal – that is, by production – and therefore means the need of more remote means of production, and, on the other hand, into a disposal of capital for the period of use, and this disposal must be regarded as a primary factor of production. The use of circulating real capital is a consumption which, by its very nature, must be replaced by production. This use requires, as a complement, a disposal of capital for waiting for the result. Consequently, it seems that real capital itself is not a separate factor of production.

But if we confine our analysis of the exchange economy to a

period that begins in the present, the real capital in existence at the beginning of the period must be conceived as a given factor of our problem, which cannot be further resolved, and must therefore be regarded as a primary factor of production. Thus our analysis of real capital as a factor of production brings us back both to the real capital in existence at the beginning of the period and the capital-disposal offered during the period, and, of course, to the other primary factors of production available during that same time. The importance of the real capital given at the beginning, or of its services in the whole pricing process, which we have substantially shown in § 12, will be more closely considered in our study of the nature of rent (§ 22 and Chapter VII.).

§ 22 *Interest as a Price*

Our inquiries up to the present have shown that capital-disposal is an indispensable factor of production. The question whether anything is to be paid for this factor is one which must not be considered from the ethical or sentimental point of view of the value of the services rendered by capitalists, but depends entirely upon whether the supply of capital-disposal is scarce relative to the demand — that is, whether it is necessary to put a price on it sufficient to check the demand and, perhaps, to stimulate the supply.

Actually, as everyone knows, a price is always paid for the use of capital. This is sufficient to prove that in our economic life there is a scarcity of it. Were there no such scarcity, it would have no price. The rather widespread belief that in our modern society excessive saving results in a superfluity of capital is therefore incorrect.

The price paid for the use of capital is called the interest on capital, or, in brief, interest. In reality this interest often includes a compensation for the risk closely connected with the loan. Such a premium on risk is regulated in accordance with its own laws, and has nothing in common with interest. The theory of interest must, on that account, disregard risk and consider only those loans where there is perfect security. In real life, of course, there is no such thing as absolute safety; it suffices however, to consider those loans where the security is, or is believed to be, so good that nothing is paid for risk. In such cases the interest agreed upon is a pure interest in the sense of the theory.

Further, in real life, the rate of interest is different in the case where the capital is loaned for a short period from that where it is loaned for a long one. The rate of interest for short-period loans varies much more than that for long-period loans. This is especially marked in the case of so-called "daily money." Thus on the New York Exchange the average rate for daily money in October, 1907, was 22 per cent.; in October, 1908, it was only 1.42 per cent. The discount rate also shows marked variations. On the Berlin Bourse it averaged 7.07 per cent. in December, 1907, and 2.92 per cent. in the same month of 1908. The London market discount rate, which fell to a minimum in 1895 with an average of 0.8 per cent., was 4.53 per cent. in 1907. Connected with such variations are the marked alterations in the rate of interest on permanent loans which occurred at the beginning of the twentieth century. German State loans fell in price from about par in 1906 to 85 in June, 1913, and this meant a rise in the real rate of interest from $3\frac{1}{2}$ per cent. to rather more than 4 per cent. In the period 1896 to 1912 the effective rate of interest on ten English public loans rose from approximately 2.7 per cent. to 3.6 per cent. [1]

We must, consequently, decide which rate to take as the subject of our study of the general theory of interest. In answer to this it might be said that a complete theory of interest should take into account all the rates and discover the determining factors of the different rates. But here, where we must limit ourselves to an elementary study of the phenomenon of interest, it seems best to choose a typical form in which capital-disposal is sold. In that case we must evidently choose the long-term loan. The greater part of capital-disposal is, as we know, required for the use of such durable goods as buildings, railways, water-works, and so on. For these

---

[1] *Economic Journal*, June, 1913, p. 284. The reason why the rate on foreign and colonial loans rose so much more slowly in the same period is that the risk attached to these fell considerably in the mind of the English public. This led to a corresponding rise in the rate of interest on English loans, as their earlier monopolistic position was in part lost.

purposes the capital-disposal must be for a very long, if not indefinite period, and for this reason we must take as typical the rate of interest on fixed loans, mortgages, and similar transactions. But we must bear in mind that the rate in question should not be raised on account of any serious risk, or reduced by any special measures – as, for instance, certain states have done by placing their own loans in a privileged position. The type of interest that best reflects the actual state of the market is, perhaps, that paid for first mortgages on land. In pre-war Western Europe this was generally between $3\frac{3}{4}$ and $4\frac{1}{2}$ per cent. [1]

If we glance at the history of the rate of interest and wish to make a comparison between old and modern rates, we must remember that the rate of interest is a market price, and so only those rates can be compared which are found in developed markets, and then only if there is no need to take risk into account. If these simple and obvious precautions had always been taken, the very exaggerated idea of the historical fall in the rate of interest would never have arisen, and the doctrine of the inherent tendency of the rate to fall would have been deprived of the greater part of the support of historical experience. In times when Canon Law was enforced, the taking of interest was often accompanied by great risk, and, in any case, by much unpleasantness. This obviously restricted to a considerable extent the number of people willing to lend money, and added a good deal to the rate of interest as compensation for risk and other disadvantages. Consequently, these rates of interest cannot be compared with ours. As soon as a true capital market began to develop in the chief centres of trade in Europe, we find rates of interest as low as those of our own time. In Holland, for example, the rate remained at about 3 per cent. in the middle of the seventeenth century, while the effective rate on first-class securities was $2\frac{1}{2}$ to $3\frac{3}{4}$ per cent. in the period before the French Revolution.

The following inquiries refer entirely to the interest paid, in fully developed markets, for long-term loans which are not particularly favourable, but which are regarded as perfectly safe.

[1] The best statistical data as to the fluctuations of the rate of interest are, perhaps, the statements given by insurance companies of the average real interest obtained by them on their funds.

As the price of a primary factor of production, interest is determined, like all other prices, as part of the great pricing process. In every period there is a limited amount of capital-disposal available, and in the same period there is a demand for it – due, in the last analysis, to the demand for finished goods – which can only be checked sufficiently by putting a definite price on that capital-disposal. In the system of equations by which the general pricing process is expressed arithmetically, one of our R is the quantity of capital-disposal available in the period in question, and one of our q is the price of it. This price is therefore determined like all the other q. (The fact that the price of a unit of capital-disposal is an abstract figure causes no difficulty here, for this price is multiplied by a certain amount of capital, and the product is a sum of money which can be added to other money costs.)

The special theory of interest can therefore be nothing but a closer examination of the pricing process considered from the point of view of the price of capital-disposal. So here we have to consider supply and demand separately. On the demand side we have to discover, first, what external factors influence this demand, and so, indirectly, the interest, and, secondly, how the price of capital-disposal – that is, the interest itself – affects the demand. In the same way we must study the supply. In our general treatment of the pricing problem we assumed the available quantities of the various factors of production to be given. In this book, however, we shall drop this assumption and attempt to discover whether and how far the supply of the factors of production is influenced by their prices. We shall do this in the present chapter in the case of capital-disposal – that is, we shall study the supply of capital-disposal as a function of the rate of interest.

Such a study will show us why capital-disposal is scarce, and how far this scarcity may be regarded as necessary. We shall thus know whether interest is merely an accidental phenomenon of our time and of our economic organisation, or whether it is rooted in objective conditions equally necessary at any future time and for any kind of organisation. Not until this much-disputed question is answered will the theory of interest have fulfilled its task. For this purpose, we must see what counterbalancing forces on the side of demand and supply would be set in action by a fall in the rate of interest. We shall find that these forces would very soon put a limit to the fall of the rate. Further, we shall have to estimate how far interest would have to be allowed for in a socialist community, and so realise that the existence of interest is independent of our particular form of economic organisation.

As interest is a price paid, like any other price, in money, its magnitude is equal to M – that of money. We found, in the preceding section, that the capital-disposal is equal to the product of MT, where T is the time dimension. The rate of interest indicates how much must be paid for a unit of capital-disposal – say, for the disposal of a capital of £100 for a year – or, in other words, that ratio of the interest paid for a certain capital-disposal to the capital-disposal itself. This rate of interest is therefore equal to $\dfrac{M}{MT}$; that is, to $\dfrac{1}{T}$. *Hence the rate of interest is the reciprocal value of a period of time.* This proposition must not be regarded as an unimportant result of a mathematical speculation. It has a real importance for the theory of interest, in that it gives a clue to the deeper nature of the phenomenon of interest – that elements of time are essential determining factors of the rate. This idea is, in reality, not strange to the mind of the average person, for the common expression of interest as "so much per cent. per year" expresses the relation between an abstract number and a period of time, or, in other words, the reciprocal value of a period of time. The character of the rate of interest is made still clearer when we consider the price of a perpetual, fixed rent. This price is a certain multiple of the rent, or the rent for a number of years, or for a certain time. If we call this time t and the fixed rent r, the price c of the rent is equal to tr. What interest does the purchaser receive on this investment? The capital is c, and the annual return r. The rate of interest is therefore $\dfrac{r}{c}$, i.e. $\dfrac{1}{t}$. So we find that the rate of interest is the reciprocal value of a period of time, namely, the reciprocal value of the number of years by which the annual rent is multiplied in calculating the purchase price. The interest may thus just as well be determined by this number of years. In earlier times, when the purchase of rents was often the predominant form of investment, this form was actually used in determining the interest. In England, when we buy land, we still speak of so many "years' purchase," and in the stock market of "years' purchase of dividend." The sum paid for a durable good that lasts for ever is not equal to the price of the annual use multiplied by an infinite number of years, but corresponds to the use of it for a definite, limited time. This time, which is the reciprocal value of the rate of interest, can serve just as well to indicate the height of the rate. The principle that the rate of interest is the reciprocal value of a definite time is, through this observation, seen in its proper light.

In connection with the position of interest in pricing, we must again distinguish between the two chief reasons for the use of capital-disposal, namely, that both the use of durable goods and production in the narrower sense take time. So we must first consider the position of interest in determining the price of durable goods and their services.

Rent, in the broadest sense of the word, is the price of the use of a durable good. The factors determining this price will be more closely considered in the next chapter, but we must introduce the idea here, for otherwise it is impossible to obtain a correct understanding of the rôle of interest in the determination of prices. When we think of the price of the durable good in relation to that of its use – that is, relating it to rent – we call the price of the good its "capital value." We come, here, to that characteristic of durable goods which most clearly shows the need for placing them in a separate category, namely, that two prices must be considered in regard to them, the price of the good itself and the price of the use of it. When this is the case, it must clearly be a particular business to buy the good and sell the use of it. The ratio between the prices must then be determined by the general laws of pricing. If, for the sake of simplification, we assume that supplying the use of it involves no other act except waiting, and, further, that the durable good lasts for ever, then the person who obtains the good need only have the necessary capital at his disposal, and therefore be paid for this service only. Then, clearly, the price of the use must be equal to the interest on the purchase price of the good itself. Consequently, in this case there is a definite equation between capital value and rent; if c is the capital value, and r the rent, and p the rate of interest, then $r = pc$.

If the durable good does not last for ever, the rent must include a proportion for the depreciation of the capital. The rent often also includes payment for special services of the landlord, such as lighting the stairs in a house split up into flats, but that is not rent in the scientific sense. Strictly speaking, the proportion for depreciation does not belong to the rent, if we take this to mean net rent, or the price of the mere use of the house after depreciation has been accounted for, but is a payment for part of the good itself. This net rent, which may be defined as the price of the use of a good which lasts for ever, will be implied when we speak of the term "rent" in what follows. Thus capital value and rent are linked up with each other and with the rate of interest by the equation we have given.

We may then ask which of these quantities is independent, and which depends upon the others. The answer to this must be different according as the durable good is reproducible or not.

If the good is not reproducible, the cost of production cannot be a factor determining price. Besides, as the demand by consumers for a durable good is essentially a demand for the use of the good and not for the good itself, no direct price is fixed for it. On the contrary, the price of the use of it is determined on the one hand by scarcity, and on the other by the demand. The price must be high enough to equate the demand with the available supply. Once the price of its use is determined in this way, the price of the good itself is settled by capitalising the rent on the basis of the current rate of interest. As there is no separate factor determining this capital value, it cannot influence the rate of interest. In order to wait for the use of a durable good, it is true that a certain amount of capital-disposal is necessary, but we do not have to deal here with a separate source of the demand for capital-disposal, for the required amount of control over capital is determined by the capital value, and this, in turn, by the rate of interest. The person who owns the good, possesses, by that very fact, the capital needed for waiting for the services yielded by that good. If another buys it, it might seem as if he withdraws so much capital-disposal from the market, for he ties up a certain amount in buying the good. This view is commonly accepted by the business world – for instance, that large purchases of land result in especially large demands on the capital market. This is obviously incorrect, for the vendor has the same amount of capital placed freely at his disposal as the purchaser tied up. The capital-disposal bound up in the good is given in the capital value of the good at the time. So the possession of the good means no special demand on the market for capital-disposal, and can therefore have no influence on the rate of interest. This is true even if the good is the subject of a rise in prices, and so of an "unearned increment." The capital value of a durable commodity which cannot be reproduced is an entirely secondary phenomenon of the pricing process.

But it is otherwise in the case of reproducible goods. The price of the commodity itself has, then, *one* determining factor – its cost of production. At the same time, in this case the price of the use of the good has only *one* determining factor, and when the existing quantity of the good is not given in advance, that factor is the demand for the use of it. Neither of these factors is, by itself, sufficient to fix the price. In these circumstances it is not possible to have a definite price until there is established a ratio between the price of the good and the price of its use. This is done by the intervention of the capitalist who buys the good in order to sell its services, or who places at the command of the entrepreneur sufficient capital for this purpose. This intervention requires a definite capital-disposal. The purchaser of the good must, in normal circumstances, pay the cost of its production. He must allow for interest on his money at the current rate, and thus, in the total cost of providing the use, the price of the use has a second determining factor. The equation between capital value, interest and rent, thus provides the necessary connection between the price of the good and the price of its use, and the problem of price-determination is settled in the ordinary way. Consequently, in this case, none of the three magnitudes – capital value, interest, and rent – is independent, but, on the other hand, none is determined by the others. They are all equally unknown quantities in the pricing process, determined simultaneously by it.

The demands that, in this case, are made on the capital market, are determined by the cost of production of the article, which must, in normal circumstances – that is, if production is to continue unaltered – be covered. These demands are new. The production of a new durable commodity naturally means a new burden on the capital market, which must be balanced by a new accumulation of capital – that is, by new savings. The demand for capital-disposal which arises because of the waiting involved in the use of reproducible durable goods represents, consequently, a separate factor in the market for capital, and must exert a separate influence on the rate of interest. The capital value of reproducible durable goods is thus not merely the capitalised value of the rent, but has its own special determining factor in the cost of production of the commodity, and itself exerts an influence on the rate of interest as well as on the price of the use of the commodity (the rent).

This connection is seen most clearly as a whole when, as we have hitherto done, we regard the services as the ultimate products; that is, when we include the waiting for the services in the productive process in the broader sense. The capital-disposal is then seen to be a factor of production, and we have only to consider a single pricing process in which the price of capital-disposal is settled in the same way as that of any other factor of production, and in which is included the prices of reproducible durable goods as well as the prices of their services. From this point of view, the cost of capital-disposal is seen to be similar to the other costs of production, the services have definite costs of production, and the general interconnection of the pricing process which adjusts the demand for finished goods to the existing quantities of primary factors of production available is again established.

In the *narrower sense*, we mean by *rent* the price of the use of a non-reproducible durable good. This price, which, as we have shown, is directly determined by the relative scarcity of services of this kind, and therefore occupies a position in the pricing process quite independent of interest, must be made the subject of a special study, and we shall devote a separate chapter to it.

With the non-reproducible goods discussed in the arguments in this section must be included those which, technically, can be produced, but which are not produced because of the lack of demand and the high cost of production. [1]

§ 23 *The Demand for Capital-Disposal*

Now that we have shown that capital-disposal is a necessary factor of production in general, we must try to get an idea of the relative importance of this factor in the different branches of production. If we could assume that this importance were the same for all products, and that the price paid for capital-disposal were always

[1] In connection with the position of interest in determining the prices of consumption goods, the following should be noted.

The condition for a continuous process of production is that at every stage the product has a price which covers the costs of production up to that point. In these costs must be included the interest which must be paid for the capital-disposal required for the continuance of production, that is, the interest on the capital represented by the product at the different stages of completion. If, therefore, the normal productive process includes, and must include, a period of waiting during which other factors of production are demanded to a less extent, the disposal of the capital corresponding to the product, which forms the chief cost, is the condition of such production, and apart from other costs the price of the product at the end of the period must include the interest which has been incurred during the period. This is the case, for instance, in the lumber industry in an organised forest administration. If a forest which can be utilised now remains untouched for another ten years, the increase in price at the end of the ten years must, besides the current costs of forestry and the rent of the land, be sufficient to cover the interest for ten years on the capital represented by the forest at the beginning of the period. If, for the sake of simplification, we ignore the other costs, we find a definite connection between the price of the forest at the beginning and end of the period and the rate of interest. The first price finds its determining factor in the cost of production and the second in the demand, but both factors are linked up by means of the rate of interest. The production requires a definite amount of capital-disposal, and this means a certain demand on the capital market; the rate of interest is therefore affected. But the result is different in the case of natural forests, where there is no need to consider cost of production as the determining factor of the price at the beginning of the period. It is then possible that this price has no separate determining factor, but represents the discounted value, at the current rate of interest, of the price at the end of the period. In this case, therefore, the required amount of capital-disposal exerts no influence on the rate of interest, but is itself determined by that rate. On the other hand, however, it is also possible that even at the beginning of the period the forest had a certain price for its immediate use. If this price is lower than the discounted value of the future selling price, it has no significance for pricing. But if the price is higher, the forest must be utilised at once. Hence the proportionate to the other costs of production, then interest would evidently play no part in determining the relative prices of the products, and we should have a pricing process in agreement with that of Ricardo (§ 31). But if, on the contrary, capital-disposal has a very different significance in the various branches of production or for different products, interest must, if it is paid, have a definitely positive influence on the relative prices of the different goods. Each rise or fall in the rate of interest must then mean an alteration in the relative prices of goods, and each alteration in the relative demand for different goods must have a definite influence on the demand for capital-disposal, and thus on the rate of interest. Capital-disposal therefore occupies the same position as any other factor of production.

In order to proceed to the first question, we must calculate the use of capital in some of the different branches of production, and

scarcity of the older stands of timber becomes more marked and the price of these may rise so much that greater areas of forest may be allowed to reach full growth. If this occurs, the normal relationship between the prices at the beginning and end of the period and the rate of interest is again restored. The price at the beginning has, in this case, a determining factor not in the cost of production, but, instead of that, in the demand for the sizes of timber which could be supplied at that time. The price at the end has, at the same time, its determining factor, namely, in the demand for the larger sizes of timber. A certain amount of capital-disposal is required to allow the forest to reach full growth, and the demand arising from this has a definite influence on the rate of interest. The price at the beginning is thus not the discounted value, at a given rate of interest, of the price at the end. As this example shows, the position of interest in pricing in all similar cases depends on whether the price at the beginning has a separate determining factor or not.

If the task of waiting consists in uniformly distributing an already accumulated stock over a given period of consumption, as, for instance, is the case with the wheat harvest, beginning and end prices are linked up with each other by the condition that the interest on the beginning-price (including the cost of storing) must be covered by the price at the end of the period. For the rest, the prices have their separate determining factors in the demand for, and the given sizes of, the harvest. The price which must be paid in August for wheat that will be consumed in January is not the discounted value of the January price, but must coincide with the price of wheat sold for immediate consumption. The connection between the different factors in this pricing is as follows: Let us imagine the price at the time of the harvest as given, then the price at any instant of the following year is settled as soon as the rate of interest is determined. Also, the amount consumed at each moment is also settled, and thus the total consumption for the year. As this latter must be equal to the harvest, we have an equation, including the price at the beginning and the rate of interest. As soon as the rate of interest is given, not only is the price at the beginning known, but also the price at any desired moment during the following year.

The continuous flow of wheat over to consumption during the whole harvest year is best regarded as a part of the process of production, in which the interest paid for waiting appears as a cost of production. From this point of view, the price-determination considered here is essentially a part of the general pricing process by which the price of wheat is settled at the different seasons of the year.

compare it with the use of other factors of production. As a measure of the importance of the other factors of production we can take the size of the total expenditure apart from the reimbursement for capital-disposal. We must then compare this expenditure with the return on the capital employed in various undertakings. We can find some statistics for making such a comparison in an English Blue Book of 1891 dealing with the relation of wages to the cost of production. [1] With the help of this material we can draw up the following table:

Trade.	Expenditure (in £1,000).	Capital (in millions).	Capital Per £ of Expenses.
Textile	25.6	0.017	⅔
Five coal companies ..	650	1.4	2
Gas (total)	11,262	60.0	5
Tramways	2,267	13.7	6
London & India Docks ..	1,188	16.1	14
Southampton Docks Co. ..	70	1.49	21
Sixteen railway companies..	36,218	718.0	20
Eight water companies ..	661	14.6	22
Canal companies (not belonging to railways)	949	24.3	26
One of these	25.7	1.57	61

From this we see that the position of capital-disposal in the different undertakings varies very markedly; the highest of the relative figures is nearly a hundred times as great as the lowest. There are certainly many industries with a lower relative capital-disposal than the textile industry, so the range between the highest and lowest relative capital-disposal is probably still greater. The burden of interest in the various trades is therefore very unequal, and the rate of interest must, in the long run – that is, if it has time – make itself felt in the supply available for the various wants, and considerably influence the prices of the different material goods and services We see, further, that capital-disposal is most important in those industries in which much fixed real capital is used, while it is far less important in those in which the capital is mainly circulating. This confirms our view that the use of durable goods is by far the

[1] *Report to the Board of Trade on the Relation of Wages in Certain Industries to the Cost of Production* (Cmd. 6536; 1891).

most important cause of the demand for capital-disposal. The statistics cited naturally include the capital necessary for the ownership of land, but this need not invalidate our results.

In this section, where we are studying the demand for capital-disposal, we shall assume the supply of this to be given. If, therefore, a certain amount of capital-disposal is available, the task of the price of this – that is, of the interest – is to limit the demand to the given supply. This is the principle of scarcity. As has been shown, the demand for capital-disposal arises for two reasons, namely, the ownership of fixed capital and that of circulating capital, and is based on the fact that the use of durable goods, as well as production in the more technical sense, takes time. In so far as the demand for capital-disposal originates in the productive process, it is a demand for a factor of production. Actually, there is also a demand for consumption purposes. This demand, proceeding from individuals who wish to extend their consumption beyond the limits of their current income, may best be regarded as a negative supply, and so need not be considered here (see § 24). Here, therefore, we may confine ourselves to the demand arising from production, and first consider the need for capital-disposal for the use of durable goods. This need, of course, originates, in the final analysis, in the immediate wants of individuals, and therefore partly in the demand for the direct services of durable goods, and partly in the demand for the material commodities which are made with the help of the services of those durable goods. Interest in this field has thus to restrict the demand for these services, whether they are desired for the direct satisfaction of wants, or for the process of production preceding this.

Consequently, a rise in the rate of interest must result from a development of the demand which makes particularly large claims upon durable goods. This was completely confirmed in the nineteenth century, since every period of specially active railway construction drove up the rate of interest considerably. Such rises in the rate of interest occurred once at the end of the nineteenth century, and twice in the fourteen years before the Great War, and were probably due, to a great extent, to the marked development of the electrical industry, and hence, in the last analysis, to the demand for electric trams, lighting, telephones, and so on – all very costly durable goods. At all such times the real scarcity of capital-disposal has made itself sharply felt. In Book IV. we shall study the fluctuations in economic activity connected with this.

The rise in the rate of interest, of which business men complain so much, and which politicians ascribe to all kinds of irrelevant factors, has a definite and very important economic task to fulfil: with its aid a selection of the various desires that make demands on capital-disposal is arrived at. Only the most important can be satisfied, and the others must, at least for a time, remain unfulfilled. Which are the most important has to be decided according to the general laws of the exchange economy; the most important are those able to pay most; that is, in this case, those which can afford the highest rate of interest. Without such a regulation of the demand the entire social economy would be placed in a completely untenable position. It is only natural that, after such a technical achievement as the electric tram, all the towns in the world should want to possess this new convenience as quickly as possible. An attempt to satisfy these requirements more or less at once, and completely, would mean a quite disproportionate demand on the productive powers of the community for this purpose, and would throw the whole world economy into disorder. In the exchange economy this is only prevented by a rise in the rate of interest, as a result of which the use of the durable goods in question is made considerably more expensive.

If we wish to study the demand for capital-disposal more closely, we must consider the various external factors which affect it. On the other hand, we must bear in mind that the demand is a function of the price, and thus of the rate of interest. We cannot be content with a study of the demand at a certain rate of interest, but, on the contrary, must make this demand in its dependence upon changes in the rate the subject of our inquiry. As we found, demand itself is never a given determining factor of price (§§ 11 and 16). The determining factors must be sought in the manner in which demand depends upon price.

Among the external factors which affect the demand for capital-disposal, the first to be considered is the growth of population. If this is to occur without any retrogression in the economic position, the quantity of durable goods must obviously be increased by the same percentage as the population. Every new family that comes into being needs a new house, with streets, water-supply, sanitation, lighting, and so on. Further, the increased population also requires a corresponding increase in agricultural buildings and equipment, factories, means of transport, and other necessities. In the uniformly progressive economy there must be a constant accumulation of capital (§ 6). The community may not consume the whole of its income, but must use part of this to increase its real capital. The growth of population thus of itself makes demands upon capital-disposal. A society with a growing population has, for this very reason, a greater need of capital-disposal than a similar society whose population is stationary. Consequently, so far as this growth occurs, the rate of interest in the former society must be higher than in the latter. A comparison of conditions in France and Germany before the war is, from this point of view, particularly instructive.

But progress does not consist merely in an increase of population; it also means a better satisfaction of wants, and for this, what is most necessary is an increase in the quantity of durable goods, that is, of fixed real capital. It is remarkable to what an extent industrial progress depends upon an ever-widening use of such capital. The greatest achievements of modern technology have generally made very large demands on the use of fixed real capital in equipment, buildings, and so on. Even to-day development continues along the same lines, and will in all probability continue in that manner. These achievements, moreover, have not been applied over the whole world with any degree of equality. In this respect there are still great inequalities between different classes of society as well as between different countries. The construction of satisfactory houses for the great mass of the inhabitants of countries with cold climates will mean further extensive demands for capital-disposal. Our old European countries are fairly well supplied with large fixed transport equipment and other installations which require much fixed real capital, but before all other countries – China, South America, Africa, and so on – can possess these things to the same extent, there will have to be an accumulation of capital to a degree that can hardly be imagined.

There is, consequently, still a very broad margin for a progress that requires an increased employment of durable material goods. [1] The constantly growing demand for capital-disposal for the purpose of utilising durable goods is based upon this progress, and is therefore intimately connected with the fundamental characteristics of the whole of our modern life.

How is this demand to be kept within the necessary limits? By making it pay a price – interest – for capital-disposal. The need to pay interest at a certain rate will always exclude a number of possibilities of satisfying man's wants by the use of durable goods. The demand for capital-disposal is thus greatly compressed, and has considerable elasticity. There is, so to speak, always a fund of latent possibilities of useful applications of capital-disposal for utilising durable goods. As soon as the rate of interest falls slightly, a certain proportion of this fund is set free, and the possibilities in question become realised. Any further fall in the rate sets free a correspondingly increasing number of profitable uses of capital. Even a slight drop in the rate is usually sufficient to liberate so many possibilities for the profitable use of durable goods that the demands for capital-disposal resulting from this completely exhaust the supply. A further fall would be met by still stronger counteracting forces. New possibilities are continually being added to this fund of possible uses of capital – by inventions, the opening-up of new countries, increases in the population, etc. Thanks, therefore, to progress, in its broadest sense, this fund is practically inexhaustible.

The rate of interest is, as everybody knows, by no means the same in different parts of the world. In the older, and politically and economically well-organised, countries of Europe, the rate is relatively low; but in countries of doubtful political stability, such as the Near and Far East, or in colonies where there is still marked

---

[1]In connection with the forces that work in this direction, as well as certain antagonistic, though definitely weaker, tendencies, see details in *The Nature and Necessity of Interest*. pp. 96 to 106.

economic insecurity, it is often impossible to obtain capital, and when it is obtainable, it is so only on unfavourable terms, or at a high rate of interest. Where such is the case, a very great number of possibilities for the profitable use of durable goods are excluded, and the demand for capital-disposal is compressed to an extraordinary degree. Every fall in the rate of interest in such countries will therefore give rise to a very considerable new demand for capital-disposal. But with the advance of civilisation these sharp differences of the capital markets in the various countries are gradually eliminated. This movement was very powerful in the last ten years before the war. However, every fall in the rate of interest in foreign markets means such an increase in the demand for capital-disposal that the European market is forced to take notice of it. The consequence of this has been a definite rise in European rates of interest, and the older States of Europe, formerly in the best position for receiving money, have been the chief sufferers. The pronounced reaction in the rate of European State loans in the period in question may, to a considerable extent, be attributed to the pressure of these circumstances. This is certainly the best evidence of the enormous extent of the unsatisfied and insatiable demand for capital-disposal on the part of those areas of the world some distance from the great financial centres, and at the same time of the actual scarcity of this capital-disposal. As the equalising movement of which we have spoken is clearly still only in its very infancy, we must count on its continuance. If, however, the demands for capital-disposal by the rest of the world are no longer restrained by appreciably higher rates of interest than those prevalent in Europe, we cannot expect any progressive reduction in these European rates.

Let us think of a self-contained community rather similar in character to present-day Europe, and let us imagine, further, that within this community there is a uniform rate of interest about as high as that considered normal in pre-war Europe. We may then ask ourselves how the demand for capital-disposal for the use of durable goods depends upon this rate of interest, and, particularly, how it would be affected by a progressive fall of the rate.

The answer is easy if we think of only some of the main sources of the demand for capital. The demand for house accommodation, strongly limited by the usual height of the rate of interest, certainly possesses an enormous elasticity, which would show itself in a marked increase in the effective demand for capital-disposal for the building of houses if there were an appreciable fall in that rate.

Europe has to some extent satisfied its need for railways. But we must remember that this was generally, though by no means always, done on the condition that the railways would pay a rate of, let us say, $3\frac{1}{2}$ to 4 per cent. If capital for the construction of railways were available at a rate of 2 per cent., we should see at once how many important railways have still not been considered. The same applies to light railways and tramways, too. What enormous amounts of capital for these purposes would be demanded if the rate were only 2 per cent. And other enterprises which even now use a great deal of capital, such as canals, docks, hydro-electric power stations, water, gas, and electricity works, sewage and drainage works, would make new demands for capital-disposal, demands which could not be satisfied. In addition, a rate of interest about half what it is now would have a very great influence upon industrial technique. We must not forget that the whole of modern industry is based on the assumption that an interest of at least about 4 per cent. would have to be paid. If we could reckon on 2 per cent. instead, industry would undoubtedly progress along lines of development now closed to it, and this progress would make very great demands upon capital-disposal.

We only need to think more carefully of these things to realise the great force of the demand upon capital-disposal for the use of durable goods, and the enormous reserves of latent and, as yet, unsatisfied demands behind those already satisfied. Anyone who has realised this has gained a real insight into the economic necessity of interest. It simply would not do to open the doors to all these demands. If there had only been a little reflection in this connection, no one would have ventured to speak seriously of the possible disappearance of interest. With the rate of interest at zero, the pure use of capital would be freely available to all men: in other words, although maintenance and renewal would have to be paid for, the use of durable goods as such would be free. But according to the principle of scarcity, which is of fundamental importance in every economy, this is possible only in the case of those goods of which there is a surplus

If capital-disposal were to be had without charge, and, consequently, there were no need to trouble about economising in its use, there would also be no limit to the demand for it. The demands for durable goods would therefore increase immeasurably. The original costs of various installations would have no significance, as there would be no need to pay interest on them. In such circumstances fantastic undertakings would naturally appear profitable, and would require the investment of stupendous sums. But it is evident that this would run the whole economy on wrong lines. If unlimited quantities of productive power were used for the manufacture of very durable equipment, they would have to be drawn, to a very large extent, from the satisfaction of current needs, and society would be reduced to a condition in which men, with tremendous efforts, and while suffering the greatest privation, would build Egyptian pyramids for the edification of future ages.

A reader with an eye to the realities of economic life will perhaps think it a waste of time to linger over such purely hypothetical situations. This would be the case if the denial of the need for interest had not played such an important part in certain economic and political programmes, and frequently found support even on the side of science.

If interest must be paid as the price of capital-disposal, it must appear in the prices of finished goods, and also in those of the services of durable goods. But the task of interest is to exert an influence on the demand for such services. A price system for the services of railways and similar installations, taking into account only current costs, and ignoring the covering of fixed costs, particularly interest, has many times been put forward as an economic ideal. Such a point of view, however, can only be defended by a person who cannot grasp the fact that the function of the pricing process is to check the demands made for consumption, and that the process is essentially determined by this function.

So far our explanation of the necessity of interest has been based entirely upon the principle of scarcity. But we must realise that a given aim of production may often be attained with the use of different proportions of durable goods – that, in other words, the need for capital-disposal is not exclusively determined by the demand of consumers, but is also partly dependent upon the choice of methods of production. Capital-disposal may, as shown in § 21 actually replace other factors of production to some extent for certain purposes. We have to study this substitution, and especially the significance of the rate of interest in this connection. Only in this way can we obtain a real insight into the type of the dependence of the demand for capital-disposal upon that rate.

Capital-disposal can be substituted not only for labour, but also for land and the raw materials of nature. If, for instance, land were so dear that it would be cheaper to construct an underground railway than to buy the more expensive land for one on the surface, there would be a real substitution of capital-disposal for the use of land. If we assume that the annual cost of maintenance and renewal is the same for both lines, then it is clear that the rent that would have to be paid by the surface railway is replaced by the interest which the underground line has to pay for the extra capital it needs, and so there is a substitution of a certain amount of capital-disposal for the use of land. If, on the other hand, in a mountain district where the cost of land is not important, the underground line is preferred because the costs of transport on this line are cheaper through the saving in coal and time, then, other things being equal, the choice of the underground line means a substitution of capital-disposal for all the other factors of production which have a part in the extra cost of the other line, such as coal, the labour of the staff, and so forth.

To what extent capital-disposal should be substituted in this way for other factors of production depends, in the first place, upon the price of it. The lower the rate of interest, the more can it displace competing factors of production. In the case considered, a higher rate of interest would probably make the construction of the underground line impossible, whereas a lower rate may make its advantages unquestionable. As the interest on the capital embodied in equipment represents the greater part of the annual cost of the underground line, a reduction of the rate of interest by half would, of course, decrease this cost considerably, and so strengthen the competitive power of the underground railway. In many cases durable equipment may be built with a solidity which varies according to the degree of permanency desired; what degree of durability is economical depends upon the rate of interest.

Modern economic life shows certain general tendencies which favour the increasing substitution of capital-disposal for other factors of production. Among these the first to be mentioned is the advance of industrial technique, which undoubtedly moves mainly in the direction of an increased use of fixed real capital. The greatest achievements of technology during the last century exhibit this characteristic very strikingly. We need only to think of the railways, the modern ocean steamers, the great canals used by world traffic, the latest developments in the field of power production – the use of hydro-electric power – the use of gas and electricity for light and heat, the other uses of electricity, and so on, as well as the constantly increasing displacement of hand labour by practically automatic machines which is the feature of modern industry, to realise the overwhelming importance of this tendency. Progress in the opposite direction, in which we can perhaps include wireless telegraphy, is undoubtedly an exception to the general rule.

In the next place we must consider the general economic tendency to concentration. The economic possibility of utilising durable means of production evidently depends upon the ability of producers to use to the full the services of these means. This ability is generally greater in large-scale industry than in a small business, though small businesses may, by co-operation, improve their capacity to utilise these services. Consequently, the increase of large-scale industry and co-operation means an extended use of durable means of production, and thus a greater demand for capital-disposal.

In this economic concentration there lies, without doubt, a tendency to an increased use of durable means of production. On the other hand, the increasing concentration in certain medium-sized businesses may improve the use of the existing means of production, such as machinery, and so reduce the relative demand for them. But at the same time other businesses grow up and begin to use machinery, and it is doubtful whether the whole movement will lead to the reduction of the group of businesses which use machines without obtaining the full benefit from them. For production as a whole, the movement towards concentration doubtless means an increased demand for durable means of production.

Thirdly, working in the same direction are the attempts to organise credit so as to place capital at the disposal of artisans and small farmers for the purchase of machines, animals, etc. Doubtless there is, in the occupations in question, much scope for the profitable use of fixed real capital. A movement which facilitates this use must lead to an increase in the demand for capital-disposal. Fourthly, it is a very general fact that machines and other equipment that would certainly yield a good profit are not used simply because there are certain difficulties in accumulating capital, or because those who control production do not follow the development of industrial technique with sufficient attention, or because, through incorrect calculation, they do not understand sufficiently well the technical and economic conditions of their business. It is easy to convince ourselves that these "frictions" still play an important part in economic life. But, on the other hand, we must admit that they are diminishing, and that the general tendency in production is to use durable goods increasingly wherever they are profitable. In so far as this is the case, it means another tendency to increase the demand for capital-disposal.

To what extent these tendencies express themselves in an increased demand for capital-disposal for the use of durable goods depends, in a certain degree, upon the rate of interest. An increased demand generally finds itself opposed by a rising rate of interest. In any case, these tendencies, ramified as they are by the tendencies of consumption which we have discussed previously, would prevent a continuous and appreciable fall in the rate of interest.

The question as to whether or not a labour-saving machine should be used in a certain factory naturally depends, to a certain extent, upon the height of rates of wages. A rise in wage-rates in that factory may decide the question in favour of the machine. It is clear, however, that rises in wages, within the customary limits, have in an individual business much less influence on the competitive power of machinery than have the other factors enumerated here. An enlargement of the business, such as occurs daily, has, for instance, a much more important effect. What applies to wage-movements may also generally apply to ordinary fluctuations in the rate of interest. The competition between machines and human labour cannot, therefore, simply be treated as a problem of pricing to be solved according to the principle of substitution. What we have said naturally applies still more to the general problem of the substitution of capital-disposal for other factors of production. The conditions which make it possible for the great transport undertakings and other large equipment of modern industry to compete cannot by any means be treated entirely as a question of the relative costs of different methods of production.

If anyone imagines it is possible to treat the whole theory of interest from the special point of view of the principle of substitution, or that the trite formula that interest is equal to the marginal productivity of capital-disposal in competition with other factors of production will allow of an exhaustive solution of the problem of interest, then he completely overlooks the fundamental importance which the principle of scarcity has in connection with that problem, as well as with every other problem of pricing. The general explanation of interest must, therefore, always be sought in the relative scarcity of the available capital-disposal in relation to the demand for it. Compared with that, the principle of substitution is only of secondary importance, and merely means that this demand is not determined solely by the demands of consumers, but is to a certain extent influenced by the conditions of production.

With regard to the conditions for a substitution of capital-disposal for other factors of production, it should still be noted that a general and uniform rise in the prices of these other factors would also have to raise the prices of durable means of production, and thus to increase the necessary quantities of capital-disposal to a corresponding extent. Thus, with an unaltered rate of interest, the substitution referred to would not be furthered. If the wages of agricultural labourers alone rise, this may lead to a more wide-spread use of agricultural machinery; if, however, all other wages rise at the same time, the price of agricultural machinery, as well as that of its annual use, will probably rise to the same extent. Thus the general rise of wages will by and of itself, with an unaltered rate of interest, cause no displacement of human labour in agriculture. But in discussing such questions we must always remember that they must be dealt with on the assumption of an unchanged value of money, and thus that an important limit is placed on the imagined general rise in prices (cf. § 35).

Thus far, we have only considered the demand for capital-disposal in connection with the use of durable goods. But capital-disposal is, as we know, also required because production, in the narrower sense of the word, takes time. The capital demanded for this purpose corresponds to the circulating real capital of the community. As for the durable goods, we only include in this connection production as far as the completion of the good itself, and so exclude the use of that good. The quantity of capital-disposal required for production is then essentially dependent upon the time taken by the productive process.

By what factors is the demand for capital-disposal for production in this narrower sense determined? What are the tendencies which apply in connection with this demand? In regard to this we must first of all note that the rate of interest is probably generally only of secondary importance in determining the length of the period of production. It is only in exceptional cases that we can assume that a fall in the rate of interest occasions an increase in the length of the productive process. Possibly, however, an increasing rate of interest may strengthen the general tendency to accelerate production. Quite apart from the actual height of the rate of interest the modern community shows a distinct tendency to shorten the productive process as much as possible. In this there is, of course, the desire to save interest on circulating real capital, but this is not the only, and perhaps not the chief, motive. This point of view is of real importance in the building trade, where a particularly large amount of capital is tied down until the actual construction is finished. On this account private builders try to shorten the period of building as much as possible. In public enterprise in this industry, it has not been sufficiently realised that the actual building costs also include the interest that is incurred during the period of construction, and so it is usual to sum up only the payments made at various times, thus leading to an uneconomical lengthening of the time of construction.

One of the chief motives behind the modern tendency to shorten the period of production as much as possible is the attempt to utilise the durable goods in the process as fully as possible. Railway directors force their goods trains to run more rapidly in order to make the line available for still more trains. Loading and unloading at the docks are speeded up with the aid of the most modern machinery, mainly in order to make as much profit as possible out of the ships' time. Everywhere, in factories as well as in the transport trades, there is this attempt to make human labour as effective as possible by speeding up the productive process.

Since the war there has been a marked attempt to shorten the period of warehousing in industry as much as possible. This has had very important results, especially in the United States. Industry in Europe might make still more important advances in this field in the direction of increased economy. In Germany alone the need for capital, according to recent calculations, might in this way be decreased by milliards of marks. A shorter period of storing means that circulating capital is used more quickly, and that, in this manner, the productive process is shortened. The higher rate of interest in post-war years has been very important in connection with these stringent economies in the demands for capital. But other factors have also entered here, and exercised a considerable influence. This shortening of the storing period must, above all, be regarded as part of the general post-war rationalisation process, and has been made particularly necessary because of the risk of falling prices, which has actually taken place frequently since the war. One important condition in this shortening of the productive process is the progress made in the methods of transport, resulting in a much more dependable and continuous supply of materials. [1]

Shortening the productive process obviously means, of itself, a decrease in the need for capital-disposal for production. But by the nature of the case this tendency is restricted. The possibilities of such development, in many fields of production, are almost exploited to the limit. On the other hand, for the increase of the demand for capital-disposal for the purpose of using durable goods, we can see no limits apart from that given by the need to pay interest. Further, since the demand for capital-disposal for the purpose of production constitutes a relatively small part of the total demand, the tendency to an increase in the total demand must, on the whole, definitely predominate.

This describes the demand sufficiently for our purpose. Its force is so great that it can only be kept within the requisite limits by putting a price on capital-disposal. Every reduction in this price tends to liberate reserves of the demand, thus preventing a further fall in the price. This is the general fact which, on the side of demand, determines the price of capital-disposal, that is, the rate of interest.

§ 24 *The Supply of Capital-Disposal*

The capital at the disposal of the exchange economy can only be increased by saving. We are already acquainted with the nature of this saving (§§ 6 and 21). The total income of the exchange economy may be divided into two parts, one of which is consumed – that is, real income is bought with it – and the other is "saved." The latter part is used directly for the purpose of buying real capital, and constitutes the new supply of capital-disposal.

The sum of the savings of individuals is, as a rule, larger than this saved part of the income of society, in the objective sense. In a

---

[1] In connection with the tendency to shorten the productive process, see further details in *Nature and Necessity of Interest*, pp. 125–7.

given period, certain persons use an amount that exceeds their income for that period. This conduct, which we may call "over-consumption," is the opposite of saving. This over-consumption is made possible, from the standpoint of the individual, partly by the consumption of one's own capital, and partly by loans which will be paid out of future income. In the first case, part of the capital is exchanged for income saved by other individuals, and it is really this latter income that is consumed. In the second case, the income is obtained by a promise to pay in the future. Any such individual over-consumption must be deducted from the savings made during the same period, and only what is left is the *net* amount of savings of the economy in that period, or the actual increase in the abstract capital (in money form) available for acquiring real capital. These net savings form, in the objective sense, the savings of the community as a whole, and thus represent the increase of its real capital during the period. In the preceding section, where we considered the demand for capital-disposal, we took account only of that demand which comes from the productive process, in the broader sense. Now that we want to study the supply, we must, to be consistent, consider this only in so far as it is of assistance to the process of production in the broader sense, or, in other words, in so far as it is placed at the disposal of the owners of real capital. So by the "supply of capital-disposal" we must understand the aggregate of net savings. In our study of the factors which determine this supply, we must bear this in mind, and must also take into account the factors which cause over-consumption.

In Book I. we accepted as given factors of the pricing problem the quantities of the available primary factors of production. As in this Book, where we are studying the pricing of the factors of production, we drop this assumption, and include in the scope of our study the influence of the prices of these factors on the supply of them, we are at once met by the question as to what importance the rate of interest has for the supply of capital-disposal. Hence in what follows we shall have to inquire not only into the independent factors – external, from the point of view of pricing – which determine the amount of saving, but also particularly the influence of the price of capital-disposal – that is, the rate of interest – on these factors, and thus on the degree of saving.

The best method of ascertaining these external factors is to analyse more carefully the forces which control saving or its antithesis, over-consumption. In this connection we must first observe that over-consumption and saving are often two sides, or, more strictly, two stages, in the same economic plan. This is true when a person puts aside part of an exceptionally large income in order to be able to increase his income in the bad years to come, or, contrariwise, when a person who has not accumulated this kind of "safety fund" has to borrow during a lean year and pay back gradually in better years. It is also true in the case where the young father of a family puts aside part of his income in order to pay for the cost of educating his children in the future, or, conversely, when a youth borrows money so as to be able to continue with his studies, intending to pay it back when he has obtained a good position. The relation between need and the means to satisfy it is, for the individual, very different at different periods of his life. This inequality of means may, however, be overcome by a proper arrangement of saving and over-consumption. Which of these is to be prior in point of time depends upon the circumstances. If saving goes first, a certain amount of capital-disposal is placed on the market for a shorter or longer period; if over-consumption goes first, a certain amount of capital-disposal will, instead, be required for some length of time.

A combination of saving and subsequent consumption of savings, which is of particularly great importance in practical life, is represented by the reserves which are put aside by many classes of our modern society in order to secure a pension, whether the pension is for the saver himself when he reaches a certain age or is ill, or whether it is for the benefit of his dependants. The large majority of employees now contribute, voluntarily or compulsorily, to funds for pensions. A great part of life-insurance is of the same character. The whole of modern social insurance is a compulsory saving from comparatively satisfactory incomes to satisfy wants in times of need. The reverse economic tendency, consumption above one's income, to be paid back later, has also, however, important instances to offer. We do not need to think only of foolish spending of borrowed money by young men who have good expectations. The bringing up of the young entails a very general, but, at the same time, a very justifiable over-consumption, which will be paid back later out of savings. The States which borrow money for current expenses are representatives of over-consumption on a larger scale. It might be thought that the States could incur this expenditure by increasing taxation, but this is frequently very doubtful. If there were no loans to be had, the expenditure of the States would probably be considerably curtailed, or, at least, their people, burdened by heavier taxation, would spend less. Consequently, the covering of current expenses by raising State loans undoubtedly increases consumption and diminishes the savings of the community, and so works in the same way as over-consumption on the part of the individual. The repayment of State loans naturally curtails the consuming powers of the taxpayers, but at the same time sets free means for the formation of new capital.

The most general reason for saving is without a doubt the feeling that provision must be made for the future. For a private household it must seem desirable to lay aside the means to pay for the customary or, at least, the necessary expenses for times when the income vanishes. So we must consider not only the general uncertainty of economic life, but also particularly old age and, to a certain extent, provision for one's dependants. This desire to save in order to provide for the future is, however, necessarily limited. An increase of saving in the community in order to make better provision for the future can only be expected in so far as the habits of saving which exist among the upper classes extend to the lower classes too. But this is certainly a lengthy process; for a long time yet, probably, increases in the income of the lower classes will be used mainly for the very desirable improvement of their standard of life.

Besides this purely personal concern for the future, which leads to private saving, there is also concern for the position of productive industry, for the industrial undertaking, a concern which leads to the laying aside of a very important part of the profits of the business. The motive behind this is to accumulate reserves for unforeseen accidents, but also to promote and to strengthen the business from the economic point of view. In both cases savings are generally employed in the business itself, although sometimes, in order to keep them more liquid, they are invested or deposited in banks. The accumulation of capital in this way is simply an economic necessity under modern conditions. In the competitive struggle between entrepreneurs, the man who cannot participate in this progress, which requires more and more capital, must go under. And the profits of the business must often be used primarily to increase the capital of that business, for only in so far as this is done will it be possible to attract further capital from outside. That accidental profits, or the profits of particularly good years, are not used up, but kept in the business, is an axiom of sound business administration. We can see this at its best in well-managed limited liability companies. In these it is also customary to create funds to equalise dividends, and so long as such funds belong to the company they naturally strengthen the business.

The internal capital accumulation of a company often assumes the form of so-called "secret balances." In favourable years the book-value of the real capital and other assets is written down considerably below the actual value. The annual profit is partly used for this purpose, and so cannot be seen in the balance-sheet. This is important, in that it makes it easier to restrain the demands of shareholders for dividends. In other words, the shareholders are forced to do some saving. If the company has losses in later, bad years, there is no need to make these public, as the secret balances can be used to cover losses. If we find, as we sometimes do in the balances of great limited liability companies, that very valuable machinery, equipment, and tools are written down at a book-value of one shilling, we can realise how important this kind of capital accumulation is in industry.

This type of accumulation plays a very important part in the provision of capital for the community as a whole. It is not, of course, limited in the same way as is the private accumulation to which we have referred. As, however, it arises from the needs of, and is directly taken up by, production, there is no reason to fear that it can be carried so far that the capital-disposal provided as a result of it will have no use.

Finally, there is an accumulation of capital which can hardly be ascribed to the motive of regard for the future. We cannot say of the great capitalists who satisfy all their wants of any importance, and possess a capital the returns on which assure a similar satisfaction to them and their families in perpetuity, and who still constantly lay aside large reserves for increasing their wealth, that they save out of concern for the future. In such cases there must be other motives causing this saving. The economic interest of the capitalist is to increase his wealth, and this gradually becomes the sole aim. There are various motives at work here; the senseless avarice that gradually and increasingly finds its sole pleasure in watching the ever-growing wealth, and which may well be described as an abnormal spiritual inertia, a pathological atrophy of the life of the emotions, is certainly not the only explanation. The desire for splendour and for the higher position in society which the possession of great wealth assures, the stimulation afforded by the jealousy of others, as well as the healthy joy of a strong man in successful work as such, in the control of large masses, above all in influence – all these are factors which we must take into account.

A more thorough analysis of this desire for an ever-increasing amount of capital must be based on the fundamental psychological fact that life always strives to attain as complete as possible a development and use of its powers. The person who really has a talent for economic activity and large-scale organisation, or for carrying on financial operations, must necessarily and naturally seek an outlet for these abilities; for him it is a duty to make the use of existing capital ever more fruitful. These motives drive him to an activity which continually extends his ownership of capital.

This craving to increase one's wealth is naturally insatiable, as no wealth is great enough for it. But the accumulation of capital in this way is restricted in other directions; first, by the income of the class concerned, and, secondly, by their consumption. The growing luxury of the rich makes their life increasingly dearer, and so correspondingly decreases their ability to save. Still, the degree of saving, the ratio between savings and the total income, will be considerably higher among the wealthy class than among the other classes, and the absolute amount of the savings of the rich will continue to form a very important part of the total accumulation of capital in the community. The aggregate saving is thus to a certain extent dependent upon the distribution of income in the community. In all probability a more democratic distribution of income would materially lower the degree of saving of the community. This would be the case particularly if the increase of income were mainly on the side of the working-classes. The latest development of income and property taxation in the direction of a more and more marked progressive gradation undoubtedly leads to a very considerable decline in saving in society.

Our observations show that in any case there is no basis for the assumption of a steadily increasing amount of saving in proportion to income in the community. The rather widespread view, found even in scientific literature, that saving in modern society is so great that sooner or later it must exceed the demand, finds no support in a careful analysis of the actual facts. Of course, absolutely, the annual amount of savings increases, but in all probability it does not increase more rapidly than income, and therefore not more rapidly than production and the demands which it makes upon capital-disposal.

If, further, we ask what influence the rate of interest has on saving, we find that it is usually assumed *a priori* that saving is a sacrifice for which a certain price must be paid in order that a given amount of it may be forthcoming, and that the supply of this sacrifice, the accumulation of capital, increases directly with the price paid for it, that is, with the rate of interest. This assumption may perhaps, on the whole, roughly approximate to reality. But a more careful consideration of the question shows that the effects of fluctuations in the rate of interest vary, and that, moreover, a fall in the rate, if it keeps within ordinary limits, may influence saving in entirely contrary ways, according to the circumstances.

The ordinary person who saves, with a moderate income, and who tries to accumulate sufficient capital in order to live on the income from it, must, if there is a lower rate of interest, save a larger amount in order to be sure of a certain annual return. So a fall in the rate may stimulate him to greater efforts, and cause him to accumulate more capital. But it is also possible that the amount he is able to save is rather limited, and that, with a lower rate of interest, he will have to be content with a smaller annual return in the future. We must also bear in mind that a person who, at a higher rate of interest, may be able to save a sum the return on which is sufficient to satisfy his year's needs, may no longer be able to do so if the rate is lower, and thus may have to choose the easier method of safeguarding his future – that is, to buy a life annuity. Such a change is not good for the capital market, and must, if it occurs to a great extent, in the course of time considerably diminish the supply of capital-disposal. That occasional large profits are not consumed at once, but added to one's wealth, is a phenomenon on which the rate of interest would probably not have much influence. The same applies to an occasional need to consume part of one's wealth; the rate of interest ought not to have any special influence on the reserves put aside for unforeseen emergencies and the consumption of capital in such cases. But on the other hand we should, perhaps, assume that a high rate of interest works against the anticipatory use of an expected future income, while a low rate makes one think less of such a use. Even ministers of finance could hardly escape that influence entirely.

In the case of the accumulation of capital in businesses, a fall in the rate of interest ought not to have an absolutely invariable effect. But as such businesses are usually big debtors, a fall in the rate may mean a greater profit and, in any case, the opportunity to accumulate more capital inside the business. On the other hand, however, we must assume that a fall in the rate makes it more difficult for the great capitalists to save, as it reduces their income. A low rate does not immediately have its full effect on the income of the capitalists, for a large part of that income consists of fixed returns (Government securities, rents, etc.) and of dividends that are partly of the same type. To some extent, however, their income consists of interest on capital that is invested over and over again, and it must therefore fall in correspondence with the rate. This is also generally true of income from newly saved capital. Gradually, therefore, a prolonged fall in the rate of interest must exercise an effective influence on the savings of the capitalist class. Small capitalists who consume their entire income are, on the other hand, merely compelled to decrease their consumption when the rate falls.

If we attempt to obtain some idea of the results of these different effects of a fall in the rate, we reach the conclusion that, as long as that rate merely fluctuates within the ordinary limits, the effects of the changes in it on the accumulation of capital as a whole ought not to be very pronounced, though we may assume that a permanently low rate rather limits the accumulation of capital in general.

We see from this how correct it is, in a preliminary survey of the pricing problem, to regard the supply of capital-disposal as a given quantity, and to trace interest primarily to the need to check demand. In a modern country where there is perfect legal security and highly developed business methods, the actual fluctuations in the rate of interest are so predominantly determined by the demand for capital-disposal that the effect of alterations in the supply is of only secondary importance, and need only be considered in a special and detailed analysis. Even if the dependence of the supply of capital-disposal on these ordinary fluctuations of the rate of interest could be regarded as a definitely established fact, this fact has no great significance in the explanation of the mechanism of pricing. The pricing process would be explained equally well, and essentially on the same lines and with the same quantitative results, if there were no such dependence, and if the supply of capital-disposal were a given quantity in the problem, independent of the ordinary fluctuations in the rate of interest. [1]

This relative independence of the accumulation of capital in regard to the rate of interest is true, as we said, so long as the rate in actual economic life moves within ordinary limits. But the case

[1] Cf. Marshall, *Principles*, Book V., chap. iii., § 2, and Book VI., chap. ii., § 4.

is quite different if the rate falls much below the usual minimum – say, much below 3 per cent. The closer examination of this hypothetical case is of great importance in connection with the theory of interest. For if it is the duty of this theory not only to explain the actual movements of the rate, but also to inquire why and to what extent interest is a necessary phenomenon in economic life, it must answer the question as to what would be the results of a fall in the rate below its usual level and almost to nothing. Only such an inquiry can show us why the rate of interest remains at the actual, arithmetically determined height of, let us say, between 3 and 5 per cent., and only by answering this question, and not by vague qualitative observations on the nature of interest, can we obtain a complete theory of interest.

A fall of the rate of interest below the hitherto customary lower limit would result in a general consumption of savings. Besides that, provision for the future would, to a greater extent than before, take the form of the purchase of annuities instead of the saving of an amount of capital with a corresponding annual yield. But as these consequences may be regarded from the point of view of a consumption of savings, we may content ourselves with an analysis of the influence of a fall in the rate of interest on the consumption of capital. We shall find that the effects of a fall in the rate of interest below the level indicated are bound to be serious for the capital market.

Let us think of a capitalist who lives entirely upon the interest on his capital. If he possesses £100,000 and has received 4 per cent. up to the present – that is, £4,000 per annum – and, further, has adjusted his standard of life to this income, a reduction of the rate of interest to $3\frac{1}{2}$ per cent. will probably make him stop some of his customary expenditure and confine his budget to the still handsome figure of £3,500. A further economy might still seem possible to him if the rate fell to 3 per cent. If we assume, however, that the rate fell to $\frac{1}{2}$ per cent., our magnate would then certainly find the reduction unbearable, and would prefer, instead of living on a paltry £500 per year, to consume his capital gradually. If he calculated that he will live for another twenty-five years, he can in this manner enjoy his original income of £4,000. If he wishes to provide for his children too, he will, perhaps, find a period of fifty years sufficient, and so consume his capital in that time – that is, at the rate of one-fiftieth per year. Without reckoning interest, that will still give him an income of £2,000 a year.

From this simple example we see how to answer the question whether a man who lives on the interest on his capital, and uses the whole of it, shall, if the rate of interest falls, live on his capital. The decisive point is, clearly, the relative increase in income he can obtain by choosing the latter course. This relative increase evidently grows much more as soon as the rate of interest falls below its usual height. It also depends considerably on the length of time his capital must last. The shorter this period, the more the man gains by living on his capital. This is the reason why, at the actual rate of interest, much of the capital possessed by elderly and not very wealthy people is used for the purchase of annuities; by using their capital, these people obtain a considerable increase in their annual income.

The relative increase of the income obtained by living on one's capital varies with the rate of interest, as well as with the length of the period for which the capital must last. [1] Whether the capital is consumed also naturally depends, to some extent, upon the absolute height of the income that can be obtained simply by using the interest on that capital. Very rich people would probably be able to bear a low rate of interest longer without drawing upon their capital. We see to-day that annuities are generally chosen by people who have a relatively small capital. If, however, the rate of interest falls sufficiently, the yield on even the largest principals must shrink a great deal and the consumption of capital appear the only possible salvation.

A general spread of the custom of living on capital in this way would obviously reduce the supply of capital-disposal to such an extent that any further fall of the rate of interest would necessarily be prevented by the acute scarcity of capital. This reaction would be felt most strongly if the rate fell so low that the majority of

[1] For some calculations in connection with this, see *Nature and Necessity of Interest*, p. 148 *et seq.*

capitalists were able, by living on their capital, more than to double their income.

Every increase in the period for which the capital must last is, of course, a factor working against the consumption of capital. If the average length of human life were increased to a considerable extent, the rate of interest would, on that account, be able to fall much more than is possible with the present average length. If we imagine people living for several hundred years, there would be no extensive consumption of capital until the rate fell to a fraction of one per cent. From this point of view there would be nothing to prevent the rate of interest being calculated as so much per thousand instead of, as now, at so much per hundred. The dependence of the rate of interest upon the length of human life is thus made very clear.

In order to realise this still more clearly, we must remember that an increase of income by the consumption of capital is most reasonably done by purchasing an annuity. The advantage of living on one's capital is then shown to be still greater than if, as above, we assume the period for which the capital must last to be fixed in advance. The following table shows the ratio between the annuity which can be bought at different ages with a given capital sum and the perpetual return obtained by putting out that capital at interest.

Age at Time the Annuity is Purchased.	Interest.										
	1%	1½%	2%	2½%	3%	3½%	4%	5%	6%	7%	8%
10	2.74	2.06	1.74	1.55	1.43	1.34	1.28	1.18	1.16	1.13	1.11
20	3.09	2.29	1.90	1.68	1.53	1.43	1.35	1.26	1.20	1.17	1.13
30	3.59	2.62	2.15	1.87	1.69	1.56	1.47	1.34	1.26	1.21	1.18
40	4.39	3.15	2.55	2.19	1.95	1.78	1.65	1.48	1.38	1.31	1.26
50	5.76	4.07	3.24	2.74	2.41	2.18	2.00	1.77	1.61	1.50	1.42
60	8.27	5.77	4.52	3.77	3.27	2.92	2.66	2.29	2.04	1.88	1.75

From this table we see that, though there is little advantage for middle-aged people in living on their capital when the rate of interest is high, this advantage increases as the rate becomes lower, and becomes important even for younger people. If we suppose that the possibility of doubling one's income through the purchase of an annuity gives rise to a certain amount of consumption of capital, this consumption will, with a rate of interest of 6 per cent., begin at the age of 60, at 50 when the rate is 4 per cent., at 30 when the rate is 2 per cent., and at 10 – that is, for almost everybody – when the rate is $1\frac{1}{2}$ per cent. Trebling the income will be possible at an age of under 60 when the rate is 3 per cent., 55 when it is $2\frac{1}{2}$ per cent., 50 when it is 2 per cent., and under 40 when it is $1\frac{1}{2}$ per cent. And the possibility of trebling one's income would, for the majority of capitalists, prove a strong incentive to use up capital, especially if their income were reduced by the fall in the rate of interest to a fraction of its original size.

At what age, in modern conditions, are people most wealthy? In connection with this very interesting question there is an instructive statistical inquiry made by the Swedish Ministry of Finance as regards hereditary wealth.[1] Although the absolute figures in this inquiry are not very reliable, the calculation of the relative distribution of wealth according to age probably approximates to the actual facts sufficiently accurately for our purpose. This material shows that, in the towns, people over 60 years old own more than half the wealth, and that this is the case with people over 50 in the country. We can calculate approximately that, as a whole, over half the total wealth is owned by people more than 55 years old. People over 40 own not less than 89.5 per cent. in the towns, and 72.5 per cent. in the country, of the total wealth.

We may conclude from this that a rate of interest that offers a strong incentive to people over 50 to live on their capital would markedly decrease the total supply of capital, and that a rate which induced people above 40 to do so would be fatal as regards the provision of capital for business. When the rate is $2\frac{1}{2}$ per cent., income can be increased by the very appreciable multiple of 2.7 for people of 50, and 3.8 for people of 60. Such a rate of interest would be bound to lead to a considerable using-up of capital. With a rate of $1\frac{1}{2}$ per cent., income could be more than trebled for people of 40, quadrupled for people of 50, and increased sixfold for people

[1] *Bouppteckninger efter avlidna* (Stockholm, 1910).

of 60, and the owners of by far the greater part of the total wealth would have a very strong, and in some cases an irresistible, incentive to live on their capital. How such a position could continue is a question the answering of which we leave to those prophets who have contemplated a fall of the rate to those levels.

Up to now, the conclusion of our inquiry is that the supply of capital-disposal depends on the rate of interest, and, indeed, generally falls with it. Within the limits of ordinary fluctuations in the rate this dependence is not very pronounced, but if the rate fell to $2\frac{1}{2}$ per cent. or less, the supply of capital-disposal would be greatly reduced.

This supply, as we have seen, is equal to the difference between saving and over-consumption. At any conceivable rate of interest these two opposite economic tendencies make themselves felt; no rate is high enough to prevent over-consumption completely, that is, over-consumption of capital or future income. There are always cases where people are willing to pay several hundred per cent. if the satisfaction of present wants can only be obtained by sacrificing, on such unfavourable terms, the satisfaction of future wants. On the other hand, no rate is low enough to prevent further saving altogether. Even if there were no interest, numbers of people would lay aside part of their income for future needs, and capitalists would not consume all their capital at once.

Present and future, therefore, have a very different significance for different individuals. It is not possible to compress these infinite variations into a single formula and describe them as a general under-estimation of future wants or future goods compared with those of the present. The actual supply of capital-disposal at any time is determined by the behaviour of different individuals at the given rate of interest, and is the resultant of a great number of partly antagonistic forces. This resultant cannot be stated in general terms, but is essentially related to, and varies with, the rate of interest. If, therefore, the supply of capital-disposal is a function of the rate of interest, this supply can only be significant for the rate in the way in which it reacts to alterations in that rate, and is expressed only through the form of that function which represents the dependence of the supply upon the rate. The theory of interest requires some knowledge of the general form of that function, and cannot be satisfied with the vague assurance that the resultant of the many varied estimates of future goods in terms of present goods is an under-estimate of the future.

§ 25 *The Determination of the Rate of Interest*

As soon as we conceive interest as the price of capital-disposal, its position in the general pricing process is at once clear; interest, like any other price, has to perform the economic function of so restricting the demand and, possibly, of stimulating the supply, that demand and supply are equal to each other. The object of the theory of interest is thus reduced to an inquiry into the manner in which the demand for, or supply of, capital-disposal varies with the rate of interest, and this has been done in the last two sections. It has been shown that the supply of capital-disposal is only slightly influenced by movements of the rate within ordinary limits, and thus is relatively fixed. In such circumstances, consequently, the main task of the rate is necessarily to restrict the demand for capital-disposal, that is, primarily, to check the demand for the services of durable goods, and, secondarily, to restrict the tendency to substitute capital-disposal for other factors of production. The first kind of restriction is directed immediately against consumption, while the second concerns the choice of methods of production. Following from our inquiry, we see that the demand for capital-disposal is so great that it can only be checked sufficiently by a rate of interest at the usual level. Any alleviation of this pressure will set free a large new demand which cannot be satisfied by the available amount of capital-disposal, even if this amount is not reduced as a consequence of the fall in the rate of interest. This, in ordinary circumstances, is the real reason why the rate cannot be lower than it actually is.

As the problem of interest has often, perhaps generally, been considered from the ethical instead of from the economic point of

view, the question why capitalists must be paid has been thrust into
the foreground. The complaint has been made that the capitalists,
by demanding interest, rob the community; or, at least, it has been
asserted that they should be satisfied with a lower rate of interest.
The whole of this kind of consideration loses its foundation when
the problem of interest is treated from the economic point of view.
It is then apparent that the capitalists proper have very little
influence on the actual height of the rate of interest. Within the
limits of the ordinary fluctuations of the rate, capitalists, on the
whole, provide approximately the same amount of capital at a high
rate as at a low one. The supply of capital-disposal from this side
is therefore rather passive in regard to changes in the rate. The
capitalists form the only economic group, in modern society, which
has no organisation for safeguarding its common interest. They
receive interest at the actual rate, not because they extract it
forcibly by some means or other, nor even because they want it, but
simply because it is economically necessary to check the demand for
capital-disposal, and because this restriction, in accordance with the
general principle of pricing in the exchange economy, can only be
achieved by placing a sufficiently high price on capital-disposal.
Even if we suppose that savers would provide the same amount of
capital-disposal without receiving any interest at all, the rate of
interest would not disappear. The scarcity of the available amount
of this capital-disposal would always make it necessary to check the
demand by a suitable rate of interest. The existence of interest is
therefore essentially independent of the demands of capitalists to
be paid interest. Another point is that, with an increased degree
of saving, the rate of interest would be lower. Those who advocate
a lower interest should, consequently, really direct their zeal not
against the savers, but against those who do not save, against
unnecessary consumption on the part of the individual or the
State.

In periods when a considerable growth of population, the opening-up of new areas, an increased demand for better living accommodation, for trams, railways, and various kinds of electrical
equipment, etc., or new inventions which substitute machines for

human labour, make more pressing demands for the use of durable goods – that is, for capital-disposal – the rate of interest rises. There are then frequent complaints in the business world that the banks, with their high rates of interest, check the spirit of enterprise and hinder economic development. Politicians lament that the heavy interest demands made by the capitalists make it much more difficult for them to carry on work for the benefit of the people, such as the building of houses for the working class; local authorities find themselves severely hampered in their economic activity, and the public denounces a bank-rate policy that stands in the way of the satisfaction of its need for new conveniences, such as railways and similar projects. All these complaints spring from the same false conception of the influence exerted by the supply of capital-disposal on the rate of interest, and testify to a lack of insight into the economic function of the rate of interest, which is to keep within certain limits all economic activity that requires capital-disposal. It is just in such periods that the rate has to dampen the ardour of entrepreneurs and slow down economic progress. The absolute necessity of such pricing lies in the scarcity of the available amount of capital-disposal. Precisely because that rate constantly keeps the fluctuating demand for capital-disposal adjusted to the limited supply, it is the universal regulator of the ups and downs of economic life, the far-reaching importance of which we shall realise better in Book IV. of this work.

The results of our study of the determining factors of interest show how little the usual notion of interest as a "cost," in Marshall's sense, or as a price which has to be paid to compensate savers for the sacrifice of "waiting," touches the core of the problem. In order to justify his conception of the nature of cost, Marshall has to lay a certain emphasis on the assumption that a rise in the rate of interest has a tendency to increase the amount of saving.[1] It is possible, perhaps even probable, that there is such a tendency in reality. But it is by no means necessarily the case. The whole theory of pricing, and, naturally, of distribution also, since it is only one side of the theory of pricing, is bound to remain the

[1] Book VI., chap. ii., § 4.

same in its essential features, even if the amount of saving were independent of the rate of interest. A small and, in any case, purely quantitative alteration of one factor in the pricing process ought not to influence our conception of the nature of this factor or our presentation of the whole mechanism of pricing.

In Book I. we assumed that the quantities of the different primary factors of production available in any unit period were given. We now drop this assumption in connection with capital-disposal, and instead we assume that the amount of capital-disposal available in each unit period is determined as soon as the price of it is fixed – that is, as soon as the rate of interest is given. For the solution of the general pricing problem, this assumption does not really matter. In our treatment of this problem the prices of the factors of production were at first assumed to be given, and we then deduced the conditions necessary for maintaining these prices in a state of equilibrium. One of these prices is interest.

In the third and fourth chapters we were obliged to assume that the sums of money available in each unit period for either saving or consumption are given with the prices of the factors of production. We were then unable to consider the special position of interest. As the price of a factor of production, interest is an element in the constitution of income as well as in the pricing of finished goods, and it has, in this connection, the same influence as the prices of the other factors of production on the extent of consumption or of saving. But interest has also a specific influence on the degree of saving, and, even if this is not particularly pronounced at the ordinary rates, it must have its definite place in our general explanation of the pricing process. However, this raises no new difficulty, as the explanation, in any case, begins with the assumption of given prices of the primary factors of production.

If we start with this assumption, we assume, consequently, that we know the continuous accumulation of capital and the rate of progress. This rate determines, again, the constant rise in the future demand, and thus the demands made upon the existing factors of production in the present unit period. As these demands must be equal to the available quantities in existence, the whole pricing problem is settled, and, through that, the rate of progress. The whole adjustment of the economy in time – the relative distribution of economic effort between the present and the future or, strictly speaking, between the immediate and the more distant future – thus appears as one aspect of the great pricing process, by means of which the exchange economy is maintained in a state of equilibrium.

The decisive influence on this adjustment of the economy is, naturally, the thriftiness of the people. The rate of progress in a community based on private property is determined by the consideration which its members have for the future. If the degree of saving is great, then there will be capital-disposal available for a considerable increase of the amount of real capital, and the demand for this capital-disposal will not need to be checked by a high rate of interest. In such a community there would be steady progress. The reverse is the case, of course, when there is little saving. Radical changes in the degree of saving would have a marked effect on both the rate of interest and the pace of progress.

If saving were so imperceptible that the people, even with the inducement of a high rate of interest, would on the whole provide no new capital-disposal, the community would be a stationary economy. Then, evidently, the demands for capital-disposal would have to be checked severely, and a very high rate of interest would be necessary for that. In view of the actual possibilities of using capital-disposal profitably for improving the satisfaction of wants, a stationary economy would only be possible if there were a rate of interest which the existing generation would consider extremely high.

Now that we have determined the position of interest in the pricing process, it is comparatively easy to glance at the effects which various external factors have upon it.

As civilisation advances, certain tendencies appear which lead to an increase of the supply of capital-disposal. Among these is, first of all, the growing safety of life and property which has accompanied the modern development of the state, and which, of course, encourages provision for the future. Moreover, the whole of economic development accentuates this provision. The more solidly built house and arable farming were the first to help to educate men in economic foresight and planning. The inclusion of the future in economic calculations of the present was further promoted later on by the constantly growing importance of durable goods in society. Working in the same direction, there has been the lengthening of human life, due especially to modern hygiene. The man who can count on living for another thirty years must definitely be more willing than a man who can only count on another ten or fifteen years to sacrifice some of his present wants so as to provide for the future.

Contemporaneously with this development leading to an increase in the supply of capital-disposal, there has been a constant increase in the demands on this capital-disposal for use of durable goods. The sources of these demands have already been fully explained; they have grown so vigorously that it has never been possible to satisfy them completely. There has always been a scarcity of capital-disposal, making interest necessary.

A comparison of the development of the supply of capital-disposal with that of the demand for it shows that it is an unquestionable fact that the former has been much more steady than the latter. The reformation of man's economic habits, his education in consideration for the future – all these are necessarily slow processes; but, in spite of occasional interruptions, especially, as we shall see, in periods of inflation, they proceed fairly steadily on the whole. On the other hand, the demand generally increases by leaps and bounds, and then falls back for a time. The increases are due mainly to such sporadic occurrences as inventions, improvements in methods of transport, and the opening-up of new countries in consequence of discoveries or political events. It follows from this that, for short periods, the influence of the demand on the rate of interest is most pronounced, and the fluctuations of the rate in such periods are usually attributable to changes in the demand. But if we consider longer periods, we perceive a real influence of the supply of capital-disposal on the rate. The increasing concern for the future which accompanies the advance of civilisation has undoubtedly, in the course of centuries, made it possible to lower the rate of interest to a certain extent – a process which may still be observed when semi-barbarous countries are lifted to the realm of civilisation. This fall in the rate, it is true, is by no means as one-sided and pronounced a tendency as was sometimes represented; it is not an unlimited tendency which we may continue to expect. As shown in the preceding sections, it is already checked by powerful forces, and has only a rather narrow margin for free play.

On the basis of these general facts we can now explain the fluctuations of the rate of interest shown by historical statistics, assuming, of course, that we know all the factors which influence the rate as shown by the analysis we have made. For shorter periods, as we saw, the tendencies on the side of the demand for capital-disposal are the main causes of fluctuations in the rate. So we must look for the causes of the ordinary variations in the rate in the changing demand for durable goods, and then in the altera-tions in the production of fixed real capital. As the rate of interest in turn regulates this demand, the whole movement of economic life appears as a continuous interaction of the rate of interest and the production of fixed real capital. The closer study of this interaction which we call the "trade cycle," belongs to the dynamics of econ-omic life, and will be the subject of Book IV.

The explanation of fluctuations in the rate is one of the chief tasks of the theory of interest. The other is answering the question how far interest is a necessary phenomenon, or merely an accidental result, of the conditions of our time, or of the arrangement of our existing economic order.

In connection with this question, we must observe the following. A fall in the rate of interest much below what is now the usual level would, as has been shown, greatly increase the demand for capital-disposal on the one hand, and very markedly reduce the supply of it on the other. These opposing tendencies, both of which are very pronounced when the rate is low, must check the fall in the rate very quickly. Let us suppose, for a moment, that there is a rate of $2\frac{1}{2}$ per cent. all over the world for a long period. Our inquiries show that there is no doubt that such a rate would give rise to enormous demands for capital-disposal for very costly equipment and construction of all kinds, and would, at the same time, cause small and also moderately wealthy capitalists to live on their capital to a great extent. We need not reflect on these things any longer to see quite clearly that the counteracting tendencies evoked by this rate would have such force as to make the maintenance of the rate impossible.

At the end of the nineteenth century various circumstances contributed to force down the rate considerably. The lowest point was attained in the middle 'nineties. It is not surprising that this led the general public to believe that the rate of interest had a general tendency to fall. But that this belief should be accepted by the foremost representatives of economic science as the result of research is not really very creditable to the science. Schmoller expresses himself rather cautiously when he says that "it is not inconceivable that the rate of interest, which fell in the eighteenth century to 3 per cent. and in the nineteenth to $2\frac{3}{4}$ per cent. may, in the twentieth century, fall below 2 per cent., and even as low as $1\frac{1}{2}$ per cent."[1] This conclusion that, because a certain movement is taking place, it is bound to continue in the same direction, is without any scientific basis. Nor is there any ground for assuming that the limit of this movement is attained when the rate of interest is $1\frac{1}{2}$ per cent. Our analysis, on the contrary, has shown that in all probability the suppositions that the rate could reach $1\frac{1}{2}$ per cent. are entirely unjustified. Before describing such a development as probable, it ought to be made clear how it would be possible to maintain a state of things in which the owners of by far the greater part of the total wealth could generally treble, and frequently more than treble, their incomes by living on their capital, and in which the actual rates checking the demands for durable goods and the requirements of industrial technique had lost most of their power. Of course, we cannot assert that a rate of $1\frac{1}{2}$ per cent. is absolutely impossible. But what kind of development would be necessary to make that rate possible? As far as we can see, it would mean an almost complete cessation both of increase of population and of every

[1] *Grundriss*, II., Teil, p. 208.

kind of economic progress that requires large quantities of durable goods, and, moreover, an extension of the duration of human life large enough to keep the consumption of capital that would occur at such a low rate within the necessary limits.

Given the actual length of human life and the present rate of increase of population and technical progress, the rate of interest cannot fall much lower than it is to-day. These are the chief determining factors of the rate. A complete stagnation of economic life all over the world as a result of external circumstances would naturally depress the rate considerably. When, however, it reached 2 per cent., the tendency to live on capital would be so great, that it seems doubtful whether the supply of capital-disposal would be sufficient even for this state of stagnation. But it is inconceivable that such a stagnation could actually occur. The demand for capital-disposal is very considerable at the present rate of interest. Besides, the entire demand for commodities, and the whole development of industrial technique, are adjusted to a certain rate of interest, and they would be revolutionised if that rate were lower – that is, in the direction of an increased demand for durable goods and so for capital-disposal.

These considerations regarding the actual conditions of a fall of the rate make a continuous downward movement such as was assumed by Schmoller and, still more, by other writers, in the highest degree improbable. At every stage, a further fall of the rate would be met by an increasing resistance. Consequently, under no circumstance is it possible to conceive a state of things where the rate of interest would be zero.

It has been repeatedly pointed out that a theory of interest must necessarily be quantitative, and must explain not only why there is interest, but also why it is generally at the actual level at which it is found. The two explanations cannot be different; the existence of interest is due to the same forces as those which make the actual rate what it is. A theory of interest must, therefore – to define the problem more arithmetically – explain why the rate is expressed as so much per cent. instead of, say, so much per mille. Why does the rate fluctuate between 3 and 4 per cent., and why can it not just as well fluctuate between 3 and 4 per mille? A theory of interest that fits either of them is, strictly speaking, no theory at all. The question has already been answered. The length of human life is one of the most important factors. At first sight, there is nothing self-evident or probable in the fact that the rate of interest varies between 3 and 4 per cent. If, however, we take the number of years' purchase of a fixed annuity instead of the rate of interest, we can show the character of the rate by saying that a perpetual annuity costs twenty-five or thirty-three times the annual value. When the matter is expressed in this way, it is easy to see that there is a definite relation between the rate of interest and the length of human life. Men, at the age at which they have control over their own capital, cannot generally count on more than another twenty-five to thirty-three years of life, and will not, consequently, sacrifice much more than twenty-five to thirty-three years of returns to secure a perpetual annuity. Those who believe an interest of 1 per cent. to be possible are really supposing that, for instance, an estate with a net yield of £10,000 would be bought at the price of £1,000,000! But the millionaire, by consuming his million, can be much better off during his remaining years than by buying an income of £10,000 a year. In reality, it is quite impossible to suppose that, with the present length of human life, absolutely durable goods would be paid for at the rate of a hundred or even fifty times their annual returns. A rate of interest of one per mille would be possible if people were inclined to save £100,000 and then give it away in order to obtain an annuity of £100. That kind of economising would only be done by a Methuselah.

In conclusion, we must again point out that what we have said about the possibility of a fall in the rate of interest applies, of course, to the typical rate which we are considering, and which is best represented by the interest on mortgages and by rents. That the rate of interest on short-term loans occasionally may fall lower is not disputed. It has already happened that the private discount rate on the chief exchanges has occasionally fallen below 1 per cent. Such a low rate is explained mainly by the fact that the lenders did not want to tie up their capital, but preferred to leave it available for a more favourable opportunity either of permanent investment or for profits from speculation.

§ 26 *Interest in the Socialist State*

The preceding inquiry has shown that interest is a necessary phenomenon of our present exchange economy. But this might merely signify that it is due to the special characteristics of our existing economic organisation, and that it might disappear if this exchange economy were freed from these characteristics. It is, indeed, undeniable that the efforts of entrepreneurs to use an increasing proportion of durable goods in production, and the tendency of capitalists to live on their capital when the rate of interest is low, have a considerable influence on the state of interest, and we might even say that the true economic task of interest is to check these tendencies. Consequently, it perhaps does not seem inconceivable that an exchange economy without private enterprise or private property would be in an entirely different position, as regards the necessity of interest, from that of our actual economy.

But such a supposition would indicate a wholly distorted conception of the nature of interest. Up to the present we have considered the phenomenon of interest in connection with our actual economic conditions. This method is quite natural in a treatment that is concerned mainly with concrete reality. Interest has then to be related to the tendencies that express themselves in the conduct of entrepreneurs and capitalists, that is to say, traced to factors which seem to depend on the particular form of our economy. But behind these tendencies are basic facts of human life which, though perhaps modified, would be present in every kind of exchange economy. In the main, interest, in another form of society, would still be subject to the same forces as in our modern organisation. To obtain a correct view of the deeper nature of these forces, and thus of the nature of the problem of interest, a study of interest in a socialist community is very useful. Such a study also affords the best opportunity to refute old erroneous ideas of the nature of interest.

The main ideas in the organisation of the socialist economy have already been given (§ 15). Even in such a community, the fundamental characteristic of the exchange economy is present, that is, the freedom of the individual to choose what he will consume, within the limits of his income. It is primarily this freedom of choice that makes interest necessary in any exchange economy, as well as in the socialist community. For if prices were calculated for the use of reproducible durable goods which would simply compensate the owner for the depreciation of these goods, but which would not include interest, the demands of consumers for these goods would increase so much that they could not be satisfied. We need only think of the demand for houses if the prices of their use did not include interest. If the socialist state wanted to fix rents on this basis, it would be met by an insatiable demand for houses, and this is true of other cases as well. In the demands of consumers there is, directly or indirectly, a demand for the use of durable goods, and consequently for capital-disposal, which has to be checked. That is possible, in the exchange economy, only through pricing, that is, by allowing for interest. For this reason the socialist state would have to permit interest. This means that every satisfaction of wants that requires capital-disposal must have a price fixed that includes a proportionate allowance for that capital-disposal in addition to the cost of labour and other factors. So the prices of different things would be raised by very different degrees – houses would cost more than clothes, and so on. Even the socialist community cannot escape the need to determine prices in this way.

The management of the socialist state, which we assume to have control of the whole of production, must, further, constantly consider which methods of production are the cheapest and, in particular, how far capital-disposal shall be used as a substitute for other factors of production. It would clearly be impossible to base this calculation on the assumption that there is no need to take account of the price of capital-disposal. Such a procedure would, as our discussion of this problem shows, place production in an untenable position. For this reason the socialist state would be obliged to base the whole of its calculations and management of production on the assumption of a certain rate of interest.

Once a rate of interest was fixed, there would at the same time be a determination of the choice of methods of production, and hence the prices of finished goods, the demand of consumers for those goods, and, finally, the aggregate demand for capital-disposal would be fixed. Let us assume that this demand makes a certain increase in the capital necessary; then the socialist state must save a corresponding amount of capital. Within certain limits the socialist community can, of course, decide itself what it will save, but as soon as the degree of saving is agreed upon, the rate of interest needed to adjust the demands for capital-disposal to the given supply is also determined. It follows from this that in a socialist community the rate of interest depends, to some extent, upon the will of the controllers of the community, in so far as it depends upon the degree of saving. It is obvious that, in this sense, the socialist state can exert a certain influence, as it has to determine the degree of saving. It is also true of the socialist economy that the more thrifty a nation is, the lower need the rate of interest be. But no conceivable degree of thriftiness would allow the community to dispense with a rate of interest altogether. The demands for capital-disposal resultant upon the abolition of a rate of interest would be completely insatiable.

How does the socialist economy have to proceed if it wants to accomplish a certain amount of saving? Evidently this must be done by making the prices of the goods which pass over to the consumers higher than the costs of labour. So the totality of claims which can be pressed by the consumers on the ground of the work they have performed will be satisfied by only a part of the total product of that work. The rest of the product goes to the state – that is, the state directs a certain proportion of its productive powers to the creation of new real capital. Capital accumulation in the socialist community is thus conducted by forcing under-consumption by raising the prices of finished goods to the members of the community, and thus freeing productive powers for increasing the real capital.

Therefore, saving in a socialist state signifies a sacrifice enforced upon the consumers, and so the question arises as to how far the community may go in making demands upon the willingness of the consumers to make this sacrifice, or, in other words, what degree of saving can be chosen. This is clearly a question which particularly concerns the socialist organised exchange economy. In our society the degree of saving, and with it the rate of progress, is determined by the economising of the mass of individual households. In the socialist community this task is concentrated in the hands of the directors of the economy, and this is the difference. But it is scarcely probable that this concentration would increase the desire of the people to save, and thus make possible a lower rate of interest.

CHAPTER VII

RENT AND THE PRICES OF RAW MATERIALS

§ 27 *The Development of the Theory of Rent*

As soon as an exchange economy is developed to the point at which large quantities of agricultural products are among the goods regularly exchanged, it is found that the prices paid for these products not merely cover the costs of labour and capital, but also yield a profit to the owner of the land. The farmer cultivating his own land will, it is true, scarcely regard this profit as a separate part of his income. But where land is leased, competition forces the holders to be satisfied with the normal remuneration for their productive activity, and to pass on profits obtained in excess of that remuneration as rent to the owner of the land. In this way rent appears as an independent type of income. Land itself is priced by capitalising its rent at the rate of interest prevailing at the time. Anyone purchasing land in order to cultivate it himself must include in his calculations interest on the purchase price paid, or, in other words, must aim at achieving a profit covering not merely the normal remuneration for his own productive activity, but also his rent. The increasing amount of debts on land makes calculations of this kind more and more imperative. Thus, from the point of view of the individual, rent appears as a part of the cost of production which must be covered by the price of the products; and the belief arises that rent raises the prices of goods. People who believe this regard it as an injustice that a group of landowners should obtain a large share of the social income simply because they possess a good which is supplied free by nature, and which cannot be regarded as the result of any productive activity. On these grounds a heavy taxation of rent-income, if not its confiscation, is demanded. On the other hand, the agrarians demand that the state should maintain the prices of agricultural products at a level which covers the costs of production, of which rent forms a substantial element. Agricultural rent has thus obtained a very prominent place in the whole problem of pricing, and economists have always given special attention to this type of income.

Following the physiocrats, who regarded the fertility of nature as the only possible reason for the surplus of production above its necessary costs, Adam Smith declared that, in agriculture, nature works in co-operation with man, and enables the agricultural labourers not only to produce the value of their own consumption and of the profit on capital, as do the workers in manufacturing industries, but also, in addition, a rent for the landlord. According to Smith, this rent can be regarded as the product of those natural resources which are placed at the disposal of the tenant by the landlord, and rises with the increase of those resources, that is, with the naturally or artificially increased fertility of the land. In manufacturing industries nature does nothing, man all, and the product is correspondingly limited. In agriculture, on the other hand, a surplus is produced through the co-operation of nature, after everything that can be regarded as the work of man has been paid for. For this reason the use of capital in agriculture is by far the most advantageous for society. [1]

This analysis was attacked by the later classical economists. In England, the limited possibility of satisfying the demand of the population for agricultural goods by home production became more and more apparent. It was therefore natural that attention was directed to the scarcity of land as the cause of rent, and this interpretation remained a fundamental element in the classical theory of rent. Ricardo worked out this theory to its logical conclusion, and the Ricardian theory of rent became later the kernel of the entire discussion on the problem.

He defined rent as that part of the produce of the soil which is paid to the landlord for the use of the original and indestructible qualities of the soil. [2] He thus wished to separate that part of the ordinary rent which is paid for the use of real capital in any form

---

[1] *Wealth of Nations*, Book II., chap. v.   [2] Ricardo, *Works* (ed. McCulloch), p. 34.

from rent proper. If land is abundant, nothing is paid for its use. Only when the best land is no longer sufficient to supply the needs of a growing population, and it consequently becomes necessary to take less fertile or less favourably situated land – in other words, land of inferior quality – into cultivation, will rent be paid for cultivating land of the best quality. And the amount of this rent is determined by the surplus product obtained by a definite expenditure of capital and labour on land of the best quality over the product obtained by the use of the same amount of capital and labour on land of the worst quality cultivated. Instead of taking land of inferior quality into cultivation, it may be possible in certain circumstances to spend capital on a more intensive cultivation of the land already in use. But if the capital applied to land of this kind is doubled, the harvest will not necessarily be doubled too, but will be merely increased to a certain extent. If the application of the second capital instalment to the land is profitable, the first instalment of capital must yield a surplus profit which is a rent, representing the difference between two products obtained by the same expenditure and which goes to the landlord. If the population grows, agricultural produce must thus necessarily be raised in one way or the other at the cost of an ever-increasing expenditure of capital and labour. Rent is the surplus product gained under more favourable conditions over the product gained under the worst conditions.

The price of the produce is always determined by the highest costs of production that must be incurred to supply the entire demand. For the sake of brevity, these costs can be called "marginal costs of production." An expansion of agricultural production necessitating greater expenditure of capital and labour relatively to the product obtained thus raises the price of the unit of the product. Those products that can be grown with less expenditure also rise in price, and this increased price makes the payment of rent possible. The cause of a rise in the price is thus to be found in the fact that the last unit of the product required necessitates greater expenditure, and not in the fact that the landlord demands the payment of rent. The price is determined by the cost of production of that unit of the produce for which no rent is paid. Under no circumstances can rent therefore be a part of the price. This general conclusion that rent is not an element in the costs of agricultural production is, according to Ricardo, a principle of the greatest importance for economic theory.

If Adam Smith's view that rent is caused by the co-operation of nature were correct, rent would rise with increasing fertility of the soil. But according to Ricardo the opposite is the case. If agricultural technique is improved so that the same expenditure of capital and labour yields a greater amount of produce on the same piece of land, it is no longer necessary to use such inferior land as previously or to expend as much capital as before on the good land. The margin of cultivation again rises, and the surplus product that can be obtained under more favourable conditions is diminished; that is, rent calculated according to the amount of produce is reduced. Since, however, the marginal product is produced at less cost than previously, and since therefore its price falls, the money rent falls to an even greater extent than rent reckoned in natural produce.

Ricardo concludes from this analysis that the incidence of a tax on pure rent must fall entirely on the landlord, and cannot be transferred by him to others. For it is beyond his power to increase his rents, since the difference in productivity between the worst land and land of any higher quality remains constant. A tax on rent, also, cannot cause a rise in the price of the product, since the product which is grown under the worst conditions, and which determines the price, does not pay any rent, and is therefore not taxed.

Ricardo assumed that the cultivation of land always commences with the best land; only if the population grows will land of inferior quality be taken into cultivation. This assumption need merely imply that the land which, under the prevailing conditions, will be regarded as the best will be cultivated first; but this does not exclude the possibility that under altered conditions of technique at a later time other types of soil may come to be regarded as the most fertile. This fact is of no consequence for the analysis of rent, but it does throw some doubt on Ricardo's assumption that with a growing population inferior land must always be taken into cultivation.

Mainly under the influence of Ricardo's theory of rent, and of the immense increase in the value of agricultural land in England, there developed a school of thought opposed to the private ownership of land. The most prominent English writer of this school was John Stuart Mill. In the United States, where extravagant rents arose on account of the rapid growth of population, and where speculation in land developed to excess, this school found its most cogent advocate in Henry George. The rise in rents was regarded as an "unearned increment" accruing to the landlords without any activity on their part, simply because of an irrational system of property rights, and the entire institution of property in land was similarly looked upon as a monopoly for the exploitation of productive labour; it was demanded that the state should appropriate rent, or at any rate its increase, by suitable taxation. The most radical representatives of this school aimed at confiscating even the already existing rents, and believed that this would suffice to supply the entire revenue of the state, and thus put forward a programme of taxation, commonly called the "single tax" programme.

The later criticism of this school was partly directed against Ricardo's theory too. In the main, two points were brought forward. In the first place, rent as actually paid is often only to a small extent "monopoly rent," i.e. rent which is entirely due to the ownership of land which is scarce relatively to the demand, but is, for the greater part, ordinary interest on capital, or, in other words, a price that must be paid, if continued agricultural production is to be at all possible. This reminder is no doubt justified if applied to certain conceptions of the land-nationalisers, but it is entirely irrelevant to Ricardo's analysis of the nature of rent. For this analysis starts from Ricardo's definition of rent which has been quoted above, and which excludes from the very beginning any rent on capital. Ricardo's analysis refers exclusively to pure rent which is paid "for the use of the original and indestructible qualities of the soil."

In the second place, it has been argued that the increase in agricultural rent is not so general and necessary a phenomenon as the classical economists and the land reformers believed. The soil which is taken into cultivation at a later stage is not always of inferior quality; it may be soil which requires high costs of cultivation, but which, as a result, yields a large net profit. The use of more distant land increases the cost of production under modern transport conditions to a far less extent than was previously assumed. The density of new settlements is in itself a factor which is highly conducive to increased agricultural productivity. An expansion of the area under cultivation need not, for these reasons, necessarily increase the marginal costs of production to any great extent. This situation becomes particularly clear if the world economy is looked at as an entity; owing to the extraordinary progress of transport technique the supply of corn to Western Europe was made possible through an expansion of the area of cultivation in other continents. Moreover, a considerable reduction of marginal costs and, in consequence, a singular fall in European rents were coupled with this expansion.

Similar facts can be adduced to refute Ricardo's assumption of a rise in the marginal cost of production in the case of an increased expenditure of capital and labour on a given area of land. Such a rise will take place if unaccompanied by improvements in agricultural technique. This "law of diminishing returns," however, need not necessarily lead to a rise in the price of agricultural produce, since it is quite conceivable that the opposing tendencies of improved technique may outweigh the other tendencies. And this, in fact, occurred on a very large scale in the last century. Thus it cannot be doubted that to-day a far greater expenditure of capital and labour can be applied to a given piece of land without increased marginal costs of production. But this argument does not imply that the law of diminishing returns loses its significance, nor is that law invalidated if the technique of production remains the same.

In general, we find that the objections which have been mentioned so far are irrelevant to Ricardo's analysis of the nature of rent, even if they appreciably diminish the validity of the assumptions made by Ricardo and the classical economists in general as to the effects of increasing population on the actual rents paid. The rapid growth of the European population in the few decades before the war was even accompanied by a contemporaneous decline in agricultural rents in Europe. The possible extension of the cultivated areas of the world, the further progress of agricultural technique, and the wider diffusion of modern technical methods, may possibly continue to prevent a rise in agricultural rents in the near future. The pronounced fall in agricultural prices since the war has shown very clearly how highly elastic, in this sense, is agricultural production. But to draw conclusions from these data of sufficient weight to stand the test of time, or even of fundamental importance to economic theory, would be an example of the common error which confuses accidental tendencies of our own time with economic principles of general validity.

From the theoretical point of view, the objections which have been raised against Ricardo's statement that rent is no part of the cost of production are of far greater importance. Thus in particular it has been argued that, even though it is true that the worst soil cultivated does not pay rent, at any rate the worst land used for more valuable crops like wheat must pay rent, and that this rent must necessarily be regarded as part of the cost of production of wheat. The truth of this objection could not be admitted without abandoning the Ricardian theory of prices in its entirety. For this theory is based, as we shall see in greater detail in the next chapter, essentially on the assumption that rent has no significance at all for the fixing of prices, and that prices are thus solely determined by the costs of production in Ricardo's sense, namely, by the remunerations of labour and capital. It was thus essential for those favouring the classical theory to maintain unconditionally Ricardo's postulate that rent forms no part of the costs of production. This was effected by the argument that the expenditure of labour and capital in every branch of agricultural production must be taken to the point at which the yield of the final unit of expenditure is zero. Even Marshall can only maintain his system with the help of a construction of this kind, a fact which is of great importance for our criticism of that system. [1] We shall have to return to this criticism, and to the conclusions which we must draw from it about the theory of prices, in the following sections.

The rental values of urban sites increased universally to a considerable degree in the last century under the influence of the growth of population and the general drift to the towns. The profits which were made during that process by the sale of sites were enormous in some cases; the desire to participate in this easy method of acquiring wealth resulted in active land speculation, through which large fortunes were made and, in cases of over-speculation and reversals, heavy losses were sustained. With the rise in site values, rents for dwellings rose, especially in the centres of large towns, to sums which were regarded as oppressive. High rents and the constant scarcity of dwellings were then popularly regarded as the results of speculation in land and of the increase in site values which this caused. This view was even supported by scientific opinion. Social scientists pointed out that the housing conditions of large sections of the community, especially those of the working-classes, were steadily getting worse, and diagnosed the cause in the rise in house-rents; this rise, in their opinion, was primarily due to the manipulations of site speculators, who raised site values artificially by keeping sites off the market, by frequently repeated sales and by high mortgaging. [2] It was argued that improvements could only be expected if site speculation were controlled or abolished; in other words, if land or increased site values were heavily taxed, or if private property in land were abolished. Concurrent with these measures a suitable control of traffic and of building was demanded. In Germany, those houses with a very large number of stories were attacked by people holding these views on the ground that through them site values had been unduly increased. In general, urban site rents were looked upon as the result of conditions which could be politically controlled, and the problem was thus treated as a political, and not as an economic, one.

Such views obviously did not promote scientific research into the

---

[1] *Principles,* Book V., chap. viii., § 3.
[2] Pohle, *Zeitschrift für Sozialwissenschaft,* 1905, p. 679.

nature and causes of urban site rents. Urban rent must be determined objectively, in the same way as any other price, by the general principles of pricing. To acknowledge this truth does not imply a denial of the possibility of consciously adjusting the level by means of such measures as local traffic policies, etc. But it is essential that any influence of this nature should be brought to bear upon rents through the medium of demand ,or supply, or, in other words, of the normal mechanism of pricing; and if that is the case, such influences must be regarded as being on a par with many other forces at work in that mechanism, and not as spontaneous acts of social reform unhampered by economic necessity and thus outside the realm of economic theory. The special difficulties surrounding the theoretical treatment of urban rents are essentially those of defining the preliminary data, for both the supply of, and particularly the demand for, urban land are highly complex phenomena. Since, however, the problem of urban rent is, from the point of view of economic theory, of a similar nature to that of agricultural rent, it is legitimate to abstain from a special investigation of urban rent in a general treatise on economic theory such as the present work. The main lines of the explanation of urban rent are given as soon as the general nature of rent in an exchange economy has been elucidated. This will be the task of the two following sections.

§ 28 *The Nature of Rent*

We have defined rent, in the most general sense of the term, as the price charged for the use of a durable good. It follows that a price paid for consumption goods cannot be rent, not even if those consumption goods are so-called free gifts of nature. Incomes derived from the sale of ore out of a mine or of wood from a primæval forest are therefore not rents proper, although, practically speaking, their nature is very similar to that of rent, provided that they are forthcoming over very long periods of time. Economists have been fully aware of this point ever since Ricardo's time. But if income derived from the sale of natural products is not rent, but is in a different category from rent, logic demands that natural products should be regarded as a separate and distinct factor of production. The traditional grouping of all forms of natural co-operation in one category which is regarded as a single factor of production can no longer be maintained, if the corresponding income is classified into two types. Having acknowledged the fundamental significance of the classification of material goods as durable and consumption goods, we have further strong reasons for advocating a division of the factor of production "nature" into *land* and *natural products*.

This distinction limits our conception of rent in one direction: rent is only paid for the use of durable goods. But rent, as predominantly used by economists, refers to payments for the use of such durable goods only as have not been produced, or, in other words, for the use of land and those of its qualities that have not been produced, or the "original" qualities of the soil. This limitation of the term rent arose from the desire of economists to regard the "rent" of a produced durable good once and for all as interest. Rent proper was not to contain remuneration for human sacrifice of any kind, but was to be regarded as the price for the use of an available durable good which in itself was not the result of human production. But since in a certain sense it is true to speak of soil as "produced," it was necessary to restrict rent to the use of "the original qualities" of the soil, or of the "natural soil."

Moreover, it stands to reason that those qualities of the soil which, when the soil is put to normal use, can only be maintained through special action directed to that end, cannot be regarded as a part of "land." That fertility of the natural soil which in agriculture is maintained by manuring, and which is lost if no manure is applied, belongs, for economics as for physics, to the same class as the minerals which are found in the soil. It follows that it must be regarded as a consumption good and not as a durable good. Similarly, relatively durable qualities of the soil which can only be maintained through constant productive activity must not be regarded as "land," but as fixed real capital. Land as a primary factor of production thus merely includes those original qualities of the soil which are not exhausted in its normal use, which are therefore in this sense, though of course not physically, "indestructible."

In accordance with Ricardo, we thus regard rent proper merely as the price charged for the use of the original and indestructible qualities of the soil Such rent cannot be regarded as remuneration for any productive activity, be that activity directed towards the creation of new goods or the maintenance of old ones. The existence of rent is solely conditioned by the necessity of limiting the demand for the use of a scarce supply of land.

The tendency of economists to regard land as not producible is primarily due to the fact that the problem was approached more from the point of view of physics than from that of economics. From the economic point of view, land is not merely a part of the surface of the globe; it includes numerous physical and economic qualities of the soil, such as its fertility, its situation with regard to markets, or, in the case of urban sites, the nature of its subsoil and its situation near the centre of favoured residential districts. Such qualities of land can, however, be largely produced, and, in fact, are produced wherever it is a paying proposition. Our own time has seen the production of fertility on the largest scale in the case of the well-known irrigation of the western area of the United States, and in that of the damming of the Nile. From the point of view of the European demand for corn, the construction of the American and Canadian railway systems and the development of large ocean steamers must be regarded as means of producing land which can enter into competition with European land on European markets. It is well known that this competition has greatly depressed rents for agricultural land in Europe. It is equally well known that the Dutch have reclaimed land on a large scale from the sea and have thus literally produced land. As regard urban sites it is a characteristic feature of our day that whole suburbs and new towns are being produced as a business proposition by entrepreneurs, who thereby compete with the owners of older urban sites. Such producers overcome the obstacle of distance by the construction of electric railways, and create fashionable residential areas by laying out public gardens, by constructing good roads, efficient lighting plant, modern hygienic services, by building and maintaining schools, and so forth. If we turn from land in the literal sense to other durable goods of nature, we find that these also are being produced in a similar sense. Thus the productive capacity of waterfalls is greatly increased by the harnessing of rivers; in fact, it is no exaggeration to speak of the literal production of waterfalls for industrial purposes. The favourable situation of a waterfall is naturally of great importance, but, even in this case, recent developments in the transmission of high tension electricity considerably widen the possibilities of competition.

The supply can similarly be increased to a certain extent in by far the greater number of cases in which land of a definite quality is demanded. As soon as the price offered for the particular quality of soil is sufficiently high, this possibility is utilised; price thus undeniably influences supply. This relationship naturally reacts on the price, in this case the rent. The rent of natural land depends, in a sense, upon the costs of production of the land produced to compete with it. Every reduction in these costs of production results in a diminution in the rent of natural land. However, what has been produced in this way is probably not so much land in the sense of a primary factor of production, but rather a product that has absorbed land among other factors of production. But this product enters into competition with natural land, and the supply of such land is therefore not fixed in the same sense that it is free from competition.

Since natural land as a primary factor of production is not merely fixed in quantity, but is also indestructible, a tax on the pure rent of this land would not influence the market position in any way, since its incidence must fall upon the rent itself and cannot be transferred. In general, it is of no consequence for the supply of an exchange economy with land of this type whether the owner of such land is paid for supplying it, and thus derives an income from his possession. The supply of natural land is not a service which need be paid for. But it is not legitimate to conclude from this that rent is of no importance for the supply of land of a specific quality. For rent, as has just been demonstrated, may stimulate the production of land which will compete with natural land, and this production of new land will be curtailed if that part of the rent of such land which is interest on the capital invested by producers is confiscated. Since it is extremely difficult in actual practice to distinguish the "original" qualities of the soil from those qualities which have been produced, it is not an easy task to exclude the results of productive activity in any attempt to place a special tax on the ownership of "natural land."

The rent of natural land is determined in the same way as the prices of all other primary factors of production in the general pricing process. The price of actual land itself is the value of the rent capitalised in accordance with the prevailing rate of interest, and, as such, is a secondary result of the pricing process. To the extent, however, that land is produced in competition with natural land, the price of natural land itself is in part determined by the costs of production of the competing produced land, and, in that way, is fixed as a direct part of the general process of pricing.

It follows from what has been said that the use of land cannot be regarded as a factor of production whose supply is absolutely fixed. The supply of this factor also is influenced by its price; and the dependence of this supply on price must be taken into account in a discussion of the general problem of pricing. This dependence of the supply on price must be regarded as one of the objective determinants of the general pricing process, instead of the supply itself.

In economic theory the notion of rent as independent of all "costs" in the sense of necessary remuneration for human sacrifice has been very important. Rent for land was taken as the typical example for pure rent in this sense of the term. But we have found that actual rent does not, in general, correspond to this ideal – this correspondence is in fact only found in those cases in which land of the same or a competing quality is not produced at the existing level of prices.

From the point of view of the pricing problem it may be desirable to argue that rent is characterised as a price not so much by the fact that the good for which rent is paid has been produced, but rather by the fact that at the present moment competing goods are not being produced, and that in consequence the price of this good has no independent determinants. This criterion of rent may under certain circumstances be satisfied by the net yield of an existing piece of fixed capital, or, in other words, by its gross yield less all costs of maintenance and replacement. For, once the real capital has been produced and the durable good is thus available, its own costs of production are a matter of the past, and as such are of no outstanding importance for the pricing process. Before the capital good in question was produced its net yield was naturally calculated to cover the interest of the capital used for its production. But in actual fact, the net yield may at a later date be larger or smaller than expected. The actual costs of production incurred have no more influence on these later events. Only to the extent to which the costs of production incurred are typical for the class of goods in question and to the extent to which further production of such goods is demanded do these costs influence the net yield of the good, and distinguish that yield as interest on the costs of production. But in cases where the capital good in question is unique, where similar goods are not produced, or else in cases where the costs of production have been considerably increased, its net yield loses all connection with its costs of production, and approximates in its economic significance to pure rent in the present sense of the term. A railway system may serve as an example. Once it has been constructed, the costs of that construction are of no more importance: the yield is entirely determined by other causes. If an adequate rate of interest is not obtained on the costs of construction, there is no help for it, since the capital has been sunk into the system and can no longer be extracted from it. If the yield exceeds the normal interest on the cost of construction, this will not, at any rate within fairly wide limits, lead to the further construction of railways. Under these circumstances the net yield of the railway partakes to a certain extent of the character of rent.

But it is necessary to remember in such cases that not merely the cost of maintaining and renewing the capital good must be subtracted from its gross yield, but also the interest which the capital thus maintained must earn, before a net yield partaking of the character of rent is obtained. For it is obvious that if no interest is obtained on the invested capital, in the long run no new capital will be applied to the maintenance and renewal of the real capital, and the latter will thus be destroyed to the extent to which it is not "indestructible." It follows that the "rent" part of the yield scarcely exists for a large proportion of capital goods, and in any case is of relatively small importance.

The proportion of rent in the net yield of a durable good is therefore smaller when the good in question is not unique, or when the number of similar goods increases, and when it is more frequently reproduced. It is also less when a growing demand calls forth an increased production of similar goods, when the relative importance of the costs of maintenance and renewal grows, and finally, when the technical conditions, and therefore the costs of production, become more stable. In the case of farm buildings, for example, all these factors will be found to be fairly prominent. In a large exchange economy regarded as a whole, the investment of new capital in such buildings is practically continuous; the net yield obtained from this form of real capital is thus essentially of the nature of interest. If the interest secured on the capital invested is insufficient, the supply will very soon be diminished, or will at any rate lag behind a rising demand. The time required for production itself is of minor importance in this case, since buildings of the type in question can usually be constructed in a few months, if not weeks. The supply can therefore follow an increase in demand with so short a time-lag that a rent, which presupposes a certain amount of stability, can scarcely arise.

The yield from improvements in the soil (such as drainage), the durability of which is great, and which require less work for maintenance and repair, is somewhat more akin to rent. Certain improvements also require so long a time to effect that the supply must for the time being lag behind the demand, and they may therefore yield income akin to rent.

Nevertheless, the fact that production takes time is in general found to be of minor importance for the formation of rent. Even in cases where this circumstance chances to work in the direction of creating rent-income, the period over which such an income

accrues is too short for it to be regarded as rent proper. Under
modern conditions the production of fixed real capital does take a
relatively very short time. The most important exceptions are
railways, water-works, and similar plant; but even for these the
period of construction is usually too brief to allow of more than a
very temporary formation of rent for existing plant of the same type.
The other factors listed above are usually decisive for the rent-
character of the yield from fixed real capital. [1]

§ 29 *The Pricing of Land*

Land occupies essentially the same position in the general pricing
process as the other factors of production. The general function of
pricing, that is, to limit the demand for finished goods by charging
uniform prices for the factors of production, and to conduct the
processes of production according to economic necessity, by
adjusting the indirect demand for factors of production with the
quantities available, is equally valid in the case of land as in that of
capital, and, as we shall see, of labour. Regarding the effects of
prices on supply, the peculiarity of land is that the land provided
by nature is in a certain sense fixed once and for all and is thus
independent of price. But, for the general pricing process, it is an
important fact that an increased price for land makes possible a more
extensive use of the land provided by nature, in some cases even
stimulates the production of new "land" which can compete with
natural land, and which thus produces reactions which have the
same significance in the pricing process as an increase in the supply
of any other factor of production caused by a rise in its price.

The general principles, according to which the price of land is
determined, are consequently already given in our general solution

[1] The fundamental significance which Marshall attributes to the distinction between
long and short periods in the formation of quasi-rent, appears scarcely justified under
these circumstances. The claim that a division of real capital according to whether or
not its supply can follow demand in a "period of moderate length" corresponds to the
profoundest and most important line of cleavage in economic theory – that the fact that
the English system of land tenure is supposed to divide the obligations of the landlord
and tenants according to this line explains the superiority of British economic theory – is
surely a slight exaggeration. *Principles*, Book VI., chap. ix., § 5.

of the pricing problem as a whole. It merely remains to study in detail the special processes peculiar to the pricing of land, or, in other words, to the formation of rent.

Let us concentrate our attention on agricultural land, and for the present accept the simplifying assumption that only a single product, such as wheat, is produced. We start with the case where a limited amount of land of uniform fertility and situation, or land of "equal quality," is available, and where the methods of production are invariable, in the sense that a fixed amount of labour and capital is required on any given portion. These abstractions are useful, since with their aid it is possible to demonstrate with great clarity the significance of the scarcity of land. If, then, the demand for wheat is so small that it can be satisfied at a price which merely covers the expenditure on capital and labour, land itself need not be priced. Under such conditions, in an exchange economy no rent will exist. If the demand is increased, the scarcity of the available land, once it has all been taken into cultivation, will necessitate a stricter limitation of the demand. In an exchange economy this limitation can only be achieved by a uniform pricing of land at a level which raises the price of the product to a sufficient height, and thus equates the demand for wheat with the quantity which can be produced on the given land with the given method of production. Thus a rent appears, determined, on the one hand, by the nature of the demand, and on the other by the available amount of land, and which thus represents a pure scarcity rent. This rent shows the fundamental characteristics of rent of land in general.

In reality, the scarcity of land is never so absolute as has been assumed in our example. It can be reduced, on the one hand, by the application of more capital and labour to the given quantity of land, or, in other words, by a substitution of capital and labour for land, thus diminishing the demand for land, or on the other hand, by the cultivation of new land, i.e. through an increase of the total area cultivated. The conditions producing such a diminution in the scarcity of land – the conditions, that is, for an increase in the harvest by means of the application of more capital and labour on a given area or of the extension of the area under cultivation – are determining factors for the price of land, supplementary to the main determinant, the scarcity of land.

Assuming that a growing population causes an increasing demand for wheat, the price of land must in general rise. The decisive question then is, What are the effects of such a rise in price? Any conceivable rise in the price of land must produce one of the following three reactions:

1. A fall in the demand for the product; or
2. A substitution of more capital and labour for land; or
3. An expansion of the area under cultivation.

The first two of these effects represent a diminution in the demand for land, while the third represents an increase in supply. All three are forces counteracting the rise in price, and co-operate in restoring equilibrium. The theory of rent consists fundamentally of a closer analysis of these counteracting tendencies. The general scheme of this theory is thus wholly analogous to that of the theory of interest.

The first of these tendencies will be stronger, the more elastic the demand for the product, i.e. the more severe the restriction upon demand which will result from a given increase in price. Now, it is well known that corn is one of those commodities for which the demand is least elastic. A very sharp increase in the price for land will therefore be required in order to achieve the required limitation of demand for this product. The usual cause of an increased demand for corn is the growth in population. There can be no doubt that a very considerable increase in the prices for both corn and land would have occurred in the past century if the second and third tendencies counteracting the rise in prices had not been as important as they actually were.

The second tendency resulting from a rise in the price of land is the greater expenditure of capital and labour on a given area. This tendency makes possible an increase in production, without increasing the demand for land, and thus neutralises the rise in the price of land. The individual farmer who is faced with the alternative of increasing his production, either by an extension of the area he cultivates (i.e. by leasing or purchasing more land), or by applying more capital and labour to his present acreage, will be induced by a rise in rent to select the latter course.

The conditions under which an increased product results from an additional expenditure of capital and labour to a given area of land are manifestly an important determining factor of rent. The examination of these conditions is thus of the greatest significance for the theory of rent.

In the first place, it is necessary to define the meaning of a definite expenditure of capital and labour. This phrase may mean a definite amount of capital together with a definite amount of labour. It may also be used in the more general sense of a unit sum, say one pound, used to purchase the co-operation of capital and labour, the prices of these factors, interest and wages, being assumed as constant.

If we imagine that on a given piece of land such units of capital and labour are applied successively, it will be found in general that, though the yield of the land is increased, it will, after a certain point, rise more slowly than the expenditure of capital and labour. If this were not the case, it would be possible to obtain any desired quantity of corn from a given area of land. This statement is traditionally known to economists as the "law of diminishing returns," and was regarded by the classical economist as "the most important law of economic science." [1]

The fact that a definitely increased return can be obtained from a given piece of land by the application of more capital and labour must be taken in conjunction with the reversed statement that a definitely increased return can also be obtained by the cultivation of a larger area of land with the old expenditure of capital and labour. We are, in fact, confronted by two competing factors of production: land on the one hand, and capital and labour on the other. The way in which they compete is determined according to the principle of substitution. In general, a certain small piece of land may be substituted for a certain small amount of capital and labour, and *vice versa*, without altering the resulting yield. The

[1] J. S. Mill, *Principles*, Book I., chap. xii., § 2.

relative amounts that can be substituted depend upon the relative total quantities that have been applied to production.

How much of each factor of production it is economical to use can only be decided if the prices of these factors are given. The principle of substitution requires that the last units of the two factors that can be substituted for one another in production should have the same price (§ 13). This condition determines, as we have seen, both the economic direction of production and the pricing problem. In the optimum combination of the two factors demanded by the principle of substitution the return per unit of total expenditure reaches a maximum. If the expenditure of capital and labour on a given piece of land is smaller than it ought to be according to the principle of substitution, the return per unit of total cost can be augmented by an increase in this expenditure. If, however, the optimum combination according to the principle of substitution has been reached, further expenditure of capital and labour must obviously diminish the return per unit of cost. In the former case, the entrepreneur is working with increasing returns, in the latter with diminishing returns. But the same is true if we take the capital and labour as fixed and the land as the variable factor. A certain area will be the cheapest for production. Every extension of the area (but also each diminution) will diminish the return per unit of cost. The complete relativity of the conception of "diminishing" or "increasing returns" is thus aptly emphasised. This relationship is, moreover, by no means peculiar to agriculture. Everywhere returns per unit of expenditure must decline in any branch of production as soon as the combination of quantities of substitutable factors of production deviates from the optimum combination under the principle of substitution, that is to say, the combination yielding the maximum return per unit of expenditure.

The proportion in which land is combined with other factors of production in any given case depends on the relative prices of land and of the other factors of production; each factor, the price of which rises, will be replaced to a definite extent by the others. If wages rise in a given country while rent remains constant, farmers will be found to reduce the number of labourers they employ relatively to the area they cultivate. An increase in rent, the prices of the other factors remaining constant, will, on the other hand, increase the expenditure of capital and labour required by the principle of substitution per unit of land: the more expensive land requires a more "intensive" cultivation. This fact is admittedly of fundamental significance for the methods of agricultural production in different countries of the globe.

This analysis of the principle of substitution leads to certain conclusions regarding our view of the pricing process as a whole, and of the position of rent within that process.

In a state of equilibrium, the unit price of a product must, of course, be equal to the total costs per unit of the product, and, as such, contains capital and labour costs as well as rent. This fact must, however, be regarded as a necessary coincidence, and must not be interpreted in the sense that the costs of production, including rent, are the causes of the price of the product. As we know, the prices of finished products and the prices of factors of production are never connected in the sense that the one is the cause of the other; both groups of prices are determined at the same moment by the independent factors of the pricing process. If, in the present case, we take the prices of the factors of production, that is, rent and the prices of capital and labour, as given, then the principle of substitution indicates the proportions in which these two groups of factors shall be combined, or, in other words, how much of each shall be used for the production of a unit quantity of the produce. In this way the costs of the production of wheat are determined, and consequently also its price. This price will limit the demand for wheat to a certain quantity, and this quantity must coincide with the quantity produced. This quantity of produce in its turn is determined by the condition that the total available area of land and a quantity of labour and capital determined by the principle of substitution shall be used. In this manner we obtain an equation determining rent in relation to the price per unit expenditure of capital and labour. (We cannot here proceed further, since the prices of capital and labour can only be determined in connection with the whole pricing process which takes account of the entire demand for these factors in all branches of production.) In this treatment of the problem, rent retains its natural co-ordination with other factors of production in the pricing process as a whole, and its direct dependence on those factors which, in the final analysis, determine all prices, becomes apparent. It need scarcely be emphasised that this conception of rent as an integral part of the cost of production approximates very closely to the current conception of the business man.

The farmer, then, cultivating a piece of land for which he pays a given rent, must, according to the preceding analysis, use labour and capital up to the point at which it becomes immaterial whether a given sum of money is applied to the acquisition of more land or to the application of more capital and labour. Given this optimum combination according to the principle of substitution, the price of the product will not merely be equal to the entire costs of production per unit of produce, but also to the costs of the additional increment of capital and labour and to the equally large cost of the additional increment of land which would be required for the production of a further unit of produce.

This truth, which is, of course, equally valid for the two competing factors of production, has in the past been inequitably emphasised in the case of capital and labour; and the attempt was made to build the whole theory of price on the statement that the price of agricultural produce is determined by that expenditure of capital and labour which is required for the final unit of produce on a given area of land. From this, the conclusion was drawn that the price of the product depends entirely on the costs of capital and labour – at the margin of expenditure of these factors on a given area – and that, therefore, the scarcity of land does not invalidate the general rule that the prices of products are determined by the price of capital and labour. The doctrine culminated in the famous dictum of Ricardo that rent is not an element in the costs of production, nor, therefore, a part of the price of the product. In this way, rent as a factor of production was placed in a separate category, and the basis for a differentiation between rent on the one hand and the prices of the remaining factors of production on the other was laid, a differentiation which later determined the whole structure of economic theory and which is perhaps most pronounced in the great work of Marshall.

The true nature of this doctrine is most clearly illustrated when one realises that it may be claimed in the same way and with the same justification that "the price of agricultural produce is determined by the cost of the additional increment of land used for the production of the last unit of produce at a given expenditure of capital and labour." From this, one could conclude that the price of products depends exclusively on the cost of the marginal use of land, and that therefore capital and labour are no part of the costs of production. No one can doubt that this line of argument is far too artificial to be taken seriously.

The equal importance which is placed here on capital and labour, on the one hand, and on land, on the other, is obvious to the practical farmer. Frequently, he may even regard the expenditure of capital and labour as the relatively fixed element and the amount of land used as the essentially variable factor. For a country as a whole, however – some may argue – the available land is fixed, while the expenditure of capital and labour on this land is variable. But this argument ignores the fact that rent can only be determined as a part of the entire pricing process in an exchange economy. If we survey an exchange economy as a whole, the quantities of labour and capital which are available are just as much fixed at any one moment as the quantity of land. The pricing process in general is based primarily on the condition that all these given quantities of factors of production are completely utilised. In this respect, there is no difference between capital and labour on the one hand and land on the other. It is an entirely different matter that the conditions of the pricing process gradually change in a closed country with a growing population and increasing wealth, and that, in such a case, the available land must be regarded as relatively fixed, and the quantities of the other factors as the predominantly variable factors. This relationship is admittedly of great importance for a historical investigation of the dynamics of price movements.

Each process of production must be regarded as an indivisible unit, for the reason that costs of production refer to the results of that process as a whole, and include all costs necessary for the production of those results. This is the natural starting-point of a theory of price. If two factors, co-operating in the process of production, may continually be substituted for one another, it is easy to conceive of the one as fixed, while, for purposes of analysis, the other is divided into minute parts of equal size and the product, too, is divided into sections, produced with the help of these successive increments. In such a case, the earlier parts of the produce will, of course, be smaller than those that follow them. The price of the last part corresponds to the price of the final increment of the second factor of production, the price of which therefore determines the price of the product. If one desires to do so, one may conclude from this that only the price of the second factor of production is a part of the costs of production and of the price of the product. The prices of the remaining parts of the product are higher than those of the corresponding parts of the second factor used for their production. Since, therefore, the entire expenditure of this factor yields a profit exceeding its own costs, it is possible to attribute this surplus to the first factor, which is assumed to be fixed, and, if that factor is durable, to call that surplus "rent"; this rent will then be excluded from the pricing process. It is not denied that, in this way, a theory of price which is formally correct can be developed. But the advantages of this highly artificial approach are dubious.

If it is said that the price of wheat is determined by the cost of that expenditure of capital and labour which is required for the production of the last bushel of wheat on a given area of land, one must beware of regarding these marginal costs as an objective cause of the price of wheat. For the marginal costs themselves are not known before the position of the margin is known, that is, before it is known how much capital and labour can be economically applied to a given piece of land. But this margin can be determined according to the principle of substitution, as was shown above, as soon as the prices of the competing factors of production, in this case land on the one hand and capital and labour on the other, are known. If this line of thought is pursued, the price of the product will again be expressed in terms of the two factors of production. It is, of course, equally possible to take two other prices as the unknown quantities of the problem. If the price of the product and the price of a unit cf capital and labour are given, the marginal expenditure of capital and labour on a given area of land will be determined, since the final increment of capital and labour must be equal in price to the part of the product produced by that increment. Thus the expenditure of capital and labour on the total available land is determined, and consequently, also, the total quantity of the produce. Since this quantity must be equal to the demand at the given price of the product, an equation can be arrived at in which the price of the product is expressed in terms of the expenditure of capital and labour, and the problem thus solved. With this method of approach, which approximates most closely to that of the classical economists, rent can only be determined after the solution of the main problem. This fact induced the classical economists to regard rent as a secondary result of the pricing process and to place the entire phenomenon of rent outside the realm of the pricing process proper.[1] It does seem that, in this case, somewhat too hasty conclusions were drawn from a purely formal treatment of the pricing problem, a treatment which, moreover, is completely unnecessary and can be replaced, as we have shown, by a different treatment approximating more closely to the facts of real life. In reality, rent occupies an essentially similar position, among the costs of production, to that of the other factors.

Finally, we come to the third tendency counteracting an assumed rise in rent. This reaction takes the form of an extension of the area under cultivation. The conditions under which such an extension is possible are also quite obviously of great significance for rent. In an old country, such an extension of the area of cultivation is generally only possible by taking land of inferior quality or of less

---

[1] See Marshall, *Principles*, Book V., chap. viii., § 2: "Restatement of the classical doctrines." As Marshall points out, it is, of course, wrong to interpret rent as a factor regulating the price of the product. The same is true of the price of every other factor of production. The prices of all factors of production and of all products occupy the same position as unknown quantities in the pricing problem, for all of them can only be determined simultaneously by the independent determinants of the pricing process. The one-sidedness of Marshall's notion of "mutual dependence" is here clearly illustrated.

favourable situation into use. In the past, probably, many different qualities of land have been taken into cultivation in this way. For the present discussion of the conditions governing the cultivation of new soil, this fact may be left out of account, and it is sufficient to compare the new land with land of a certain quality already under crops. The first fact which will then arise is that the costs of production on the new land, though it bears no rent, will exceed the costs of production on the land already under cultivation, including its rent. If this were not the case, farmers would prefer to cultivate the unused land rather than make the payment of rent for the old land.

It obviously follows that the strength of the reaction against an increase in the old rents will be the greater, the smaller the amount by which the costs of production on the new land exceed the costs of production on the old land bearing rent, and the larger the area the cultivation of which has become possible by a certain small increase in the old rents. If the reaction is very strong, a considerable rise in the old rents will be impossible. If, on the other hand, it is very weak – if, in other words, a considerable expansion of the area of cultivation is only possible by taking land with appreciably higher costs of production into use – then there will be little resistance from this side to a rise in the old rents; rents will be determined almost in the same way as they would be if there were an absolute scarcity of land.

Consequently, an increase in the old rent is the normal condition for an expansion of the area of cultivation. Nevertheless, the cultivation of new land may, under certain circumstances, be possible without affecting the old rent. The clearing of new land usually requires capital investment for draining, cleaning, deep ploughing, roads, etc., and thus partakes of the character of land production. These costs may be so high that, in the past, at a time of a pronounced shortage of capital and of high rates of interest, they were excessive, and the land in question therefore remained unused, while only such land was taken into cultivation which could be made arable at a smaller initial cost. This state of affairs is what one might expect, particularly, in the first period of the colonisation of new countries. If, later, the rate of interest falls from, say, 10 per cent. to 5 per cent., a considerable extension of cultivation may become possible. The costs of production on the new land need, then, not exceed those on the old land; it is even conceivable that an expansion of cultivation takes place accompanied by a fall in the old rents. At any rate, this possibility of clearing new and fertile land will be a strong obstacle to an increase in the old rents.

Similarly, improvements in agricultural technique may enable the cultivation of new land to be undertaken without raising the old rents; new inventions may be made which considerably reduce the costs of production on land of certain qualities hitherto unused, and these lands will then also compete with the land so far cultivated. It cannot, therefore, be taken for granted that different areas of land were drawn into cultivation in the sequence which would correspond to the degree of quality assigned to them under the present conditions of technical knowledge and social organisation.

If land of varying quality is cultivated simultaneously, rent appears as *differential rent*, based on the different quantities of produce resulting from the application of the same amount of capital and labour to different pieces of land. Considering the large numbers of factors determining the quality of land and the great expanse of all available land, as well as its extremely varying nature, it is generally safe to assume that land of all qualities is available. The worst land cultivated is free from rent, and the rent of any piece of better land is determined, in accordance with Ricardo's formula, by the difference in the quantity of produce which can be gained by the application of the same amount of capital and labour to this more fertile land on the one hand and to rent-free land on the other. This general theory of rent, however, greatly lacks precision. For it remains uncertain how much of both kinds of land shall be cultivated with the same expenditure of capital and labour. One might assume that the comparison refers to two equal areas of land. But this assumption is impossible, for, in general, the area which would be suitable for the given expenditure of capital and labour in the one case, would probably be entirely unsuitable in the other. It is obviously necessary to assume in any comparison of productivity of two types of land that, in both cases, the most advantageous combination of land with capital and labour expenditure has been chosen. But which is the most economical combination cannot be determined for the better, rent-bearing land before the rent (or what is the same thing, the price of the product) has been given. The apparently simple interpretation of rent as a differential sum is therefore complicated by the simultaneous action of the principle of substitution. It follows that we do not progress very far with the idea of the difference between the quantity of produce on the better and the worse land as a determining factor of rent.

But even if this complication were absent, and even if we accepted the extremely simple assumption that the amount of labour and capital which can be used on a given area is absolutely fixed for all types of land, we would nevertheless not be able to accept the surplus of produce of the rent-bearing land above that of the rent-free land as an independent determinant of rent. For the area under cultivation, and, therefore, the margin of cultivation and the quality of rent-free land, is just as much determined by the rent, as rent is determined by these factors. In general, the explanation of rent as a surplus above the produce of the inferior land is not very satisfactory. The rent of any piece of land of a certain quality is, on final analysis, a scarcity price referring in the first place to this land itself, and is determined by its supply and demand. The existence of land of inferior quality which can compete with the better land may somewhat reduce that scarcity price, but it certainly cannot fundamentally change the nature of rent. The over-emphasis of the differential factor easily leads to the misconception that the existence of worse land is of primary importance to the rent of the better land. In reality, however, the existence of this rent does not depend at all upon the existence of worse land, but, on the contrary, it is even reduced thereby! If, in a country, the most inferior type of land already under cultivation is scarce relatively to the demand, and the unused land is of appreciably lower quality, that inferior land used must bear rent, and the nature of this rent as a scarcity price is clear. We must insist that our theory of price covers a case such as this, which is quite conceivable. It is of no fundamental significance to the real nature of rent whether rent-free land exists at the margin of cultivation or not. If this latter characteristic is an essential condition for the validity of any theory of price, it is the clearest proof that that theory is highly artificial, and we can be certain that, despite its formal validity, it misses the core of the problem.

Let us now approach closer to reality by noting the fact that the same land can be employed for the production of several different kinds of products. Thus the worst land on which wheat is grown still bears a rent, for it can also be used for other crops, such as potatoes. The classical economists were never able to explain this fact in a satisfactory way. Certainly, the doctrine that rent forms no part of the price of the produce can be formally maintained even for this case. We need merely assume that the expenditure of capital and labour for the cultivation of wheat is taken to its economic margin in accordance with the principle of substitution. It is particularly clear in this case that a theory which concentrates in this way on the margin of production must lose sight of an essential part of the pricing problem. For the economic significance of the pricing of the factors of production is most clearly shown in the resulting uniform regulation of the demand for the different products which can be produced by means of the co-operation of these factors, and in the optimum use of the factors of production thus combined. Rent therefore fulfils the highly important function in the pricing process of limiting the demand for different products of the land, according to their different requirements of land, and thus of regulating the use of land for different purposes. Rent fulfils this function in its capacity as an integral part of the cost of each product of the land. A series of different agricultural products is competing for the use of one and the same piece of land. The fact that this land bears a certain rent if used for growing potatoes is not without significance for the price of wheat. Indeed, rent, which must be equal in all branches of production, is equally significant for the prices of all products which are produced on the same land. It seems quite impossible to obtain a clear view of these very important processes and relationships if rent is not regarded, in conformity with the present argument, as a factor of equal significance with other prices for the pricing process.

The preceding analysis of rent refers directly to an exchange economy in which there is private property in land. But our proofs rest essentially on the necessity for limiting the demand for products of the soil through a uniform pricing of the factors of production, particularly rent, in accordance with the general principles of the pricing process. Since, as we know, this necessity is vital for every exchange economy, our general results remain valid for all exchange economies. A socialist society, owning all the land and carrying on agricultural production on its own account, would have to maintain rent in its pricing system in the same manner as an exchange economy based on private property in land, and it would similarly derive an income in the shape of rent. "Unearned income" can be abolished in this case by a socialist system of production and property with just the same difficulty as in the case of capital. That the socialist state may perhaps alter the use to which this income is put, does not alter its nature. The significance of rent as a regulator of the economically best expenditure of capital and labour on land, of the extension of the area under cultivation, and of the relative prices for different products of the soil, would be the same in a socialist community as in the present system.

§ 30 *The Pricing of Natural Materials*

Since natural materials are not durable goods, we need not, in their case, distinguish between the price of their use and the price of the goods themselves. The prices of natural materials are simply prices of consumption goods found in nature. If such materials – coal or ore, for example – are mined and taken to the consumers, their prices consist, for by far the greater part, in remuneration for the capital and labour expended, and only as to a small part in payment for the materials as found in nature. This latter part of their price will be the subject of the following analysis.

The total amount of ore in a mine cannot be brought to the

surface all at once; usually, a fairly long period of time is required to do this. The total value of this quantity of ore is therefore not simply equal to the total quantity multiplied by the price per unit. The value of the ore which will only be mined in the future must rather be reduced to current terms according to the present rate of interest, or, in other words, the value of the total ore in the mine is equal to the present value of all the ore which will be mined in the future, calculated according to the present rate of interest. Thus, the annual production of the mine represents the interest and sinking fund on its capital value. As in the case of any amortisation, interest on capital value represents, during the early years, the larger part of the annuity, and therefore of the price at which the material mined is sold, while in later years the redemption predominates. In the case of a mine with a very long period of productivity, the price of the material annually mined is thus essentially of the nature of interest on the capital value of the mine, and, therefore, so to speak, akin to a price paid for the use of a durable good, or, in other words, rent. This explains why the income which a mine-owner derives from his property in free gifts of nature is frequently regarded as a rent, and placed on an equal footing with the rent of a landlord. A scientific analysis of the pricing problem involved must not, however, rest satisfied with an analogy of this sort. It must refer directly to the price of the material, and must regard the price of the mine merely as a secondary phenomenon.

The price of the material as a primary factor of production must be determinable by the general pricing process. The price must therefore be regarded essentially as a price determined by the general principle of scarcity; and the special study of the prices of natural materials can be confined to a study of those circumstances which regulate the supply of these materials in an exchange economy.

The statement that the prices of natural products are determined by the scarcity of their available quantities may at first sight appear to be completely out of touch with the conditions of reality. For, in general, there are much greater quantities of natural materials available than we can use at present, say during one year. If that is true, how can it be said that natural materials are only available in such scarce quantities that a scarcity price must be placed on them in order to limit the demand?

In answering this question, it is necessary to remember in the first place that natural materials, such as the ore in a mine, cannot be made available all at once. The exhaustion of a mine always takes time, generally very many years. The annual production of ore is thus in any case far more severely restricted than the total quantity of the ore. The period of production is not, however, definitely fixed beforehand by technical factors; it can be shortened, provided the owner is prepared to bear the costs of the required extensions of plant, means of transport, sources of power, etc. Thus, even the quantities of these new materials, available within a certain period of time as primary factors of production are not absolutely limited, but are, in a sense, determined by the pricing process. If technical equipment is available in such quantities as to be sufficient for the mining and transportation of the whole ore deposit during a certain period, any increase for the purposes of quick mining will increase the costs chargeable to the whole quantity of ore. On the other hand, assuming that the price of ore at the place of consumption remains constant, and that the entire sales revenue is thus determined, there is the advantage that the owner receives his return at an earlier date. The owner working his own mine must balance these advantages and disadvantages against one another. He can do this only by reducing all income and expenditure for the whole period of the productivity of his mine to their present value. Every increase in the present value of the capital and labour cost, which produces a still greater increase in the present value of the sales revenue, is of advantage to him. The owner must therefore invest so much capital in his mine that the last increment of the present value of the capital and labour costs is balanced by the final increment of the present value of the sales revenue produced thereby.

An increase in the capital and labour cost cannot, of course, enhance the mass of ore contained in the mine, but it does make that ore available at an earlier date, and thus produces a saving in interest. If the sales price is fixed, the present value of the total sales revenue is equal to the total sum actually realised in sales multiplied by a factor which is determined only by the rate of interest and the period of production – if, for simplicity's sake, we assume that production is spread evenly over the whole period – and which grows with every diminution in that period. A diminution in the period of production thus always implies an increase in the present value of the sales revenue. Since this increase is obviously proportionate to the sales price, every rise in that price must correspondingly increase the advantage of the reduction in the period of production, and thus, prices of capital and labour remaining constant, provide a further inducement for reducing that period. Each rise in the price paid at a given moment at the place of consumption thus stimulates the supply.

But there is another side to the question of how quickly the natural resources should be made available for human consumption. While regulating present consumption, we must not lose sight of the needs of the future. If there is danger that the natural resources will be completely exhausted at the present rate of consumption within a short period of time, it is obviously desirable to limit present consumption as far as possible. In an exchange economy based on private enterprise, such a limitation upon the present consumption is actually brought about by the fact that the rise in the prices of raw materials which must be expected to occur in the future as a result of their increasing scarcity must permit a certain amount of saving in the present to appear to be to the advantage of the entrepreneur. If a sufficiently substantial rise of prices is expected within a reasonable period of time, entrepreneurs will reduce the volume of their production and thereby increase the present price. Prices will not therefore remain constant at first, only to rise suddenly to immense heights, but will show a far more uniform, though still marked increase. The prospect of a future scarcity does not merely affect future prices, but is of great importance even for the prices charged at the present.

The degree to which the private entrepreneur takes account of future needs depends upon the rate of interest, in addition to the circumstances already mentioned. The higher the rate of interest, the higher must the future rise of prices be in order to counter-balance the loss of interest involved in a saving of natural resources; and therefore so much the more amply will the present be supplied in comparison with the future. It is, moreover, necessary to remember that there can be no certainty regarding the future market. For, on the one hand, new deposits may be discovered, and, on the other, demand may fall as a result of the invention of substitutes or of new methods of production; thus, for example, the demand for firewood for the production of iron practically vanished for the purposes of large-scale production after the inventions enabling the use of coal. As a result of this uncertainty regarding the future market, the saving of natural resources becomes economically advisable only if the expected rise in prices includes a premium for risk, usually very considerable apart from the interest on capital. This is another factor working in the direction of the more ample supply in the present. If the supply of natural raw materials in an exchange economy is in the hands of a single monopolist, it may pay him to restrict present output more severely than under the conditions we have assumed. For, through his restriction of output, he will correspondingly restrict the supply in the exchange economy as a whole and thereby raise present prices, which cannot be undercut by competing entrepreneurs but will correspond entirely to the degree of his restriction. Monopoly control of raw material resources is thus a factor acting in the direction of a greater regard for the needs of the future. Any rise in the prices of raw materials which is due to the formation of trusts leads to a greater economy in the available resources.

If an organised society itself own the resources of raw materials, whether that society is socialistic in other spheres or not, it is always faced with the problem of regulating the relative present and future supplies. If the society in question is part of the world economy, or, in other words, is in contact with other societies, it will probably regulate the consumption of natural materials in accordance with essentially the same principles, and especially with the same regard for the rate of interest as in the case analysed above, although perhaps somewhat greater regard will be taken for the needs of the future. But in the closed socialist economy it is scarcely necessary to regulate the raw material supply of the present and of the future with regard to the dominant rate of interest. Just as a socialist society must choose the rate of economic progress and thereby must fix the conditions determining the rate of interest, it must also decide upon the time-element in the distribution of the available raw materials, and the pricing problem cannot be solved before this choice has been made.

We have described the regulation of demand, in accordance with the available means for its satisfaction, as the general economic function of pricing. But we have now seen that, in regard to natural materials, pricing has the further special task of bringing about a desirable temporal distribution of consumption, or, in other words, of limiting consumption in such a way that a certain degree of uniformity in the supply is maintained, at least over a certain period. In cases where the resources of nature are strictly limited, this problem can only be solved in a very relative sense. In general, we find that it has not the same determinateness as the general problem of pricing.

Under present economic conditions the scarcity of natural materials is essentially determined by the objective economic factors mentioned above. But direct state action to protect the needs of the future or, at least, to regulate the temporal distribution of consumption by the indirect method of raising present prices is not a rare occurrence. Even certain policies of taxation, such as the taxing of nitrate exports by the Government of Chile, work in that direction. There are, however, examples of policies aiming more directly at this goal, one of which is the regulation of iron exports from Sweden. The present scarcity of raw materials under such circumstances is, so to speak, artificially increased by state action.

The scarcity of natural materials does not merely depend upon the degree to which a deposit is exploited, but also upon the degree to which activities are extended to deposits of varying quality. It two mines with the same quality of ore supply a smelting works, the prices of the ore at the mines must be such that prices at the smelting works are equal, and thus the differences in mining and transport costs balance. If there are only two mines in existence, the ore in its natural state must be priced even in the mine which, from the present point of view, is less valuable, when only a correspondingly high price at the works can bring about a sufficient limitation of the demand. The intensity of mining is in that case determined by the price obtained at the smelting works, for the reasons which have been stated above. Although, therefore, the differential principle is at work in the pricing of the ore from the two mines, both prices are, in principle, scarcity prices.

If there are a great number of mines, and if we assume that the price at the smelting works just covers the capital and labour costs of mining the ore of the least remunerative mine, i.e. of the "last" mine which is actually used, then the price of the ore in that mine will be nil, and the prices of the ore in the others will correspond to the difference by which the capital and labour costs in those mines are lower than in the marginal mine. This does not, of course, alter the fact that the prices of the ore from such mines are scarcity prices which are primarily determined by the scarcity of supply in relation to demand. If one were to approach this problem in a way analogous to the old theory of rent, one would conclude that the price paid for the ore in its natural state does not enter into the price at the smelting works, nor therefore into the prices of iron products. For the price of the ore at the works is solely determined by the capital and labour costs of the marginal mine where no price is paid for the ore. The formal correctness of this statement is just as unassailable, and the resulting picture of the pricing process is just as much distorted, as in the case of the traditional theory of rent. In any case, Marshall's attempt to maintain the distinction between these two instances, and to regard the prices paid for natural materials as parts of the prices of the products, while this is denied of the price of land, is undoubtedly unsuccessful. [1] But that even Marshall finds reason to regard the prices of materials in their natural state as integral parts of the price of the product is very instructive. For, in this manner, the foundation of his entire

[1] Marshall, *Principles*, Book V., chap viii., § 4.

dualistic representation of the pricing problem is proved to be wholly inadequate. The price of natural materials is a pure scarcity price which need not be motivated by any service or sacrifice. If such a price must be acknowledged as part of the costs of production, Marshall's conception of those costs can no longer be maintained. The necessity of the general and objective conception of productive costs which is at the basis of the present treatise of economic theory now becomes manifest.

If an increased demand for iron enhances the price for ore at the place of consumption, the price of the ore in every mine will be raised. If there are several deposits in existence with heavier mining and transport costs, the rise in price will cause these also to be worked. The consequent reduction in the scarcity of supply will put a stop to the rise in prices. A rise in prices thus reacts not merely in the previously discussed direction of a more intensive working of the existing mines, which thereby reduces their periods of exhaustion, but also leads to an extension of mining to deposits which, owing to their heavier capital and labour costs, were previously valueless and, therefore, not operated. This reaction can be observed at the peak of every trade cycle, when previously unexploited deposits are opened or old mines which had been closed owing to low prices are again worked.

The effect of the prices paid by consumers for raw materials on the supply of such materials is most clearly seen when the quantities which can be produced at any given price are stated, or, in other words, when the total production is regarded as a function of the price. In order to judge the development of pricing, we must know the shape of this function, at any rate in the neighbourhood of the existing price. Above all, the elasticity of production as a whole, or, in other words, the increase which results from a given small rise in prices, is of great importance. The greater this elasticity, the stronger the reaction counteracting the rise in price, and the greater, therefore, also the stability of prices.

The effect of pricing on our supply of natural materials having thus been stated, it remains to indicate shortly the importance of the external factors for this supply. We refer to the development of technique. Technical progress in mining, such as the introduction of pneumatic drills and the utilisation of water-power for the supply of electricity, has reduced the costs of production, while the progress in the means of transport has so far reduced costs of shipping and rail transport that a material as cheap as iron ore is now largely transported even between continents. At the same time, recent interesting metallurgical developments have made possible the exploitation of poorer ores or ores of inferior quality. The introduction of the basic process in the iron and steel industry has made the numerous deposits of phosphoric iron ore available for the production of iron. The exploitation of deposits of ore with a low content of iron has become economically possible through the new methods of crushing and separating. The immense importance of technical improvements of this type for the supply of raw materials to the civilised world is obvious, since nature abounds in low quality ores or, more generally, in materials of inferior quality.

CHAPTER VIII

WAGES

§ 31 *Ricardo's Theory of Price and the Socialist Theory of Value*

IN attempting a critical review of the bewildering mass of contradictory but vague and uncertain opinions which have been expressed on the problem of wages, and which emerge at the present time not merely in political and social discussion, but even in scientific studies, it is necessary to go back to Ricardo's theory of price, which is the source of so many of the lines along which modern economic thought has developed. We have already made several references to this theory, but have only now reached a position where we can obtain a more complete impression of it. [1]

To be able to understand the Ricardian theory of price properly, one must first of all remember that it is put forward as a cost of production theory, and that such a theory is logically only possible when there is simply one factor of production to be taken into account, or at least when the various co-operating factors of production bear prices which are given and fixed relatively to each other in advance. Otherwise, every cost of production theory must leave open the question as to the way in which the relations of the prices of the factors of production to each other are determined, and consequently can never be a complete and self-contained theory of prices. Ricardo therefore set out to reduce the different factors co-operating in production to one single factor, thereby to be able to explain the prices of commodities by their cost of production.

English political economy has, since Adam Smith, as we have shown (§ 18), distinguished three factors of production – land, capital, and labour. We saw in the previous chapter how Ricardo succeeded in eliminating the first of these factors from the problem of pricing. At the margin of production no rent at all is paid, and

[1] Cf. Cassel, "Die Produktionskostentheorie Ricardos," *Zeitschrift für die Gesamte Staatswissenschaft*, 1901, pp. 68 ff.

it is at the margin of production, according to Ricardo, that the entire pricing process is carried out. Consequently, the use of land is not a factor in the pricing process at all, and the chief categories into which the factors of production fall are thus reduced to two in number.

It is clear that the use of capital cannot be removed from the pricing problem in the same way. Here Ricardo, in order completely to reduce the number of factors of production to one, had recourse to an even bolder assumption, in that he assumed that the capital required to be employed in any branch of production is always proportional to the labour employed in it. On this assumption, commodities would obviously be exchanged in proportion to the amount of labour expended on them. The prices of commodities would be proportionate to these amounts of labour, and could be expressed in terms of the unit which serves as a measure of labour. From this it would follow that the theory of pricing need have no further regard to capital as an independent factor of production.

But to trace the entire pricing process to a single factor of production yet another step is necessary, namely, the reduction of all the different kinds of labour to a common measure. That labour varies considerably in quality is, of course, a fact which cannot be disregarded. A theory which would put all labour on the same footing, and would therefore assume that any quantity of labour could simply be measured by the number of hours worked, would obviously be far too remote from reality. Such an assumption, however, is not necessary for the purpose Ricardo had in view. He was content to assume that it is possible to reduce labour to a common measure, by using a given and invariable scale of reduction. Superior work is then merely to be calculated as a certain multiple of "normal labour," and all costs of production can be expressed in terms of a quantity of normal labour. The assumption of a fixed scale of reduction thus means the elimination from the pricing problem of the fixing of relative prices for the various kinds of labour.

Thus, by means of three substantial simplifications – by eliminating rent, postulating proportionality of the use of capital to the quantity of labour, and assuming a fixed scale of reduction for the various kinds of labour – Ricardo succeeds in reaching a theory of price which can be expressed in the simple statement that the prices of all products are proportionate to the quantities of the labour necessary for their production, and in which the quantity of labour therefore appears as the general measure of price. According to Ricardo, the price of the product includes both wages and "profit" (i.e. reward for the co-operation of capital), but does not include rent. The rules by which the price of the product is divided between labour and capital form the subject of special studies by Ricardo, to which we shall return in the next section.

This very abstract but logically thorough and acute theory of prices of Ricardo's seems, however, to have been generally misunderstood. Ricardo himself clearly realised that his assumptions could only be valid as approximations, which he regarded as permissible when it was a question of obtaining a broad preliminary view of the course of the social process of pricing.

This relativity in his assumptions, and in particular the purpose of his whole method of approach, were lost sight of by readers who could only grasp the barest outline of the Ricardian system. Where Ricardo had perceived a proportionality of commodity prices to the necessary quantities of labour as a general result of the action of supply and demand, his followers saw a necessary equality of value and quantity of labour. Ricardo's theory was used to support the theory that labour is the source of all value, and value gradually came to be conceived as a quantity of labour embodied, like some mysterious fluid, in commodities. The "labour theory of value," which was based upon such complete misunderstanding of the Ricardian theory of price, gradually hardened into a lifeless dogma, in which form it was taken up by the early Socialists and was made the basis of a so-called socialistic theory of value with scientific pretensions. In view of the ridiculously exaggerated importance which has been attached to this theory not only by the apostles of Socialism, but also by its opponents and scientific critics, it appears to be not unimportant to explain the true origin of the theory.

In Ricardo's theory of price the "hour of work" serves as the unit of price in much the same way as the shilling or the franc does in real life. Every commodity costs as many hours of work as were necessary to produce it. Of this quantity of hours of work the worker receives a part as his wage, while the remainder goes as profit to the capitalist. The worker who has worked for one hour thus receives a wage equivalent to, say, three-quarters of an hour of work, and the value of the remaining quarter of an hour of work is paid for the use of capital. Socialists have used this theory of Ricardo's to support their assertion that the worker has a "right to the full product of his labour," but they have been completely in error in so doing. It cannot in any way be represented as a consequence of the Ricardian theory that the wage for an hour of work shall be a full hour of work. The assertion that value is equal to work expended, and the claim based thereon that labour should receive as wages the whole value of the product, are, whether we consider them justified or not, on an essentially different plane from that of the Ricardian assumption of an approximate proportionality between the use of capital and the quantity of labour, and consequently between commodity price and the quantity of labour. This was for long obscured by the fact that German scientific circles, in spite of hostile criticism of the Socialists, clung to the belief that the latter were only drawing conclusions from the Ricardian theory of value. Even an expert like A. Menger and a critic like Böhm-Bawerk have lent a certain measure of support to this erroneous idea. [1]

The Socialists were much more justified in claiming the authority of Ricardo for the reduction of the various kinds of labour to a common denominator. By his assumption of a given and invariable scale of reduction, Ricardo in fact excludes all competition among workers in different occupations and localities or among skilled and unskilled labour as an element to be considered in connection with prices. But Ricardo is merely studying how prices vary with the general development of society, and to that end he assumes that the relation between the prices of different kinds of

---

[1] A. Menger, *Das Recht auf den vollen Arbeitsertrag* (2nd edition, Stuttgart, 1891), p. 54. Böhm-Bawerk, *Kapitalzinstheorie* (Innsbruck, 1885), p. 362.

labour may, in that development, be taken as being approximately invariable. For the Socialists, the theoretical assumption here again becomes a practical postulate: labour of different qualities shall be valued on some objective basis, and not according to the conditions of the labour market. This is, in effect, the deeper meaning of the demand for the abolition of the wage-system contained in the socialist programme.

Socialism condemns the whole of the present wage-system as immoral because it treats the worker as a commodity on the market, in that it determines the wage of the individual worker not solely by his ability or by the amount of work he does, but also according to the number of other workers who are seeking employment in the labour market. In contradistinction to this regulation of wages according to the state of the market, Socialism demands for the worker an income fixed on objective ethical grounds. The principles whereby this income from work is to be determined are, for the most part, very vague and uncertain. A reduction of skilled labour to "normal labour," with greater or less regard to the claims of superior work, is set up as the standard for the payment of the workers; or else it is claimed that the worker should receive for his labour a return that will provide him with the necessary means of subsistence, and thus wants are set up as the correct standard for wages. Under these systems, a particular gradation of wages, for example, according to different degrees of skill and vocational training, may be recognised as justified, but justified only on objective and ethical grounds and not in any circumstances in relation to the state of the market. It is directly opposed to the fundamental tenets of Socialists that any considerations whatever of the supply of, and demand for, labour of a particular kind should bear any weight in the determination of wages.

Having thus shown the real meaning of the Ricardian theory of price and of the socialist theories of value which are wrongly based upon it, we shall now turn to the criticism of these theories. Ricardo's theory of price, as we have shown, claims to be not an accurate picture of reality, but a much simplified presentation of it, obtained by means of a series of abstractions. Such a theory cannot be condemned on the ground that it does not completely harmonise with our observations of reality. Any theoretical investigation must begin with certain abstractions. The value of the theory depends largely on the question as to whether it is possible to build further on the foundation provided: whether the modifications of the theory which are required to adapt it to reality can be effected without involving any contradiction of the fundamental ideas underlying the theory.

This, however, is not possible in the case of Ricardo's cost of production theory. This theory, as we have seen, is based essentially upon the reduction of the various factors co-operating in production to a single factor. We have already indicated the assumptions necessary for this purpose. With regard to the significance and the admissibility of the first of these – the elimination of rent from price – we have but to refer to the previous chapter. As regards the proportionality of the use of capital to the use of labour, reference should be made to the facts given in § 23. They show clearly that the relative employment of capital in modern production diverges very considerably from such proportionality. The assumption of a fixed scale of reduction for different kinds of labour entirely excludes from the theory of price the important chapter on the relative pricing of those different kinds of labour. It is clearly impossible to retain such assumptions; and the moment we abandon them the essential basis of Ricardo's entire theoretical structure is destroyed. For the reduction of the factors of production to a single factor, which is the essence of the theory, is then no longer possible. Thus, as soon as we recognise that different branches of production work with different relative quantities of labour and capital, we have to deal with at least two factors of production, labour and capital. Every further approximation to reality increases the number of factors of production which enter into price. This is true of the recognition of a difference in types of human labour, and is also true with regard to those cases in which land has a real scarcity-rent and in which therefore rent appears as an integral part of price. Any theory of price is bound to take into account the existence of several factors of production, each of which occupies a more or less independent position in the pricing process. For a theory of this kind, Ricardo's cost of production theory is of no value whatever. The path taken by Ricardo does not get us anywhere. We have to turn back, give up all thought of a cost of production theory, and, as we have done before in the present work, choose an entirely different method which takes into account the existence of a number of independent factors in price.

It follows as a matter of course that, with this recognition of the complete and fundamental inadequacy of the Ricardian cost of production theory, the caricature of it – the socialist theory of value – falls to the ground, and we will not waste any time on the subtleties of this theory.

The socialist demand for the abolition of the wage-system is based, as we have seen, on the theoretical view that it is possible to have an exchange economy in which the prices of the different kinds of labour would be fixed regardless of the state of the market; regardless, that is to say, of the relative scarcity of the available supplies of labour in relation to the demand for them. This view is in contradiction to the principle of scarcity, and therefore to the fundamental conditions of any exchange economy which is organised on the general economic principle. Things are excessively simplified if labour is treated as a homogeneous factor of production. Moreover, some of the most important aspects of the wage theory can only be understood if the diversity of labour is taken for granted. An up-to-date theory of price must, above all, pay special attention to the relative pricing of different kinds of labour. Different kinds of physical labour, too, occupy greatly different positions as regards price. Particularly since the war, the conflict of interests between industrial workers and agricultural workers, as well as between workers in sheltered trades and workers in unsheltered trades, has become accentuated.

§ 32 *Pessimistic Theories of Wages*

The development of theories of wages in the first half of the nineteenth century was largely dominated by a desire for extremely simplified general formulæ, preferably mathematical in character, for which the authority of Ricardo was claimed.

According to Ricardo, the marginal product is divided between capital and labour, the precise division at any given moment being determined by the state of the market. The share of the worker, wages, is therefore primarily governed by the state of the market. But there is also a *normal price* of labour, which is determined by its cost of production. This normal price, or "natural wage," is equal to the cost of subsistence of the worker and his family, and this cost is, in turn, determined by the worker's customary standard of living. If the market wage is higher than the normal wage, the worker is in a position to support a larger family, which leads to an increase in the supply of labour. This increased supply depresses the market wage, if at the same time the demand for labour, by reason of an augmentation of capital, has not increased by a greater amount. This, however, is possible over quite a long period in a progressive society. Under such conditions, therefore, it is possible for the market wage to be permanently at a higher level than the normal wage. Under less favourable conditions, however, the market wage is forced down to the level of the normal wage, and, at times, even below that level. But this has the effect of checking any further increase in the working population, and thus, if demand increases as capital increases, of again improving conditions in the market. The market wage cannot remain permanently below the level of the normal wage.

But as population increases, the margin of cultivation too, according to Ricardo, must shift, so that recourse is had to increasingly inferior land. Let us assume that the product of ten hours' work on the margin of cultivation was previously divided so that the worker received the product of seven hours' work as his wage, while the capitalist kept the product of the other three hours as his profit. As it becomes necessary to cultivate inferior land, the product per hour of work diminishes and the product of seven hours' work is perhaps no longer sufficient for the worker's subsistence. As a result, the normal wage of seven rises to, let us say, eight hours, and profit is thus reduced to two hours. This reduction of profit cannot, however, be continued indefinitely, for in that event any incentive to further capital creation would necessarily vanish. The insufficiency of new capital creation in these circumstances forces the market wage gradually down to the level of the normal wage. A growth of population which necessitates the bringing into cultivation of inferior land is, for this reason, detrimental to the workers. As long as necessary foodstuffs can be imported from abroad, however, this effect of an increase in population can be avoided. The insistence of the workers on a customary high standard of life may also to a certain extent prevent the use of high market wage from giving rise to a harmful increase in the population.

Subsequently, the Ricardian theory, particularly under the influence of the collaboration of the German Socialist, Lassalle, was transformed into a sterile dogma, according to which wages under the prevailing social system had a necessary tendency to fall to a bare subsistence level. This so-called *iron law of wages*, as we know, could not, naturally enough, be entertained in our present-day social democracy, since it laid down that only a restriction of births would help the workers, and that all other efforts to improve the position of the workers would be futile.

The actual development of the standard of living of the workers in the nineteenth century in countries with a Western civilisation gives little support to the iron law of wages. Wages have risen, and the rise has not by any means been exclusively devoted to a more rapid increase of population. On the contrary, there is apparent, at least among the higher grades of workers, an unmistakable tendency to restrict births and to devote wages to an improvement in their standard of living. We must not, however, forget that these desirable developments are confined for the most part to the most highly civilised countries, the people of our own race, and to a certain extent to the higher grades of workers in those countries. In the whole of the rest of the world, as Marshall has rightly observed, the iron law of wages still prevails, and wages generally only cover the cost of rearing and maintaining a class of workers of inferior ability.[1] The possibility of raising the worker's standard of living

---

[1] Cf. Marshall, *Principles*, Book VI., chap. ii., § 3.

above a bare subsistence level is conditioned by such a large number of individual and social factors that any attempt to deal exhaustively with this subject by means of a simple formula should be given up as being unscientific and entirely profitless.

Once we have made it clear that the "working-class" is not the homogeneous body upon which primitive theory and political rhetoric like to base their discussion, but is in reality composed of a very large number of different strata of the population, with widely differing standards of living, the untenable character of the old conception of the subsistence level, or, more particularly, of the "cost of production of labour" as the lower limit of wages, is immediately apparent. Under modern economic conditions it is quite possible that a particular class of labour may be permanently condemned to a wage which does not allow the worker to have a family, bring up children, and fit them for work: a wage, in effect, which may not even cover the worker's current cost of living. Obviously, the "cost of production" of such labour must be covered in some way or other. It may be borne, either wholly or in part, by higher grades of the workers, by the farmers, or by middle-class families, or, finally, by the state or the municipality. There are undoubtedly many occupations in modern society, particularly women's occupations, which scarcely supply the workers in them with their necessary subsistence, and certainly are not in a position to pay the cost of production of the workers, but must be continuously fed by supplies of labour from other grades. In these occupations, therefore, the payment of a "natural wage" in the Ricardian sense is not necessary. Such circumstances, which are essential for an appreciation of the true nature of some very important problems in connection with the theory of wages, are bound to be completely hidden from us as long as we adhere to the fiction of "labour" as a homogeneous factor

With regard to the *market price* of labour, Ricardo had, as we have seen, taught that this depends upon the state of supply and demand at any time. In so doing, he conceived of the demand as a magnitude determined by the quantity of capital in the country. According to Ricardo, the demand for labour grows in the same proportion as capital. In times when capital increases more rapidly than population, the market price of labour is therefore higher than its cost price. If, on the other hand, capital increases more slowly than population, the market price of labour may for a time fall below its cost price, and this in turn must then retard the growth of population.

Ricardo's conception of the importance of capital as a regulator of the market price of labour was similarly transformed into a dogma by his followers, and was expressed in much simplified arithmetical formulæ as a universal, natural law of economic life. This was the origin of the *wage-fund theory*, about which so much has been written. Capital was regarded as a given fund at any time, out of which wages are advanced; the average wage must therefore be determined simply by dividing the wage-fund by the number of workers. The divisor, the number of workers, is in the long run, in conformity with the view of Ricardo, determined by the cost of production of labour. Thus the wage-fund theory does not displace the older theory of the "natural wage" or cost price of labour. It only has reference to the market price of labour at any time, but states that this is absolutely determined by the wage-fund. Extremely far-reaching practical conclusions were drawn from this doctrine. The workers can influence wages only by regulating their own numbers. Any other attempts on the part of the workers to raise their wages, especially the formation of trade unions, can at best only help small bodies of workers, and this only at the expense of the other workers, whose share in the wage-fund is then correspondingly diminished. It was but natural that organised labour should refuse to be convinced of the necessity of this pessimistic view.

Criticism of the wage-fund theory must proceed from the fundamental fact that the whole theory is founded upon utterly confused ideas as to the nature of the productive process. A study of the history of the wage-fund theory is useful, in so far as it brings out clearly the fundamental importance of representing the productive process as a continuous process, as we tried to do in § 4. The wage-fund theory is still dominated by the old idea of Adam Smith that an accumulated stock of goods is a necessary requisite of production. All attempts to give more precise expression to the conception of a wage-fund have been unable to meet the need, from which the wage-fund theory suffers, of a clear analysis of the productive process itself.

Again, the view taken by the wage-fund theory, that the quantity of labour which can be employed at a given rate of wages is arithmetically determined by means of the quantity of capital, is fallacious. Against this view it should be emphasised, in the first place, that labour can be employed in branches of production which require a greater or smaller relative use of capital. The distribution of the workers among these different branches of production is itself a problem in the pricing process, and cannot therefore be regarded as given in advance. But it is clear that upon this distribution depends the number of workers who can be employed at a given rate of wages according to the wage-fund theory. Secondly, the fact must be stressed that, in accordance with the principle of substitution, labour and capital can be combined in different proportions to produce the same product.

As an objection to the wage-fund theory, it is often asserted that labour is remunerated not by capital, but by the result of production. This objection, however, does not go to the root of the matter. It is of course correct that the workers, like all other members of society, are enabled to live only by the finished products made by current production and, in so far as they have claims to such products, are paid with these for their share in the process of social production. Continuous payment of such a wage, however, is primarily dependent on the maintenance of a continuous productive process, and that process is only possible if, in each unit period, the necessary capital to be employed is made available. In this way, of course, the continuous employment of the workers is dependent upon the continuous inflow of disposable capital.

The wage-fund theory is much too primitive and weak to be able to withstand serious criticism. It leaves us nothing which might be utilised in a positive theory. None the less, we must not forget that the wage-fund theory proceeded from a correct theoretical basis, inasmuch as it understood, or, perhaps more correctly, felt, that at a given size of population wages bear a certain relation to the capital wealth of the exchange economy, and, moreover, rise and fall in common with that capital wealth. The precise relationship, however, is of a kind widely different from what the wage-fund theory conceived it to be; capital and labour, in our view, are competing, but also co-operating and complementary, factors of production, the prices of which are determined by the general pricing process, and thus, of course, the relative scarcity of these two factors of production is of primary importance in determining their price. It is from this point of view only that the influence of the quantity of capital upon wages can be analysed.

§ 33 *Optimistic Theories of Wages*

Adam Smith opens his chapter on wages with the remark that the produce of labour constitutes the natural recompense or wages of labour. Under modern conditions, the worker has to give up part of his product in the form of rent and profit to the landowner and the capitalist. The remainder of the product of labour constitutes wages. In this conception there lay already the essence of a theory which sees in the productivity of labour the essential determinant of wages, and which therefore puts in the foreground the dependence of wages upon the product of labour. The more recent development of the theory of wages is in effect substantially conditioned by this method of approach.[1] This clearly attributes to the workers themselves some influence on the level of wages, in that they can improve their position by their own efforts and skill. The optimistic colouring which is thus given to the theory of wages is in contrast to the pessimism of the earlier wage theories, according to which the level of wages was essentially fixed by external circumstances and the workers could exert no influence upon it except by restricting births.

---

[1] Among early exponents f this view may be mentioned the following: Leroy-Beaulieu in the 'sixties (*Traité d'économie politique*, Paris, 1896, Vol. II.); Walker in the 'seventies (*Wages Question*, London, 1891, chaps. viii. and ix., and p. 411).

That wages must in some way depend upon the product of labour is a very natural and, as we shall see, a very useful idea. But we must take care not to regard the connection so simply as to represent wages as the product of labour after deducting what must be paid for the co-operation of the other factors of production. This kind of reasoning leads to a one-sided "residual theory," according to which wages are regarded as the "residue" remaining from the result of production after the entrepreneurs and owners of land and of capital have received their due share.[1] If such a residual theory is to have any meaning at all, it must assume that the shares of the other factors of production can be independently determined before the residue itself is fixed. In view of our inquiries into the nature of the general pricing process such an assumption is impossible. In reality, all the factors of production are on the same footing in the pricing process, and their shares in the total product are simultaneously determined when all the given factors in pricing are operating. Only the profit of enterprise, which is, of course, not to be regarded as a normal price for the co-operation of a factor of production, could possibly be described as a residual income.[2]

In further elaborating the theory of labour productivity as the factor determining wages, we are met with the difficulty that, in actual fact, an augmentation of product brought about by an increase in labour efficiency does not necessarily accrue entirely to labour as wages, but is in general also credited to the remaining factors of production. As a rule, there arises, as a result of an increase in the efficiency of labour, a new market situation with a relatively greater demand for the other factors of production, and thus with a relatively worse position as regards labour. In that case, labour cannot keep the whole of the increase of product for itself. Thus wages depend not on labour alone, but on the other factors of production too, particularly on the relative supply of the different factors of production in the exchange economy – in a word, on the

---

[1] Cf. Jevons, *Theory of Political Economy* (London, 1879), pp. 292–6: "Every labourer ultimately receives the due value of his produce after paying a proper fraction to the capitalist for the remuneration of abstinence and risk." (See Walker, *Political Economy*, 3rd edition, London, 1889, chap. v.)

[2] Cf. Clark, *Distribution of Wealth* (New York, 1908), p. 204.

state of the market. The productivity of labour, therefore, is not
an objective factor conditioned solely by the nature of the labour,
and accordingly is not to be regarded in that sense as the determinant
of wages. Once this fact is realised, the productivity theory loses
its direct theoretical simplicity and practical applicability.

More recent economic theory has attempted to elaborate the
productivity theory by trying to ascertain the share of every single
factor of production ,n the productive output by determining its
"marginal productivity." This attempt has led to the principle of
substitution being placed in the foreground in the treatment of the
pricing prob.em, and to the assumption that one factor of production
can continually displace another which is being allotted an undue
importance. Statements ,n text-books which adopt this line of
reasoning frequently give one the impression that this assumption
is a necessarv condition of determinateness in the pricing problem.
As we have already sa.d, however, we must require of any theory
of price that it shall be able primarily to explain a pricing process,
determined solely by the principle of scarcity, in which, in particular,
the possibility of substitution is disregarded.

A further objection which has to be made to a theory of wages
based upon the conception of marginal productivity, as indeed to any
marginal productivity theory, is that marginal productivity itself
is not an objectively ascertained factor in the pricing problem, but
is in fact one of the unknowns in the problem, and is in the same
position as the other unknowns. As long as we confine our attention
to one definite branch of production, in which only a single product
is produced, it is possible to regard marginal productivity as at least
a clearly determined conception. The "marginal product" is a
certain concrete portion of the total product. If, however, the same
labour is used in a number of different branches of production, this
concrete conception of the marginal product is clearly no longer
possible. The marginal productivity must be the same in each
branch of production, and accordingly can only be conceived as a
part of the prices of the various products. These prices are, however, subject to the condition, among others, that the labour in
question must have the same price in all the different branches of

production. Its marginal productivity, then, cannot be defined as anything other than this price, for this price represents precisely the contribution of the labour in question to the price of the product. The statement that wages are determined by the marginal productivity of labour thus loses all independent meaning.

Finally, it should be borne in mind that to trace wages to the marginal productivity of labour throws no light on the dependence of wages upon the exertions and efficiency of the workers. For the effect which an increase in the efficiency of labour has on its marginal productivity is certainly not clear as a matter of course, but is rather a question appertaining to the very essence of the problem of wages. The efficiency of labour is a conception which has reference to the technical suitability of labour. "Productivity," too, is largely understood in this sense. Marginal productivity, however, has reference to the state of the market, and is only determined by pricing. There is always the danger that this essential distinction may be forgotten, and that an increase in the marginal productivity of labour may immediately, without further thought, be inferred from an increase in the efficiency of labour. [1]

That an increase in the efficiency of labour brings about an increase in the worker's income is only one aspect of the optimistic theory of wages. The theory often adopts the further thesis that the capacity of the worker increases as his income increases. Thus, according to this view, there exists a reciprocal action between the efficiency and the income of the worker. This reciprocal action gives rise to the possibility of a progressive rise in the standard of living of the workers, and the assumption of such reciprocal action thus gives the wages theory an even stronger tinge of optimism.

The socio-political tendency which raises the worker's income to the position of primary determinant of his efficiency has been chiefly emphasised in the writings of Brassey and Schoenhof. [2] A scientific criticism of this school must, in the first place, point out

---

[1] Cf., e.g., Seligman, *Principles of Economics* (4th edition, London, 1909), § 177: 'Anything which tends to enhance the productivity of labour in itself will increase the product of the marginal unit and thus raise the rate of wages."

[2] Brassey, *Work and Wages*, London, 1872; Schoenhof, *The Economy of High Wages*, London and New York, 1892.

that the effect of wages upon the standard of living of the worker, and thus upon his efficiency, depends upon a large number of factors (e.g. climate, race, the mental outlook of the society, the individual character of the worker, etc.), and that, therefore, an increased effectiveness of labour in consequence of an increased income can only be expected in a conjunction of favourable circumstances, in addition to the fact that any improvement of the individual worker and still more of a whole section of workers as producers must, as a rule, take quite a considerable time. On the other hand, we must probably – at least in Western civilisation – lay some stress on the importance of high wages, as manifested in a keener selection of the best workers and in the consequent stimulus to greater efficiency. In this, however, we must be on our guard against a naïve belief in a spontaneous development of greater efficiency in the workers. That result is to-day best secured by deliberate and scientifically thought-out schemes on the part of those in control of industry.

It should not be overlooked that the optimistic theory of wages which we have here described can also be examined from the opposite standpoint: if wages fall, efficiency must in the long run be diminished, and thus a tendency for a further fall in wages would emerge. This cumulative reciprocity may thus have effect in a negative direction too.

After the wage-fund theory had fallen into discredit in the 'seventies, the general trend of thought was very little inclined towards a belief in objective determinants of wages. In the absence of a satisfactory economic theory of wages, it was but natural, at a time when the combination movement was becoming more and more prominent, that support should be given to the view that wages are essentially a product of the conflict of interests between workers and employers and are in the main determined by the relative strength of the two parties. This view was naturally very prejudicial to the development of a science whose task was to represent wages as the product of economic necessities and objectively ascertained factors. It represented the wage problem essentially as a matter of power, and was therefore fatal from a practical point of view, in so far as it helped to shift the efforts to improve the position of the workers from the sphere of economic inquiry to the sphere of the development of power. The tendency to discredit every established economic theory, and the efforts to keep alive the view that, in economic life, "everything flows," "everything is subject to change," are partly responsible if the workers look upon their unfavourable position as being entirely due to the imperfections of the present social system or to exploitation of the workers by modern capitalism, and, since matters might equally well be different, if they believe in the possibility of a complete reversal of the position of the working-classes and seek the means whereby to achieve this reversal in industrial or political power or even violence – anywhere, in fact, except in the economic sphere.

It should not be overlooked here that the school of thought that wished to extend the study of the wages problem to a study of the "social question" has, despite its conspicuous lack of a sound economic theory, despite even its manifest under-estimation of the importance of such a theory, achieved something of importance, in that it recognises, as important factors in the wage problem, social position, composition of the population, industrial organisation, and the legal system of the society, and has included a study of these factors and their effects on the position of the workers in the wage problem. There is no doubt that the whole problem was far too greatly simplified and schematised by the old economics. In particular, it was necessary to study the supply of labour, which it had hitherto been considered sufficient to characterise as a purely arithmetical magnitude, from the angle of its dependence on the composition and recruitment of the body of workers, on their education and vocational training, and on the improvement which is largely effected by the organisation of production, and of the labour market, of the worker and his productive efficiency – in short, that is to say, from the angle of its dependence on social factors.

It is not enough, however, merely to introduce these considerations in the treatment of the problem. They must be subordinated to a coherent economic theory of wages. The thesis that wages are determined by economic necessities must be placed in the foreground. The nature of the economic relationship which links wages with the given factors in the wage problem must be investigated, so that we may discover the framework within which alone a proper knowledge of the effect of these factors, and of the significance of each of them in relation to the whole, is possible. The socio-political theory of wages, if such a name may be applied to what is more or less an indefinite tendency, may be described as an optimistic theory in so far as it lays particular emphasis on the possibility of an improvement in wages or, more generally, of an improvement in the position of the workers by means of socio-political measures which lie within human power. It should not, however, be forgotten that such measures affect wages only through the mechanism of pricing, and that their aim can only be achieved, at least in general and in the long run, if they permit of a real change in the market situation. Consequently, the socio-political theory cannot in the least be recognised as a theory of wages as long as it disregards the study of the market situation and imagines that it can deal with the social aspect of the problem in complete isolation from its economic aspect. There is apparent, too, the great practical importance of a correct view of the true position of the social factors in the process of the pricing of labour, as regards the rational direction of trade union policy and, in particular, of the efforts of the workers, as well as of general Government and municipal social policy. Everyday experience tells us how extremely necessary it is that our social policy, in the widest sense of the term, should be permeated and governed by the consciousness that it cannot put the economic necessities on one side, but must operate within the framework determined by those necessities.

The trade union movement itself has, of course, always subscribed to our optimistic view of the wage problem, in so far as it has always believed in the possibility of raising wages, or, more generally, of improving the conditions of labour, through trade union action. Partly, of course, under the influence of the earlier pessimistic theories of wages, but also as a result of mediæval tradition, the older trade union movement confined its iam to the furtherance of the interests of its own trade and only considered it possible to achieve that aim by a monopolistic separation of it from the rest of the general body of workers. In this respect the trade union movement has more recently manifested a substantially more optimistic feature, inasmuch as it has been found that an artificial limitation outwards is not necessary and that it may be sufficient to maintain a common high standard; this standard itself has somewhat the same effect as a restriction on the supply of labour in the trade in question. For it is only the worker who can offer a standard of ability corresponding to the standard of wages, who finds it possible to obtain a situation in that sphere of production in which the trade union standard has secured recognition. At a time of rapid economic progress, during which, particularly, every kind of skilled work, generally speaking, was always in considerable demand, an "open" trade union policy of this kind was shown to be quite compatible with the aim of protecting the interests of the members of the trade union. It then appeared as though the trade union movement was no longer confined to furthering the interests of individual trade unions, but, as it was open, in theory at least, to the whole body of workers, was a common means towards the improvement of the position of all workers. But in fact, in most countries numerous elements of the working-class have remained outside the trade union movement. Some of these could definitely have derived no benefit from the trade union movement, and were even directly harmed by it.

The earlier closed policy of the trade unions, as indeed the whole of the earlier economic policy, had been developed on the assumption of a given but strictly limited market, and, on the whole, invariable conditions of production. On this assumption a dividing up of the market, together with a firm restriction on entries into any trade, was but a natural policy. The assumptions of the open policy of trade unions are generally quite different. The whole of modern economic life is characterised by far greater mobility. The market can never be regarded as a given quantity. Every trade must in general compete with all other trades for the purchasing power of consumers, and, in particular, must compete with other trades which satisfy the same or similar wants in other ways. Besides this, there exists in general within every trade a competition between producers in different places, and particularly in different countries. The extent of the market or of employment, in these circumstances, is not given in advance. It can be increased if the efficiency of labour is increased and the product thereby improved or made cheaper. It can, however, be diminished too, if efficiency lags behind that of competitors. The producer of to-day can never rely on the quantity of employment he has at any time remaining with him. The closed policy which formerly was justifiable, or at any rate understandable, in these circumstances lacks a fixed starting-point, and must be replaced by a policy aiming at the greatest possible efficiency; that is to say, at meeting the wishes of customers in the most perfect way. What is, in this way, true of productive activity in general also has particular validity for the wage-earning class, and the trade union policy of the latter has had to make allowance to a certain extent for this fact.

Mr. and Mrs. Webb have built up what may be termed an ideal theory of modern trade union policy. [1] According to this theory, the essence of trade union policy is to be found in the standardisation of the conditions of labour in every occupation. This standardisation does not exclude competition between the workers. Rather, it substitutes regulated competition for the earlier "free" competition which was frequently very detrimental in its effects. Whereas the earlier unregulated competition in many cases led easily to under-bidding by the acceptance of lower wages and inferior conditions of work, competition regulated by standardised conditions is competition for employment which is only to be had upon those conditions, a rivalry, in other words, in the matter of efficiency, the effect of which must tend to improve the workers as regards both their standard of life and their productivity. The policy of standardised conditions also has a favourable effect for entrepreneurs, in so far as it drives out of business those undertakings which are unable to pay standard wages or generally to maintain the standard conditions, and which hitherto were only able to continue in

[1] *Industrial Democracy*, London, 1897.

business by means of underpaid labour, cheaper but inferior factories, and so on. The necessity for observing the standard conditions compels the adoption of the best possible organisation and the greatest technical perfection in industry.

This ideal theory, as we see, is pursued in a highly optimistic vein, and its conclusions would scarcely ever be completely realised in practice. The Webbs' theory,[1] however, has the great merit of focussing attention on the influence of the forms which we give to competition in the labour market, on the wage-earners themselves, and on the direction of the moral, intellectual, and physical forces which ultimately determine the supply of labour. In this way a very valuable impetus is given to a change in the study of the supply of labour from a pure computation in terms of arithmetical magnitudes to an examination of the underlying economic and social processes which determine the supply of labour.

The Webbs' theory is of interest from the point of view of the formal theory of pricing, too. As long as a certain product, using labour which differs in quality and to a corresponding extent in wages, can be produced at approximately the same cost, the problem obviously remains indeterminate from a theoretical standpoint also. If, however, we assume a standardisation of wages, and thus also, broadly speaking, of efficiency, it is possible for the theory of pricing to proceed from the assumption of a uniform price for each different kind of labour. This assumption clearly means a substantial simplification of the theory of wages. Let us observe how the Webbs' system can be introduced into the complete pricing process: if the wage for each kind of labour is fixed, and if we assume that the prices of the other factors of production are also given, then the prices of finished products, and hence the demand for them, are also given, and thus also the demand for each different kind of labour. That demand then, must correspond to the supply of labour. Herein is to be found the criterion as to whether the level of wages imposed by the trade unions is the correct one: a superfluity in the supply of labour indicates that wages are too high and must be

[1] See also, *The Public Organization of the Labour Market* (Part II., Minority Report, Poor Law Commission), London, 1909.

reduced. If the trade unions have to support their own unemployed, this will constitute a powerful incentive towards such a reduction in their wage claims. If there is equilibrium, the level of wages of the different sections of labour must be so adjusted that there is everywhere an appropriate supply of labour, and that demand is simultaneously regulated to an adequate extent and in proper proportions by means of the prices of labour and of the prices of products thereby determined.

This ideal system of price-fixing had, of course, never been completely realised, and unfortunately it broke down after the war. The trade unions in the naturally sheltered trades reverted, in large numbers, to a monopolistic policy. Building operatives, municipal workers, tramway and railway employees, and generally workers in trades which are protected locally from external competition, were able, by means of a closed trade union policy, to raise their conditions considerably above the average level of the other industries, which were exposed to effective competition. The products of these monopolistic trades also became considerably dearer relatively to those of the non-monopolistic trades, as can be seen in the movement of price index numbers in a number of highly industrialised countries. Again, the cost-of-living index number, as compared with the position before the war, is as a rule considerably higher in such countries than the index number of wholesale prices. That serious disadvantages not only for individual countries, but also for the world economy, are present in such a distortion, achieved by monopolistic power of the entire pricing process, and that unemployment has been greatly increased by this isolation of certain industries, should now be reasonably clear.[1]

Government measures for the relief of the unemployed have been enormously extended since the war, and have led to the trade unions being able easily to raise their wage demands, without thereby being subject to the same deterrent as formerly, when they had to bear greater responsibility for their own unemployed. A consequent extension of public relief of unemployment in the

[1] Cf. Cassel, *Recent Monopolistic Tendencies in Industry and Trade*, Memorandum to the International Economic Conference in Geneva, 1927 (League of Nations, 1927, II. 36). Also *Quarterly Journal of Skandinaviska Kreditaktiebolaget*, Stockholm, July, 1931.

direction demanded by organised labour must result in a situation in which the natural counteraction to excessively high wage demands is removed, and in which, therefore, the wage-fixing process becomes indefinite and, in the long run, cannot economically be maintained. Recent experience in England and Germany, in particular, has shown in a most disquieting manner to what an insupportable level unemployment may rise under such conditions.

§ 34 *The Place of Labour in the Pricing Process*

Any general theory of wages must proceed from the fact that labour is a factor of production, and that wages are the price of that factor of production in the general pricing process. Only in this way is it possible to fit in the theory as an organic part of a homogeneous theory of price.

The demand for finished products is, in this light, directly or indirectly, in part a demand for labour. Wages are thus an expression of the valuation placed upon the labour in question by consumers or, more generally, by demand. This view-point must constitute the basis of the theory of wages. Now, in each unit period the aggregate demand for the primary factors of production is equal to the total income; equal, that is to say, to the aggregate productive output. This total income, or output, is distributed in the same proportions as the demand for the various factors of production. We are, therefore, justified in stating that the total income from work is equal to the share in the total productive output corresponding to the co-operation of labour. This method of expressing the matter has the advantage of bringing out the dependence of the income of labour upon the result of production. But we must take care to understand the word "share" aright; that is to say, we must conceive the share as a magnitude which can only be determined through the pricing process. Thus stated and explained, the productivity theory is in no way opposed to a theory which treats wages as a result of the general pricing process.

The price of labour, like the price of any other factor of production, is determined by its relative scarcity, or, in other words, by the supply of labour relatively to the demand for it. Hence this scarcity cannot be judged purely from the point of view of the supply of labour, but must always be considered in relation to the demand. T'.e total demand depends upon the total production, which in turn depends upon the total amount of work done. It is particularly necessary, in studying wages, to bring to the fore this general dependence of the income of the individual factor of production upon the total output of production, because the total amount of work done in society is not given when the number of workers is given, but is dependent upon the will of the workers, and because a lack of precision as to the dependence of wages on the total productive output frequently leads to a misdirection of the efforts of the workers.

In the most general sense, the factor of production, "labour," is to be regarded as one of the two main categories of personal services, the other including saving or the provision of capital. Labour in this general sense, however, is very far from being a homogeneous category. In addition to wage-labour, it includes work done by entrepreneurs – the price of which, theoretically, can easily be distinguished from pure entrepreneur's profit, though in practice it often approaches it very closely – and also the work of the independent artisan and of the farmer, as well as the services of the liberal professions and of domestic servants. Even "wage-labour" is not by any means a homogeneous factor of production. It includes the labour of employees in both technical and commercial occupations, as well as the labour of the great mass of what are usually described as wage-earners. Even this last category is by no means so homogeneous as is largely assumed in theoretical and political discussion. The variations in wages and work even within this class are very great. Standards of living, moral, intellectual, and social standards, all reveal marked differences. Wage theory must take these factors into consideration if it is to avoid the fatal error into which it has fallen by reason of the fact that, in its efforts to achieve as great a degree of simplicity as possible, it treated labour as a single factor of production and the wage-earning class as a homogeneous body. There is no doubt that we get a far more accurate presentation of reality if we regard the supply of labour, in the same way as the supply of land, as a mass which is split up into such an infinite series of types and qualities that it is possible, roughly speaking, to pass continuously from the lowest stage to the highest.

Work is done partly directly for consumers and partly primarily for entrepreneurs. The distinction is not an important one as regards price theory; for even in the second case the demand for labour is, in the main, ultimately determined by the demands of consumers. In the first case, the truth of the statement that the price of labour is the expression of its valuation on the part of consumers is at once clear. But the statement is substantially applicable to the second case, too. The entrepreneurs then appear, of course, directly as buyers of labour. They may, however, even when, as we shall see in the next section, they have a certain influence on the nature of the demand, be regarded to a certain extent purely as intermediaries between the workers and the final purchasers. In an ideal pricing system, entrepreneurs merely receive the necessary return on their necessary services, and labour, like the other factors of production, receives the price which has of necessity to be paid in accordance with the principle of scarcity. In this sense the wage paid by the employers, in the same way as the wage directly paid by consumers, is determined by the scarcity of the labour in question relatively to the demand for it. Naturally with the incessant movement of actual economic life, there occur deviations from this ideal determination of prices, and in such cases wages may, at times, in particular industries, places, or undertakings, be higher or lower than they should be according to the ideal price-fixing. Labour, as an element in the pricing process, undoubtedly possesses certain special features which conduce towards such irregularity in pricing. Just as the state of our imaginary ideal market, however, is of great practical importance as regards actual wages, so too in theory we have primarily to keep in mind prices in the ideal market, and to ask what wage such and such a class of labour would obtain if it were to get just what the market permits and no more.

It is not possible here to give a theory of wages elaborated in

every detail. We must confine ourselves to a statement of the
general outline of such a theory. The work of filling this in with a
detailed description of reality, based upon a comprehensive mass of
data (in which we are unfortunately still largely deficient), must
be left to special research. Our main task must be to present the
theory of wages in its organic connection with the general theory
of price, to consider wages from the angle of their dependence
upon the entire pricing process, and, in particular, upon the other
factors of production. In this section we have first of all to settle
more accurately the general position of labour as a factor of production and as an element in the pricing process.

For this purpose it is first necessary to emphasise the distinction
between labour and the worker. Labour is the service rendered by
the worker. There exists here, therefore, a distinction analogous
to that between durable goods and the utilities they provide. We
have already seen how great an importance attaches to this latter
distinction. The distinction between work and the worker is
scarcely less important, and neglect of it leads to a great deal of
confusion in research into wages. The relation between work and
the worker, however, has certain peculiar features. Whereas the
quantity of the utilities yielded by a group of durable goods is
determined by the quantity of the goods themselves, this is not so
with regard to labour; for the extent to which the worker is made
use of depends in part upon his own will. The quantity of labour
offered is thus, to some extent, an independent magnitude determined not only by the number of workers, but by other factors
over which the workers have control.

The utilities provided by durable goods cannot, therefore, in
dealing with the general pricing process, be treated as primary
factors of production, since they can be imputed back to the durable
goods themselves and to the capital-disposal required in order to
benefit by them, and the durable goods themselves can in their turn
be imputed back to the factors of production required to produce
them. This connection is essentially economic in character, and
constitutes a necessary part of the pricing process. With regard
to the relation between labour and the worker, matters are different.

The connection between the amount of work done and the number of workers is not purely economic in character, nor can the worker himself be regarded solely as the result of an economic productive process. Labour, therefore, can and must, in any preliminary treatment of the pricing problem, be regarded as a primary factor of production; and the quantities of the available labour of different kinds must be treated as objectively given elements in the pricing process. It then remains to complete this theory by a study of the general factors which connect the quantity of work with the number of workers, or which actually determine the number of workers. This will also afford an opportunity of investigating the ultimate effect of the level of wages itself on the supply of work and workers. We thus have here to proceed in our usual way – in the first stage of our treatment of the pricing process, as it affects a particular factor of production, to assume the quantity of that factor to be given, and then to show the factors which influence that quantity, including eventually the price of the factor of production too, and to determine their significance as regards pricing.

If labour takes part in the pricing process as a factor of production, it must be measured quantitatively, and a particular unit must be selected for the measurement of the work done by the worker. With regard to the production of goods in the narrower sense of the term, this unit is generally a definite piece of work done, such as the digging of a ditch one yard long, the weaving of a yard of cloth, the setting of a line of type in a printing-works, the cementing-in of a brick, etc. But in many cases, too, the unit of work done can only be expressed as a particular time taken by the work. This is in general true of the work of superintendence, of the supervision of other workers, and is in particular true of work in transport undertakings. In this latter case wages are naturally measured in terms of the time devoted to work – in terms, that is to say, of hours, days, months, or years, and are, therefore, *time-wages*. In the first case, in which the unit of work is a definite act of production, wages can be reckoned as *piece-wages*. Even then, however, time-wages are still possible, and are paid in a number of cases, as, for example, where the measurement of the work done presents especial difficulty, or where the quality of the work might suffer from the quickness to which piece-wages give rise, or, finally, where the worker is prevented by causes beyond his control from making full use of his productive capacity.

None of these methods of measuring the work done by the worker, however, is of any importance other than for the practical calculation of wages. The factor of production, labour, cannot in any circumstances be regarded purely as an aggregate of productive acts.

Even from the point of view of the entrepreneur, labour is not completely characterised by its productive work. Thus, for example, the unit of productive work does not, as we might be inclined to think, possess the same value to the entrepreneur, whether it is performed in a short period or in a long period; for the entrepreneur usually has a strong interest in seeing that his fixed capital shall be used to the greatest possible extent; the cost of using the factory premises, machinery, etc., and, in addition, the cost of supervision, heating, lighting, etc., are all fixed per hour, and it is thus desirable that the workers should make the utmost possible use of their valuable time in the factory; in the construction of a building there is also the consideration that the work shall be carried out as quickly as possible, and, as there is room for only a limited number of workers, the contractor must attach importance to securing the performance of the greatest possible amount of work per hour, even though he pays piece-wages.

For the rest, it follows too that the value of the unit of work done, even in those cases where the resulting product is exactly the same, can be affected in a variety of ways by the quality of the work. It is thus of importance to the entrepreneur that machinery should be wisely and economically used, for example, with the minimum expenditure of mechanical power, and that materials should be carefully and intelligently handled, with a minimum of waste. In many occupations, the reliability of the worker is of decisive importance to the entrepreneur, such as when the worker has to tend very expensive or dangerous machinery or to superintend dangerous operations. The absolutely dependable worker is in such case worth infinitely more than the worker who, on the whole, it is true, does the same amount of work, but who cannot be relied upon to the same extent. In those cases in which the worker's employment at the same time includes training for superior work, the employer often has an interest in seeing that the worker is disposed to remain in that industry, and in effect concerns himself with his training. In this connection we frequently find a definite distinction between men's work and women's work – the fact that women workers usually give up their employment on marrying should in itself be a factor lowering their wages even when they do the same work as men.

If, then, it is not possible for entrepreneurs to measure the price to be paid for labour solely according to the workers' productive work, still less is it possible for the workers to agree to a price for their labour which is determined solely according to their productive work. For the total productive work done is not exclusively dependent upon them, but is also substantially dependent upon the entrepreneurs, upon the management and organisation of the undertaking, upon the equipment of the factory with machinery and tools, and so forth. The workers place their labour on the market. The use to which the entrepreneurs – or consumers, if work is done directly for them – are able to put this labour is their own concern. The general measure of labour as a factor of production is thus not to be found in the product of labour.

Following on from what we have just said, the factor of production, "labour," must be regarded essentially as *the power of disposal, during a certain period, of labour of a certain quality. Wages* constitute the payment for this disposal. This definition holds good even where various methods of computing the wage are adopted, such as piece-wages or wage-bonuses of one kind or another, aiming at providing the greatest possible incentive to an intensification and an improvement of effort.

The worker who sells his labour thereby derives an *income*. This income must be rigorously distinguished from wages. Wages do, it is true, form a very important factor in determining the worker's income, but there are other elements too, notably regularity of the worker's employment. This latter element, again, clearly depends upon the worker himself, upon his moral and physical capacity and his health, as well as upon demand, and thus ultimately upon consumption; moreover, it is also directly dependent upon the management of the undertaking in which he is employed, and is in addition – a fact which is often disregarded – largely affected by the entire organisation of the labour market and the methods of covering the demand for labour. The worker's income may be reckoned in terms of a day, a week, a year, or in terms of his whole lifetime. With regard to the size of his income over the whole of his life, the duration of his full capacity for work is obviously an important factor.

In an ideal market there is one uniform price for a uniform factor of production. A general tendency towards such uniformity of price is to be observed in the actual labour market with regard to the "disposal, during a certain period, of labour of a certain quality"; though, naturally, there are always a number of tendencies working in an opposite direction and other obstacles in the way of complete uniformity. On the other hand, there need be no such uniformity at all with regard either to the prices of productive work or to the incomes of workers who earn the same wage. This again shows that the factor of production, labour, can only be taken as having the sense in which we have here defined it.

The wage and the income of the worker are accordingly two different magnitudes which do not necessarily move in unison and which occupy different positions in the pricing process. The true significance of wages is, as an item in cost of production, in their effect on demand, and also, of course, as an element in the worker's income. Just as the employer naturally concerns himself with limiting his cost of production and only reduces wages in so far as it is necessary for that purpose, so too the interest of the worker is necessarily primarily directed to the income which he can get by his work. If we wish to regard labour, or the worker himself, as the result of a process of production, and so connect the supply of labour with its cost of production, then the worker's income is clearly the decisive factor, and we must ask how far this income covers the cost of production of labour.

With regard to wages, we distinguish between *wages paid in kind* and *money wages*. The payment of wages in kind has, with the development of a money economy, been gradually replaced by the payment of money wages. This development was supported by socio-political legislation, owing to the fact that payment in kind made it very difficult to understand the actual terms of the contract of service, and also restricted the economic liberty of the worker. It must, however, be remembered that, even where wages are paid wholly in money from a popular point of view, labour nevertheless receives certain additional benefits which economically must certainly be included in wages, although the individual worker has no right of choice as to the form they take. In this class may be mentioned, for example, house accommodation, either free or at reduced rents, free heating, baths, medical attendance, etc., and also insurance contributions, pensions, and similar allowances on the part of the employer. The cost of all these benefits is naturally, from the point of view of the employer, to be regarded as wage-costs. That these items in wages are only available in a definite form, and are not simply paid in money, shows that in this way it is expected more effectively to promote the worker's real welfare, and thus in the long run to be able to get better work done in return for the money expended.

Employees of larger undertakings, and in particular employees of public bodies, receive in addition to this actual wage various benefits, such as regular holidays, wage-increases according to age, continuous payment of wages – either in whole or in part – during illness, pension, provision for orphaned children, and so on, not to mention greater security of employment. The sum of these benefits must be manipulated for each job so that an adequate supply of labour of sufficiently high quality may be permanently relied upon. The appropriate distribution of these benefits has the result that people in the same employment often receive widely differing total benefits relatively to the work done. That such a system of wage-payment for employees should have proved to be expedient may be concluded from its generality as well as, in particular, from the fact that increasingly large classes of other workers are aiming at securing the status of salaried employees, and do, in fact, attain that status to a greater or less extent. The whole of social insurance may be regarded as an attempt to give to all wage-earners the most important advantages of the system of salaried employment.

A distinction is also drawn between *money wages* and *real wages*. The basis of this distinction is to be found in the fact that the commodities which the worker buys are subject to price fluctuations, and that therefore the same money wage may vary in its significance for the worker's household. If we wish to ascertain the effect of the level of wages on the position of the working-class, it is necessary to concentrate our attention upon the worker's real income, or in other words, to refer money income to a certain average price-level of the goods consumed by workers. In our theoretical treatment of the pricing process, however, we work on the assumption that the average price-level remains constant. The importance of this assumption lies in the sphere of monetary theory, and can only be more closely examined in connection with a discussion of that subject. On this assumption, however, it is possible, at least approximately, to disregard the distinction between money wages and real wages. The following studies will accordingly have reference throughout to money wages alone.

§ 35 *The Demand for Labour*

We must now first study the pricing of labour on the assumption that the quantity of labour of every kind and quality, which is for disposal in the labour market, is a given magnitude in the problem – is independent, that is to say, of price. The pricing problem thus defined will be elucidated by special consideration of the factors operating on the side of demand.

The pricing of labour, like all pricing, is governed primarily by the principle of scarcity. Labour of every kind and quality is thus given a price which must be just high enough to restrict the demand for it so as to coincide with the available quantity of the labour in question. If we assume these prices to be known, we can, with their help and that of the prices of the other factors of production, calculate the prices of the products. We thus determine the demand for the various products, and hence, too, the demand for the various factors of production, in particular the demand for labour of each kind and quality. This demand must coincide with the supply. If the demand for any particular kind of labour is inadequate, it is a sign that the price of it is too high and – if there is no way of restricting the supply – must be reduced if an increased demand is to be brought about. Conversely, if the demand exceeds the supply, wages must be raised.

Wages are thus essentially determined by the competition of the purchasing power of society for labour, and must to that extent be regarded as the expression of the valuation placed by consumers upon the labour in question. This thesis in effect constitutes the central substance of the whole theory of wages, and any discussion of practical wage problems must be intimately related to it.

In practice, wages are usually settled by fixing the wage for a particular kind of labour at a level which appears to be necessary in order to attract an adequate supply of labour with the requisite qualifications. The answering of the question as to whether the correct level has in this way been decided upon must be left to subsequent experience: a scanty supply will necessitate a rise in wages, while an excessive supply must sooner or later bring wages down. This is the procedure adopted by every large undertaking, which of course cannot negotiate separately as to wages with every individual worker it engages. The same method must, in principle, be followed in the wage-policy of public undertakings. On the largest scale wages are settled in this way, and from time to time revised, by negotiation between trade unions and employers' associations.

If we take the total quantities of labour of every kind and quality as given, this pricing process clearly means only a distribution of the given quantities of labour among the various branches of production, according to their ability to pay, or, ultimately, according to the demands of consumers. The same method, in effect, is adopted in practice as that which we followed in our theoretical analysis – prices for the various kinds of labour are fixed experimentally, so to speak, and on the basis of these prices the prices of the finished products are calculated, the way being left open, however, for a revision of all these prices in accordance with the indications given by the actual demand. The prices which the various categories of labour receive in this way are clearly determined by the scarcity of the given quantities of labour relatively to the demand, in exact conformity with the principle of scarcity.

If we speak of wages as the "share of labour in the result of production," it must be remembered throughout that this much-discussed concept can in effect only be defined as a consequence of the pricing process determined in the manner we have described. Any conception of the share accruing to labour as a technically and objectively determined portion of the product is absolutely excluded. The frequent attempts to calculate the "share" of labour objectively, technically, with the aid of the "marginal productivity" of labour, have already been critically examined above (§ 33).

The principle of scarcity makes it clear that the main reason for a particularly low wage is primarily to be sought in a relative surplus of labour of the particular kind and quality – in other words, that a restriction of the supply is in general the first condition for improving the situation. When the needs of consumers for a particular kind of labour are satisfied to a certain extent, then, as a rule, consumers can find room for more labour of that kind only if the price of it is appreciably lowered. This is merely an indication that the demand has a limited elasticity. The acceptance of an abnormally low wage is a desperate way of creating employment for a quantity of labour of the particular kind, for which there would not be sufficient room, given a normal level of wages. Any attempt to improve the position of such workers which does not proceed from a clear recognition of this aspect of the problem must be doomed to fail. Any assistance in the nature of an improvement of wages can obviously only have the effect of aggravating the overcrowding in the particular trade and making the situation chronic.

On the other hand, of course, particularly high wages may

greatly restrict the demand for a particular kind of labour, and, consequently, the area of employment open to it. From the point of view of labour, the best situation is, on the whole, achieved when the supply of labour corresponds as closely as possible to the demand, and thus when the prices of the various kinds of labour are merely the expression of their inevitable, natural scarcity.

If we assume such correspondence, then the "value" of labour, apart from this natural scarcity, is substantially determined by the nature of the demand. Changes in habit, taste, and purchasing power on the part of consumers naturally constitute independent factors in shaping demand, and may have considerable and some-times – when the supply can adapt itself either not at all or only with insufficient rapidity to these changes – fatal effects on the state of the market for particular kinds of labour.

The demand may also turn out to be more or less favourable for the factor of production, labour, in general. In the first place, society's demand may turn more directly to labour or more to products in the production of which other factors of production co-operate in a considerable degree. The demand of the wealthier classes turns, to a particularly great extent, directly to personal labour, such as domestic work, the products of handicrafts, and so on, whereas the great mass of people are more inclined to consume standardised goods produced by highly specialised machinery. A democratic distribution of income should from this point of view tend towards a relative intensification of the demand for capital-disposal, and thus towards a relative diminution in the demand for labour.

If we disregard fluctuations in this general distribution of demand among different factors of production, the development of the total demand for labour depends entirely upon the volume of social purchasing power, that is, upon the community's aggregate income. Any circumstance that increases the efficiency of social production, then, will also increase the general demand for labour, and thus tend to raise the general level of wages. To this extent "labour" has a common interest – in practice a very real one, though it is only too often forgotten – in securing the highest possible degree of efficiency throughout the process of production. It is precisely this dependence of wages upon the output of the entire process of social production that is brought out by the conception of wages as a definite share in the total outcome of social production.

If the intensity of the total demand is determined by the total result of social production, any diminution in the total amount of work done must obviously have the effect of diminishing social demand. If, however, we are considering a particular kind of labour, which plays a minor part in the productive process as a whole, a diminution in the supply of that labour will in most cases have no appreciable effect on the total income of the exchange economy. This is not the case where a diminution in the total quantity of personal labour in the exchange economy is concerned: a diminution of this sort will indeed give an advantage to personal labour as compared with the other factors of production, but, at the same time, it also means a considerable diminution in the social income, that is to say, in the purchasing power possessed by demand as a whole, and thus a substantial decline in the labour market. There is always the danger that this unfavourable effect may outweigh the benefit of the former effect.

Even in those cases, however, where a definite diminution in the supply of labour will result in a certain rise in wages for a particular class of labour, the effect on the income and standard of life of the workers is still undetermined. A diminution in the supply of labour may come about in two ways – in a diminution in the number of workers or in a diminution of the average amount of work done per worker. If the greater scarcity of labour is due to the latter cause, the rise in the rate of wages is to be set off against the decrease in the amount of work done. The final result would then in exceptional cases only be an increase in income (cf. § 37). The prospects are obviously much more favourable as regards obtaining an increase in income for workers through a diminution in their number, especially within a particular industry. These prospects are most favourable if the diminution in the number of the workers in an overcrowded industry is achieved not by means of an absolute decrease in the total number of workers in society, but as a result of a transference of workers to branches of production which were hitherto unable to satisfy completely their own demands for labour, or, in other words, when it is achieved side by side with a positive increase in total production in society.

Thus far, we have been proceeding on the assumption that the demand for finished goods determines absolutely the demand for the various kinds and qualities of labour also. In practice, however, there are various exceptions to this rule, modifying the principle of scarcity as the determining factor of wages. The same productive result can frequently be obtained in different ways, so that one particular kind of labour may be replaced by another, or that the factor of production, labour, may be partly displaced by the other factors of production, land and capital. We have now to consider more closely the conditions for and effects of such substitution, beginning with the cases of a

Substitution of Different Kinds and Qualities of Labour for Each Other

There is, in the first place, a certain amount of competition between different trades which ultimately satisfy the same want on the part of consumers. Thus, for example, workers employed in the production of tile stoves compete with workers engaged in the provision of central heating and in the branches of the iron and steel industry which provide their raw material. The level of wages prevailing among the one or the other group of workers is always a factor in the competition between the two systems, and it is not improbable that the high wage demands of the tile-workers have in places led to a more extensive use of central heating. Where there is competition of this kind between different trades, there are as a rule cases in which the two competing methods are of equal value and in which a change in wages therefore turns the scale on one side or the other. There is thus a certain connection between wages in different trades.

We have further to consider competition between labour of different qualities within the same occupation. It is often possible to produce the same commodity with labour of different qualities.

We may use dear and efficient labour or we may use cheaper and less efficient labour, and the economic results may be so nearly the same that undertakings of both kinds can exist side by side. The wage problem is thus to a certain extent indeterminate. Capable entrepreneurs may achieve better results by employing efficient workers at good wages, and thus displace other entrepreneurs, so that the same demand for the finished goods is concentrated upon a higher class of labour. It is possible for much the same thing to be done by the workers if they are able, by combining, to prevent wages from falling below a certain level. This is the way in which the trade union policy of standardised conditions works, namely, by preventing labour of inferior quality from attracting consumers' purchasing power to itself. In this connection trade custom, too, is undoubtedly of considerable importance. A traditionally high standard of living in any occupation will in some measure be a protection against any possible competition with it on the part of the workers lower down in the scale. On the other hand, labour of a lower grade also shows a tendency to keep an occupation tenaciously for itself, and to protect itself against any possible competition on the part of superior labour, even to the extent of still further lowering its standard of living. In those cases in which the wage problem is thus indeterminate, there is clearly always the possibility that a policy aiming at an amelioration of the position of the workers can achieve its aim by suitable measures. The wage problem, then, is not simply a theoretical problem of pricing, but also a practical problem of social policy.

Finally, in this connection, we must mention competition between male and female labour. Much has been written about the inequality of the wages which men and women receive for allegedly the same work. The explanation is sought in different social circumstances, particularly in the traditionally smaller demands and wants of women, and also in the surplus of female labour, or else the whole phenomenon is ascribed to the familiar but uninformative reason of general social injustice. But all this leaves the essential question unanswered. How is it possible for female labour in general permanently to receive a lower wage than it is worth – that is to say, a price below that which would be fixed for it in the pricing process by equilibrium between supply and demand and would therefore correspond to the valuation placed on this labour by demand? It is undoubtedly true that female labour may occasionally not get its real market price owing to the weakness of its powers of resistance or to a lack of information or of mobility, but only when there is no fully effective competition between employers for the available female labour. But when it is said that it is unjust permanently to pay women lower wages than men, it is still not clear why the employer who employs both kinds of labour for the same work does not increasingly substitute the particularly cheap female labour for the costly male labour. Therein lies the essence of the matter. If the employer – and we must assume that he acts from a purely business point of view – does not do this, we must conclude that for some reason or other he attaches a higher value to the male labour, in spite of the supposedly equal work done. Clearly, practice does not admit the equality of work affirmed by theorists. In practice, demand makes a very definite distinction between male and female labour, and this is the decisive factor. Where men and women work together in a particular trade, there is in the vast majority of cases some differentiation in their employment. The rule is that men and women in the same trade do different kinds of work, and so also receive different wages. But even where the employment is, to outward appearance, the same, the demand turns definitely, for various reasons and within certain limits, to male labour. There are certainly numerous sound reasons for this differentiation. Some of these reasons, which have a certain material significance, we have already mentioned. Objectively considered, however, they need not even be logical. Thus in a certain trade – banking, for example – there may be a long-standing custom of employing only male workers in certain posts. It would, perhaps, not be considered *comme il faut* if female employees were engaged in their stead. Such ideas, which we may perhaps be inclined to describe as prejudice, but to which the business man does not willingly run counter, may result in the male worker receiving a higher market price, no matter how equal the work may be objectively. There are also a number of considerations, which cannot be denied some objective justification – such as considerations of security against thieves or of the necessity of maintaining discipline – that may help to bring about a similar result. Until we have adequately examined and tested all these and similar factors, we should not jump at the theory that female labour is generally "underpaid," having regard to the actual market situation.

The demand, however, for the payment of equal wages to men and women, regardless of the state of the market, on some theoretical "grounds of justice," is in principle on the same plane as the usual socialistic wage policies.

Substitution of Land and Labour for Each Other

We discussed this type of substitution in the preceding chapter. A large quantity of labour may be employed on an acre of land, or a small quantity may be employed. If the price for the use of the land – that is, the rent – and wages are given, the economically most profitable combination of labour and land is thus determined too. The demand for labour is thus not absolutely determined by the demands of consumers and the level of wages. It is also affected to a certain extent, as we can now see, by the price of a competing factor of production, land. The effect of this is a modification of the scarcity of labour, but it does not in any way eliminate this scarcity as the essential factor determining the price of labour.

The question as to how a larger available supply of land affects wages is of great practical importance. If the quantity of a factor of production – in this case, land – is increased, the relative share of each unit of that factor of production, calculated in accordance with the principle of scarcity, in the result of production is diminished. For this reason alone there is already a tendency for an increase in the available supply of land to raise wages. The increased supply of available land, however, leads to that factor of production being substituted for labour. This to some extent counteracts the fall in rents, though it does not entirely prevent it. Further, as a result of the more extensive use of land per unit of labour, production is increased, and thus the national income is augmented and the purchasing power of consumers is increased, which in turn tends to raise wages.

Thus although, on the whole, a rise in wages must follow from an increase in the supply of land, nevertheless agricultural labourers cannot claim for themselves the whole benefit of falling rents in the form of a rise in wages. There must generally be a relative fall in the prices of agricultural products. If the general price-level is to remain unchanged, the prices of industrial products must rise correspondingly, so that industrial workers, too, benefit by the increase in the supply of land. The wage of the agricultural worker must in any case correspond to the standard of living which such a worker can attain by acquiring and cultivating his own land.

Substitution of Labour and Capital for Each Other

That capital competes with labour and can be substituted for it at many points in the process of production has already been seen (§ 23). At those points the prices of the interchangeable quantities of the two factors of production must obviously be equal. This requirement represents a condition which operates in determining the pricing process. Here again we find that the demand for labour is not determined wholly by the demands of consumers, but is also in part dependent upon the supply of a different factor of production, namely, capital. Even the possibility of a modification of the demand for labour in consequence of a substitution of capital, however, should not be allowed to obscure the fundamental significance of the scarcity of labour in determining its price.

The importance of a country's capital wealth in regard to the general level of wages is seen most clearly if it is considered primarily according to the principle of scarcity, and if the principle of substitution is regarded simply as a modification of that principle. An increase in capital wealth increases social productivity and, hence, the national income, and thus increases demand in general. An increased supply of capital, unaccompanied by any change in the labour supply, also improves the relative state of the labour market at the same time. These two facts combine to raise wages as determined by the principle of scarcity.

It has thus to be pointed out, in opposition to the wage-fund theory, that it is not capital, but income, that is the source of the social demand for labour or the social capacity to purchase labour. An increase in capital wealth affects this demand mainly by increasing production, and, consequently, the income of the community, and also by relatively improving the state of the labour market, which it does by adding to a competing factor of production. From this point of view the workers undoubtedly have a strong interest in maintaining and increasing society's capital wealth.

The substitution of capital for labour, as was shown in § 23, is determined by a number of different circumstances, of which the pricing of the particular factors of production scarcely, in practice, plays the chief part. Other things being equal, however, a low rate of interest must always favour such substitution. A rise in wages in a particular branch of production or in a limited area of production has the same effect, as long as it does not extend to the production of the machinery, equipment, etc., which are to replace manual labour in the branch of production in question. If it does, the rise in wages must lead to an increase in the demand for capital, and thus to a corresponding increase in its cost. A general and uniform rise in wages throughout the whole of the exchange economy therefore has, in any case, only a subordinate effect as regards the possibility of substituting capital for labour. (If, apart from capital-disposal, there were no other factor of production than "labour," such a rise would clearly have no effect at all on the possibility of substitution. The imagined increase would then, after all, merely mean a fall in the purchasing power of the money-unit, since the price of capital-disposal, as we know, does not include the dimension of money.)

With regard to the problem of competition between machinery and labour, we have still to make the following observations. Inventions which render the application of capital in the form of machinery, etc., more productive, and thus more capable of competing with manual labour, at first clearly have the same effect in the branches of production concerned as a relative increase in the demand for capital and a relative diminution in the demand for labour, and therefore as a tendency towards the reduction of wages in the trades affected. But, at the same time, the prices of the products are for the most part greatly reduced, so that the demand for them rises. This rise may go so far as to bring about also an absolute increase in the demand for the labour in question, which of course means a tendency towards an increase in wages.

On the other hand, the assumed technical progress results in an increase in the total production of society and thus an increase in its total income. From this there results a general increase in the demand for labour. If this demand is distributed among all kinds of labour, the workers as a whole derive some benefit from this technical progress. It always remains doubtful, however, whether the particular labour that is employed in that branch of production in which technical progress has been made gains or loses by that progress. This will depend upon whether the favourable tendency towards an increase in the demand for the particular product or the unfavourable effect of the relative displacement of labour by machinery will prevail.

If labour-saving machinery is introduced in a relatively small branch of production, and the ability of that industry to expand is not particularly great, then, in the short run at least, the demand for the labour in question will be diminished. If in that case the friction involved in transferring that labour to other occupations is not overcome – if, that is to say, the supply remains on the whole unchanged for some time – it is inevitable that the workers in the industry concerned will be harmed by the introduction of the labour-saving machinery. The injury may, according to the particular circumstances, take the form of a reduction of wages or of an insufficiency of employment for the workers. In these circumstances technical progress may easily be bought at the expense of a degradation of human labour. Such consequences can be avoided, or at any rate modified, if the workers maintain a sufficient degree of mobility and adaptability, as regards place and occupation, to changing market conditions. Instead of this, however, trade unions frequently seek a solution in open or concealed resistance to technical advances. There is always the danger that resistance of this kind may be continued for a much longer period than would be necessary to overcome the friction of the transitional process, and that as a result economic development will suffer a serious check.

The effects of the substitution of machinery also depend largely upon the kind of labour which the machines require. The earlier machinery generally required only labour of very inferior quality, and was for that very reason fatal to the development of the workers' standard of living and to the quality of their work. The new machinery, on the other hand, often, though not always, makes great demands on the quality of the workers – for example, on their reliability, attentiveness, intelligence, and nervous strength. On the whole, therefore, it means a growing demand for labour of that quality. If the production and training of workers to meet these requirements does not keep pace with the demand, the general level of wages for the labour in question is bound to rise.

After the war, "rationalisation" took place on a vast scale in almost every sphere of production. This process of rationalisation had its origin in the revolutionary advances in the sphere of machine tools, and particularly in machine manufacture, as a result of which productive capacity was increased to an extraordinary extent. Rationalisation, however, also includes any considerable advances in organisation, both in production proper and, perhaps most important of all, in transport. The economic and social significance of this process of rationalisation has been vigorously discussed in all countries. Rationalisation has often been held to be responsible for the extraordinary increase of unemployment. On the other hand, it has been urged in opposition to this view that only by means of a comprehensive and thorough process of rationalisation was it possible to find markets, and thus, in particular, to provide employment for workers. If we now consider this movement, there appears to be no possibility of doubt that the post-war rationalisation means a considerable advance for mankind, an advance which was an essential condition of a higher standard of life. That unemployment should have appeared as a result of this advance was in no wise in the nature of things, but must be essentially ascribed to a lack of economic mobility. Of the factors which have obstructed the way, the following are the most important: the monopolistic policy of the trade unions in locally sheltered industries, which has already been mentioned; the great extension of protective tariffs and the consequent isolation of the various markets of the world; Government measures for the relief of the unemployed, which have substantially decreased the mobility of the workers and appear to be leading to a state of affairs in which a considerable proportion of the workers will normally be permanently employed on public relief works. Monetary instability (to which we shall return in Book III.), particularly during 1929–30, has had a very disturbing effect on production, and has caused the evil results of the reduced adaptability of the labour market to stand out more prominently.

One consequence of rationalisation, however, which is certainly assuming permanent importance, is that the demands on the quality of labour have been raised to a high degree. Rationalised industry can only find use for the best labour. Labour of inferior quality will meet with greater and greater difficulties in its attempts to obtain work, and the future is faced with the great problem of how it may be made possible to find employment for second-rate labour, and to make such labour of some use in society, without adversely affecting the normal market for labour which yields full value.

§ 36 *The Supply of Labour as Determined by the Number of Workers*

For the theory of price which regards cost of production solely as a price which has to be paid in order that certain sacrifices shall be made, it necessarily appeared to be essential to represent labour as a sacrifice of that kind and wages as the price which alone could attract the necessary supply of labour. It is clear that, merely in order to provide a foundation for this theory, the dependence of the supply of labour upon its price has frequently been emphasised in a way that does not seem to be justified by the relevant facts. On the other hand, it has also been sought to deny the position of labour as a primary factor of production, and the supply of labour has been represented as a quantity dependent upon a particular kind of productive activity and consequently determined only by the process of production; and, in conformity with this, the normal determinant of wages has been found in the so-called cost of production of labour. In contrast with these arguments, which have for the most part been adduced to support a particular theory, we must try to represent the supply of labour as it appears in fact in its essential characteristics, and with the most important of the factors which determine it. It is then scarcely possible to doubt that the supply of labour must primarily be regarded as a given quantity in the pricing problem, independent of the ordinary variations in the price of labour. This assumption must accordingly be made the basis of a preliminary study of the theory of wages. In any case it corresponds so closely to actual fact that the ultimate complete theory is bound to retain its validity for this conceivable case too. The theory of wages must, therefore, in its first stage rest upon the assumption that the quantity of the factor of production, labour, in its various kinds and qualities, is given.

For the study of the supply of labour this means that we must first form a general idea of the composition of this labour supply, so that we may then proceed to examine the external factors – i.e. the general social factors – which determine the supply, and finally make an analysis of the ultimate effect of wages themselves on the quantity of labour offered. Here we can indicate only the general outline of this study.

The scarcity of labour is obviously conditioned by two factors – first, the scarcity of actual workers, and, secondly, the limitations on the amount of work per worker. In this section we shall first deal with the *scarcity of workers*. If we regard the whole of the working-class as a single homogeneous body, it must, in view of widespread unemployment, seem somewhat remarkable that we impute wages to the scarcity of workers. It is not possible, however, to form at all a correct idea of the labour market until we are quite clear about the real composition of what we call the working-class. The workers, as we have already emphasised, actually constitute a very heterogeneous body, in which every conceivable kind and quality is represented, and in which transition from one group to another is in most cases practically continuous. Differences of age alone mean a considerable gradation of workers. Only a few decades in the prime of life represent full working capacity; juvenile workers form a distinct class, and at quite an early age, especially in modern industry, the ageing workers are declassified. With regard to health and, in particular, general physical ability, the variations are again very large, and in practice there is a continuous transition from those who are perfectly capable and efficient to those who are only semi-capable and to those who are completely unfit, the invalids in the literal sense. Further, we must have regard to the very complex gradation of natural gifts and aptitudes in moral, intellectual, and physical respects. Here, too, the whole gamut is represented, from those who are exceptionally reliable. energetic, and ambitious, intelligent and efficient, to the opposite extremes. These natural differences are exceedingly marked, even within any one nation, but they are even more sharply emphasised when different races are compared.

These differences in innate qualities are to some extent removed, but perhaps to a far greater extent accentuated, by education and training, and above all by differences in social environment and in the conditions of employment. That inadequate education and training, poor nourishment, and similar disadvantages, as well as dissipation and lack of foresight and such habits as develop under a certain social pressure, such as gambling and, in particular, drinking, can cause men to deteriorate as workers, and even completely destroy their powers, hardly needs to be enlarged upon. But it is probably the conditions under which he earns his living – particularly the regularity and permanence of his employment – which have the greatest influence in determining the fate of the worker. The grave social evils which exist in this sphere must not infrequently overshadow all the others.

In the very interesting Minority Report of the English Poor Law Commission, Mr. and Mrs. Webb[1] have made a more detailed

---

[1] The second part of the Minority Report is also published under the title of *Public Organisation of the Labour Market* (London, 1909). Compare also Beveridge, *Unemployment, a Problem of Industry* (London, 1909 and 1912).

analysis of the composition and recruitment of the large army of those in need of relief. They reach the conclusion that this army, which by itself would rapidly die out, is constantly being fed with new recruits, that modern industrial society is incessantly producing new paupers solely as a result of its organisation of the labour market. The most important sources of this recruitment are provided in the first place by those in irregular employment – in other words, those workers who, like those in the building industry, after each period of employment have to spend a shorter or longer period seeking further employment; and, secondly, and most important of all, by the permanently under-employed, including in particular the casual labourers employed in ports, docks, iron-works, etc. The demoralising effect of such systems of employing workers is, on the whole, seen to be irresistible. Through them the position of the workers is depressed bit by bit until they sink for ever among the body of unemployables. A further source from which this body is fed is the employment of boys in occupations in which they receive no form of training for a future occupation, their capacity as workers simply being used out and wasted.

If, then, the "working-class" is composed of such widely different elements, and if the lower grades are constantly being recruited anew through the operation of various factors, it no longer seems a mystery that there exists a scarcity of labour of a particular high quality side by side with permanent unemployment. Only when we have a correct idea of the real composition of what we call the working-class can we gradually understand the true nature of the much-discussed phenomenon usually described as "the industrial reserve army." Under normal conditions workers of different quality are employed in any particular occupation up to a certain point. When reductions of staff become necessary, it may be taken as a general rule – though not by any means without exceptions – that the inferior workers will be the first to be dismissed, and the better workers will, as far as possible, be retained. If the demand for labour rises again, it must as a rule be met to a great extent by taking on workers of inferior quality.[1] One consequence, among others, of this is that labour costs rise during the boom, this being a generally observed phenomenon. The process we have described bears a certain resemblance to that of the extension of the area under cultivation when the demand for foodstuffs increases – in which case land of increasingly poorer quality has to be taken into cultivation. But just as the existence of inferior unused land does not prevent an actual scarcity of land and does not prevent rents being mainly based on that scarcity, so, too, the existence of unemployed workers of considerably lower quality cannot prevent an actual scarcity of suitable workers from making itself felt in industrial life and from being one of the principal factors determining wages.

This analogy between the pricing of labour and the pricing of land is not a perfect one. The usual assumption that the last piece of land taken into cultivation does not yield a rent is scarcely tenable in practice, but is nevertheless possible in theory; whereas a similar assumption with regard to the last amount of labour taken on is entirely out of the question, even in theory. Even the worst worker who is required must receive a wage. How this can be reconciled with the fact that there is at the same time a certain amount of labour of equal or inferior quality without employment is, in effect, one of the main problems of the theory of wages. The explanation of the fact that a scarcity of labour may exist simultaneously with a certain surplus of workers lies in the fact that the individual withholds his labour, and a discussion of it therefore belongs to the next section.

Wages in each individual trade are, as we have seen, as a rule uniformly fixed. It is, then, obviously in the employer's interest to employ the best possible workers at the wage he has to pay. In times of labour shortage, however, when he has to engage workers of inferior quality too, he usually has to pay these inferior workers at the same rates as the more efficient workers whom he already

[1] The satisfaction of the demand for labour during a boom period cannot by any means be entirely explained in this way. The chief reserve upon which industry drew during the last century in periods of extensive development was quite different. We shall return to this question in Book IV (chap. xv).

employs. By means of piece-wages and more intricate wage-systems he tries constantly to adjust the pay as nearly as possible to the value of the work done. But, as this is never completely successful, the differences in the remuneration of labour will not, for the most part, correspond exactly to differences in labour productivity, as is generally assumed in the case of the rents of different pieces of land.

In periods of depression workers of normal efficiency, too, often fall out of employment, and there is then undoubtedly a surplus of workers in a certain sense. This is also to a great extent true in the case of workers in seasonal occupations during the slack season; and to an even greater extent in the case of workers in trades which are subject to great day-to-day fluctuations in their demand for labour. As opposed to the fluctuating demand for labour there is, on the supply side, a relatively constant number of workers which is large enough, at any rate by means of extra work (overtime, etc.), to meet the maximum demand, but is, on that account, also too large to be completely employed in periods of decreasing demand. This phenomenon is not peculiar to the labour market – industry has also to arrange its plant and machinery, shipping companies their tonnage, railways their rolling-stock, if not to meet the maximum demand, then at any rate to meet demand during the busier period; and this fixed capital can thus be only partially made use of in less busy periods. A detailed study of these facts belongs to the dynamics of economic life, and has its place in Book IV. Here we need only remark that in the cases mentioned the supply of factors of production can, on the whole, hardly be described as excessive; this does not prevent the fact that it is impossible during a depression to make full use of the factors of production already devoted to production from being very unpleasant for the owners of those factors. Naturally, this must be particularly true of the workers who find no use for their labour in periods of declining demand. For them there is, then, a real, if temporary, over-stocking of the market. That, simultaneously with this over-stocking of the market with workers, there is a scarcity of labour, is clearly a necessary condition of any wage being paid at all. The interesting question as to how it is possible to realise this condition belongs, as we have said, to the next section.

Here we only make the further observation that a small amount of unemployment as revealed by statistics does not necessarily prove that there is an excess of workers, for in the labour market both supply and demand are so differentiated in point of quality, time, and place, that there must always be a certain maladjustment. The frequent change of job which is inevitable in the present organisation of many industries, such as the building industry, is bound to appear in the statistics in a certain not inconsiderable percentage of unemployment, but this does not mean that employers then have no difficulty in meeting their demand for labour. Much the same is true of other industries too, though to a less extent. A well-organised labour exchange will reduce this type of unemployment to a minimum, but can never completely eliminate it. [1]

The number of workers is of course primarily determined by the increase of population, which is usually not uniform, however, but differs in different classes of the population. Whereas there is a certain degree of abstinence among the wealthier classes, among the poorer classes the rate of increase is at times exceedingly high. The large number of children in certain sections of the working-class makes it difficult to rear them and educate them properly, and in this way also makes it difficult for them to rise to a higher level. The inevitable result is an over-stocking of the market for unskilled workers and workers of inferior quality. If, at the same time, the higher classes and the upper grades of the working-class rear relatively too few children, there may be relatively too great a scarcity of skilled workers, particularly in managerial posts, in which a higher degree of education is required. The state of the market, then, is very unfavourable for the lower grades of the population, and it is inevitable that wages in these grades should be very low. That the unequal distribution of the increase in population means also an extra burden on the lower classes, and a worsening

[1] It is well known that complete utilisation is not possible in any sphere of economic life. Given even the most intensive traffic, only a fraction of the passenger-mileage of the railways is really used. Even in a large town with a decided housing shortage there is always a certain proportion of the houses standing vacant.

of their position, is just as obvious as the fact that it is injurious to the interest of the producing community in the proper education of their children.

Passing over these inequalities in the increase of population, and considering the increase as a whole as an expression of the supply of workers, we have first to turn our attention to the relationship between this increase of population and the simultaneous increase of the other factors of production, land and capital. If we consider first the scarcity of workers relatively to the scarcity of land, it is at once clear that the state of the market must be unfavourable for the workers when population is increasing, if land is limited in extent and if the methods of cultivation are practically fixed. If, on the other hand, the land can be increased by the opening-up of new districts or countries, or made more productive by means of technical improvements, it is clearly possible for there to be an increase of population without adversely affecting the labour market, or the latter may even be improved. In the first case, a pessimistic view of the population question will prevail; in the second, an optimistic view.

The scarcity of workers must, however, also be considered in relation to the scarcity of capital. An increase of population at a more rapid rate than the increase of capital must inevitably have an adverse effect on the state of the market for the factor of production, labour. Every economic advance depends upon the supply of workers being more and more restricted in relation to the supply of capital. Hence a more uniform distribution of income does not of itself suffice to improve the position of the working-classes. It is only when we can assume it to be accompanied by a sufficiently large creation of capital and an adequate degree of restraint with regard to the increase of population that there is a permanent gain to the working-class. The conditions in certain colonial countries with a democratic distribution of income should not mislead us in this respect. Given an abundance of land and a plentiful influx of capital from older countries possessing great capital wealth, it is of course always possible to have a profitable scarcity of workers together with a considerable increase of population.

Undoubtedly, the increase of population is largely determined by factors which lie outside the pricing process. Yet, even with regard to the factor of production we are now considering, pricing is by no means entirely without influence on supply, and, primarily, on the supply of workers. The attempt to regard the worker as a product, the supply of which depends solely on the cost of production being covered by the income from work, fails entirely, however. Men are not produced for economic reasons. The results of the sacrifices made for the education of the new generation accrue for the most part to others than those who bore the cost. The cost of producing and maintaining men of a particular degree of efficiency must naturally be paid; but it is, in fact, paid out of the current national income, not simply out of the income which these men earn themselves, still less necessarily out of the income from their work. In a progressive society a larger sum is spent on the education of children than would correspond to the repayment of the cost of education by the working generations. In a community with a declining population the reverse might happen. There is, therefore, no direct connection whatever between the cost of production of workers and their wages.

Neither can it be asserted that there is always produced just the number of workers that could possibly be permitted by the income from work of the existing generation, or that an increase in income from work always and of necessity brings about an increase in the production of new workers. The production of new workers does not, in fact, follow the income of the workers. The higher grades of the population, as well as the higher grades of the working-class proper, often have relatively few children, and the same is true of wealthy nations. The prosperity of a particular section of the population, especially under modern conditions, has no marked effect on births within that section, even though periods of prosperity may give temporary stimulus to marriages and to the growth of population, although this is due less, in all probability, to wage-increases than to the greater ease of finding regular employment. Similarly, with regard to infant mortality, the level of wages should have less direct effect than hygienic knowledge and measures of public hygiene. The greater the care taken of neglected children by public authorities, the smaller will be the direct significance of the level of wages with regard to the growth of population in an advanced country with a modern civilisation. No doubt the level of wages is of fundamental importance to the standard of life of the working-classes, but its effect on the supply of workers in the society is conditioned by so many factors that we are not even in a position to ascertain generally the direction in which that effect tends.

If we consider the separate grades of the population, we find that the supply of labour is still less determined by the extent to which the cost of production is covered by the income from work. Workers of a certain quality can, as we have seen (§ 32), be kept even permanently at a wage which does not cover their cost of production. The various grades of the population are not sharply marked off from each other, and are not, therefore, merely recruited from themselves. The income from work of a certain class of workers need not, then, necessarily cover their cost of production.

Such a state of affairs in the sphere of production proper would naturally be a contradiction of the principle of cost, and thus of the general economic principle. But, as we have already observed, men are not produced for economic reasons, and, in the present social order at any rate, we cannot avoid men being born and brought up who, for reasons to be found in themselves or in the labour market, will afterwards prove to be of inferior quality, and will never be able to cover their cost of production by their labour. At the same time, however, these workers contribute to the social labour supply. It is here eminently clear that the theory of pricing in the exchange economy, as we have repeatedly urged, must regard the supply of workers primarily as a factor of the problem determined on independent grounds, and thus a given factor, and that in any case it can never place this supply on an equal footing with the supply of products of various kinds as one of the unknowns in the pricing problem.

Up to the present we have only considered the number of workers in general, or the number of workers of a certain quality. Now let us turn to a study of the supply of workers in particular occupations or places. A correct distribution of the workers among the different occupations and localities clearly assumes a certain degree of mobility on the part of the workers, and the greater the mobility of industrial life and the less the uniformity of the increase of population in different countries and localities, the greater must the mobility of labour be. In practice, however, this mobility is restricted by various factors. A person who has prepared himself for a particular occupation, settled in a particular place, perhaps founded a family, acquired his own house, will not easily be induced to change his occupation or the place in which he lives. Generally speaking, mobility is considerably lower in the higher age-groups. It is only natural that there should always be difficulties in the way of a change of occupation. These difficulties have, it is true, under modern conditions, been diminished over fairly large areas by the substitution of machine-minders, who can change over from one branch of production to another with comparative ease, for the old highly trained and specialised craftsmen. There are, however, still many obstacles in the way which cannot, in fact, be surmounted.

In the original choice of occupation there is certainly a somewhat greater degree of freedom, but the choice is for the most part considerably influenced by environmental conditions and more immediate possibilities. In localities which have specialised industries, freedom of choice is often extremely limited. The great industrial concerns which, as is frequently the case in Sweden, are situated in isolation in the country offer few possibilities of choice to the rising generation of workers. Women workers everywhere are to a great extent tied to their families, and are therefore confined to the particular labour market which is in the immediate vicinity of the place of work of the head of the household. These obstacles to mobility on the part of the workers may easily bring about a certain overcrowding in a particular labour market, and so exert a certain pressure on wages. The relatively greater immobility of women workers must frequently be responsible in no small measure for their relatively low wages.

Free choice of occupation is further substantially restricted by the cost of training for particular occupations. It is often found that the differences between these costs bear no relation to the differences in earnings in the different trades or in the different occupations within the same trade. From a purely business point of view, training for a better trade or a higher position would be very profitable. The explanation generally is that the cost, though small in proportion to the gain, is an insurmountable obstacle for the working-class family or for the young worker himself. By facilitating and improving vocational training, it is possible to promote a more uniform distribution of the workers among the different trades or grades of employment and thus to prevent a disproportionate reduction of the wages of particular groups. On the other hand, such a distribution is rendered more difficult by a lack of interest on the part of parents, a lack of a sense of responsibility on the part of the youth, and thus also by all measures of a fallacious social policy or of charity which can in any way assist these tendencies.

Migration from one locality to another within the same country is to-day a much simpler matter, and is also directly facilitated by the labour exchanges. Although much has been done in this respect, as compared with the position formerly, to secure an economic distribution of the available workers among the different localities within any one country, nevertheless the difficulties in the way of a similar distribution of labour among different countries, or even different parts of the world, are still very great, and have an unfavourable effect not only on the position of the individual groups of workers, but also in particular on world productivity. In this respect conditions since the war have unfortunately deteriorated to a considerable extent on account of the short-sighted restrictive immigration policy, particularly of the United States and other colonial countries.

The delimitation of the various trades from one another is accentuated by protectionist efforts within the world of labour itself. The economic significance of such restrictions will always depend upon whether they are merely to the advantage of casually separated groups of workers or whether, in a general way, as shown in the previous section, they direct the demand preferably to workers of higher quality, and thus give these workers preference in employment, make the continued existence of the lowest grades of inferior labour more difficult, and thus help to improve the position of the working-classes.

As the uniform distribution of the workers among the various occupations is restricted by so many circumstances, it is to be expected that in practice inequalities of wage-rates and other conditions of employment will be met with which cannot be explained entirely by the requirements imposed upon labour and the natural scarcity of workers who are able to satisfy those requirements. In branches of production which are particularly capable of development, in which the demand for labour has grown much more rapidly than the working population as a whole, we frequently find a higher wage than would appear to be warranted by the nature of the work. On the other hand, we find that unprogressive industries, which could not enlarge their markets perhaps in decades, offer their workers terms below the normal. The fate of the worker is thus to a certain extent bound up with that of the industry or firm in which he is employed. The view that employers only prosper at the expense of the workers, and conversely that the workers can only make progress at the expense of the employers, is strikingly robbed of much of its validity by these facts.

The flow of workers into the different occupations is in the main determined by these external factors. Wages themselves are, of course, of importance in attracting labour to a particular occupation in so far as that occupation competes with others for labour of the same quality. With regard to the total supply of workers of each particular quality, however, the wages paid for the different qualities do not, as we have shown, act as a directly effective regulator. The immediately deciding factors in this case lie outside the sphere of pricing.

§ 37 *The Supply of Labour as Determined by the Supply of Work per Worker*

The scarcity of the factor of production, labour, depends not only upon the number of workers, but also upon the amount of work done on the average by each individual worker. We have here to consider those factors which regulate this individual supply of labour.

The actual amount of work done by the individual is at any given moment generally much less than it could be, over a short period at any rate. Men have learnt that they must economise their effort. The greatest individual economic result is obtained, as a rule, not by the greatest possible effort at any moment, but rather by a wise distribution of work over the day, week, or life. This economic regulation of the individual performance of work is of fundamental importance as regards the social supply of work per worker. Modern industrial development has generally led to a considerable shortening of the working-day simultaneously with an intensification of work. In this the efforts of the workers to secure time for recreation and protection against uneconomic use of their powers, and the recognition by public bodies of the necessity for regulating hours of work in the interests of national health and strength, have had their part; but these tendencies coincided at least in part, particularly in those large-scale undertakings with the best technical equipment, with the interests of the employers in making economies in overhead costs by getting the maximum of work done in a short working-day. Under the influence of these tendencies, the length of the working-day is usually fixed in different industries either by custom or by agreement between the organisations of the parties concerned or finally by legislation, which is being increasingly influenced by international agreement.

The amount of labour actually offered by the individual worker further depends upon the permanence and regularity of his employment. A worker who, by reason of defective endowment, inadequate education, or the effect of bad organisation of the labour market, only obtains irregular work, and in the intervals wanders about idly for some length of time in search of new employment, provides much less than the normal individual's supply of labour. In certain industries in which there are very frequent changes of employment, such as the building industry, a considerable proportion of the possible number of working-days is regularly lost. Such factors as these clearly have a very appreciable effect on the actual "supply of labour per worker." The general external factors which govern the supply are thus fairly clear.

Again, we have to consider the deliberate regulation of the supply of labour by the workers themselves with the intention of protecting or improving the market situation. If a certain amount of unemployment is caused as a result of a decline in demand, one would think, on general grounds of price theory, that the excessive supply of labour must bring wages down, and that this pressure on wages would not cease until unemployment was somewhat diminished by the stimulus given to demand or, if this result could not be brought about, until wages had fallen to zero. In practice, however, matters are not so. The unemployed resist with all their power any reduction of wages, and are extremely reluctant to offer their labour at a lower price. In withholding their labour they are further supported by the popular view, among advanced peoples at least, which sees in low wages a tendency towards personal degradation. The unemployed are also morally and materially supported by their fellow-workers in their insistence on full pay. Not infrequently, too, these same fellow-workers forcibly prevent them from undercutting in the labour market. It is often found that there are higher wages paid in seasonal trades than in regular trades of a similar nature. This higher wage is to some extent a payment for the period of waiting, which explains how it is possible for the workers to withhold their labour in a sufficient degree during slack periods. Thus there takes place a considerable artificial limitation of the supply of labour, by means of which the workers succeed in maintaining a certain scarcity of the factor of production, labour, even during periods when there is a surplus of workers and consequently a certain amount of unemployment. This is always happening, but the attempt naturally succeeds more completely in the case of organised workers, particularly if they have funds for maintenance. It is only by an artificial scarcity of labour brought about in this way that we are at all able to explain theoretically a state of equilibrium existing simultaneously with the payment of wages at a certain level at a time when there is unemployment.

We also find within the labour world attempts to effect a

permanent increase in the scarcity of labour, and so to obtain higher
wages by restricting the available supply of labour. The demands
for a reduction of hours, which, as we have just seen, are substantially different in their aim, are also occasionally based on such
considerations. To put ourselves in a position to judge the prospects
of such attempts theoretically, let us assume that the group of
workers which seeks in this way to raise its wages is fully employed.
A restriction of the individual amount of labour must in that case
reduce output. The assumption that the efficiency of labour is
increased in proportion to the smaller number of hours worked is
out of the question here, since it is inconsistent with the assumption
of an increased scarcity of labour. If, on these assumptions, it is
desired to bring about an increased scarcity of labour for the purpose
in view, we are bound to include a reduction of output in our
reckoning. What then will be the probable effects of such tactics?
If the group of workers in question meets with competition within
the same trade, or in trades which cater for similar needs, its efforts
will naturally be quite futile. If, on the other hand, the group is so
comprehensive that by restricting its labour it is able to bring
about a real restriction of the supply to consumers, the prospect is
rather more favourable. If the elasticity of the demand which is
thus restricted is not particularly great, the labour in question will
soon receive an increased price per unit of work. But even in cases
where an increase of time-wages or of piece-wages can be obtained
by artificial restriction of the hours of work or of the amount of
work done per hour, it still remains doubtful whether the increase
will outweigh the reduction in the amount of work done per day.
If it does not do so, the income of the worker is bound to be reduced
by this policy.

The diminution of output brought about by the restriction of the
amount of work done must obviously reduce the total purchasing
power of the community to a certain extent. Thus the possible gain
of a limited group of workers is bought at the expense of a downward movement in the market for labour as a whole. If the group in
question is very large, covering, let us say, all manual workers, this
last effect will, as we have observed (§ 35), generally prove to be of

predominant importance. That a diminished income for the workers would be the result of a *general* restriction of hours of work unaccompanied by an increase in the efficiency of labour is beyond all doubt.

It is sometimes put forward as an aim of the restriction of the worker's daily output that the available employment shall be spread over all the workers in the trade. This object is clearly essentially different from the one we have just considered, and it was precisely for that reason that the assumption from which we now proceed – namely, that there is a certain amount of unemployment – could not be made in the preceding case. If, in accordance with our present assumption, the total amount of labour available is not reduced by the limitation of the amount of work done by each individual, but is merely spread over a larger number of individuals, then clearly the scarcity of labour and the price of labour cannot be affected by the change. The total income of labour remains the same, and is merely shared by a larger number of workers. The earnings of each individual worker, however, must be reduced in the same proportion as that in which the hours of work are reduced. In temporary crises, and also in the slack periods of seasonal trades, it is often profitable to spread out the diminished volume of employment in this way. But as a normal remedy for unemployment this method is very dangerous, as it keeps an unnecessarily large number of workers within a trade and puts them in a position of chronic under-employment and a correspondingly low standard of living.

Let us now see what effect wages themselves may have on the individual supply of labour. The theory which regards wages as a price that must be paid in order that a certain amount of work may be done, and which therefore treats wages theoretically as an element in cost corresponding to the sacrifice involved in performing the work, places an emphasis on the dependence of the individual's work on his wages, which is, in practice, without justification. First, as regards the hours of work, it follows from what we have said that they are essentially determined by factors other than wages. At all events, there can be no question of an increased wage leading to longer hours of work. On the other hand, we can state as a normal feature of development, that as wages rise demands for shorter hours are intensified and are able to be carried into effect. What is known as the "disutility theory," according to which wages must cover the disutility of the last extension of the working-day and are determined by this condition, appears to be a quite meaningless theoretical construction, especially in view of the fact that the individual, who alone can have a real perception of that disutility, has practically no influence over the length of his working-day, as we saw previously.

On the other hand, the quality of the labour offered undoubtedly depends to a certain extent upon wages. The intensity of work to-day necessarily implies a correspondingly high standard of living on the part of the worker, and wages may thus in some measure be compared with the necessary cost of maintaining and running machinery. It must be remembered, however, that a rise in wages does not by any means certainly, still less immediately, bring about an increase in the efficiency of labour. Such an effect of higher wages is rather due in the main to other conditions, such as national character, the system of education, the general direction of consumption, and so on. A rise in the standard of life of the worker, and therefore in the efficiency of his work, is, for the most part, merely the outcome of a gradual development, and cannot simply be purchased by a rise in wages. The socio-political value of an increase in wages appears to be largely dependent on whether the increase is effected gradually or suddenly. Too rapid an increase of wages may easily reduce the worker's diligence and regularity or lead him to an uneconomic consumption which even at times injures his own working powers, and may thus engender habits that will be prejudicial to his whole future and perhaps quite outweigh the benefit of the rise in wages. The rapidity with which the young worker attains his highest income under modern conditions often has bad effects for these reasons. From what we have said, then, high wages are a necessary condition of efficient work, though by no means a sufficient condition.

Nor can it be generally stated that wages must necessarily cover the current cost of maintenance of labour. In actual fact, there are such large numbers of poor and economically inferior workers that their wages, in accordance with the principle of scarcity, are in many cases reduced to an amount that does not even suffice to cover the bare cost of maintaining their labour power. This again lends special support to our view of the supply of labour as a factor in the pricing problem determined essentially by independent factors.

It may become necessary to supplement such very low wages by a subsidy from the family, and also in special cases by charity or by public provision for the poor. Consequently, it is not possible to secure strict adherence to the principle of cost in the cases of human labour. On the other hand, however, it is clear that assistance of this kind must invariably have a bad effect. Any sound social policy must aim at educating people as far as possible to be self-reliant, and will therefore attempt to maintain the principle of cost as strictly as possible in the case of labour, too. A theory of wages that attempted to proceed from the assumption that these effects had already fully achieved their purpose would, however, be too remote from reality.

It follows unquestionably from what we have said that, like the supply of workers, the supply of work per worker, too, is primarily to be regarded as a given factor in the pricing process. Both the hours of labour and the regularity and intensity of the work are essentially determined by general factors which lie outside the pricing process. The influence of wages themselves sinks entirely into the background, or at any rate can only make itself felt after a long interval, and with the co-operation of other factors. That, in these circumstances, the correct first approximation of the theory of price lies in the assumption that the work performed does not depend upon the wages is clear. In making this assumption, the scarcity of labour as the first determining factor of wages is clearly brought out, whereas the conception of wages as a necessary compensation for some work done is completely forced into the background.

Finally, we may observe that, although the wages themselves have only a very limited influence on the work done, the form in which they are paid may nevertheless have a considerable direct effect on the work. Those forms of wages which give not merely the hours of work or the amount of work done, but also the amount of work done per unit of time a certain influence on wages, undoubtedly have a great effect on the intensity of the work. (They may at times have too great an effect, which may imperil the economic use of labour power.) The methods of wage-payment, therefore, have a not unimportant place among the factors which determine the supply of labour, and which the theory of price thus has to regard as given elements.

§ 38 *Wages in the Socialist State*

Socialistic views of the problem of wages have not been built into a consistent, and generally recognised, logical system. It is nevertheless not difficult to get an idea as to what constitutes the main substance of these views. The principal defect of the present social system with special reference to the labour question lies, in the opinion of Socialists, as we have already seen (§ 31), in the fact that both the wage and the employment of the worker depend upon the state of the market, and are determined by commercial factors. Under this system, labour is reduced to the position of an ordinary commodity, which is not consistent either with the worker's dignity as a human being or with his rights as a member of the productive society. Socialism challenges such a social system and demands, in addition to full employment for the workers – that is to say, the elimination of unemployment – also in particular the determination of wages on objective grounds. In fixing wages, regard may of course be had to the worker's efficiency, the length of time necessary for his training, the difficulty or unpleasantness of his work, and so on, but in any case only on objective grounds, based on the nature of the work, and, fundamentally, not on the state of the market, the number of competing workers, or similar factors. In these demands we have, as we observed in § 31, the main substance of the socialist programme for the "abolition of the wage-system."

These demands, however, clearly establish an entirely new object for pricing. Whereas, according to our basic studies, the chief object of pricing in the exchange economy is to restrict consumption and to direct the use of the productive forces of the exchange economy, and ultimately also to stimulate the supply of factors of production, in such a way as to produce equilibrium of supply and demand, the socialist demand imposes upon the pricing process the requirement that it shall regulate the social distribution of income, and this again must be done on independent, objective, and ethical grounds, altogether apart from any considerations of the state of the market. This demand, however, as can easily be seen, is inconsistent with the general economic aim of pricing. Pricing, as our studies have shown, is largely determined by this aim, and cannot therefore be subjected to any second condition. Given a pricing process that wishes to effect a certain distribution of income, it is obviously not possible to maintain at one and the same time freedom of consumption as well as freedom of choice of occupation, freedom of choice of locality, and freedom of propagation; in a word, freedom of the supply of labour, and a realisation of the wishes of the Socialists, would thus mean an abandonment of certain essential values of the exchange economy.

It is inherent in the nature of the exchange economy that both wages and employment are expressions of the demand for the performance of work at the existing supply. The much-discussed "value" of labour can, in effect, only be defined as the price of labour in the ideal pricing process, governed by the principle of scarcity, which we examined above. This definition indicates clearly all there can really be in such vague but popular expressions as "the full produce of labour," "the real share of labour in the proceeds of production," etc. A pricing process which fixes wages in accordance with the principle of scarcity is indifferent to the distribution of income in the community. If it is desired to modify this process in favour of one group of workers or other, while preserving the fundamentals of the exchange economy, no way is open other than that of regulating the "value" of labour; in other words, of influencing the market in such a way that the price of labour is raised.

According to the result of our inquiries, there are in our present exchange economy various methods of regulating the labour market in this way. These include socio-political measures for preventing overcrowding in badly paid trades, for dealing with cases of obviously underpaid labour in certain trades by fixing minimum wages, and, in general, measures rendering it as difficult as possible to have a standard of living which does not cover the real cost of living. A national system of education, particularly vocational training, helps positively to strengthen the position of labour in the labour market, as do also a well-organised and rationally conducted system of labour exchanges, a suitable local distribution of population, a limitation of the increase of population in those classes of society in which it is excessive, and, in certain circumstances, a certain general restriction of the growth of population relatively to the possibilities of increasing the other factors of production, land and capital. Finally, the state of the labour market is in general improved by an increase in social purchasing power – by an increase, that is to say, in the productivity of labour, and thus in total social production.

The socialist state would in fact have to proceed in the same way; that is to say, it would have to try to influence the labour market by means similar to those we have indicated or by other means which might prove to be suitable, in order that labour might obtain a fair value. If the socialist state were to succeed in this, it would be superfluous to attempt to regulate wages in any other way conflicting with the principle of scarcity. In any such attempt the socialist state would run counter to its former programme of realising the right to the full produce of labour. For if this right is secured for the workers by the ideal pricing process on the basis of the principle of scarcity, any arbitrary encroachment for the purpose of regulating wages in accordance with other views will deprive some workers of part of the full produce of their labour, and give others an amount over and above the full produce of theirs.

It might now be objected that the socialist state has, by abolishing private ownership of the material factors of production, taken over the "unearned income," and must therefore be in a position to improve the situation of the poorer classes without touching the higher incomes. The socialist state, however, must itself take care of the necessary formation of new capital, and besides this must satisfy a large number of purely collective wants. It must also provide the necessary funds for education, art, and so on, which are at present paid for out of the larger private incomes. If, after paying for all these things, the socialist state still has some money over, this simply means that the prices of finished goods in general can be reduced to a certain extent. This must, then, be done, since the object of pricing is after all to effect the necessary limitation of consumption. The fixing of higher prices than are necessary is equivalent to taxation, but taxation of larger incomes in order to supplement the lower incomes is, nevertheless, a violation of the programme of the right to the full produce of labour.

Moreover, even in a socialist state, any attempt to supplement low earnings must necessarily make it easier for the lowest workers to remain in inferior employment, and this will inevitably make the market still worse, and wages will be further reduced. The result in this case is bound to be the same as it is in every case when it is attempted to supplement low wages out of public contributions. The socialist state would thus find that real social progress could be secured not by transferring income from one class in society to another, but simply by such measures as would raise the value of inferior labour.

This conclusion might with advantage be taken as the guiding line of all rational social policy in our existing society.

BOOK III

MONEY

CHAPTER IX

ANALYSIS OF THE MONETARY SYSTEM ON THE BASIS OF ITS EVOLUTION

§ 39 *The Origins of Money*

THE origin of money is most intimately connected with the development of exchange of goods, and exchange itself is a comparatively late outcome of economic evolution. Long before it had become the general custom to exchange goods, it was possible in various ways to obtain commodities from other communities. They might be acquired by robbery, for instance, or they might be more or less regularly secured in the form of tribute by the exercise of some kind of authority. The custom of giving and returning presents has been of direct significance in the evolution of exchange. [1] It is only reasonable to expect that the present made in return should bear a certain relation to the present given, and it may be safely assumed that such relations were fixed and recognised by custom at very early stages of development. It would then be possible to stipulate a certain return-present in advance, and so the needs of exchange were able for a long time to be satisfied in the old form of present and return-present. Wherever exchange had developed into a normal economic procedure, it was conducted for a long time according to traditional standards, which, perhaps, had

[1] We get a good idea of the frame of mind which is at the root of this custom from the ancient Scandinavian poem "Havamal" (in the earlier Edda). It runs :

> Never did I find a man so generous,
> Or so hospitable,
> That he would not take what was offered him;
> Or with his treasures
> So lavish to his friends
> That hateful to him was the reward he received.
>
> . . . . . .
>
> With weapons and garments
> Do thou gladden thy friend,
> And the like will be done to thee,
> With gifts and return gifts.
> Friendship grows old.

been defined by the priesthood or other high authorities. The paying of tribute of various kinds made it necessary, at a very early stage, to draw up tariff schedules of the various commodities accepted in payment. For it is clear that, as a rule, the various peoples, or tribes, or separate communities, would have to be allowed to pay the tribute in those commodities that they were best able to produce.

For these two reasons, schedules fixing the relative values of different commodities are economic necessities which must have made themselves felt in the earliest stages of the development of forms of exchange. That such schedules actually did exist is shown from ancient inscriptions, as well as from those primitive economic systems which have survived down to the present day. Probably the custom soon arose of settling the value of various commodities by reference to a "standard commodity." This might be done either by establishing that a unit of the standard commodity should be equal to so many units of the other commodities; or by taking a unit of each of the other commodities as equal to so many units of the standard commodity. However, in primitive conditions the valuation of commodities by reference to a standard commodity is carried out only for distinct and separate groups of commodities, and each of these groups has its own standard commodity. In early stages of cultural evolution, the very natural feeling predominates that commodities of great value should not be exchanged for others which are of considerably less worth. Thus, for example, it is said that in Africa ivory could be exchanged for certain highly valued goods, but not for others whose value was considerably less. This idea retained its influence long after the development of a money economy, as is shown by Mercantilist policy.

Although the earlier schedules for the valuation of commodities fell into various separate parts, the necessity of uniting these incomplete schedules into a coherent whole gradually made itself felt. This was attained as soon as definite ratios of value were established between the various standard commodities. Thus there resulted a uniform scale of reckoning, by means of which the value of all goods could be estimated. These scales of reckoning often consisted of a whole series of units which were connected with each other by simple numerical relations.

Ridgeway reproduces a scale of this sort, with five different units, from Annam.[1]

> 1 slave (male) = 6 or 7 buffaloes.
> 1 buffalo = 7 jars.
> 1 jar = 4 *muk*.
> 1 *muk* = 10 *mats*.

The meaning of the word *muk* seems to have been lost, and it is now merely a unit of account. The smallest unit, the *mat*, was an iron hoe used in agriculture. All other commodities were reckoned in terms of these five units, and occasionally several of these units would be employed in succession in order to express a precise value: for example, 1 good sword = 1 jar, 1 *muk*, 3 *mats*. Of course, the existence of such a scale of reckoning does not prove in itself that the most valuable commodities were exchanged for the cheapest. It was, however, a formal unified scale by means of which the value of all sorts of commodities could be reckoned.

The use of different units to express the value of dear and cheap commodities has obstinately persisted through all stages of the development of an exchange economy. The division of our modern currency systems into marks and pfennigs, francs and centimes, etc., originates from this custom. The three units of the English coinage are a particularly good example of the persistence of this point of view from ancient times.

Each unit of such a scale of reckoning must necessarily be an abstract unit of account. Thus, if a value is expressed in dried fish, the calculation must be based on fish of "average size and quality," or some other definite standard. A store of one hundred fish does not then necessarily represent a hundred fish in the sense of the unit of account. This is still more apparent when we consider what is by far the most important of such units of account – that is, cattle. When "an ox" is used as a unit for reckoning value, it perforce

[1] Ridgeway, *Origin of Metallic Currency and Weight Standards* (Cambridge, 1893), pp. 23–4.

obtains a purely abstract meaning. A real ox, just like other commodities, will be valued in these units, and in greatly varying amounts, since even primitive people compute the value of an ox very exactly according to its age, etc. The abstract nature of the unit of account can clearly be seen in those cases where the unit chosen has entirely lost its original meaning. In the Hudson Bay regions, payment was made for a long time in "skins." Skins originally were taken to mean a beaver pelt, but gradually the unit of account took on the fixed value of two shillings, while the real beaver pelts were probably valued higher. [1] Not infrequently, the original meaning of the unit of account has been completely forgotten, as we saw in the case given above.

The sum at which a commodity is valued in such an abstract unit of account is clearly a price. The unit is a price unit, and the whole scale of reckoning is a price-scale. Thus, the calculation of price is from the beginning a calculation in an abstract unit, which has always an independent existence, detached to a certain extent from the standard commodity.

Whenever a scale of reckoning of this type is drawn up, the numerical valuation of commodities is obviously made easier, and so furthers the extension of exchange. This development of barter must, in its turn, give more scope to the scale of reckoning and strengthen the position it holds in the mind of the community. This barter and the scale of reckoning develop hand in hand, and there has probably never existed anything like a developed barter trade without a scale of reckoning.

When the value of commodities is expressed in terms of a common unit of account, an exchange may take place such that, first, the prices of the two commodities to be exchanged are fixed, and then the goods in question will be exchanged in such quantities as will yield the same price for both; that is to say, such quantities as will represent the same number of units of account. The transaction then falls into two separate acts, which have to a certain extent the character of a purchase and sale: A buys from B the commodity b for the sum p; at the same time B buys from A the commodity a

---

[1] Jevons, *Money* (London, 1899), p. 21.

for the sum p. A then pays the sum p by delivering the goods a, which B has engaged to accept for the sum p. Here, however, the buying and selling transactions are still bound up together. They have not the complete freedom which will only be attained when they take place quite independently of each other.

In unilateral transactions – taxes, fines, etc. – the scale of reckoning serves to fix the extent of the obligation. It is by no means necessary that the payments should be made in the standard commodities of the scale. It is more usual, rather, for the debtor to be allowed to pay in certain other goods, or even *in quo potuerit*.[1] Of course, these other goods must have definite values in the scale of reckoning.

Thus the scale of reckoning may play an important part both in exchange and in unilateral transactions, without it being necessary for the standard commodities to be utilised in their material form.

When one country sells its products in another country, where it cannot obtain in payment any commodities that it needs, the purchasing country may be able to give in settlement a commodity for which there is a demand in a third country. This commodity will then be taken in payment and exchanged in the third country for some other commodity, perhaps, which the first country greatly values. This country then obtains possession of the goods it really desires by means of an *indirect exchange*. The detour described is the only possible way of attaining the object, when there is no demand in the third country for the goods produced by the first, or when the demand is so small that the seller would obtain no advantage through a direct exchange. Hence indirect exchange must greatly extend the possibilities of exchange, and so be most instrumental in promoting barter.

Although indirect exchange is of prime importance from this point of view, it would, however, be incorrect to regard it, and the use of means of exchange, as constituting in themselves the beginnings of a monetary system. For in a real monetary system there must be a *common* medium of exchange, that is, a commodity which

[1] Cf. Bücher, *Die Entstehung der Volkswirtschaft* (1904), p. 131.

will be used by *all* as a medium of exchange, and which will therefore be regularly accepted in settlement for other commodities.

General media of exchange seem to have come gradually into use in connection with the development of calculation in prices. It is certain that the introduction of general media of exchange can never precede calculation in prices, for the reason that the use of a general medium of exchange presupposes a price-schedule in this self-same medium, except in so far as other price-schedules do not already exist. It is not vital that the general media of exchange should be identical with those standard commodities which are the basis of the price-schedule. The need for some standard commodity to serve as a unit in calculating prices, and the need for a general medium of exchange, are two distinct necessities of economic life, and they may be met in different ways. Indeed, the qualities demanded of a general medium of exchange are in part different from those demanded of a standard commodity. If a commodity is to develop spontaneously into a general medium of exchange, it must be in itself an object of general demand. When the commodity has already been elevated to a general medium of exchange, and is commonly recognised as such, it necessarily acquires a new value in virtue of its new property. The essential qualities demanded of a general medium of exchange are three; it must be easy to *store*, easy to *transport*, and easy to *divide*.

If a commodity is to be taken in exchange merely to be used later for exchange with another commodity, it must clearly be one that is easily stored. It must be such that everyone can take it and store it without any special difficulties or arrangements. This requirement naturally takes on a different interpretation in different stages of economic development. Among pastoral peoples, one can generally say that cattle will be accepted by every household, but this is by no means the case among more advanced peoples who practise division of labour. The property of general storability postulates also a permanency, which, carried to its highest degree, amounts to indestructibility.

That a general medium of exchange must also be easy to carry about is obvious. The requirement of transportability brings with it, in its more refined stages, the requirement also that large values should be represented by objects of as small a weight as possible. This can be achieved only when the commodity serving as a medium is at the same time one of great rarity.

Finally, divisibility is an essential requisite of a general medium of exchange, for if it is to carry out its object it must be capable of being delivered in any desired quantities. Perfect divisibility includes among its qualities that of uniformity, guaranteeing as it does that pieces of equal size may be treated as being identical in value.

The necessity of having all these requirements embodied in a common medium of exchange makes one realise how it is that, though commodities may be chosen as standard for the price-schedule, because of their high economic importance, it does not follow that they will always be found suitable as media of exchange, and other commodities will have to perform that function to some extent. We have already seen that cattle, which was the most important and most general standard commodity of primitive stages of culture, is not suitable as a medium of exchange for more advanced stages, because of its defective "storability." It does not at all fulfil the requirement of divisibility, and its transportation, especially by sea, must for a long time have been on a very small scale.

It is only natural, under such conditions, that, as soon as the need for a general medium of exchange was more strongly felt, the old major units of the price-schedule were not chosen to fulfil this want, but, instead, other commodities – especially metals, and, above all, precious metals, were employed. From what has already been said, the special advantages of the precious metals as general media of exchange are quite obvious. In addition, their use for ornament gave them that general attractiveness which alone in primitive stages of culture raises one commodity to the position of a general medium of exchange, and makes it easy to understand why the precious metals have come to be preferred to all others as such media. At the same time, other metals, especially copper (bronze) and iron, were used to represent the smaller values.

If commodities other than the standard commodities of the price-schedule are to be used as general media of exchange, their value must be expressed in the then obtaining price units; that is to say, they must have a generally recognised price. In view of the great stability of prices in primitive economic systems, this requirement is probably as a rule easily fulfilled. The regulations made by the priesthood and other high authorities as to which goods will be accepted in discharge of existing unilateral obligations have probably been of great importance in fixing the value of suitable media of exchange.

As soon as a general medium of exchange is expressed in the existing price-schedule, it obtains the character of a *general medium of payment*. It is now possible, thanks to a general medium of payment, to carry through the sale of a commodity as an isolated transaction. The obligation which the purchaser assumes – that of accepting the goods in exchange for a certain sum reckoned in price units – can now be directly carried out, without it being necessary for the sale to be completed by a purchase to the same amount. The normal method of transferring goods is now the one-sided method, in which the rendering of an equivalent value consists of a *payment*. Also, all one-sided obligations can now be met by payments made in the general means of payment.

When the use of general means of payment becomes well established, it is natural that the old price units should lose their connection with the standard commodities and gradually become abstract units for estimating values. The economic significance of these price units is clearly determined through the general price-level, and is fixed to the extent that the price-level is stationary. But the valuation of the general medium of payment has an especial influence on the value of the unit of account, in so far as this valuation is subject to the arbitrary decision of some ruler. When a definite *"legal tender power"* is assigned to a certain means of payment – that is to say, when it is provided that obligations to pay in the existing price unit shall be met with a certain means of payment according to a definite ratio – this must ultimately influence all prices, and thereby also give a new material significance to the price unit itself. As soon as a State reserves to itself the right of regulating the means of payment, the economic significance of the price units becomes, in the long run, completely dependent on the value that is ascribed to one or other of the means of payment.

The price-schedule and the general means of payment together make up the *monetary system*. Thus the monetary system has arisen from two natural requirements of trade by what was probably a very slow process of development. This development has no doubt kept pace with the development of exchange at all its stages. Already in the earliest sources where there is mention of trade we find a price-schedule, and there is no doubt that the general media of payment were in use wherever trade got beyond the elementary stage. Even in later stages, the development of barter was never in advance of the monetary system. When, finally, in the nineteenth century, barter, driving out the old self-contained patriarchal system, set up a developed barter economy in its place, this only occurred in conjunction with a further great development in the monetary system.

This attempt to reconstruct analytically the main lines of evolution of the monetary system receives a good confirmation in the account that Ridgeway gives of the corresponding development which took place in the ancient world. This distinguished scholar informs us that the ox was for thousands of years a chief unit for the settlement of prices in the whole of the Mediterranean region, from the Atlantic Ocean to Central Asia. At the same time, subunits were used, such as the sheep, and possibly a slave (whose value equalled three oxen) was used as a higher unit. It is at a quite early date that other commodities, the metals, came into use as general means of exchange or payment. In the earliest stages, metals were valued according to their bulk. They were drawn out into bars, and measured with a unit of length derived from the human body. Gold was used as an ornament in the form of bracelets (often spiral-shaped), but, if necessary, it was also used as a means of payment, the form making it easier to estimate the different amounts. To facilitate their use as means of exchange, the metals were moulded into pieces of a definite size in the shape of rings, nails, needles, etc. The first weights were grains of wheat and other seeds, as is demonstrated by the English unit of weight, the "grain," and the "carat" (which signifies *keration*, the seed of the carob), still used in weighing gold. It is particularly noteworthy that gold was always measured in a unit which corresponded to the value of an ox. This unit had a weight of about 130 grains troy ($=$ 8.4 grammes). Even before measurement by weight was invented, gold was probably shaped into pieces which represented the value of an ox. The system of weighing then simply adhered to this tradition, and the first unit of weight was that piece of gold which has been regarded since the earliest times as the gold unit, and which represented the value of an ox.

There can be no doubt that this quantity of gold was used as a medium of payment in the much older price-schedule founded on the ox unit. The custom of counting in "oxen" was long retained, and the ox-scale was turned into a purely abstract scale of reckoning, the original meaning of which was probably entirely lost, real oxen being priced by it and paid for in gold. In such circumstances it is natural that the quantity of gold which represented an ox should be known as an "ox," and that the name should be retained after the quantity of gold in question had been given the form of coin. The essential feature of the development was that a definite quantity of gold, the value of which was taken to equal that of an ox, was generally recognised as a medium of payment with a fixed value. This power of payment was made legal when the power of the State developed. In the course of these changes the connection of the unit of account with the live ox was lost.

Other metals have also been used as means of payment in quantities which were suitable for the earlier units of account. In Rome, for instance, copper was used, 100 *as* representing the value of an ox, and 10 *as* the value of a sheep.

The conception of a monetary system is necessarily connected with the existence of a scale of reckoning, and also with a medium of payment reckoned by this scale. With the presence of these two elements, a monetary system already exists. Lack of clarity on this point is largely responsible for the unsatisfactory treatment which money received at the hands of archæological and ethnographical research; undoubted indications of money were not recognised as such, and so its early evolution was, for the most part, ignored. It is greatly to be desired that the attention of investigators should be more sharply drawn to cases exhibiting the existence of a money economy, as well as to those showing signs of the use of a means of payment. In this first respect, the system of book-keeping should be especially noted, as it is developed even in the earliest stages of primitive society that have been discovered by archæologists. As soon as such a system of book-keeping is carried on in terms of a common denominator, a system of money-reckoning exists. With regard to the second point, special attention should be devoted to the use of ornaments of exactly uniform size, or having an easily measured shape, as such ornaments have been probably used also as means of payment.

Recent research has shown that the system of money-reckoning reached a surprisingly high standard even in early civilisations. In ancient Babylon payment was made by means of orders drawn on credit balances, even for distant places. This system of payment was actually so highly developed that it must be regarded as a genuine system of payment by cheque. Highly developed, also, was such a system of cheque-payment in ancient Egypt, on the basis of grain stored in the big granaries. We know, too, how actively trade, on the basis of payment in uncoined pieces of metal, manifested itself. Gold, either in the form of rings or spirals, was by no means such a primitive medium of payment as people to-day are inclined to think. Actually, the use of gold as a means of payment in the form of rings or spirals was so popular that it persisted for more than a thousand years after the invention of coins in the seventh century B.C. It is easy to understand why the Nordic people, in their relations with Mediterranean peoples, after discovering the variety and complications of the then existing monetary system, still preferred to employ gold as a means of payment in the shape of rings and spirals. Such "ring money" has also been found in large quantities in Swedish soil. The diagram gives a good representation of the use of this money for payments in different amounts.

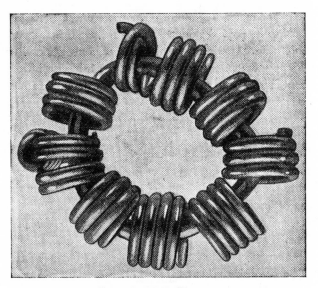

FIG. 1.—RING MONEY.

It might be disputed which of the two elements of the monetary system is the more important. The scale of reckoning could probably claim precedence, on the ground that it is possible to have an estimate of value in terms of a definite unit of account, and this may serve as basis for an exchange of goods, although there is no general medium of exchange or payment; whereas the creation of the latter necessarily presupposes the general use of a unit of account. However, both elements are definitely indispensable to our existing monetary system, so that a comparison of their relative importance is out of the question.

The theory of money has directed its attention mainly to the analysis of the nature of *money*. As, however, money was primarily conceived as a material commodity, the material medium of payment has been given undue prominence. It was asked what characteristic requirements had to be fulfilled before an object could be defined as money, in this material sense. It is clear that the concept of money must be defined not by the properties of any particular thing, but with reference to its essential functions. It follows from this conception that the analysis must be brought to bear directly on the essential functions of money. It is the co-ordination of the institutions which fulfil these functions that constitutes the monetary system. The question of what is to rank as material money is only of secondary interest. It can be answered in the most general sense by saying that every general medium of payment which is recognised as such is "money." Nevertheless, it is clear that the monetary character of such a money is the more strongly pronounced the more exclusively it is used, or is capable of being used, as money – that is to say, the more the "money" divorces itself from the "commodity."

For theoretical economics, our analysis of money has a special significance. Just as the fixing of prices is a primary practical need of every system of exchange, so also must the fundamental treatment of the theory of exchange be carried through as an analysis of the determination of prices. It has been shown in the first two Books of this work that such a theory can be worked out as a theory of the determination of prices without it being necessary for special attention to be devoted to the part played by the existing means of payment. The analysis of the origin of the monetary system shows that this rôle, by its very conception, is distinct from the part played by the price-scale. For the purposes of theoretical treatment, it is natural that the part played by the means of payment, and especially its significance for the price-scale, should be made the object of a special inquiry. This gives us the task of Book III.

§ 40 *The Minting of Money and its Significance*

When once the use of metals as a means of payment had been established, the creation of *coinage* was sure to follow. This development was due to two important advances. In the first place, at a very early date, even before the invention of the weighing scale, the metals were made into pieces corresponding to the units of account or fractions and multiples thereof, in order to facilitate payment. Secondly, the need was felt of stamping the pieces of metal in order to indicate and guarantee their weight and fineness, so as to avoid the constant process of weighing and assaying, which was always troublesome and, for most people, quite impossible.

Each of these advances was in itself important enough; but it is the combination of the two which was of decisive and one might even say, of epoch-making importance. It led to the appearance of *coinage*.

The introduction of coinage marks a new stage in the history of money. It would be wrong, however, to regard the whole development of the monetary system as being solely or principally that of a history of coinage, as people were formerly inclined to do. First, as has been demonstrated above, the monetary system is thousands of years older than the institution of coinage. Secondly, the development of money after the Great War has gone in the direction of doing away with the use of coins as full-bodied money. Probably the use of coins as the basis of the monetary system will be henceforth a closed chapter in the history of money.

As a result of technical improvements, it was gradually possible to attain an increasing uniformity in the minting of coins, so that variations between different coins could be confined to a very small proportion of the whole. The stamping developed until it extended over the whole surface of the coin, so that every holder could verify whether the coin had retained its original metal content.

For practical purposes, it is of fundamental importance that the various coins of the same denomination should be taken indiscriminately in payment. This ideal of reciprocal equivalence in value, or "fungibility," of the circulating coins has been gradually attained by the methods mentioned.

In the earlier stages it was possible only through legislative authority to require that individual coins should be ranked equally as means of payment. The State early reserved to itself the right of minting coins, and gave the coins a certain power of legal tender in a definite scale of prices. All coins, irrespective of their denominations, receive this quality of legal tender, as long as they are recognised bv the legislature as being valid. In payment transactions, therefore, no attention need be paid to variations in single coins of the same denomination. In cases where the coins are used as metal, a distinction will most likely be made among coins according to their metal content, but as long as they remain coins they are to be regarded as identical.

This legal identity of the coins is of supreme significance. The price-scale, as we saw, is always reckoned in units supposed to be identical. By means of coinage a material medium of exchange is created, possessing the same validity as that of the unit of account of the price-scale.

The currency unit is named either after the old unit of account or after the weight of the metal (mark, pound, lire), or from some chance reason. The word "crown" is very expressive, since it emphasises the minting authority of the State. Assuming that the currency unit is called a crown, and also that the price-scale will be based on this unit, then in the country in question all prices will be expressed in crowns. As always happens to the units of a price-scale, the crown will also become a purely abstract and independent unit of account without having a direct or necessary connection with its original material basis. The connection between the price-scale, that is the reckoning in crowns, and the means of payment is established by the legislative enactment that debts in crowns shall be paid by the coins called crowns. Through its power of determining what shall be legal tender, the State has complete control over the price-scale, and can materially alter its actual significance, though maintaining its formal identity.

In the course of time, such changes have been constantly occurring. As bad coins rank equal with the good ones, there is always the temptation to debase the coinage and thereby make a profit. In spite of such currency debasements, carried out for thousands of years by those in authority, the identity of the price-scale could generally be maintained. Furthermore, the State has at times replaced the metal which should serve as the basis for the price-scale by another metal, without, even then, destroying the identity of the scale. A case in point is the modern change-over from the silver standard to the gold standard. The State, indeed, can deprive the price-scale of any metallic basis, and declare paper notes to be legal tender, and still maintain the legal identity of the price-scale.

In this development, the price-scale, as always, appears as an abstract scale of reckoning, which is only more definitely fixed through establishing a medium of payment which is to have a settled purchasing power in it. When we tackled the problem of the general fixing of prices in Book I., we reckoned all prices in a common abstract unit. We found then that prices as a whole were determined except for a multiplying factor. This signified that only the relative values of different prices could be determined by price-fixing in an abstract scale of reckoning. The fixing of prices in absolute amounts presupposes that, besides the internal equilibrium requirement of the pricing process, prices are subject to another condition which gives them a relation to money. Such a condition obtains when a certain means of payment receives a definite purchasing power in the price-scale. It is, however, required of the means of payment that there shall be a certain limit to the supply of it for the purposes of trade; that is, that the means of payment should be relatively scarce. When once this requirement is met, the determination of the legal tender value of the means of payment is clearly sufficient to do away with the arbitrariness of the pricing system with regard to the absolute price-level and, in this sense, to fix the price-scale. Thus the economic significance of the unit of account is primarily dependent on the scarcity of the means of payment recognised as legal tender in the price-scale.

When coins are recognised as being means of payment, the significance of the unit of account is determined by the limitation of the supply of these coins. As the coins are not only employed as means of payment, but can also always be used as metal, a distinction is drawn between their *metal value* and their *nominal value*. The relation which exists between the nominal value and the metal value is always of great importance in a monetary system of this kind, and hence the factors determining this relation deserve particular attention. The relation obviously determines in what form the coins are to be used. The metal value cannot exceed the nominal value, as then the coins would be melted down and used as metal. It is certainly true that, in exceptional cases, when such a process is effectively forbidden, the nominal value can fall below the metal value. On the other hand, the nominal value can, under certain conditions, exceed the metal value, because the State, as minting authority, can restrict the amount of coinage.

As the mint price of the coins is formally fixed by their legally established validity in the price-scale, their value obviously cannot be expressed in this scale as a price. All that concerns us here is that the relation between the nominal and the metal value has a definite significance. Clearly, it is determined by the ratio of the quantity of the metal offered on the market for the coin, to the quantity of the same metal contained in the coin. In other words, the ratio between metal value and nominal value may be defined as the price of the metal in terms of the current price unit.

If we wish to give the general factors which determine the nominal value of the coin, we must assume that it is not convertible into another coin, and does not acquire its value from that other. For the sake of formal simplicity it is assumed that the coin represents the unit of price.

We must distinguish three cases:

I. Let us suppose that the circulation consists of a single medium of payment of completely homogeneous quality. If there is a certain scarcity of this medium, its exchange value may possibly rise above its intrinsic value. When, however, the medium is available in sufficient quantities, its exchange value must sink to its intrinsic value. It is obvious that a surplus of coins which cannot be used in payment for transactions can then only be valued as metal. On this supposition, however, the nominal value must equal the metal value. For the nominal value to rise above the metal value, there must be a sufficient scarcity of the means of payment, which thus causes demanders for money to offer more than the value of the coin's metallic content. Experience has repeatedly confirmed that such a scarcity of the means of payment may exist, with the result that they are valued above their intrinsic value.

II. Let us imagine, secondly, that two media of payment A and B are present, each of which, in itself, is of homogeneous quality, and that the same legal validity is assigned to each. Let us suppose that, of the two, A has the greater intrinsic value. We have now to distinguish two main contingencies. Either there is a sufficiency of medium B, or there is not. In the first case, the currency value of B will be determined by its intrinsic value. Accordingly, A has then a higher metallic value than nominal value, and must therefore be treated as metal. The overvalued coin is in the circumstances then displaced by the undervalued coin, and disappears from circulation. This result conforms to the so-called *Gresham's Law*, which is popularly, though not quite accurately, expressed in the phrase "Bad money drives out the good."

In the other principal case, when there is a sufficient scarcity of B, its nominal value can exceed its metal value. Nevertheless, the value of the price unit can be lower than that of the metal value of A, or it may be equal to, or even exceed it. This last contingency will clearly occur when A and B together form a supply of means of payment of sufficient scarcity.

III. Thirdly, let us assume that there is a whole series of different means of payment, in which every quality from the best to the worst is represented, and let us assume further that the need for means of payment is amply satisfied. Under these conditions, the value of the price unit will clearly be determined by the metal value of the best of the means of payment which must still be used as such in order to meet the demands of trade. Those coins having a higher metal content will be melted down and withdrawn from circulation.

Thus we find that the currency value is regulated by the principle of scarcity and the differential principle. In the latter case, the value of the currency is determined by the dearest of the coins which has to be taken into consideration. The three principles we have expounded are of useful guidance for the judgment of the various problems of the monetary system.

The creation of means of payment with a definite legal validity, and with a scarcity regulated by some means or another, gives the price-scale of a country its fixed significance on the lines we have stated. When we wish to express this price-scale in its connection with the entire system of means of payment that are valid in it, we speak of the *standard* of a country.

By means of minting, *money* is created which is essentially only money, and from which the metal is clearly distinguished as a *good* or *commodity*. It is true that the coin can be melted down and used as metal, but then it ceases to be a coin. It may also happen that, though having the form of a coin, it can be treated as a commodity, as indeed the not uncommon use of coins as ornaments in certain countries (India) proves. On the other hand, the metal itself can be turned into coins only by means of minting, on conditions imposed by the State at its discretion. However, as the State makes minting easier and more accessible, the difference between money and metal tends to disappear. Pure money, detached from any kind of material good, is found only in the case of paper notes recognised as legal tender.

§ 41 *The Problems of the Coinage Circulation*

The process of payment has been facilitated to a high degree by the invention of minting, and this step forward has had, without doubt, a great significance for the development of trade. But, in the first place, the use of coined money instead of uncoined metal has great disadvantages which have been completely overcome only after thousands of years of unfortunate experiences and fruitless endeavours.

The possibility of debasing the coinage, that is, minting it with a smaller metal content than originally but with unaltered nominal value, in conjunction with the continual wearing-away of the coins, has led, in all countries, to a more or less extensive and constant depreciation of the coinage. Attempts made from time to time to check the depreciation of the coinage have failed, because the problem involved was not properly understood, and also because the conditions necessary for a correct handling of the problem did not yet exist. It has only in modern times been possible satisfactorily to solve this problem of maintaining unaltered the metal content of the coinage, which may be termed the "*problem of the invariability of money.*"

Secondly, in ancient times it was not possible to bind together into a uniform system those coins which, though of the same metal, were minted in different denominations. It is of the nature of coins, if they are to satisfy the needs of trade, that they must be minted in various denominations bearing certain simple relations to each other. These unequal coins of the same currency were differently debased by wear in the course of time, so that the original relations between them were altered, and became variable. In this way, the originally unified money fell into a number of independent "varieties." This disadvantage was also clearly connected with the transition to coined money, for in the use of the uncoined metal a hundredth part of a certain weight of metal always remains a hundredth part. The disintegration of the coinage entrained with it also a disintegration of the price-scale into various independent scales, among which no definite relations could be maintained. Here, again, attempts to improve the situation were for a long time unavailing.

A similar difficulty is common to the use of coined money and the use of uncoined metal. The difficulty arises from the fact that various metals are used as a means of payment side by side, and, in view of the need to represent the most diverse sums of money, must be used in this manner. The coins minted from different metals, if they are to be combined into a unified monetary system, should have a fixed relation to each other. If the metals themselves do not provide this, then experience has shown that the fixed relation between the coins cannot be maintained without resorting to special regulations. It is not possible to bring together coins of different metals into a unified monetary system.

The two last-mentioned difficulties have only been overcome in the last century, by the solution of the big problem which may be designated as the "*problem of the single standard*." As we have seen, this problem has two sides, according as one takes into consideration one or more of the coined metals.

Progress in the field of money was greatly hindered in ancient times by political conditions. Because of the divisions existing in the organisation of the State, there were a large number of minting authorities, each of which minted its own coins, and allowed them to fall into different varieties, even putting into circulation coins of different types. The power of the minting authority was generally not strong enough to exclude foreign coins from circulating in its own territory. The result was that the circulation consisted of a miscellaneous medley of all types of money, having no connection whatever with each other. Naturally, in such circumstances no unified scale of prices, having exclusively the recognised means of payment in it, could be maintained. Nor could as a rule, a special mint value exist, the coins being generally valued, at least in large-scale trade, according to their metal content. This condition of the monetary system, where there is no question of a standard and where the use of coined money appears to be particularly disadvantageous, has rightly been characterised by Helfferich,[1] under the title of *Sortengeld* (variety money), as a particular phenomenon. It was not until the rise of the modern national State, capable of maintaining a monopoly of coinage within its territory and of excluding foreign money from circulation, that the basis was created for a monetary policy on rational principles.

Such a policy demands, further, that the State shall recognise its important task in the sphere of the monetary system, and that it shall be willing to make sacrifices for this, if necessary. A conception of this nature was more or less alien to the older State, which generally saw a means of profit in the system of coinage. The progress in this part of the monetary system is probably due, in the first place, to the general development of political life.

Along with this, one must take account of the development of the technique of minting, which has rendered possible a constantly increasing uniformity in the coining of money, and which has, at the same time, reduced minting costs. Finally, of prime importance, also, has been the growing scientific insight into the nature of monetary problems.

On turning to the solution of the various problems of the monetary circulation, we must first notice, with reference to the *problem of the invariability of money*, that the *constant debasements* of the

[1] *Das Geld*, 2nd edition, 1910.

coinage of ancient times were not only due to the greed of the currency authorities, but were also caused by objective conditions which these authorities could not control. The difficulties which occur in this respect are of three different kinds; they arise partly from the high cost of minting, partly from the lack of uniformity in minting, and partly from the wearing-out of the coins.

The high cost of minting accounts for the readiness with which the metal content of the coins is reduced by an amount corresponding to those costs. As the currency value cannot be maintained above the metal value, it must gradually fall to this level. The next large issue from the mint leads similarly to a further fall of the value of the currency unit, and so on. The difficulty touched upon here is, however, considerably lessened by the fact that costs of minting are reduced to a minimum by the technical improvements in machinery.

Lack of uniformity in minting, which, too, was a result of the imperfect technique of coining in ancient times, also led to a depreciation of the currency, in that the best coins were picked out and used as metal. According to the third principle enunciated in the preceding section, this could happen as soon as the stock of money exceeded the demand for means of payment. Selection of this kind, which was especially practised in connection with payments abroad, clearly produced a fall in the average metal content. This unsatisfactory condition, too, has been largely remedied through the improvements in minting technique which enable coins to be produced with a high degree of homogeneity.

The means by which the modern State has succeeded in effectually stopping the steady depreciation of the coinage consists in abolishing the legal tender power of those coins which do not come up to the *required standard of fineness.*

As a rule, these coins will always be accepted by the State treasuries at their nominal value. It is by this means that the regulations regarding the standard of fineness are made effective. If it is possible for everyone to get rid of those coins which do not come up to the required standard, without making a loss, then such coins will not remain long in circulation.

The exact minting of the coins according to the legally determined metal content, the fixing of a narrow limit of wear and tear
beyond which the coin loses its property of being legal tender, and
the effective calling-in of coins which do not conform to the standard
requirements – these are the means whereby the coins are maintained at their defined metal content, and, by so doing, ensure for
the money, as far as possible, an invariable ratio of value to the
metal.

When a full-bodied coinage circulation is assured in this manner,
the currency value can only fall below the metal value if the use of
the coins as metal is prevented, particularly if melting down is forbidden. The *"free right to melt down"* is therefore a necessary
guarantee for the maintenance of the currency on a par with the metal.

The theoretical possibility of a *rise* in the currency value above
that of the metal, as a result of a restricted coinage, had no practical
significance in the earlier minting policies, which aimed at producing as much money as possible. The right of private persons to
have the principal coins made for their own account by the State
mint in any required quantities against delivery of the metal, and
possibly against payment of a certain minting fee (the right which
has been generally recognised in recent times, and which is known
as *"the right of free coinage"*), effectively prevents any rise of the
currency value of the principal coins over that of their metal
content, at any rate, to not more than an amount corresponding to
the costs of minting. Where, as is the case in England, no minting
fees were charged, and the right of free coinage is gratuitous, the
conversion of metal into coins means, at the most, a slight loss of
interest. The upper limit of the fluctuations of the currency
value is then greatly reduced.

The free right to melt down and the free right of coinage as
supplemented by the right of unrestricted import and export of the
metal are, in a full value circulation, the guarantees of the maintenance of a constant metal parity of the unit of account.

Let us now turn to the problem of the single standard, and let
us first consider the case where there is only one coined metal.
The three factors which have contributed to the progressive

depreciation of the coinage are particularly active in the case of the smaller coins. As the costs of minting various coins are approximately the same, they must be relatively higher for the smaller coins than for the larger. It is for this reason that the smaller coins are habitually minted at considerably less than their face value than the large coins. Also, the lack of uniformity in minting is relatively greater in the case of the smaller coins than it is for the larger. The same condition obtains with regard to deterioration from use, since the smaller coins circulate much more than the larger ones. The continuous depreciation of the metal content of the coins, caused by these factors, must necessarily occur more markedly in the case of the smaller coins. As, on account of this, the coins which were minted in different denominations from the same metal lost, in the course of time, varying fractions of their metallic content, clearly no fixed value relation among them could be maintained. Thus the original connection of the various coins of what was, at first, a single monetary system had to be severed, and the monetary system as such destroyed.

To counteract these influences and to find a means of maintaining a unified monetary system has been at all times one of the great problems of monetary policy. The problem was to find a means by which the smaller coins which could not be coined or kept full-bodied could yet be kept at their full face value. This was possible only when the minting of the smaller coins was sufficiently restricted. As a result of this, the minting of the smaller coins has been reserved to the State, and has been restricted to an amount which does not exceed the needs of trade.

In employing this method, the difficulty of foreseeing, more or less accurately, the needs of trade for the smaller coins is encountered. That modern currency policy has not been able to do this is certain. The German coinage law of 1873 restricted the issue of Imperial silver coins to 10 marks per head of the population. In 1900 this maximum was raised to 15 marks, and in 1908 to 20 marks per head. It is improbable that an exact fulfilment of the requirements for silver coins was ever achieved by these figures. When such a provision is strict enough, a time will quickly come when the permitted circulation becomes too small, and the scarcity of the smaller means of payment will be felt irksome by traders. An exact fulfilment of the changing requirements of trade is only attained when the opportunity is given to trade of returning superfluous amounts of small coin to the central issuing offices, whilst the demand for such means of payment is always adequately met. In Germany, it fell to certain Reichsbank offices to redeem silver, nickel, and copper coins in gold coins. As long as such a redemption is effectively carried out, it is hardly possible for trade to be burdened with an excessive quantity of small coins. When, under these conditions, small coins are minted in sufficient quantities and placed at the disposal of trade, the amount of the small coins in actual circulation will always correspond to the needs of business.

The redemption of the undervalued small coins is the necessary condition for the maintenance of the uniform value of these coins in relation to the principal coins. A money, the value of which is maintained only by the State's promise to redeem it in a money of full value, has clearly the nature of a credit money. The value of such a money must, in the last resort, always be determined by the capacity and willingness of the State to fulfil its obligations.

Currency legislation has determined that such small coins shall be legal tender only to a limited extent. Coins, the intrinsic value of which is less than their face value, which have restricted legal power, but yet which can be exchanged for higher coins, are designated *token coins*. In contradistinction, these principal coins with unlimited power of legal tender are called *current coins*. As long as the State effectively redeems any surplus token coins, the limitation of the legal tender power of these coins has only the result of enabling the payee to refuse a means of payment which is too bulky and inconvenient.

Let us consider, finally, the problem of the single standard for the case in which coins of two different metals circulate together.

The relative value of gold and silver has undergone important fluctuations in the course of the last few centuries. On the whole, there has been, since the beginning of the sixteenth century, a considerable increase in this ratio, from about 11 to 1 at the beginning of the sixteenth century to about $15\frac{1}{2}$ to 1 in the first three-quarters of the nineteenth century, and about 34 to 1 at the end of the century. However, the rise has not been uninterrupted; in certain periods, such as the middle of the eighteenth century and also in the 'fifties of the nineteenth century, the ratio of gold to silver fell a little.

These variations in the relative value of the two precious metals were bound to cause similar variations in the relative value of gold and silver coins. As we have seen, the value of both the principal gold and silver coins could, on the whole, so long as their minting was not subject to any special restrictions, only be determined by the metal value of the respective coins. With a fluctuating ratio between the metals, a stable relationship between gold and silver coins could not be maintained. The gold and silver coins appeared as two different monetary systems, and the corresponding price-scales as two different standards. When a country, in this manner, has a gold currency and a silver currency, with free right of coinage for both, but without a fixed relation between the two, although each is recognised as legal tender in its respective price-scale, it is said that the country is on a *parallel standard*. The expression is not a happy one, because the country has really two standards.

The practical disadvantages of such a double system, which occasions constant changes from one type of money to the other as the ratio between the two varies, are perfectly obvious. It is no wonder, therefore, that great efforts were made to put an end to this state of affairs. At first, it was attempted to lay down a legal ratio between gold and silver. In this way, at all events, a single monetary system was obtained for the time being. Under this system, both gold and silver are full legal tender and are used as means of payment in a legally fixed ratio. When there is free coinage of both metals in this system, the country is said to have a *double standard*.

However, in accordance with the second of our principles regarding the coinage circulation stated above (§ 40), such a monetary system has no stability. For, as soon as the ratio of gold and silver on the open market alters, either gold or silver money will be treated as metal, and so disappear from circulation. The right of free coinage is naturally made use of in such wise that the metal which has fallen in value will be presented for minting. As a result of the unrestricted coining of this metal, the value of the unit of account in the price-scale will be determined by the value of the quantity of the said metal corresponding to this unit. The metal which has, relatively, risen in value will, therefore, possess a higher value as metal than as money, and will thus disappear from circulation, being driven out and replaced by other metals.

It is conceivable that the legal determination of the ratio of gold to silver will exercise a certain influence on the relation between gold and silver on the open market. This is because the double standard affords a great opportunity, to the metal which has fallen in value, of being used as money, thus increasing the demand for this metal and counteracting its fall in value. The efficacy of this counter-effect is clearly dependent on the importance of the country which has a double standard, as well as, more generally, on the relationship between the monetary and industrial demand for the metal in question. These questions, however, do not concern us. It is sufficient in this connection to observe that when the ratio between gold and silver on the open market is altered, the double standard will then lose one of its two kinds of money. It is easy to see that the disappearance of the gold or silver coinage entails disadvantages which, in serious cases, may become quite intolerable. It is very inconvenient, for big business, to have to dispense with gold coins when once such a coinage has come into use. The loss of the silver money is even more strongly felt, as only with difficulty can it be replaced for small payments. It is therefore but natural that great efforts are made to get beyond the stage of the double standard.

The solution of the problem to which historical development has led consists in making gold coins only the principal coins with unlimited legal tender and with free coinage, whilst silver coins are reduced to token money, whose minting is reserved to the State. These token coins must be minted below their value to such an extent that, in the case of the price of silver rising, there is no fear of their disappearance from circulation. Currency legislation has been content with minting them at a small percentage below their nominal value. This initially somewhat narrow margin has been considerably widened, because of the heavy fall in the price of silver since the 'seventies. The metal value of silver coins before the war was generally not more than half their nominal value.

A single standard, in which only gold coins are unlimited legal tender and in which there is a free coinage right for gold bullion and a free melting right for gold coins, and, in addition, freedom for import and export of gold, is called a *gold standard*. This name must not be taken as meaning that gold is the price unit of the standard. The former German gold standard was a mark currency. The unit of account was the mark – prices were quoted in marks and payment made in the same. The mark standard, which in itself was only an abstract scale of reckoning, was, however, more closely fixed, in that 279 ten-mark pieces were coined from a kilogramme of gold, and also in that these gold coins were unlimited legal tender. It is the fact of the mark standard being more closely defined by this connection with the metal, gold, that we mean to express when we call it a gold standard. Similarly, England has a pound sterling standard.

The relation between the former mark standard and gold can be best expressed by saying that the price of a kilogramme of gold is fixed in the mark-scale. The price of gold should normally be 2,790 marks per kilogramme. This price is not absolutely fixed, but it is so fixed within certain rather narrow limits. The rule set out for the minting of gold coins cannot be followed with perfect accuracy. Therefore, a certain margin of error is allowed in minting, amounting, for single coins, to 2 per mille in respect of fineness and $2\frac{1}{2}$ per mille in respect of weight. These limits apply only to single coins; for the coinage taken as a whole, an "absolute accuracy" is required. The limit of deterioration is 5 per mille below the normal weight. If it is wished to obtain gold from coins which have been in circulation, allowance must be made for a certain average amount of depreciation in the coins. The loss may be from 2 to 3 per mille. The upper limit of the price of gold lies therefore some 2 to 3 per mille above the normal price of 2,790 marks.

The lower limit of the price of gold is determined by the costs of minting. In Germany, a minting fee of 6 marks per kilogramme was charged, and a certain loss of interest also had to be considered. As, however, the Reichsbank was obliged to accept all gold offered to it at the price of 2,784 marks per kilogramme (that is the normal price, less the minting costs), this price always fixed the lower limit of the price of gold. Thus the price of gold could fluctuate from the normal price of 2,790 marks by rather more than 2 per mille downwards and 2 to 3 per mille upwards.

Conditions were similar in other gold standard countries. In England, the normal gold price was 77s. 10½d. per standard ounce (11/12 fine). The lower limit of the gold price was 77s. 9d., at which price the Bank of England was obliged to purchase gold at all times. The upper limit may be placed at 78s. in normal conditions, although higher prices were paid in isolated cases. These limits correspond to deviations from the normal price of roughly 1½ per mille in an upward and downward direction.

It might be said that an ideal gold standard requires an absolutely fixed price of gold. Such stability is, however, unattainable in practice. Any large deviation from the normal price is to be regarded as an imperfection of the gold standard. A variation upwards is to be regarded as equivalent to an imperfection of coins in circulation; a variation downwards is equivalent to the making of a minting charge. Every reduction of such variations means an advance in the direction of a consistently carried out gold standard.

The possibility of a variation in the price of gold is of theoretical significance, in so far as it shows that the price-scale has an independent existence even under a gold standard, and that the unit of account even here is a purely abstract unit, and not a definite weight of gold. The fundamental part of the former German currency system was the reckoning in marks. The unit of account, the mark, was an independent magnitude. The price-system was made up in it, and all debts were paid in it. The settlement of prices in such a unit is, however, restricted by the fact that it must not cause the price of gold to fluctuate beyond certain limits. The variations in the price of gold under a gold standard have also a practical significance, as we shall see when studying international payments (§ 60).

The gold standard was introduced by England at the beginning of the nineteenth century, and since the 'seventies it has been gradually adopted, first in the Western European countries, and then all over the world. In certain countries, however, people did not want to do away entirely with the full legal tender power of silver money. Thus in France, the silver five-franc piece retained its property of being full legal tender for any amount. Although this silver money was not convertible, as a rule it maintained its parity with the gold currency, even though, for making payments abroad, a small premium was generally paid for gold money. That this parity should be possible is due to the scarcity of the silver money, which was very far from satisfying the need for means of payment. But as gold must always be in demand, the value of the currency is determined by the metal value of the dearer coins (see our second principle on the coinage circulation). A gold standard in which an inconvertible silver currency with full legal tender power is retained, is known as a *limping standard*.

The sharp fall in the price of silver which has taken place since the 'seventies as a result of greatly increased production of silver, and the relative contraction of the monetary uses of silver as a result of the change-over to a gold standard, has led to certain efforts to "rehabilitate" silver on the part of those interests which have been injured by the fall. These efforts were supported by those people who saw a proof of the inadequacy of gold as the sole standard metal in the fact of the increasing scarcity of gold and the fall in the general price-level which was undoubtedly provoked thereby. These efforts culminated in the demand for a restoration of the double standard on an international basis. It was held that the wider basis of the double standard would offer such a wide monetary use for whichever of the two metals was in less demand at the time on the open market, that any considerable fluctuations in the relative value of gold and silver could be avoided.

This programme of an international double standard is known as *bimetallism*. Bimetallism is an attempt to solve the problem of a single standard on the basis of two standard metals. The possibility of such a solution is for the most part a political question which cannot be discussed here. There is no doubt that a considerable stabilisation of the relative values of gold and silver could be attained, if the whole world could agree upon a bimetallic system. Whether this stabilisation would be sufficient to maintain the two metals constantly in circulation together is an open question. It must, therefore, remain uncertain to what extent bimetallism can be regarded as a practical and satisfactory solution of the problem of the single standard.

It is certain, however, that bimetallism, under the pressure of accidental circumstances, has introduced into the problem of the standard an element which is, strictly speaking, foreign to it. Our general treatment of the pricing problem has shown that prices are determined but for a multiplicative factor. It follows from this that a *single price* may be determined in any way. A *new* condition *must* enter before the problem of the determination of prices is finally settled. The condition, which means the fixing of the price-scale, may take different forms, one of which is the settling of the price of one particular commodity. This method is followed by the gold standard, and also by the silver standard. The double standard, however, results in the attempt to fix *two sets of prices*, that is, first the absolute price of a commodity, and then the price relationship between two different commodities. The task of fixing the relative prices of two commodities clearly lies outside the sphere of the monetary system, and must, when coupled with the problem of a standard, greatly complicate that problem and obscure its essential features.

With the introduction of the gold standard the development of the monetary system is completed, in so far as we have arrived at a solution of the currency question which has completely removed the disadvantage at first involved in the use of coined, instead of uncoined, metal, and also the disadvantage of a fluctuating relationship between the two precious metals. We have succeeded in obtaining an "invariability of money" as well as a "unity of standard." There still remains to examine, however, whether the binding of the price-scale to the metal, gold, will guarantee a sufficient stability in the settlement of prices. It is conceivable that gold, apart from the formal fixing of its price under a gold standard, is subject to important fluctuations in value in relation to other commodities, and this would naturally lead, under a gold standard, to corresponding changes in the level of commodity prices.

This problem cannot be fully stated here, but it will be made the subject of a thorough examination in Chapter XI. As has already been mentioned, the scarcity of gold at the end of the nineteenth century brought about a fall in the general level of prices under a gold standard. Bimetallism wished to combat this fall in prices by abolishing the gold standard and creating a standard which should be plentifully supplied with the means of payment. At the beginning of the twentieth century the greatly increased output of gold caused prices under the gold standard to rise once more. In this way, the need which bimetallism wanted to satisfy was satisfied, at least for the time being. The supply of gold was sufficient to allow the world to maintain a gold standard and a gold coinage, without in itself exerting a pressure on the price-level. If, in the future, this should no longer be the case, or if, on the other hand, too much gold should come on the market, we shall be faced with a problem of monetary policy which will be of a much more general and fundamental importance than can be solved by merely reverting to bimetallic ideas.

§ 42 *Free Standards*

The metallic standard, which fixes the price-scale by fixing the price of a metal, is not the only solution of the problem of the stabilisation of the price-scale. Experience has already shown, by a number of instances, that a certain stabilisation of the price-level can be attained without binding it to a metal or, indeed, to any commodity.

The fixing of the price-scale is accomplished, as we have seen, always by designating some medium of payment as unlimited legal tender in the scale. A necessary condition for the stability of the price-level is clearly a specific quantitative limitation of this medium of payment. If the means of payment could be procured in any desired amounts without difficulty, then any price might be offered, and the stability of the price-level would cease.

If the means of payment is a freely mintable coin, its scarcity is guaranteed by the scarcity of the coinage-metal. As the latter has other uses also, the scarcity of the medium of payment is, it is true, secondary, but is at all events determined by objective conditions.

When the State reserves to itself exclusively the production of the coinage, it can restrict this coinage to whatever amount it wishes and so regulate the price-level. The requisite stabilisation of the price-scale will be attained in this instance by a direct quantitative limitation of the means of payment. A standard that rests upon this basis and, therefore, is not bound to a metal, is called a *free standard*.

Holland, until 1873, had a silver standard (guilder standard), but in that year, on account of the threatened depreciation in the price of silver, it suspended free coinage. The former metallic base of the currency was thereby done away with, inasmuch as the currency value of the coin could exceed its metal value. The scarcity of the means of payment, which up till then had been regulated by the scarcity of silver, now became more accentuated because of the progressive development of Dutch industry and commerce; and the value of the guilder not only rose above its falling silver metal content, but also rose above its former gold parity. During the early 'seventies, until the beginning of 1875, the London price of silver fell from approximately $60\frac{1}{2}d.$ to about $57\frac{1}{2}d.$ per ounce, whilst the London rate of exchange fell from 12 guilder to 11.6 guilder to the pound sterling. Thus the value of the Dutch guilder had risen considerably above its silver content.[1]

If, on the contrary, the need for means of payment in Holland had diminished, the value of the guilder could not have fallen below the value of its silver content, as the guilder could always be treated as metal. The former connection of the guilder with the metal, silver, still set a lower limit for the movements in value of the guilder. In practice, this limit never came into effect. The

[1] Helfferich, op. cit., p. 80.

Dutch coinage had its value determined, in the period under review, exclusively by the scarcity of the guilder as a means of payment in the Dutch national economy; and so the Dutch monetary system was actually on a free standard. This standard fixed its price-scale by an authoritatively determined scarcity of the valid means of payment in it. By calling it a free standard, that does not imply that the value of the standard unit was less definitely fixed than would be the case under a standard based on metal.

A freely minted gold coin, the ten-guilder piece, having full legal tender at its nominal value, was introduced in 1875. As, however, the Government was not obliged to convert silver guilder into gold guilder, there was always the possibility that the Dutch standard currency unit would fall in value below that of the gold guilder. Actually this never happened. The silver coins were sufficiently scarce to maintain the standard currency unit at a parity with the gold guilder, and thus the Dutch monetary system got into a condition that was much akin to a gold standard.

India, after it suspended the free coinage of silver in 1893, was also for a time on a free standard. The value of the rupee rose above its silver value and was exclusively determined by the scarcity of Indian means of payment. At the same time the Indian mints were directed to exchange on demand English sovereigns against rupees, at the rate of 1 sovereign = 15 rupees. In other words, rupees were to be sold at 16*d.* each. Thus an upper limit was set to the value of the Indian currency unit. These regulations, however, had at first no practical significance, as the rupee rate of exchange remained in the years following a good deal under the rate of 16*d.* The rupee currency was therefore on a free standard, with a limitation of the fluctuations in value of the currency unit in the two directions. The lower limit of the value of the rupee was the value of its silver content, while the upper limit was the gold value of 16*d.*

Moreover, there are standards which have no connection whatever with a metal. These are the *paper standards.* A paper standard generally originates when bank-notes, which are no longer convertible into metal money, are declared to be legal tender, and become *"forced currency."* If paper money is issued in sufficient quantities, then, since it has no intrinsic value, it must necessarily drive out all metal money. The value of the unit of account will then depend entirely on the scarcity of the paper means of payment.

A paper standard, without any connection with metallic means of payment, may be regarded as being theoretically the simplest standard of all. The various standards are differentiated according to the manner in which the scarcity of the means of payment is regulated. Under a pure paper standard the scarcity of the means of payment is determined by two factors – on the one hand, by the quantity of the paper money, and on the other hand, by the need for means of payment within the economic system in question. Under a metallic standard the regulation of the scarcity is much more complicated. In this latter case, the available amount of the means of payment is no given quantity in the problem, but, through the right of free minting, depends on the world supply of the mint metal, which in turn bears a certain relation to the cost of producing the metal. Under the head of demand one must not only reckon the monetary demand of the economic system concerned, but also that of the remaining economic systems, and, still further, the total world industrial demand for the metal.

For the clarification of the connection existing between the value of the standard currency unit and the scarcity of the means of payment, the existence of a pure paper standard is a phenomenon of the greatest interest.

If paper money is issued in unlimited quantities, the unit of account will depreciate to an unlimited extent, and prices will rise without limit. The paper economy is then bound to end in a catastrophe. We have an older example in the case of the issue of notes by Law's notorious bank in France, which issued notes to the stupendous amount of roughly three thousand million livres, but failed in the great crash of 1720. There was also the even greater, and just as fatal, issue of assignats during the French Revolution.

In recent times, there has often been a paper standard with a definite limitation of the paper money. The paper money has then maintained a definite value, though it has undergone some fluctuations as compared with metallic standards. The object in view in regulating the paper money was generally the resumption of cash payments at a definite rate – that is, the eventual return to a metallic standard based on the original metal or a transference to a new metallic standard (gold instead of silver). In the meantime, however, the paper standard was essentially determined by the scarcity of the circulating paper means of payment in relation to the demand for them, although the expectation of an imminent change to a metal standard may have influenced the value of the paper currency to a certain extent.

During the period of the Napoleonic Wars, the Bank of England could not redeem its notes in gold as from 1797. As the notes were forced currency, and were thus legal tender, they displaced gold money. England, therefore, was on a paper standard, in which the unit of account, the pound sterling, had an independent value, determined only by the amount of currency in circulation – that is, bank-notes. Gold became a commodity, with a price, like that of other commodities, reckoned in pounds sterling. In this case, the independent existence of the price-scale is clearly seen. After the end of the war the pound sterling was gradually, by strict limitation of the note issue, brought to parity with the sovereign, and so finally the gold standard was restored.

In recent times, there have been numerous instances of deliberately regulated paper standards. The history of the Austrian paper currency system since 1848 is perhaps the most interesting for throwing light on the problems of monetary systems. During the 'fifties and 'sixties, Austria made fruitless attempts to return to the original silver standard. While it was not possible for the Austrian Government to raise their paper money to parity with the silver currency, this parity was finally reached automatically by the fall in the price of that metal. By the beginning of 1879 the premium on silver had disappeared. As, however, the depreciation of silver threatened to continue still further, and as, thanks to the right of free coinage, silver would have forced its way into the Austrian circulation (thus dragging the unit of account down with it), the

Government, wishing to change to a gold standard, decided in 1879 to suspend the free coinage of silver. Previous to this year the silver value of the silver guilder set an upper limit to the movements in value of the Austrian unit of account. After the suspension of the free coinage of silver, this limit was no longer valid. Austria had a pure paper currency without any connection with the precious metals. Actually, the Austrian guilder in the ensuing period of the sharp depreciation of silver maintained its value increasingly over the silver value of the silver guilder. [1]

All earlier experiences of paper currencies have been eclipsed completely by the train of events which, after 1914, turned all the currencies of the world into paper currencies, some of which suffered a fantastic depreciation. The belligerent countries issued notes, printed both by the State and the banks, in order to meet their obligations, while the neutral countries followed suit, partly on account of their own State expenses arising out of the war, and partly because they were more or less forced to grant credits to the belligerents. Attempts were made everywhere to veil the true significance of these proceedings, and to justify them on the grounds that the new means of payment were required solely in order to cover the growing needs of trade. The Governments, however, as we shall see in greater detail later, constantly created new purchasing power for themselves, either in the form of bank credits or by directly printing paper currency. By their action, they caused prices to soar, and the value of the currency unit to fall correspondingly.

The enormous increase in the world supply of the means of payment had an effect even on the value of gold itself, which, in 1920, fell to as much as 40 per cent. below its pre-war value. Later, the value of gold was stabilised for some years at a level corresponding to approximately 67 per cent. of its pre-war value. It was, therefore, not necessary for the purpose of restoring the gold standard that the value of the paper currency should be raised to the former gold value; it was sufficient if roughly 67 per cent. of its former value could be attained. This greatly facilitated the restoration of the gold standard at its old parity, and a number of countries

[1] Helfferich, op. cit., p. 82.

– first the United States, and, in Europe, Sweden, followed by England, Holland, and Switzerland – were thus successful in returning to their former gold standard. In certain other countries, especially those where the currency depreciation had been the greatest, stabilisation of the monetary system was reached by means of a financial administration based on the creation of new media of payment, with strict limitation of their quantity, so making it possible to give the currency a new parity with gold. In Germany, where the old mark depreciated to a billionth part of its former value, as a result of the issue of paper currency, the currency was stabilised at this level, and, in so doing, a new unit of account, the Reichsmark, equivalent to the former gold mark, was introduced. In many countries, however, the stabilisation problem remained unsolved for a long time. People dreamed of restoring the old gold parity, but with justice hesitated to undertake the necessary, and often very considerable, restriction of the supply of the means of payment, from which would ensue a fall in the price-level. In the end, people had to be content with a stabilisation which placed the gold parity in the neighbourhood of the actual gold value of the currency in question. The experience gained during this period has demonstrated the absolute and decisive influence which the quantitative factor of the supply of the means of payment has on the value of the currency unit. [1]

[1] For a detailed discussion of these revolutions in the world's monetary systems, the reader is referred to my specialised works, viz.: *The World's Monetary Problems* (two memoranda, London, 1921); *Money and Foreign Exchanges after* 1914 (London and New York, 1922); *Das Stabilisierungsproblem* (Leipzig, 1926); *Post-war Monetary Stabilisation* (New York, 1928); regular articles in the *Quarterly Report of the Skandinaviska Kreditaktiebolaget* (Stockholm), from 1920 onwards.

CHAPTER X

BANK MONEY

§ 43 *The Concentration of Cash Balances in Banks*

MONEY is accepted as a general means of exchange in order to carry out a further exchange. This second exchange transaction may take place a greater or less period of time afterwards. It is not possible to say definitely in advance when the money will be used again as a means of payment. In the meantime, the supply of money forms the *ready cash* of the individual household. In general, every household that is not very poor has at all times a larger or smaller fund of ready cash. The sum total of all the cash reserves in a national economy, at a given moment of time, represents the *demand for money* of the country at that moment. The amount of money demanded depends on the habits of the people, and also on the organisation of the monetary system.

In primitive economies, the money is stored until it has been decided how to use it, either as such or as metal in the form of ornaments. If the money is not required at all for current consumption, this storing of it assumes the character of a treasure hoard. Such hoarded means may, in cases of emergency – such as a bad harvest, as happens periodically in India – be applied for purposes of consumption, or be used for any other special object; Lord Cromer's story of the Egyptian who bought an estate for £25,000 and half an hour later appeared with a string of asses carrying the money, which he had unearthed from his garden, illustrates this aptly. [1]

Under modern conditions, ample opportunities for making safe and profitable capital investments are afforded, even to people who are not themselves entrepreneurs, and the possibility is maintained of

[1] *Annual Report of the Director of the Mint,* 1911 (Washington, 1912), p. 55.

re-converting the capital into money whenever unforeseen circumstances make it essential. This has led everyone who has no special use for his money in the near future to invest it. By this means, the community's demand for money is clearly reduced considerably. Cash balances now consist mainly of those means which are destined to be used in the immediate future for payments, either for capital investments or for consumption by the individual or in the current management of a business.

The course of development, however, shows a progressive diminution even of this demand for money in proportion to the total volume of payments. The endeavour to find profitable employment for the cash funds, which after all represent capital, makes itself increasingly felt, and is reflected in the reduction of the individual's need of cash and in the diminution of the demand for money by the community as a whole. Four stages may be distinguished in this development.

The *first stage* is the concentration of the cash funds of several separate households in a bank. The individual entrusts his cash balances to the bank and withdraws money when he needs it. This concentration of cash balances represents already an important saving of ready money, for, although by the nature of the transaction the balances are repayable on demand, the bank does not need to keep a cash reserve as large as the sum total of private balances entrusted to it. The individual depositors will not all demand the return of their money at the same time. One individual has a payment to make to-day, another has one due to-morrow. It will be some time before a sum equal to that of the balances is paid back, and in the interim, under normal conditions, the bank will have received fresh cash. If there is a large number of depositors, the payments and withdrawals every day will be approximately equal. The bank then will need its cash reserve only in case of any excess withdrawals. The more the payments and withdrawals balance, the smaller will be the average level of the bank's cash reserve in comparison with the deposits of the public. Nevertheless, the bank must always be prepared to meet demands for repayment which may be greater than usual, and hence, usually, its reserve must never fall below a certain level. If it is possible for the bank to keep a cash reserve smaller than the total of the balances deposited with it, then the bank can use a portion of the deposits, and invest them in interest-paying enterprises. The bank will be able to make a profit out of the transaction, and will endeavour to attract as much cash as possible. To this end it may possibly pay interest on deposits, though, naturally, at a relatively low rate. The convenience and security of keeping balances at a bank are often a sufficient inducement to attract deposits. Thus the concentration of individual balances in the banks is in the interest both of the banks and of the public.

As a result of this development the money stock of the national economy is divided into two parts, one of which lies in the banks as a *reserve*, and the other remains in the hands of the public, and is known as the *circulating* volume of money. When the habit of depositing funds with the banks has become widespread, the community will be satisfied with a relatively small quantity of circulating cash, but, in addition, the bank reserve will have to be kept at a certain level. This reserve will be drawn upon as soon as the total demand for circulating money happens to rise above its normal volume. On each of these occasions money will flow out of the reserves into circulation, only to return to the reserves when the demand subsides. The size of the cash balances which must normally be held as reserves will be accordingly determined by the extent of the fluctuations in the community's demand for circulating money.

Nevertheless, as a result of this concentration of cash balances, a considerable reduction in the community's demand for money must on the whole be attained. Looking at it from another standpoint, an increased volume of payments will be effected by means of a given quantity of money. In other words, the concentration of cash balances diminishes the scarcity of money.

We have taken bank deposits into account here only in so far as they represent cash balances repayable on demand. As has been shown, these deposits are received by the banks, partly from business concerns requiring a cash fund for current purposes, which, however, prefer to keep a portion of this fund in a bank, and partly from private persons who have means at their disposal for a short time either for consumption or investment purposes.

The banks also receive deposits of a quite different nature. Sometimes, a man who has saved money entrusts the investment of it to his bank. He lends his savings for a long period to the bank against payment of interest. The bank has then to find an investment for this capital. The finding of suitable investments for the capital of the public is a specialised business, which is undertaken partly by the banks and partly by special institutions set up for that purpose. For small savings, the savings banks are specially indicated. Naturally, besides these main types of deposits, there are also intermediate forms; in these cases, the balances are repayable at short notice and are allowed only a low rate of interest. It is not clear whether they are to be regarded as temporary investment or as so much cash. In a study of the nature of money we must clearly leave out all deposits which represent capital investments, and confine ourselves to pure cash balances, entrusted to the banks on current account.

The second and third stages in the rational utilisation of these balances are reached when cheques are introduced. The bank will then be able to authorise a depositor to use his balance by means of a *cheque*, that is, an order on the bank, payable at sight. In what follows, such balances, which may be drawn upon by cheque, we will for brevity call "deposits." A payment by means of a cheque tranfers to the payee a sight claim on a bank for money. The payee may pass on the cheque to some other person, instead of paying it into a bank, but this use of cheques is not the customary procedure. Here we assume, as is generally the case, that the cheque is used only for a single payment between members of the public.

This payment, however, may be effected in several ways. If the cheque is presented for payment by the payee himself, then, in respect to the payment itself, no essential advance has been made upon the first stage. Payment by cheque is, in this case, no substitute for a money payment. But even then the possibility of being able to pay at any moment by means of a cheque enables the usual cash balance of the depositor to be considerably reduced. When the receiver himself has an account, he may simply let the cheque be placed to his credit. In this connection two cases must be distinguished. The holder of the cheque either has his account at the same bank as the drawer or at another bank. In the first case, there is clearly involved only a transfer in the books of the bank. The payment is effected without the use of cash. This process of transfer, which, if the bank has a network of branches, can be used for payments between different places, and thus greatly facilitates the settlement of accounts, is the *second stage* in the development of the holding of cash balances.

In the second case, however, the bank of the holder of the cheque would have to cash it at the bank of the drawer, and so the payment would have to be effected by using money. This is avoided by the system of compensation between the banks, which is known as the *clearing system*; and this is to be regarded as the *third stage* in the development of the holding of cash balances.

The introduction of cheques, coupled with the development of the clearing system, has enabled the banks to meet the demands of their depositors, mostly without having to pay out cash. Every bank, however, must keep a cash reserve in order to satisfy the demands of its customers for ready money, and also in order to meet any unfavourable balance at the clearing house. These funds must bear a definite relation to the total amount of its deposits.

The *fourth stage* is the concentration of the cash balances of the banks in a central bank. Of course, the banks retain an amount sufficient for their daily needs. Additional cash, needed to serve as a reserve fund for greater security, is deposited with the central bank as a "clearing reserve."

For the clearing system, this means that any differences may be met by transfer from one clearing reserve to another. The stage is then reached when cheque payments between the holders of bank deposits are effected without resorting at all to ready money, and thus no cash reserves need be held for that purpose.

Nevertheless, in order to be able to meet their deposit liabilities at all times in cash, the banks must hold certain reserves in cash. The concentration of part of these cash reserves in a central bank has the same effect as the corresponding concentration of the cash of individuals in the ordinary banks – that is, a saving in the total demand for cash. Probably this saving is relatively smaller, as the cash requirements of the different banks are generally subject to the same influences, both seasonal and cyclical. The demands of the banks for money occur mainly at the same period of time, and the central bank has to meet these demands in full. The periodic compensation of the demands for money of a number of banks will rarely be so complete as the corresponding compensation of the demands for money of a much larger number of bank customers of the most diverse occupations and in the most varied economic circumstances. The central bank is therefore obliged to keep a relatively greater cash reserve against its deposits which can be drawn on by cheque, and it can invest only a relatively small proportion of the funds deposited with it in remunerative transactions. Naturally, the clearing reserves at the central bank do not bear interest.

The process described above is of prime importance with regard to economy in means of payment. As credit balances may be disposed of by means of cheques, and as, therefore, payments may be effected without resorting to cash, the deposits assume the character of independent media of payment, being substitutes for money. The deposits have this character only in so far as they exceed the cash reserve held against them, for the remainder of the deposits merely represent the cash held as reserve. The main point, however, is that, through the use of cheques, certain demands for money payable at sight are used as media of payment, side by side with money, and compete with money, thus reducing the scarcity of the means of payment.

Up to the present, we have so represented matters as if deposits always arose through the public's entrusting its surplus funds of cash to the banks. This, however, is only one side of the process. In practice, deposits are also created and constantly fed by the bank's granting advances to its customers, either by discounting bills or by making loans and then crediting the clients with the amount in their accounts. The difference between these two methods of creating deposits is by no means as great as people seem to imagine, in the lively discussions on the subject. In the first case, the cash flowing into the banks is lent out again, the banks thereby granting new advances. The final result in both cases is that new advances are granted to the public so that its balances, against which cheques may be drawn, rise correspondingly, whilst the supply of circulating money remains unchanged. The crux of the proceeding is, therefore, an increase of deposits whilst the public's supply of cash remains unchanged, and this results in an increase in the total supply of the means of payment. However, as we shall see presently, such an increase in the supply of the means of payment is generally not possible without a corresponding increase in the demand for circulating money. It is the difficulty of satisfying such demands that limits the apparently unrestricted power of the banks to create deposits.

In practice, cash constantly flows into the accounts of depositors, since every business pays all surplus cash into its banking account. On the other hand, cash is always drawn out in such amounts as will meet the needs of trade for such means of payment. Thus constant equilibrium is maintained in supplying a country with the media of payment of the two different kinds. As a result of drawing cheques, deposits are transferred in large quantities to other banks. This may force single banks to place restrictions on their creation of new deposits; but these transfers have no effect on the total sum of deposits, nor on the supply of the means of payment of a country.

Deposits can never completely replace actual cash as means of payment. Even when the use of deposits is highly developed, actual cash is used on a large scale in certain spheres and for certain kinds of payment. The whole of the working-class, the majority of artisans, and also small traders and the large majority of farmers, are as a rule entirely outside the cheque-using public. But the holders of accounts which can be drawn on by cheque also require ready cash to a great extent for their daily personal expenses (in restaurants, theatres, trains, taxi-cabs, etc.).

The quantitative relation existing between deposits and money in a nation's supply of means of payment varies considerably from country to country, and even in any one country is subject in the long run to variations, generally in the direction of extending the use of deposits as media of payment. At any given moment, however, this relation is determined by the habits of the people, and is therefore to be regarded as a fixed quantity. The public will deposit on cheque-account a sum which bears a definite relation to the actually circulating quantity of money, neither more nor less. If, therefore, the banks, through their advances, create a surplus of deposits, they will at once be faced with demands for payment in cash. The ratio of deposits to money is, of course, not absolutely fixed. In certain circumstances the demand for means of payment applies specially to deposits, but in other circumstances the demand applies to money; but even these variations relate to independent causes, which, in the main, are outside the sphere of influence of the banks.

§ 44 *The Limitation of Deposits*

Deposits against which cheques may be drawn are, as we saw, a special medium of payment competing with money. At first sight, it would appear that banks are able to increase these deposits as much as they please. The bank's customers, who wish to extend their businesses and therefore require further means of payment, receive these means in the form of deposits either by discounting their claims on others, or by obtaining advances against securities, or simply on the security of their reputation. As long as the banks grant new loans, new deposits can be created. Such an unlimited creation of means of payment which are used to a great extent in the modern economy, and which are ranked equal to money, must be regarded as impossible. If the price-scale is to have any stability at all, there must be a definite scarcity of the total supply of means of payment, and, hence, of each particular medium of payment. Actually, as has already been emphasised, a medium of payment attains its proper character only by virtue of the way in which its relative scarcity is determined. This applies also to deposits.

The scarcity of this medium of payment is determined by the liability to pay out deposits in cash on demand. In dealing with this question it is better, at first, to leave out those claims to money

which are destined for payments abroad, since international payments are best dealt with as a separate subject (Chapter XII.). We
shall, therefore, not deal with foreign payments, and shall confine
our considerations to "the closed economy."

We have seen that, at every stage in economic development, the
total needs of trade for means of payment are divided in a definite
ratio between money and deposits. With a plentiful supply of means
of payment the demand of trade for circulating money increases,
and this increased demand turns to the cash funds held by the banks.
It follows that banks cannot supply means of payment to traders in
unlimited quantities without being faced with demands for ready
cash.

As long as these demands are confined within narrow limits,
they can be satisfied with the aid of the cash reserves of the banks,
but if the demand for money continues to increase it is clear that
this will become impossible. The banks are therefore compelled to
impose special restrictions upon their activities in connection with
supplying trade with means of payment. On the whole, these
limitations must be of such a nature that the reserves are drawn on
only occasionally; over a long period of time they must remain
largely intact. This results in a certain scarcity of deposits and in a
definite limitation of the supply of means of payment.

As a result of the general restriction of the supply of means of
payment, the demands of trade for cash are perhaps not entirely
prevented, but, still, they are limited to such an extent that they
can be satisfied with the help of the cash reserves of the banks. The
purpose of the total cash reserves of the banks is, therefore, to
satisfy those demands for money which arise even though the terms
on which the banks grant loans result in correctly limiting the
total supply of means of payment. The level of the cash reserves
must be determined with this end in view.

It must be noticed that the community's demand for money is
by no means constant, but undergoes considerable variations from
causes which are beyond the control of the banks. In the first
place, the demand for means of payment rises above its normal
level at certain seasons of the year. For instance, on every quarter

day large sums of money become due. Rents, salaries, interest of all kinds, are then paid on a large scale. Means with which to make these payments must be held ready for some days previously, and it is not until some days after the quarter day that the demand for money sinks to its normal level. In autumn, large sums of money are necessary to pay for the harvest, and similarly for purchases made at Christmas, and for the especially lively tourist traffic which occurs at certain seasons. In the second place, the demand for money is influenced by the state of trade at the time. If boom conditions prevail, an increase in the turnover of the whole economy occurs, and consequently the demand for money is often considerably enhanced. Such a rise also takes place in periods of crisis. As a result of the cessation of buying, anticipated sources of income do not materialise, or, at least, not at the expected time, whilst, on the other hand, means of payment must be held ready in case of unforeseen expenses, such as honouring protested bills.

Under such conditions, everyone will seek to strengthen his cash reserve as much as possible. Thus there arises in times of crisis an abnormal demand for means of payment, which may rise to dizzy heights if it is feared that the banks will soon refuse to grant further advances.

In all such fluctuations in the demand for means of payment, it is a great advantage that deposits can be easily increased by further loans and thus represent a very elastic media of payment. It is neither feasible nor desirable to regulate the supply of means of payment (by varying the terms of bank advances) so strictly that no play is left for independent variations in the demand for money. But, if an increase in deposits takes place, there generally follows a corresponding, though perhaps not strictly proportional, rise in the demand for circulating money. The reserves of the banks must then supply the means necessary to satisfy this demand.

There must, therefore, be present in the national economy a reservoir of cash, out of which trade can draw enough to cover its occasional extra demand for circulating money, and into which money will flow when the demand falls. This purpose is served by the total bank reserves. With this end in view, a minimum level is required in normal conditions for the reserve, determined by the amount by which the maximum demand for cash exceeds the normal demand. This difference is naturally dependent on the regulation of the total supply of means of payment on the part of the banks and, by a suitable strictness in these regulations, may be reduced to a certain minimum.

Naturally the margin within which the amount of circulating money varies widens in direct proportion to this actual quantity of money, and the normal reserve must therefore be regarded as a definite quota of the quantity of money in circulation. As, however, at a given time, this quantity of money bears a definite relation to the total deposits, the normal reserve which is held to cover cash withdrawals of deposits may also be expressed as a ratio of the total deposits. It must be noticed that this ratio becomes progressively smaller the more deposits are used as media of payment in preference to money. In this way, a community in which the use of deposits is highly developed, and in which the actual cash circulation is relatively small, is able to carry on with a relatively small cash backing for deposits, as is shown by English experience.

The means by which the banks succeed in protecting their reserves, and thereby attain a certain scarcity in the supply of the means of payment, are found, as we have seen, in a limitation of the advances, by means of which new deposits are created. Nowadays, however, no large bank – least of all a central bank – will grant advances up to a certain limit and then suddenly refuse its customers any further accommodation. The limitation which may become necessary is enforced rather by means of a suitable tightening-up of the terms for discounts, loans, etc.

Hence the real regulation of the creation of new media of payment in the form of deposits is to be found, not in a rigid restriction of the total amount of advances, but by controlling the conditions on which the banks grant advances. What exactly are the effects of these conditions we shall see later (§§ 46–8). Here it is sufficient to recognise the *fact* that the loan conditions of the banks are the means by which the necessary limitation of the deposits, and thus of the total supply of means of payment, is effected.

The mechanism by which the community's supply of means of payment is regulated is as follows. By means of the conditions on which they will grant loans, the banks largely regulate the total demand for the means of payment, although there remains a margin for independent fluctuations of this demand. The demand for means of payment is distributed in a certain ratio (subject to slight variations) between money and deposits. Thus the quantity of circulating money, as well as that of deposits, is, subject to slight variations, determined by the conditions on which loans are granted. The demand for money which is still possible is met by the money stocks of the banks. The loan terms must be so framed that the reserves are always able to fulfil this function. To this end, the regulation of the supply of deposits to the business community must broadly be made so that business on the whole does not demand repayment of the deposits in cash. Only then will the maintenance of cash payments over a long period of time be made possible.

Thus, through the terms on which they will grant loans, banks are able to impose a certain limitation of deposits which, at first sight, seem to be a medium of payment which can be increased indefinitely, and by this means the banks can maintain the deposits at a certain approximate parity of value with actual money. If this restriction is sufficiently severe, and if, in addition, a sufficient supply of ready cash is kept, it is always possible to satisfy the demands of trade for cash, and thereby to bring about the absolute parity between deposits and money.

In the modern economy, as we have seen, the power of correctly limiting deposits, and thereby of regulating the total supply of the means of payment, is placed in the hands of the directors of the banks. The guarantee that the banks will carry out this task properly is to be found in the fact that it is only in this way that they will be able to fulfil their obligation to redeem the deposits in cash on demand.

One might expect that a function which is of such importance to the community at large would be subject to State supervision.

Against such a legal regulation of reserves which would fix a minimum ratio of reserves to deposits is the fact that these reserves would be immobilised also in the case of an abnormal need and, therefore, their main purpose defeated. In most countries, the State has refrained from imposing such restrictions. The influence in the opposite direction, which originates in the United States and which, in recent years, has grown in strength, hardly appears favourable to a rational regulation of the supply of means of payment.

§ 45 *Bank-notes*

The bank-note is an order for a round sum drawn on a bank, and payable at any time to the bearer. Bank-notes, in so far as they are sight demands for money, are ranked equal to deposits. This comparison is made particularly clear in those cases where the bank-note originally arose from an acknowledgment by a bank of a sum of money deposited with it. Both notes and deposits serve as media of payment, but fulfil this function in somewhat different ways. When payment is made by a bank-note, a money claim on a bank is directly transferred to the payee, whilst the corresponding transfer of a deposit balance postulates the drawing of a cheque. In reality, the process is the same in both cases. The bank-note, however, which itself is the certificate of a money claim, is a means of payment much nearer to actual money than are deposits. A bank-note, like a coin, can effect any number of payments one after the other, whilst payments through the transfer of deposit balances require a new cheque to be drawn each time.

Further, it must be noticed that bank-notes, especially when they have been issued by a large central bank, possess a greater and a more generally recognised security than a cheque. For the security of a cheque depends not only on the bank on which it is drawn, but also necessarily on the drawer. Only he who knows the drawer personally will take the cheque in payment, whilst everyone who has confidence in the bank will accept a bank-note. In the physical sense, the bank-note can circulate quite in the same way as a coin. In this respect, the cheque is inferior to the bank-note.

Further, bank-notes resemble coins, in that they represent round sums, and, therefore, as soon as available in suitable denominations, can be used with advantage for payments of any amount. These two properties – a generally recognised value, and a round sum value – as we know, are those which distinguish minted coins from the raw metal as means of payment, and make them money. These self-same properties enable the bank-note to take over the special money functions of cash.

If the bank-note is issued by a respectable bank, it is willingly accepted by everyone in payment, and thus serves equally with money as a general means of exchange and medium of payment. It is a universally recognised rule of law that a debt is regarded as paid when once payment has taken place in bank-notes. Notes of the central bank are generally even declared legal tender. The bank-note thereby approaches so closely to the conception of money that the general public regard it as such. Only the circumstance that the bank-note is only the certificate of a claim to money prevents us from recognising the bank-note as money. The moment that the obligation of banks to convert their notes into money is suspended, bank notes are transformed into actual money. The country has then a system of paper money, and the inconvertible notes which are now legal tender in this system have a "forced currency." Such bank-notes no longer represent claims to money, but are actual money. It must be noticed however, that as long as there is a prospect of a resumption of cash payments, the notes retain a certain latent character as claims to money.

The circumstance that convertible bank-notes are simply claims to money, and not actual money, has not diminished the practical utility of the legal tender notes of central banks as circulating media of payment. Experience shows that, on account of their convenience, notes are actually preferred by the public, and therefore drive out hard cash as a means of payment. If such a displacement were regarded as undesirable, steps would be taken to set a lower limit to the face value of the notes. Thus, before the war, the Bank of England was not allowed to issue notes of a denomination of less than five pounds, and so gold coins were kept in general circulation.

The German Reichsbank, which formerly was not allowed to issue notes of smaller denomination than one hundred marks, received in 1906 the right to issue notes of fifty and twenty marks, so that the bank was enabled to attract to itself a quantity of gold corresponding to the amount of the note issue, or at least to satisfy in part a rising demand for circulating money by means of these notes. In Sweden, where the Riksbank's notes are issued in denominations down to five kroner (a little more than five shillings), no gold whatever circulates, and the whole stock of gold is concentrated in the Riksbank.

Bank-notes, therefore, fulfil the need for cash balances just as well as actual cash. In this respect, the effect of bank-notes is somewhat different from that of deposits. Deposits replace to a certain extent the private holding of cash balances, whilst, in those private balances that are still necessary, bank-notes replace actual cash. The bank-note is thus suited to satisfy the demand for money which remains after the development of cheque transactions, at least in so far as payments of somewhat large amounts are concerned. How far bank-notes will displace actual cash depends, as we have seen, chiefly on the denominations in which they are issued. If notes are issued, in sufficient quantities, down to the denomination of the smallest gold coin, the whole current circulation may be replaced by notes, so that, finally, only token coins circulate alongside of the notes.

The power of replacement of money by bank-notes is specially significant when it is necessary to deal with fluctuations in the demand for actual cash. As has been mentioned in previous paragraphs, a rising demand for circulating money directs itself to the reserves of the banks, and ultimately to the central bank. This demand may be satisfied by an increased issue of notes, at least to the extent to which notes make up the regular circulation. Generally, when there is an increased demand for money, the relative share of notes in the total circulation rises, so that the abnormal demand may be satisfied to a still greater extent by means of notes. The right to issue notes replaces, to a greater or less extent, the reserve that the central bank must hold against its deposits.

To the extent that bank-notes displace money from the circulation, whether as a result of the issue of notes of smaller denominations or as a result of changes in the habits of the public, the note circulation can be increased without augmenting the total supply of means of payment. If, however, this displacement of money by notes comes to a stop, and money henceforth maintains, on the whole, a fixed relative share of the total circulation, every increase of the notes must produce a corresponding relative rise in the demands of home trade for cash. The effect of an increased note issue is then the same as that of a further creation of deposits.

Actually, notes and deposits together form a group of means of payment that we may suitably call "*bank money*," the common features being that they are created by the banks and supplied to the public, and that their requisite quantitative limitation is determined by the same factors. As we have seen in the case of deposits, this limitation is necessary because any excessive creation of bank money gives rise to demands for cash, which are directed against the reserves of the banks, and these demands can only be prevented in the long run by a suitable moderation in the creation of new bank money.

However, in a country where notes form a relatively large proportion of the total circulation, these demands are fairly small, and they practically disappear completely when notes have totally displaced full-bodied money from circulation. In the closed economy to which our study has hitherto been confined, an indefinite increase in bank money would certainly occasion an increased demand for small token coins, but would not be checked by the demand for standard money. Under a gold standard, however, there is always a demand for gold for non-monetary purposes, and, as a rule, this demand will increase in proportion to the increase in the supply of means of payment, and will be directed at the bank reserves, thus preventing an increase in bank money (see § 50).

The obligation to redeem notes in gold imposes on the banks under all circumstances the necessity for a certain moderation in the creation of bank money, and especially in the issue of notes. This necessity furnishes a guarantee to the community that there will be a suitable restriction in the total supply of the means of payment. If banks were to satisfy demands for media of payment without limit, the total reserves would soon be exhausted, and convertibility could no longer be maintained.

As we have seen in the case of the limitation of deposits, the function of the reserve, given a sufficient restriction of the note issue, is to form a fund capable of satisfying the periodically recurring increase in the needs of trade for money. As far as home trade is concerned, the cash reserve of the central bank does not serve in the main, as is often supposed, for the conversion of the notes or of other daily liabilities, but, rather, it renders possible the extension of these liabilities and thereby the satisfaction of all the legitimate needs for payment of a business activity of a changing volume.

The means for retaining the note circulation, as well as deposits, within suitable limits are given by the conditions under which bank money is supplied to the public. As the banks can only supply their customers with bank money in general, and can exert no influence as to the type of means of payment which is demanded, clearly the conditions are the same for both types of means of payment; therefore, they will be treated together in what follows.

On account of the great importance that the note circulation has for all sections of the population, and in view of the resemblance of bank-notes to actual money, which constantly deceives the average politician, it is easy to understand why the legislature has deeply occupied itself with the regulation of the note issue, whilst, as we have already seen, there has generally been no corresponding regulation of deposits. It must be noticed that the legislature can regulate only the right to issue notes and not the actual note circulation, which will always have to be controlled by the bank itself, according to the economic situation at the moment. We shall now see that the legislature in these endeavours has been unsuccessful, as is often the case in the economic field, in trying to reach the direct realities of life.

In regulating the note issue, either a maximum limit was set to the note circulation, as was formerly the case in France, or, as in most other countries, a direct relationship was established between the total note issue and the reserve. In the latter case, two chief methods have been employed.

The first method, which originated in the regulation of the note issue of the Bank of England, consists in setting a limit to that portion of the notes not covered by the reserve; that is, in the fixing of a certain maximum amount by which the note circulation may exceed the cash reserve. The principle underlying this is that there may be a certain minimum of notes in circulation, without any gold cover, because trade cannot dispense with them, and for the remaining notes there must be a reserve exactly corresponding to the sum needed for their redemption. If the note issue is regulated according to this method, new notes may be issued only to the extent to which the cash reserve increases. The elasticity which the note issue should give to the total supply of means of payment is therefore very limited, and is present only in so far as the right of note issue is not fully made use of. The great disadvantage of this method, that it does not provide the elasticity which is essential in times of crisis, has been overcome in England simply by suspending, when necessary, the relevant clauses of the Bank Act. The pre-war German banking law, which took over the English principle of a fiduciary issue, attained a more regular elasticity of the note circulation, in that, apart from the raising of the fiduciary limit at the quarter days, introduced in 1909, issues in excess of the fiduciary limit were sanctioned on payment of a tax in proportion to the excess note issue. This taxation, although it might have had a certain influence on private banks, probably had no influence on the note-issuing policy of the Reichsbank. Hence the fixing of a fiduciary limit hardly resulted in a real restriction of its notes by the Reichsbank. [1]

The second method of legally regulating the note issue in relation to the reserve consists in fixing a certain percentage cover. This method has also been incorporated in the German banking law – the note circulation must be covered to at least a third by the cash reserve. Such a cover was recognised for a long time by the

---

[1] Cf. the relevant passages in the memorial publication of the Reichsbank (*Die Reichsbank*, 1870–1900, p. 219), where it is said that "the Reichsbank in its discount policy has never let itself be mechanically influenced by the intentions of this system."

private English note-issuing banks as a suitable average, and was endorsed by practical experience. The reserve so calculated is clearly there to be made use of in bad times, either for the conversion of notes or for increasing the note issue beyond that permitted by the normal cover requirements. If, however, the law fixes the cover requirements, then those requirements thereby cease to be a practical rule for the limitation of the note issue. Thus, if the State attempts to fix the normal relation between note issue and reserve, the bank will be prevented from disposing of these reserves, at the very time when they should be put to practical use. If, however, the law fixes a percentage cover which is lower than what may be regarded as normal, it clearly furnishes no guarantee of a sufficient cover in normal times and, perhaps, puts obstacles against a rational employment of the reserve in times of need. In any case, the rule of keeping a cover of one-third has never been, under normal conditions, the guiding principle of the Reichsbank in its note issue, as the bank before the war generally kept a cover in the neighbourhood of two-thirds.

Thus we see that the direct limitation of the note issue lies in no case in the legal prescriptions as to the size of the cash reserve. The banks will always strive after another, and better, reserve proportion, and thereby will take care to be able at all times to comply with the legal provisions, without letting themselves be exclusively guided by this consideration. But even in these endeavours of the banks there is no direct and effective means for regulating the note circulation. No central bank will issue notes up to a certain limit and then turn away any further demands. The real limitation of the note circulation always lies in the concrete conditions under which notes are supplied to trade in general.

In this respect, therefore, notes resemble deposits.

The one-sided interest of the legislature in the maintenance of the reserves gradually led to the reserves being regarded as the principal thing, while the convertibility of the notes which should be guaranteed by the reserves, and the limitation of the note issue which should render convertibility possible, have been accounted only of secondary importance. This view-point found its expression in the idea that in all circumstances a minimum reserve had to be maintained, which could therefore never be made use of. In order to protect the reserves of the central banks, on the outbreak of the war, the obligation of conversion was actually suspended, or other measures having the same effect were introduced. By those means, however, the way was left clear for an unlimited increase in the note issue. In spite of the fact, therefore, that the holding of reserves had failed in its main object, people still sought to retain the reserves and to reinforce them as far as possible. Attempts were made to convert the public to the idea that the reserves still formed a certain "cover" for the notes, and gave them a security which they no longer possessed in a definite limitation of their quantity. In what follows, we shall see that the dishonesty of the official announcement, by which the public, with the aid of a distorted statement regarding prevailing conditions, was deceived, was fatal for the entire European monetary system.

§ 46 *The Cover of Bank Money and its Reflux*

It is of primary importance, with regard to the conditions of the supply of means of payment by the banks, that bank-notes as well as deposits, when they are not simply exchanged against cash or money claims that have fallen due, should come into the possession of the public only in the shape of *advances* made by the banks. This fact is important in connection with the limitation of the supply of means of payment mainly from three different points of view. First, because a regular *reflux of bank money* is set up; secondly, because the *cover for the bank money* is determined through selection of the securities offered for the advances; and thirdly, because the *interest* charged on the advances limits the demand for them, and thereby indirectly limits also the supply of the means of payment. In this section we shall consider the first two of these factors.

When granting advances which serve for the creation of media of payment, emphasis must be laid on the speedy repayment of the advances. Such advances are not willingly made for periods longer than three months. Among central banks the average time in which the securities held have yet to run is kept very short. Such a liquidity of the advances has the result that a large part of them must be repaid each day.

The liquidity is in itself important in so far as it enables the banks quickly to adapt their advances to alterations in the solvency of their customers, to changes in the conditions of the various branches of industry, and also to changes in the quality of the real security offered them. Thus bad investments may be got rid of as quickly as possible, and so the value of the bankers' portfolio is maintained at its highest practical level.

Moreover, a greater liquidity of the assets serves to maintain as great as possible the reflux rapidity of the bank money. The reflux rapidity is of great significance for a well-ordered supply of the means of payment of a community, and thereby also for the preservation of a stable monetary system. Here, two view-points must be considered.

In the first place, a sound supply of the means of payment requires that their amount shall be reduced automatically and as quickly as possible when a falling demand for money occurs. We know already that the demand of the modern community for means of payment is subject to important fluctuations, for example, according to the seasons. A fortuitous increase in the demand for money should be completely satisfied by the banks. As soon, however, as the demand falls off, the bank money so created must be withdrawn as quickly as is practicable. If this is not done, a condition must arise in which the quantity of the bank money outstanding exceeds the real demand for it. Such an unjustified extension of the money supply of the community has always a tendency to depreciate the value of the currency unit, and for this reason should be avoided as much as possible.

In the second place, the regulation of the supply of means of payment by the terms on which banks grant advances becomes effective to the extent that changes in these terms quickly obtain general applicability. If advances are granted only for thirty days, clearly it can take only thirty days before changes in the terms for the total quantity of advances are put into effect. If, instead of this, advances were granted for periods of three months, then the corresponding interval would be three times as long, which would obviously greatly weaken the influence of the banks on the market.

The banks must be able at all times to control the supply of money to trade, and therefore must have adequate opportunity to exert as great an influence as possible on the community's supply of money, by restricting advances. This can occur only through a tightening-up of the terms on which new advances are granted. Such a restriction exerts a sufficiently powerful influence on the total monetary supply only if a relatively large share of the advances outstanding falls due for repayment each day.

The advances, by means of which new bank money is put into circulation, are granted as a rule only against security. These securities form the cover for the bank money. As the maintenance of the requisite liquidity of the claims held by the banks makes it necessary for advances to be granted only for short periods, temporary capital requirements alone can be met by bank advances, while the whole of the demand for permanent capital resources must be excluded. Within the banking profession itself, those concerned do not wish, as a rule, to tie up the resources of the bank for periods longer than three months. This restriction on the nature of the capital requirements which may be met by the creation of bank money results naturally in a certain limitation of the total supply of means of payment.

The securities which are used in such circumstances as cover for the bank money are principally composed of bills and securities serving as collateral for loans.

In its various forms, the *trade bill of exchange*, regarded from an economic point of view, is a promise by the purchaser of a commodity to pay a certain sum of money, the price of the commodity, after a definite period.

The goods are undoubtedly paid for provisionally by the bill. For the time being, therefore, the bill serves as a means of payment, and the possibility of being able to pay with bills temporarily increases the purchasing power of the buyer of the commodities. A promise to pay, however, is in itself no real substitute for a medium of payment. If the seller retains the bill until it falls due, and if the bill is honoured, then the final settlement will take place after all in the usual media of payment. The bill of exchange only postpones this payment, and does not render it superfluous. The employment of bills in this case does not diminish the necessity for media of payment. The same is true when the seller of the commodities does not retain the bill himself, but sells it before maturity to his bank.

The bill may serve as a genuine means of payment when, after endorsement, it is handed on in settlement to other persons. In earlier times this use of the bill was general, and large quantities of bills were in circulation, bearing whole series of endorsements. Now, however, inland bills are mostly used only once in payment. If they are not retained by the receiver of the payment, they are sold as claims to money, but are generally not employed as media of payment. In the sphere of international payments, the bill is still widely used as a means of payment. We shall deal in a later chapter with the case of payments by means of foreign bills. At present, we are concerned with explaining theoretically the internal supply of the means of payment of a national economy, and shall ignore the employment of a bill as a means of payment; and assume that it serves as payment only on its creation.

What principally causes the bill to be less suitable as a means of payment is that it is payable not on sight, but only after a certain time. In this respect, the bill differs essentially from bank-notes and deposits, which while being equally claims to money, are due at all times. As a result of this disadvantage bills are exchanged against these particular means of payment or against money. This takes place when the bill is *discounted*, that is, when it is sold to a discounter, who charges the discount to compensate himself for the loss of interest suffered from the day of purchase till the day the bill falls due. The amount charged as discount corresponds to the difference in value between a sight claim and a claim to the same amount which falls due only after a certain time.

From an economic standpoint, the discounting of a bill amounts to a loan to the person who draws the bill. The discounter normally supplies the purchaser of a commodity with the capital resources which he requires for the period that he must keep the commodities in his business. In a certain sense, the commodities can be regarded as real security for the bill. Normally, therefore, the sum total of bills in circulation is covered by a quantity of goods in various stages of production. However, there can be no talk of an exact correspondence between the time that a commodity remains in the process of production in the purchaser's business and the currency of the bill he has accepted. For instance, though the currency of the bill may be three months, the process of manufacture or of sale may take four months. Thus, clearly, the total value of commodities in the process of manufacture is greater than the value of bills then outstanding. This means that industry itself possesses part of the capital resources necessary for its circulating capital, and has only to procure part of it by discounting bills. But it may happen that the average currency of the bills of a concern is greater than the average period of production of that concern. If, for example, the currency of the bills is three months, but the commodities, which are sold for bills, are, on the average, produced and sold in a month and a half, the total of bills outstanding is obviously double that of the total market value of the commodities which have been bought by bills. In this case, industry has acquired capital resources through discounting, not only for its circulating capital, but also for a part of its fixed capital. It is, therefore, not quite accurate to maintain that the total bills in circulation are completely covered by circulating capital used in the process of production; but in normal conditions it is approximately true. There is no doubt, however, that the total circulating capital of a community is much greater than the total value of bills concurrently in circulation.

As bank money is covered by bills, which themselves are covered by circulating capital, the real cover of bank money consists of circulating capital. From this point of view, bank money is to be regarded as claims on the circulating capital of the community. This renders bank money especially suitable as a means of payment. For by far the greatest employment of the means of payment consists precisely in payments for circulating capital, advancing in the process of production towards the consumer. When this circulating capital is bought with bank money, this merely signifies that a general claim on the circulating capital of the community has materialised in a concrete form. The seller who accepts the bank money in payment employs it when necessary in redeeming bills, and in this way bank money returns to the banks.

The covering of bank money by circulating capital is also important, because in this way the community's supply of money is adapted to the changing volume of production. When bank money is exclusively covered by short-term bills, this adjustment of the supply of means of payment to the actual volume of production, and consequently to the actual demand for money, is very effective·

Genuine commercial bills, which represent circulating capital in the process of production, supply the banks with a particularly suitable cover for the bank money outstanding. This is not because commercial bills represent a better security than sound Government stock or similar gilt-edged securities, but because the discharge of a commercial bill belongs, so to speak, to the normal course of the process of production. The process of production itself provides, normally, the means for settling those bills which are covered by the commodities worked-up in the process. Hence, when the banks seek the settlement of the bills which they hold, they need not necessarily exert a disturbing influence on the normal life of the community.

Besides commercial bills, *loans* come into consideration as cover for bank money. The pledge for the loan may consist partly of goods and partly of securities. In the first case, the real backing for bank money consists of circulating real capital. In the second case, the nature of the real cover of the bank money depends on the nature of the securities. These may be mortgages, shares, etc., representing fixed capital. This fixed capital must then be regarded as the real cover for bank money. If, however, the security for the loan consists of Government stocks or similar securities without real cover, there is no material cover for the bank money.

As a rule, only such commodities and securities as are dealt in on the Stock Exchange are used as cover for bank money. Stock Exchange transactions result in the mobilisation of a type of capital which is not mobile in itself – that is to say, which may not be transferred in the normal course of the productive process. This mobilisation naturally increases to a great extent the suitability of the type of capital in question as cover for bank money. It means that, in normal conditions at least, the pledge may be sold at any time. As, in the case of loans granted against securities, the pledges are valued at a rate appreciably under that of the daily Stock Exchange quotation, it may be taken that claims for pledged loans are exceptionally suited to act as cover for bank money. However, it must be remembered that the normal course of the process of production does not guarantee in itself the repayment of these loans against pledges. Hence, when, in certain circumstances, banks are compelled to assert their loan claims by a forced realisation of the pledges, this is often impossible without producing disturbing influences which may become particularly harmful to the community in times of crisis, and, therefore, should be avoided by the banks as much as possible. In this respect, loans on pledges are greatly inferior to good commercial bills as a cover for bank money.

From the aspect of the monetary supply of the community, it may be justifiable to a certain extent for bank money to be covered by pledged securities, and therefore ultimately by fixed capital. For bank money is also used, to a certain degree, for the purchase of securities and fixed capital. As, however, this employment of bank money is of much less significance than its employment in the purchase of circulating capital, it is probably in the interest of a proper regulation of the monetary supply that the pledged securities should not be ranked equal to bills as cover for bank money. For example, covering a note issue by pledged securities should not be permitted, and the rate of interest on advances should be regularly kept above the discount rate. This side of the problem of suitable cover is often overlooked when people wonder why the banks, when seeking to find cover for their notes and deposits, give preference to the bills of a small trader or manufacturer over the much better security afforded by the debentures or shares of large concerns, or even over bonds issued by powerful States. The banks' action in covering the money they create should not only provide security, but the nature of the cover required should, incidentally, provide a natural general limitation of the supply of means of payment. The total production of a community, but not the total wealth of a community, is suitable as a general limitation of this kind; the supply of commercial bills is suitable, but the supply of securities is not, because these represent fixed capital or mere promises to pay. The consequences of this are by no means generally followed up. Thus, in the case of England, where the employment of bills originated, we find that claims against loans play an important rôle as cover for bank money, especially in the case of the Bank of England.

In no circumstances, however, could a sufficiently strict limitation of the supply of means of payment be attained merely through the nature of the claims used as cover. As a rule, the bill circulation is probably considerably greater than the demand for media of payment. The total amount of circulating capital is even greater, and might therefore serve as cover for a still more extensive bill circulation. The aggregate value of securities pledged is naturally many times greater than the bill circulation. The actual circulation of bank money at a given moment corresponds only to a small fraction of the securities which might be used for issuing bank money.

§ 47 *The Limitation of the Supply of Money through the Rate of Interest*

The fact that trade obtains bank money only in the form or interest-bearing advances by the banks is significant for the limitation of the supply of money in so far as, in such circumstances, only that amount of bank money can be put in circulation which corresponds to the needs of trade for advances. A bank, therefore, cannot force its notes and deposits upon trade; so the relation of the bank to the public is different from that of the State, which pays for goods or services by means of inconvertible paper money specially created for the purpose. The public can always rid itself of superfluous bank money by depositing its balances with the banks at interest, or it may pay off its maturing debts to the bank without taking up advances to the same amount. A certain limitation of notes and deposits is provided for by the manner of their origin, as described above. It would, however, be too precipitate to draw the conclusion from this that it is impossible for banks to issue too much money.

The demand of trade for bank advances depends to a great extent on the rate of interest charged for these advances. The rights to command capital are bought and sold on the capital market, as we already know. These rights are at first supplied and demanded in the shape of money, and therefore the immediate object of the capital market is the control over money. As, however, banks can, within certain limits, create constantly maturing money-claims on themselves to any amount, the objectively determined scarcity of command over capital on the market is destroyed.

In general, the capital market is controlled by the rate of interest. If the rate is kept too low, the demand for capital will exceed the supply, and a scarcity of capital-disposal will arise, which will cause the rate of interest to rise again. This normal self-regulation of the capital market is disturbed by the intrusion of the banks with their supplies of bank money. If the banks maintain a rate of interest for their advances that is too low, and if the equilibrium of the capital market is thereby disturbed, this equilibrium may be restored simply by creating new bank money. As long as the scarcity of capital-disposal is relieved in this way, a rate of interest can be maintained that is too low and that does not tally with the real situation of the capital market.

Such conduct on the part of the banks must, if persisted in, extend its effect into the whole capital market. It is true, however, that the immediate interference of the banks is confined to the short-loan market. If the demand for short-period advances is amply satisfied, the result is usually that the supply of capital furnished by the public is diverted to a greater extent to the market for long-period or permanent capital-disposal, and this will express itself in a keen demand for mortgage securities and shares. Such a demand must result in depressing the rate of interest for the capital-disposal in question. The banks' low rate of interest will thus influence the whole capital market, and will have the same effect as if a genuine increase in the supply of capital had occurred.

The result of such conduct on the part of the banks will clearly be the creation of an artificial purchasing power, which does not correspond to any increase in commodities that may be purchased. A rise in prices must be caused thereby, and this means a reduction in the purchasing power of the unit of account. A position of equilibrium requires a definite restriction of the supply of means of payment, and this restriction can only be brought about by means of an interest-rate policy which is a true reflection of the real scarcity of capital.

A falsification of the capital market's situation through too low a rate of interest cannot arise without a reaction setting in. The appearance of counteracting forces is the necessary stipulation for any sort of stability of industrial life. In this case, the reaction is to be found essentially in the sphere of production. It is the function of the rate of interest to bring the demand for new capital-disposal into harmony with the supply – that is, with the newly-saved capital. As, however, the rate of interest has, as a rule, little influence on saving, its rôle as regulator of the capital market consists primarily in the correct restriction of the demand for capital-disposal – that is to say, in directing the process of production. If the market rate of interest is kept too low, the mistake will reveal itself in a relatively increased production of capital. Such an abnormal increase of the production of capital must gradually restrict the possibilities of remunerative employment of capital, and thus render new capital investments less profitable. Under normal conditions, this should bring about a fall in the rate of interest. However, when the rate of interest is already too low, the effect of the increased production of capital is to bring the situation of the capital market gradually into correspondence with the prevailing low rate of interest. But thereby the capital market is once more brought into a position of equilibrium. The disturbing influence of the banks' rate of interest ceases after this rate of interest becomes the normal rate. At the same time, the special competitive power on the capital market, which the banks have acquired by their low rate of interest, comes to an end, and the causes of the abnormal increase of bank money are removed. Only if the banks fix their rate once more below that of the capital market can this increase in their money be continued. The artificial reduction of the interest-rate has, then, led to an artificially reinforced capital production, which is tantamount to a forced increase in the national savings. This is a reminder that one can speak of "too low a rate of interest" only in relation to the prevailing situation of the capital market.

We find, therefore, that excessive reduction of the rate of interest on the part of the banks brings with it an increase in bank money. Conversely, a rise in the rate which is not warranted by the situation of the capital market must result in a reduction of the circulation of bank money. Savings from income which are present in bank money flow into the banks, attracted by the high rate of interest, and are used by them merely to reduce the total amount of bank money. From this we may conclude that it must be possible to regulate the supply of means of payment through the rate of interest. Given a suitable interest-rate policy on the part of the banks, any desired limitation of bank money can be attained.

Under a gold standard, the creation of bank money is, as already seen, set an upper limit by the obligation of conversion. This conversion is, however, only to be regarded as a last resort for limiting an excessive amount of bank money. Normally, the supply of bank money to trade is regulated only by the banks' rate of interest.

In a country where the central bank issues notes with a forced currency, the quantity of notes may be increased indefinitely and, if all metallic money is abolished, may also be diminished indefinitely. The central bank in this case can regulate at will the supply of its notes, and thereby, indirectly, the total supply of the means of payment.

Of course, every important alteration in the supply of money takes a certain amount of time. The result of the rate of interest policy on the quantity of means of payment can only gradually take effect, but any desired effect can be attained. This assumes that the banks retain full control over their grants of advances and over their interest policy. If the State makes some sort of claim on the banks which cannot be rejected, then the problem ceases to be one of purely monetary policy.

The question then arises: How shall the banks' interest-rate be fixed when it is desired to maintain a position of equilibrium? It could be replied that the bank-rate shall equal the real rate of interest on capital. It must, however, be noticed that a "real rate" in a sense other than that of the market rate is a very unreliable indicator for the banks' interest policy, since the market is, as already shown, directly and powerfully influenced by the banks' interest-rate.

The general answer to our question can only be that the banks at all times may increase their advances only to the extent which corresponds to the total of the savings which at that time have been placed at their disposal. If advances are increased still further, the increase can only take place by means of an increase in bank money. Such an increase is permissible to the extent that the general progress of industry means a greater demand for money, but otherwise the increase amounts to an unjustified creation of artificial purchasing power, which will depreciate the value of the unit of account.

In practice, the bank-rate, under a gold standard, is regulated mainly to protect reserves. The interest policy of the banks is then completely determined with reference to the maintenance of the gold standard. Where the gold standard has been thrown over and the notes of the central bank circulate with forced currency, the guiding principles for the interest policy are generally sought for in the maintenance of a definite relation between the domestic currency and the gold coinage of foreign countries. In both cases, the interest policy is set the task of maintaining the price of gold within certain limits. Naturally, this is possible only if the prices of commodities in general can be maintained at a certain level. It is also obvious that, in the last resort, the interest policy of the banks signifies a regulation of the general price-level. This connection, however, can only be explained by means of a theory of the value of money, to which we shall proceed in the following chapter.

§ 48 *The Significance of the Means of Payment in regard to the Utilisation of Income*

In § 8 we defined money income as being the remuneration, reckoned in money, which the individual receives for his contribution to the process of production. As we then ignored the existence of media of payment, we came to the conclusion that every item of income that the community receives is, right from the time of its creation, invested in real capital, and that for every period of time the total money income of society amounts exactly to the sum needed to purchase the total production in that period.

But when we have taken into account the use of media of payment, we are faced by the question of what is the significance of the existence of media of payment in regard to the utilisation of income. On that account we must investigate thoroughly whether and to what extent our earlier conclusions regarding the utilisation of income must be modified. It is at once obvious that income may either be drawn in media of payment or may later be exchanged against them. Income may therefore be used to acquire media of payment, or, in other words, may be invested in media of payment. This conception approaches the one which holds that income thereby loses its property of acting as purchasing power for goods. This conception is very widespread, and the most far-reaching conclusions have been drawn from it. Especially in America, the supposed existence of unused income has, in a dilettante fashion, been made the starting point not only for most questionable theoretical speculations, but also for far-reaching practical demands relating to industrial and monetary policy. Similar points of view are continually expressed in the writings of the financial Press throughout the world.

It is therefore necessary to examine further the question of the utilisation of income. If *A* invests his income in media of payment, and thereby increases his cash balance, this arises from his selling a commodity to *B*, whereby *B*, being a buyer, naturally diminishes his cash balance correspondingly. It is true that *A* has invested his income in media of payment, but at the same time *B* has realised his investment in media of payment, and by doing so has rendered possible the purchase of the commodity. The employment of media of payment signifies not only that a part of income may be invested in them and so withdrawn from purchasing goods, but also that already existing cash funds appear, together with the newly-formed income, as a demand for goods. These remarks should be sufficient to dispel the most elementary misconceptions concerning the effect of investing income in media of payment.

If we survey a definite short income period, we find that the exchange economy at the end of the period has a certain amount of income bound up in media of payment. Normally, this amount is approximately the same as at the beginning of the income period. At the outset we may assume that this is exactly the case, that is, that the supply of the media of payment of the exchange economy has remained unaltered. If a certain part of the income arising during that period is invested in media of payment at the end of the period, and thus loses its purchasing power in respect of commodities, then, on the other hand, a corresponding purchasing power, which at the beginning of the period was tied up in media of payment, is now set free, and so the sales of goods are able to attain the same proportions as they would have done if no income during the period had served to acquire means of payment, but the total income had come forward as purchasing power for commodities. In itself, therefore, the investment of income in media of payment means no diminution of active purchasing power, and does not invalidate our general principle, that in every period the total income of an exchange economy exactly suffices to purchase the total output of production.

In a progressive economy the demand for money normally increases at the same rate as the general progress of the community. This increasing demand is satisfied by the creation of new media of payment. During such a constant expansion of the monetary supply, portions of income are constantly invested in the newly created media of payment. On the other hand, however, means of payment are also created which represent a corresponding amount of active purchasing power. When, for example, a central bank increases its note circulation by means of an increased discounting of trade bills, these new notes represent for the first holder a cash fund for the time being. As long as this fund is not utilised, the note issue has clearly no effect on the sale of goods. It only serves to satisfy an increased demand for cash balances. If a certain commodity is bought with these notes, then the seller has invested a certain amount of income in bank-notes, and has withdrawn some purchasing power over goods for the present. For this the newly-created notes themselves have exercised a corresponding purchasing power. The sale of output has at no moment been hindered by the increase in the holding of money. Also, in a seasonal increase of the demand for money, such an increase in the supply of money may take place, and so portions of income may be invested in increased cash funds without the total sale of the output of production being thereby affected.

The condition is only that the supply of means of payment is widened in accordance with the increased demand. The same holds true when the increase in the need for means of payment is due to an inclination of the savers to postpone the investment of their savings and, therefore, to keep them in the form of money until a later period. If only the supply of means of payment is correspondingly widened, the total output of production can be sold in any income period.

It must, however, be noted that changes may take place in the supply of means of payment as well as in the demand for them. Such changes will increase or diminish the active purchasing power which is exercised during a given period, and thus the amount of this purchasing power may differ from the money income flowing in during the period. In such circumstances there is no reason for expecting the money income and the real income to correspond exactly to each other. This lack of agreement is, in this case, to be ascribed to changes in the relation between the supply of and the demand for means of payment, that is, a purely monetary phenomenon. This conclusion is important, because it dispels, once and for all, the general conception, according to which such disturbances in the normal flow of real income are to be ascribed to deeply rooted faults in the whole economic and legal organisation of our present society. It is also important because it points the way towards a full explanation of the disturbances in question, and to the method by which they could be completely avoided. Two chief cases of such disturbances must now be examined.

First, let us consider the case where an abnormally increased supply of means of payment creates extra purchasing power, which, in accordance with the findings of the foregoing pages, must cause a rise in commodity prices. Equilibrium will be brought about, as we have found, by the fact that the results of production in a period are no longer bought entirely by the money income, but also in part by the newly created means of payment. In this case, the money income does not suffice to purchase the whole of the real income.

The contrary case is that where the supply of media of payment is reduced through debts being repaid to the banks, thus causing commodity prices to fall. A part of the money income will therefore be used in repaying these debts, and is not available as purchasing power for goods. Only the remainder buys the real income, which is, of course, only possible if prices are lowered.

An excess of means of payment can also arise when an abnormal fall in the demand for them is not accompanied by a corresponding reduction in the supply. The results will be the same as they were in our first principal case. On the other hand, a scarcity of means of payment can be caused by an abnormal rise in the demand for means of payment which is not met by any corresponding increase in the supply. In this case, the same consequences will ensue as in our second principal case.

According to this plan, we may form an estimate of the various disturbances which happen in actual practice, in that the active purchasing power will deviate from the total money income as a result of alterations in the relative supply of means of payment.

The widespread view that the money income does not suffice to purchase the total results of production during an income period, and that this is the general cause of reductions in turnover and thus of unemployment, is based, in reality, if it has any justification at all, on the consideration of a state of affairs which corresponds to our second principal case. In an economic depression, entrepreneurs will repay their debts to the banks, and for this purpose will use bank-notes or will draw cheques on their bank accounts; in this way, the supply of means of payment will be reduced. Consequently, commodity prices will begin to fall. The recipients of income will then adopt a policy of holding back their money. They reduce their outlay in the hope of having the opportunity later on of buying more cheaply, and they tend, for the time being, to keep their savings in money form, as they fear that, on account of a continued fall in prices, any real investment will result in losses. Thus at the same time as the supply of money is reduced the demand for money increases. There arises a scarcity in the supply of money, which exerts a pressure on the prices of commodities. The banks usually try to reduce this pressure by creating more money by means of a more liberal credit policy. However, as long as they do not perform this task with sufficient energy, or if they proceed at too slow a rate, the fall in prices will continue. Confidence cannot be restored; the depression, with its accompanying phenonema of reduced turnover and unemployment, deepens. The view becomes general that this is all due to deep-seated defects in our economic and legal organisation, which cause purchasing power to lag behind productive capacity. In reality, the fall in the general price-level which plays the central part in the whole process is a purely monetary phenomenon due solely to an insufficient supply of money. If the banks were only to increase the supply of money sufficiently through issuing more notes and creating more cheque means of payment, then they would be able to prevent a fall in the general price-level. It would then be far easier to overcome the remaining difficulties and to restore confidence once more. But we can never hope for such a rational bank policy as long as the misconception prevails that it is inherent in our economic system for purchasing power to be insufficient to purchase the total production.

The popular conception that saving is carried too far and that the complete sale of the results of production is prevented by an "under-consumption" can now be fully explained. If we assume the supply of money to be normal, such a result is impossible. Under this assumption the total money income always purchases the total real income; only it is divided into two parts, one of which buys consumption goods and the other capital goods. The theory of "over-saving" assumes, in its more elaborate form, that the savers do not invest their savings for some reason or another, so that the active purchasing power is thus reduced and the complete sale of the results of production is rendered impossible, with the result that saving beyond a certain limit does not give rise to any commodity production, but that it simply disappears as income. In this representation of the case, one overlooks the fact that the increased demand for money should be satisfied under an enlightened banking policy. Then there would be no reduction in active purchasing power, and the act of saving need not result in reduced sales or falls in prices.

The developments here considered are essentially a result of a supply of money that is too small, and to that extent are monetary phenomena. From a practical point of view, it must be emphasised that the supposed attitude of the saver is usually occasioned by a general fall in prices which could have been prevented by an extension of credit if carried out early enough. Complaints about excessive habits of saving are in such circumstances calculated to confuse the mind of the public and to distract attention from the shortcomings of monetary policy.

CHAPTER XI

THE VALUE OF MONEY

§ 49 *Introduction*

OUR study of money has shown that the scale in which all prices are reckoned, and which in itself is an abstract scale of reckoning, can possess stability only when there is a certain scarcity of the media of payment valid in the price-scale. If media of payment were available in unlimited quantities, any price could be offered for goods and services. A certain quantitative limitation of the supply of the media of payment is the indispensable condition of a stable price-system – that is, a definite equilibrium between money and commodities. It is also clear that the quantity of money must exert a certain effect on the price-system, in the direction of a greater monetary supply having a tendency to force prices to a higher level. With a greater supply of money one receives less for the unit of money. The *value of money* is lower.

The scarcity of the supply of money, which is necessary for the maintenance of a stable value of money, naturally applies to the whole supply of the means of payment. For money to have a stable value, there must be not only a definite scarcity of money in the narrow sense, but also of other means of payment which, although not money, can be used for payment of sums reckoned in money; and the value of money must be dependent to a certain extent on the quantitative limitation of all these means of payment. Actually, every means of payment, as we have found, is primarily distinguished by the characteristic limitation of its quantity. In the two preceding chapters we have seen the special way in which the limitation is applied to metallic money, paper money, and bank money. In the study of the individual forms of money, as well as that of means of payment which are not money, this factor limiting the supply of the means of payment came always to the forefront. Then, however, we could consider this limitation only as a necessary condition of a stable value of money, and we had to leave for the time being its effect on the value of money – that is, of the quantitative dependence of the value of money on its quantity. What remains now to bring our description of the monetary system to a logical conclusion, and thereby to attain a sound theory of money, is a detailed examination of the connection between the value and quantity of money.

As the value of money, to be stable, requires a definite restriction of the supply of the means of payment, every increase in a means of payment which takes place without a corresponding driving-out of other means, must exert an influence on the value of money. An inquiry into the value of money must therefore take account of the total supply of means of payment. Hence it is not possible, as is so often attempted, to treat means of payment which are not money apart from the treatment of money. The central point of the study of money, the problem of the value of money, can be completely examined and answered only if account is taken of all means of payment which are actually used for payment in the respective price-scale.

It must have been observed at an early date that an increase in the media of payment brings about a general rise of prices – that is, a falling value of money. After the discovery of America the European stock of the precious metals increased to such an extent that the resulting rise in prices must be noticed and ascribed to the proper causes. The history of earlier paper currencies was especially suited to make clear the fact that an unlimited increase in a means of payment must lead to an unlimited rise in the price-level, and thereby to a depreciation of money to the point of complete worthlessness. In the so-called bank-restriction period in England, at the time of the Napoleonic Wars, when the notes of the Bank of England had forced currency, there was finally shown, after much dispute, the nature of the effect which an arbitrary increase of banknotes exerts on the monetary system, and especially on the value of money. From this time a real theory of money began to develop.

In the centre of these theories there are always found inquiries into the connection between the quantity and the value of money, and in this respect scientific thought has come to fairly definite conclusions. How little, however, the scientific view on this connection was accepted by the general public, and in particular by political leaders, not to speak of the directors of the central banks, was clearly shown after the outbreak of the Great War. Official pronouncements sought to maintain as long as possible the fiction that, in spite of any increase in the means of payment, the currency unit remained unaltered. The eyes of the public were opened only by the unfortunate experiences of those countries where the supply of money was at last increased a million- and even a billionfold and where the value of money fell correspondingly, and this catastrophe finally caused the point of view advocated by science to be accepted. This success, however, is not complete, for in countries with moderate currency depreciation the old misconceptions are still sought to be maintained.

It is clear that scientific analysis cannot content itself with the fact of a connection between the quantity and value of money and with the truism that a certain value of money postulates a definite limitation of the supply of money. Therefore, we must attempt to express numerically the effect of the quantity of money on its value – that is, to express arithmetically the value of money as a function of its quantity. To this end a clear definition of the value of money is especially needed.

The concept of the value of money, like the concept of value in general, is not fixed. However, the concept of value could, in so far as it is a question of goods and services, be replaced by the exactly determined concept of price. This method of fixing the concept of value is not possible in the case of the value of money, for, as prices are measured in the unit of currency, the price of the unit of currency is always equal to one, and so the value of money is always formally constant. An idea of the value of the money of a country may be obtained when it is measured in another currency. The value of the money is then clearly seen to be determined by the quantity of goods or commodities which may be obtained for it. The unit of currency represents a greater or less quantity of goods according to whether prices are low or high.

These reflections show the way that must be taken to attain a clear idea of the value of money in a closed economy. A falling value of money expresses itself in a general rise in commodity prices. We have, then, simply to define the value of money as the reciprocal of the general price-level. Of course, the problem of defining the value of money is not yet completely solved, for there always remains the difficult question of how the general level of prices is to be defined in order to reflect as truly as possible general movements of prices. We shall deal with this problem more closely later on (§ 52), but will presuppose at present the concept of the general price-level as being already known. The whole theory of the value of money then reduces itself to a theory of the changes in the general price-level.

§ 50 *The Quantity Theory of Money*

It was natural to suppose that money, as such, has no other task than to purchase commodities or to make general payments, and that for this task any given quantity of money must suffice if only prices stand at a suitable level. This conception is expressed in the *quantity theory*. In its primitive form, the theory is reduced to the statement that money buys commodities. The total quantity of money buys the total quantity of goods. The total value of money equals the total value of commodities, and is thus independent of the quantity of money. From this it follows that the value of the unit of money is inversely proportional to the quantity of money. This is the substance of the quantity theory of money as it is repeatedly given in the older economic literature.

It is, however, easy to understand that an exchange between all commodities on the one hand and all the money on the other hand cannot be taken as given. The quantity theory has therefore been more exactly formulated in the proposition that the general price-level is determined by the relation between the money in circulation and the commodities which come upon the market. Money and goods have an influence on each other only when they come into contact. Let T be the total quantity of goods on the market, P the general level of prices, and M the quantity of circulating money; then the quantity theory may be expressed by the formula:

$$PT = M.$$

It must be specially noted that this proposition relates to a *given point of time*. The quantity of commodities and the quantity of money are two conceptions which contain no time element, and may therefore be thought of only at a given moment. If, however, the conception is strictly confined to a given moment, one cannot explain why the money should purchase the total quantity of commodities. The process under which this purchase is completed takes time. If one wants to take account of the result of this process, it is obviously necessary to base the inquiry on a definite *period of time*. The commodities which are sold within this period must be paid for with the money in circulation during the period. This alteration of the proposition brings a new difficulty into the problem. As soon as one considers a period of time, the possibility is always present that in this period several payments will be made by one and the same coin. The volume of payments is no longer measured by the quantity of money alone, but also with reference to the number of payments made in the period by each unit of money. This brings one to the concept of the *velocity of circulation* of money. In order to give a definite meaning to this concept we may assume that each piece of money makes the same number of payments within the period. Let V be the number of payments which are made by each piece within the period, and let T be the quantity of commodities which are sold within the period; then the quantity theory would be expressed in the formula:

$$PT = MV.$$

This equation, which must be applied to the total of all payments (and not only of commodity payments), and in which T is to be taken as a measure of the real turnover, states that the volume of payments which have to be made within a certain period is equal to the volume of payments which can be made with the given quantity of money within the period.

Clearly, one cannot generally assume such an absolutely uniform utilisation of all the pieces of money. The payments made by the total quantity of money are in reality equal to the sum of the payments made by the individual pieces of money, the payments effected by an individual piece of money being determined by the product of its nominal value and the number of times it effects payments within the period. Let m stand for the nominal value of the single piece of money, and v for the number of payments effected by it. Then the total payments effected is given by the expression Σmv. The average velocity of circulation of money can be rendered by the equation $V = \dfrac{\Sigma mv}{M}$, that is, by dividing the total of the payments effected by the quantity of money. This, however, presupposes that the quantity of money remains unaltered within the given period. For one must note that the payments made by the total quantity of money refer to a definite period, whilst the quantity of money must be taken to refer to a given moment. A comparison of these two quantities must tacitly assume that the quantity of money remains unaltered during the whole period. If (as in reality) this is not the case, the average velocity of circulation of money can be defined only by taking, instead of the real period, a fictitious one in which all conditions remain constant and in which the payments within the period may be compared with the quantity of money at the commencement of the period. The quotient obviously gives the average velocity of circulation at the beginning of the period.

The velocity of circulation of money is to a certain extent an independent factor of the pricing problem. The frequency with which a coin is used in payment within a given period depends on the habits of the people regarding the holding of cash balances, on the degree of development of the exchange economy, on the density of the population, on the development of the transport system, etc.; in sum, on the factors which, in the theory of money, have to be taken as given. This, of course, does not exclude the possibility that changes in the general price-level or in the quantity of money may have a certain influence on the velocity of circulation of money. When this velocity is represented as an independent factor, this only signifies that it has independent causes outside the pricing problem.

The substance of the quantity theory is always that the actual quantity of money will occasion a certain number of payments and that the price-level is forced to adapt itself to it. In the primitive quantity theory, this point of view is expressed in the proposition that the total quantity of money in existence must buy the total quantity of goods. In later forms of the quantity theory, this proposition is modified by the assumption that the velocity of circulation of money remains constant. This means that in the unit period there must be a definite volume of payments determined by the quantity of money. It is of the essence of the quantity theory to attempt to make changes in the general price-level dependent on changes in the quantity of money.

If, however, the quantity of money is taken as an independent factor in the determination of prices, it is naturally necessary to take the quantity of money itself as determined by objective factors, lying outside the determination of prices, or at least as equally determined by these external factors. The problem of finding the determining factors of the general price-level or of the value of money is, of course, not solved until one has got down to factors which themselves may be regarded as objectively given.

With reference to the quantity of money, it must be noted in this connection that the quantity theory ascribes to the *circulating* quantity of money alone the rôle of exerting an influence on the fixing of prices. This circulating quantity of money is, however, not independently determined, since it is never definitely distinguished from the quantity of money lying in the reserves of the banks or from any hoards of money in private hands. The money goes into circulation from the reserve stocks, and, conversely, according to the daily needs of trade. The statement, then, that the circulating quantity of money determines the general price-level is, in such circumstances, devoid of any meaning. Rather, the general price-level is one of the factors which determined the actual circulating quantity of money To that extent the quantity theory leaves the problem of the determining factors of the value of money still unanswered.

If it is wished to ascribe changes in the general price-level to objectively given factors, the general price-level must be linked up with the *total* quantity of money. This can be done if, in the equation $PT = MV$, M represents the total quantity of money, whilst V represents the velocity of circulation of this quantity of money – that is, the average amount of payments effected in the period by each unit of the total quantity of money. If two cases are compared in which the payments effected by a given quantity of money are the same, and where the volume of the real turnover T is also equal, then the general price-level P is directly proportional to the quantity of money M.

This proposition is of definite significance as long as the total supply of money can be taken as a given quantity. This is the case with a paper currency, where the State has fixed the amount of the paper money. If the paper money is issued in the form of bank-notes with forced currency, then, as we found in our inquiry into bank-notes (§ 45), the direct effective limitation of paper money is found in the credit terms of the banks. Here, at any rate, we strike upon an objective factor which can be considered as a cause determining the value of money. If all independent limitations on the issue of paper money cease, the determination of prices becomes an entirely vague problem, and, as painful experience shows, prices can rise indefinitely.

On a gold standard, conditions are different. Even the total quantity of money is then no independent factor of the problem. For the quantity of money is not separated from the total supply of gold, but rather does gold flow from the monetary to the non-monetary gold supply, and conversely, and these movements to and fro continue all the time. The amount of gold that is put to monetary uses may depend, among other things, on the needs of trade for money, and thus on the general level of prices. The existing monetary gold stock thus provides no objective basis for the determination of the value of money. As a matter of fact, it is only possible to relate the general level of prices to objective determining factors when the price-level is regarded in its connection with the total stock of gold. This stock is either given absolutely, or, if gold is continually produced, it is determined also by the technical conditions of production, and thus in both cases the explanation of the general price-level is carried back to objectively given factors.

In the equation $PT = MV$, M must now represent the total supply of gold, and V the payment effectiveness in this period per unit of this supply of gold. If we consider two cases where the payments effected per unit of the total supply of gold is equal, and where real turnover is the same, then the quantity theory can be expressed by saying that the general price-level is directly proportional to the total supply of gold.

Thus far, we have assumed that all payments are made in money. There still remains the problem of how the value of money is determined when, besides actual money, bank-notes and bank deposits are reckoned as media of payment. A theory of the value of money which places the price-level in relation to the volume of payments made within a given period must clearly add to payments made by ordinary money all those payments made by bank money. We have, then, $PT = Z_1 + Z_2 + Z_3$, where Z_1, Z_2, Z_3 represent respectively the volume of payments made by cash, by bank-notes, and by cheque. Exactly as we replaced formerly Z_1 by $M_1 V_1$ we may now replace Z_2 by $M_2 V_2$, where M_2 represents the circulating quantity of notes, and V_2 the velocity of circulation of the notes. If the velocity of circulation is assumed to be equal in both of the cases contrasted, our equation shows how an increase of the note circulation leads to a proportional increase in the payments effected by the notes. Similarly, we can substitute $M_3 V_3$ for Z_3, where M_3 represents the total amount of those bank deposits upon which cheques may be drawn. As a physical velocity of circulation of bank deposits is impossible to define, V_3 must be defined as the payments effected in the period per unit of deposits. If the payment effectiveness of deposits is assumed to remain unaltered, a rise in the total volume of deposits will occasion a proportionate increase in the payments effected by them. By assuming the number of payments effected to remain unaltered, and also that the utilisation of media of payment remains the same, fluctuations in the general price-level are occasioned by three variables, namely, the quantity of money, the note circulation, and the volume of deposits.

These variables, however, are not completely independent. The volume of the notes and deposits, with a given quantity of money, is regulated by the credit terms of the banks. These terms are thus an independent factor in the pricing process. On the assumptions given above, the general price-level is determined by two factors: the credit terms of the banks and the circulating quantity of money. As, however, under a gold standard, the circulating volume of money is not an independent variable, but depends on the total supply of gold, we reach the conclusion that fluctuations in the general price-level, when the real turnover is constant, are determined by the total supply of gold and the credit terms of the banks, as well as by the degree to which the media of payment are utilised. This result may be best expressed if we return to the original formulation of the quantity theory, letting M, in the equation $PT = MV$, equal the total supply of gold and V the total payments effected in the unit period per unit of the supply of gold. In the relative effectiveness of the media, the most important factors are the more or less extended use of bank money and the correlated utilisation of the gold reserves of the banks, as well of the total supply of gold for monetary purposes. These two factors are at all times directly influenced by the credit terms of the banks. Alongside must be considered fluctuations in the degree of utilisation or the various media of payment. If the relative effectiveness is equal in both cases to be considered, it follows that the general price-level is proportional to the total supply of gold.

For the present we shall not inquire into the correctness of the propositions formulated in the preceding paragraphs. Our task has been to ascertain clearly what is precisely the substance of the quantity theory on different assumptions; or, rather, what must this substance logically be. With this reservation we shall take the analysis of the quantity theory a step further.

In its classical form the quantity theory links the value of money directly with the volume of payments. We ourselves have stated the theory in this way, but this manner of viewing it is not absolutely necessary. The value of money may be considered in its connection with the existing demand for cash balances – that is, the demand for money. There is, however, a difference between these two methods as regards the time limits of the problem. The volume of payments must necessarily refer to a definite *period*, whilst the demand for cash balances refers to a *point of time*. It is natural for a theory, which wishes to explain the dependence of the value of money on its quantity, to concentrate upon a definite point of time, as the quantity of money itself must, by definition, refer to a definite period of time. The exchange economy, with definite habits of payment, needs a definite stock of money at the beginning of the period in order to carry out, in a certain period of time, a certain volume of payments. There exists, therefore, a definite relation between the demand for money at a given moment and the payments effected in the subsequent unit period, and it is quite as natural for the theory of the value of money to proceed from the demand for money as from the payment effectiveness of money.

If we wish to examine the value of money in connection with the demand for it, we may treat the problem of the value of money in the same way as we have treated the general problem of pricing (Chapter IV.). The variable which must be determined in the present case is the general price-level, which we term P. For the present this variable may be taken as given. The general problem of the determination of prices is then completely solved, for the prices can be determined even as to their absolute amount. From the view-point of pricing, the demand for money is then determined. We will assume that the demand for money, in conditions which otherwise are equal, is proportional to the general price-level. This signifies that when two independent cases are compared, in which all of the other factors influencing the demand for money are equal, the demand for money is in direct proportion to the general price-level. The demand for money may then be given as the product of two factors – the general price-level and the demand for money at a price-level chosen as normal.

With a price-level which is to be taken as normal or basic, the demand for money is a variable independent of the price-level, and primarily depends on, and is proportionate to, the volume of the real turnover T – that is, the turnover measured in money at the normal level of prices. At the beginning of a unit period with a volume of turnover which is selected as representing the normal, the demand for money is determined by the degree of development and the organisation of the money economy. The demand for money when the price-level is 1 and when the real turnover is 1 may be termed the relative demand for money, and expressed by the letter R. R then equals the demand for money, at a certain point of time, per unit of the payments effected in the ensuing unit period – that is, PT multiplied by the relative demand for money R, and thus equals the product PTR.

We have dealt at length with the determining factors of the relative demand for money in the previous chapter. The relative demand for actual cash depends on various factors, as we have seen, especially on the concentration of cash balances in the banks and on the replacements of money in private funds by bank-notes. We found that the relative demand for money is diminished in the higher stages of economic development. At a given moment and in a given country this relative demand for money may be taken as given.

When the demand for money is given, equilibrium requires the demand for money to be equal to the total quantity of money present M – that is, that $PTR = M$. This equation suffices to determine the unknown – the general price-level. The dependence of the general price-level on the quantity of money and the relative demand for money is thereby shown, and, by a comparison of the two independent cases, where R and T are unaltered, we find that the general price-level is directly proportional to the quantity of money. This result brings us back to the quantity theory.

If we compare this equation for determining the general price-level with the earlier equation $PT = MV$, we find that $R = \dfrac{1}{V}$, or in other words the demand for money per unit of the payments effected in the unit period is the reciprocal of the velocity of circulation of money – that is, the reciprocal of the payments effected by the unit of the quantity of money in the unit period, which is self-evident. The two equations given for the determination of the general price-level are identical, which is natural, since an unknown can only be determined by *one* equation.

The equation which states that the demand for money equals the quantity of money, determines the price-level only when the quantity of money can be taken as given. On a gold standard, there is no sharp division between the quantity of money and the stock of gold. In order to base the general price-level on objectively determined factors, the total demand for money must be compared with the total supply of gold. The following procedure must then be adopted. In the first place, the general price-level must be assumed as given. In this manner, all prices are settled, and the demand for gold for industrial purposes is known, as is also the demand for gold for monetary purposes. Thus the total demand for gold is known This, however, must equal the total supply of gold, and through this equation the general price-level is determined. We may assume here, in order to uphold the quantity theory, that not only the demand for gold for monetary purposes, but also the industrial demand, is proportional to the general price-level. If this is the case, the total demand for gold is clearly proportional to the general price-level, and as this demand must equal the total supply of gold, the general price-level is proportional to this supply; this once more agrees with our conclusions above.

The assumption that the non-monetary demand for gold is proportional to the general price-level, is not in itself improbable. For as gold is used for purposes of ornament, it is chiefly desired on account of its value and not on account of its quantity. Then the value of a unit of gold should, other things being equal, be inversely proportional to the total quantity of gold. If it has been assumed that the monetary demand for gold increases proportionately to the general price-level, the assumption that the industrial demand for gold is also proportional to the price-level means only that the relation between the monetary and the industrial demand for gold is independent of the general price-level; in other words, that the quantity of gold distributes itself in the same proportion between its two chief uses independently of the size of the total quantity of gold. It must be noticed, however, that it is sufficient, for upholding the quantity theory, to assume that the *total* demand for gold is proportional to the general price-level, and to leave open the possibility of changes in the monetary and industrial demand.

§ 51 *The Significance of Changes in the Quantity of Money*

The theory of the value of money is of direct significance as regards practical monetary policy only in so far as it is able to explain how *changes in the quantity of money* react on the general price-level. It is usual, in the teaching of economics, to represent the effect of changes in the quantity of money by the popular formula that "if all the cash balances of the community were to be doubled at a given moment, then, *ceteris paribus*, the general price-level would also be doubled."[1] This proposition is clearly quite outside the results of our analysis of the quantity theory up to now. For it is here assumed that an increase in the quantity of money takes place in a given national economy, and a definite statement is made regarding the result of this alteration. From a comparison of two given independent cases one comes to the problem in which the inner relations of the whole process of economic change must be considered; that is, from a static problem one comes to a dynamic one.

This formulation of the quantity theory necessarily assumes that all other factors are unaltered, and this assumption is generally made without considering its justification. But it must be clear from the first that an increase in money may also exert an influence on the "other factors," especially on the velocity of circulation of money and on the relation between bank money and cash, and perhaps also on the total sales of commodities. The reservation of *ceteris paribus* is here quite inadmissible. If one cites the quantity theory, including this reservation, as being obviously correct, then attention is diverted from very important sides of the problem before us. Such

[1] Mill, *Principles of Political Economy*, Book III., chap. viii., § 2.

a procedure hardly promotes the development of sound scientific criticism.

As long as we consider two distinct and independent cases, as we have done in the preceding paragraphs, the assumption that the "other factors" are equal is justified, for we can select the two cases to be compared as we wish. If, however, in a given case we assume that the quantity of money is suddenly increased, we are not justified in making an indefinite number of assumptions about the new situation which results. What may be assumed is that no new disturbing factors of an external kind arise, but no further assumptions may be made regarding the effects of the supposed increase in the quantity of money, for precisely those effects have to be studied now.

When we pass from the static to the dynamic treatment of the problem of the dependence of the value of money upon its quantity, we encounter difficulties of quite a new nature, for whose solution the methods used hitherto are insufficient. Already by our treatment of the static side of the problem of the value of money we have found that the quantity theory is not so self-evident as people sometimes profess, and that, to support the theory, it is sometimes necessary to make certain assumptions, in themselves not exactly improbable, but whose study lies outside the scope of purely theoretical analysis and requires an examination based on the actual facts of economic life. Even more defective are the expedients of pure theory when we turn to the dynamic problem. The effect of an increase in the quantity of money upon its velocity of circulation, upon the extension of the use of bank money, or upon the volume of the turnover, and thus the final result on the general price-level, are all problems which cannot be finally solved by the expedients of theory.

If one seeks to attain a notion of the direct effects of a rise in the quantity of money, assuming that no further independent factors come into play, one must assume that there will be a decrease in the velocity of circulation of money, a relative increase in the use of cash in relation to the use of bank money, and a rise in the cash reserve of the banks, and perhaps also an increase in trade activity. These are, however, effects which result in a rise in the demand for money, and thus counteract the rise in the quantity of money. If the demand for money is in this way increased to the same extent as the quantity of money, clearly the effect of the rise in the quantity of money is completely counterbalanced, and the effect on prices, which should take place according to the quantity theory, does not come into play. If there is only a small rise in the demand for money, a rise of prices is to be expected, but not to the same extent as the simple quantity theory would lead one to expect. The opponents of the quantity theory have repeatedly drawn attention to the results of this nature, which must follow from an increase in the quantity of money, and have emphasised that these results are too important to be neglected, and that they must always in practice cut across the effects, according to the quantity theory, of an increase in the quantity of money. From this people have concluded that the whole of the quantity theory must be rejected as a theoretical speculation unfit for any practical application. The defence of the quantity theory against these attacks has generally been carried on in a very feeble manner. Even Fisher, who proclaims with such emphasis the quantity theory as an obvious truism about which no doubt is to be allowed, has not been able to do more than represent these effects of an increase in the quantity of money as merely temporary disturbances without great significance; and, although he makes many valuable observations in support of this view, he is prevented by his method in general from making even an approximate estimate of the extent and duration of these effects. In such circumstances it is still an open question how far the quantity theory holds good.

It is clearly outside the powers of pure theory to state the quantitative extent of the above-mentioned effects of a rise in the quantity of money. It is equally impossible for theory to solve the problem of how far these effects will extend into the future. It is perhaps probable that their immediate importance will predominate and that they will lose their power with time, and that, therefore, in actual fact the rise in the quantity of money will gradually result in a corresponding rise of prices. For if the effects now under review are simply the results of a transition, one would expect that the prophecies of the quantity theory would be the better fulfilled the longer the transition period, and the more the two cases to be compared may be considered as independent of each other. Such discussions, however, have no real power to prove anything. They only show how indispensable it is to treat empirically the entire theory of the value of money on the basis of facts systematically collected for this purpose.

Such an inquiry must first ascertain changes in the general price-level during a certain period, in order to proceed to an analysis of the probable causes of these changes. The available data about the quantity of money and its utilisation by means of bank money, as well as about the volume of the real turnover, must be brought together, and in suitable form they must then be compared with the general price-level. The inquiry must be conducted, paying, naturally, special attention to the gold standards of the pre-war period, and also to the later paper standards. As, in the case of the gold standard, the quantity of money is not sharply divided from the stock of gold and is not an independent magnitude, it is necessary, as has been mentioned above, to compare the development of the general price-level with the development of the total stock of gold in order to examine how far changes in the general price-level may be traced back to changes in the quantity of gold, and what variations in the general price-level remain to be explained by the effects of the other variables of the problem.

This shall form the subject of the following inquiry. First of all, we must focus our attention upon the methods to be used in ascertaining changes in the general price-level.

§ 52 *The Measurement of the Price-level by Index Numbers*

The movement in prices may appear either as a change in all prices, or at least in the vast majority of them, in one and the same direction, or as a series of changes in the different prices relatively to one another without a perceptible movement of the whole mass of prices in either direction. Only movements of the first type are reckoned as changes in the value of money, whilst movements of the second type are possible with an unchanged value of money. In practice, price movements of both kinds occur simultaneously. In an inquiry into the value of money, it is necessary to distinguish the two kinds of movements, and to ascertain to what extent a general change of prices has occurred in a certain direction; or, in the language of mechanics, how far a shifting of the centre of gravity of the price-level has taken place. This is the problem the solution of which has been attempted by the formation of index numbers for the general price-level.

In order to form an index for this general movement of prices in one direction, we must first select a group of representative prices, since in such a calculation it is practically impossible to take account of all prices. We must confine ourselves to typical standard commodities of a practically fixed quality. In this respect, retail prices are less suitable, because, among other things, the conditions of sale alter considerably (delivery of the goods, credit, etc.). Services and immaterial goods, generally, cannot as a rule be taken into consideration. Rents, for example, even when paid for the same house, are the prices paid for a convenience of very changeable real content, for the district may become more or less modern, central, easily reached, and so forth. Wages cannot be included, because, being the share of the worker in the total fruits of economic production, they normally rise in a progressive economy, even if commodity prices remain unchanged. Therefore, only the wholesale prices of the most important commodities may be considered.

After a group of standard commodities has once been selected, the individual prices are expressed as a percentage of the prices of a certain base year, and thus the absolute prices are replaced by index numbers. We then have to calculate a certain average of the index numbers so determined. This average must be chosen so that relative changes of prices in relation to one another have the least possible effect on it; that is, so that changes in the average express as faithfully as possible changes in prices in one direction.

In order to minimise the effect of chance occurrences, it may be desirable to cause the more important commodities to have a greater influence on the index number. This is done by calculating a "weighted" average of the price index figures; each price index figure is included once, twice, thrice, etc., according to the relative importance of the corresponding commodity, and the general price-level is then shown by the average of the total number of items.

One may also seek to ascertain changes in the general price-level by observing the effect of price movements upon the collective price of a certain quantity of commodities. If the selected group of commodities is sufficiently comprehensive and representative, one can assume that relative price movements neutralise each other in their effect on the collective price, so that changes in the collective price of the group of commodities only reflect real changes in the general price-level.

The technique of calculating index numbers has been treated in detail in the most recent literature. Special notice must be taken of that most meritorious book by Irving Fisher, entitled *The Making of Index Numbers*. We may content ourselves here with a description of the index numbers which we shall use in what follows.

The well-known index numbers compiled by Sauerbeck[1] for the period 1846–1912 are not "weighted," but account is taken of the relative importance of the commodities included, by taking the prices of several qualities or stages of production in the case of the more important commodities. For each of the 45 articles the yearly average of the monthly market prices is reckoned and expressed as a percentage of the corresponding average prices for the period 1866–77. The sum of the 45 price index numbers divided by 45 is the Sauerbeck index of the general price-level. The various commodities are grouped in the following way: vegetable foodstuffs (8 articles), animal foodstuffs (7 articles), sugar, coffee, and tea (4 articles) (total foodstuffs, 19 articles), minerals (7 articles), textile materials (8 articles), various materials (11 articles) (total materials, 26 articles). For each of these groups a special index number is also calculated. The numbers of the articles in each group show the relative weight that is assigned to each individual group in the calculation of the total index. In order to obtain an insight into this

[1] *Journal of the Royal Statistical Society*, 1886–1913.

method of weighting the individual articles, the 8 articles of the first group are given. They are: English wheat, American wheat, wheat-flour, barley, oats, maize, potatoes and rice. Wheat, which is very important in English trade and consumption, thus has in this group a relative importance of $\frac{3}{8}$, and in the total index a relative importance of $\frac{3}{45}$.

To obtain a fairly accurate idea of the movements of the general level of prices, expressed in *gold*, since the middle of the nineteenth century, we may use the fairly reliable Sauerbeck index numbers. English index numbers are to be preferred in this connection, for three reasons: first, because England in the period under review – the period after the middle of the nineteenth century – was mainly a free trade country; secondly, because the English market in this period was pre-eminently the market for world trade; and thirdly, because England throughout the period maintained an effective gold standard. For the problem with which we are here especially concerned, that of the influence of the gold supply of the world on the value of money under a gold standard, the last-mentioned circumstance is naturally of decisive importance.

For these reasons, we shall base the following inquiry on the Sauerbeck index numbers. [1] In order to obtain a rough idea of the development of the general level of prices throughout the nineteenth century, we shall add to the series of the Sauerbeck index numbers, which start from the year 1846, the index numbers calculated by Jevons [2] for the period 1800–45. Jevons's index numbers extend to the year 1865. Thus the two series cover the twenty-year period 1846–65. The average number for this period according to Jevon's index is 75.3, and according to Sauerbeck's is 93.1. These two series will probably best be represented on one and the same diagram if one chooses such scales that these average figures are in agreement.

On studying Sauerbeck's index numbers, one is struck by the fact that the general price-levels for the two years 1850 and 1910 were very nearly identical. The index number for 1850 is 77, and

[1] These are reproduced in Table I. in the Appendix.
[2] *Wholesale and Retail Prices*, 1903 (321). p. 450.

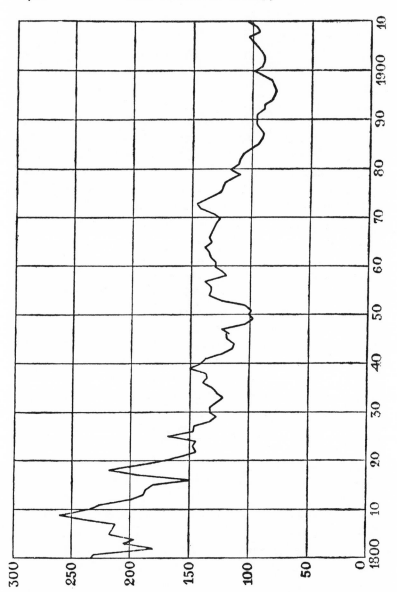

FIG. 2.—INDEX CURVE OF PRICES, 1800-1910

that for 1910 is 78. In making such a comparison, it is important not to be content with contrasting two isolated years; the years following should also be taken into account. We find that the average of the index numbers for the four years 1848–51 which followed the crisis of 1847 amounted to 76, whilst the corresponding average for the four years 1908–11 following the crisis of 1907 amounted to 76¼. The coincidence between the general price-level for 1850 and that for 1910 is thus very marked. We shall take this common price-level as our normal level and make it equal to 100. The scale for Jevons's index is adapted to the selected scale so that the average figures for the period 1846–65 correspond for both series.

The diagram (Fig. 2) is drawn according to these principles. All figures for the general price-level are therefore expressed as percentages of the normal level, which corresponds to the Sauerbeck figure of 76.

§ 53 The Price-level and the Relative Stock of Gold

We have found that the analysis of the factors which produce changes in the general price-level, as long as the gold standard comes into consideration, cannot stop at the quantity of gold money, but must be extended to the total gold supply of the world. It is thus necessary to make a general survey of the development of the gold stock of the world. The total gold stock of the world for the year 1850 may be estimated to have been about 10,000 million marks (about £500 millions). If Lexis's[1] estimate of 9,560 million marks for the total gold supply in 1848 is approximately correct, the above figure for 1850 (at the end of the year) may be accepted. According to Lexis, in calculating later increases in the gold stock, a total annual loss of 2 per mille of the actual total stock must be assumed. Account has been taken of the production for the period 1851–75 in five-yearly totals and for the period following in yearly totals (as given by Helfferich and the *Statistical Year-book for the German Reich*). A loss equal to 1 per cent. of the total stock

[1] *Handwörterbuch der Staatswissenschaften* (2nd edition), article on "Gold und Gold-währung."

at the beginning of the period has been assumed for the five-yearly intervals, but after 1875 the yearly gold loss of 2 per mille has been subtracted from the stock at the commencement of the year. In order to maintain a continuous record for the period before 1850, the gold production in ten-yearly totals has been subtracted from the gold stock of 1850, and, in so doing, a loss has been reckoned of 2 per cent. of the stock at the beginning of each period of ten years, in addition to a loss of 2 per cent. of half the production of the period. The figure of 7,535 million marks thus obtained for 1800 is somewhat lower than that of 7,940 million marks given by Lexis, but the difference is of no considerable importance. For 1890, Lexis's estimate is 28,560 million marks, whilst our calculation gives a figure of 28,775 million marks.

The results of our calculation are given in the Appendix, in Table II. ("The Gold Supply of the World"), under the heading "Actual Gold Stock," and are also graphically represented in Fig. 3. In accordance with our method of calculation the figures relate to the gold stock at the end of each year.

We find that the actual gold stock from 1850 till 1910 rose from 10,000 million marks to 52,000 million marks – that is, it has multiplied 5.2 times in 60 years. This rise corresponds to an annual increase of 2.79 per cent., or approximately 2.8 per cent. Thus, if the gold stock had increased annually by 2.8 per cent. from 1850, it would have reached by 1910 the actual level of the gold stock of that year.

If we now proceed to compare the development of the general price-level over a longer period with the corresponding growth of the gold stock of the world, we have to note initially that the general economic development makes room for a certain increase in the stock of gold, and that this increase will not occasion a change in the general price-level. In order to find the effects of changes in the gold stock on the general level of prices, we must first know what increase in the stock of gold was necessitated by the general economic progress in the respective period. It is helpful in this connection if we can so choose the period under review that the general price-level is the same at the beginning and at the end of the period. For then, clearly, the increase in the stock of gold during the period has occurred without influencing the price-level, and merely corresponds to the increase necessitated by the course of economic progress.

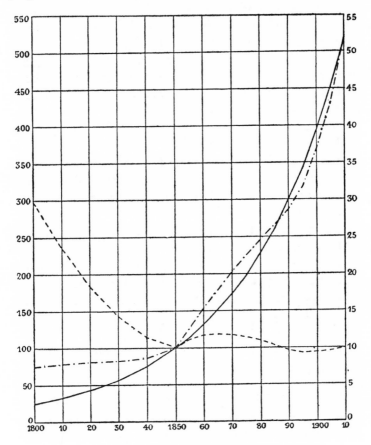

Fig. 3.—World's Actual Gold Stock —·—·—·—·
Normal Gold Stock ————·
Relative Gold Stock ——————·

These conditions, as we have found in the preceding section, have been very fortunately realised in the period from 1850 to 1910. The price-level for 1910 was practically the same as that for

1850. From this we may conclude that the increase in the gold stock from 1850 to 1910 was necessary and sufficient to maintain the price-level the same in 1910 as in 1850, in face of the continual economic expansion. This increase, as we have already found, corresponded to an average annual increase of approximately 2.8 per cent. throughout the whole period. If the gold stock of the world had increased constantly by this 2.8 per cent., then clearly no one would attempt to ascribe any changes in the general price-level to alterations in the gold stock. An absolutely uniform increase in the world's stock of gold would then have taken place, and this increase would have been sufficient to maintain prices at the end of the period at the same level as at the beginning. People would not then be able to say that the increase in the gold stock as a whole had been too great or too small, or that irregularities in the increase had caused changes in the price-level. A uniform increase in the gold stock which, after the elapse of a certain period leaves the price-level unaltered, may be termed a *normal* increase for that period, and the stock of gold at any given moment, assuming a normal increase, may be termed the *normal gold stock* for this period. The normal gold stock for the period 1850–1910 is obtained by starting from the stock of 10,000 million marks at the beginning of the period and reckoning with a uniform annual increase of 2.8 per cent. The figures for the normal gold stock in Table II. of the Appendix are calculated in this way. (The figure for any one year is obtained by multiplying the figure for the preceding year by $\sqrt[60]{5.2} = 1.0279$.)

The normal gold stock, thus calculated, for the period 1850–1910 is represented on the diagram (Fig. 3) by the thick line. The calculation is carried back to the year 1800, using the same formula, and the curve on the diagram is correspondingly continued.

From what has been said, it follows that, in so far as changes in the general price-level for the period 1850–1910 may be traced to changes in the gold stock, they refer exclusively to deviations of the actual gold stock from the normal stock. If no such deviations had taken place, then, as already pointed out, there would have been no occasion to ascribe any changes in the general price-level to fluctuations in the gold stock. It must not be concealed, however, that this problem is to a certain extent one of definition. It can always be said that changes in the general price-level need not occur, at least not on a large scale, if only the gold stock were kept at a suitable level. In this way, it would be possible to lay the blame on the gold stock for every change in the price-level. Such an explanation of the cause would, however, satisfy nobody. When other factors exert an influence on the general price-level, and, in conjunction with the gold stock, determine it, changes in these factors are regarded as independent causes of changes in the price-level, even if their effect may be neutralised by opposite changes in the gold stock. If it is wished to ascribe to each of the various factors a definite share in changes of the price-level, this is possible only by considering a certain development during the period in question as being the normal course of development, so that the general price-level remains unaltered as long as all of the factors remain normal. It is the decision as to what constitutes a normal development that has been described above as a problem of definition. It would be difficult to find a definition of "normal," as applied to the gold stock, which would be more natural than the one given here.

If we are agreed, then, in regarding as normal, in this sense, a rise of 2.8 per cent. per year in the gold stock during the period 1850–1910, we must regard every deviation of the actual gold stock from the normal as *pro tanto* the cause of a change in the general price-level. These deviations of the actual gold stock from the normal are clearly shown on our diagram. From 1850 till 1887 the actual gold stock was greater than the normal stock, whilst from 1887 till 1910 it was smaller. We should therefore expect a rise of the general price-level above the normal level in the first period, and a fall below the normal level in the second period.

In order to be able directly to compare deviations of the actual gold stock with the development of the general price-level, the actual gold stock is expressed as a percentage of the normal stock.

The relation of the actual and the normal gold stock, which we term the *relative gold stock*, is given numerically in Table II. of the Appendix, and is represented on the diagram (Fig. 3) by the line – – –. This relative gold stock increases, as may be seen, during the middle of the 'sixties to a maximum of 1.18 – that is, 18 per cent. above the normal level – and falls in the years 1896 and 1897 to a minimum of 0.92, or 8 per cent. below the normal level.

To obtain an approximate idea of the gold supply before 1850, the relative gold stock for the first half of the nineteenth century has also been calculated and put on the diagram. It must, however, be noted that the figures for the earlier period have not the same value as those for the later period, since the normal gold stock is defined only for this later period.

Let us now bring together on one diagram (Fig. 4) the curves of the relative gold stock and of the general price-level. One glance at the diagram suffices to note the general correlation between the price-level and the relative gold stock. It is, however, noticeable that the price-level is subject to variations of two kinds. A distinction must be made between "secular" and "annual" variations in the general price-level. The secular variations correspond on the whole to the simultaneous variations of the relative gold stock, although the secular price-level of the period 1850–80 was clearly somewhat higher, and in 1890 perhaps somewhat lower, than it should have been according to the relative gold stock. Our comparison suffices at any rate to demonstrate that for the period under review (1850–1910) *the chief causes of the secular variations of the general price-level are to be found in changes in the relative gold stock,* and that the quantity theory is correct in so far as the general price-level, although influenced in addition by other factors, is *directly proportional to the relative gold stock.* This very real connection could not be observed so long as, in the comparison of the price-level with the gold supply, one was content to have quite vague criteria as to the abundance or paucity of the gold supply. The problem of the dependence of the general price-level on the gold supply has a definite significance only if the conception of a normal

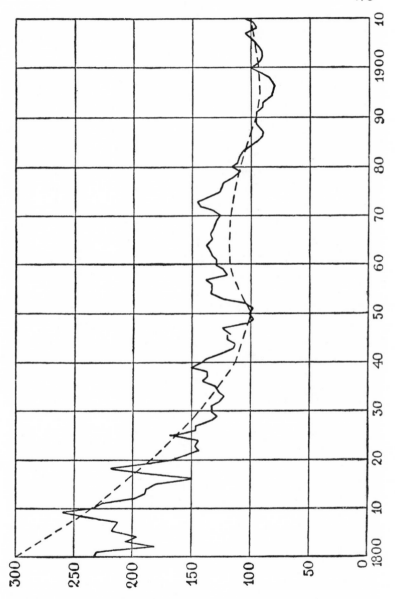

Fig. 4.—General Price-level and Relative Gold Stock.

gold stock is adopted, but then the problem can be at once solved by a careful investigation of the facts.

The diagram teaches us, further, that the general price-level is subjected also to *yearly variations, which,* however, *have no connection whatever with the gold supply.* This is a very important result, which forces us to seek the causes of these variations in other factors; this will be done later.

The deviations of the relative gold stock from unity show to what extent deviations of the actual price-level can be attributed to changes in the gold supply. Of the great rise in the price-level during the 'sixties (about 30 per cent.), a rise of 18 per cent. may be attributed to the abundant gold supply. The much-discussed scarcity of gold in the 'eighties and 'nineties is responsible for a fall in the general price-level to 8 per cent. below the normal. From the point of view of the gold supply, the general price-level from 1886–7 was probably at the normal level, as the relative gold stock had a value corresponding to unity. However, this could apply only if the secular variations of the general price-level are considered, to the exclusion of yearly variations. Now, the years 1886 and 1887 occur in a depression period, and, therefore, it is to be expected that the general price-level should be abnormally low; this is borne out by the diagram. A curve representing the secular changes of the general price-level would cut the normal level somewhere about the year 1886. This fact is important in so far as it demonstrates that the gold stock which we have defined as normal is, in the same sense, normal for the periods 1850–86 and 1887–1910. An increase in the gold stock of 2.8 per cent. annually would have left the secular price-level unaltered in both periods. This furnishes a good proof of the trustworthiness of our methods, and of our statistical material.

With reference to the trustworthiness of the material, the following remains to be said. The least reliable of our statistics is, of course, the estimate of 10,000 million marks for the gold stock in 1850. If we suppose an error of 5 per cent. in this estimate, so that the actual gold stock was 10,500 million marks, instead of 10,000 million, this would mean that the normal increase of the gold stock was 2.72 per cent. instead of 2.79 per cent., which is only slightly different. If we assume the figure of 10,000 million marks for 1850 to be correct, an error of 1,000 million marks in the estimate of the gold stock for 1910 results in an error of only 0.03 per cent. in the increase factor of the normal gold stock (that is 2.82 instead of 2.79 per cent.). If we assume the curve of the normal gold stock to be correct, an error of 100 million marks in the estimation of the actual gold stock towards the end of the period would cause an error in the relative gold stock of 2 per mille, and so would have no significance whatever. We may assume, accordingly, that the figure of 2.8 per cent. represents fairly exactly the true increase of the normal gold stock for the period 1850–1910, and that the curve of the relative gold stock gives, broadly speaking, a true picture of the development of the gold supply.

For the period before 1850 the curve representing the relative gold stock is of value only in so far as it shows the general direction of development. This suffices to make apparent the sharp bend which the curve describes in 1850, and which is accompanied by a remarkably similar bend in the secular trend of the general price-level curve. In all probability general economic progress was considerably slower during the first half of the nineteenth century than during the latter half, but nevertheless the growth in the stock of gold from 1800 to 1850 was quite insufficient for the progress that took place, and the general level of prices was bound to fall. A curve representing this fall would be less precipitate than the curve of the relative gold stock of our diagram, but would leave practically the same impression of the general development of the gold supply during the nineteenth century.

Even if our figures are uncertain within fairly wide limits, it seems far better to give, by correct treatment of the available materials, a quantitative statement of the true position of the gold supply than to create vague impressions, which various text-books, according to their point of view, try to strengthen by using a large number of favourable adjectives.

In order that the general price-level shall remain constant, it is necessary that the gold stock should increase at a fixed yearly rate of 2.8 per cent. It is, however, quite immaterial how large the gold stock is at the initial moment. If, for the moment, it is above the normal, and if the price-level is thus correspondingly above the normal level, an annual increase of 2.8 per cent. will maintain general prices at a constant level, but a slower growth in the gold stock will gradually lower the price-level. Conversely, a growth of somewhat more than 2.8 per cent. in the gold stock will suffice gradually to raise a price-level that is too low.

As the yearly loss of gold may be estimated at 0.2 per cent. of the gold stock, an annual gold production amounting to 3 per cent. of the gold stock at any time is the condition for keeping the general price-level constant, in so far as it depends on the gold supply. Thus we have secured a firm basis on which to estimate the sufficiency of the gold production, a question which people have been chiefly content to discuss in vague and general terms, the gold output being described as "too small," or "huge," "enormous," etc.

As long as the world demand for gold at a constant price-level increases 2.8 per cent. per annum, the stability of the price-level requires that the annual production of gold should amount to 3 per cent. of the increasing gold stock, and thus itself grow by 2.8 per cent. annually. This means that, if the supply of gold equals the demand at a particular moment, a production which is maintained at a constant level will gradually become insufficient. This fact, that the gold output must steadily increase, is very important in connection with the question of the future gold supply. Unless, *pari passu* with economic progress, unexpected possibilities of increasing gold output arise, the world will inevitably be faced with a scarcity of gold which will make the maintenance of a given price-level a most difficult task.

If a gold production amounting to 3 per cent. of the existing stock of gold is necessary to maintain the price-level unaltered, this means that the actual gold stock must be thirty-three times as large as the annual gold output. Writers on the subject generally state that the price-level, under a gold standard, is maintained fairly stable because, through the centuries, the total stock of gold has risen to an enormous amount in comparison with annual output, or, in other words, the annual output is insignificant in relation to the accumulated stock of gold. Such statements are as superficial as they are misleading. In reality, as we now know, stabilisation of the general price-level by no means requires the gold stock to be "enormous," in relation to the annual production, but simply that it should be thirty-three times as large, neither more nor less.

The great changes that occurred in the sphere of money during the war, and more especially after it, have completely interrupted the continuity in the development of the world demand for gold. As a result of the competition of paper money issued with little or no gold backing, and particularly as a result of the withdrawal of gold coins from circulation, there arose a superfluity of gold, which raised the price-level, after the resumption of the gold standard, by roughly 50 per cent. as compared with the pre-war level. (This figure is based on the average price-level of the United States for the period 1927–8.) As a matter of fact, the superfluity of gold was so great that an even greater rise of prices would have taken place if the United States had not kept a part of the surplus gold as a reserve for the future, the Federal Reserve System allowing its gold stocks to reach the abnormally high level of 70–80 per cent. of the notes and deposits outstanding.

The stability of the general price-level, assuming no new alteration in the relative demand for gold, requires an annual gold production which allows the world's total stock of gold to increase at the same rate as economic progress in general. If the future rate of progress is to be as rapid as that in the period 1850–1910, the present gold output is decidedly too small. The world production of gold, after reaching its maximum in 1915, fell rapidly, and at present amounts to hardly more than 2 per cent. of the total stock (see table below). In fact, for more than ten years we have lived in a period of insufficient gold production. The maintenance of a stable price-level, in such circumstances, is the most important economic task which the world has to face to-day. We shall return to this question in § 58.

The World Gold Supply Since 1910

	Annual Output of Gold. (Million Marks.)	Actual Gold Stock at end of year. (Million Marks.)	Production as percentage of the gold stock at the beginning of the year.
1910	1,912	52,004	3.81
1911	1,935	53,834	3.72
1912	1,953	55,679	3.63
1913	1,927	57,495	3.46
1914	1,839	59,219	3.20
1915	1,971	61,072	3.33
1916	1,903	62,853	3.12
1917	1,757	64,484	2.72
1918	1,607	65,962	2.49
1919	1,532	67,362	2.33
1920	1,403	68,630	2.09
1921	1,383	69,876	2.02
1922	1,337	71,073	1.91
1923	1,541	72,472	2.17
1924	1,630	73,957	2.25
1925	1,655[1]	75,464	2.24
1926	1,675	76,988	2.22
1927	1,687	78,521	2.19
1928	1,705	80,069	2.17
1929	1,705	81,614	2.11
1930	1,700	83,151	2.08

§ 54 *The Price-level and the Cost of Production of Gold*

It was natural for the classical economists, who assigned to cost of production a key position in their system of value, to attempt to base the value of money also on the costs of production of the precious metals. According to Adam Smith, the value relationship between these metals and other commodities depends on the relation between the amount of labour necessary to bring a certain quantity of gold and silver on the market, and the amount necessary to bring a quantity of other commodities on the market. [2] Ricardo followed the same line of thought when he stated, in accordance with his general theory of value, that the value of the precious metals was

---

[1] Production figures from 1925 onwards, according to Kitchin. Those for 1929–30 are estimates.

[2] *Wealth of Nations*, Book I., chap v., and Book II., chap. ii.

proportionate to the amount of labour required to produce them. [1]
Mill brought it into line with his quantity theory, by asserting that
the quantity of gold indeed governed the actual market price of
gold, but that the normal price must in the long run be determined
by the cost of production of gold. [2]

This theory of the value of money, which states that under a
gold standard the general price-level is determined by the cost of
production of gold, and which is so often regarded as a self-evident
and definitive solution of the problem, suffers from the same errors
as the general cost of production theory. In practice, there are
generally no fixed costs of production. If we take the theoretical
case where gold can be produced only at a certain fixed cost price,
there is no reason why this price should not be lower than the market
price, if the opportunities for production are sufficiently restricted.
In this event, the producer would, as monopolist, make a profit
containing certain rent elements. On the other hand, it would be
quite possible for the costs of production to exceed the market price,
in which case obviously no gold would be produced. In practice,
there is a whole series of gold-mines with varying costs of production, and this series may practically be regarded as continuous.
If, because of this, it is wished to replace the conception of costs of
production by the conception of "marginal costs of production,"
then it must again be remembered that these cannot be held as
factors determining the price, since the extension of production,
and therefore the marginal costs of production, themselves depend
equally on the price. Nevertheless, there is clearly a certain connection between the possibilities of producing gold and the general
price-level. If the general price-level rises, the costs of production
of gold, reckoned in money, rise also, whilst the nominal price of
gold remains unaltered. The result is a shrinking in the possibilities
of profitable production, and therefore also in the total production;
thus the supply of gold becomes less, and a further rise in the general
price-level is prevented.

How, now, can the effect of the costs of production be linked up
with the available supply of gold, and how is the general price-level

---

[1] *Works*, ed. McCulloch, p. 213.   [2] *Principles of Political Economy*, chap. ix., § 3.

determined by the combined effect of these two factors? This question is most easily answered, if, in accordance with our general theory of pricing, we regard the price-level as an unknown in the equation which states that the demand for gold must equal the available supply of it. If the available supply of gold is known, then the price-level is known also. If, on the other hand, the supply of gold is increased by production, then the conditions of production exert a certain influence on the price-level, which through our equation is given its correct connection with the influence of supply and demand. Assuming the general price-level to be given, the demand for gold as well as the extent of production, and thereby the gold supply, is determined. In equilibrium the supply must equal the demand – that is, the supply of gold must increase at the same rate as its demand, assuming an unchanged price-level, and it is through these conditions that the general price-level is determined.

We are now in the position to relate exactly the influence of the conditions of production on the price-level and to ascertain numerically the conditions prevailing before the war. If the possibilities of production are such that at the existing price-level the production of gold corresponds to 3 per cent. of the available stock of gold, there is equilibrium, and the price-level, in so far as it depends on the gold supply, remains constant. If, however, the possibilities of gold production are so abundant that at the prevailing price-level the production exceeds 3 per cent. of the stock of gold, the general price-level rises by a percentage corresponding to the excess by which the relation of the annual gold production to the stock of gold exceeds 3 per cent. Conversely, the general price-level falls if the possibilities of production at the prevailing price-level do not permit of a gold production amounting to 3 per cent. of the stock of gold.

The influence of the gold production upon the general price-level thus depends on the *quantity of gold which can be produced at the prevailing price-level*, not on the "cost of production," which is an entirely vague concept.

The quantity of gold which can be produced at the prevailing price-level is naturally dependent on the price-level, rising when the latter falls, and conversely. As an increase in the production of gold tends to produce a rise in the general price-level, and conversely, the production of gold serves to a certain extent as a regulator of the general price-level. This regulator is naturally the more effective, the more the production of gold is dependent on the general price-level. For the practical consideration of this problem it is necessary to note that the price-level in the gold-producing countries may deviate greatly from the world price-level. In the most important producing country – South Africa – the price index for 1926 was only 123, whilst the world price-level was somewhere in the region of 150. According to this point of view, the South African production should have been not nearly as restricted as the high level of world prices would have led us to suppose. On the other hand, it must be noted also that the cost of production of gold may be strongly influenced by factors other than the wholesale price-level of the country in question. Such factors, are, in South Africa, particularly the restricted influx of black labour, high taxes, as well as rising expenditure for social purposes. In addition, there is the progressive exhaustion of the mines and the necessity of working at great depths, and this naturally makes production more expensive.

§ 55 The Price-level and Bank Money

As we have determined, in the last section but one, the effect of the relative gold stock on the general price-level, it is useful, in the further analysis of the factors which determined the general price-level, to picture to ourselves how the curve of the price-level would have looked if a deviation of the actual gold stock from the normal had not taken place during the period in question – if, that is to say, the relative gold stock had remained equal to one during the whole period. We obtain an idea of this in the following diagram (Fig. 5), in which the Sauerbeck index numbers are divided by the relative gold stock and represented by the thick line. The thin line represents the general price-level according to Sauerbeck (for the relevant figures see Table I. in the Appendix).

The price-level so reduced is, as one can see, much smoother in its secular movements than the price-level itself. The annual fluctuations remain, however, and it will be our task to find an explanation for them. Everyone who is familiar with the history of general economic conditions in the period in question will see at once that these annual fluctuations are connected with the cyclical movements of trade. In order that this connection may be clearly seen in the diagram, the years in which a boom period has reached its height are distinguished by a thick line. A glance at the diagram shows that the peaks of our curves coincide regularly with the peaks of the booms. An exception to this is found only in 1882, when the conditions of good trade were not very marked. It is also

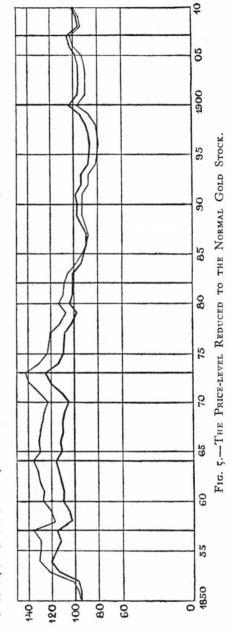

FIG. 5.—THE PRICE-LEVEL REDUCED TO THE NORMAL GOLD STOCK.

clear that there exists a definite correlation between the various phases of the trade cycle and the annual fluctuations of the price-level. Why a period of very good trade should lead to a rise in prices, and a period of trade depression to a fall in prices, are questions which we shall reserve for the next Book, in which we shall deal especially with the trade cycle (§ 70). For a closer study of the times of trade booms in the past we must refer to the same Book (§ 62).

It has long been a very disputed question whether non-monetary factors, also, exert an influence on the price-level. It was always brought up against the monetary theories of the value of money which we have set out, that other real economic conditions may influence the price-level. Thus, for example, a lowering of the costs of production through the introduction of labour-saving machines, a general reduction of transport costs through the extension of railways, the development of the modern great steamship lines, the competition of new producing countries, cheaper labour – all these, and any other elements which make for cheapness, would, in the opinion of the critics, lower the price-level. On the other hand, wage-increases engineered by workers' associations, modern social and tariff policy, etc., would, they said, raise the general price-level. Such explanations do not merit being called theories of the value of money. They overlook completely the fact that the value of money cannot be determined without the co-operation of the decisive factors on the side of money. A change in the general price-level always presupposes a corresponding change in the total payments made, and therefore, in any case, changes in the supply of money or in the use of the existing means of payment. If the co-operation of the monetary factors breaks down, if the monetary factors show independent and perhaps antagonistic changes, the ultimate effect on the general price-level must be different.

It must always be the primary aim of a theory of the value of money to establish the changes of the monetary factors and to make clear the connection between these changes and the simultaneous changes of the general price-level. We have already done this in regard to the secular changes, when we showed the effect of the gold supply on the general price-level. Before we proceed further with this analysis, we have to inquire into the annual fluctuations of the general price-level and to examine how far they are due to monetary or other economic factors. We then come across the striking fact that the various phases of the trade cycle exert a decisive influence on these annual fluctuations. This, however, by no means completes the explanation of these annual fluctuations. Still another problem comes to the fore, a problem which may be formulated thus: In periods of very good trade the turnover is greatly increased, and, therefore, also the demand for money; the immediate result should be a *fall in prices*. If, nevertheless, there occurs a *rise in prices*, how will the demand for money, increased as it is from two causes, be met? If the increased demand for money is not satisfied, then those causes which originate in other factors cannot produce a rise of prices.

The general answer to this question can only be that the existing supply of gold in times of brisk trade is used to a greater degree for purposes of payment. This can happen in various ways. The velocity of circulation of gold coins can be increased. The volume of gold coins can be increased at the expense of the bank reserves, as can the total monetary gold supply at the expense of the non-monetary supply. Above all, bank money may be created on a large scale and used more intensively. All such changes are equivalent to an increase in the payments effected by the existing gold supply. If we call the payments effected per unit of the existing gold stock the "relative payment effectiveness," we may lay down the proposition that annual fluctuations in the general price-level are due to changes in the relative payment effectiveness.

When we examined the effect of the gold supply upon the general price-level, it was natural to compare the existing supply of gold with the demand for it (§ 50). Now, when we have to determine how changes in payment effectiveness affect the general price-level, we must compare this payment effectiveness in relation to a certain unit period with the extent of the payments to be effected in that period. The aggregate of these payments equals the product PT, where T represents the volume of the real turnover, and P the general price-level.

We do not possess any reliable statistics relating to changes in the real turnover. We know, however, that the real turnover rises in periods of brisk trade, and at a more rapid rate than usual. From this we may conclude that the total payments effected in periods of brisk trade must show a bigger increase than the general price-level. In those cases where the maxima of the price-index and of the real turnover exactly coincide in point of time, the increase in the total volume of payments effected must be particularly clear.

In order to be able to test these conclusions we require some measure of the changes in the total volume of payments effected. In the present state of statistical science we must not press our claim for such a measure too far. However, we have in the clearing house figures for the United States and England an index of changes in the total volume of payments which will suit our purpose.

The clearing figures may, on the whole, be regarded as a measure of payments by cheque, and in the countries named these payments form by far the greater part of all payments. As the other payments generally have to follow the movements of the payments by cheque during the various phases of the trade cycle, these cheque payments may, without risk of appreciable error, be used as an index of the total payments in the countries in question. This, of course, is only permissible in regard to short period variations of the volume of payments, or when we study the movements of the volume of payments in connection with the phases of the trade cycle.

To obtain an index of total clearing transactions capable of being directly compared with the curve of the reduced price-level, we may divide the clearing figures by the actual gold stock for each year. We thereby eliminate the influence of secular movements of the general price-level upon the clearing figures, in so far as these movements depend on the relative gold stock. At the same time, as we shall see directly, the increase in the clearing figures throughout the whole period is eliminated, so that the annual variations of the clearing curve may be directly compared with the corresponding variations of the general price-level. To achieve this, all that is necessary is that the clearing figures be given as percentages of a

certain normal level. Accordingly, the London clearing figures for
the period 1870 to 1910 are first divided by the actual gold stock
of each year; then the results are expressed in percentages of the

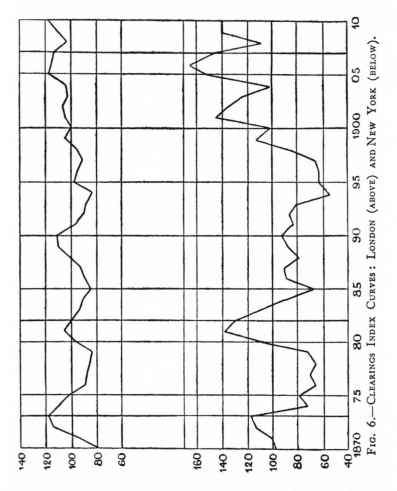

FIG. 6.—CLEARINGS INDEX CURVES: LONDON (ABOVE) AND NEW YORK (BELOW).

average for the whole period. The New York clearing figures are
treated in the same way.[1] The results are given in the diagram
(Fig. 6). (For the figures, refer to Appendix, Table III.)

[1] *Statistical Abstract of the United States*, 1910, p. 570.

For short periods these curves may be regarded as indices of the volume of payments of the countries concerned. The two index curves show, on the whole, similar movements, although the American curve, corresponding to the far greater industrial fluctuations of that country, generally shows more violent variations.

If we now examine more closely, say, the English index of payments, we find that the increases always coincide with periods of brisk trade, although its peaks occur sometimes rather earlier than those of the trade booms. On the whole, the index of payments shows considerably greater variations than the reduced price-level. Wherever the highest point of the payments index coincides with the peak of the boom and also with the maximum of the price-level, as in 1873 and 1890, the rise in the index is particularly pronounced. The index of payments shows, therefore, the very movements that our theoretical considerations would lead us to expect.

After this study there can be no doubt that the occasional rises in the price-level, which we have here considered, are made possible by a rise in the payment effectiveness per unit of the available gold supply, and that this increased payment effectiveness is for the greater part caused by the increase in bank money and its more intensive use, also by the release of gold coins from the reserves of the banks, and perhaps by increased velocity of circulation of the circulating coins. Thus sympathetic action by the banks results in the supply of money to trade during a boom period being increased not only in the same proportion as the real turnover, but even more, and this leads to a general rise in prices. In the succeeding depression, the fall in prices is determined by a corresponding restriction of the supply of media of payment on the part of the banks. Even if all these "annual" fluctuations of the general price-level are influenced also by other factors inherent in the trade cycle, they are possible only on the assumption of a corresponding supply of means of payment provided by the banks, and must therefore be ascribed first of all to the policy pursued by the banks.

The line of study pursued in these sections has produced certain other results also. A glance at the diagram shows that the English curve as a whole – if we neglect the influence of the trade cycle –

is almost perfectly horizontal, so that the volume of the payments effected in London during the period in question increased, on the average, at the same rate as, or perhaps a little faster than, the gold supply of the world. The synchronous development of the total volume of payments of the country was probably about the same. We must, perhaps, assume that the circulation of other media of payment grew somewhat more slowly, but, as cheque payments undoubtedly predominated throughout the whole period, this fact could not have had much influence on the development of the total volume of payments.

However, we are now in a position to obtain an approximate idea of the average increase in the real turnover in England, and thereby of the rate of the total economic development of the country during the period in question. For this it is necessary only to reduce the established rise in the volume of payments to a constant price-level, which may easily be done, as we know that the secular price-level at the beginning of the period stood roughly at 30 per cent. above our normal level (§ 53), but, at the end of the period, coincided with the normal level. According to these principles, the average rise in the real turnover of England during the period 1870–1910 works out at 3.05 per cent. The increase in the absolute gold supply is therefore taken as the basis. Taking into account that the rise in the payment effectiveness was somewhat greater, we arrived at a figure which is, perhaps, one- or two-tenths of one per cent. higher. This figure agrees very well with our general estimate of the rate of economic progress in the Western world (§ 6).

The development in the United States was unquestionably much more rapid, but, on account of the changing monetary conditions, can hardly be numerically evaluated in the same way. On the other hand, certain other countries developed much more slowly. We may perhaps be justified in regarding the development of England in the period under review as an approximate average for the whole world (cf. recent investigation of the New York Federal Reserve Bank, *Monthly Review*, 1931).

§ 56 The Price-level and the Demand for Gold

As it is now settled that the annual fluctuations of the general price-level are explained by the trade cycles and by the elasticity which the banks give to the supply of means of payment, we may confine our attention to the secular variations of the general price-level. The general agreement between these variations and the corresponding variations of the relative gold stock, which we established in § 53, is at first sight to be regarded as a mere fact. If, however, in accordance with the general quantity theory as developed in § 50 and in accordance with our analysis of the effects attributable to the gold supply, we assume that changes in the relative gold stock result in proportionately similar changes in world prices, expressed in gold, then the secular movements of the general price-level are substantially explained.

It is remarkable that in this way all changes of the general price-level may be traced to causes which, in so far as they are of a monetary nature, belong to the sphere of the monetary supply, in this case particularly the gold supply. Have, then, the great changes in the demand for gold during the period exerted no effect at all on the general price-level? We have based our study on English prices, because they are the prices of world commerce, and because England throughout the period was on a gold standard. We have compared the price-level so calculated with the gold supply of the whole world, because of the circumstance that a gold supply less broadly conceived would not have furnished an objectively given magnitude in the problem. It may now be asked: Did not the greatly increased world demand for gold during the whole period exert such a strong influence on prices, that the connection between the general price-level and the world gold supply was completely obscured? During the period in question, all the civilised countries, one after the other, went over to the gold standard, and therefore new claims on the gold supply of the world were continually being made. Have not these claims then, left strong traces on the curve of the general price-level? It is natural for such questions to be asked, but our inquiry has shown that, in the main, they are to be answered in the negative. After we have examined the effects of variations in the relative gold stock and in the fluctuating supply of bank money to trade, there remains to explain only a relatively unimportant secular variation in the general price-level.

The world demand for gold, during the period 1850–1910, reduced to the normal price-level, must have increased fairly uniformly at the same rate as the normal gold supply – that is, at the rate of 2.8 per cent. per annum. This figure is somewhat lower than that which we found to be characteristic of the general economic development of the world for the period 1870–1910. It is also not improbable that the development of bank money had the effect of causing the demand for gold to rise somewhat more slowly than the real turnover.

The somewhat peculiar fact of the uniform increase of the demand for gold can be explained if it is noted that a country's transition to the gold standard results in by no means so great an increase in the demand for gold as one would, perhaps, be inclined to expect. Frequently, gold was already extensively circulating in the country, either because of a double standard or as trade coins, or it had been accumulated for years in large reserves, either by the State or the central banks. In other cases, either the full gold standard was not at first introduced, or an effective gold circulation was dispensed with. Under such circumstances the demand for gold resulting from a change of standard may be spread over a fairly long period. So late as in the years immediately preceding the war the Bank of France was gradually improving the relation between the gold and silver in its vaults, and, to this end, was buying gold. Nevertheless, a transition to the gold standard means to a certain extent an abnormal increase in a country's demand for gold, but this need not exert an appreciable effect, if only other countries in the meantime reduce their demand for gold to a corresponding extent. For the individual countries, the demand for gold has certainly not increased so uniformly as for the world as a whole. A country may, for a time, be content with a relatively small increase in its gold, if payments effected with bank money are proportionately increased. These circumstances show how hopeless it must be to trace changes in the general price-level to changes in the gold supply of a particular country. The demand for gold of a particular country, which is determined by monetary and bank policy and similar factors, is certainly a component factor in the determination of the value of gold on the world market, but only the total world demand determines, in conjunction with the total supply, the value of money – that is, the general price-level.

It is natural to suppose that periods of exceptionally abundant gold production have especially accelerated the transition to the gold standard and gold circulation, and that on this account room was made for the new gold. In the period under review, however, this has not been the case. The demand for gold showed none of the elasticity which would have partly prevented a rise in prices. On the contrary, in both periods of exceptionally large gold production – the Californian-Australian period from 1850 on and the Transvaal period from the middle of the 'nineties – the rise of prices was, as the diagram (Fig. 4) shows, distinctly greater than the rise in the relative gold stock would have led one to expect. Even if our statistical material contained relatively large errors, this result, as can easily be seen, would remain. The whole of the extraordinary increase in the gold production has been absorbed in both cases by the rise in prices. The demand for gold during this period increased at the most by its normal percentage of 2.8, rather less if anything. Precisely because the abnormally increased gold production could not be absorbed by the demand at an unaltered price-level, prices had to rise.

The fact that the secular price-level in the 'fifties and 'sixties was above and in the 'nineties below the relative gold stock, suggests, however, that certain secular variations occurred in the generally uniform development of the demand for gold. The situation cannot very well be explained otherwise than by a somewhat less than normal increase in the demand for gold previous to 1870, and a somewhat more than normal increase after 1871. Such an assumption appears very natural in view of the great changes in the sphere of monetary policy which characterised the 'seventies. People, and especially bimetallists, have been inclined to ascribe to this demand for money a somewhat exaggerated share in the determination of prices. Probably the transition to the gold standard, which certain European countries made during the 'seventies, was carried out so gradually that in itself it was not able to exert much influence on the general price-level. The later transition of Russia and Austria-Hungary to the gold standard left, as we have already remarked, no recognisable trace of pressure on the price-level.

Even if the European currency reforms of the 'seventies may have had a certain small share in the resulting fall of the general price-level, probably another circumstance must be held primarily responsible for this fall, in so far as it was not caused by the simultaneous fall in the relative gold stock. This circumstance is the enormous increase in the demand for gold in the United States at the end of the 'seventies and at the beginning of the 'eighties, which was caused by preparation for, and the carrying into effect of, the resumption of cash payments. The paper currency of the Civil War was declared convertible from 1879 onward. In the period from the middle of 1875 till the end of 1887, the monetary gold stock of the United States grew from 89 million dollars to 650 million, which is more than a seven-fold increase in $12\frac{1}{2}$ years. The increase was particularly marked from the middle of 1876 till the end of 1881, namely, from 99 to 485 million dollars – that is, nearly five-fold in $5\frac{1}{2}$ years. These demands were made at a time when the world supply of gold was already so scanty that it was bound to lead to a considerable reduction in the general price-level. The sum of 386 million dollars, which the United States acquired in this period of $5\frac{1}{2}$ years for its monetary gold supply, amounted to no less than 64 per cent. of the world's gold production at that time. As under normal conditions the remainder of the gold production would be required for non-monetary purposes, there was nothing left to satisfy the monetary demand of the rest of the world. Clearly, there must have taken place a rise in the value of gold considerably above that warranted by the small output of gold alone. A doubling of the monetary demand for gold in 12 years may perhaps be regarded as normal for the United States, in view of the rapidity of its economic development. But, in addition to this, the United States in the period

1875–87, acquired approximately 2,000 million marks (nearly £100 million) for monetary purposes. The fall in the price-level caused thereby may be estimated at roughly 7 per cent. [1]

Another factor acting in the same way, though to a less extent, on the side of demand, was the greatly increased gold import of India in the first half of the 'eighties. The effect of this demand in lowering prices may perhaps be estimated at 2 per cent. [1]

These irregularities in the development of the demand for gold are quite sufficient to explain the fall of the general price-level from the 'seventies to the middle of the 'nineties, apart from the fall caused by the reduction in the relative gold stock. *The secular variations of the general price-level are in the main to be ascribed to the fluctuations of the relative gold stock and for the rest to certain irregularities in the otherwise practically uniform rise in the demand for gold.* This completes our analysis of the causes of the secular variations of the general price-level.

All the factors used in this explanation belong, as may be seen, to the monetary side of the problem. They are based on the conditions of gold production or on monetary policy, and therefore may be primarily regarded as independent factors determining the value of money. There is, therefore, no room for an explanation of the secular variations in the value of money in the period in question in terms of other causes of a general economic nature. In the period under review the secular movement of the general price-level was exclusively a monetary phenomenon.

Under the influence of the trade cycles, general economic progress naturally exhibits fluctuations; the rate of progress must, in the upward swing of the trade cycle, be greater than normal. Such an increase in the rate of development should of itself cause a fall of the price-level. But the supply of the media of payment by the banks in such periods is so abundant that, even though trade increases, it is sufficient for the needs of a higher price-level, and thus prices are pressed up.

Hence the rapidity of the general economic development in the

[1] For the statistical data which are the basis of the calculations see the *Report of the Director of the Mint* (Washington, 1911), pp. 21, 43, and 37.

period in question did not affect the general price-level in either its secular or annual variations.

It must be especially noted that a general cheapening of commodities, which one is so often inclined to expect from a great increase in the productivity of human labour, has not taken place. The provision of the world with means of payment has been sufficient to counteract the tendency.

§ 57 *The Regulation of the Price-level by the Bank-rate*

We have established the fact that, given a gold standard, secular variations of the general price-level are determined by the varying scarcity of the supply of gold in relation to the demand. The question, how the gold supply is able to exert such an influence on the general price-level, is not yet answered. The new gold, as a rule, passes from the areas of production to the great trade centres, particularly to the London market, whence it is distributed all over the world. In so far as it is not acquired by industry or the Oriental markets, it is at first generally purchased by the big central banks and the treasuries of the various States. There, perhaps, it will remain for some time without exerting any direct influence on the price-level.

Now, we know (Chapter X.) that in a country on the gold standard the volume of all the means of payment at the disposal of trade always bears a certain, though also very elastic, proportion to the gold reserves of the banks. As fairly great fluctuations may take place in this proportion, an increase of the gold reserve need not necessarily exert a direct effect on the general price-level. But there is no obvious reason why an increase of the gold supplies should cause a permanent alteration in the average proportion between means of payment and bank reserves. Rather, it is to be expected that the more abundant gold supply will gradually bring about a corresponding extension of the supply of money to trade. We shall, therefore, find it quite natural that the gold supply completely controls the secular variations of the curve of the general price-level.

As the gold supply influences the secular variations of the general price-level only through the policy of the banks, and the annual variations of the price-level, in so far as they depend at all on monetary factors, are likewise determined by bank policy, it is found that at any given moment banking policy alone, on the monetary side, is directly responsible for changes in the general price-level. Now, in this bank policy – that is, in their regulation of the total supply of means of payment – the bank-rate appears as a factor of such prime importance, that it may be regarded as being representative of the whole policy of the banks.

The bank-rate, of course, is not arbitrarily fixed, but is regulated with a definite end in view. As we have seen, in a gold standard country the bank-rate must always be so fixed that the demands of domestic trade on the banks' reserves (indicating an increased demand for money) are only temporary, and, on the whole, leave the reserves untouched. Only by means of such a bank policy is it at all possible to maintain the gold standard. Further, the bank-rate has to be regulated so that the reserves are protected against too great a demand for payments abroad – that is, against an occasional unfavourable situation of the foreign balance of payments. In both cases, the endeavour to maintain the currency at par with gold is the decisive factor in the regulation of the bank-rate.

Experience shows that this can be done if the correct rate policy is pursued, but the rate policy alone is not enough for this purpose. For the maintenance of the gold parity of a currency, there must be, in addition, a supply of means of payment according to the actual needs of trade. This involves the use of elastic bank money to take the place of gold, as otherwise the demand for gold might become too great if there is a pressing need for means of payment. But even gold itself must, to a certain small extent, be released from the reserves, since no effective demand for gold may be left unsatisfied. One might be inclined to say that this constant convertibility of bank money is the only necessary condition for a gold parity. Convertibility, however, is possible only on the assumption, on the one hand, of a rate policy which keeps the demand for money within certain limits, and, on the other hand, of the satisfaction of this demand by means of bank money in so far as these will be accepted in lieu of gold. By helping out the gold circulation with bank money, and by the release of gold or foreign bills from the reserves of the bank, the demands of commerce for gold are reduced and the supply is increased. In periods of pressing demand for money, this acts as a preventive against a rise in the value of gold.

By this means, it is actually possible to maintain the value of money in a country at the same level as that of a certain metal, or more exactly, to fix, within certain narrow limits, the price of a certain metal expressed in the currency of the country. This fixing of the price of a metal, namely, gold, has been represented (§ 41) as the central feature of a gold standard. This factor distinguishes the gold standard from a free standard. Even on a gold standard, the currency (such as the pound sterling) has its independent existence. It is bound to the metal, gold, only by the fact that the price of gold is fixed within certain limits. The regulation of the currency is carried out by the bank-rate and the utilisation of the bank reserves, with this condition as their object.

The gold standard may thus be regarded as a free standard under which the price of gold is determined within certain limits. The fixing of the price of gold is effected during secular periods by the regulation of the price-level according to the gold supply, but for short periods by regulating the gold market according to the general price-level.

It may now be asked to what extent the general price-level is controlled by a rate policy which has as its object the maintenance of the gold parity. The answer is supplied by our inquiries above: the rate policy has been able to regulate the general price-level in its secular variations according to the world's gold supply, and consequently in agreement with a certain price-level which is determined exclusively by this gold supply in accordance with the quantity theory. On the other hand, the rate policy of the banks has not prevented "annual" variations in the general price-level.

A bank policy which aims at maintaining the gold parity of a currency – that is, at maintaining a constant price for gold – will produce a price-level having its secular variations in inverse proportion to the value of gold, and having, besides, yearly variations which are to a certain extent independent. It would hardly be presuming too much to infer from this that a bank policy, which aims at the fixing of any other price, could produce the same result. As an object of bank policy there should be considered above all the fixing of the average, calculated in a definite manner, of a certain group of commodity prices, or, what comes to the same thing, the fixing of the price of a definite collection of commodities. With a suitable bank policy it should thus be possible to maintain a price-level having its secular variations in inverse proportion to changes in the value of this collection of commodities relatively to all commodities. If a sufficiently representative collection of commodities were chosen, such fluctuations in value could not take place to a marked degree, and it would thus be possible by means of an enlightened bank policy to stabilise the general price-level so far as to eliminate secular variations.

If we compare what has been said in the previous chapter about the effect of the bank-rate as a regulator of the supply of the means of payment with the conclusions drawn in this chapter, we can answer the question in what way the general price-level is influenced by the bank-rate. A lowering of the interest rate of the banks means a keener competition of the banks on the capital market, as newly created bank means of payment compete with the real savings of the public. The demand for capital-disposal, increased through these favourable conditions, is in part satisfied merely by the release of newly created bank money. An extra purchasing power is thereby created, against which there is no increase in those objects that may be purchased. This purchasing power competes with the genuine purchasing power on the market. The inevitable consequence is then a rise in prices, which must continue until the total nominal purchasing power is completely absorbed. As a result of this rise in prices, room is made for a certain quantity of bank money which is then retained by commerce.

These considerations lead to a final solution of a controversy which from early times has been the centre of discussions relating to monetary policy. At every opportunity, the banks urged against the quantity theory that control over the volume of means of payment did not lie with them, as the public would never absorb more money than it actually needed. We now see that the banks, by fixing too easy terms for advances, can cause the public to absorb an increased quantity of money, and that such an increase of nominal purchasing power must result in a rise in prices. This rise in prices increases the real demand for money in the same proportion, and therefore the public must retain a corresponding amount of money. It is not certain that every arbitrary increase in the quantity of money will be taken up by the public. But it is certain that the increased quantity of money will result in a rise in prices, and a rise in the demand for money corresponding thereto. Any money in excess of this will be returned to the banks by the public. If, however, the credit terms continue to remain so attractive that the demand for capital is in part satisfied by the creation of new bank money, the same process must be continually repeated. The price-level is raised, and the demand for money must rise correspondingly. What we are able to observe statistically in such conditions is a constant rise in the general price-level and a parallel increase in the supply of money. These two quantities increase proportionally to each other. But we now know where the cause lies. The activating factor of the whole movement is furnished by the constant creation of artificial purchasing power. We thus arrive at a satisfactory formulation of the quantity theory.

A depreciation in the value of money caused through too abundant a monetary supply is commonly termed *inflation*. The opposite process is termed *deflation* – that is, an appreciation in the value of money caused by an excessive scarcity in its supply. If the credit terms of the banks are too severe – always, of course, in relation to the actual situation of the capital market – the public will pay off its debts to the banks, means of payment will be destroyed, and the scanty supply of money will force down commodity prices. This process is continued as long as the interest rates of those responsible for creating money (in its widest sense) are kept higher than the interest rate required at any given moment to maintain the capital market in equilibrium.

The extent of the inflation or deflation is measured arithmetically by the rise or fall in the general price-level. It is quite conceivable, and indeed has happened in abnormal circumstances, especially during the Great War and the years immediately following, that a rise in the price-level has been caused through a diminution in the supply of commodities. Such a rise of prices must, however, be restricted within narrow limits. If we take the normal supply of commodities to be 100, and if we suppose that this supply happened to fall to 80, which would be a very serious occurrence indeed, then a rise in prices would occur in the proportion of 80 to 100 – that is, only from 100 to 125. Such a rise in prices can, however, never be a ground for an increase in the supply of money, as the central banks maintained so often during the big inflation of the war-years and after. For, according to our assumption, the commodity turn-over has fallen in the same proportion as the price-level has risen, and so the demand for money should remain unchanged. Strictly speaking, the supply of money should be reduced whenever the supply of commodities is curtailed, and at the same rate. If this is done, the scarcity of commodities cannot cause prices to rise. Thus, on strict monetary principles, every rise in prices must be termed inflation, as it is clearly based on a too abundant supply of money, having regard to the circumstances of the case.

The rise in prices in an ordinary boom period is, in strict accord-ance with this view-point, to be regarded also as inflation. It is true that non-monetary factors also may be cited as causes col-laborating in the price movement. If, however, the supply of money were limited exactly according to the needs of the growing volume of real trade, then no general rise in prices could take place. The rise comes about only because the banks, during the upward swing of the trade cycle, stiffen their credit terms insufficiently and at too slow a rate, having regard to the prevailing conditions. Thereby inflation is caused. There is no doubt that the price movement could be considerably reduced if a stronger bank policy were ap-plied. To what extent it might be practicable to manipulate bank policy skilfully enough to prevent any rise in prices in the upward phase of the trade cycle, and any fall of prices in the depression, can be decided only by future experience. In order to get this experience central banks, however, must unequivocally recognise the maintenance of an invariable price-level as their function, and direct all their efforts towards the realisation of this aim.

If the banks are compelled by the State to provide bank money for State expenses, the responsibility naturally falls on the State. This does not prevent the consequent rise of prices from being caused by an increase in bank money, as in the previous case, and also from having the character of an inflation. In actual practice, the worst cases of inflation are of such a nature. The economic possibility of providing the State with a source of income through inflation is explained by the fact that wages, interest, rents, and other more or less fixed incomes, do not rise to the same extent as the supply of money or commodity prices. Inflation is then a means of exploiting a large section of the population, the State actually robbing them of a substantial part of their real income. If the State afterwards deplores and condemns this exploitation, this is pure hypocrisy, for which a defective understanding of the true nature of inflation is a rather poor excuse.

In the theoretical representation of the quantity theory, attention must of necessity be paid to changes in the velocity of circulation of money. To the extent that such changes appear of themselves, their effect on the price-level must be measured, and theoretically this presents no especial difficulty. More important are those cases where the velocity of circulation is influenced by an alteration in the supply of money. One might be inclined to suppose that an increase in the supply of money would cause a reduction in its velocity of circulation, which would prevent a rise in prices, at least in part. As a rule, this is not the case. On the contrary, the increased supply of money generally seems to result in an increased velocity of circulation. In the normal boom periods, this is a result of the general stimulating effect of the brisk state of trade. In the worst examples of extensive inflation by the State, the velocity of circulation of money reaches abnormal heights, on account of the fear that the value of money will soon fall still further. If this fear has reached such a pitch that no one will hold money even for a very short time, then, as the experience of Germany has manifestly taught us, money nearly ceases to be of any use at all.

In the previous chapter, we were content to say that the "true" or "normal" rate of interest could not be defined as a "real rate of interest," a "marginal productivity of capital," or such-like, for the rate is by its very nature a market price, and the market is always strongly influenced by the rate-policy of the banks. It is, therefore, quite clear that the "real interest on capital" can be defined only as a market rate of interest formed in certain definite conditions of the market. Our latest results now allow us to fix the conception of the real interest rate for capital more precisely.

In our theory of capital, we defined the interest on capital as the price which is paid for the right of disposing over a unit sum of money during a unit period. In this, the sum of money could be conceived only as an abstract sum expressed in the scale of reckoning formally taken as unchangeable. Now, as we consider the possibilities of a change in the value of money, the concept of a rate of interest on capital must be determined in regard to those changes also.

If the bank-rate is kept so low that the value of money falls, then the person who advances money will, when his loan is repaid, receive a smaller real capital than he originally lent. He sold capital-disposal on the market and stipulated for a certain interest. The bargain, however, turned out otherwise. He has not received back his capital undiminished. The interest, then, is not a sufficient compensation for his sacrifice. For the lender, too, to be compensated for the loss of capital caused through the fall in the value of money, a higher rate of interest would have to be paid. If we suppose the market rate of interest to be raised for this reason, we approach a rate of interest which will not cause any further fall in the value of money. If this rate is attained, the lender will sell a mere capital-disposal, and will get the price of it in the market rate of interest.

The true interest on capital might therefore be defined as that rate of interest at which the value of money remains unaltered. At this rate of interest just so much new bank money will be put into circulation as corresponds to the growing needs of trade, the price-level remaining constant. The competition of bank money with savings on the capital market may be considered as normal, and the rate of interest which keeps the capital market in equilibrium may be defined as the "natural rate of interest." The rate-policy which, under a free standard, strives to keep the price-level constant would then be identical with a rate-policy which seeks to bring the bank-rate into harmony with the natural rate on capital. This lays down what is to be understood by a sound direction of the capital market and a correct distribution of productive forces between the present and the future. Nevertheless, there is inevitably something conventional in all these attempts to define interest on capital. For it is assumed in the definition that the invariability of the price-level is to be taken as "normal," and this is by no means self-evident (§ 58); in addition, the concept of a general price-level always contains a certain conventional element in the construction of index numbers.

§ 58 *The Stability of the Value of Money*

The considerable secular variations in the value of money since the middle of the nineteenth century have naturally raised the question of whether it would not be possible to avoid such variations and to create a monetary system in which, on the whole, the value of money would remain constant. As variations in the value of money were rightly ascribed to fluctuations in the supply of gold, this question was bound to lead to a demand for the substitution of a more perfect monetary standard in place of the gold standard.

The great fall in prices from the beginning of the 'seventies to the middle of the 'nineties was used by the bimetallists as the starting point in their endeavours to create a monetary standard on the basis of two metals instead of one, in order to be more independent in the case of an eventual scarcity of one of the metals. We have already demonstrated in § 41 that a foreign element was thus introduced into the problem of the stability of the standard. The problem in itself required only the fixing of *one* price, or, what amounts to the same thing, an average of a certain group of prices Bimetallism requires, in addition, the fixing of a relation between two prices, a matter that lies quite outside the problem of the standard.

Fisher has submitted a proposal to create a "standard dollar" which should represent a constant gold value but a variable quantity of gold. The gold-content of the dollar, or rather the amount of gold which lies at the back of that abstract currency unit, "the dollar," should be varied from time to time in accordance with the state of the gold supply, and, in this manner, it should be possible to maintain a constant price-level.

This much-discussed plan is exposed, to some extent, to the same objections as bimetallism. Binding the standard to the metal, gold, has a purpose so long as it is thereby possible to maintain the price-level substantially unaltered, or as long as we abstain from using better means of regulating the price-level. If, however, the short-comings of this method of regulating the general price-level are recognised, and an attempt made to keep as constant as possible a price-level defined by a definite index number – that is, the collective price of a certain group of commodities – we are really again introducing a foreign element into the problem, when we attempt to fix the price of gold from time to time under a standard regulated in this fashion.

If we wish to create a monetary system with the value of money invariable, this object must be our sole aim, and other outside problems must not be merged with it. The solution of the problem, according to what has been said above, lies in starting from a completely free standard, and then attempting to stabilise it by fixing the collective price of a definite group of commodities. The only possible means for doing this is the rate-policy of the banks. There is no doubt, from the point of view of monetary theory, that it is possible by this means to create a standard in which there would be no important secular variations in the general price-level.

During the Great War, not only was the gold standard generally abolished and replaced by paper standards, but, as shown in § 42, there took place, as a result of these changes, a big change in the value of gold itself. After the United States had restored the gold standard, the general price-level, expressed in dollars, rose to a maximum of 272 in May, 1920, compared with 100 before the war. The value of gold at that time was hardly 40 per cent. of its pre-war value. The ensuing process of deflation raised the value of gold to roughly 67 per cent. of its pre-war value. Later, it stabilised itself at this level, since the general price-level in the United States until the middle of 1929 remained in the neighbourhood of 150 (Bureau of Labour). This stabilisation is the result of American banking policy. The value of gold has, since the war, been determined to a great extent by the value of the dollar. The gold standard has thus lost an essential characteristic of the typical old-fashioned gold standard. A country which formerly went on to a gold standard thereby bound its money to a commodity the value of which was determined by external objective factors. The individual country's monetary demand for gold, of course, exerted a certain influence on the value of gold, but this influence was not very great and could be neglected. This was not the case, however, in the period when a single great country, the United States, had a gold standard, whilst the rest of the world remained on a paper standard. Many countries were at that time dubious about returning to a gold standard, which, in effect, would signify only a linking to the dollar, and which would bring their own standard into subjection to American banking policy. It was clear, however, that were a number of countries, more especially England, to return to the gold standard, the value of gold would receive a broader basis.

The return to the gold standard was undoubtedly the only solution if the world wanted to have an orderly monetary system within a short period of time. Nevertheless, it could not be overlooked that gold had a much less stable value than before the war. One could not be content, therefore, with simply restoring the gold standard, but conscious attempts would have to be made to supply gold in the future with a satisfactorily stable value. As the gold supply of the world had become decidedly too small, as we have already seen, prices could be maintained at their existing level only if the world's monetary demand for gold were systematically restricted.

In my memorandum to the League of Nations for the International Financial Conference at Brussels in 1920, I drew attention to this problem in the following words: "It thus appears that the whole world has a direct common interest *in preventing a further rise in the value of gold.* The present low value of gold is principally the result of a relatively diminished demand for it for monetary purposes. The actual circulation of gold has been suspended fairly generally and the big central banks have considerably reduced their requirements for relative gold-cover. If a return to pre-war conditions were to be made in this respect, the inevitable consequence would be that the value of gold would be raised. In order to avoid this, it is necessary for all countries to refrain from measures directed towards re-introducing an actual gold circulation, and they should content themselves with their present standard of gold-cover as the basis of their paper circulation. Countries which are able to attract gold from the rest of the world must refrain from doing so. Thus the stabilisation of the value of gold during the coming years clearly requires a close co-operation between all countries."

At the International Financial Conference at Genoa in 1922, it was not possible to obtain recognition for the first of the points of the programme referred to. Later developments have demonstrated, however, its unavoidable necessity. The act of Germany, when it restored the gold standard in 1924, in renouncing the circulation of gold coins, could well be regarded as a temporary expedient. But it was of decisive significance that England in 1925 went on to a gold standard without a gold circulation. The new English gold standard has retained only the essential crux of the old gold standard, whilst all subsidiary details have been discarded. It is the typical standard as represented in this book, namely, a gold standard which is nothing more than a paper standard in which the price of gold is fixed within certain narrow limits. As England, which first set up the gold standard and which still remains the centre of the world's monetary system, was content with a gold standard of such a nature, it was no longer possible to regard it as a standard of second-rate quality. The example of England was soon followed by a number of other countries, and the circulation of gold coins has now ceased to play a practical part in the world economy. In this respect, it was of greatest significance that India was successfully dissuaded from introducing gold coins into circulation, and thus a new demand for gold which would have been fatal to the policy of economising gold was averted. It is true that from time to time a restoration of gold coins into circulation is spoken of, but on the whole we may take it that such a use of gold belongs to the past. Thus the coinage system, which used to have ascribed to it such an excessive importance in the monetary system that these two concepts were even regarded as identical, has now ceased to be a factor in the monetary system, at least in so far as full-bodied coins are concerned. Coinage, as a matter of fact, is for the future a closed chapter in the history of money.

The second point in the programme for economising gold was unanimously adopted by the Genoa Conference, whereby a concentration of the holding of cash balances of central banks in large financial centres, such as London and New York, was recommended as a suitable measure. A certain amount of co-operation between the central banks to reduce the demand for gold actually took place in the years following, although not in the official forms originally proposed.

By means of the policy of economising gold described above, the value of gold has actually been maintained at a fairly satisfactory stability until the middle of 1929. Professor Fisher's index number for the wholesale prices of the United States remained for the five years 1924–8 around 150. The annual index was 149 for 1924 and also for 1928. Even in July, 1929, the index was at this figure. It was thus demonstrated that a conscious regulation of the demand for gold could result in a certain stability of its value, and also of the whole gold standard system of the world.

The restrictive banking policy of the United States, which had as its object the damping down of the excessive speculation on the New York Stock Exchange, caused a depression of commodity prices from the middle of 1929, which was to lead to dire results.

Confidence disappeared, and with it the spirit of enterprise, and very strong and speedy measures became necessary in the way of easing credit to combat the continued fall of prices. In fact, such measures were taken when the discount rates of the Federal Reserve Banks were gradually reduced, and when large quantities of Government securities were purchased by the system. Action, however, was taken far too slowly, so that two years were lost without success having been attained in checking the fall in prices.

At the same time, a breach was made in the policy of economising gold, in that two countries – France and the United States – attracted tremendous quantities of gold to themselves and thereby aggravated the scarcity of gold in the rest of the world. The large imports of gold into these two countries took place on account of their favourable balance of payments, artificially increased by war debt payments. Such a movement of gold could only be prevented by an export of capital on a large scale. But during the period of falling prices the necessary confidence was lacking. The central banks of the countries in question have not done what was required of them in the way of reducing discount rates and taking other measures for easing credit, in order to encourage the export of capital. It was especially noticeable in France how a lack of freedom on the part of the central bank, and an ineffective and politically influenced organisation of the capital market hindered the pursuit of a sensible monetary policy.

The consequences of this course of development on the world economy have been injurious to a degree rarely attained earlier. The number of unemployed in the leading industrial countries has risen to fantastic figures, and all countries have been hit by a devastating industrial crisis. The fundamental importance of a stable monetary system for the well-being of mankind has never been so obviously demonstrated as in these hard times. But even now the explanation of the causal connection and of the essentially monetary character of the whole crisis has met with strong opposition. All possible kinds of explanations for the fall in prices have been advanced, but wide and influential circles have obstinately refused to see that the explanation lies in a defective monetary policy. A correct understanding of the deeper roots of the world economic crisis has been exhibited by only a few leading personalities, most of whom are English.

The League of Nations set up in 1929 a Gold Delegation to study the problem of the scarcity of gold. In its first memorandum, the delegation drew up calculations for the probable world gold supply during the next ten years. Two different calculations of the future production of gold are reproduced. According to the first, the gold production will fall off from 405 million dollars in 1930 to 314 million dollars in 1940. According to the second estimate, it will fall from 404 million dollars in 1930 to 370 million dollars in 1940. In its further calculations, the delegation bases itself on the more favourable estimate. It estimates the non-monetary demand for gold in 1930 to be 180 million dollars, and assumes that this demand will increase at the rate of only 1 per cent. per annum, which is clearly a very low estimate when it is assumed that economic progress will be at a rate of 3 per cent. per annum. On the basis of these particularly favourable assumptions, the delegation comes to the conclusion that in 1930, 224 million dollars of gold will be available for monetary purposes, but in 1940 only 170 million dollars.

At the end of 1928, the gold reserves of the central banks amounted to rather more than 40 per cent. of the liabilities falling due daily. If such a gold cover is maintained, and on the assumption of an annual progress of 3 per cent., the annual demand of the central banks for new gold will rise from 303 million dollars to 408 million dollars in 1940. One would, therefore, have to reckon with a deficit, rising from 79 million dollars in 1930 to 238 million dollars in 1940. At the end of the period, then, substantially less than half of the monetary demand for gold would be satisfied. Even if the central banks were to reduce their requirements for gold cover to 33 per cent. of their daily liabilities, there would be a deficit of 170 million dollars in 1940, and only half of the demand would be met.

Bearing in mind the fact that the assumptions for these calculations of the possibilities have been made on an especially favourable basis, one must conclude that the prospects for a satisfactory gold supply are very bad; in other words, equilibrium is possible only if the claims to gold reserves are radically reduced. The calculation appears much more favourable if we assume a rate of progress of the world economy of only 2 per cent. per annum. But, even then, there will result a deficit at the end of the period, even if the central banks are content with a cover of only a third. The practical problem which arises is what restrictions are necessary in the monetary demand for gold in order that the increasing scarcity of gold will not stand in the way of a normal rate of progress of 3 per cent. per annum in the world economy. Our measures must, of course, be planned in such wise that the general price-level may be maintained unchanged on this assumption of a rate of progress of 3 per cent.

The Gold Delegation published a second memorandum in 1931, dealing with the policy of central banks and especially with their requirements for gold cover. The most important recommendation which the delegation made was for a general reduction in the legal requirements for gold reserves, which should be carried out on the basis of an international agreement. We have already seen that the legislature is never in a position to regulate either the actual supply of money or the actual gold backing, but that it only stands in the way of a rational central bank policy. This being so, all legal regulations regarding gold-cover should be rather removed, and the full responsibility for the regulation of the supply of money, and for the maintenance of gold reserves, should be laid on the banks. It would seem, moreover, that an international agreement would be more easily reached in this direction than one dealing with specific figures for gold-cover. On the other hand, the legislature should lay on the central banks the absolute obligation of maintaining the gold parity of their respective currencies in all circumstances.

In conclusion, we must say a few words about the object to be kept in view, when we once obtain command over the value of money. In an economy in which productivity increases by a certain annual percentage, it may be assumed either, on the one hand, that commodity prices remain unaltered, and that consequently the incomes of the producers increase at the given percentage, or, on the other hand, that the producers' incomes remain constant but commodity prices fall by the given percentage. This problem is of primary importance with regard to the relation between borrower and lender. If commodity prices remain constant with increasing productivity, a lender will receive back a sum of money which represents the same real quantity of goods as the original loan. He will draw no benefit from the increased productivity; relatively, he will be worse off. The whole benefit goes to the borrower who, if he is a producer, as is generally the case, profits directly by the increased productivity, production costs remaining constant; or if, for example, the borrower is a State, which borrows for the purposes of consumption, it sees its financial strength increased by the increase in the national dividend. If, on the other hand, commodity prices fall at the same rate as productivity increases, the lender receives his share of the increase, whilst the borrower receives no benefit in respect to the loan from the increase in productivity.

Which alternative is to be preferred, or whether a middle course should be adopted, is a question in which great interests are opposed to each other, and to which a deduction from an abstract ideal of justice cannot supply an answer. In such circumstances, the deciding view-point must be the general well-being of the society. Now, there can be no doubt that a monetary system with a constant price-level is incomparably better for the development of economic life than a monetary system in which one must always reckon with a fall in commodity prices, and which therefore must inevitably exert a restrictive tendency upon production. Consequently, a constant value of money is to be decidedly preferred in the mutual interest of all who benefit from as high a state of industrial activity as possible. It must also be taken into account that the regulation of the general price-level is made much more difficult as soon as an object other than the maintenance of a constant price-level is aimed at, and if a fall of the price-level in a certain proportion to the increasing productivity is sought. For then it must be constantly ascertained how great the increase in productivity is at any moment, which, of course, is a very difficult problem.

From what has already been said, it may be seen that the only practical indicator of a constant value of money is the index of wholesale prices calculated on similar lines to the one now in use. This becomes more evident when one considers that it is not only a question of uniting the various interests in any one country, but also a programme must be drawn up which will meet with the approval of the whole world. The interminable discussions over the best method of calculating indices, which have attracted so much attention, in reality serve no practical purpose. A currency system, in which a good index of wholesale prices would remain constant, would be such an immense improvement on the existing conditions that disputes about the hypothetical advantages of other methods of calculation could be simply ignored. In this problem, we must never lose sight of the fact that monetary policy involves, above all, a practical task of fundamental importance for the whole world economy.

CHAPTER XII

INTERNATIONAL PAYMENTS

§ 59 The Adjustment of the Balance of Payments
First Case: Free Independent Standards

So far, we have generally ignored international payments in the course of our study, and have concentrated our attention on the functions and position of money within the community, partly for the sake of the simplification of monetary theory which is then attained, and partly because, above all, it is necessary to show how money functions in a closed economy, and especially how a definite value of money is maintained – because, in other words, the soundness of a theory of money must first be tested in the simplest case of a closed economy. We have now to take into account the international functions of money. We shall see that the treatment of this question is considerably simplified by the preceding study of money in a closed economy. However, we shall deal only with the technique of international payments in so far as it is indispensable for a complete explanation of the theory of money; for the rest, readers should refer to the specialised text-books on the subject.

First, let us consider two countries having free and mutually independent currency systems. Clearly, payments between these countries can be effected only through the cancelling out of mutual claims. How does such an adjustment take place?

The regular international medium of payment is the bill of exchange. The following is the simple scheme of the adjustment of international obligations by means of the bill: The exporters of commodities in country *A* sell commodities to country *B* against bills drawn in the currency of *B*. These bills are sought after in country *A* by the purchasers of the commodities of *B*, and then are sent by them in payment to country *B*. In country *B* these bills are redeemed by the acceptors. It is clear that, according to this scheme, all payments are effected in the currency of country B. It should be noted that payments between two countries may actually be effected, as they are in this scheme, from the point of view of country B. As long as there is equilibrium between the claims on both sides, this system is clearly sufficient for settling all payments between the two countries.

What is paid in country A for bills on country B? The reason why there is a demand in country A for bills drawn on country B is that they represent purchasing power on the market of country B. This purchasing power is clearly valued in A, on the one hand, in proportion to the lowness of the general price-level prevailing in B (in other words, in proportion to the value of money in B), and, on the other hand, in direct proportion to the height of the general price-level in country A itself. Thus the price of the bill on country B must, as an expression of the value of the currency of country B in terms of the currency of country A, be directly determined by the relation existing between the value of money in countries B and A respectively. This relation is the *purchasing power parity* of the two currencies.

The price of the unit of currency of country B in terms of the currency of country A is called in country A the *rate of exchange* on country B. (In England, on the contrary, the rate of exchange is, in most cases, given as the amount of foreign currency that can be bought by the unit of the home currency, the pound sterling.) The essential factor determining the rate of exchange is therefore the purchasing power parity, which in practice represents the normal level of the rates of exchange.

It is not possible to determine exactly the purchasing power parity on the basis of the definition here given. That is to say, the price-levels in two countries having different paper currencies are not exactly comparable. It is true that we can ascertain that the prices in one country are, on the average, roughly ten times as high as prices in the other country. An exact comparison would, however, be possible only if the various prices in the one country bore the same relation to each other as they did in the other country.

But then no exchange of commodities would take place between the two countries. International trade postulates that in this respect there shall be a marked inequality; thus, in the example given, certain commodities must be more than ten times as dear in one country as in the other, and other commodities must be less than ten times as dear. In such circumstances, as we shall see in Book V., where we have to study the theory of international trade more closely (§ 82), an exchange of commodities will take place between the two countries at a suitable rate of exchange. This rate is fixed by the requirement that there must be equilibrium in the exchange of commodities, so that one country may pay for its imports from another country by means of its exports to the latter. The rate of exchange so determined clearly represents its normal level, and may thus be taken as a more exact definition of the purchasing power parity.

A shifting of the general price-level in the one country in relation to the price-level of the other must obviously alter the purchasing power parity and thereby also the normal level of the rates of exchange. This has been particularly clearly demonstrated during the great changes since 1914 in the internal purchasing power of various countries. If two countries, A and B, have both experienced a period of inflation, but in A the general price-level has only doubled, whilst in B the price-level has increased sixfold, then the purchasing power parity of the currency of B, reckoned in the currency of A, represents only one-third of its former amount. The normal level of the rate of exchange on B must similarly have fallen to one-third of the former normal level. The new normal level of a rate of exchange may be obtained by multiplying the former level by the ratio between the degrees of inflation in the two countries. In this way, a new purchasing power parity may be determined on the basis of a known old purchasing power parity.

This deduction from theoretical analysis, which aroused so much opposition in the first years of the monetary upheavals, since it was such a great departure from the traditional points of view, has now been completely vindicated by abundant practical experience. After more or less normal conditions had reappeared in the sphere of world trade, it became clear that the rates of exchange of the various currencies tended to oscillate round normal levels, which were determined by their new purchasing power parities, calculated in the manner described here. Strictly speaking, one must take into consideration the possibility that the normal levels might be altered somewhat as a result of changes in the entire economic situation of the countries in question, and also in the conditions of trade between them. The actual movements of the rates of exchange show, however, that such changes do not play a great part in determining the new normal level, except perhaps for countries with a very specialised trade.

The normal level of exchange rates is, in fact, determined by the purchasing power parity. It is not certain, however, that the prevailing rate of exchange will always coincide with this normal level. In actual practice, deviations from the normal level fall into two categories, the first consisting of the effects of external circumstances which arise only by way of exception, and the second resulting from constant fluctuations in the market situation.

Among the exceptional factors which result in a big deviation of the rate of exchange from its purchasing power parity, there is, above all, the undervaluation of a currency as a result of an anticipated internal depreciation. Such an undervaluation amounts only to the discounting of an expected diminution in value. In those cases where the currency underwent a continuous and severe process of inflation, the international undervaluation of the currency assumed at times large proportions. The antithesis of such an undervaluation is, of course, the overvaluation of stable currencies in such an inflated currency. An independent overvaluation of a currency may occur – as the experiences of Denmark and Norway in 1925 and 1926 demonstrated in particular – when the world anticipates that, as a result of a systematic deflation in order to restore the former coinage parity, the currency will attain a greater internal purchasing power.

A second cause of the undervaluation of a currency lies in measures taken to hinder its export, such as export embargoes, high export duties, special high prices for foreign buyers, and so forth.

The depressing effect of such measures on the international estimation of the currency becomes at once clear when we recognise
that other nations as a rule buy the currency principally because it
re͜ esents purchasing power on the internal market. Strictly speaking, every one-sided hindrance to the trade between two countries
must affect the rate of exchange between them. The ordinary
commercial-political measures, such as tariff charges, etc., do not
seem to exert a great influence on the rate of exchange.

An international undervaluation of a currency will result in
giving an especial stimulus to exports, and at the same time will
restrict imports. The premium which exporters enjoy as a result of
the abnormal rise in the rate of the foreign exchange increases their
power of competition in the foreign markets, with a result that
foreign producers often complain. The so-called exchange dumping
has repeatedly led to tariff measures to prevent the entry of imports
specially favoured in this way. In dealing with such problems, it
must always be borne in mind that the exports of a country are
specially favoured only as a result of an international undervaluation
of the currency, and that a low-value currency does not particularly encourage exports as long as foreign valuation of it corresponds with the purchasing power parity.

According to the point of view which used to prevail, the rate of
exchange between two countries was determined solely by the
market situation – that is, by the demand for, and supply of, bills.
The complete inadequacy of this theory, which was quite unable to
give any factors determining the normal level, was demonstrated
during the upheavals in the monetary system after 1914. Only
when one recognises that the purchasing power parity is decisive for
the normal level of the exchange rates can one conduct an inquiry
into the influence of the market situation on the exchanges with
any hope of success.

There is no doubt that temporary fluctuations in the exchange
rates may be caused by temporary maladjustments in the balance of
payments. Such maladjustments in the balance of payments are
occasioned in the main by a disequilibrium in the demand for, and
supply of, bills of exchange. As soon as bills upon country B become

scarce in country *A* – that is, as soon as, at the prevailing rate of exchange, the demand for bills exceeds the supply – then clearly the rate must rise. It appears that people have generally deluded themselves into thinking that this explanation provides a satisfactory theory of the rates of exchange. This is, of course, not the case. In such a problem as this, it is always necessary to make clear how a position of equilibrium does come about, and in what way the rise of prices contributes to establish an equilibrium.

The stability of the price-system always presupposes that a rise in prices diminishes the demand or increases the supply, or results in producing both effects at the same time, so that equilibrium is again restored between supply and demand. In what way can a rise in the rate of exchange reduce the demand for means of payment on country *B* or increase their supply? This is the question which the theory of the foreign exchanges has to answer.

The problem is closely connected with that of how temporary irregularities in the international balance of payments are smoothed out. Such an adjustment takes place in two main ways: by transferring payments in one direction or other, and by altering the balance of claims. Under the heading of *"Transference of Payments,"* we may include the following operations:

(*a*) Deferring payment (prolongations, transferring payment from present to future).

(*b*) The discounting of claims not yet due, chiefly bills of exchange (transferring payment from the future to the present).

(*c*) Loans proper, often in the form of accommodation bills of exchange, Treasury bills, and such-like (synonymous with a transference of payment to the future).

Loans for adjusting temporary fluctuations in the balance of payments consist chiefly of short-term loans, whilst a permanent unfavourable balance must be made up by means of fixed loans.

Further, an adjustment of an unfavourable balance is often arrived at by creating new claims on abroad by means of increased commodity exports or exports of securities, as well as by restricting the creation of new debt obligations through reducing commodity and security imports.

It is obvious that an unfavourable balance may be improved by these means. They will all be made more effective by a rise in the rates of exchange for foreign currencies, although their degrees of sensitiveness to fluctuations in the rates of exchange vary greatly. With a high rate of exchange, payments will be postponed to a certain extent and thereby the demand for means of payment at that moment will be reduced. This, however, in all probability, does not play a very great part in adjusting the balance of payments. In the main, this adjustment is brought about through the creation of sight means of payment on abroad. The fact that a rise in the rate of exchange stimulates the discounting abroad of claims not yet due, as well as the raising of foreign loans, is explained by the higher prices which foreign balances accumulated in this way yield in the home market at the higher rate of exchange. In the same way is explained the effect of the rates of exchange upon exports. As long as the general price-level remains constant within the country, the home producers have the opportunity, through exporting commodities and selling the foreign currencies on the home market, of turning to account the rise in the rates of exchange. Similarly, speculators can purchase securities on the home stock exchanges, and export them and sell in their own country the foreign currencies so obtained, and so again make a profit from the rise in the rate of exchange. Naturally, the traffic in securities is much more sensitive to fluctuations in the exchange rates than is the commodity trade.

It must further be noted that the stimulating effect of a higher rate of exchange upon the exports lasts only as long as the internal price-level does not rise. If there has been a rise of prices within the country, corresponding to the rise in the rates of exchange, any special advantage to the exporter disappears. The higher rates of exchange are, then, simply an expression of the disparity in value which has come about between the home currency and the foreign currencies. Such a disparity is of no significance for the balance of payments of the countries; it signifies only that the purchasing power parity – that is, the normal level of the exchange rates – has undergone a displacement.

Any discussion about the determination of the exchange rates by the market situation must base itself on the fact that any irregularities in the balance of payments must always be adjusted, so that the balance of payments must always finally show a complete agreement between the debit and the credit sides, and this not only for long periods of time, but also for each single day. A displacement of the rates of exchange is thus not to be explained away as a result of defective agreement between the supply of, and demand for, foreign means of payment, but must be regarded rather as a means which helps the market to adjust the balance of payments so that an equilibrium is secured.

§ 60 *Second Case: Metallic Standards*

We now turn to the case in which the two countries are on metallic standards. These standards, in the first place, may be different. Let us suppose that one country has a gold and the other a silver standard. The standards are no longer completely independent of each other as they were in the previous section. The holder of gold currency may change it for bar silver and have it coined in the silver standard country. The value of the silver currency expressed in the gold currency thus depends on the price of the metal silver. From this there arises a definite connection between the two currency units; the value ratio between them is, to a great degree, determined by the value ratio of silver and gold upon the open market, and the rate of exchange cannot differ widely from that rate which corresponds to the value ratio between gold and silver. Deviations of the rate of exchange from this normal level are of the same nature as deviations from the parity rate in the case where the two countries are on the same metallic standard, and thus do not need to be specially explained.

Still closer is the connection between the two standards when they are based on one and the same metal. Let us suppose that both countries are on a gold standard. This means that movements in the price of gold in the two countries are confined between two fairly narrow limits. It is, therefore, always possible for the holder of currency A, by buying gold in country A and selling it in country B, to obtain the currency of B. The highest costs of acquiring B currency in this way occur when the gold price in country A is at the upper limit fixed by the gold standard of A, and when at the same time the gold price in country B is at its lower limit; the lowest costs arise when the price of gold is lowest in A and highest in B. The outlay which arises in country A in acquiring the unit of currency B by sending gold is termed *the gold export point* of country A, or the *upper gold point* for A. This upper gold point can vary within certain limits. In addition to the buying and selling prices of gold, it is determined by the costs of transhipment.

On the other hand, it is always possible for the holder of B currency to acquire A currency by buying gold in country B and selling it in country A. But what he receives for the unit of B currency depends on the price of gold in the two countries. He receives the most when the price of gold in country B is at its minimum, and when at the same time the price of gold in country A is at its maximum; and he receives the least when the contrary conditions obtain. The amount which may be obtained for the unit of B currency by sending gold from B to A is termed the *gold import point*, or the *lower gold point* for country A.

Both gold points are therefore variable within certain limits. At any given moment, however, they are fixed, and indicate the extreme limits of fluctuation in the rate of exchange. The price of the unit of B currency cannot rise above the upper gold point, as then, instead of buying bills, people would export gold, or, rather, speculators would export gold, draw bills upon it, and sell these bills on the market; this process, as a result of competition, would clearly bring down the rate of exchange to the gold point. On the other hand, the rate of exchange cannot fall below the lower gold point. For the holder of a bill upon B would not content himself with such a low price, but would rather sell his bill in country B and draw the proceeds in gold, or arbitrage operators would buy the bills on B and, by importing gold, convert them into A currency;

and so as a result of competition the rate of exchange would be forced up to the lower gold point. Thus, from the point of view of international payments, the gold standard is to be regarded as a free standard, in which the movements of the rate of exchange with another gold standard country are confined within two slightly variable, but always rather narrow, limits. This limitation will exist as long as the gold standard is effectively maintained in the two countries – that is, as long as gold may be bought and sold at a price within the legal standard limits. As long as the rate of exchange varies within the gold points, the gold standard, with respect to international payments, is to be regarded entirely as a free standard, and the rate of exchange is regulated in exactly the same way as in the case of free standards. A rise or fall in the exchange rates, occurring as the result of a temporary inequality in the balance of payments, the value of money remaining constant, will set up those counteracting forces mentioned in the preceding paragraphs for the adjustment of the balance of payments and the restriction of the movements of the rate of exchange. If, in spite of this, one of the gold points is reached, a gold movement from one country to the other begins, which is thus a commodity export of a special kind, being calculated to restore equilibrium in the balance of payments. The gold supply of a country thus acts as a reserve for adjusting a temporary deficit of the international balance of payments. If this reserve is completely exhausted, there remain only the usual means for adjusting the balance of payments – the floating of loans abroad, and the export of commodities and securities. In that case, however, the gold standard is no longer effective.

These means are naturally much in demand as soon as the rate of exchange approaches or even exceeds the upper gold point. This automatic regulation of the balance of payments takes place only on the assumption that the value of money of the country is not lowered below that obtaining abroad. If, on the other hand, the unfavourable balance of payments and the rise in the rate of exchange are the result of a general rise in domestic prices in comparison with prices abroad (in other words, a shifting of the purchasing power parity), the rise in the exchange rates will meet with no such hindrances. But even then the stock of gold, as long as gold is sold freely at the legal par rate, affords a temporary obstacle to a further rise in the exchange rate, but not against a continuous rise in prices. If the gold supply is completely exhausted, or if the convertibility of notes is suspended, the rates of exchange and prices may continue to rise indefinitely.

The stabilisation of the rates of exchange is, in the last resort, completely dependent on the stabilisation of the relative value of money – that is, on the factors which regulate the value of money in the two countries.

According to the classical theory, the supply of gold must be distributed among the gold standard countries according to their needs, so that the price-levels of the various countries will be much about the same. If the price-level were to rise in one of the countries, commodity imports into this country would be stimulated, commodity exports, on the contrary, would be discouraged, so that gold would leave the country, and thus the gold stock would be reduced and the price-level would fall in accordance with the quantity theory. This would furnish an automatic regulator of the distribution of gold and of the price-levels in the various countries. This theory would be true, on the whole, if the currency consisted entirely of gold. In reality, this is not the case; even in gold standard countries the currency has its independent existence, and is connected with gold only in the way we have already described. The nucleus of truth which the classical theory contains must have been correctly represented in the arguments of this paragraph.

This so-called currency theory, which was the basis of Peel's Bank Act of 1844, and which is the starting point for the "fiduciary" limitation of the note issue, was a practical consequence of this classical theory of the international distribution of gold and the regulation of the value of gold. If bank-notes circulate alongside of gold, this should be permitted only on the assumption that the total quantity of the circulating media shows the same changes, under the influence of fluctuations in the price-level, as a pure system of gold circulation would have shown. Therefore, every diminution of the gold supply of a country should bring about an absolutely equal reduction of the supply of means of payment. Such legislation suffers not only from the same defects of principle as every legal fixing of the note reserves (§ 45), but, in addition, suffers from the mistaken idea that the gold standard is a system of actual gold payments.

The practical effect of the gold standard is that the central bank of the country buys gold at a certain price and sells it at a somewhat higher price. Between these two prices there is a small margin which, in most cases, rarely exceeds 1 per cent. One may ask whether this margin should not be made still smaller, and whether it ought not to disappear completely with an ideal gold standard. There seems to be a fairly widespread impression that, through the creation of an international bank, which should serve, so to speak, as a central bank for central banks and should accept gold deposits from them, the margins for the fluctuations of the rates of exchange could be reduced to zero, and thus complete stability of the exchanges could be brought about.

Let us first assume, in order to answer this question, that the internal value of the currency is maintained, and that, therefore, its purchasing power parity corresponds to its legal parity. As we have seen, temporary fluctuations in the rate of exchange will call forth strong counteracting forces which generally suffice to restore the equilibrium of the balance of payments. Only by way of exception will it be necessary to resort to gold exports for this purpose.

A diminution of the margin between the buying and selling prices of gold would restrict the scope of the effectiveness of these natural forces counteracting a deviation of the exchange from its purchasing power parity, and so a correspondingly heavier burden would be laid on the gold exports. Such a change in the international system of payments would not be economical. A central bank which bound itself to buy and sell gold or gold exchange at fixed prices could demand with justice that these prices should afford a certain opportunity for profit-making, which would be sufficient to cover the chief expenses.

The most important temporary deviations from the purchasing

power parity are, in normal currency conditions, caused through international movements of capital. It then seems a very natural consequence for such deviations to call forth counteracting forces in the form of the capital movements described above. This natural reaction against abnormal unilateral capital movements might be used with advantage before the central bank is called on for capital transfers in the shape of gold.

If the international value of a currency falls as the result of a depreciation in its internal purchasing power, it is an advantage that the central bank is not forced to export gold at once, but has time to bring in measures to raise the internal purchasing power of the currency. According to the old theory, gold exports in such a case would force the central bank to reduce the internal supply of means of payment, and thus the purchasing power of the currency would be brought to its proper level. In practice, this decrease in the supply of money does not take place so automatically, as the central bank has, as a rule, a free gold reserve which can be reduced without producing an effect on the actual supply of money. On the other hand, a sensible central bank policy should feel it necessary to inquire into the situation and to take the requisite restrictive measures, even without being forced to do so by the necessity of an immediate export of gold. It is too much to require the central bank to restore equilibrium without allowing for a small margin within which the exchange rates may rise.

§ 61 The Significance of Banking Policy with regard to International Payments

With regard to internal payments, banking policy, as already seen, has the task under a gold standard of regulating the supply of money so that the money is kept as near as possible at parity with gold. For this purpose, banking policy alone is not sufficient. In general, even in order to avoid a temporary premium on gold, it is necessary to keep a gold reserve to satisfy temporary increases in the demand for gold. If gold does not actually circulate, this reserve will not be used for internal payments, but, for the domestic economy, represents only a means of satisfying the non-monetary demand.

Similarly, banking policy must occupy itself with the maintenance of the currency in regard to international payments. This task has already been partly fulfilled by a banking policy which keeps the currency at a parity with gold on the internal market. For, thereby, those changes in the general price-level are avoided which drive the exchange rates to the upper gold point and thus cause gold exports. Internally as well as externally, it must be the endeavour of banking policy to avoid claims being made on the gold reserve as much as possible. Even for an enlightened banking policy this is not completely attained. The gold reserve must be kept to satisfy those demands for gold which will arise in spite of everything. With respect to external payments, the gold has the task, described in the preceding sections, of making up the deficit of foreign means of payment in the external balance of payments. Banking policy has to see that this task, like the corresponding task in regard to home trade, arises only occasionally, and that, as soon as the balance of payments corrects itself, the gold will flow back into the country and into the bank reserves. It is only when the general price-level is properly regulated by banking policy that the bank reserve can thus be protected against home or foreign demands, and be preserved for its purposes.

We have seen that, in respect to the domestic demand for money, the gold reserves of the central bank can be greatly reduced if gold does not circulate within the country. Similarly, claims on the gold reserves may be greatly reduced if other means of payment are used instead of gold for settling international payments. As such, there are, as far as central banks are concerned, mainly sight claims on foreign banking houses, contango loans employed on the principal stock exchanges, and, above all, first-class bills on those places. These bills may be drawn in part by people inside the country on people abroad, but they may be bought particularly in the foreign centre in order to employ the bank reserves profitably. A central bank which has at its disposal sufficient quantities of such credits on the chief world centres of payments can always satisfy demands for foreign means of payment by issuing orders on these credits, and thus avoid gold shipments. This way seems to be the most natural and the most convenient, as, in the last analysis, it is not gold, but foreign means of payment that are demanded. If demands for gold for export are thus avoided in all ordinary cases, and if no gold at all circulates within the country itself, the central bank can content itself with a comparatively small gold reserve. This idea found expression in the proposals, which we have already discussed, of the International Financial Conference at Genoa, 1922, regarding a concentrated holding of the cash balances of the central banks in the great financial centres.

Whether the reserve consists of gold or of foreign credits, it must in any case be protected from excessive claims. As has already been emphasised, this is done primarily through a banking policy which aims at keeping the general price-level as much as possible in agreement with the relative gold supply of the world. Let us assume for the sake of simplicity that the gold supply has remained constant during a period of time; then banking policy must endeavour also to keep the price-level constant. Let us assume also that this has been completely successful for a period. The means to this end is the credit policy, especially the discount policy of the banks. So that the general price-level shall remain constant in the period taken, a quite definite discount policy must also be pursued. Let us assume, further, that the price-level abroad remains unaltered. On these assumptions the domestic discount policy will protect the reserves against all claims which would otherwise arise from an increase in prices and an increased demand for domestic or foreign means of payment. The demands for means of payment which, nevertheless, are made by the home market arise from a marked increase in trade activity at certain seasons of the year, or from periods of brisk trade, and are primarily satisfied by increasing the supply of bank money. Similarly, special demands for foreign means of payment will arise from an occasional excess of foreign liabilities. Such an occasional negative balance of payments may easily arise without a change in the general price-level; it may also when on the whole there has been equilibrium in the balance of payments over a long period, and again as a result of the lending of capital to abroad or a bad harvest, etc. Such occasional demands for foreign means of payment are primarily satisfied by the means discussed in § 59 – that is, especially by the discounting of bills, sales of securities, and the floating of loans abroad. Generally, these measures are successful in bringing the balance of payments into equilibrium and thus in protecting the reserves against the demands of foreign trade, just as the employment of bank money is successful in turning away the domestic demand for means of payment.

It is within the power of a central bank to accelerate and to strengthen these self-acting measures for correcting the balance of payments. This is accomplished by measures which, in this connection, are simply designated as "discount policy." If the discount rate in Berlin is raised above the rate prevailing in similar foreign centres, foreign capitalists will, in normal conditions, willingly invest their money in Berlin for the time being. This may cause gold shipments to Berlin, but it generally is done through the purchase of claims falling due on Berlin. In this manner, payment obligations are transferred to the future and the German balance of payments is improved for the moment. Germany will also discount bills drawn on foreign centres at a lower rate, and by means of this anticipation of claims will create credits for the temporary relief of the balance of payments. Or, in order to avoid the high German discount rate, bills are sent by Germany to abroad *en pension*, and this is synonymous with the taking up of a short-period loan. The high discount rate, and the resulting high rate for contango loans, has a depressing effect on the Berlin Bourse, thus causing sales of securities to abroad, and this again relieves the German balance of payments. The methods may differ greatly, but the crux of the matter remains the same: the high interest rate attracts capital and thereby improves the balance of payments.

We must note, however, that this discount policy, which we may perhaps term "external discount policy," bears a character quite different from the discount policy of a central bank which regulates the value of the money of the country, as we have already seen (§ 48). According to the simplifying assumptions which we have just made, the latter kind of discount policy is completely controlled by the endeavour to keep the price-level constant. This does not prevent irregularities arising in the external balance of payments, which may thus cause the central bank to pursue a discount policy with special reference to the situation of the balance of payments at that moment. But thereby the bank runs counter to its fundamental discount policy of regulating the value of money, and, as a rule, this policy, as well as the capital market, has to suffer from the new objectives imposed on the discount policy. The external "discount policy" thus signifies a disturbance in the proper and central discount policy.

The external discount policy by its very nature is a differential discount policy, which primarily has to take account of the differences in the discount rates of the various money centres. If Berlin raises its rate in order to attract money, London will often be forced to adopt a counter-measure and to raise its discount rate also. As a result, the discounting of sterling bills in London is made more difficult, and the transfer of money from London to Berlin is hindered. If London raises its discount rate above that of Berlin, the latter will be quickly compelled to raise its rate once again. In this way there takes place a kind of race, and in the process the discount rate may be forced up considerably higher than is necessary from the point of view of regulating the internal value of money. Nevertheless, it must be borne in mind that such increases in the discount rates, if they occur in times of trade booms, hardly go too far, as the general price-level in any case is not prevented from undergoing what is often an excessive rise. On the other hand, in times of crisis a feverish raising of the discount rates, under the pressure of international competition, in order to obtain gold is hardly reconcilable with a rational monetary policy.

The disadvantages of frequent and violent fluctuations in the discount rate, arising from the "external" discount policy, have resulted in the formulation of a policy which, instead of raising the discount rate, seeks to protect the gold reserves of the banks by releasing gold for export only on payment of a premium. This "gold-premium policy," although the pure gold standard is maintained, is often carried so far that the price of gold is driven up to the highest limit allowed by the currency regulations. The gold-premium policy can go still further in countries having a "limping" or otherwise imperfect gold standard. As soon as a gold-premium policy is introduced, the rates of exchange on abroad may exceed the normal gold points. Thus the gold-premium policy results in fluctuating exchanges instead of fluctuating discount rates, and it may be disputed which of the two alternatives is the lesser evil. In the one case trade has to put up with a discount rate which is justified neither by the situation of the capital market nor from the point of view of regulating the supply of money, and in the other case there arises a depreciation of the currency with a temporary abandonment of the rigid gold standard. The best policy is of course to avoid both.

Assuming that a country always charges a constant premium on gold, this measure has essentially only the significance of a reduction of the gold parity of the currency, and there is no reason why this reduction could not just as well be carried through directly. Such a premium on gold has as little effect on the balance of payments as it has for protecting the gold reserves.

In order to avoid an unnecessary aggravation of the international competition for gold, with the resulting injurious disturbance of the internal discount policy, occasional inequalities in the international balance of payments should be settled for preference without gold shipments. This may be rendered possible to a certain extent if every country keeps a reserve of short-term claims on abroad. In the last resort, it is a question of being able to mobilise international credit quickly when necessary. This is once more a question of the effective organisation of the international capital market, and of the maintenance of economic and political confidence.

BOOK IV

THE THEORY OF TRADE CYCLES

CHAPTER XIII

INTRODUCTION

§ 62 *The Nature of the Problem*

IN the first two books of this work we have ignored, as far as we could, the possibility of change in the economy. To show as clearly as possible the simplest theoretical principles, we first of all considered the stationary State and then introduced the concept of the uniformly progressive economy, which allowed us to study the simplest and most important kind of change. In all these inquiries a strictly deductive procedure was necessary, for we were dealing with imaginary pictures having no exact counterpart in reality. If we wish to approach a step nearer to reality, the deductive method must be replaced by an inductive one. So we have to see how far the actual economic development diverges from the previously assumed uniformity of progress. Such divergencies can, of course, only be established by a study of the actual facts.

The divergencies which are most noticeable and, at the same time, which show the greatest regularity, are the so-called trade cycles. The study of these movements will form the subject of Book IV.

Out of all the phenomena of trade cycles it is but natural that most attention has been drawn to the crises. The public finds a dramatic element in them which attracts interest. For the business world, the crisis is the period of danger, of great losses, and of ruin, and science, too, has particularly devoted itself to the study of these crises. Economists have specialised in theories concerning crises, and have attempted, by means of a mass of historical material, to establish the characteristic features of crises, and to gain some knowledge of their causes and effects by comparing the peculiar phenomena of the crisis with incidents of the boom and depression periods. This method has certainly not been unfruitful, but from its very nature it is bound to pay attention chiefly to those external characteristics of crises which seem to be most interesting, and which thus have a greater objective importance from the point of view of the business world or of a more or less predetermined scientific theory. A really systematic and impartial study is hardly possible in such circumstances, or is at least made considerably more difficult.

We shall adopt a different method here. We shall not study crises as isolated phenomena, but shall consider the trade cycle as a whole, as a single continuous movement of the national economy. Thus our attention will not be mainly directed to a few arbitrarily chosen phenomena. Instead, we shall systematically investigate the real changes which the economy undergoes in the boom and depression periods. This systematic study of economic movement will gradually afford us a deeper insight into the nature of trade cycles and of the causal connection between the different factors which are responsible for the cyclical movements in the economy, and which are in turn affected by them. In this way the study of trade cycles will lead to the consideration of the dynamics of the economy, which will serve as the necessary supplement to our earlier treatment of economic life as a static phenomenon or a uniform development.

In our study of the fluctuations in economic activity under the influence of trade cycles, we shall, as far as possible, go from the concrete to the abstract. We shall therefore, consider first the changes in material production and the accompanying changes in the factors of production. We shall then pass over to the fluctuations in prices and income, and shall conclude with a study of the changes in the condition of the capital market. At every stage we shall try, as far as possible, to establish the actual incidents statistically, so as to bring to light the reciprocal action of the various lines of movement and reveal the inner connection. It is evident that, in such a treatment, the graphic method can be of great service, especially when a comparison of two different movements is made.

It is clearly an advantage to be able to follow the lines of development of economic activity for as long a period as possible. Only a curve which includes a series of cyclical changes can give us a satisfactory picture of the way in which these changes act upon a certain factor, and only a comparison between two such curves enables us to obtain a more or less definite insight into the reciprocity or parallelism of different factors.

However, a study of this kind, which is to be valid for the whole of Western Europe, cannot, in general, go back further than the beginning of the 'seventies. Such a limit is fixed by the nature of the available statistical material. There are, however, also deeper grounds for it; only since that time has there developed a world economy of so uniform a kind that it is possible to regard it as an entity. Only since that time have the older types of economy generally and definitely been surmounted and replaced by the modern exchange economy, with its division of labour and its "capitalistic" methods of production and transport. From that time onward, certain old forms and causes of crises seem to have been mainly overcome, and the modern type of crisis and of boom and slump periods, with all their characteristic features, have emerged.

Crises, in the general sense of violent disturbances of economic activity, may be of very different kinds. Historically, they appear chiefly in connection with great economic revolutions or new organisations and conditions, the proper handling and control of which man must learn from long experience. Thus, for instance, the development of the monetary system led to innumerable crises which may be traced to the misconceptions as to the use of coinage or the issue of notes. Further crises arose through the misuse of credit, perhaps especially of State credit or of special instruments of credit such as bills of exchange. The widespread opportunities of speculation afforded by the stock exchanges or the newly arisen limited companies were at first subject to many abuses, and these caused the most violent crises. The extension of the sphere of European trade to the whole world involved such an alteration of existing economic conditions as to lead to many crises before the business world had really grasped the new conditions of trade and adjusted itself to them. The beginning of exportation from Europe to the colonies was characterised by an absolutely astonishing lack of knowledge of the needs and purchasing power of distant parts of the world. This fact, together with the slowness of means of communication was responsible for the series of great commercial crises both in the eighteenth and in the first half of the nineteenth centuries. Revolutions in the conditions of importation of commodities from abroad also resulted in crises, the most important and best known of which was that of European agriculture at the close of the nineteenth century. It is but natural that the great modern changes in the technique of production could not take place without serious disturbances, especially in a number of trades which underwent the change from manual labour to machine production.

Besides these circumstances, there are also series of smaller, and less important, disturbances of economic life to be taken into account as causes of crises. They can generally be traced back to an occasional scarcity or surplus of commodities, and arise, for instance, from very good or very bad harvests, or during a period when the scarcity of raw material is of such a nature as to bring industry to a standstill, or on account of changes of fashion which make stocks of goods unsaleable, and so on. Finally, war must also be included among the general causes of economic crises.

It is at once evident that no general or single theory is valid for so varying and varied a phenomenon as crises, in the sense in which we have here described them. What we wish to study in this Book is not the generality of possible disturbances of economic life, but, as we have suggested, the general up and down movement of economic activity, particularly the features it has presented since 1870. Since that time, many of the older causes of crises have ceased to be active. The crises which fall within that period have to some extent a common character, and they are in the main an outcome of the causes which are responsible for the ordinary and increasingly interdependent fluctuations of economic activity; the more casual conditions which generally gave rise to the older crises, however, disappear more and more into the background. The careful observer of the economic history of the nineteenth century cannot fail to recognise a gradual change in the type of phenomenon we call a crisis. Not until the 'seventies, however, did this change proceed so far as to show clearly the new type of crisis and trade cycle. On this ground, there are objections to theories of modern trade cycles which are based too much on material from the history of the earlier crises, and it is quite justifiable to limit our inquiries to the period after 1870.

Of course, there are, in this limited period, certain casual disturbances of the kind we have mentioned, although, as we have said, many of the causes of earlier crises are now effective in only a small degree. But as we are here directing our attention to the larger up and down movements of the world economy, we ignore, as far as possible, all casual and small disturbances, all that are local in their effects, and all that are confined to particular industries.

We cannot overlook the fact that the period under consideration also represents one of transition which involved far-reaching economic changes. That period saw the end of the old self-sufficing agricultural economy, and the perfection of production based on division of labour and the system of exchange connected with it. It is only to be expected that a revolution of this character should entail great economic disturbances. So all views of modern fluctuations and crises as necessary concomitants of the modern productive and social order are on that account premature. Theory must not start with the assumption that it must find the complete and conclusive explanation of the movements in question in the nature of the economic order which we have attained, but must pay attention to the importance of the transition to this order. We are still in a period of transition, and must wait to see what effect the end of the transition period will have upon the movements in question. The old belief that crises were progressively more devastating in their effects is, at all events, now obsolete. In the most progressive and economically best educated countries, where some of the worst of the earlier causes of crises (as, for instance, an unsound bank-note policy) have been overcome, the available material points rather to a weakening of crises. Consequently, we must at present leave open the question of how far the great economic fluctuations which we are to consider are connected with the revolution in the social and economic system – a revolution in itself unique – and how far we should expect a decrease in their strength at the close of it.

In the main, I leave these observations as they were drawn up before the war. It is undoubted that the World War means an interruption of the economic cyclical movements which we are about to study in this Book. The economic development of post-war times has been so strikingly dominated by great monetary disturbances that trade cycles of the earlier kind are no longer applicable. Also, other extraordinary disturbing factors, such as the political insecurity, the burden of war debts, and the universal return to a protectionist commercial policy, as well as the increasingly monopolistic character of labour organisations in the sheltered industries,[1] and the State maintenance of the unemployed, have introduced into the economic life of the post-war period a very marked element of instability. A satisfactory study of the economic history of the last decade must be primarily directed to the explanation of these disturbing factors. Not until this has been achieved, and – we may assert this – not until we have, on the basis of such an analysis, in the main surmounted these disturbances, shall we again be confronted by the question of how far the term trade cycles in the sense of this Book is still valid, and what significance they still have for economic life.

At present, there is a prevailing belief, especially in the so-called *Konjunkturinstituten*, that everything that occurs in economic life is determined by mathematical curves, and that we have only to discover these to be able to learn our predetermined fate. This modern Western form of an ancient Eastern fatalism must be fought and overcome. The study of the disturbances which prevent a uniform development of economic life must always be directed to the discovery of these disturbances, and must follow the practical aim of suppressing them as much as possible. From this point of view, the study of the cyclical fluctuations during the period 1870–1914 is very instructive. We shall find that these fluctuations have no absolute necessity, but are to a great extent caused by factors which represent passing phenomena of economic history, or which may be, if not eliminated, at least to a great extent controlled.

[1] Cf. Cassel, *Recent Monopolistic Tendencies in Industry and Trade*, Geneva, League of Nations, 1927.

Before we pass on to the study of the movements of economic activity under the influence of trade cycles, we must come to an agreement as to the chronology of these fluctuations – that is, we must decide in which years the trade cycles changed from a period of increasing activity to one of depression. In such a decision no

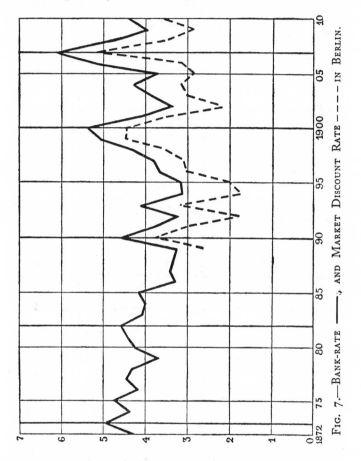

Fig. 7.—Bank-rate ———, and Market Discount Rate – – – – in Berlin.

a priori position is taken up in regard to our problem. The assignment of a point of time to which we have to trace back economic changes is really a question of terminology. In deciding the question, we must only lay stress on our determination to keep as closely

as possible to what is generally recognised. Fortunately, there is
no difference of opinion on that point. In what follows we shall
take 1873, 1882, 1890, 1900, and 1907 as years of crisis, or, in
order to emphasise the change from advance to decline, "transition

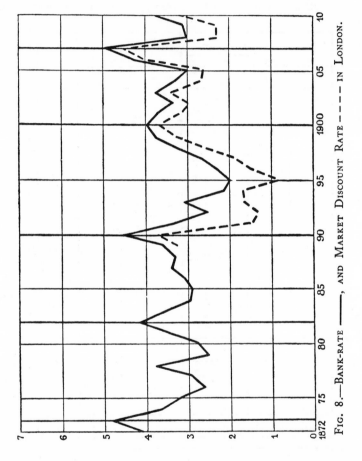

FIG. 8.—BANK-RATE ———, AND MARKET DISCOUNT RATE – – – – IN LONDON.

years." In our diagrams, we shall indicate these years, following
Lucien March in the *Bulletin de la Statistique Générale de la
France*,[1] by thick vertical lines, which we may call "transition
lines."

[1] Vol. I., Paris, 1911–12.

In thus determining the crisis years, we must, however, note that in different countries there may be differences in the dates at which the crises occur. The differences are only of material importance in the case of the United States, where the crises of 1890 and 1900 were delayed until 1893 and 1903 respectively.

Although this chronology is generally accepted, it might not be out of place to justify this acceptance. If we define the crisis as a time of general inability to meet obligations which fall due, we must take, as the first external sign of the crisis, an extraordinary tension of the money market, and so a tightening of the rates for short-period loans, especially the discount rates. The statistics of the discount rates show infallibly that the maxima of these rates always occur in the crisis years we have enumerated. The simplest way to convince ourselves of this is to glance at the diagrams (Figs. 7 and 8), in which the continuous line represents the bank-rate, and the dotted line the market discount rate, for Berlin and London.[1]

The closer study of the relation between trade cycles and discount rates properly belongs to a later stage of our inquiry. Here we need only note that the extraordinary tension in the money market which is always connected with the idea of a crisis did actually occur in each of the crisis years we have enumerated.

[1] The figures on which the diagram is based are given in Table IV. in the Appendix.

CHAPTER XIV

THE INFLUENCE OF TRADE CYCLES ON PRODUCTION

§ 63 *The Chief Branches of Production during Trade Cycles*

WE now pass on to the study of those changes in economic production which appear during the various phases of a trade cycle. For this purpose we must divide productive activity into its main branches and observe the particular effect of trade cycles on the different kinds of production.

Production, as we know, falls into two main branches – the production of fixed capital and the production of goods which pass directly into consumption. In both cases, there is, as an intermediate stage in the process, the production of materials, semi-manufactured goods, and those things actually used in the productive process. These materials and semi-manufactured products, such as pig-iron and rails, cotton and cotton-yarns, and material like coal for providing power, which we have put together under the head of "circulating capital," are, so to say, only symptoms of the continuous productive process which finds its technical goal in the creation of fixed capital or of a commodity that passes into the consumption system. We may therefore assume that the production of circulating capital orientates itself to one or the other main branch of production, at least in the first place, according to the volume of this branch. So in our study of the influence of trade cycles on production, we have only to distinguish between the production of fixed capital and that of goods which pass directly into consumption. For the sake of brevity, we shall call these two branches of production "production of capital" and "production of consumption goods." As to the extent of each kind, the production of certain kinds of circulating capital will, as we shall soon see, be our best measure.

Let us consider the production of capital first. The most important fixed capital in the modern community consists, as we have seen, of buildings and railways. Hence, if we wish to ascertain the direct influence of trade cycles upon the production of capital, we must examine the statistical data of the construction of houses and railways.

In the case of houses we have, for the United States, statistics of the sums devoted annually to building in the fifty-two chief cities. The figures are for calendar years, in millions of dollars. [1]

Year.			$ mill.	Year.			$ mill.
1904	..	..	.. 469	1909	..	..	.. 772
1905	..	..	.. 645	1910	..	..	.. 726
1906	..	..	.. 679	1911	..	..	.. 688
1907	..	..	.. 646	1912	..	..	.. 739
1908	..	..	.. 566	1913	..	..	.. 660

The figure for 1907 is increased by $20,000,000 through the inclusion of three new cities in the statistics. But it is clear from the table that there was a great increase in building in the years preceding 1907. The maximum year is the one before the crisis year of 1907. During the following depression the amount of building decreased rapidly. In a single year the sums invested fell by $80,000,000, or 12 per cent. of the amount that had been reached in 1907.

During the following year, when, in the United States, there was an advance as sudden as it was brief, the amount invested in building rose by no less than $106,000,000. With the next two years came a severe reaction. However, a new maximum was reached in 1912, once more in the year before the transition year of the trade cycle of 1913. The upward movement is therefore characterised by an increase in building activity, and the depression by a decrease. The peak of production is reached a little before the end of the upward movement.

A similar effect of trade cycles upon building activity can also be traced in the case of Germany. The volume of memoranda to the Imperial Finance Reform of 1908 gives *statistics of the amounts*

[1] *Statistical Abstract of the United States.*

insured in the public fire insurance companies with compulsory rights. [1]
(The figures are given, abbreviated, in millions of marks.) The
changes in these figures from year to year may give us a general
idea of the changes in the rate of building. [2] It can be seen that the
increase in the amounts of insurance reached a pronounced peak in
1882, 1891, 1901, and 1904, and that, consequently, the highest
points almost coincide with those of the boom periods. In some cases,
however, the peak is a year late; this means that a brisk trade in the
building industry in one year is only shown in a corresponding
increase in the insurance figures in the following year. The
maximum of the year 1904 points to a special advance outside the
broad general trade cycle.

Year.	Amounts of Insurance.	Year.	Amounts of Insurance.
1875	14,281	1891	22,742
1876	15,135	1892	23,120
1877	15,756	1893	23,836
1878	15,696	1894	24,572
1879	16,079	1895	25,275
1880	16,293	1896	25,639
1881	16,681	1897	26,500
1882	17,983	1898	27,529
1883	17,478	1899	28,520
1884	17,868	1900	29,349
1885	18,314	1901	30,780
1886	18,719	1902	32,123
1887	19,487	1903	33,667
1888	20,151	1904	35,414
1889	20,855	1905	36,792
1890	21,445	1906	37,209

The extent of railway construction has long been regarded as a
good measure of trade cycles. But it is unmistakable that the economic character of railway building in the most advanced countries of
Western civilisation has changed to some extent. To-day, the
centre of interest in these countries lies in increasing the transport

[1] *Reichstag*, 12 Legislatur Periode, I. Session, 1907–9, Nr. 1,043, Teil III., "Materi-
alen zur Beurteilung der Wohlstandsentwicklung Deutschlands im letzten Men-
schenalter," p. 35.

[2] The average percentage growth of the amounts of insurance in the thirty-year period
1876–1906, is 3.05. This figure agrees with the percentage of the general economic
progress which we have found to be characteristic of the period.

capacity of the old lines, rather than in constructing new ones. This change seems to have considerably decreased the effect of trade cycles upon this type of construction.

Special interest lies in the development of railway construction in the United States. [1] Since the middle of the nineteenth century the history of railway construction in that country has also been the history of crises. Construction in the 'fifties, which reached its peak with 3,642 miles of new lines in 1856, was retarded by the crisis of 1857, and sank annually, reaching its lowest point (660 miles) in 1861. With the close of the 'sixties, the building of railways became active again. In 1871 the newly opened lines rose to 7,379 miles. From this peak, there was a decline until 1873, when a little over 4,000 miles of new lines were opened. For 1875 the figure had dropped to 1,741 miles. At the close of the 'seventies and the beginning of the 'eighties, railway construction increased, until, in 1882, the enormous figure of 11,569 miles was reached, followed by a drop to 2,975 miles in 1885. These figures show very clearly the relation between railway construction and trade cycles. The boom periods are characterised by unusual activity, which attains its maximum point in or just before the crisis year. But, on the other hand, in what we have called the slump periods, railway construction falls to a minimum.

After the depression in the middle of the 'eighties, there was a great increase in railway building in the United States, culminating in a total of 12,876 miles in 1887, and continuing with a considerable amount of new construction until 1893. With the 'nineties, however, the increase of the transport capacity of the old systems seemed to gain considerably in importance compared with the opening of new lines. The statistics published by the Interstate Commerce Commission of railways opened since 1890 give us some insight into this development. [1] These statistics give the total length of tracks laid down, and the figures are given separately for the first, second, third, and fourth tracks and for station tracks. The annual increase (in thousands of miles) of the total length of

[1] *Statistical Abstract of the United States.*

tracks for each of the years 1891 to 1907 is, on this material, as follows (fiscal year to June 30th):

Year.	Thousand Miles.	Year.	Thousand Miles.
1891	7.6	1901	6.6
1892	3.6	1902	8.8
1893	10.8	1903	9.6
1894	7.9	1904	13.3
1895	3.5	1905	9.7
1896	5.9	1906	10.3
1897	2.9	1907	10.9
1898	3.3	1908	5.7
1899	4.8	1909	8.7
1900	8.6	1910	9.4

It must not be forgotten that the years given in the figures end on June 30th for each year. It then appears that the three boom years which end in the crises of 1893, 1903, and 1907 are characterised by a great increase in length of tracks, while the slump periods after the crises are just as clearly marked by a reverse movement. In the period covered by our statistics, the length of the first track has fallen much below half of the total length, so that the additional and station tracks surpass it. Thus, for example, the length added to the first track in 1907 amounted to only 5,100 miles, while the addition to the others was 5,800 miles. This shows that statistics which refer only to the length of the newly built first line are not sufficient for testing the effect of trade cycles upon railway construction.

The new character of railway construction appears not only in the extended demand for additional tracks, but also in the general development of the old systems, by which the gradient of the lines is improved, sharp curves abolished, and wooden bridges and viaducts replaced by steel. The annual reconstruction of bridges and viaducts alone must be reckoned in miles in the case of the larger systems. All this work was evidently necessitated by the great increase of traffic. It has, consequently, much less of a speculative character than the building of railways in earlier times, when the object was primarily to open up new districts as rapidly as possible. It is therefore justifiable to assume that the change in the character of railway construction that has taken place will gradually decrease the influence of trade cycles upon the sphere of production we are now considering.

In a country like England, railway building has certainly not yet come to a standstill, but the development is less marked than formerly. The annual increase of paid-up capital of the English railways is now often less[1] than 1 per cent. of the whole, and in the period 1901–11 it never exceeded 2 per cent. The fluctuations from year to year show no striking connection with the movements of trade cycles. In earlier periods, however, railway construction in England is very significant in connection with the study of trade cycles.

In many new countries, railway construction has, of course, the same character as it had during the earlier period in our older countries. Hence statistics giving in kilometres the length of new lines opened throughout the world do not convey an accurate idea of the importance of railway construction. This becomes still clearer if we bear in mind how much the cost of construction per kilometre varies in different countries. A general account of the influence of trade cycles upon railway construction is thus made very difficult.

While, therefore, we can demonstrate that trade cycles have a definite influence upon the building of houses and railways, even in the sense that the production of capital in these branches increases during a boom period and decreases during the depression which follows, this result is still obtained from isolated observations which are possibly not representative, in the selection of which different conditions cannot all equally be taken into account, and which, above all, provide no measure of the influence of trade cycles. We must rather try to find a type of production which can represent the entire production of fixed capital, which gives a quantitative reflection of the fluctuations in the production of capital, and from the variations in which we can deduce corresponding variations in the production of capital. To attain this, we must

---

[1] "Paid-up Capital of Railway Companies" (*Statistical Abstract for the United Kingdom*).

turn from the production of definite concrete capital goods, and direct our attention to the materials which are generally used in such production.

If we therefore ask ourselves what, in the modern economy, are the most important materials embodied in fixed capital, we easily find that among these iron, wood, and stone (including bricks and cement) are of the greatest significance. Of these, again, iron undoubtedly takes the first place. Modern technical development has given it this paramount importance as material for fixed capital. In earlier times, it was mainly used for making tools. Technical advances in its manufacture made it possible, by the first half of the nineteenth century, to use it for building purposes, but it was not until the Bessemer, Siemens-Martin, and Thomas processes were introduced that the economy entered upon the "iron age" in the modern technical sense. From the 'seventies onward, it was used to an increasing extent for construction of all conceivable kinds. It is now the chief material not only for railways, in which it is used for bridges, viaducts, stations, and rolling stock, but also for ships, not excepting sailing vessels, buildings, factories, and even houses. Since, through the Thomas process, it is possible to produce iron girders cheaply, it has been used considerably in the building of houses. Even a small house can hardly be built nowadays without the use of iron girders. Then there is also the extensive use of iron for pipes, either in the house itself or in the streets leading to it. When we consider all the uses of iron, we see clearly that it is not only unequivocally the most important material of fixed capital, but is so generally used as such that the consumption of it is a very good measure of the entire production of fixed capital. It might be objected that a certain amount of iron is used in the manufacture of consumption goods, but if we calculate the consumption of iron not in value but in tons, the quantity that is used for making razors, skates, etc., is insignificant, and need not be considered. The annual production of iron may therefore be taken as a measure of the annual production of fixed capital.

Iron assumes a great variety of forms. In practice, however, all iron, at least under pre-war technical conditions, passes through the stage of pig-iron. Here the statistics of the production of pig-iron afford the measure we need of the total production of capital. The statistics have the further advantage of including fairly reliable

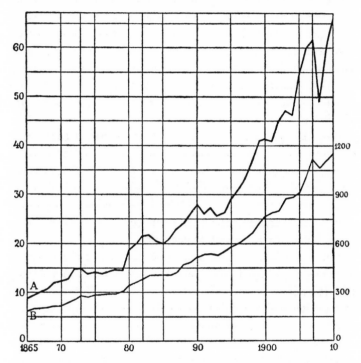

FIG. 9.—WORLD PRODUCTION OF PIG-IRON (A) AND COAL (B) IN MILLION TONS.

figures covering the whole world, and thus enable us to construct a curve that reflects the world production of fixed capital.

In our diagram (Fig. 9)[1] the world production in pig-iron is represented by curve *A*. A glance at this curve shows that its highest points regularly coincide with the turning points of the

[1] The numbers on the left of the diagram represent the world production of pig-iron in millions of tons. The statistical data on which the curve is based are reproduced in Table V. of the Appendix.

trade cycles; in other words, that the maxima of iron production occur at the busiest periods of the trade booms. Before each line marking the turning point in the cycle, there is a considerable increase in the output of iron, and, after it, a fairly regular diminution of output. And as the production of iron represents the entire production of fixed capital, we see that there is a special increase in capital-production before each turning point, a decline afterwards. This justifies our use of the terms "periods of boom and depression." We may now define, with precision, these conceptions. *A period of boom is one of special increase in the production of fixed capital; a period of decline or a depression is one in which this production falls below the point it had previously reached.*

Altogether, the production of pig-iron in the period 1865–1910 rose from some 9 million tons to about 66 million tons, which means an average annual increase of 4.5 per cent. The increases in the periods of increasing trade activity amount to as much as 30 and even 40 per cent. The decline in the periods of depression is usually smaller, and remains as a rule below 10 per cent.; only for 1908 does it reach about 20 per cent.

It may thus be considered as definite that trade cycles influence the production of fixed capital, and the way in which they do so is clear. It is not, however, sufficient to know the effect of trade cycles; we must know also whether their effects on other production are identical or different, perhaps contrary. It remains for us, therefore, to investigate how the production of commodities which pass immediately into consumption behaves in the various trade cycles. We might attempt to select various commodities and subject them to such an examination. But this method would, to a large extent, expose us to the danger of our choice depending too much on coincidences, and consequently our conclusions concerning the dependence of the output of consumption goods on trade cycles would not be convincing enough. In this case, too, it is essential to select one individual article to represent the entire production.

Before we proceed on these lines, we must remember that one large field of production for consumption is excluded from the outset, namely, the whole of agricultural production. In the case of agriculture, weather conditions play the leading part. Agricultural production fluctuates with the harvests and shows no direct connection with the movements of trade cycles.

Excluding, therefore, all agricultural production, we have, in the case of the remaining production, a commodity of such universal importance that it can be employed as a measure of production. This commodity is coal. Coal, it is true, is used to a great extent for the production of fixed capital, and the curve of the coal output will not supply us with an individual picture of the production of consumption goods, but a comparison of this curve with that for pig-iron will nevertheless be instructive. Coal is used not only for actual material processes of production, but also for the immediate satisfaction of definite needs, such as the heating and lighting of our houses, and passenger-transport on train and tram. From our point of view, this is an advantage, since the coal output thus becomes a measure for the great sphere of production to satisfy immediate immaterial requirements. In our diagram (Fig. 9) the world production of coal is represented by the curve B, which gives the production in millions of tons (numbers on the right).

This curve represents regular increases for the boom periods, but, in general, no decreases or only insignificant decreases in periods of depression. As is immediately observed, it has, on the whole, a far more regular course than the pig-iron curve. The influence of trade cycles is suspected, but it is extremely probable that this influence would disappear, or, at least, be partly neutralised if we could deduct the coal output which is employed for the production of pig-iron and the whole allied iron industry. We seem, therefore, justified in our conclusion that the coal output which is used in the production of consumption goods really grows steadily and shows no dependence on trade cycles. The only really important decline in the coal output is to be found in 1907. It is, however, obvious that the decline is essentially to be ascribed to the huge decline in the pig-iron output for the same year, and that, therefore, the coal output for purposes other than the iron industry was practically unaffected even by the boom in 1907 and the subsequent depression.

The comparison between our two production curves thus leads us to the conclusion that trade cycles have a marked influence on the production of pig-iron, but that, in the case of coal which is employed in the production of goods for consumption, a similar influence is almost non-existent. This result can, after what we have said concerning the significance of our curves, be further taken as indicating that, while the production of fixed capital depends essentially on trade cycles, *the production of consumption goods shows no marked dependence on trade cycles. This means that the alternation between periods of boom and slump is fundamentally a variation in the production of fixed capital, but has no direct connection with the rest of production.*

This statement is obviously of such vital importance for the whole theory of cyclical fluctuations that we must not fail to test it by all the means at our disposal. First, we are going to draw our comparison between the output of pig-iron and that of coal in a single country – Germany. The corresponding curves are reproduced in the diagram (Fig. 10)[1] As far as the production of pig-iron (curve *A*) is concerned, it shows, in the case of Germany, a relative advance which exceeds the corresponding increase in the world output. The periods of increasing trade activity are, therefore, very pronounced in the German production of pig-iron. Again, after the turning years of the trade cycles, 1873, 1900, and 1907, we find marked depressions. On the other hand, no decline takes place after 1890; after 1882, a decline is not found till 1886, and that is but an insignificant one. The coal curve runs very evenly on the whole, showing in fact only a few important declines, namely, 2.7 per cent. in 1876–7, 1.8 per cent. in 1891–2 and 1.5 per cent. in 1901–2. The comparison between the German coal and iron outputs may be looked upon as ample confirmation of our result.

In the United States, the fluctuations in the pig-iron output have, it is well known, been great for a long time past. From 1890 to 1894, for example, the production of pig-iron fell from 9.2 to 6.7 million tons. But the coal output of the United States has become

---

[1] Figures in Table V. of the Appendix.

steadier. In the period 1870–1907 it shows no decline of more than
9 per cent. In the year 1908, when the iron output fell 38 per cent.
below that of 1907, an important decline in the coal output naturally took place, but even then only 13.4 per cent.[1]

It is natural that England must, on account of its large exports

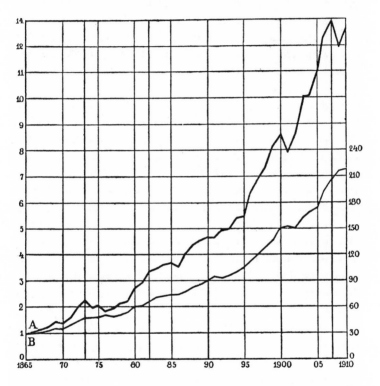

FIG. 10.—PRODUCTION IN GERMANY OF PIG-IRON (A) AND COAL (B)
IN MILLION TONS.

of coal, show proportionately large fluctuations of output. The
worst decline in coal production was from 1891 to 1893, and
amounted to 11.4 per cent. The production of pig-iron had, however,
fallen by 19.4 per cent. from 1889 to 1892. The decline of 18.3

[1] *Statistical Abstract of the United States.*

per cent. in pig-iron output from 1882 to 1886 is accompanied by a fall in the coal output of 3.8 per cent. from 1883 to 1886.

Now let us test our conclusion in another way. The statistics of the railway goods traffic in certain countries enable us to divide the total tonnage according to the classes of goods. We may make the division in such a way as to keep, on one side, the commodities which serve mainly as the material of fixed capital, and, on the other side, all the remaining commodities. For Germany, we have done this by including under one head cement, iron, wood, and stone (classes of goods 7, 11–20, 31 *a* and *b*, and 59 in the official statistics) as material of fixed capital. The tonnage for these is subtracted from the total tonnage of the goods conveyed. We thus get the tonnage of "capital goods" and "other goods" (see Table VI. in the Appendix). If we examine these statistics, which go back to 1886, we find the capital goods rising considerably until the year 1889, and no decline after the turning year 1890; a result that agrees with the German curve of pig-iron production. For the group "other goods" we notice a decline of 127,087 to 124,766 tons from 1891 to 1892, or about 1.8 per cent. For the period from 1885 to 1889 the development is shown on the diagram (Fig. 11). The lower continuous line represents the tonnage of "capital goods" in millions of tons. The upper dotted line shows in the same way the tonnage of the "other goods," but for convenience it has been lowered by 100. This latter curve indicates, as we see, no reaction, while the curve of capital goods has pronounced reactions after the turning years of the trade cycles, 1900 and 1907. The diagram therefore confirms the connection which we found to exist between the movements of the trade cycles and the production of fixed capital, and it also clarifies how much less the remaining production is influenced by trade cycles, although the group "other goods" is naturally not altogether free from fixed capital goods.

A similar investigation may be made for the United States.[1] We will consider only the trade booms of 1904 to 1907. We find an increase in the tonnage of goods traffic from 1,310 million to 1,796 million tons, or 37 per cent. Of the various classes of goods which

[1] *Statistical Abstract of the United States.* Note that the year ends at June 30th.

the statistics specify, those given in the following table show an increase above this average by the percentage stated:

Goods.			Per Cent.	Goods.	Per Cent.
Coke	..	..	.. 75%	Machines, etc. ..	.. 49%
Ore	..	..	.. 92%	Iron bars and tin	.. 76%
Stone, etc.		..	.. 54%	Cement, bricks and lime	58%
Rails	..	..	.. 42%	Coaches and tools	.. 48%

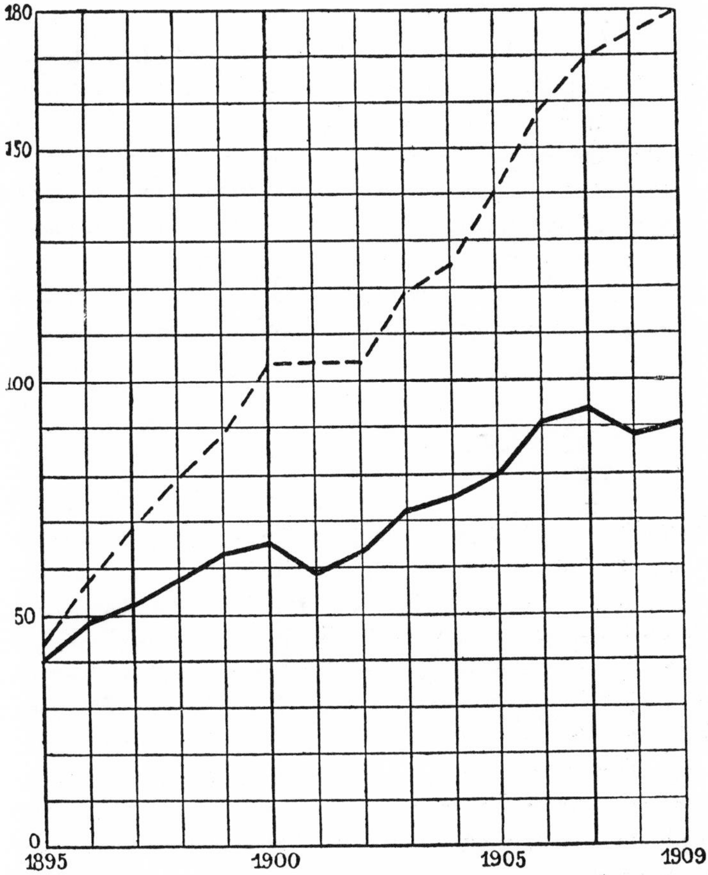

FIG. 11.—GOODS TRAFFIC ON GERMAN RAILWAYS, IN MILLIONS OF TONS.
———— CAPITAL GOODS.   ———— OTHER GOODS.

Below the average increase are the great groups of agricultural and animal products, with 21 and 9 per cent. respectively. For domestic and such-like articles the increase is 21 per cent. Sugar even decreased by 3.5 per cent. Unfortunately, we cannot follow the matter any further, as the statistics were changed in 1908. The figures quoted, however, confirm the fact that the rising period means a considerable increase in the production of capital goods, but the remaining production shows scarcely any advance beyond the normal.

Now that we have established that the production of fixed capital reflects the trade cycles in their periods of boom and depression, it remains to show as accurately as possible when the decline in production begins. The culminating point of a crisis can generally be determined with some precision. The question is whether capital production – and, firstly, the production of pig-iron – falls just at the highest point of the crisis, or a little earlier or later.

According to the data collected by Pohle,[1] the output of pig-iron in the German tariff area was, in thousands of tons:

Year.					Tons in 1000's
1906	..	..	..	..	.. 12,422
1907	..	..	..	..	.. 13,046
1908	..	..	..	..	.. 11,814

Thus the annual statistics show no decline for the year of crisis. When we study the statistics for the individual months, we find that in 1907 the production for each month is higher than for the corresponding month of 1906. The output for January, 1908, is practically equal to that of the corresponding month in the previous year. For February, 1908, the output is higher than for February, 1907. Not until March is there a slight decline of some 52,000 tons, and in April there is a considerable drop (98,000 tons) as compared with the same month in the previous year. On the other hand, the daily output declines from as early as December, 1907. It is as follows:

[1] *Monatliche Übersichten über die allgemeine Wirtschaftslage* (Supplement to the *Zeitschrift zur Sozialwissenschaft*).

	1907.			1908.	
September	..	.. 36.4	January ..	..	.. 34.2
October ..	..	.. 36.7	February	..	.. 34.3
November	..	.. 37.1	March ..	..	.. 33.8
December	..	.. 35.7	April ..	..	.. 32.7

It is clear, then, that the decline in the output of pig-iron did not occur until some months after the crisis, which, as is well known, began in September.

In the United States, where the crisis originated and was also very acute, the decline in the production of pig-iron followed rather more rapidly on the crisis. The pig-iron production in thousands of gross tons per day came to 72.8 in September, 75.4 in October, 60.9 in November, 39.8 in December, and reached its minimum of 33.7 in January, 1908. As the crisis broke out in September and was very severe in October, even in the United States the decline in the production of pig-iron came somewhat later.

CHAPTER XV

THE INFLUENCE OF TRADE CYCLES ON LABOUR

§ 64 *Changes in the Numbers of Workers in the two Chief Branches of Production*

IF the essential element of a trade cycle is the extraordinary production of fixed capital and the subsequent considerable decline in that production, these movements are bound to be reflected in changes in the number of workers employed in this production. If it is true that the trade cycles exert no material influence on the rest of production, this fact should come to light in a more uniform rise in the number of workers in these other industries. In this connection, the old question arises: Where do the industries producing capital goods obtain the additional labour which they need during the trade booms, and what happens to those workers whom the same industries are unable to employ during the depressions? We are obviously broaching here the whole subject of a general inquiry into the movements of labour under the influence of trade cycles.

Unfortunately, this point, important as it is for our knowledge o trade cycles, as well as from the general social point of view, does not appear to have been specially considered in official statistics. We can, however, get certain statistical data for some countries which throw considerable light on the phenomena under consideration.

In the case of Sweden, the official factory[1] statistics for each year give the number of workers divided into various groups of industries. We can therefore include here those groups of industries which in the main serve for the production of fixed capital and thus calculate the total number of workers employed in these industries. The industries in question are the timber, stone, and building material, and iron and steel industries. The total number of workers

[1] *Sveriges officiella Statistik* D., "Fabriker och Handtverk."

employed in these industries can be calculated from the available statistics for each year after 1896. This number is shown on the diagram (Fig. 12) by curve *A*. Curve *B* indicates the number of workers in other industries, and curve *C* the total number of industrial workers, or the sum of *A* and *B*.[1] Curve *C* shows, for the two turning years of the trade cycles, 1900 and 1907, the characteristic sharp points of a trade boom. When we examine the causes of these peaks we find that they are almost entirely due to fluctuations in the number of workers in the capital-producing industries. The curve of these industries shows very marked drops after both 1900 and 1907, while the curve of the other industries maintains its advance after 1900, though at a more moderate rate, and only falls a little after 1907. The fluctuations in the industries producing capital goods as shown by the curve are here expressed in figures:

Year.	Rise.	Year.	Fall.
1896–1900	29.5%	1900–1902	5.1%
1902–1907	12.9%	1907–1909	10.0%

Curve *B*, of the other industries, shows not a single fall before 1907, and in the great strike years of 1908–9 a fall, as against 1907, of only about 1,000 workers, or about 0.56 per cent.

Thus the conclusion at which we have already arrived, that the movements of the trade cycle are merely expressions of the fluctuations in the production of fixed capital, is fully borne out by the statistics of the number of workers in Swedish industries.

A similar study may be made in the case of Germany by examining the number of persons in the various trade associations who are insured against accident. The figures are given in the official reports of the Imperial Insurance Authorities in the *German Statistical Year-book* (*Statistiches Jahrbuch für das Deutsche Reich*).

Regarding the character of these figures we may quote the following remarks of the officials[2]: "The object of the returns is to give annually an approximate idea of the number of employees

---

[1] The figures are given in Appendix. (Table VII.) Miners and foundry workers are not included among the industrial workers.

[2] *Official Reports of the Imperial Insurance Authorities*, 1902, p. 629, No. 4.

and workers who are covered by insurance against accident. It is, therefore, not a question here of average figures in the strict statistical sense. For this reason, we have not to work out an accurate mean of the number of insured employees and workers actually

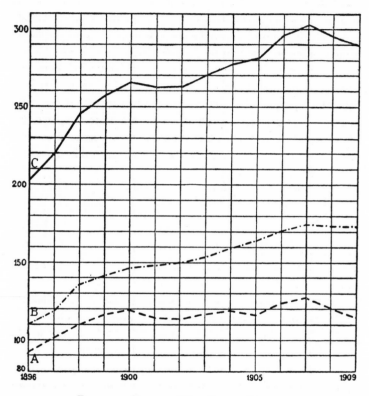

FIG. 12.—FACTORY WORKERS IN SWEDEN.
A. CAPITAL-PRODUCING INDUSTRIES.   B. OTHER INDUSTRIES.
C. TOTAL INDUSTRIES.

engaged in the year above or below the number of regular workers, but have to give the number of persons which the trade has regularly kept in full or current (normal) occupation in the year of our calculation. A spinning mill, for instance, which needs to employ as a rule 200 (though sometimes more, sometimes less) insured officials and workers daily to produce what is taken to be the normal daily output during the year in question will . . . be taken as employing 200 persons. . . . Moreover, the introduction of additional help to assist the average working staff for a short time is only left out of account if done every year. . . . Trade unions, which know the total number of days worked during the year, can ascertain the average number of insured by dividing the total number of working days on which, as a rule, work is done in the branch of industry in question."

This characteristic of the statistics of insured persons in the associations seems, on the whole, suitable for our purpose. We want really to know how the large movements of the trade cycle affect the number of employed workers from year to year, and not how the number varies from day to day.

In order to obtain an idea of the number of workers employed in the industries producing capital goods, we have to add together all the persons insured through the associations of the iron, steel, quarrying, brick-making, and building industries. By subtracting this sum from the total number of insured persons in the industrial unions, we arrive at the number of insured persons in the "other" trade unions.

This division of trade unions into "capital-producing" and "others" does not pretend to be accurate. For instance, the iron and steel industry produces some goods which cannot be reckoned as fixed capital. On the other hand, there are among the "other" industries several which produce, to a greater or less extent, fixed capital or the materials therefor. Among such may be mentioned the mining, fine engineering, electrical, chemical, and smelting industries. But for our present purpose it is sufficient to be able to separate the great mass of the workers engaged in the capital-producing industries from the other workers. The different sensitiveness of the two main branches of industry to movements of trade will become quite clear even in such a broad division of workers.

The workers in the capital-producing industries are about 40 to 50 per cent. of the total number of workers insured through their trade unions. If the division were more accurate, they would probably prove to be about one-half of the total number of industrial workers. A more accurate study, based on a thorough knowledge of the various trade unions, of the effect of trade cycle

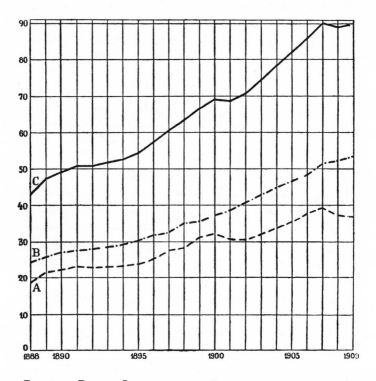

Fig. 13.—Persons Insured by the Industrial Trade Unions.
A. Capital-producing Industries.   B. Other Industries.
C. All Industries.

upon the number of workers would certainly prove interesting from many points of view.

On our next diagram (Fig. 13) curve *C* indicates the total number of insured persons in the industrial trade unions for every year from 1888 to 1909.[1] The trade booms of 1900 and 1907 can be

[1] For the figures, see Table VIII. in the Appendix.

clearly traced in the relevant points of the curve. The 1890 boom seems to continue into 1891, but no reaction is perceptible afterwards. But if the curve C is broken up into curves A and B, of which it is the sum, A representing the capital-producing industries and B the others, we find that the peaks in C correspond exclusively to those in A, while B shows us no points at all, and runs as smoothly on the whole, as any course of economic development can ever be supposed to do.

Thus the effects of the trade cycles, so far as they exert an influence on the number of employed workers, and so far as Germany is concerned, are scarcely noticeable in the group of "other industries," but are very pronounced in the "capital-producing industries." The descending parts of curve A after the trade booms clearly signify a corresponding amount of unemployment in the industries in question. In the "other industries," taken as a whole, no unemployment occurs, as the diagram shows, in consequence of the general trade fluctuations. We shall presently investigate more closely the unemployment attributable to such trade movements, but we may state here that, like the general trade cycles themselves, it must on the whole be ascribed exclusively to the production of fixed capital.

Let us examine a little more closely the development of the capital-producing industries in Germany. In the three trade booms included in our statistics, the number of workers employed increased as follows: from 1888 to 1891 by 24.49 per cent. (that is, an annual average of 8.16 per cent.), from 1894 to 1900 by 38.29 per cent. (6.38 per cent. per annum) and for 1904 to 1907 by 16.05 per cent. (5.35 per cent. per annum). For the other industries, the increases for the same periods were 12.6 per cent., 27.4 per cent., and 12.3 per cent., these being much lower in every case than in the capital-producing industries. The latter experience a period of unemployment after a trade boom, in that the number of employed workers is then smaller than the maximum number reached in the preceding trade boom. At the beginning of the revival in trade, not only are the unemployed absorbed, but new workers too are taken on in large numbers. Where do these come from? The natural increase of population in the groups of workers in question is insufficient. In the entire German Empire the births exceeded the deaths per 1,000 inhabitants by 11.7 in 1881–90, by 13.9, in 1891–1900, and by 14.3 in 1901–10. In the twenty-one years from 1888 to 1909 the average annual increase in the population was 1.34 per cent. As the number of workers in the capital-producing industries increased yearly by 5 to 8 per cent. during the trade booms, we can see that during these periods of trade activity an influx of workers from outside must have become necessary. After the trade boom of 1891, there was a period of unemployment, which lasted over 1892 and 1893. It ceased in 1894. In 1895 the natural increase in population among the groups of workers in question was sufficient to meet the demand for labour, but from 1896 to 1900 there must have been an influx of labour from other industries. The depression at the beginning of the present century was accompanied by a spell of unemployment that continued throughout the period 1901 to 1903. But the unemployed were absorbed in 1904, and the trade revival of the three years 1905 to 1907 necessitated a considerable influx from outside to meet the demand for labour.

It follows from this that the demand for workers at the beginning of the trade boom may be met by the absorption of the unemployed of the preceding period of depression, or that, at all events, the process may be conceived arithmetically in that way, and that the real trade boom depends essentially upon an influx of additional labour from outside to cover its demand for labour.

This result, which puts the theory of the "industrial reserve army" in its proper light, is confirmed by the study of the various industries in which we can ascertain statistically the number of workers employed. The pig-iron industry, which, following upon the conclusion drawn from our investigations, may be taken as representative of the entire production of fixed capital, shows the following development since 1885 (in the average number of employed workers [1]:

[1] *Statistisches Jahrbuch für das Deutsche Reich.*

Year.	Employed.	Year.	Employed.
1885	22,768	1898	30,778
1886	21,470	1899	36,334
1887	21,432	1900	34,743
1888	23,046	1901	32,367
1889	23,985	1902	32,399
1890	24,846	1903	35,361
1891	24,773	1904	35,358
1892	24,325	1905	38,458
1893	24,201	1906	41,754
1894	24,110	1907	45,201
1895	24,059	1908	43,532
1896	26,562	1909	42,227
1897	30,459	1910	45,324

We see that the unemployment of 1886–7 had disappeared by 1888, and that the two years of the trade boom of 1889 and 1890 necessitated additional labour being brought in from outside. The period of 1891–5 was one of unemployment, but this was absorbed by the brisker trade of 1896. During the period 1897–9 additional labour from outside was required. The subsequent trade slump made itself felt in a spell of unemployment that lasted from 1900 to 1904. In 1905, both the unemployed and, for the most part, the natural growth in population were required; the active development of trade in 1906 and 1907 plainly called for a considerable influx of labour from outside. This additional labour flows back into the unemployed when the subsequent depression arrives.

The same is true of the iron foundry industry. The average number of employed workers (in thousands) during the present century was as follows:

Year.	Employed (in 1000's).	Year.	Employed (in 1000's).
1900	95.9	1905	109.6
1901	85.7	1906	117.5
1902	84.5	1907	119.8
1903	87.8	1908	113.8
1904	104.6	1909	112.1

We see that not only were the unemployed workers of the 1901–3 depression absorbed in 1904, but so was, without doubt, the entire natural increase in population since the trade boom, and additional labour as well was drafted in from outside. This need of outside labour lasted during the whole of the trade revival until 1907. In the subsequent depression, a small proportion of this additional labour was again thrown out of work.

§ 65 *The Agricultural Population as a Source of Additional Labour to Industry*

As it is now settled that the periods of keen trade activity are made possible only by the influx of additional workers to the capital-producing industries, the question arises as to where this additional labour comes from, and whether these industries can rely upon such movements of labour in the future.

It is well known that, ever since the rise of modern industry, the agricultural population in the industrial countries of Europe has been in a position to supply a substantial addition of workers to other branches of industry. But the stream which brought these additions to industrial labour did not flow evenly. The capital-producing industries could not, as a rule, absorb any outside labour in times of depression, but on the other hand considerable increases of labour during trade booms were indispensable to them. Consequently, the surplus agricultural population was kept, to some extent, on the land during periods of depression – stored, so to say – until it could be absorbed by the capital-producing industries in times of trade revival. These readily available reserves of labour in agriculture constituted the real "industrial reserve army" of the capital-producing industries. It was these potential industrial workers who enabled trade booms to assume the proportions they have hitherto attained. This is not true of the "other industries," or at least to anything like the same extent. The flow of outside labour to these industries has been much more smooth and even.

Let us now see how this process goes on in different countries.

In Germany, in the three census-years 1882, 1895, and 1907, the "industrial population" was divided into the three main occupations *A*, *B*, and *C* as follows (in thousands):

Occupation.				1882.	1895.	1905.
A. Agriculture, etc.	..	..	..	19,225	18,501	17,681
B. Industries, etc.	..	..	..	16,058	20,253	26,387
C. Trade and Transport		..	..	4,531	5,967	8,278

The agricultural population thus decreased absolutely in the periods 1882–95 and 1895–1907. The entire natural increase in population, and a not inconsiderable part of the agricultural population of 1882 in addition, definitely abandoned agriculture. By far the greater part of this surplus rural population joined classes B and C. We can obtain a rough idea of the proportions of this movement. The total population of the German Empire increased by 14.5 per cent. in the period 1882–95, and by 19.22 per cent. in the period 1895–1907. If we assume that the agricultural population increased at the same rate in the periods in question, in 1895 it should have amounted to 22,000,000, whereas the actual figure was 18,500,000, a loss of 3,500,000, or 270,000 a year. In 1907, the agricultural population, if it had increased after 1895 at the annual rate of 19.22 per cent., should have been 22,850,000; as a matter of fact, it stood at 17,680,000, so that between 1895 and 1905 it lost 4,370,000 persons, or 365,000 a year (1,000 a day). It is not necessary to point out that the sole object of these calculations is to obtain just a general idea of the extent of the migration from agriculture to those other occupations which we have under consideration.

This rural migration has not been steady, but has, for the most part, been greatest during the trade booms. For instance, none of the industrial trade unions was able to absorb any outside labour from 1892 to 1895, but from 1896 to 1900 they must certainly have attracted a million workers from outside, or about 200,000 a year, which obviously meant a greatly increased population in these industries. It is only this reservoir of potential industrial labour in agriculture during trade slumps that makes it possible to meet this extraordinary demand for labour during trade booms.

In this connection it is particularly interesting to examine which sections of the agricultural population migrate to other occupations. According to the 1895 and 1907 censuses of occupation, there were in class *A* (agriculture, etc.) the following number of "dependants without special occupation" in the *a* and *c* classes of population, which correspond to the independent class and working-class (in thousands):

			1895.			1907.
a	..	..	6,550	..	..	5,144
c	..	..	3,141	..	..	2,350

or for every 100 self-supporting persons:

			1895.			1907.
a	..	..	255	..	..	205
c	..	..	56	..	..	32

We see that the *c* class of population had reduced the number of its "dependants without special occupation" to such an extent that any further diminution would appear to be impossible, at least for a considerable time. A population that has only 32 dependants to every 100 self-supporting persons will obviously not be able to spare as much labour in the future as it did when it had a far larger number of dependants. The *a* class of population also lost a large number of its dependants. If the class of independent farmers is to continue to increase by natural growth and have a proportionate share in the growth of the population in Germany, it does not seem possible to go much below the figure of two dependants to each self-supporting person. For the whole population of Germany the number of dependants to each 100 self-supporting persons fell from 131 in 1882 to 120 in 1895, and 100 in 1907.

In the aggregate, dependants without any special occupation in agriculture fell by about 2,200,000 from 1895 to 1907. During the same period, the class of "servants living at place of work" fell from 375,000 to 164,000, a decrease of 211,000. Thus these two classes together show a decrease of 2,411,000 persons. On the other hand, the class of persons actively employed increased by 1,590,000 between 1895 and 1907 (8,293,000 to 9,883,000). The net diminution in the total agricultural population therefore amounted to 820,000.

The process that is reflected in these figures is, clearly, a partial break-up of the agricultural family, a process that has gone farthest among agricultural labourers, but is now also in an advanced stage among the farmers themselves.

In Sweden, the changes in the agricultural population are demonstrated by the following figures[1]:

Year.	Agricultural Population (in 1,000's).	Per cent. of Population.
1870	3,095	72.1
1880	3,093	67.7
1890	2,943	61.5
1900	2,795	54.4
1910	2,674	48.4

In Sweden, too, therefore, there has been a considerable relative decrease in the agricultural population since 1870. Since 1880, there has been a marked positive reduction. The phenomenon is due primarily to a decrease in the more fecund classes of the agricultural workers. In these classes, the number of married males was considerably reduced in the period 1870–1900, whilst the number of unmarried workers increased appreciably in the same period. Among the class of independent farmers, the number of whom went up considerably, the number of completely dependant members of the family, which, in the main, means children under fifteen, diminished to a marked extent, as was also the case with the agricultural population as a whole. Completely dependant persons in the total agricultural population numbered:

Year.	Male.	Female.
1870	549,803	563,357
1900	474,349	498,761

The relative decrease in the class of agricultural workers accustomed to rear families, and the general change in the size of agricultural families, were, in the case of Sweden, the chief causes of the diminution in the agricultural population. However, the

[1] *Statistisk årsbok* (Stockholm).

independent farmers and unmarried workers increased in number in the period 1870–1900.[1]

In the case of England, the following table shows the number of persons employed in the main branches of industry in the various census-years (in thousands)[2]:

Industries.	1851.	1861.	1871.	1881.	1891.	1901.
Agriculture	1,905	1,803	1,424	1,200	1,100	988
Building Trades ..	399	472	583	687	701	946
Mining	193	271	315	384	519	649
Cotton Industry ..	415	492	509	552	606	582
Woollen Industry ..	256	230	247	240	258	236
Silk Industry	131	116	83	65	52	39
Iron and Steel Industry	95	130	191	201	202	216
Engineering and Ship-building	81	124	173	217	292	—
Tailoring	139	143	150	161	209	259
Boots and Shoes ..	244	256	225	224	249	251
Printing and Book-binding	33	47	64	88	122	150
Furniture	48	64	75	84	101	122

These figures illustrate in the clearest fashion the enormous reduction in the number of people employed in agriculture in the second half of the nineteenth century. The table also indicates which industries received the largest additions of workers from other occupations during the same period. They were the industries producing capital goods – namely, the building, iron and steel, engineering, and shipbuilding industries, as well as the printing, bookbinding, and furniture trades.

When we go more deeply into the problem of how the composition of the various groups employed in agriculture changed, we find that the number of female workers decreased far more than the number of male workers, and that the number of persons under twenty fell a little more rapidly than the total number. The number of females employed in agriculture in 1851 was 436,174, and by 1891 it had fallen to 46,001. During the same period, the

[1] Wohlin, Den Jordbruksidkande Befolkningen i Sverige, 1751–1900: "Emigrationsutredningen," Bilaga IX. (Stockholm, 1909).

[2] Board of Trade, British and Foreign Trade and Industry, Cmd. 1761, 1903, p. 362.

number of male workers fell from 1,468,513 to 1,053,371. These decreases, however, carried the disproportion between the sexes too far. By 1901 the number of females had risen to 52,459, and the number of males had fallen to 935,881.

A study of the migration of labour from agriculture up to the present time shows, therefore, that the movement cannot go on indefinitely, but in the most advanced countries must nearly have reached its limit. There are two things to be noticed. On the one hand, if agriculture is not to go backward, it can scarcely spare any more labour. On the other hand, the size of families among the agricultural population has already diminished to such an extent that the natural rate of increase of this particular class of the population can no longer be maintained at the former high level. At the present time, industry, in attracting labour from agriculture, clearly relies upon the growth of the agricultural population as it was fifteen to twenty years ago. In another fifteen or twenty years, industry will begin to feel the consequence of the present diminution in the size of agricultural families in the form of a reduced volume of additional labour coming from agriculture.

The question as to how far we should expect these results to be modified by a progressively wider distribution of land and a considerable development of smallholdings must be left open for the present. The temporary nature of the migration of labour from agriculture in the nineteenth century, which we have pointed out, is instructive enough when we consider this migration as a link in the great process of transformation which has led to our system of division of labour and modern industrialism. The very extensive emigration from Europe to countries overseas constitutes part of this development, as we all know, and this makes it difficult for us to grasp the essential features of the development. We simplify our task, and get a broad and general view by regarding the old Europe and the new countries overseas as a whole, and by asking what influence the transition to industrialism has exercised upon the agricultural population of the whole region.

We then notice that the transformation of the productive process that has taken place in our time contains two features of importance to agriculture. In the first place a large proportion of the domestic production of the old household economy has been extinguished and transferred to the modern industrial system. The occupations that have thus been transferred are partly those which we do not now regard as in any way agricultural and partly those which are more directly connected with agriculture. To the first group belong spinning and weaving, the making of clothes and boots, and a thousand and one small domestic activities. In the second group we have butter-making, cheese-making, slaughtering, baking, and so on. In this way the old type of domestic production has been gradually reduced to agriculture alone. The latter has thus been converted into a sort of trade. In proportion as industry took over these occupations from the domestic sphere, it deprived the older family of its now superfluous labour and applied it to industrial purposes. It is clear that this development represented a change that had to be completed within a certain period of time. Our present-day agriculture is rapidly approaching the limit of its capacity to supply more labour to industry.

The second element in the transformation of the productive process is the development of the technique of agriculture. This was due partly to the improvement in agricultural methods, such as the progress of agricultural chemistry, botany and zoology, etc., and partly to the introduction of machinery. These two progressive factors gave industry something new to do, while at the same time the latter innovation served to lessen the need for labour on the land. As long as technical advances of this sort occur, we can imagine a further transfer, within certain narrow limits, of workers from agriculture to industry.

Let us continue with our inquiry. The cause of the migration from agriculture to industry has been due, for the most part, to a revolution in our entire economic organisation. This revolution has, broadly speaking, been spread over the last hundred years, and has already reached its final stage. Consequently, we must expect that in the immediate future the movement of labour from agriculture will materially diminish.

The last century was also the period which saw modern industry begin on a large scale, the period in particular during which the capital-producing industries made extraordinarily rapid progress. This progress, as we know, was not steady and continuous; it was an advance by leaps, and was concentrated in the trade booms. It was made possible by the extraordinary additional supply of labour that could, when occasion demanded, be recruited from agriculture. If it is clear that the capacity of agriculture to meet this industrial demand for labour will be substantially curtailed at the end of the industrial revolution, we reach the important conclusion that *the trade cycles are, to a very great extent, a phenomenon of the period of transition from the old economic forms to the modern.* If outside labour can no longer be attracted, or only to a slight extent, trade booms cannot occur again with anything like their former intensity. But if the curve depicting trade cycles graphically can no longer have such peaks, it will obviously not be exposed to such violent reactions, and must progress more smoothly than has hitherto been the case.

We get an idea of the changes which take place in this sphere when we consider the actual features of trade cycles in different countries. These cyclical fluctuations are most acute in the United States, where an almost unlimited supply of labour can be drawn upon in a boom. The source of this labour in the United States is immigration. It is exceedingly instructive in this respect to study the relations between immigration and the production of fixed capital, with the latter represented by the output of pig-iron. We find that the maxima of immigration coincide with the maxima of pig-iron production, and that the minima of immigration usually take place at the close of the periods of depression. The table below brings out this fact very clearly.[1]

Year.	Immigration (in 1,000's).	Pig-Iron Production (in 100,000 tons).
1891	560	83
1892	623 max.	92 max.
1893	503	71
1894	314	67 min.

[1] *Statistical Abstract of the United States.* The figures of pig-iron production refer to the calendar years, and those of immigration to the fiscal years (to June 30th of each year).

Year.	Immigration (in 1,000's).	Pig-Iron Production (in 100,000 tons).
1895	280	94
1896	343	86
1897	231	97
1898	229 min.	118
1899	312	136
1900	499	138
1901	488	159
1902	649	178
1903	857 max.	180 max.
1904	813 min.	165 min.
1905	1,026	230
1906	1,101	253
1907	1,285 max.	258 max.
1908	783	159 min.
1909	752 min.	258
1910	1,042	272

The time-lag characterising the minima of immigration is due to the fact that an addition to the labour already employed in the capital-producing industries cannot be absorbed by them until the depression is over: that is to say, until these industries have again absorbed the maximum number of workers which they employed during the last boom. It is plain that such enormous and sudden augmentations of fixed capital, like those that occur in the United States, are only possible in a country where the capital-producing industries can attract outside labour to practically any extent. In Europe, where the possibility of this happening is now very remote, we can hardly imagine such a trade boom as that which the United States experienced from 1905 to 1907. And as in Europe the movement of outside labour to the capital-producing industries is now slower than ever, we must expect a considerable contraction of the booms. This must lead to a corresponding mitigation of the slumps While the prodigious fall in the pig-iron output in the United States in 1908 (from 25,800,000 to 15,900,000 tons) and the corresponding fall in the total production of fixed capital have no counterpart in Europe, we may look forward to a time when European slumps will be even less pronounced than they are at present.

It goes without saying that the development which we describe as probable may follow a very different path if the great capital-producing industries of the Western world in the future obtain their labour to a greater extent from among the foreign races.

§ 66 *Unemployment*

In the two preceding sections we learned something of the manner in which the flow of labour into the two main branches of industry is influenced by trade cycles. It was necessary for this purpose to use statistical data which included, at least approximately, the total number of workers in the various industries. It was only from such statistics that we were enabled to compare the number of workers employed from year to year in any particular trade.

We found that the industries producing capital goods, which in time of trade boom attract labour from other sources, dismiss some of it during periods of depression, and so cause unemployment. This does not necessarily mean, of course, that these dismissed workers will be really unemployed, for it is conceivable that to some extent they will return to agriculture, from which they had recently come, and, for the time being, again find employment there. In Sweden, as a matter of fact, this is a fairly common practice. The capital-producing industries are able to take agricultural workers or members of peasant families directly from their rural occupations. This applies, of course, particularly to the timber industry, but also, to a considerable degree, to the building industry. When these workers find no further employment in industry, they frequently return to their former occupations.

It is obvious, however, that these conditions cannot obtain in highly industrialised countries, at least not to the same extent, and in them the workers dismissed during periods of depression do, on the whole, face real unemployment. The decrease in the number of workers normally employed by their respective industries, which we have proved for Germany, should give a true general indication of the extent of unemployment caused by industrial fluctuations.

But the statistics which we have hitherto used give no idea of the temporary variations in the amount of employment. If we are to study the problem of unemployment from this point of view, to obtain a sort of barometer of the development of trade fluctuations, we must employ different methods. We must turn, in the first place, to the unemployment statistics of those trade unions which give regular returns of their unemployed members. The chief defect of these statistics is that they are usually able to include only a small part of the total number of workers.

Let us first consider the results obtained in England. The report of the *Labour Gazette* in 1893 embraced trade unions with 336,000 members, and by 1903 this number had risen to 560,000. The statistics differentiate the main groups of industries; in fact, the engineering, shipbuilding, and metal industries are specially treated. Unemployment figures are also given separately for the building trade. We are thus able to examine what proportion the unemployment registered by the trade unions in the specified industries producing capital goods bears to the corresponding unemployment in other industries.

	A.	B.	C.	D.	E.
1872 min.	0.9	1.2	2.4	1.5	0.0
1879 max.	15.3	8.2	8.3	4.0	3.3
1882 min.	2.3	3.5	2.5	2.4	0.9
1886 max.	13.5	8.2	4.7	2.6	5.2
1890 min.	2.2	2.2	2.5	2.2	1.6
1893 max.	11.4	3.1	4.1	4.1	2.6
1899 min.	2.4	1.2	2.1	3.9	1.2
1904 max.	8.4	7.3	6.8	4.7	3.0
1906 min.	4.1	6.9	4.8	4.5	1.9
1908 max.	12.5	11.6	8.3	5.5	2.9

This table, based on Board of Trade statistics,[1] presents unemployment in the trade unions as a percentage of the total membership, divided into the following groups:

A. Engineering, shipbuilding, and metal industries.
B. Building industry.
C. Timber and furniture industries.

[1] *Fourteenth Abstract of Labour Statistics of the United Kingdom,* 1908–9.

D. Printing and bookbinding industries.

E. Coal-mining, textile, clothing, paper, leather, glass, pottery, and tobacco industries.

The figures are reproduced only for those years in which the average percentage for all the trade unions was either a maximum or a minimum. We see that in the "minimum years" unemployment for all the groups is usually very small. But in the maximum years we see very clearly how depressions influence capital-producing industries (*A* and *B*) much more than they do the others. During the severe depression of 1879, for instance, when unemployment reached 15.3 per cent. in group *A* and 8.2 per cent. in the building industry, it was confined in group *E* to 3.3 per cent. Similarly in 1908, when unemployment in groups *A* and *B* was 12.5 per cent. and 11.6 per cent. respectively, while only 2.9 per cent. in group *E*. These figures are obviously a strong confirmation of the results to which our previous investigations led us, namely, that movements of trade cycles are, in essence, fluctuations in the production of fixed capital, and have only a secondary influence at the most on the other branches of production. It is in the nature of these statistics that they allow this difference in character of the two principal groups of industries to be seen only in periods of depression, for in times of booming trade real unemployment falls practically to zero in all industries, and the unemployment statistics conceal the great rise in the number of employed workers which the capital-producing industries in particular experience in times of boom.

The British Board of Trade also publishes monthly statistics of unemployment in certain trade unions which give their members unemployment relief (see table below). The real significance of these statistics is that they are a symptom of trade cycles, and represent a kind of barometer of crises. For example, when the unemployment figures in the second half of 1907 are seen to exceed the corresponding figures for the previous year, this must be taken as a sign of the turn in the trade cycle, even though this turn was not fully visible in the figures of unemployment until the beginning of 1908. On the other hand, a fall in the unemployment percentage indicates an improvement in the trade cycle. From August, 1909, onwards there was such a fall, and, in fact, a period of improved trade did follow. Unemployment naturally varies with the time of year, the highest figures being usually reached at the end of the year. And so, as a rule, the December figures are higher than the average figures for the whole year. When there is an exception to this rule, as in 1905 and 1909, this seems a very reliable omen of an upward swing in the trade cycle.

MONTHLY RETURNS OF UNEMPLOYMENT BY THE BRITISH
BOARD OF TRADE, 1901–11 [1]

Year.	Jan.	Feb.	Mar.	Apr.	May.	June.	July.	Aug.	Sept.	Oct.	Nov.	Dec.	Average for year.
1901	3.5	3.4	3.1	3.4	3.0	3.0	2.9	3.4	3.2	3.2	3.3	4.2	3 3
1902	4.0	3.9	3.2	3.4	3.5	3.7	3.5	4.0	4.5	4.5	4.4	5.0	4.0
1903	4.9	4.3	3.9	3.6	3.5	3.9	4.4	5.0	5.2	5.6	5.5	6.3	4.7
1904	6.1	5.6	5.5	5.5	5.8	5.5	5.6	5.9	6.3	6.3	6.5	7.1	6.0
1905	6.3	5.7	5.2	5.2	4.7	4.8	4.7	4.9	4.8	4.6	4.3	4.5	5.0
1906	4.3	4.1	3.4	3.2	3.1	3.2	3.1	3.3	3.3	3.9	4.0	4.4	3.6
1907	3.9	3.5	3.2	2.8	3.0	3.1	3.2	3.6	4.1	4.2	4.5	5.6	3.6
1908	5.8	6.0	6.4	7.1	7.4	7.9	7.9	8.5	9.3	9.5	8.7	9.1	7.8
1909	8.7	8.4	8.2	8.2	7.9	7.9	7.9	7.7	7.4	7.1	6.5	6.6	7.7
1910	6.8	5.7	5.2	4.4	4.2	3.7	3.8	4.0	4.3	4.4	4.6	5.0	4.7
1911	3.9	3.3	3.0	2.8	2.5	3.0	2.9	3.3	2.9	2.8	2.6	3.1	3.0

For Germany, the *Reichs-Arbeitsblatt* has published since 1903 continuous statistics of unemployment in the German trade unions. The number of unemployed (at home or travelling) in proportion to the number of members of the unions which send their reports is given for the end of the last week in every month. The figures for March, June, September, and December since the beginning of the statistics are reproduced here:

Year.	March.	June.	September.	December.
1903	—	3.2	2.3	2.6
1904	2.0	2.1	1.8	2.4
1905	1.6	1.5	1.4	1.8
1906	1.1	1.2	1.0	1.6
1907	1.3	1.4	1.4	2.7
1908	2.5	2.9	2.7	4.4
1909	3.5	2.8	2.1	2.6
1910	1.8	2.0	1.8	2.1
1911	1.9	1.6	1.7	2.4
1912	1.6	1.7	1.5	2.8 [2]

[1] *Fourteenth Abstract of Labour Statistics*, p. 7, *Labour Gazette*, 1911–12.
[2] *Reichs-Arbeitsblatt*, X. Jahrgang, Nr. 4, p. 264.

The low figures for 1905, 1906, and 1907, clearly reflect a trade boom, and the subsequent depression is just as clearly seen in the high figures for 1908 and 1909. The significance of these statistics, however, lies only in their use as general symptoms. Comparison between the different years, and especially between the various trades, becomes, owing to the nature of the material, much more difficult. The number of workers considered has increased four-fold since 1904, having risen from about half a million to about two millions. The various trades are very unequally represented, and the data for several important industries, such as mining and building, happen to be very defective.

In order to obtain an idea of the duration of unemployment, the *Reichs-Arbeitsblatt* calculates for every quarter the proportion of the total number of unemployed days to the total number of "member-days" – that is, the number of members multiplied by the number of working days in the quarter (possible working days). Out of every hundred possible working days the following were "unemployed days" [1]:

	1st Quarter.	2nd Quarter.	3rd Quarter.	4th Quarter.
1909	3.2	1.9	1.6	1.4
1910	1.7	1.4	1.2	1.2
1911	1.8	1.0	1.1	1.1
1912	1.8	1.1	1.1	1.4
1913	2.1	1.8	2.1	2.5

The figures show that the period of depression was definitely over by 1910, and that the end of the subsequent period of favourable trade is clearly indicated by the growing unemployment in the fourth quarter of 1912.

To illustrate the extent of employment among German workers, the *Reichs-Arbeitsblatt* also publishes statistics of the changes in the number of employed members under the sick-insurance scheme, subtracting the increase in this number which is due to the growth of population. These statistics can, naturally, be used only as a barometer for the labour market, but as such they can claim a certain value, as the returns include about 5,700,000 members (March, 1912).

[1] *Reichs-Arbeitsblatt.*

The work of the labour exchange, as an intermediary, is also given to illustrate the state of the labour market. But the number of those seeking work as compared with the number of vacant situations is far too complicated a problem to afford any help to the theoretical explanation of the changes in the labour market.

§ 67 *Changes in Working-time*

So far, we have examined those changes in the number of employed workers which correspond to the fluctuations in production brought about by trade cycles. We found that, during a trade boom, the industries producing capital goods partly re-absorb those workers who had been thrown out of work in the depression and partly attract outside labour, only to dismiss some of it again in the next depression. But there is another method of adjusting labour to the requirements of varying productive activity, and that is to increase or curtail the daily working-time or the number of working days in the week.

This latter method is employed in the English coal-mines, where its operation can be followed statistically. The annual average of the number of working days in the week is given in the following table[1]:

1895	..	..	.. 4.74	1903	..	..	.. 5.09
1896	..	..	.. 4.92	1904	..	..	.. 5.07
1897	..	..	.. 5.13	1905	..	..	.. 5.03
1898	..	..	.. 5.25	1906	..	..	.. 5.26
1899	..	..	.. 5.46	1907	..	..	.. 5.51
1900	..	..	.. 5.47	1908	..	..	.. 5.22
1901	..	..	.. 5.12	1909	..	..	.. 5.14
1902	..	..	.. 5.22	1910	..	..	.. 5.19

We see that the working-time per week rises from a minimum in 1895 to a maximum in 1900, falling again to a minimum in 1905, and rising once more to a maximum in 1907. The differences between the maxima and the minima are, as can be seen, fairly significant.

[1] Board of Trade, Memoranda, etc., Cmd. 2337, 1904, pp. 80 and 94, *Fourteenth Abstract of Labour Statistics.*

The working-time in 1907 was greater for every month than in the corresponding month of the previous year. It is not until the beginning of 1908 that a decrease takes place, and not until the last quarter of 1908 that the working-time falls below the 1906 level.

In iron-mining, too, this method of adjusting requirements to the amount of labour is employed. The average number of working days in the week in iron-mining, from 1896 to 1910, was as follows:

1896	..	..	.. 5.72	1903	..	..	.. 5.72
1897	..	..	.. 5.76	1904	..	..	.. 5.79
1898	..	..	.. 5.75	1905	..	..	.. 5.77
1899	..	..	.. 4.76	1906	..	..	.. 5.78
1900	..	..	.. 5.65	1907	..	..	.. 5.81
1901	..	..	.. 5.58	1908	..	..	.. 5.69
1902	..	..	.. 5.74	1909	..	..	.. 5.76
	1910	..	..	..	..	5.77	

Here, the fluctuations are, as we should expect, smaller, but they bring out clearly the upward movement from 1901 to 1907, and the subsequent decline in 1908.

In iron and steel works the number of working shifts is adapted to varying requirements. The average number of shifts worked by one man in a week was, in the following years[1]:

1901	..	..	.. 5.32	1906	..	..	.. 5.57
1902	..	..	.. 5.36	1907	..	..	.. 5.58
1903	..	..	.. 5.39	1908	..	..	.. 5.36
1904	..	..	.. 5.40	1909	..	..	.. 5.38
1905	..	..	.. 5.51	1910	..	..	.. 5.50

Here again the trade boom of 1907 is conspicuous.

When we multiply the average shifts worked by the number of men employed, we obtain a correct measure of the extent of employment in the iron and steel works. The percentage increase or decrease for every month in comparison with the corresponding month in the previous year is regularly published by the *Labour*

[1] *Fourteenth Abstract of Labour Statistics.*

Gazette. The percentages for the years 1906 to 1909 are as follows [1]:

	1906.	1907.	1908.	1909.
January	+13.3	+2.9	− 6.6	−5.8
February	+10.1	+3.4	− 8.3	−7.8
March	+10.7	+3.1	− 10.0	−4.1
April	+ 8.4	+5.5	− 12.8	−4.1
May	+ 7.0	+5.4	− 13.9	−0.4
June	+ 8.5	+5.2	− 14.7	+1.4
July	+ 5.6	+4.1	− 14.0	+0.9
August	+ 5.4	+4.4	− 13.3	+3.2
September	+ 4.2	+2.5	− 12.3	+3.7
October	+ 4.6	−1.9	− 11.2	+6.3
November	+ 3.1	−4.9	− 9.0	+6.5
December	+ 3.1	−4.0	− 11.4	+9.6

These figures are sufficiently suitable to inform us accurately of the time of the beginning and end of the depression. We find that it is not until October, 1907, that a decrease takes place in the employment induced by the trade boom as compared with the corresponding month in the previous year. It is not until November that the decline exceeds the increase of the previous year, and not until May, 1908, that the whole increase of the two years of boom is balanced. Thus the iron and steel industries were very busily employed up to the last moment of the trade boom; and this is in accordance with the results we reached above (§ 63, at the end) in our inquiry as to the time of the commencement of the decrease in the production of materials of fixed capital.

[1] From Pohle, *Monatliche Übersichten.*

CHAPTER XVI

INFLUENCE OF TRADE CYCLES ON THE DURABLE MATERIAL MEANS OF PRODUCTION

§ 68 *Changes in the Quantity and Efficiency of the Factors of Production*

THE changes in production which appear in the various stages of the trade cycle point to changes in the employment not only of labour, but also of the material means of production. Increased output during a trade boom is inconceivable without an increased use of these. The greater demand for them during a trade boom can be met in two ways:

1. By the manufacture of new means of production, thus increasing the total supply, or, at least, raising its efficiency.
2. By the better use of the existing means of production.

Let us consider the former alternative first. In the first place, we can leave out of consideration those material means of production which we have lumped together under the name of "circulating capital." For an increase in the production of circulating capital is to be regarded, as we know, as an accompaniment of every extension of the economic processes of production. We may therefore limit our investigations to the increase in the durable material means of production, or of fixed capital, involved by the increased production during a trade boom.

Where does this increase in the durable means of production, which the trade boom necessitates, originate? The production of fixed capital is, as we have seen, continuous, and, although it proceeds at a slower rate during periods of depression than in times of brisk trade, yet even then it goes on to a considerable extent. The fall in pig-iron production during periods of depression may amount to several per cent.; in exceptional cases it may be much greater (in the United States in 1908 it was 38 per cent.), but the production nevertheless, even in severe depressions, is substantially maintained. We have reason to suppose that what applies here to pig-iron production applies equally to the entire production of fixed capital. The construction of new railways goes on, as the statistics show, at all times, even though it varies in extent. The re-equipping of the railways in order to increase their efficiency is also continued during periods of depression, as we may best observe in the United States, with its system of private railways, and its severe trade cycles.[1] The annual increase in the length of railway track, which had amounted to 2,644 miles in 1892–3, fell to 1,240 miles in the depression of 1894–5. This is undoubtedly a significant decrease, but it demonstrates nevertheless that the construction of railway stations continued on a considerable scale during the whole period of depression. During 1903–4, a year of trade prosperity, the construction of new railway track reached the total of 4,932 miles. This figure was reduced in the following year of depression merely to 3,450 miles. The construction of second, third, and fourth railway tracks was also continued during the periods of depressions, and reached a minimum of 880 miles in 1905–6, for instance, and 1,485 miles in the following year. We thus find constant work being done, continuing right through the slumps, to improve the traffic capacity of the railway system. The same may be said of rolling stock. The number of trucks in 1903–4, roughly 1,654,000, was increased by 38,000, and in 1904–5 by a further 39,000. At the same time, the average carrying capacity rose from 29 to 30 and 31 tons. This shows that a considerable scrapping of old trucks took place, and that the number of new trucks must have been much greater than the number quoted. The increase in the number of coaches during the depression is very small in proportion to the enormous increase in the subsequent trade boom, when it amounted to 107,000 in 1905–6, and 153,000 in 1906–7; yet it shows that in this respect, too, the depression period added a contribution, by no means insignificant, to the improvement of the traffic capacity of the railways.

[1] *Statistical Abstract of the United States.*

What we have established in figures as regards the railways holds good for the entire sphere of economic production. At the end of a depression the economic system of the country is essentially better equipped with durable material means of production than at the beginning, and is thus well prepared for the approaching upward trend of the trade cycle. This equipment facilitates the increased production during the period of expanding trade, but it is not nearly sufficient to meet the extraordinary demand created by the expansion. By far the greatest part of the new means of production which are required during the trade boom must be produced within its duration; and this is the reason why the production of fixed capital, too, as we have seen, increases during a boom. It is just this significant increase in the production of material means of production above the normal rate which, in particular, creates the trade boom.

We have already seen, in one example, that during a depression the antiquated equipment of production is discarded and replaced by a new and better one, so that average productivity is improved. It is very interesting to observe these changes in the case of pig-iron production, which is indeed the most important basis of the production of fixed capital.

It is a well-known fact that blast furnaces have been considerably enlarged during the last generation. This change was effected by the constant construction of new blast furnaces and scrapping of old ones. This, however, was not a uniform development. The demolition of the old furnaces evidently took place to a larger extent in times of depression. During trade booms it was more often necessary to re-employ furnaces which had been abandoned during the depression, even if they were perhaps considered out-of-date.

The German statistics of the industry give, in addition to the total production of pig-iron, the time (that is, the number of weeks) during which the blast furnaces were in operation. We can thus calculate the average pig-iron output per working week. If we multiply this figure by fifty-two, we obtain figures which may serve as a measurement of the average annual productive capacity of the active blast furnaces, assuming that they are in constant operation (see Table IX.). The productivity of German blast furnaces, thus reckoned, rose in the period 1872–1909 from 7,560 tons to 51,320 tons. The increase, however, slackens considerably during periods of depression. For the whole time, we can count some nineteen bad and eighteen good years. In the bad years, the increased productivity averages 1,555 tons, and in the good years it is, on the contrary, only 789 tons. This is due to the fact that the old blast furnaces were overwhelmingly thrown out of use or definitely abandoned in the periods of depression. The building of new furnaces seems to have been carried on more uniformly. The face that more or less antiquated furnaces are again brought into use during expanding trade counteracts the increase in productivity which is bound up with new construction. In 1880, with the trade cycle moving upwards, and when pig-iron production rose from 2,227,000 tons to 2,729,000 tons, the number of working blast furnaces increased from 210 to 226, and as a result the average productivity even suffered slightly, falling from 12,934 to 12,930 tons. Apart from this instance, the tendency towards increasing productivity prevails, although, as stated, the increase is always much slower during a boom than during a depression. In the severe depression after 1900, when the output of pig-iron declined from 8,520,000 tons to 7,889,000 tons in 1901, and reached only 8,530,000 tons even in 1902, the average productivity of the blast furnaces rose from 33,430 tons to 35,580 tons and 40,520 tons; this particular change is clearly connected with the fact that the number of existing furnaces fell from a maximum of 309 in 1901 to 289 in 1902, and the number of furnaces in operation fell from a maximum of 274 in 1900 to 241 in 1902. In 1908 there were seven more blast furnaces in existence than in the previous year, but the number in operation had decreased by twenty-three, both of these changes together causing an increase in the average productivity from 45,298 to 48,733 tons.

We may accept it as a rule that the discarding of antiquated means of production generally takes place during periods of depression, while, on the other hand, the production of new means of production is carried on more vigorously during expansion of trade. An increased productive capacity is always a result of the development during periods of depression, on which the coming trade boom can rely. It is also very probable that during depressions old methods of production are abandoned. In part this is directly connected with the creation of new means of production, but to some extent this improvement in methods has its foundation in the sphere of organisation. The periods of slackened activity allow the business men time to effect a comprehensive reorganisation of their concerns. In this way, too, in all probability, a very general increased productive capacity is obtained.

The multiplication of durable material means of production, which we can prove takes place during a depression period, represents naturally an accumulation of capital during the period. But it is not the accumulation of capital in "money form," or of "free capital" waiting for investment, assumed by certain theorists and financial journals. The formation of capital is, during the depression as at all other times, a real increase in invested capital, and in particular of fixed capital. This accumulation of capital is scarcely to be considered as a condition of a trade boom, and is, in any case, far from being a sufficient basis for the increased production. To a considerable extent, this expansion of production must always depend, as we have seen, on means of production which the trade boom itself creates.

The expansion of capital in a depression is also in part an accumulation of circulating real capital – that is, of stocks of commodities which do not find purchasers in the depression. These commodities may be materials for fixed capital or for products which pass into consumption, or consumption goods properly so called. Apparently, it is sometimes imagined that the boom is made possible only through such an accumulation of stocks. This view has at least the advantage of assuming a concrete basis for the capital accumulation, which is definitely to be considered as a preliminary condition of the trade boom; and, according to it, the exceptional increase in the production of fixed capital, which distinguishes the trade boom, is facilitated, partly directly by the stocks of materials for such real capital, and partly by the fact that productive forces could, thanks to stocks of consumers' goods or materials from which these can be produced, be diverted from the immediate supply of goods to the consumers to the production of fixed capital. In this conception there lurks a trace of the old theory of Adam Smith, according to which "a stock of goods must be stored up somewhere" before any production of capital can begin (cf. p. 38). We may now stress the point that the existence of stores of this description can have no material significance for the trade boom, since, as we know, the production of materials and consumption goods during the boom is extended beyond the normal in every sphere, and thus the boom itself covers in the main its demand for these articles. Whether the preceding depression has left stores of, say, pig-iron, is really a matter of indifference to the development of the boom, since the extra supply that will be taken from such stocks to meet requirements is, in any case, of little consequence in comparison with the enormous production in the boom itself.

Although it is difficult to compile really adequate statistics of the accumulated stores during periods of depression, yet we may venture to assert that the depression is characterised, above all, not by "overproduction" (that is, a production of goods which cannot be sold for the present), but rather by an incomplete utilisation of the existing factors of production. The stocks which are accidentally left over here and there by the depression form no general or necessary condition of the origin of the trade boom, nor any essential element in explaining the possibility of its occurrence.

§ 69 *Variations in the Use of Factors of Production*

The other chief method of facilitating an increased production during a boom is the better utilisation of the existing factors of production.

This better utilisation may, so far as the circulating capital is concerned, be attained by accelerating the whole process of production and thus increasing the "velocity of circulation" of circulating capital. This is clearly equivalent to reducing the stores of circulating capital relatively to the extent of production. During a boom, when production is pushed forward with the greatest possible intensity, every intermediate product is, as a rule, passed on with all haste to the next stage of production, and does not remain long in store. It may be generally assumed that, in this sense, a better use of circulating capital is a feature of the boom. But it would certainly be an error to see in this an essential element in the explanation of the increased production of the boom.

There is no doubt that better use is made of the durable material means of production during a boom, and that this conduces, to a certain extent, to increased production. In periods of depression, the durable means of production are either badly used or not used at all. The changes in their use are partly connected with the fluctuating employment of labour. When a factory works overtime or employs extra shifts, there is obviously a better use made not only of the machines, but also of the whole plant. If new workers are taken on, new machines will to some extent become necessary, but the existing machines are often sufficient for the larger number of workers. In such cases, the increased production is partly made possible by the more intensive use of the machinery. This is likewise true of the factory buildings and the rest of the plant.

But, quite apart from the changes in the number of workers or working hours, there are considerable fluctuations in the employment of the durable means of production; as, for instance, when a ship makes a voyage on one occasion with a full cargo and on another with only half a cargo.

In certain cases we are in a position to illustrate statistically these variations in the use of the durable means of production and so to get an approximate idea of the extent of the fluctuations, and a more accurate conception of the time when they occur. Railway statistics are particularly suitable for this purpose. Below are submitted several tables showing the use of the existing railway stock on the German railways. Taking 1,000 "kilometres of use" to one locomotive, the average is [1]:

[1] *Statistisches Jahrbuch für das Deutsche Reich.*

Year.	Kilometres of Use (in 1,000's).	Year.	Kilometres of Use (in 1,000's).
1888	22.4	1900	27.4
1889	23.4	1901	26.8
1890	24.4	1902	26.5
1891	24.6	1903	27.4
1892	23.4	1904	28.1
1893	23.3	1905	28.9
1894	23.4	1906	29.8
1895	23.9	1907	30.1
1896	24.9	1908	28.1
1897	25.6	1909	26.5
1898	26.7	1910	26.5
1899	27.0	1911	27.4

It is seen that there is, in general, an improvement in the use of the locomotives, but this takes place only during periods of boom, and must give way to a certain retrogression during depressions. Thus the rate of use reached in 1891 was not maintained in the subsequent depression, and was not exceeded until 1896. Then there was a sharp rise until 1900, which, however, was interrupted by the depression that followed, and was only resumed in the later 1907 trade boom. The subsequent depression again caused a considerable decline in the rate of use.

Similarly with the use of railway coaches. The following figures represent (in 1,000's) the number of "wagon-axle kilometres" to one wagon-axle [1]:

1895	..	..	.. 19.1	1903	..	..	.. 20.1
1896	..	..	.. 19.3	1904	..	..	.. 20.6
1897	..	..	.. 19.5	1905	..	..	.. 21.4
1898	..	..	.. 19.7	1906	..	..	.. 22.0
1899	..	..	.. 19.9	1907	..	..	.. 22.2
1900	..	..	.. 19.6	1908	..	..	.. 20.7
1901	..	..	.. 18.9	1909	..	..	.. 20.5
1902	..	..	.. 19.2	1910	..	..	.. 21.1
	1911	..	..	.. 21.7			

The changes in the conditions of trade can easily be traced in these figures.

The whole railway system is of course much better utilised during

[1] *Statistisches Jahrbuch für das Deutsche Reich.*

a trade boom than at other times. This is clearly seen in the statistics showing "ton miles" per mile of track which are published in the United States. The goods traffic on the Swedish State Railways in tons per day and kilometres of line shows the following development in the period 1870–1910, taking only the maxima and minima[1]:

1870	..	..	.. 1.56	1894	..	..	.. 2.98
1876	..	..	.. 2.85	1900	..	..	.. 4.99
1879	..	..	.. 2.22	1901	..	..	.. 4.85
1883	..	..	.. 2.77	1907	..	..	.. 6.68
1887	..	..	.. 2.49	1909	..	..	.. 6.13
1889	..	..	.. 3.26	1910	..	..	.. 7.28

In order to determine the point of time at which a change in the use of fixed capital takes place, we may consider the monthly revenues of the railway systems of the great industrial countries. In Germany, the income in marks from goods traffic per kilometre of working line was, in the following months[2]:

1907.				1908.			
July	..	..	.. 2,696	January	..	..	2,493
August	..	..	.. 2,819	February	..	..	2,526
September		..	.. 2,745				
October	..	..	.. 3,085				
November		..	.. 2,903				
December		..	.. 2,525				

In each of these months, the income was greater than that of the corresponding month of the preceding year. There is no reaction in this respect until March, 1908, and it is only in the fourth quarter of that year that the revenue falls below the figure for 1906.

For twenty of the leading British railways, the return from goods traffic shows an advance for each month of 1906 and 1907 upon the corresponding month of the previous year, an advance which even in December, 1907, is more than £120,000. There is no decrease until January, 1908, and it is not considerable enough until February to counteract the whole increase of the preceding year.

[1] *Statens Järnvagstrafik*, 1910, pp. 187–8.
[2] These and the subsequent monthly figures are taken from Pohle, *Monatliche Übersichten.*

For the United States, figures are published showing the percentage increase or decrease in the net working revenue in comparison with the corresponding month of the previous year. These statistics show a continual rise until December, 1907, when the first set-back takes place, which, however, does not overbalance altogether the increase of the corresponding month of the previous year. From the beginning of 1908 onwards, however, the decrease is very marked.

Thus, in all these cases, the fall in revenue did not occur until after the commencement of the crisis. Throughout the boom period, until the crisis, the railways were very busy. In many cases, their capacity for transport could not satisfy the demand, as we may infer from the reports of the prevailing scarcity of trucks.

The varying utilisation of the durable means of production may sometimes also be statistically confirmed by the production of consumption goods, as, for instance, when we compare, in the English cotton industry, the consumption of raw cotton with the number of spindles at work during the year. The consumption of raw cotton shows the following fluctuations since 1880, giving only the pronounced maxima and minima [1]:

Year.	Absolute Consumption (in 1,000 cwts.).	To One Spindle (in 1,000 cwts.).
1880	12,300	310
1883	13,400	319
1885	11,900	277
1891	14,900	332
1893	13,200	292
1899	15,700	347
1903	13,900	295
1907	17,600	338

It can be seen that the maximum consumption of raw cotton coincides approximately with the turning years of the trade cycle, and that highest and lowest rates of this consumption correspond respectively with the highest and lowest rates of utilisation of the spindles. The rise in the rate of utilisation during the trade boom is

[1] Board of Trade, *British and Foreign Trade and Industry,* 1909, Cmd. 4954, pp. 153 and 157. The proportions have been calculated.

certainly considerable, but is by no means sufficient to meet the demand, and must be supplemented by simultaneous additions to the number of spindles. For example, the number grew from 47 million spindles in 1903 to 52 millions in 1907.

That considerable fluctuations occur in the use of the durable means of production in the case of the pig-iron industry, we have already seen in dealing with the German blast furnaces. Many blast furnaces which are not employed during a depression were again brought into use during every boom. This is particularly clear in the United States. On December 31st, 1902, 307 furnaces were active, and on the same day in 1903, after the arrival of the crisis, there were only 182 in use. The number in use at the end of 1906 was 340, and at the end of 1907, only 167.

The partial utilisation of the durable material means of production, which we have shown to take place during periods of depression, is really the most characteristic feature of a trade slump. The definition of a depression is, in general, a period of relative unemployment of the durable means of production. But, as we have found, the general broad movements of the trade cycle consist essentially of a variation in the production of fixed capital. Hence depressions must make themselves chiefly felt in a relative unemployment of those durable means of production which serve for the production of fixed capital. The quantity of such means of production is determined by the highest demand during a trade boom. As the production of fixed capital falls off after a crisis, these means of production must be only partly employed, precisely because they are durable and fixed. It is just this feature which most surely characterises the depression.

We can follow this phenomenon in the case of the production of pig-iron, which may, as a matter of fact, be considered as representative of the whole production of fixed capital. In the diagram (Fig. 14) the pig-iron output of the world is presented. At the time when the output is at its maximum there must clearly be such a quantity of durable means of production used in the pig-iron production as will suffice for the maximum production. All these durable means – blast furnaces, iron-mines, equipment, etc. –

which are necessary in the trade boom are still in existence during the depression, and represent the productive capacity of the community in this field.

This productive capacity is shown on the diagram by a horizontal

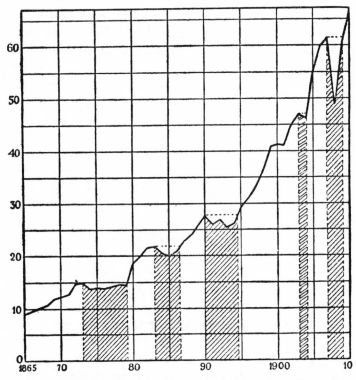

FIG. 14.—GRAPHIC REPRESENTATION OF THE PERIODS OF DEPRESSION. THE WORLD PIG-IRON OUTPUT IN MILLIONS OF TONS.

dotted line which starts from the peak of a trade boom. So long as the output of pig-iron remains below this productive capacity, a certain amount of unemployment of the means of production prevails. This output exceeds the previous productive capacity, that is, until the curve cuts across the dotted line. In this way, we can indicate graphically the periods of depression. They are shown, on our diagram, by shaded areas.

This diagram gives a correct and concrete conception of the nature of depressions. *A depression is a period in which the demand for durable material means of production is smaller than in the boom which precedes it.* "Overproduction" is not necessarily a condition of the depression. It is enough that the actual production is less than is possible with the existing means of production. The part of the productive capacity which stands idle usually amounts, as we can see in the diagram, to only a small percentage. But, for all that, it means a considerable loss to the owners, a loss which is aggravated by the fact that competition keeps down the prices of such work as is still available. Moreover, the workers are bound up, to a certain extent, with production, and for them, too, the depression means comparative loss of work, or unemployment and pressure on wages. Thus the slight dip in the curve of pig-iron output, since this output represents the total production of fixed capital, is sufficient to cause severe disturbances in the whole economic system.

A glance at the diagram shows us that the periods of depression have a tendency to become shorter. This tendency must obviously continue so long as the pig-iron output curve follows the same upward movement as it has, in the main, done since 1870. We cannot, of course, predict the future trend of this curve.

Since the production of fixed capital continues steadily, the community is better provided with durable means of production at the end of the depression than at the beginning. The relative idleness of the factors of production is, therefore, greater than it would appear from the diagram. But as soon as production again reaches the level of the previous boom, the depression, as experience shows, is over, and an upward trend in the trade cycle is started. Thus our method of constructing the periods of depression is satisfactory.

The results which we have reached in this section bring out clearly the significance, in the fluctuations of the trade cycle, of the durability of the means of production. It is often asked, Why cannot productive forces be perfectly adjusted to demand? This question is sometimes made the starting point of an adverse criticism of the whole modern economic system. But it overlooks the fact that the durable means of production must be adapted to the highest point in the demand, and thus, precisely because they are durable, they must be in excess at every decrease in demand. They could be permanently and fully employed only if the demand for their employment never fell off.

In regard to the effects of the fluctuations in demand, we must distinguish between those durable means of production which work directly for the consumer and those that are employed in producing further instruments of production. A fall in the demand of consumers means a corresponding idleness for the first group of means of production, but possibly complete idleness for the second group, since there are more than enough means of production available for the first group.

In order to bring about a certain amount of unemployment of the means of production of the second group, it is not even necessary that there should be a fall in demand for consumption goods on the part of consumers. If it is thought that demand will remain constant for a time, the creation of more means of production of the first group ceases, and those of the second group have nothing to do, unless they are employed in repairing or replacing the worn-out equipment of the first group. Even if the consumers' demand is not constant, but increases only a little more slowly than the normal, it will not be necessary to make more than a slight additional quantity of the means of production of the first group, and those of the second group will be only partially employed.

It follows from this that the production of durable means of production must be, on the whole, much more sensitive to the fluctuations of the demands of consumers than the production which works directly for the needs of consumers. In such circumstances, it is only natural that the production of fixed capital should show more pronounced fluctuations than the rest of production, a fact which we have already ascertained in various ways.

How far the employment of the means of production of the higher order can be influenced by the fluctuations in the demand of the final consumer is seen, particularly when one considers those means of production that serve only a very special purpose.

Consider, for example, English shipyards. The vessels which they produce are durable means of production, and the demand for them may be represented by the extent of the freightage. The fluctuations in this demand need not be great in order to cause violent

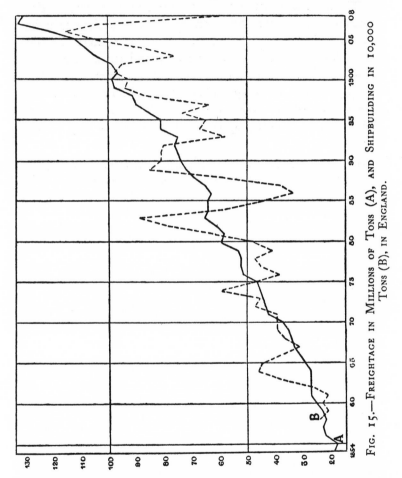

FIG. 15.—FREIGHTAGE IN MILLIONS OF TONS (A), AND SHIPBUILDING IN 10,000 TONS (B), IN ENGLAND.

fluctuations in the extent of employment of the yards. In the preceding diagram (Fig. 15), curve *A* indicates the total tonnage of ships entering English ports annually, and thus gives us an idea of the development of freightage. Curve *B*, on the other hand, shows, in tens of thousands of tons, the total tonnage of new ships built annually in English yards. [1] As we can see, curve A needs to dip very slightly, or even remain horizontal for a time, to provoke a startling reduction in the employment of the shipbuilding yards.

The freightage curve must be regarded, on the whole, as being very uniform. It will be difficult to attain greater uniformity in this and in similar lines of development in the near future. Yet the slight deviations from the steady proportional rise are enough to cause grave disturbances in the shipbuilding industry. According to this, therefore, the prospect of ever attaining completely uniform activity, not exposed to the fluctuations of the trade cycle, in the sphere of the capital-producing industries, seems very remote indeed.

[1] For the figures of this diagram which are repeated in Table X. in the Appendix, see Board of Trade, *Statistical Tables and Charts*, Cmd. 4954, 1909, pp. 97 and 104.

CHAPTER XVII

THE INFLUENCE OF TRADE CYCLES ON THE
DETERMINATION OF PRICES AND INCOME,
AND ON CAPITAL CREATION

§ 70 *The Prices of Commodities*

TURNING now from the concrete processes in the sphere of production to the process of exchange, we have first to consider the influence of trade cycles upon the determination of prices. For this purpose we must at first confine ourselves to materials and consumption goods, the prices of which are precisely the prices for the use of them. We cannot deal until a later stage with the determination of the prices of those durable goods which are fixed capital, as we have already seen that this is a complicated phenomenon in which the price of the capital-disposal, or the rate of interest, plays a part.

The commodities to be considered here fall into two main categories: materials of fixed capital and other commodities. Let us see how the prices of the goods in these two groups are determined during the phases of the trade cycle. The course of prices since 1871, according to English statistics, for three of the most important materials, namely, pig-iron, bricks, and timber, is shown in the diagram (Fig. 16). [1] The prices are calculated as percentages of the 1900 prices. It is seen that the maximum prices stand out sharply, and that, in general, they coincide with the turning years of the trade cycle. During periods of trade boom we find, as a rule, a rise in the prices of the materials of fixed capital. This is a generally recognised phenomenon, and can be observed in all countries.

It is not sufficient to know, however, that the movements of the trade cycle influence the prices of the materials of fixed capital.

[1] The figures are reproduced in Table XI. in the Appendix, Board of Trade, Cmd. 4954, 1909, pp. 184 and 190.

We must discover whether the determination of the prices of other goods depends in the same way and to the same extent upon the trade cycle. Unfortunately, different index numbers for the materials of fixed capital and for other commodities have not been

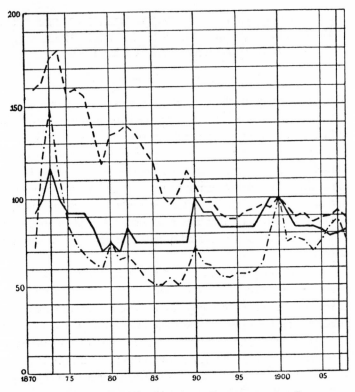

FIG. 16.—CURVES REPRESENTING THE INDICES OF THE PRICES OF PIG-IRON (–·–·–·), BRICKS (————), TIMBER (– – – –).

published; which is regrettable in view of the extraordinary importance of this division. However, in order to obtain at least an approximate solution to the problem, we can break up the Sauerbeck index number in such a way as to have, on the one hand, the index numbers which Sauerbeck gives for his "minerals" groups, and, on the other hand, the numbers for all his other groups. To eliminate the disturbing influence of the fluctuations in the gold output, we shall divide the index number by our figures of the relative quantity of gold.

The index numbers thus obtained for minerals and other commodities form the basis of the accompanying diagram (Fig. 17). [1] The thick black curve indicates the fluctuations in the prices of minerals, while the dotted curve indicates those of the other commodities. A glance at the diagram shows how much more clearly the movements of the trade cycle are reflected in the prices of minerals than in those of other commodities. The rise in prices of minerals during a boom is usually very steep, and is followed by a fall which is just as pronounced. Other commodities show similar movements, though essentially of a modified nature.

The movements in the prices of commodities under the influence of trade cycles, which we have examined in the case of the free trade English market, should be characteristic of the world market as a whole. We should certainly reach the same conclusion if we were to make a similar analysis of the German index number of prices.

We thus find that even in the sphere of the determination of prices the movements of the trade cycle have a very intimate connection with the production of fixed capital. This confirms the conclusions we reached in our investigations regarding the influence of trade cycles on production and labour. But we can draw even more important conclusions from the movement of prices during the various phases of the trade cycle.

We find, first, that the trade boom causes a rise in prices not only of the materials of fixed capital, but also of other commodities. The rise in prices of the materials of fixed capital is not offset, as one might perhaps expect, by a reduction in the prices of other goods. What is noticeable is not merely a relative change in the prices of various commodities, but, in fact, a general rise in the price-level. This is not due to the fact that the rise in the prices of materials of fixed capital outweighs a contrary movement in the

[1] The figures are reproduced in Table XII. of the Appendix.

prices of other commodities, but that the group of "other commodities" shares, though to a much slighter extent, in the general advance in prices. This general advance cannot be attributed to

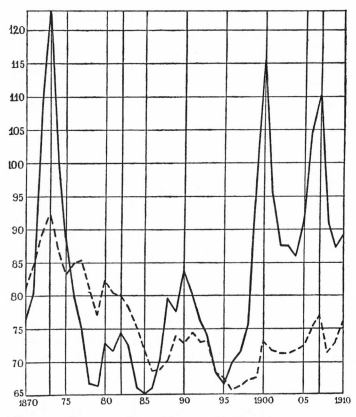

FIG. 17.—SAUERBECK INDEX NUMBERS DIVIDED BY THE RELATIVE STOCK OF GOLD. ——— MINERALS, − − − − − OTHER COMMODITIES.

changes in the gold supply, for it is still manifest in our diagram, where we have eliminated the influence upon prices of changes in the gold supply. We must conclude, therefore, that the trade cycle has a special influence in the purely monetary sphere.

We have already settled what this influence is (§ 55). During a trade boom, there is a rise not only in the prices of goods, but also in the volume of actual transactions, and consequently in the whole volume of payments. This increased volume of payments is made possible partly through an acceleration in the circulation of existing means of payment and partly through an increase in the means of payment issued by the banks. The increased velocity of circulation of the means of payment is a direct effect of the greater vitality of trade which characterises a boom. But the ampler provision of means of payment, on the other hand, implies a definite co-operation on the part of the banks, and thus depends on this co-operation – particularly on the interest policy of the banks. The trade boom means accordingly not a mere change in the relative prices of goods based on the conditions of the market, but also a definite rise in the general price-level which can be explained only as an outcome of a superabundant issue of means of payments by the banks.

Secondly, the extraordinary height which the prices of materials of fixed capital reach during a trade boom points to a great scarcity of these materials. Although they are produced on a large scale, the demand for them can only be satisfied if it is restricted by the extremely high prices. The increased production of materials of fixed capital during the boom does not signify overproduction. On the contrary, during a trade boom there is a real, and by no means a merely speculative, demand for the materials of fixed capital, which originates from the producers of fixed capital themselves. At the peak of a trade boom, this demand, as a rule, is considerably in excess of the supply, and therefore equilibrium has to be achieved by means of a rise in prices. This fact is also confirmed by the market reports during any trade boom – that is, scarcity of materials puts a brake on the increase in the production of fixed capital.

Thirdly, during a trade boom a certain scarcity of those factors of production which are employed in the production of the materials of fixed capital must always exist. When the prices of these materials rise rapidly, as is usually the case, the producers will, in these circumstances, undoubtedly do their utmost to derive the maximum profit from the favourable trade movement. If, however, the market is inadequately supplied for some considerable time, this may be explained by the fact that the factors of production are functioning to their full capacity. This applies equally to labour and to the durable means of production. As regards the workers, we have already shown that during a trade boom the industries we are considering experience a shortage of labour that can only be partially met by working overtime. We have seen, for instance, in the working of the transport system, that the durable means of production are used to the fullest extent. But the steady rise in the prices of the products of these industries clearly proves that their productive capacity is, in general, exercised to the full. Thus, during the trade boom there are no more workers or durable material means of production than are needed for the production of that quantity of materials of fixed capital for which there is an effective demand.

This is particularly true of the production of pig-iron. During a trade boom the existing blast furnaces, mines, transport equipment, etc., cannot produce a greater quantity of pig-iron than they have actually produced. The peaks of the curves on the diagram (Fig. 14) indicate the maximum production that can be achieved with the existing durable material means of production. The productive capacity that is attained at the height of the trade boom remains possible throughout the subsequent depression, and is the standard by which the actual production must be judged if we wish to have a definite idea of the falling-off in employment during the depression.

We can use the monthly index numbers of the prices of commodities in Germany in order to obtain an accurate idea of the times when price movements took place during recent trade cycles. [1] For the group of articles referred to as "metals," the index number rose from 123.83 in February, 1906, to a maximum of 163.35 in January, 1907, to fall again to a minimum of 119,31 in July, 1908. This fall in prices did not take place steadily. In the first of the three half-years, that is up to July, 1907, the fall in prices was 8.26, whereas in the second half of the second year it

[1] Pohle, *Monatliche Übersichten.*

was 29.88, and in the second half of the third year it was 5.90. We see, therefore, that the greatest fall in prices occurred in the second half of 1907, and was most pronounced during the last quarter of the year. The lowest figure for 1906 – that quoted for February – remained the minimum until December, 1907. The decline from the highest point that prices reached during the boom began quite a considerable time before the crisis (October, 1907), but prices as a whole did not fall to a normal level until after the crisis. Similarly, the index number reached a maximum of 166.27 in October, 1912, whereas that particular trade boom lasted till the autumn of 1913, when the fall in prices also took place for the most part (154.20 in September to 137.05 in December).

The total index number rose from 109.33 in February, 1906, to 122.40 in July, 1907, and then fell to 107.79 in December, 1908. From this point it again rose to a maximum of 132.54 in May, 1912. We can see that the prices of metals were more markedly affected during the trade cycles than the total index figures.

Similar conclusions may also be reached with regard to the United States of America. The monthly average price of Bessemer pig-iron in Pittsburg[1] rose from a minimum of 18.10 in May, 1906, to a maximum of 24.27 in June, 1907, and fell to a minimum of 15.71 in October, 1908. It is very remarkable that the violent crisis of the autumn of 1907 sent the price of pig-iron down only to 19.34 (December, 1907); this price had not been reached in the first half-year of 1906, and was only exceeded in September, 1906, during a period of marked trade activity. The next trade boom raised the price again to a maximum of 18.15, a figure reached in December, 1912.

We have thus established the fact that high, or at least good, prices are paid for the materials of fixed capital up to the last moment of a trade boom, and even for a certain time afterwards. The turning point in the movement of the prices of these materials is reached a considerable time before the crisis begins, and may serve as a sure indication of the approaching end of the upward trend of trade. These prices reach their minimum only in the course of the slump.

[1] Ibid.

From this minimum point there is a more or less steady upward movement, until a new maximum is reached a few months before the next period of depression sets in.

§ 71 *Wages*

The average wage per shift of a coal-hewer in the Dortmund area has been subject to the following variations since 1872, taking only maxima and minima:

Year.			Marks.	Year.			Marks.
1872	..	..	.. 4.50	1893	..	..	.. 3.71
1873	..	..	.. 5.00	1900	..	..	.. 5.16
1879	..	..	.. 2.55	1902	..	..	.. 4.57
1883	..	..	.. 3.15	1907	..	..	.. 5.98
1886	..	..	.. 2.92	1909	..	..	.. 5.33
1891	..	..	.. 4.08				

The dependence of this wage upon trade cycles is evident. The highest wages coincide with the transition years, though sometimes, as in 1883 and 1891, a noticeable delay occurred in this respect. In order to fix times of the changes in wages more closely we can resort to the following data concerning the average earnings per shift of all the miners in the mining district of Dortmund (the figures indicate the number of pfennigs in excess of the sum of 4 marks)[1]:

Year.	Quarter.	Pfennigs.	Year.	Quarter.	Pfennigs.
1906	1st	17	1909	1st	56
	2nd	26		2nd	45
	3rd	43		3rd	48
	4th	59		4th	48
1907	1st	70	1910	1st	48
	2nd	81		2nd	51
	3rd	94		3rd	57
	4th	99		4th	61
1908	1st	87	1911	1st	64
	2nd	82		2nd	66
	3rd	82		3rd	72
	4th	76		4th	75

[1] Pohle, *Bevolkerrungsbewegung, Kapitalbildung und periodische Wirtschaftskrisen* 1902, § 70. The latest figures are taken from the *Reichsarbeitsblatt*.

The highest figure, 4.99 marks, was reached in the fourth quarter of 1907. There was a considerable decrease in the figure in 1909.

Thus wages seem to possess a certain power of resistance to the effect of a trade depression. Statistics of wages per shift do not give us an accurate idea of the real earnings of labour. We know that the number of shifts per worker varies considerably during trade cycles. From this we may assume that the actual average wage decreases more rapidly when the trade cycle enters upon the downward trend than the rates of time-pay suggest.

In Belgium, Mahaim has obtained index numbers of wages by dividing the whole annual amount paid out as wages by the number of workers.[1] He thus found for the whole class of coal-miners in Belgium the following variations, again giving only the maxima and minima:

1883	..	..	..	84	1893	..	..	..	74
1886	..	..	..	65	1900	..	..	..	118
1890	..	..	..	93					

The figures apply to from 103,000 to 135,000 workers, and bring out very clearly the fluctuations in yearly wages. The wages of the 8,000–10,000 workers of the Cockerill Works actually fluctuated from:

1883	..	..	..	86	1894	..	..	..	85
1885	..	..	..	74	1901	..	..	..	114
1890	..	..	..	93					

The British Board of Trade publishes statistics of wages in the most important industries (coal-mining, building, engineering, and textile industries). These figures, given below, are based mainly on the rates of pay accepted by the trade unions, showing the maxima and minima reached since 1874[2]:

1874	..	..	..	91.36	1895	..	..	88.23
1879	..	..	..	81.16	1900	..	..	100.00
1882	..	..	..	84.41	1904	..	..	95.56
1886	..	..	..	81.12	1907	..	..	101.79
1891	..	..	..	91.13	1909	..	..	99.41

[1] *Journal of the Royal Statistical Society*, 1904.
[2] Board of Trade, *British and Foreign Trade and Industry*, Cmd. 4954, p. 212. (*Fourteenth Abstract of Labour Statistics.*)

We see that the highest wages again occur in the turning years, though in 1891 there was the same kind of delay that we observed in the case of the wages of German miners.

The Board of Trade also publishes periodically statistics regarding the increase in the total weekly wages in industrial occupations due to changes in wages. The following figures show, in thousands of pounds, this increase (+) or decrease (−)[1]:

Year.	£1000's	Year.	£1000's
1894	− 45	1902	− 73
1895	− 28	1903	− 38
1896	+ 27	1904	− 39
1897	+ 32	1905	− 2
1898	+ 81	1906	+ 58
1899	+ 91	1907	+ 201
1900	+ 209	1908	− 59
1901	− 77	1909	− 69

The careful investigations made by Bowley and Wood on the wages of English workers have furnished us with the following facts. The average wage since 1850 in the shipbuilding and engineering industries shows the following maxima and minima (the index number for 1900 equals 100)[2]:

1850	..	..	.. 68	1882	..	..	.. 88
1854	..	..	.. 76	1886	..	..	.. 84
1860	..	..	.. 73	1890	..	..	.. 93
1866	..	..	.. 79	1893	..	..	.. 91
1867	..	..	.. 77	1899	..	..	.. 00
1877	..	..	.. 88	1903	..	..	.. 99
1879	..	..	.. 83				

The index number of the average weekly wage in the cotton industry shows the following fluctuations since 1863[3]:

1863	..	..	.. 62	1884	..	..	.. 85$\frac{1}{4}$
1868	..	..	.. 74	1886	..	..	.. 83$\frac{1}{3}$
1869	..	..	.. 72$\frac{2}{3}$	1901	..	..	.. 100$\frac{2}{3}$
1877	..	..	.. 88	1903	..	..	.. 99$\frac{1}{2}$
1879	..	..	.. 78$\frac{1}{2}$	1906	..	..	.. 107$\frac{1}{3}$

[1] *Abstract of Labour Statistics.*

[2] *Journal of the Royal Statistical Society*, 1906, p. 185. The figures relate to the whole United Kingdom.

[3] *Journal of the Royal Statistical Society*, 1910, p. 599.

Wages in the cotton industry remained unchanged after the depression of 1901, but in the shipbuilding and engineering industries they suffered a definite, though not a large, reduction.

We need not quote any further figures. Although even the most accurate statistics of wages may be liable to error, the facts given regarding the short period of a trade cycle should give a good idea of the trend of the level of wages. We may also regard as a settled fact that a trade cycle always leads to a rise in the wages, whereas a depression is usually accompanied by a fall. These variations affect not only wages in the capital-producing industries, but also, though perhaps to a less noticeable degree, wages in other industrial occupations, and even, according to English statistical data, the wages of agricultural workers.

It would be exceedingly difficult to compare wages in different occupations in order to prove the dependence of wages upon trade cycles. Besides, the conclusions arrived at would hardly be relevant to our purpose. The results already obtained are of great importance for a correct understanding of the nature of trade cycles. Rising wages are paid only when an increasing scarcity of labour make them necessary. We may conclude from the statistics of wages that during a trade boom there is a perceptible scarcity of labour. This is a valuable confirmation of the results already obtained in earlier sections in relation to the supply of, and demand for, labour.

The rise in the general level of wages during a trade boom is in itself a phenomenon of great practical importance, materially influencing the whole nature of the trade boom. This increase clearly means an increased purchasing power for the most essential articles of consumption on the part of the working-classes, and is thus an important factor in determining the production and pricing of these articles.

The question whether *real wages* do or do not rise during a trade boom has often been discussed. We cannot give a definite answer to this question, because the issue depends upon which of the tendencies at work get the upper hand. With the aid of statistics, we can give many examples of every conceivable relationship between the increase and decrease in wages on the one hand, and the rise and fall in prices on the other. We may, under these circumstances, dispense with a more detailed investigation of the changes in real wages.

§ 72 *Income*

The study of the influence of trade cycles on the national income is, naturally, a very important aspect of our subject from the practical point of view, but it also affords an opportunity for observations of some theoretical importance. In order, however, to clarify the problem from every point of view, we must not be content with a survey of the changes in the national income as a whole, but, where we can, must also separately consider the various chief parts of this income.

In such an inquiry we must scrutinise not only the statistics relating to wages, but also those of income tax. As the income of any year is, in practice, mostly subject to income tax only in the following year, we should bear in mind, in the course of our researches, that the yearly income is best computed on the basis of the subsequent year's income tax statistics. This method is far from being infallible, but, nevertheless, it gives, on the whole, the closest idea of the real position.

In England the working-classes were not subject to income tax, and, therefore, the information we can derive from the income tax returns concerns only the income of the middle and upper classes. In order to get an idea of the changes in the income of the working-classes we must refer to the statistics relating to wages. The gross amount of income subject to tax varied from 1870 onwards as follows[1]:

Year.	£ Millions.	Year.	£ Millions.
1870	482	1893	694 min.
1874	579 max.	1899	868
1875	570 min.	1900	902
1883	631 max.	1901	915
1884	629 min.	1902	938
1891	718 max.	1905	979

We find that the maximum amounts of income coincide with the

[1] Board of Trade, Cmd. 4954, 1909, p. 136.

peaks of trade booms, though they are generally a little retarded. The decline during the period of depression is, in every case, very small, and amounts, at the most, to about 3 per cent. (1891–3). After the trade boom of 1900 there was no decrease at all, but only a retardation in the upward movement.

The influence exercised by the trade cycles upon the classes of incomes which the English income tax law groups under Schedule D is much stronger. The variations are as follows[1]:

Year.	£ Millions.	Year.	£ Millions.
1870	203	1893	341 min.
1874	272 max.	1899	466
1875	257	1900	488
1878	250 min.	1901	492
1883	293 max.	1902	502
1885	286 min.	1907	566 max.
1890	369 max.	1908	559
1891	367		

In 1891 another small group of incomes was included under Schedule D, though this did not prevent the income already taxed from falling. The real diminution in income from 1890–3 was, therefore, rather greater than is shown by the figures. We find that the fall in Schedule D incomes, reckoned as a percentage, is much greater than that in the total income – in fact, many times greater. Schedule D is not comprised of a homogeneous class of incomes. It includes certain salaries and dividends, though it should consist primarily of income derived from business. Thus we may conclude from the available data that income from business undertakings is affected by trade cycles more than any other class of income. When we consider the different types of income from business mentioned in the statistics, by far the greatest fluctuations are found, characteristically enough, in incomes from iron and steel works, which have varied as follows (in thousands of pounds)[2]:

Year.	£1,000's.	Year.	£1,000's.
1890	2,979	1904	2,684
1892	1,832	1907	5,101
1900	6,600	1909	3,233

[1] From the same source. Figures for 1907 and 1908 are taken from the *Statistical Abstract.*

[2] *Statistical Abstract.*

The table which follows is based on the Prussian income tax statistics, the figures referring partly to incomes ranging from 900 to 3,000 marks, and partly to incomes over 3,000 marks, classified according to the source of income. The figures are given in millions of marks.

INCOME OF ACTUAL TAXPAYERS IN PRUSSIA
(in millions of marks).

Year.	Income from 900–3,000 Marks.	From Investments.	Incomes over 3,000 Marks.		
			From Land.	From Commerce, Trade and Mines.	From Occupations.
1891	2,912	892	755	982	594
1892	2,969	887	746	960	615
1893	3,027	888	742	954	633
1894	3,134	904	739	963	660
1895	3,197	912	855	1,019	685
1896	3,318	943	785	1,106	729
1897	3,472	966	816	1,206	818
1898	3,685	1,081	867	1,304	892
1899	4,011	1,141	921	1,418	964
1900	3,328	1,208	968	1,497	1,037
1901	4,460	1,237	996	1,475	1,084
1902	4,616	1,243	1,007	1,424	1,132
1903	4,895	1,300	1,049	1,439	1,189
1904	5,209	1,380	1,109	1,507	1,261
1905	5,551	1,473	1,171	1,623	1,354
1906	6,592	1,610	1,185	1,744	1,500
1907	7,344	1,702	1,233	1,833	1,622
1908	7,642	1,731	1,269	1,809	1,732
1909	7,676	1,797	1,348	1,859	2,052
1910	8,078	1,915	1,426	1,946	2,205

The income derived from business, given under the heading "Commerce, Trade, and Mines," clearly decreased from 1891 to 1893, and only rose above its former height in 1895. It then increased rapidly during the trade boom of 1900, and fell considerably for three years in the subsequent slump. It again rose rapidly in the trade boom of 1907, and once more declined a little in 1908. The increase during the years 1896–9 amounted regularly to about 100 million marks per annum, that is, 8–10 per cent., but there was a fall in 1900. In 1905 and 1906, too, there was a considerable increase in this type of income, but a considerable reduction took place in 1907. The maximum amounts of income from business also occur in the turning years, though the greatest increase occurs in the earlier years of the trade boom. The other classes of income show no fall in the depressions after 1900 and 1907. In the depression following 1891 the income derived from investments underwent a slight reduction, and income from land a rather greater reduction, though this must be attributed to the particularly bad state of agriculture at the time. Thus we can see that the influence of trade cycles is by far the greatest in the case of income from business undertakings. In the other classes of income the trade slumps are felt only to the extent of a slight modification in the rate of increase.

The following income tax statistics of Saxony have the great advantage of including incomes down to 400 marks. The variations in the various classes of income are as follows[1]:

RESULTS OF THE ASSESSMENTS FOR INCOME TAX IN SAXONY
(in millions of marks).

Year.	Landed Property.	Investment Income.	Salaries and Wages.	Commerce and Trade.	Total Income
1877	214	109	334	357	1,014
1878	218	112	365	350	1,045
1879	222	116	380	353	1,071
1880	225	123	403	360	1,111
1881	229	129	422	371	1,151
1882	233	135	450	378	1,196
1883	233	142	465	395	1,236
1884	237	151	492	408	1,288
1885	241	158	521	418	1,337
1886	242	162	552	430	1,378
1887	247	168	584	444	1,443
1888	255	178	619	468	1,519
1889	263	187	665	496	1,611
1890	271	200	701	517	1,689
1891	277	205	714	516	1,713
1892	283	214	738	521	1,756
1893	287	220	771	528	1,806
1894	289	229	800	541	1,860

[1] *Jahrbuch für das Königreich Sachsen.*

Year.	Landed Property.	Investment Income.	Salaries and Wages.	Commerce and Trade.	Total Income.
1895	293	237	851	562	1,943
1896	300	250	913	596	2,059
1897	307	263	972	626	2,168
1898	318	276	1,041	653	2,288
1899	329	289	1,103	682	2,403
1900	377	291	1,144	693	2,465
1901	343	300	1,158	700	2,502
1902	349	304	1,182	712	2,548
1903	356	303	1,234	703	2,597
1904	365	307	1,283	720	2,675
1905	373	321	1,338	738	2,770
1906	380	333	1,416	775	2,904
1907	388	348	1,515	813	3,064
1908	401	364	1,577	846	3,188
1909	413	379	1,644	873	3,309

The total income in Saxony did not, as we can see, suffer the slightest reduction, but the income derived from commerce and trade fell slightly in 1891 and 1903. A corresponding decrease occurred in respect of investment income in 1903, alone among all the other classes of income, and this only to a small degree. Income from landed property, together with salaries and wages, continued to grow, even during periods of depression, though at a slower rate. During the trade boom which culminated in 1900, the greatest rise in income from business occurred during the years 1896 to 1899. This increase slackened to some extent in the subsequent years, until in 1903 it was completely suspended.

The income figures for Sweden are very characteristic. Income from agriculture, landed and house property, as well as incomes below 500 kronor (about £27), are exempt from voluntary assessment. The estimate of income from business, from which income from agriculture is excluded, is arrived at on a basis of 5 per cent. of the capital value of the land, premises, etc., of the aggregated undertakings, and this sum is deducted as a profit from the total value of capital. The increase or decrease (–) in income from business and from salaries and wages is given below (in millions of kronor), as compared with the previous year[1]:

[1] From *Generalsammandrag öfver Bevilningen*

INCREASE AND DECREASE (−) OF INCOME VOLUNTARILY ASSESSED FOR
INCOME TAX IN SWEDEN
(in millions of kronor).

Year.	Service (including Pensions).	Business and Professions.
1883	0.3	− 0.9
1884	6.2	9.7
1885	3.9	− 7.7
1886	3.6	1.7
1887	2.7	3.0
1888	2.8	23.1
1889	5.7	24.4
1890	7.7	− 1.0
1891	7.0	− 0.8
1892	13.3	− 7.8
1893	7.3	8.8
1894	6.6	10.5
1895	10.4	20.1
1896	12.7	29.3
1897	20.4	41.0
1898	26.7	27.9
1899	21.5	32.0
1900	29.7	15.9
1901	15.1	− 15.0
1902	43.1	11.3
1903	34.5	27.5
1904	26.3	20.2
1905	29.5	40.1
1906	48.2	73.7
1907	123.1	31.7
1908	56.8	− 37.9
1909	10.4	− 22.1

The large increase in wages in 1902 and 1907 must be ascribed to the introduction and, later on, the extension of self-assessment. This is also true to some extent regarding the increase in income from business in 1902.

We find that while income from business has decreased during every depression, wages have steadily risen. The chief increase in income from business always takes place in the early years of the upward movement of a trade cycle, whereas when the trade boom proper is taking place, the increase in the income from business is already somewhat reduced. In the turning years themselves there is a decrease, or at least a considerable weakening of the upward tendency. The increase in wages is always substantially smaller than the increase in income from business at the beginning of an upward trend, and reaches its highest point only during the trade boom proper. During the turning years and the subsequent depressions wages show a steady increase. There is thus an important difference between the income of the entrepreneurs and that of the workers, in that the former obtains the benefit of the earlier years of the increased activity in trade, whilst the latter is favoured during the actual trade boom and perhaps still more in the depressions.

We thus find that the relatively steady increase in wages, especially in the case of Saxony and Sweden, where the assessment for income tax includes the large class of industrial workers, is a phenomenon of great significance, and probably of fairly general occurrence. The wages of the workers represent, together with the income derived from land which also increases comparatively steadily, a real burden upon enterprise, for if they continue to increase in bad times they are bound to bring down the profits of entrepreneurs. The beginning of a trade boom is a particularly favourable time for the profits of entrepreneurs. They increase rapidly, as a rule, but this is soon counteracted by the steady rise in wages. As soon as the rate of increase in profits begins to slow up, or even disappears, the turning point of the trade cycle is at hand. It is obvious that the profits of entrepreneurs must form a larger part of the total national income at the beginning of a trade boom than at the peak. During a depression the income of entrepreneurs and the remaining shares of the national income are subject to inverse variations.

Our investigations of the real processes of production led us to distinguish only between periods of advance and decline. A closer analysis of the fixing of prices and income makes it necessary, as we now see, to divide the former period into two stages. We may call the first of these stages *the period of the beginning of the advance*, and the second the *trade boom proper* in the narrower meaning of the term.

§ 73 Consumption

We have seen that the increased production of fixed capital, which is the chief feature of the trade boom, brings about an increase in the number of workers, and usually an increase in hours of work. The new workers are recruited from among the ranks of the unemployed, from young people hitherto not employed, or from the agricultural population. In each case the employment of fresh labour and the increase in working hours denote the creation of new income. This income represents an additional purchasing power, and, as it is doubtless absorbed for the most part in consumption, it creates new demands upon the industries which supply the working-class with ordinary necessities. Those industries are to some extent also capital-producing – for instance, in so far as they help to provide new houses for the workers. The industries which work along mass production lines must also be considered here. As there is an increased activity in all these industries on account of the greater demand, new workers are required and longer hours must be worked. This steadily increasing demand for labour in the capital-producing industries, as well as in mass production industries, gradually forces wages up, and thereby increases the purchasing power of the working-classes.

This revival of industrial activity is especially favourable to the textile industry. The working-classes demand for clothing is particularly elastic. When times are bad the worker must remain content with satisfying his need of food and a roof over his head, while clothes must be worn as long as possible. Hence a demand for clothing at the commencement of the trade boom is so much greater, and the textile industry enjoys a brisk demand. We have already shown that the textile industry is particularly sensitive to the great movements of the trade booms. This fact is substantiated by the figures of textile workers insured through their trade unions in Germany, and by the trend of cotton yarn production in England.

The revival of industrial activity, which begins in the capital-producing industries, spreads also, though in a progressively declining degree, to other branches of industry. This increases the money income not only of the working classes, but also of other sections of the population. That is why the trade boom has so deep a significance for the entire community.

The increased production of consumption goods that obviously takes place during a trade boom is naturally consumed. This proves that consumption really increases during a trade boom. Production is now, as we can prove statistically, mainly a mass production of standard articles. As there is no doubt that industrial production increases considerably during every trade boom in order to meet the needs of the large number of consumers, we must conclude that the total real income of the working-classes increases in proportion during the trade boom.

The increased purchasing power of the working-classes enables them to purchase a larger quantity of goods. But on the other hand an increased purchasing power leads to a rise in prices. It follows that the real income of the workers does not increase in the same proportion as their money income.

This rise in prices is a fact which we can prove statistically in the case of the principal industrial consumption goods. However, as compared with the increase in the prices of the materials of fixed capital, this increase is entirely a secondary phenomenon, which takes place only in a relatively slight degree. We already know, particularly from the diagram (Fig. 17), that this is the case.

After what has been said, we ought to be able to state with a great degree of certainty that the total real income of the working-classes increases during a trade boom. But this is mainly due to the fact that the new workers employed in industry formerly earned nothing at all, or earned much lower wages in agriculture. With regard to the development of the real income of the individual workers who were already employed in the industry, it is, as we said before in § 71, not possible to give a general answer.

The conclusions arrived at in this section apply only to industrial production. We find that the same tendencies occur in the sphere of agricultural production, but they are modified to a considerable extent by the variable conditions of agriculture, and therefore can rarely be fully realised. The prices of agricultural products, which normally should rise during a trade boom, may be neutralised by good harvests, or even fall below their former level.

On the other hand, the prices of agricultural products may, owing to bad crops, go up to such an extent that they directly affect wages. There is an interdependence between wages and the amount spent on consumption goods, which in this case would be a cause of the diminution in the real income of the workers. Thus, in the question of the fluctuations of real income, there is the play of certain factors lying outside the movements of the trade cycle, in the sense in which we have used this term. The theory of trade cycles cannot, therefore, furnish a definite answer to this question.

§ 74   *Capital from Savings*

The total sum of the annual savings of the community can hardly be determined statistically, as a large part of them is, as a rule, used directly in special enterprises. Every employer must, in order to keep his works up-to-date, annually set aside considerable sums out of his income. In the case of limited companies a part of these savings go to build up the "secret reserves," the amount of which is not divulged to the public. In agriculture, too, large sums, which cannot be given in accurate figures, are taken from the annual income in order to improve the land, and for similar purposes. This direct formation of capital by entrepreneurs must, on the whole, be very considerable, but it cannot be included in any statistical calculation of capital-formation.

Private individuals, who are in no way entrepreneurs, are constantly on the look-out for remunerative forms of investment of their savings. A large part is always invested in mortgages, and thus promotes the development of agriculture, and particularly of building. Another part is entrusted to banks of all types, and so indirectly placed at the disposal of production. The third and remaining part goes to pay for new issues of stocks and shares. It is true that certain statistical data are published in connection with the latter two groups of savings, but they are always incomplete and unreliable. We cannot obtain an exact idea from them as to the amount of total savings, for we never know what the ratio of bank deposits and securities is to the other kinds of savings. Probably this ratio varies considerably in different countries and during different trade cycles. We know also that bank deposits vary a good deal, and play quite different parts in different countries. Similarly, the share issues do not, for various reasons, give a clear idea of the formation of capital. In this respect we observe only that a considerable part of these shares is used to cover floating debts, or to purchase existing real capital, and therefore does not actually increase the capital of the community. Issues, for example, which serve for the conversion of private enterprises into limited companies, or for merging different companies, must not be included in the statistics of the actual formation of capital. We cannot ascertain, moreover, to what extent the shares issued will really be paid for in the current year, and still less whether the payments effected are covered by existing savings or by loans. Indeed, the figures regarding issues of shares show considerably greater fluctuations than can be supposed to occur in the actual formation of capital.

We must not limit our studies of the formation of capital to a single country, but must take into account the important international movements of capital. If we consider all these complications, we may conclude that the figures published regarding the formation of capital do not supply us with reliable information as to the fluctuations of the amount of savings which are offered on the capital market from year to year. We are thus compelled to form in an indirect way an approximate idea of the variations in the formation of capital during different stages of a trade cycle.

We found in § 72 that the national income increases on the whole very steadily, but that it falls a little in a depression, or is, at all events, checked in its rate of increase. In all probability the movements of the trade cycle have a rather more pronounced influence on the formation of capital.

As entrepreneurs are compelled by economic exigencies to save, they put aside, as savings, a part of their profits. The proportion of these savings to profits usually largely exceeds the savings from other groups of income. When the proportion of savings set aside from the profits of entrepreneurs is greater than the average rate of savings, the community's formation of capital is greater in these times, which are therefore particularly favourable from the entrepreneur's point of view. Such a time is the period at the beginning of renewed trade activity. From this we may assume that at the beginning of a trade boom a relatively large amount of capital is formed. But then, in all probability, the rise in wages and prices brings about an immediate decrease in the formation of capital relatively to the national income. For the working-classes certainly consume a comparatively larger part of their income, particularly when there is a rise in the prices of ordinary necessities. Simultaneously, the income of the entrepreneurs begins to fall owing to the rise in wages, or, at least, the rate of increase is diminished, and thus this important source of new capital tends to be diminished. Thus the end of a trade boom should be characterised by a relative stringency in the supply of capital. It is quite obvious that, during the depression, the entrepreneur's profits can contribute very little to the formation of capital. But during a depression, on account of the lower cost of living, and particularly when the worst times are over, the other classes of income ought to contribute considerably to the formation of capital.

In the light of these considerations, we may assume that the formation of capital is, relatively to the national income, greatest at the beginning of a period of trade revival, that it does not diminish considerably during the trade boom, and that, after being seriously impaired at the time of the crisis, it gradually recovers during the downward phase of the trade cycle.

CHAPTER XVIII

THE INFLUENCE OF TRADE CYCLES ON THE CAPITAL MARKET

§ 75 *Supply and Demand*

THE foregoing inquiry has shown that the production of fixed capital is subject to certain variations during the various phases of the trade cycle. During the depression there is a reduction in output and during the boom an increase above the normal. This fact, which is of fundamental importance for the whole theory of trade cycles, is, on the whole, directly confirmed by the data which we have given in connection with production, and also indirectly by our study of the movements of labour and of commodity prices. The chief point is that this effect of trade cycles is peculiar to the production of fixed capital, and is not felt, or at least not to the same extent, in the sphere of production for consumption. From this it follows that during a trade boom the production of fixed capital represents a greater part of the total production than during a depression. In other words, during the boom the total production shifts in the direction of a relatively greater production of fixed capital. During the depression there is a drift in the opposite direction.

Income is divided into what is consumed and what is saved. The first part is employed in purchasing articles of consumption; the other part, the savings, is used to purchase the newly produced real capital. On the capital market the savings appear as supply, and, on the other hand, the real capital produced appears as a demand for capital-disposal.

We must now investigate the changes which the capital market experiences during the various phases of the trade cycle. To get a clear idea of these changes, we will first assume that there is no change in the use of the income, or, in other words, that the ratio of the income consumed and the income saved remains unchanged. In that case both the income consumed and the newly created capital increase at the same rate as the total income. But during the trade boom the production of fixed capital increases at a faster rate than the total income, and the production of consumption goods at a slower rate. Owing to this a maladjustment occurs between the distribution of production and the distribution of income. In the sphere of consumption income predominates, and the result must be a rise in the prices of goods for consumption. We have already been able to prove that this is really the case. This increase is generally a very moderate one, and is due to the fact that the displacement in the sphere of production is relatively unimportant as regards the production of goods for consumption, which represents the far greater part of the total production. On the capital market production predominates, and there the movements of prices must, therefore, take an opposite direction. These, however, must necessarily be more pronounced, on account of the relatively greater change in the range of capital production. If we regard the capital market as a market on which the fixed capital produced is offered for sale, the prices of the material capital goods must obviously fall in the conditions supposed. This movement will continue until equilibrium is restored between the total value of the newly produced real capital and the income available for the purchase of it. Possibly the upward movement of the prices of consumption goods will be followed by a similar movement in the price of the services of capital. In that case, the ratio of the price of fixed capital to the price of using it will fall, which is equivalent to an increase in the rate of interest.

Again, if we regard the capital market as one in which the supply of, and the demand for, capital-disposal meet, under the conditions assumed the demand will tend to predominate, and the price of capital-disposal will rise, or, in other words, the rate of interest will go up. As securities become capitalised at this higher rate of interest their capital values decline. This reduction in the price of capital goods diminishes the capital-disposal required to produce them to such an extent that equilibrium is soon restored on the capital market.

It is obvious that any displacement in social production in favour of the production of capital, if unaccompanied by a corresponding change in the use of income, must bring about changes in prices which are unfavourable to fixed capital, but favourable to consumption goods. It is only the new prices that can restore equilibrium between income and production in their principal sections.

Depressions must clearly have an opposite effect. As the production of fixed capital decreases relatively to that of consumption goods, the prices of the latter must fall and the prices of goods which are fixed capital must go up – that is to say, the rate of interest must fall.

We must now consider the fluctuation in the formation of capital under the influence of trade cycles. We have seen in the previous chapter that trade cycles have some influence on the use of income, and cause changes in the direction of a rise or a fall in the amount of saving effected. At the beginning of an upward movement in trade, when entrepreneurs' profits have risen rapidly, the creation of capital is comparatively large. Subsequently, a change takes place in the use to which income is put in the direction of increased savings. This raises purchasing power in respect of capital goods, and generally to a greater extent than the production of such goods. Thus, during a period of this kind a general rise in the prices of fixed capital must be expected. The fluctuations in the rate of interest will depend upon the profits made on this capital.

During the real boom, on the other hand, entrepreneurs' profits diminish and the saving tends to fall off, but the production of fixed capital maintains its upward movement, and sometimes even increases in intensity. The stringency of the capital market is accentuated, the prices of capital goods fall, and the interest rates must rise still higher than was necessary on our first assumption.

During the depression, when the production of fixed capital decreases, there is, at first, less capital on the market in search of investment than would be the case if there were a normal amount of saving. This modifies a little the rise in the prices of fixed capital and the fall in the bank-rate, but does not altogether eliminate them. In the later phase of the depression, when capital is again formed more freely and an increase in the production of fixed capital has not yet begun, the position of the capital market is particularly favourable.

These movements are also influenced by the increased return on fixed capital which characterises the period of trade revival. This increased return is the result of both the more complete use to which we are able to put existing fixed capital at this period and the opening-up of new and very remunerative uses of capital, which is the starting point of the whole upward movement. At first, this increased return is probably greater than the rise in the price of fixed capital which we also found to be characteristic of the earlier part of the upward course of trade. This is why the rate of interest rises, though rather slowly, during this period. At the time of the trade boom proper, the large return on fixed capital combines with the factors already mentioned to raise the rate of interest yet higher. During the depression the unfavourable return on fixed capital helps to keep the rate of interest at a low level.

A study of the influence of trade cycles upon the capital market must take into account still another factor, namely, the attitude of the banks. At the very outset of a trade revival they generally continue to supply means of payment at the earlier rate of interest, or, at all events, hesitate to raise the rate as quickly as the growing scarcity of capital-disposal would require. Consequently, the capital goods are capitalised at too low a rate of interest, i.e. their prices are pushed upward. Hence the production of capital goods appears to be particularly profitable, and the entrepreneurs make free use of the purchasing power which the banks put at their disposal so cheaply. This leads to a diversion of the community's purchasing power in the direction of capital goods. There ensues a corresponding change in production, so that the consumers' demands cannot be fully met. Thus this action of the banks has the same effect upon the distribution of the community's total purchasing power between capital goods and consumers' goods as an increase in the savings of the community.

The newly created purchasing power which the banks put at the disposal of business men must naturally bring about a rise in prices and this must spread until it results in a rise in the general price-level. Trade then requires a corresponding increase in the supply of means of payment, and the banks satisfy this demand. During the period of trade revival both the quantity of bank-notes and the general price-level go up. During the depression, however, banks' advances are repaid to a great extent, the general provision of means of payment becomes more stringent, and the general price-level falls again.

The movements we have described – namely, the change in the relative scale of the formation of capital, the fluctuations in the amount of the savings of the community, the variations in the return on fixed capital, and the changes in the supply of bank-notes – collectively bring about fluctuations in the rate of interest and in the prices of capital goods. We see these phenomena occurring during the various phases of a trade cycle. We can show them statistically, as we shall endeavour to do in the subsequent sections.

§ 76 *The Rate of Interest*

It is a generally recognised fact that the rate of interest rises sharply at the peak of a trade boom. We made this fact the basis of our definition of the critical phases of trade cycles, the "turning years." Our diagrams in connection with the variations of the discount rate in Berlin and London (Figs. 7 and 8) show how pronounced this rise in the rate of interest is at the highest point of a trade cycle. After the crisis the rate of interest, as a rule, falls rapidly, usually much more rapidly than it rose. It is interesting to follow these movements month by month. In London, the market discount rate stood, on the average, at 2.66 per cent. in 1905, but rose in 1906 to an average of 4.05 per cent. In November, 1907, the maximum rate of 6.61 per cent. was reached. It then fell very rapidly in the following months, and in July, 1908, reached the minimum of 1.30 per cent. In November, it stood at 2.27 per cent. On the Berlin Bourse the maximum rate of 7.07 per cent. was reached in December, 1907. In July of the following year the rate dropped to 2.75 per cent., and in December it stood at 2.92 per cent.[1] There is no doubt, therefore, that the capital market is rapidly and considerably eased by the reduction in the production of fixed capital during the depression, in spite of the simultaneous, but less important, reduction in the formation of capital.

During boom periods that have lasted for some considerable time we can see how the rate of interest remains at first very moderate, and does not alter much until the later years of the boom. In England the upward movement of the 'nineties began in 1896, when the output of pig-iron reached the figure of 8,799,000 tons, as against 8,456,000 tons at the height of the preceding boom (1889).[2] The average market discount rate was only 1.52 per cent. in 1896, and during the two following years it remained at the moderate level of 1.87 and 2.65 per cent. It rose to an average of only 3.29 per cent. in 1899, and in the turning year, 1900, it reached an average of 3.70 per cent. In Berlin the discount rate in 1897, when the German output of pig-iron had risen to 6,881,000 tons as against 4,658,000 in the turning year, 1890, stood only at an average of 3.09 per cent. In the following years, 1898–1900, the average rate rose to 3.55, 4.45, and 4.41 per cent. After the crisis of 1900 and the subsequent depression a substantial increase in the production of fixed capital occurred in 1903 and 1904, though the market discount, however, did not exceed the average of 3.14 per cent. (1904). In 1906 and 1907, when the boom entered upon its second phase and the production of fixed capital was still very considerable (the pig-iron output amounted to 12,875,000 tons in 1907 against 8,521,000 in 1900), the average discount rate rose to 4.04 and 5.12 per cent. Thus the first years of an upward movement of the trade cycle may enjoy a moderate rate of interest. It is only in the last years of the revival of trade, during the trade boom proper, that the rate reaches such a height that it points without doubt to an increasing shortage of capital. The fluctuations in the capital market, which theoretical consideration compel us to assume, are thus completely confirmed by the movements of the discount rate.

[1] Pohle, *Monatliche Übersichten.*
[2] These and the following figures are taken from the *Statistiches Jahrbuch für das Deutsche Reich.*

In order to make the connection between the rate of interest and the production of fixed capital quite clear, it is useful to compare the changes in the rate of interest with the output of pig-iron at identical periods. Let us first try to make this comparison for the whole world. As the standard of the rate of interest we use the average market discount rate in London, Paris, Berlin, and New York.[1] The changes in the output of pig-iron and in the rate of interest in the four trade booms coming after 1873 are shown in the following table:

	Year.	*Rate of Interest.*	*Pig-Iron Output.*
	1873	6.3 max.	15.1 max.
	1879	3.5 min.	14.4
1st Period	1880	3.8	18.6
	1882	4.5 max.	21.6
	1883	4.1	21.8 max.
	1886	3.5 min.	22.8
2nd Period	1887	3.8	27.9 max.
	1890	4.5 max.	29.4
3rd Period	1895	2.8 min.	41.3
	1900	4.3 max.	54.8
4th Period	1905	3.0 min.	61.3 max.
	1907	4.83 max.	

We see that the maximum outputs of pig-iron and the maximum rates of interest fall, as a rule, in the same years. Only in 1883 did the maximum outputs of pig-iron extend to another year, but the figure of the preceding year was not exceeded by much. On the other hand, the minimum outputs of pig-iron do not, as one would be inclined to expect, correspond to the minimum rates of interest. As may be seen from the table, it is not until the beginning of a new period of trade revival, reckoning this period from the year when the pig-iron output first exceeds its old maximum after a depression, that the rate of interest reaches its minimum. The revival of trade activity, defined in this way, begins for the first period in 1880, for the second period in 1887, for the third period in 1895, and for the fourth – if we take into account the maximum of 46.6 for 1903,

Pohle, *Statistische Unterlagen* (MS.).

which is not given here – in 1905. We have found, in the case of the first two periods, that the minimum rate of interest falls in the year preceding the commencement of the upward phase of the trade cycle, but in the case of the latter two periods in the first year

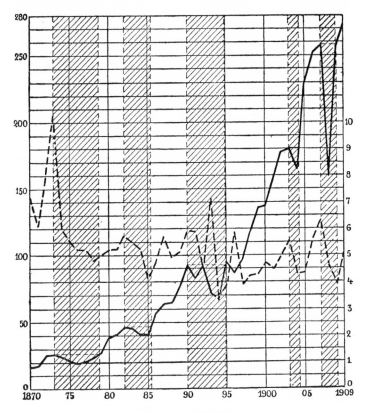

FIG. 18.—UNITED STATES.
PIG-IRON OUTPUT (IN 100,000 TONS, FIGURES ON THE LEFT) (————),
AND MARKET DISCOUNT RATE (FIGURES ON THE RIGHT) (– – – – –).

of the trade revival. These differences obviously depend upon the season of the year in which the changes take place, as well as upon other minor circumstances. We are therefore justified in drawing up the following general rule: The rate of interest passes from a fall to a rise when the pig-iron output reaches its old maximum, and from a rise to a fall when it establishes a new record.

This rule, within certain limitations, is also valid for other countries. The case of the United States is demonstrated on our diagram (Fig. 18). The thick black line indicates the pig-iron output (in 100,000 gross tons, figures on the left), while the dotted line shows the market rate of discount in New York (figures in percentages on the right). The periods of depression are illustrated in accordance with our usual method (§ 69). We see that the minimum rate of interest always falls at the end of the period of depression. As a rule the rate of interest continues to decline during the whole period of depression.

This rule does not apply to the economic development of England in the 'eighties, as the pig-iron output decreased and was considerably smaller in the minimum year, 1889, than in the preceding maximum year, 1882. On the other hand, the rate of interest fell to its minimum in 1879, in the depression of the 'seventies, in the year before the beginning of a new revival. Similarly in 1895 the rate of interest fell to a minimum, and the new trade revival began in the following year. In 1905, when the pig-iron output in Great Britain exceeded its previous maximum after the depression at the beginning of the new century, the rate of interest was at its minimum.

In Germany the beginning of an upward movement, as we have defined it, coincides, as a rule, with the minimum market discount rate, except that in the 'eighties the rate did not reach its minimum until 1888, though the period of revival started as early as 1887. Regarding the maximum rates of interest and pig-iron outputs, one detects small discrepancies when separate countries are considered. Nevertheless, our rule should be regarded as adequately confirmed by experience. It appears to merit attention both on theoretical and on practical grounds.

§ 77 *The Changes in the Value of Stocks and Shares*

It is not an easy matter to give a general idea of the fluctuations of the prices of fixed capital, for there is no proper market for the commodities in question. The greater part of fixed capital is, however, represented in paper values of one kind or another on the Stock Exchange. The demand for savings capital with which to purchase the fixed capital that has been produced is expressed partly as a demand for the means of buying shares, and partly as a demand for loans. The ownership of fixed capital is directly represented by shares, but the loans which reach the Stock Exchange in the form of bonds bearing a fixed interest also serve, from the economic point of view, as means for taking over the newly produced fixed capital. Loans are wanted not only by ordinary entrepreneurs, but also by public bodies. However, a substantial part of these public loans, particularly those of municipalities, is used for acquiring fixed capital. There are important differences between the movements of the prices of securities bearing fixed interest and those of ordinary shares, and these are based upon the fact that the value of shares does not depend merely upon the rate of interest, but also very materially upon the profits of undertakings.

The scarcity of capital which makes itself felt throughout the period of trade revival is bound of itself to reduce the value of all stocks and shares, particularly during the real trade boom, when the shortage of capital is generally very acute. But in the early part of the trade revival this tendency is counterbalanced, as regards shares, by the excellent profits that are earned on them. Hence, at first, shares increase in value, and the upward movement reaches its maximum at about the beginning of the boom proper. In consequence of the shortage of money on the capital market, the fixed interest bearing securities must, at the same time, fall a little in value. Though at first this decline may be very slow, these securities will probably pass their highest point while shares are still rising. It is clear that the value of the securities bearing fixed interest must be, to some extent, inversely proportional to the rate of interest. Their movements are, however, under normal conditions, somewhat slower than those of the rate of interest. When the rate of interest is low the Stock Exchange must always count upon a possible rise in the rate, and, consequently, upon a decrease in the value of securities bearing fixed interest, and thus it is only natural that the latter should usually reach their highest value when the rate of interest has already passed its minimum – that is, somewhere about the beginning of an upward movement of trade. The maximum for the shares usually comes still later, as will be understood from what we have said.

During the trade boom proper, when the return on fixed capital already often shows a downward tendency, and the scarcity of capital is felt very acutely, shares are bound to be affected, and generally begin to decline in value. Hence the maximum value of the shares is to be found at a point somewhere near the beginning of the boom period. Even the securities bearing fixed interest will now, on account of the acute scarcity of capital, begin to decline rapidly in value, the culminating point being reached during the crisis itself. It would, therefore, be wrong to assume that it is the crisis which provokes the fall in values. The shortage of capital is in fact so acute for some time before the crisis that it is bound to lead to a considerable decline in values.

During the depression, when the rate of interest is low, the securities bearing fixed interest usually recover rapidly, moving steadily in an upward direction. In the case of shares, however, a poor return is generally the chief feature, and, though they recover a little after the crisis, it is not until the end of the depression that they begin to rise again.

From our knowledge of the condition of the capital market during various phases of the trade cycle we can deduce the following general rule regarding the movements in the value of stocks and shares: Both securities bearing fixed interest and ordinary shares touch their minimum at the time of the crisis; after this they both rise, but, in the case of the securities bearing fixed interest, only until the beginning of the next trade revival, when they both reach a maximum. The shares continue their upward course and attain their highest point at the onset of the trade boom. The downward movement starts at that point, soon extending to all classes of stocks and shares.

Now let us test these results.

That a fall in the value of stocks and shares occurs before the crisis sets in – even to such an extent that we may speak of a crisis on the Stock Exchange as a forerunner of the economic crisis proper – is a fact generally known from the history of crises.

We will first consider the fluctuations in the quotations of shares on the Berlin Bourse in 1909. The index number of the *Frankfurter Zeitung*[1] stood on the last day of December, 1906, at 162.68, and on the last day of January, 1907, at 160.59, after which there was a sharp decline which reduced the index number by the last day of March to 152.61. Thus in the months of February and March eight points were lost. The next marked decline did not take place until October – the crisis month – when the index number fell from 149.10 to 143.90, or about five points. If we calculate from the maximum price of shares which stood in September, 1905, at the index number 175.60, we see that by far the greater part of the downward movement had ended before the crisis proper began. The crisis only brought down their value to a minimum of 142.91 (February, 1908).

We will now consider the movements of the $3\frac{1}{2}$ per cent. Inconvertible Imperial Loan in Berlin, with a view to following the fluctuations of fixed interest bearing securities through a series of trade cycles.[2] The annual averages after 1889 were as follows:

Year.	Annual Average.	Year.	Annual Average.
1889	103.70 max.	1901	99.54
1890	100.45	1902	102.06
1891	98.39 min.	1903	102.30 max.
1892	99.97	1904	101.94
1893	100.38	1905	101.33
1894	102.39	1906	99.54
1895	104.44	1907	94.65
1896	104.58 max.	1908	92.61 min.
1897	103.59	1909	95.14 max.
1898	102.65	1910	93.17
1899	99.77	1911	93.46
1900	95.80 min.	1912	89.79

The minima, as we can see, occur regularly in the crisis years, and the maxima in one of the earlier years of the trade revival.

[1] That index gives the average price of one half of the issues officially quoted on the Berlin Bourse (*Volkswirtschaftliche Chronik*).

[2] *Denkschriftenband zur Reichsfinanzenreform*, Part IV.; Pohle, *Monatliche Übersichten*

It is very interesting to compare the course of the share quotations with these movements. The above-mentioned index number of the *Frankfurter Zeitung* enables us to make this comparison from the year 1904. From that date the exchange level of share quotations developed along the following lines[1]:

Year.	Index No. of Shares.	Year.	Index No. of Shares.
1904	153.92	1909	156.96
1905	168.82 max.	1910	162.77 max.
1906	163.25	1911	162.45
1907	149.29	1912	158.78
1908	145.32 min.	1913	157.59

It is remarkable that the share quotations do not reach their maximum until 1905, or at the beginning of the trade boom proper, and two years after the culminating date of the Imperial Loan. This occurs again in the upward phase of the next trade cycles. The Imperial Loan reached its highest point in 1909, but share quotations do not appear to have reached their maximum until February, 1911. This was just at the time of the beginning of the boom proper.

It is particularly interesting to study the movement of those shares which specially represent the production of fixed capital. According to *Volkswirtschaftliche Chronik*, the following annual averages may be given for the Berlin Bourse:

Shares.	1904.	1905.	1906.	1907.	1908.
Gelsenkirchen Bergwerk	219.18	230.21	224.84	198.50	189.33
Harpener Bergwerk	205.45	215.47	214.34	203.89	198.07
Bochumer Gussstahl	200.90	247.78	244.79	217.47	212.75
Dorntmund Union	83.40	93.67	86.50	71.02	58.54
Königs- und Laurahütte	243.37	261.72	243.86	225.51	207.09
Berliner Maschinenbau	238.35	251.88	243.89	220.09	232.55
Allgem. Elektr. Ges.	219.64	234.23	217.80	198.14	212.79
Siemens und Halske	148.79	186.71	187.35	169.71	183.79

We see that, as a rule, these shares, too, touched their highest average point in 1905. In the case of the last share quoted, however, there is a slight exception to this.

[1] From the *Volkswirtschaftliche Chronik*, 1913, p. 1067.

§ 78 *The Scarcity of Capital during the Trade Boom*

During the last stage of a trade boom it is not only in the rise of the rate of interest and the fall in the value of stocks and shares that the tension of the capital market manifests itself. Every similar period presents us with an opportunity of directly observing a real dearth of capital. This scarcity makes itself felt in the growing difficulty which even very profitable concerns experience in raising funds.

These difficulties naturally react upon the production of fixed capital. Not every kind of production of this type, however, can be directly curtailed. The sphere in which a falling-off in production on account of the increasing stringency of capital may first be expected is clearly the building industry, in which the various contracts are completed relatively quickly, and in which, therefore, the contraction of production is easiest. The scarcity of capital makes itself felt in this industry in an increasing difficulty to sell completed houses, or to secure credits whereby to continue building operations. As building depends to a very great extent upon securing capital to assist these objects, and as builders can easily refrain from commencing new buildings, it should be regarded as a normal thing that the tension in the capital market causes building activity to slacken off even during the trade boom, and that, therefore, the maximum activity in this industry is attained some time before the end of the boom. This is confirmed by the American statistics of building which we have previously given (§ 63).

It is quite otherwise with the railways and similar large undertakings. The railways are not built for sale. The owners have, as a rule, a considerable command of capital, and can procure what is needed even in difficult circumstances. This is, of course, particularly true of State railways. Moreover, the construction of a new railway takes a much longer time than the building of an ordinary house. Again, a railway in course of construction must be completed even if the capital required should become slightly more expensive. It is, therefore, quite conceivable that in spite of the stringent condition of the capital market the work will be prolonged for a considerable time. What we have said about railway construction also applies more or less to other enterprises, such as tramways, canals, electricity generating stations, etc.

Thus we see that the production of fixed capital and of the materials required for it maintains its upward movement for a time in spite of the difficulty of getting capital. In the later stages of the boom we must expect to find that the development of the building industry and its subsidiary industries will not be the same as that of the other kinds of production of fixed capital.

In Germany this difference became very clear in 1907. From the very beginning of the year the building trade was announced to be in a bad way, and the situation was ascribed to the dearness of money. The branches of the iron and steel industry which experienced a decline in comparison with the previous year were precisely those which supplied materials for the building trade. The output of the Stahlwerksberband of primary materials and moulded articles in 1907, as compared with that of the previous year, showed only a slight decrease, whereas the output of railway materials rose considerably. The difference is clearly seen in the following figures (in thousands of tons)[1]:

Products.				1905.	1906.	1907.
Primary materials	..	..	..	..	1,911	1,862	1,558
Moulded articles	..	..	..	..	1,673	1,936	1,699
Railway materials	..	..	..	..	1,631	1,936	2,327
			Total:	5,215	5,734	5,574

The greatest difference in development took place in the last months of 1907, when the output of primary materials, and especially of moulded articles, fell very considerably, whilst the output of railway materials continued to increase.

Owing to the difficulty of raising capital during the height of a boom, the big transport undertakings are often compelled to reduce their demand for capital. The management must then limit itself to what is indispensable with regard to the improvement and enlargement of the equipment and to the construction of rolling stock. This is still more necessary in the case of the smaller concerns. But as the means of transport are, as we saw, used to a very great

[1] *Volkswirtschaftliche Chronik*, 1907, pp. 695 and 772.

extent throughout the whole of the boom period, the larger undertakings will make certain sacrifices in this effort to get the necessary
capital for their requirements. This is, of course, easiest in the case
of States, which are on this account least disposed to reduce their
demands for capital.

A consideration of the case of the United States enables us to see
how great are the difficulties of raising capital during a trade boom.
In 1907, the American railway companies were forced to limit
themselves, to a great extent, to short-term loans instead of a
regular issue of debentures. That part of the funded debt of the
railways which is given in the statistics as "Miscellaneous Obligations" rose from $974,000,000 in 1906, to $1,616,000,000 in
1907, and $2,181,000,000 in 1908, though in the latter year the
range of the statistics was curtailed. At the same time the
bonded debt rose from $6,267,000,000 to $6,472,000,000 and
$6,610,000,000.[1] These figures show an enormous demand for
capital, as well as the great difficulty in getting it. In the following
year, 1909, the amount of "Miscellaneous Obligations" rose by only
$86,000,000, while the bonded debt increased by $332,000,000.
These figures clearly illustrate a profound disturbance of the capital
market.

The American statistics also give the amount which the railways
have to pay annually as interest on their floating (unfunded)
debts.[2] This charge amounted, in millions of dollars, to:

Year.	Interest Charges.	Year.	Interest Charges.
1890	8.1	1901	5.5
1891	8.2	1902	7.7
1892	7.9	1903	9.1
1893	8.0	1904	13.9
1894	10.2	1905	11.5
1895	7.9	1906	11.7
1896	8.5	1907	16.7
1897	7.8	1908	31.3
1898	7.1	1909	24.2
1899	7.1	1910	16.5
1900	4.9		

[1] *Statistical Abstract of the United States.* It must be remembered that the years quoted
end on June 30th.

[2] Ibid. Here again the years end on June 30th.

We see how considerably the interest on the unfunded debts rises in years of crisis. Even in the preceding year there is an appreciable rise. This demonstrates that the railway companies, during the last phases of the boom, were unable to raise regular loans to a sufficient amount. This again confirms the very important fact that during a trade boom there is a scarcity of capital.

From the foregoing it follows that the diminution in savings during the last part of a trade boom makes itself felt first in a limitation of the kind of industrial activity in which the separate undertaking, as in the building industry, is completed comparatively quickly, and then in an increasing difficulty which large transport concerns experience in raising capital, until at last, in the case of private companies at least, this can only be done at the cost of substantial sacrifices. Governments and municipal bodies are least affected in the production of fixed capital by the increasing stringency in the capital market.

CHAPTER XIX

THE DETERMINING FACTORS OF TRADE CYCLES

§ 79 *The Principle of Action and Reaction*

IN our studies of trade cycles, we have so far confined ourselves to the actual processes and their immediately connected problems. Now let us look more closely at those factors which, acting as driving or restricting forces, determine the movements of the trade cycle.

Of these forces, interest on capital occupies the central place. The low rate of interest which prevails during the depression obviously leads to a greatly increased production of fixed capital. Given a certain return, the lower the rate of interest, the higher is the value of fixed capital. Hence the low rate of interest is equivalent to high prices for the capital already produced. At a time, therefore, when a low rate of interest has been maintained for a long period, prospects of considerable profits await those entrepreneurs who are prepared to undertake building contracts, railway construction, or other works which require a large amount of fixed capital. The profits can be realised by selling the houses or the shares of the undertakings to the public in search of investments.

We have already seen (Chapter VI.) that there are always potential undertakings which require a good deal of fixed capital, and which are, therefore, not remunerative when the rate of interest is high. Directly the rate falls, however, a certain proportion of these undertakings become remunerative. It will then not be long before the possibilities begin to be translated into realities. If, for example, a railway from which we estimate a net annual revenue of £400,000 requires an outlay of £10,000,000, it cannot be constructed as long as the rate of interest is 5 per cent. But if the rate falls to 3 per cent., the construction becomes profitable and will, in all probability, be carried out. Thus the rate of interest is, to a great extent, the decisive factor as regards the economic possibility of providing permanent productive equipment. But, as we know, it has nothing like the same importance in connection with the current production of consumption goods. A low rate of interest which is maintained for some time ought, therefore, to accelerate the production of fixed capital much more than any other kind of production, and so bring about gradually that adjustment in social production which, favourable to the production of fixed capital, we described as an essential characteristic of the trade boom.

A high rate of interest, on the other hand, must reduce the value of fixed capital and cause loss to entrepreneurs who are engaged in producing this type of capital. Many undertakings can hardly be completed as long as the rate is high. The economic possibilities of an increased production of fixed capital are greatly restricted by a high rate. Only undertakings that promise an exceptionally high profit can be considered. But if they prove less remunerative than was anticipated, and unable to bear the high interest demand for the disposal of capital, this must have a depressing effect upon any new projects for the production of fixed capital.

This explains why a prolonged high rate of interest leads to a fall in the production of fixed capital. The production of consumption goods, however, does not suffer to anything like the same extent from a high rate of interest. When it too declines a little, together with the production of fixed capital, this must not be regarded as a direct consequence of the high rate of interest during a trade boom, but rather as a secondary phenomenon. However, the direct effect of the high rate of interest on the production of fixed capital is enough to convert the trade boom into a depression.

Thus the rate of interest has a very definite effect on the course of the trade cycle, an effect that is always in the opposite direction to that course. During the depression there is a low rate of interest which has a restorative effect upon enterprise: during the boom there is a high rate of interest which acts as a brake. On the other hand, the rate of interest is itself affected by the trade cycles. The depression brings down the rate of interest, which in turn leads to the end of the slump. A parallel to this is the rise of the rate during a boom to a level which cannot be maintained for long, and the boom itself is bound to come to an end. There is thus a reciprocal action between the rate of interest and the progress of the trade cycle.

This reciprocal action is only an instance of the general principle of action and reaction. If there is to be any stability at all, all action, in the economic as well as the physical world, must provoke a reaction. The fluctuations in the rate of interest, however, are not the only reactions that serve to check the trade cycles. Among other factors which restrict the boom there is, in the first place, the rise in the prices of the materials of fixed capital, which, as we have seen, may be very considerable, and must naturally greatly hamper the further production of such capital. A second factor modifying the boom is the rise in wages. Both these influences tend to make the production of fixed capital dearer; houses, railways, factories, etc., will cost a good deal more to build than was allowed for in the plans. This phenomenon, which takes place almost without exception during the boom, has naturally a very disturbing effect upon the chances of profit, even upon the enterprise of many firms, and clearly gives little encouragement to further enterprise. Even if there is a fall in the value of the fixed capital already produced, on account of a high rate of interest, we quite understand how the rise in wages and prices, together with the rising rate of interest, must act as a powerful brake upon the trade boom. It is not at all surprising that these restricting factors put an end to the abnormally large production of fixed capital, and consequently to the whole trade boom.

It might rather have been asked how it is possible that in the boom period proper, when the prices of fixed capital have begun to decline, the high prices of the materials and labour required to produce the fixed capital can be maintained for some time. This may be explained by the fact that the equipment, buildings, etc., in question promise for the most part an exceptionally high profit, and, therefore, leave a certain margin for the increase in cost; again the undertakings in question, when once begun, must be completed even at a sacrifice.

The depression also creates corresponding forces which tend to counteract it: there are then low prices for materials of fixed capital and low wages. These factors cheapen the production of fixed capital, at the same time as the low rate of interest, itself a result of the depression, raises the value of the completed capital goods. The co-operation of these forces overcomes the depression and leads to an upward movement in trade.

The rate of interest has, of course, a certain importance in connection with production itself, just as have the prices of materials. But we may leave this element out of consideration in order to bring out more clearly the essential effect of changes in the rate of interest.

The fluctuations of trade cycles are, in general, somewhat accentuated by the action of the banks which we mentioned previously. If the banks keep the rate too low at the beginning of an upward movement in trade, this acts as a special encouragement to the production of capital, and helps to intensify the boom. The rise in the general price-level which is caused by the unduly low rate of interest ought to act at first in the same direction.

§ 80 *Further Explanation of Trade Cycles*

From what we have said, cyclical fluctuations of trade must be regarded as a result of the reciprocal action of the enterprise of business men and the great regulative factors of the social economy which have their roots in economic scarcity – the prices of materials, wages, and the rate of interest. After this explanation, there still remain a few questions that require further elucidation.

In the first place it might be asked: Does not the reaction produced by the various restricting forces make itself felt at once, so that any increase or decrease in the production of fixed capital is prevented from the start? It might be supposed that in this way we could gradually bring about, at least for the most part, a state of constant equilibrium.

But we must bear in mind that the reactions in question always take some time to make themselves felt. The decrease in the production of fixed capital that characterises the depression generally continues, as we saw, for some time before its effect on the rate of interest is fully felt. The rate of interest in turn must remain low for a time in order to restore and strengthen the confidence of entrepreneurs in the capital market. Moreover, the entrepreneurs, too, need some time to prepare new plans, adapted to the changed conditions, and to get to work on them. As long as the production of fixed capital remains below its previous maximum, the rate of interest continues to fall, giving an increasing incentive both to the public with money to invest and to entrepreneurs to enter upon new ventures. As soon as the reaction induced by the low rate of interest sets in, and the production of fixed capital consequently begins to rise above its last maximum, the rate of interest changes its direction, but still remains for a time too low to be able to check the beginning of an upward swing in trade. Our studies have also shown that the rate of interest does in fact reach its minimum at the end of the depression, that it rises slowly in the period of trade revival, and that it rises rapidly only during the trade boom proper.

The length of the trade cycle is also connected with the fact that the production of fixed capital requires time. The undertakings which are planned during the depression or at the beginning of the revival generally require several years for their completion. Comparatively little time is necessary for erecting houses. One or two years generally suffice. Railways, canals, water-power stations, etc., require a much longer time. Hence a brisk activity in this sphere cannot be checked at once by the restrictive forces. Thus the length of the trade cycle is to some extent connected with the length of the period of production of the undertakings in question. It is, therefore, not altogether improbable that the general tendency, so characteristic of our day, to shorten the time required for building and other constructions has also helped to shorten the periods of trade cycles, a phenomenon that seems to have manifested itself in the twentieth century.

Add to this the fact that the increased production of fixed

capital requires on its own side enlargement of all plant and means of transport needed for this production. Even the production of goods ready for consumption, which has its share in the trade boom, though in a slighter and secondary degree, will need new machinery and larger plant. This expansion of the trade boom naturally takes some time. The profits that are made on account of the high prices of products prevailing at the beginning of a trade boom lead to the establishment of new undertakings or enlargements of existing businesses based on the expectation that the high prices will continue. The prolongation of the trade boom depends largely upon the expectations inspired by the first and really profitable part of the trade revival, which, however, cannot be realised during the later part of the boom on account of the counteracting forces, the latter being constantly ignored or under-estimated by the public. But these forces become the more impelling the more they are over-looked. They may succeed in exercising a restraining influence at the right time in some spheres, such as building. Generally, however, there has to be a more or less violent crisis before the public learns not to lose sight of the laws of economic limitation.

In the second place it might be asked: If it is quite clear that the trade cycle must spread itself over a number of years, why is there not at least a gradual levelling-out of the upward and downward movements as a result of the reactionary influences? To this we can reply: This would undoubtedly be the case but for the events taking place from time to time which cause a renewal of the whole trade cycle.

Technical progress is one of these events. We have already seen that modern technical progress has mainly expressed itself in an increased use of fixed capital. The best instance of this is the railways. In the nineteenth century railway construction was always the form of activity that mainly characterised the trade boom. But in the last boom of that century, as well as in the first of the present one, this leading position passed, at least in part, to another sphere of enterprise, namely, the electrical industry. In the middle of the 'nineties, when the rate of interest was, perhaps, lower than ever, the widespread application of various electric inventions was apparently the immediate cause of the enormous demands on fixed capital, which led to a new boom and thus started once more the fluctuations of a trade cycle. The construction of electric tramways, electric lighting installations, large power stations, telephones, and so on, necessitated a vast production of fixed capital. In the present century all these improvements have become the objects of a keen demand. No country, no district, no town, could be satisfied without making some use of these new achievements in the application of electricity. The communities were not intimidated by the possibility of a shortage of capital until it was impressed upon them by an exceptionally high rate of interest, or even the impossibility of getting capital at all. In this competition, State and municipal authorities have been at least as keen, and as regardless of the state of the capital market, as private individuals.

Under such circumstances a trade cycle that is already much attenuated is bound to be restored to full strength by some new technical advance, and will then continue in the form of a fluctuation for some time.

Among other events having the same effect we must include particularly the exploitation of new countries. When an uncivilised or semi-civilised country is opened up to civilisation, there is immediately a considerable new demand for means of transport, bridges, hydraulic works, lighting installations, and, above all, houses for a rapidly growing population – in a word, for fixed capital. The pronounced booms since the middle of the 'nineties have clearly been due to a great extent to the diffusion of Western civilisation. The economic exploitation of the whole of the Far East, particularly China, is bound to give rise once more to new large demands for fixed capital and will in all probability lead to fresh trade booms. But, naturally, the stimulation of trade which originates in the exploitation of new countries will tend to disappear altogether when the world is more or less uniformly equipped with the material foundations of Western civilisation.

Every new opportunity to use fixed capital profitably on a large scale acts as a stimulus to trade. Society, as we have repeatedly pointed out, always has a large number of such opportunities, but they can only be used to a limited extent on account of the rate of interest. If this number is increased by more such opportunities to use fixed capital which remain profitable even when the rate of interest is high, there will inevitably be an extraordinary increase in its production, or a new trade boom. Anyone who complains of trade cycles, and condemns a social order that facilitates or tolerates their existence, is really complaining of the advance of our material civilisation. Here again we notice how the critics of our social order conveniently overlook progress and all the difficulties it entails for the community by means of a facile abstraction, so simplifying the matter for themselves. But in so doing they make it impossible for themselves to understand the true facts.

Progress cannot be absolutely uniform. Every development, intellectual or material, has its specially active periods and its reactions. As far as material production is concerned, we have particularly to bear in mind that every unevenness in production for current consumption is always bound to lead to much greater unevenness in the employment of the durable means of production of a higher order. As these represent fixed capital, and as the trade cycles are, in essence, merely fluctuations in the production of fixed capital, we can hardly conceive a complete elimination of trade cycles in a progressive economic system. In proportion, however, as progress is retarded or made more uniform, we may expect a certain modification in the amplitude of the trade cycle. In accordance with this observation, it is only natural that at the time of the great industrial revolution, when society took the decisive step from the old to the new economic order, there had to be a series of pronounced booms and subsequent depressions.

When we speak of progress in the economic sense, we must always include in this term the growth in population. Every increase in population necessitates a corresponding increase in the fixed capital of the community. An increase of fixed capital above the average must clearly afford more room for the play of trade cycles. On the other hand, a generally weaker increase of fixed capital is bound to some extent to have a restrictive effect on trade cycles. A community with a constant population might succeed in keeping the trade cycles within narrow limits. We might even discover the existence of such a correlation between the growth of population and trade cycles by comparing different countries. It is at once noticeable how much more important Germany and the United States, with their huge growth of population, are in connection with world-wide trade cycles, and how much more they are affected by them than a country like France, with a relatively stationary population.

Thus we come to the conclusion that the future of trade cycles depends essentially upon the future of material progress, viewed qualitatively as well as quantitatively.

In this connection what place ought we to assign to speculation, which is very generally held to be an essential factor in trade cycles? Naturally, we ought not to overlook the part which speculation plays in a trade boom. The exaggerated ideas and hopes of the public concerning the economic possibilities are powerful impelling forces in every boom. But, at bottom, speculation, apart from its excesses, is only an expression of the zeal of entrepreneurs to obtain a profit by meeting the increased demand of the community for fixed capital. As this demand has its roots in the desire of the community to utilise technical discoveries or new lands – the determination of the nation to grow: in a word, the national will to progress – we may say that speculation is only a reflection of the general will to progress in the economic field. The fluctuations of trade cycles are a result of the struggle of this will to progress against the economic scarcity that it encounters in all points. Under modern conditions, speculation has its place in this struggle, but does not represent an essential feature of it.

Such being the case, the trade cycle is not bound up with a social order based upon private enterprise. As long as there is a will to progress, and as long as the physical satisfaction of this will requires the use of a large amount of fixed capital, we must expect the same kind of fluctuations in the productive work of the community that occur in the modern trade cycle.

Socialists believe that the socialisation of the means of production, in putting an end to private enterprise, will also put a stop to trade cycles. This contention appears to be based on a very inadequate analysis of the trade cycle. The possibility of diverting social production too much in the direction of an increased production of fixed capital is present in every social order. If these changes are, in the long run, due to a will to progress and a desire to profit without delay from new possibilities, they will hardly be more successfully avoided in a socialistic community than in a capitalistic system of private enterprise. All experience up to the present has shown that it is particularly difficult under a democratic régime to resist the demand made upon the State and the municipality. Public bodies already have very wide productive functions, and these require a great deal of fixed capital. As producers they have scarcely helped to lessen cyclical fluctuations of trade. Indeed, their increasing demands have only made the boom periods more acute. Thus a further transfer of fixed capital into the hands of the State and the municipality is hardly, in itself, a means of mitigating the trade cycles.

Another question which we cannot answer here is whether public enterprise, through a more far-sighted policy, based on a thorough knowledge of the nature of trade cycles, could not bring about a certain modification of trade cycles. It remains to see what will come of the various experiments made recently in this direction. But in most countries the conditions for such a policy are entirely wanting. [1]

§ 81 Crises

Why cannot the trade boom, when the conditions for its continuance no longer exist, pass gradually into the depression, much as it itself gradually developed out of the depression? Experience shows that this is not the case; that the boom collapses suddenly, and often ends in a catastrophe. This catastrophe, which we call an economic crisis, is characterised chiefly by a general inability to

[1] The present Five Year Plan of the Soviet Republic is a most gigantic example of an increased construction of fixed capital under the leadership of a socialist Government, eager to attain the highest possible progress within a short time. Such exaggerated sacrifices for progress are unthinkable in a society founded on private enterprise. This experience is a good confirmation of the views of the text formulated before the war.

meet existing liabilities. Its well-known symptoms are great losses, compulsory sales, an abnormal increase in the number and extent of bankruptcies, and a general lack of confidence.

Such a situation shows that the business world must have gone astray on some point; it must have made some calculations that have proved unsound. What is this point?

According to a very widely accepted view, the crisis must be regarded as a result of over-production. It would therefore be due to a miscalculation of the demand, an over-estimate of the real needs of the community. We cannot deny that wrong calculations and over-estimates of this sort do commonly play a part in every boom, and intensify the crisis. This was particularly the case with the older forms of crises. But in modern crises it is not primarily a question of over-production in this sense. As the boom is distinguished by an extraordinarily increased production of fixed capital, it would appear that we should look to this sphere in particular for the over-production. But, as we have already seen, it seems that the services of fixed capital, which are the object of the demand of the consumers, are generally not at all in excess even in the last part of a boom; that, on the contrary, the fixed capital has to be used to the utmost to meet the demand. Even the materials of fixed capital are not produced to excess during the trade boom. Indeed, the boom commonly shows an unmistakable scarcity of these materials – a scarcity which becomes particularly apparent through the extraordinarily high prices of these commodities. We must, therefore, entirely reject the theory that the crises are caused in the main by an over-production of the materials of fixed capital.

Hence it seems that no link is missing in the chain that normally connects the producers with the consumers. Why, then, in spite of this, does the chain break? The answer is: *The typical modern trade boom does not mean over-production or an over-estimate of the demands of the consumers or the needs of the community for the services of fixed capital, but an over-estimate of the supply of capital, or of the amount of savings available for taking over the real capital produced.* What is really over-estimated is the capacity of the public to provide savings in sufficient quantity. We must bear in mind that this capacity has to be estimated many years in advance, since, on the average, there are several years between the time when the work is planned and the time it makes its full demand upon the community's savings. The individual entrepreneur has no other means of judging the condition of the capital market except the rate of interest. The rate, however, is low, or at least moderate, during the depression and the first part of the trade boom, since the demands for capital-disposal which result from the increased activity of entrepreneurs in the production of fixed capital, do not yet make themselves fully felt. It is therefore quite possible that undertakings, such as the building of houses, railways, etc., will be planned, and even begun, in such numbers that, when their need of capital makes itself fully felt, it cannot be satisfied.

If the boom is pressed continually onward in this way, there must, at last, come a time when it is clear that the market cannot find a sufficient quantity of savings with which to purchase the real capital produced. There must then be a sudden fall in the value of fixed capital, and entrepreneurs must find it extraordinarily difficult to get the capital they need, either by loan or selling securities. They undoubtedly have not counted upon such an event while incurring their various liabilities in the course of their productive work. When it becomes clear that they have been mistaken in this respect, there is bound to follow a widespread inability to meet the liabilities incurred. This situation gradually becomes worse, since the whole business world depends to a great extent upon the punctual discharge of obligations that fall due. There is bound to be a general economic crisis.

Clearly, this wrong estimate of the future condition of the capital market would not lead to such a catastrophe if the individual entrepreneur secured in advance the whole of the capital he needs to carry out his plans. But this can rarely be done. The capital subscribed by shareholders for commencing a large undertaking generally represents only a part, sometimes only a very small part, of the whole of the capital needed. As to the remainder, business men usually reckon upon procuring it in the future by the issue of debentures, by bank credits, etc. Moreover, the capital is, as a rule, not paid up by the shareholders all at once. The payments are often deferred for long periods. Here again, therefore, calculations are based upon the capital market of the future. In addition, shareholders usually go beyond their own means and need capital, which they have to get by means of loans, often only of short duration. It is clear that subscriptions of this sort do not, from the economic point of view, represent a real actual command of capital on the part of the entrepreneur. But, even in the case where a business has secured capital in advance, this capital will be temporarily invested at interest until it is used in the business, and will be placed at the disposal of the community through the banks or in some other way. It will, in that case, be used in other undertakings, and, from the economic point of view, will be no longer available for the construction in question. In these complex circumstances we can easily understand why the demands made by existing business undertakings upon the capital market of the future cannot be satisfied in their entirety, and why the possibilities of this future market of meeting the demands are over-estimated. An entrepreneur whose aim is to put his business on a sound basis can, if he so wishes, possibly secure the whole of his capital from the start. If the primary cause of crises is a wrong estimate of the possibilities of obtaining, on the capital market of the future, the funds necessary for completing an enterprise that has been begun, the best means of avoiding the danger of a crisis is in such a policy. Obviously, however, it can only be done in practice to a limited extent. Calculating in advance the future capital requirements of an undertaking is a difficult proposition, because the rise in prices and wages that accompanies a trade boom often adds considerably to the costs of the business, so that the future requirements of capital, both of the individual concern and the entire business world, will be greater than was estimated. To avoid unpleasant surprises of this kind it would be necessary to take into consideration the imminent rise in prices at the commencement of a boom.

The question of the provision of capital during a boom cannot, therefore, be examined entirely from the angle of private enterprise. From the general economic ponit of view there can be no such thing as a securing of capital in advance; the capital that is used to-day must always be taken from the social income of to-day. In actual practice, therefore, the only course left open to us is to attempt to make a correct estimate of the whole of the demands for capital which arise at the same time during the boom; and it is not an easy matter to make such an estimate.

That the crisis really consists in an acute shortage of capital – that is, savings needed for purchasing the real capital produced – is partly shown by the great difficulty of selling the fixed capital already produced or obtaining the means to cover the costs of its production, and partly by the very general inability to complete undertakings that have been begun. In either case, the lack of capital must mean heavy losses. They are bound to be particularly severe when constructions already begun cannot be completed, and must suffer damage or even be entirely destroyed and abandoned. Examples of both effects of the lack of capital may be witnessed during every severe crisis.

The increasing scarcity of capital during a boom is hidden in a confusing way from the business world by the usual large increase of bank means of payment at such a time, which are naturally regarded by the business man as capital. Later on, when the banks find it necessary in their own interest to cut down this excessive supply of means of payment, the real scarcity of capital is felt suddenly and acutely. It is obvious that this may precipitate and greatly aggravate the crisis.

BOOK V

INTERNATIONAL TRADE

CHAPTER XX

THEORY OF INTERNATIONAL TRADE

§ 82 *International Trade as a Problem of Currency*

BY international trade we mean trade between two or more regions which regard themselves as independent economic units. Such a view is expressed by the idea of a certain economic community of interests within the regions, and this idea is able to make itself felt to such an extent that it causes a conscious representation in one form or another of these common interests. If it is sought externally to influence this consciousness of common trading interests in any way whatsoever, there arises an international commercial policy. The most effective means for carrying out a commercial policy is a definite tariff boundary, and, according to modern conceptions, the territory which is bounded by a tariff barrier is the essential commercial-political unit. According to this concept, international trade is trade between different tariff areas. It is clear, however, that such a definition lays undue weight upon a technical factor. Tariffs are by no means a necessary condition for the existence of international trade. Indeed, for purposes of theoretical study, it is the most natural course to assume at first that no such artificial obstacles are placed in the way of international trade. The characteristic feature of international trade must therefore be sought in the essential nature of the economic independence of the areas in question.

Now the theory of international trade, like every economic theory, must be primarily a theory of the fixing of prices. As soon as we wish to study the price-structure in two different countries as influenced by the trade passing between them, we must postulate a monetary system for each country. The most general assumption is that these monetary systems are independent of each other. We may, therefore, base our reasoning on the fact that the economic independence of every country is shown primarily by an independent currency. We may think of this currency as a free paper currency autonomously controlled by a suitable regulation of the supply of means of payment. International trade is, then, to be regarded essentially as trade between two countries with independent currencies. By means of this definition we are able to strike at the roots of the new phenomena which we have to analyse if we wish to extend the study of price-structures beyond the limits of a unified territory. Thus it appears that this view of the basic principles underlying international trade is very suitable for a representation of the theory of international trade, and we shall select this definition as the starting point of the study that follows.

Countries on a gold standard have, to a certain extent, a common basis for their currencies. From the point of view of the principles of this book, such currencies are to be regarded purely as independent paper currencies which are consciously regulated so that they are maintained at an approximate parity with gold, and thereby with other gold standard currencies. This case is, therefore, to be treated as a special case of our general assumptions, a special case which is distinguished by the fact that a definite aim is set for the regulation of the currency.

It sometimes happens that independent countries have a so-called common currency. This was the case, for example, in the Scandinavian countries before the war, as well as in the countries of the Latin Monetary Union. In reality, such countries have each an independent currency. Each country is responsible for the maintenance of its currency at the given parity, and must pursue a monetary policy specially to this end. Even when uniformity in the sphere of monetary systems goes so far that the various currencies of the Union are always bought and sold at par, as in the former Scandinavian Currency Union, on the basis of an agreement between the central banks, the characteristics of an independent currency remain. The various German States are not independent entities in the sense understood above, for actually they have a common currency which is governed by a single organisation – the Reichsbank. The United States of America has, it is true, a uniform currency. For a long time, however, it was quite a problem to maintain the dollar currencies of the various States at a parity with one another. Since the creation of the Federal Reserve System this problem has been gradually solved. For, as this system is under the supreme direction of the Federal Reserve Board, there is a common currency within the Union, although the twelve different Federal Reserve Banks are so far independent that each one has a monetary policy more or less of its own, with its own discount rates to maintain the parity of the dollar. It would certainly be very interesting to study the trade between the various Federal Reserve districts and its significance on the maintenance of the dollar parity; such a study would throw much light on the closely related problem of international trade. In what follows, a region having an independent currency will be termed simply a "country."

Let us now consider the simple case where there are only two countries, A and B, trading with each other, and where the trade between them is exclusively in commodities; further, let us assume that the rate of exchange between the two countries is expressed as the price of B currency in terms of A currency. If this rate of exchange is high enough, then all commodities of country B will be too dear for country A, and a commodity import from B into A cannot take place at all. On the other hand, the commodities of country A will be very cheap in country B, and, if the rate of exchange is sufficiently high, people in B will import all their commodities from country A, instead of producing them themselves.

If the rate of exchange is high, without, however, reaching the level that prohibits the import of commodities from B into A, it must nevertheless greatly restrict these imports, and at the same time encourage exports from A. The result is, then, that A constantly has a substantial surplus arising from its trade with B. Conversely, a very low rate of exchange must result in a constant deficit in A's balance of trade. Clearly, there must be a position between these two extremes where A will buy from B exactly as much as it sells to B, and where the balance of trade will be in equilibrium. We assume that all commodities are immediately paid for; in other words, that the one country extends no credit to the other, at least not for a period longer than is technically necessary for adjusting the mutual payments. This position, then, represents the equilibrium position for the rate of exchange, for in any other position a constant scarcity of foreign currency would be felt in one of the countries, and the price of this foreign currency would of necessity rise. Only a rate of exchange at which the balance of trade is in equilibrium can possess a permanent stability. This rate of exchange is termed the *purchasing power parity* (cf. § 59).

From these simple considerations we reach at once an important conclusion. A country, in its trade with another country, can never have an all-round superiority, and can never be so inferior in competition that it can sell no products at all to the other country. There is no such thing as an absolute superiority in the sense that one country produces more cheaply than the other. Such a comparison can only be made at a definite rate of exchange. Let the one country be inferior to the other in technique and organisation, let it be worse equipped with capital, land, and skilled labour; nevertheless, there exists a rate of exchange at which it can sell as many commodities to the richer country as it buys from it, and thus equilibrium will come about in its trade with that country. There are always branches of production which are relatively more favourable for the poorer country, and in these branches the country will necessarily be able to export at a suitable rate of exchange. Costs of production are a conception that refer to the internal price-system of a country, and a comparison of the costs of production of two countries is only possible at a definite rate of exchange. The rate of exchange must so be fixed that advantages and disadvantages in respect to costs of production are so compensated that the balance of trade is brought into equilibrium.

This line of reasoning not only sets out the classical theory of "comparative costs" in its most simple and, at the same time, most general form, but also clears the ground for answering a series of questions which generally have a prominent place in discussions of commercial policy. The widespread impression that an undeveloped country needs tariff protection to allow it to compete with an economically advanced country, now appears as a misconception of the elementary conditions of international trade. The same applies to the idea that a rich country which has high costs of production as the result of a high standard of living must be inferior in competitive power to countries with a lower standard of living. We shall return later to these practical questions.

It is necessary in the first place to define more closely the significance of the term "purchasing power parity." A direct comparison between the purchasing power of money in two different countries is not possible in an exact sense. If, however, we are content with a rough and ready estimate, there is no difficulty in seeing that the purchasing power of money is distinctly higher in one country than in another. If everything in France is nominally – that is, reckoned in the currency unit of the country – about one hundred and twenty-four times as dear as in England, then it is obvious that the public will find that the French currency is only a hundred and twenty-fourth part as valuable as the English; in other words, a pound sterling will be ranked equal to one hundred and twenty-four francs. The natural rate of exchange for the pound sterling, measured in French francs, thus lies in the neighbourhood of 124. At this rate of exchange the purchasing power of money in the two countries is approximately the same, so that for a certain sum of money one obtains just as much, whether it be changed into French or English currency. In this rough sense we can say that the rate of exchange results in a parity of the purchasing power of money in the two countries, and so the term "purchasing power parity" is justified. It is obvious that this purchasing power parity must be the fundamental factor determining the rate of exchange. A direct comparison of the purchasing power of money in the two countries does not enable us to calculate exactly the rate of exchange, but it does bring out clearly why the pound sterling cannot be equal to *one* franc, but must be in the neighbourhood of *a hundred and twenty-four francs*. If the English were to reckon in shillings instead of pounds, the rate of exchange would be reduced to a twentieth of its former equilibrium level, because the English currency unit would have only a twentieth of its former purchasing power.

The rate of exchange must therefore fix itself in such wise that when one currency is changed into another a certain sum represents approximately the same purchasing power. The idea that a sum of money has a much greater purchasing power in one country than in another, the exchanges remaining at their equilibrium level, is in most cases an erroneous conclusion drawn from cursory observations. If, for example, tourists observe that living in a rich country is much dearer than in another country, and from this form the hasty conclusion that the purchasing power of money in the former country is distinctly less than in the latter, this conclusion is based substantially on the fact that the travelling expenses of tourists are dependent to a great degree on the price of personal services, and must therefore be particularly high in a country with high wages. If one believes that a large and representative quantity of commodities is dearer in one country than in another, one must always inquire whether there are also some important commodities or services which are cheaper. For if this were not the case it would be impossible to explain why equilibrium in international trade should come about at the prevailing rate of exchange.

On the other hand, as already emphasised, an exact comparison between the purchasing power of money in different countries is not possible. We have no trustworthy measure for the absolute purchasing power of a currency in its own country. With index numbers, we are only able to determine the relative changes in this purchasing power from time to time. If such changes in the purchasing power of the currencies to be compared have taken place, they must be reflected in the rates of exchange. If we base our inferences on the assumption that, with a constant purchasing power of money in the two countries, the rate of exchange between them has remained for a long time in equilibrium, then we may regard this rate of exchange as a purchasing power parity based on practical experience. If changes in the internal purchasing power of the currencies take place, the new purchasing power parity arising out of these changes may be calculated by multiplying the old purchasing power parity by the ratio of the changes in the internal purchasing power of the currencies. This method naturally presupposes that no changes in the conditions of international trade have taken place in the interim which would have altered the equilibrium level of the rates of exchange – that is, the purchasing power parity – even if the value of money had remained constant. Important changes in the internal purchasing power of money have a much greater influence on the rates of exchange than any other alterations in the real conditions of international trade which come into consideration. The arithmetical process reproduced above is therefore satisfactory for a first rough calculation of the new equilibrium level of the rates of exchange after big monetary changes have occurred.

The changes in the equilibrium level of the rate of exchange which take place between two countries whilst the value of money remains constant are, in the nature of things, generally on a small scale. For, if a country carries on a brisk trade with another country, there are then a large quantity of commodities which may possibly be imported or exported. At the prevailing rate of exchange, imports or exports only take place to a certain definite extent. Let us now assume that, whilst the value of money remains unchanged, a small shifting occurs in the rate of exchange. Then a relatively important change is made in the volume of imports actually possible, and simultaneously exports are affected in the opposite direction, so that a relatively large shifting of the balance of trade from its equilibrium position will take place. Strong forces will then be set up to bring back the rate of exchange to its former equilibrium level. This signifies that the rate of exchange in its equilibrium position – always on the assumption of a constant value of money – possesses a great stability, that is, a great power of resistance against changes in the real conditions of international trade which tend to shift the rate in one direction or the other.

The supposition of a constant internal value of money in each of the countries under consideration is here of great importance. For the rate of exchange has no powers of resistance against changes in the internal purchasing power of money in one or other of the countries, but must passively allow itself to be adapted to such changes. If we term the equilibrium position of the rate of exchange as here defined, "the purchasing power parity," this designation is also justified by the fact that, from the point of view of its effectiveness, by far the most important factor in the determination of the rate of exchange is the internal purchasing power of the currencies in the two countries. If we suppose that, whilst the price-level remains constant in A, all prices in B rise ten times, so that the internal purchasing power of the B currency is reduced to a tenth without any changes taking place in the relative level of the various prices, then the conditions of trade with A will remain exactly the same as before if the rate of exchange is lowered to a tenth of its former value. The rate of exchange must, in the given circumstances, rise or fall proportionately with the internal purchasing power of B currency. Similarly, the rate must change in inverse proportion to the internal purchasing power of A currency if any change in the value of money occurs. If there are big changes in the internal purchasing power, as happen during periods of heavy inflation or deflation, then, as already pointed out, the corresponding changes in the equilibrium position of the rates of exchange are far greater than any changes which may be caused by other factors. Of course, this conclusion as to the final results of changes in purchasing power in the two countries does not prevent the movements from having in themselves temporary effects of a purely dynamic character, which will prevent the final results from making themselves clearly felt at once.

The rate of exchange will thus be primarily determined by changes in the purchasing power parity of the two currencies to be compared. After the theory of purchasing power parity focussed attention on the significance of the relative price-level of the two countries in question, it was often pointed out, especially by statisticians, that the equilibrium position of the rate of exchange must be determined exclusively by the price indices of commodities imported and exported. We now see where the error of this reasoning lies. If we assume that prices of all the export commodities of country B are doubled, whilst all other prices in B remain unchanged, it would not be possible for the rate of exchange to be reduced by a half, as a much smaller fall in the rate would bring out the latent export possibilities of a mass of other commodities of country B, and would prevent a further fall in the exchange. This restrictive influence is reinforced through the difficulties placed in the way of imports from A by the fall in the rate of exchange, and its combined effect is so great that the doubling of the prices of exports in question is unable, by a long way, to depress the rate of exchange to half its value. However, the general internal purchasing power of the B currency has, of course, fallen, and to that extent one must expect a corresponding fall in the rate of exchange. Over and above that, there will perhaps take place a further fall in the rate as a consequence of a distribution of the general rise of prices which may be particularly unfavourable for the external value of the B currency.

If we now wish to consider the specific problem of international trade apart from changes in the value of money, we must assume that the purchasing power of money remains constant in each of the countries to be considered. This assumption, however, cannot be expressed in absolute terms. It can only be so expressed that the general price-level must remain constant. The general price-level is a statistical conception, and, as such, is more or less imperfect. It must be specially noted that we have no opportunity of fixing the conditions for a constant price-level for two different countries in an identical manner. Nevertheless, we may formulate our assumption with sufficient exactness – at least, if there are not too great or far-reaching changes in the economic life of any of the countries in question – so that the problem of international trade is allowed to appear as an independent problem, while the value of money remains constant.

We should make it a rule, when analysing theoretically an economic problem of a non-monetary nature, to introduce from the start the assumption of an unaltered value of money, and in so doing we must presume the money to be a rationally regulated paper currency. As a matter of fact, in the first two books of this work we have treated the entire theory of the determination of prices in this way. Such an assumption signifies that the supply of means of payment is regulated in such a way that the general price-level remains constant in spite of all economic changes. In this manner the influences of all economic phenomena on the value of money are excluded from the first. If, therefore, in any particular study we come to the conclusion that a rise in certain prices must take place, we must conclude from this that this rise is neutralised by a fall in other prices. Even when we cannot state exactly which prices are so influenced the necessity for such a fall in prices remains.

What has just been said applies also to the theory of international trade. If we wish, in this connection, to study phenomena which have their foundation in non-monetary causes, then, in each of the countries in question, we must assume an unaltered value of money. Changes in the real conditions of international trade cannot then have any effect on the general price-level in any of the countries. On the other hand, they may always exert an effect on the rate of exchange, and the study of these effects, which we may term "inter-valuta" effects, naturally belongs to the theory of international trade.

Formally, this problem appears in a different light when we consider countries on a gold standard. It is true that the gold standard, according to the point of view expressed in this book, is a paper standard also. This paper standard, however, is regulated not with the idea of keeping the internal purchasing power of money constant, but with the idea of maintaining the gold parity of the currency. Let us assume that country B is a large country which always maintains the gold currency intact, and, for the sake of simplicity, let us assume that this is carried out under a constant price-level, so that country A will only have to see that its currency is kept at a gold parity, as shown by the constancy of the rate of exchange on B. Those factors, which under our previous assumptions would have produced changes in the rate of exchange, will instead now result in changes in the general price-level in country A. This new formulation does not alter anything in the essential causal sequence of the case previously considered. If, under the assumption of a paper currency with a fixed internal purchasing power, the rate of exchange on B had risen as a result of an alteration in the conditions of international trade, then the same cause, under a constant rate of exchange, would have led to a fall in the general price-level in country A. We may, therefore, study the "inter-valuta" effects of international trade under a gold standard also, which in many cases is clearly necessary if we wish to examine the problem on the basis of actually existing material. But for the theoretical explanation of the problem the assumption of a paper currency with a fixed internal purchasing power is much more advantageous.

§ 83 *Pricing under International Trade*

The necessary condition for international trade to take place between two countries is that a certain inequality exists in the relative prices of commodities, and that in certain directions this inequality is strong enough to overcome the obstacles of the costs of transport. The driving factor of international trade is thus the inequality of prices in the various countries, which is based on the differences in the given factors of the price-structure; that is, in the supply of primary factors of production, of technical coefficients, and in the nature of the demand. International trade, as we shall see in more detail later, has certainly a tendency to smooth out inequalities in commodity prices. But this never actually happens, for the whole price-system will reach an equilibrium position, where the differences in the economic factors in the two countries are proof against the tendency of international trade to equalise prices. We shall now study this position of equilibrium more closely.

When two previously isolated countries enter into commercial relations with each other, there is a fairly far-reaching change in all economic conditions. In country A the branches of production which work at a relatively high cost are given up, and by way of compensation other branches of production, in which A has a relative superiority, are more intensively exploited. The same takes place in country B. The primary result is thus a division of labour. This need not embrace all the branches of production, for as a rule there are branches where no exchange at all is possible between the two countries. This division of labour leads to a far-reaching change in the whole price-structure in the two countries. For in country A

prices of commodities imported from *B* must, allowing for the transportation expenses, coincide with the prices prevailing in *B*, and are thus different from what they were before international trade took place. Also, the prices of goods exported to *B* are generally changed, since they are now the subject of demand from *B*. If, however, such important changes take place in the price-structure, then the whole structure changes, and we have an entirely new process of pricing.

Commodities which may be exchanged are generally not only finished products, but also primary factors of production and intermediate products of all stages. The requirement for the exchange is that the expenses of transport can be covered. This requirement varies according to the nature of the commodity. For a whole series of commodities transportation is impossible. This applies to a primary factor of production such as land, and also in a great degree to finished products such as houses. If we consider that production, according to our view-point, is not finished until the finished product is placed at the disposal of the consumer, then, in most cases, a transfer of finished products in the strict sense is impossible. The prepared meal served in a restaurant may contain substances coming from nearly all foreign countries, but in its final form it is a home product. International trade is thus, to a predominant degree, carried out in intermediate products.

The theory of international trade for the most part has been built upon the assumption of a complete immobility of the primary factors of production, together with a more or less perfect mobility of finished products. It has thus undertaken the task of studying directly the levelling effects of trade on the prices of finished products, and, from this, on the prices of the primary factors of production. Such a conception of the problem is in no way justified by the nature of things. An exchange between the two countries may take place in all stages, from the primary factors of production right up to the finished products, and this exchange has everywhere a certain price-levelling effect. If this effect acts directly on the prices of the primary factors of production, then it brings about indirectly a corresponding adjustment of the prices of finished goods produced with their help. As we shall see more closely below, there are characteristic differences between such an adjustment in the direction of production and an adjustment in the opposite direction. The latter is weaker than the former. The problem is symmetrical in so far as all the prices have the same position in it. The problem of pricing under international trade does not differ in this respect from the problem of pricing in an isolated country. As we know, this may be represented only by a system of simultaneous equations. The same necessarily holds good for the problem which now confronts us. It is our task to adumbrate the general character of the system of equations that represents the price-structure under international trade.

We must start from the assumption that trade between the two countries A and B has reached a position of equilibrium, and we have to examine the conditions for the continuation of such an equilibrium. As in our treatment of the general problem of pricing we may then assume the prices of the primary factors of production to be our unknowns. We have, then, two series of such prices, namely, one for country A and one for country B. There now arises a further unknown, namely, the rate of exchange between the two countries. The appearance of this new unknown, as already pointed out, is what actually characterises the pricing of international trade as an independent problem.

Let us assume for the time being that all these unknowns are given; then we may calculate the costs of production and also the prices of the finished goods, assuming that they are produced both in A and in B. We can thus see which is the lower price for every finished commodity. If costs of transport are taken into account, we may add these costs to the prices of the imported commodities. We shall then know whether the home products or the imported products are cheaper, and we may then choose the lower price. The higher price concerns us no further. In this way we may calculate all the prices of the finished commodities for A as well as for B. In so doing the demand is determined. We know how much of each commodity is demanded in A and B, and we know also how much of the various primary factors of production are used in the two countries to satisfy this demand. In equilibrium, these quantities must agree with the given quantities of the primary factors of production in each of the countries. We then have a number of equations corresponding to the unknown prices of the primary factors of production. However, we need still another equation, because, as we have already pointed out, we have yet another unknown – that is, the rate of exchange. This new equation represents the condition that A buys exactly as much from B as it sells to B, so that the balance of trade is in equilibrium. We now have just as many equations as there are unknowns, and so the system of equations is determined. As we have assumed that each individual country, as such, maintains a constant value of money, all prices are also absolutely determined.

This solution which at once clears up the essential nature of pricing under international trade,[1] has been built up entirely upon the principle of scarcity; that is, it is assumed that the costs of production are determined in every single case as soon as the prices of the primary factors of production are given. In those cases where this is not so, we must make use of supplementary principles of pricing in order to make the problem definite. These supplementary principles modify the conclusion which has been reached but alter nothing of the principle underlying the chain of causation represented by our system of equations. The demand for finished products in A is indirectly a demand for primary factors of production in A as well as B. The same applies, of course, to the demand in B. There is, therefore, a collective demand for factors of production in A and a collective demand for factors of production in B. These demands must be limited by sufficiently high prices being charged for the various factors of production. In this way an equilibrium position is attained for both countries, the whole of the factors of production are in full employment, and the demand in the two countries is satisfied according to the willingness to pay.

This position of equilibrium is naturally quite different from that

---

[1] Bertil Ohlin, of the Stockholm Commercial Academy, in his doctor's dissertation, was the first to give such a solution of the problem of international trade, and I am indebted to this work for many suggestions. However, in the text I do not follow his treatment of the problem.

which would have arisen in each country had there been no international trade. On the whole, a certain adjustment has taken place between the prices in the two countries; that is, a certain *rapprochement* has been achieved between the relative prices in the two countries. As has already been emphasised, the price adjustment is partly direct and partly indirect. A direct adjustment, excluding costs of transport, takes place for every commodity which can be directly exported from one country to another. An indirect price adjustment takes place in two different directions; first, in the direction of production, or from commodities of an earlier stage in the process of production to commodities in the later stages; and secondly, in the opposite direction – that is, from finished products to their means of production situated more or less far back.

The nature of the first process may be best appreciated if we assume that the primary factors of production can be transferred without expense, but that there are no other possibilities of transfer. The price adjustment is then perfect for the primary factors of production, and every country will be equipped with them according to its willingness to pay. If we now suppose the state of technique to be the same in both countries, then the equality of prices of the primary factors of production results in a complete equality of prices of the finished products.

The adjustment of prices in the opposite direction is not so effective. We obtain the best idea of it if we consider the simplest case, in which the elementary factors of production are not transferable at all, but, on the other hand, finished products may be transferred without expense. The effect of international trade is, then, to bring about a division of labour. Each country produces only those commodities for whose production it is especially favourably situated; the remaining commodities are imported from the other country. The price of a commodity which *A* imports from *B*, it is true, is equal to the price prevailing in *B*, but cannot be compared with the domestic price, as this commodity is not produced in *A* at all. With regard to the factors of production, a certain price adjustment takes place. A factor of production which is particularly abundant in A must, in a condition of isolation, make place for itself in the demand, in that its price is kept very low. An exchange of finished products having been established, this factor of production will be an object of demand on the part of B also, originating in the demand for commodities produced with the help of this factor of production in A. The total demand is therefore now greater than before. This does not signify that the demand can be satisfied to a greater extent, for the supply of the factor of production in A is fixed. It does signify, however, that a higher price must be charged in order to restrict the demand. If B is especially poorly equipped with this factor of production, then, in a condition of isolation, its price must be raised to a very high level in order to limit the demand sufficiently. After international trade has been established, this factor of production need no longer bear the full brunt of the total demand for itself in country B, as this demand can be satisfied with the aid of the corresponding factor of production in A. It may be that it will be demanded by branches of production which work also for the demand in A, but which require only a small quantity of this factor of production. On the whole, the demand will be less than formerly, and may be kept within the necessary limits at a lower price.

The price of the factor of production has, then, risen in A, but has fallen in B. Simultaneously, there has taken place a corresponding price adjustment in the opposite direction for the other factors of production. A complete adjustment, however, does not take place. The relative scarcity in each country of the various factors of production maintains an influence on pricing which counterbalances, in the equilibrium position, the price-adjusting tendency of the exchange of finished products.

Let us assume for the sake of simplicity that only three factors of production – land, labour, and capital – are present in the two countries, and that both countries are approximately equally well supplied with capital, but that A is rich in land and poorly supplied with labour, whilst B is poorly supplied with land and well supplied with labour. Before international trade takes place, A has low prices for land and high rates of wages, whilst B has high prices for land and low rates of wages. Such a comparison is naturally quite relative. We have no opportunity of comparing rates of wages and prices of land in B directly. Only when we consider them from the standpoint of A are we able to state that there is an inequality in the price-structure of the two countries. If international trade takes place, there is a division of labour, whereby A prefers to concentrate on those branches of production which require much land and little labour, whilst B prefers those branches which require much labour and little land. Land in A will then be the object of demand not only from A, but also from B. This demand is directed in all cases on finished products which require especially large amounts of land for their production, and thus represent in their entirety a greater demand for land in country A than did the previously existing demand. As a result, the price for the use of land in A rises. The small supply of labour in A will be utilised in those branches of production in which relatively little labour is required. In spite of labour in A being demanded by A as well as by B, this total demand is weaker than previously, and rates of wages fall in A. An opposite movement takes place in B. It is in this way that the price-adjusting tendency of international trade operates.

In equilibrium, the price of land in A is, of course, still lower and the rate of wages still higher than in B. A more extensive exchange of commodities cannot take place, for the reason that the countries have now fully concentrated on those branches of production which are most advantageous to them. If A were to attempt to monopolise yet another branch of production from B, it would have to be a branch where relatively little land and much labour were necessary – that is, a branch of production which is not particularly suited to A. Having regard to equilibrium under international trade, this could not take place without B monopolising a branch of production from A, which would also be less suitable for B. These conditions give a definite stability to the position of equilibrium. Thus we see that the inequality in the distribution of primary factors of production, which must result in a corresponding inequality in the price-structure as long as the countries are isolated, represents a factor which is also effective after international trade has arisen, and which can only be partly eliminated by the exchange of finished products.

The advantage derived from international trade consists primarily of the fact that demand is confronted with a more varied supply of primary factors of production. It is not necessary, therefore, for demand to be restricted so narrowly or for prices to exert such a great pressure as in a condition of isolation; demand may be satisfied in a more varied and harmonious manner. It is easier to conform to the principle of scarcity under international trade, and its rigour is mitigated.

Also with regard to the supplementary principles of pricing, the situation is more favourable under international trade than in a condition of isolation. For example, the principle of substitution is better applied, because the production of a commodity may be transplanted to a country where the requirements for a technically favourable co-operation of the factors of production are best realised or because mobile factors of production may be assembled in a country where the best possibilities of substitution are to be attained. International trade thus promotes the most effective – that is to say, the cheapest – production.

International trade has a similar effect when it renders possible a concentration of production in large-scale units, which work with less expense than the relatively small firms which would exist in isolated countries. Thus, through international trade, the principle of the diminution of costs through aggrandisement of the business unit obtains a wider and more productive scope.

The benefits accruing from international trade consist, as we have seen, of the mobility it introduces into regions which were formerly isolated. If there were complete mobility and no costs of transport, we should have the state of affairs from which we started out in our fundamental treatment of the general theory of pricing – that is, a state of affairs in which there was a uniform price for each type of commodity. This would mean the greatest economic effectiveness. Now, international trade can never bring about complete mobility, nor totally eliminate the condition of isolation. The economic effectiveness which it produces is thus only relative, and represents a stage lower than the ideal economic effectiveness of complete mobility. Nevertheless, the effectiveness attained is the greater, the greater the mobility, and every diminution in mobility signifies a reduced effectiveness in the whole economic system.

It must be noted that the benefits of international trade can only be judged socially – that is, for the whole country. From the point of view of the individual, international trade results in losses as well as profits. As prices are increased or decreased for certain primary factors of production, so different vested interests are affected in different ways. One group may see its income increased whilst another group may suffer great losses. This is, of course, the reason why the benefits of international trade are judged so differently. Everyone bases his opinions on his own private experience, and from this makes up his mind about the advantages or disadvantages of international trade and also of the correct commercial policy. Naturally, it is impossible to reach a conclusion in this way. The effects of international trade must necessarily be judged from a general social economic standpoint.

§ 84 *The Significance of International Movements of Capital*

We have studied the problem of equilibrium in international trade on the assumption that no credit is given and that a country must pay for its imports over a period entirely by its exports. We found that, on this assumption, a definite rate of exchange is established and that, generally, the entire price-structure of the countries trading with one another is determined. If international movements of capital were actually to exercise a material influence on the rate of exchange, our solution would clearly have only a very limited value and would scarcely get to the root of the problem of equilibrium in international trade. We shall soon see that this is not the case, but that, in reality, a transfer of capital from the one country to the other has no material significance as far as the rate of exchange is concerned.

Let us first consider the simplest case of a direct transfer of capital. We shall, therefore, assume that the savers in country A have a certain purchasing power at their disposal which they are willing to invest, not as usual in newly produced real capital, but in a loan to country B. We shall also assume that B uses this to buy a newly produced capital good from A – a ship, for example. In A the means provided by the savings in question thus serve to buy newly produced real capital just like any other kind of savings. The total production of real capital is therefore maintained at an unchanged level, and consumption is not diminished in the slightest degree. Country B has acquired a new piece of real capital, but has paid for it with the means provided by the loan. This transaction leaves the economic life of the country, for the moment, completely undisturbed. The remaining trade between the two countries is likewise left undisturbed, and the condition of equilibrium in this trade is the same as before. The rate of exchange is therefore unaltered.

Let us suppose that country B raises a public loan in country A. We can say that B's securities are exported to A as payment for the import of real capital. If we look at these securities as objects of international trade we can thus formally uphold the principle that equilibrium in international trade is attained when both countries buy exactly the same amounts from each other. We find by means of this that we can preserve a formal unity in our treatment of the theory of international trade. It is then easy to see how the enlargement of international trade which occurs as a result of the transfer of capital in question does not exercise a material influence upon the trade already existing, and consequently, also, on the rate of exchange.

The case which we have discussed is a good theoretical example of how a transfer of capital takes place. But in practice complications arise which modify the transaction somewhat, without, however, altering the principle. Let us suppose that B constructs a railway with the help of a loan from A. The means provided by the loan can be utilised in several different ways. In the first place, as in the case considered above, B can import real capital in the shape of locomotives or rails, etc., for the new undertaking, and pay for it in securities. Secondly, *B* can reduce its exports to *A* and in this way release productive powers which can help to build the railway. This happens, for example, when wood, instead of being exported as before, is used to erect railway-station buildings. The same thing also happens as soon as workers are attracted from an export industry to the new railway under construction. The total exports from *B* to *A* are reduced in this way. The deficit in the balance of trade that arises from this is, however, set off by the means provided by the loan in country *A*. Thirdly, *B* can also increase its imports of consumption goods from *A*, and pay for these surplus imports with the help of the means provided by the loan. This takes place, for example, when agricultural labourers leave their work in order to find employment on the railway which is being built. In that case the production of corn will probably be diminished, and *B* will have to import a corresponding quantity of corn from *A*. In all these three cases a deficit in the balance of trade will result. The total deficit, however, is covered by the loan. *B* exports a quantity of securities, which corresponds exactly to the deficit that has arisen in the balance of trade. Equilibrium is then maintained, and there is no question of an alteration in the rate of exchange taking place. The same holds true when *B* raises a loan for purely revenue purposes, in order to meet national expenditure. The vital point in the concept of a transfer of capital is clearly the transfer of purchasing power: it is a relatively minor matter what products *B* buys from *A* with the help of this purchasing power.

Meanwhile, we must take into consideration the fact that the transfer of capital envisaged above may lead to certain changes in demand and thus also to certain internal price adjustments in both countries, and that, as a result of the change brought about in the conditions of equilibrium in international trade, a definite alteration in the rate of exchange may take place. But such adjustments are, as a rule, undoubtedy of very little importance. In country *A* the loan represents a sum of savings which, if they had remained in the country, would have had to be used to purchase newly produced real capital. If *B* uses the loan for the same purpose, a procedure which may be regarded as the normal course, its special demand for capital goods will certainly alter the production in A to a certain extent, but for all that there will probably be no visible changes in the price-structure in A. For, on the whole, it must almost be a matter of indifference to the price-structure whether demand is directed at ships, or locomotives, or agricultural machinery, and so forth. If A is a well-developed industrial country, possessing an economic life which is richly varied and highly advanced, its industries will certainly be marked by such a great capacity for adaptation that they will be able to satisfy every demand that arises as a result of loans made abroad, without internal prices being affected to any noticeable extent. In country B small adjustments in prices are perhaps to be expected. The transfer of labour from one trade to another (which we supposed to take place above) cannot in all probability be accomplished without the workers in question demanding definite increases in wages. Their purchasing power is thereby increased, and this will probably have some effect on the internal price-level in B. But if B is at all a developed country, a foreign loan will very seldom produce such a revolution in its economic life as to cause a material alteration in its entire internal price-structure. If, however, only smaller relative adjustments occur in the internal price-structure of each of the two countries, these will not produce a noticeable alteration in the rate of exchange between the countries, for we know that the rate of exchange has a high degree of stability, and that, consequently, when there is a small fluctuation in it, strong tendencies arise in practice to offset this fluctuation.

There is a widespread notion that a loan from one country to another must, in consequence of the transfer of purchasing power, lead to alterations in the general price-level in both countries. It is thought that the total purchasing power of A must be reduced and that of B increased, and that, as a result, a fall in the general price-level in A and a rise in that in B are to be expected. This notion is clearly wrong. A transfer of capital to B is only possible if B buys goods in A and pays for them with the means provided by the loan; on this account the transfer of capital can neither reduce the purchasing power in A nor increase it in B.

As long as we maintain our assumption of a constant money value in each of the two countries, fluctuations in the general price-level are naturally formally excluded. The assumed effect of the transfer of capital must then, instead of altering the general price-level, find its expression in a corresponding alteration in the rate of exchange. But as the whole reasoning rests upon a misunderstanding of the nature of international capital movements, there is no ground for assuming that such an effect will take place.

The examples which have been adduced to demonstrate the tendency of an import of capital to raise prices are not susceptible of proof, and can scarcely withstand detailed criticism. The commonest error in connection with this is that the capital is conceived as being imported into an undeveloped country. In such cases, a fairly general rise in the prices of the commodities produced in the country itself may very well take place. This rise in prices, however, results from the fact that the country attains a more intimate economic contact with the outside world, and it therefore cannot be regarded necessarily as a result of the import of capital. Nor is a rise in prices so general that it can be regarded, in any strict sense, as a diminution in the value of money.

It is, however, conceivable that a large loan should exert a certain influence for a time upon the rate of exchange. If, that is to say, B possesses for the time being a very large credit balance in A currency as a result of a loan made by the latter, and if the individuals holding this credit balance are eager to realise it in order to acquire B currency, a definite pressure can undoubtedly be exerted during this period on the value of A currency, which will therefore cause B's rate of exchange to rise. As a rule, such a pressure will soon weaken, on account of B's purchases from A increasing and sales to A decreasing. An actual levelling-out of total payments between A and B must, under all circumstances, be accomplished for each day's transactions. No more purchasing power can therefore be transferred at any time than the surplus purchases allow. A transfer of capital *in abstracto*, as the public delights to think of it, simply does not take place. The necessary settlement of payments, however, can sometimes only be brought about when where is a definite pressure on the value of *A* currency. This pressure naturally increases the difficulty, under which the recipients of the loan labour, of transferring the loan, and constitutes an inducement for them to delay the transfer, at the same time as it is also naturally an incentive for other people who have *B* currency at their disposal to take over credit balances in *A* as a speculation for a profit on the exchange, thereby enabling the owners of such credit balances to exchange them for *B* currency.

What we have said here with regard to the case of a fixed loan is naturally also valid in the case of short-term movements of capital which are always taking place between big financial centres, on the ground, for example, of a difference in the interest rates. We must expect such capital movements to bring about transitory, though fairly limited, fluctuations in the rate of exchange.

The whole question of the actual formation of the rate of exchange and its deviations from the purchasing power parity can naturally only be studied in an empirical manner. In such a study we have to choose two countries which possess comparable indices of the movements of the general price-level, so that possible changes in the internal value of money in the one or other country can be eliminated. I made an investigation of this type with regard to England and the United States for the period extending from the beginning of 1919 up to October, 1924.[1] The fact emerged that, during this period, the dollar was alternately over- and undervalued. Let us reckon a value corresponding to the purchasing power parity to be equal to 100; an overvaluation of the dollar occurs when the value exceeds 100, and an undervaluation when it is less than 100. On calculating the average of this percentage value we find that, over the whole period, there was an average overvaluation of the dollar amounting to 0.3 per cent. This deviation from the purchasing power parity is extraordinarily slight, and in fact is kept entirely within the limits of error of the material from which the calculation is made.

We thus arrive at the conclusion that the rate of exchange, apart from occasional fluctuations, corresponds exactly to the calculated

[1] *Quarterly Report of the Skandinaviska Kreditaktiebolaget*, April, 1925.

purchasing power parity, or, in other words, that the new equilibrium level of the rate of exchange deviates from the former equilibrium level only to the extent of the alteration it has caused in the relative value of money. This means that the equilibrium level of the rate of exchange, if reduced to terms of an unaltered relative value of money, has remained unchanged in spite of all economic disturbances. The experience gained since England returned to the gold standard has shown that the validity of this conclusion is also upheld by a comparison between the pre-war era and the present time. At any rate, by virtue of the same general rise in prices, the equilibrium level of the rate of exchange between the two countries is now the same as before the war. The view taken here, that changes in the economic conditions of international trade have only a slight influence on the equilibrium level of the rate of exchange, is confirmed in a striking fashion by these facts.

A closer study of the value of the dollar in pounds sterling during the period 1919–24 shows that the origin of the deviations of the actual rates of exchange from the purchasing power parity is to be found essentially in international movements of capital. In periods of particularly liberal granting of American credit to Europe a definite undervaluation of the dollar has conclusively taken place, while in periods when the Americans have stopped granting credits to Europe a definite overvaluation of the dollar has occurred. The relation between interest rates in New York and London is of some importance, too, as regards fluctuations in the value of the dollar. Thus, as soon as interest rates are lower in New York than in London, liquid American capital tends to flow to London. Undervaluation of the dollar may then well ensue. Deviations of the dollar exchange from the purchasing power parity amount as a rule to less than 5 per cent., but in exceptional cases exceed even double this percentage. For the most part, however, their duration is a matter of a few months only.

This should suffice to explain the general nature of the influence of international capital movements on the rate of exchange. Our conclusion undoubtedly has substantially the same validity for an outflow of capital to less highly developed countries, although in such cases we must expect greater and, perhaps, somewhat more lasting deviations from the purchasing power parity.

From our study of the movements of the dollar exchange over the period in question we are able to draw yet another important conclusion. In September, 1922, the new highly protective Fordney Tariff was introduced in the United States. In accordance with the customary view, it was expected that, as a result, the exchanges remaining constant, there would be a considerable rise in the general price-level in America; in other words, that the dollar would be considerably overvalued. This was not the case. It is true that the dollar was substantially overvalued in the autumn of 1922, but this overvaluation is explained quite naturally by the decrease which then occurred in the amount of American credit granted to Europe. After a few months the dollar exchange returned more or less to normal, and in 1924 the dollar was undervalued for some time. This fact is calculated to destroy the basis of the popular view of the effects of an increased protective tariff upon the general price-level. The statistical data usually quoted to support this view cannot, speaking generally, stand serious criticism.

In the years 1929–30, American grants of credit to other countries underwent a considerable reduction. During that period, too, there occurred from time to time a substantial overvaluation of the dollar, to which the breakdown of international confidence also contributed. In view of these extraordinary disturbances it is not possible to make any study of the effects of the intensification of American Protection brought about in 1930. Not until normal conditions are restored in the international capital market shall we be able to form any judgment as to these effects.

§ 85 *Practical Conclusions*

We have now reached a point at which we are able to indicate the general framework for dealing with practical problems of international trade. Such problems arise chiefly in determining the effects of changes in the terms of international trade, and in this the effects on prices in particular come to the fore. The question of the effects of a protective tariff upon prices constitutes the most important group of such problems from a practical standpoint.

In discussing such questions, the need for drawing a sufficiently sharp distinction between relative changes in prices and changes in the general price-level is usually neglected. It is seldom laid down with sufficient clearness that changes of the latter kind are monetary in character, that they imply changes in the monetary unit in which prices are reckoned. Consequently, too, the change in relative prices, which is something quite different in character, does not stand out as an independent phenomenon. In addition, there is the fact that the effects on the general price-level are generally greatly over-rated, both as regards their extent and their economic significance. In all these respects our theoretical presentation of the problem of international trade is designed to prepare the way for a clear and accurate treatment of the relevant practical questions.

We thus suppose that a certain change has occurred in the conditions of international trade, that, for example, a certain country has adopted a higher protective tariff. The problem is to determine what effect this change has on prices. We have first of all to state that the effects on the general price-level of the country, or on the international value of its currency, are purely monetary phenomena, and as such are to be dealt with and judged in isolation. On the whole it may be assumed that such effects, if they do appear, will only be small in extent, and further, that, once a new position of equilibrium has been reached, they cannot have any greater economic importance.

These effects vary, as to the form they take, with the currency laws of the particular country. We may assume for purposes of simplicity that the rest of the world has an unchanged currency, and, if it has a gold standard, that gold itself has a constant value. If the country we are considering has an independent paper currency, any change in its general price-level must be regarded entirely as an independent change in its monetary unit. This change is an arbitrary one, and could be avoided by means of a suitable monetary policy. We have therefore to eliminate this type of change, which we do by reckoning all prices, including the price of foreign currency, in terms of an unchanged price-level; it may then perhaps be revealed that a certain slight change has occurred in the international value of the currency – that is, in the rate of exchange. This change is the actual monetary effect of the assumed change in the terms of international trade. A change of this kind in the foreign quotation of the currency, which has taken place while the price-level remained unchanged, naturally possesses a certain significance as regards international trade in that it affects the terms both of importation and of exportation. In most cases, however, these effects are, of course, of minor importance.

If the country has a gold standard, and that gold standard is so rigidly maintained that the rate of exchange remains practically constant, it is possible that, as a consequence of a change in the terms of trade, an alteration, let us say a rise, may take place in the general price-level. In most cases this rise is very limited. It makes no difference whatever to the internal market once a new position of equilibrium has been reached, since it does not matter what monetary unit is the basis on which prices are reckoned. As regards external trade, a rise of this kind in the general price-level clearly means an encouragement of imports and a discouragement of exports. These effects, however, are only minor reactions against the direct effects of the change in the conditions of international trade. If, for example, the change consists in a higher tariff wall, the direct effect is a discouragement of imports; this effect is somewhat diminished as a result of the rise in the price-level.

In any case, the raising of the general price-level is a phenomenon apart which must be isolated from the relative change in prices. This can best be done by dividing all prices by the increase in the general price-level, that is to say, by reducing the country's internal prices, as in the case of the paper currency, to a constant money value. We then see that price increases are exactly counterbalanced by price diminutions. Relative price changes which come about as a result of the changed terms of trade thus exist to an equal extent in rises in prices and in reductions in prices. It is these changes which, in practice, are of importance. They imply a change in the distribution of income which, naturally, is advantageous to some of the population and disadvantageous to others. As regards the whole national economy a change has taken place in the bias of production, as a result of which the national income is affected. Nothing can be said in general with regard to these effects. If the change in the terms of trade consists of some arbitrary interference, such as an intensified tariff policy, it may as a rule be safely assumed that production will be diverted into less profitable channels, and that the present aggregate income of the country will consequently be diminished, but this does not prevent the possibility of gaining other advantages.

Any calculation of the ultimate result, by aggregating the changes which it is thought possible to ascertain in regard to individual prices, is in any case impossible. In particular we may stress the fact that calculations of the "burden of the tariff," to which it is usual to attach such great importance in politics, are without any foundation whatever. It is, of course, recognised for the most part that the statistical data available for making such a calculation are inadequate, and that the rise in price which the tariff brings about in the case of every protected commodity cannot always be properly estimated. These deficiences are, however, of secondary importance compared with the fact that the "burden" which it is desired to calculate has no definite conceptual meaning. If, for every article, the rise in price is multiplied by the quantity consumed, and all these "burdens" on consumers are added together to give a total burden, we are overlooking the fact that, if the value of money does not change, rises in prices must be offset by approximately the same amount by reductions in prices and that, therefore, the addition, if it be extended to those objects which have fallen in price, would in fact have to yield a sum in the neighbourhood of zero. The fact that a tariff which brings about rises in prices must also result in falls in prices should be rather illuminating if one considers that rises in prices necessitate heavier demands on the purchasing power of the population, so that there necessarily remains a smaller amount of purchasing power for other commodities. If the rises in prices were not counterbalanced by any diminutions in prices, this could only mean an increase in aggregate nominal purchasing power, which, however, would be tantamount to inflation of the currency. If in fact such a change in the value of money has occurred, and a position of equilibrium has been reached on the basis of the new value of money, the higher figures in which prices are henceforth reckoned do not imply any "burden." Accordingly, any change in the value of money must at once be eliminated from a discussion of the effect of the tariff; that is to say, the discussion must be conducted on the assumption of a constant money value. But if this is so, rises in prices and reductions in prices must in the aggregate counterbalance each other. Any calculation of the total burden of the tariff is therefore completely meaningless.

In any practical treatment of questions of tariffs, the effect of Protection on the general price-level may as a rule be ignored, without thereby giving rise to any appreciable error. From this it also follows that the motive behind a particular tariff policy cannot be to protect a higher price-level as against countries with a lower price-level. Protection of this kind clearly cannot be achieved to any considerable extent. And if it is actually achieved, it is insignificant in the long run.

The argument in favour of a general protective tariff which is of the greatest importance at the present time is expressed in the view that it is necessary in order to protect a country with a high labour standard against countries with a lower standard. This view forms the basis, on the one hand, of a policy of high protection in a number of countries which have a high labour standard, and, on the other, of the attempts to secure uniformity of labour standards throughout the world. By the term labour standard we are to understand not only the general level and effectiveness of labour legislation, but also the conditions of labour which are maintained by the trade unions. The term labour standard further embraces not only the regulation of hours of labour and other technical conditions of labour, but also the regulation of wages themselves.

Attempts to protect the labour standard naturally imply that a higher labour standard will raise costs of production. If this were not the case, no special protection would, of course, be necessary.

It would, however, be giving a very bad recommendation of the
efforts to raise the labour standard if we were at once to assume that
such a rise must inevitably raise costs of production. In practice,
of course, this is not so. A reasonable rise in the labour standard
should, in the long run at any rate, be followed by a corresponding
increase in the productivity of labour. On the whole, too, the
economic possibility of the higher labour standard becoming permanent depends upon a corresponding increase in efficiency.

The protecting of a high labour standard by means of tariffs
necessarily implies, as we have said, that in some cases at least
production will be made dearer as a result of the higher labour
standard, and will not be able to compete with production which is
carried on under a lower labour standard. The question then arises
whether such a branch of production shall be maintained in the
country with the higher standard. It may be better to give up that
branch of production and leave it to a country which has a lower
labour standard, and to concentrate on those branches of production
in which, despite the higher labour standard, the first country
possesses a certain superiority. The advantage of international
trade consists, as we know, in the division of labour and in the
concentration of production in each country on those branches of
production in which it has some superiority. This generally
recognised advantage, however, does not depend upon the causes of
that superiority. International division of labour finds its economic
justification not only in differences in natural resources, climate,
etc., but also in differences in labour standards. It is possible, for
example, that a country with a nine-hour day may possess a certain
superiority in particular branches of production, but that another
country with an eight-hour day may with advantage concentrate
upon branches of production in which it is not particularly hampered by the shorter working-day and in which, despite the eight-
hour day, it possesses a measure of superiority. This latter country
will then have to leave over certain branches of production to the
country with the nine-hour day, and will have to acquire those
particular goods by exchange. In this way it is possible for international division of labour to arise between countries with different

labour standards, to the advantage of all the countries concerned. The existence of some industry abroad which, by reason of its low labour standard, competes at an advantage is therefore not an adequate reason for the introduction of a tariff.

If we assume that the labour standard in a particular country is continually being forced up, that country will at first lose one branch of production after another. But it will regard the loss of these inferior branches of production with equanimity, and will instead concentrate its productive powers on other branches of production. This re-direction of production cannot, of course, be continued indefinitely. There comes a time when a further rise in the labour standard will jeopardise the existence of a branch of production which simply cannot be given up. The highest labour standard possible under the given conditions has then been reached, and the efforts to raise the labour standard further have reached their natural limit. This salutary regulation of the labour standard is rendered inoperative if competition on the part of countries with a lower labour standard is eliminated by means of a tariff. In those industries which are protected in this way, the labour standard can still be raised without there being any direct reminder that a level has been reached which cannot be maintained, and the only effect of Protection will thus have been to help to break down the natural uniformity of labour conditions and to produce an artificial distortion in the economic life of the country.

Changes of this kind do not, of course, arise solely in consequence of a tariff; they arise equally as a result of other protectionist measures which are in principle comparable with a tariff, such as the relief of the unemployed. As long as one is prepared to assist in the raising of the labour standard by relieving the unemployed, the efforts to raise the labour standard will not meet with any definite obstacle, and it will be impossible for a natural economic equilibrium to be reached.

The second principal method of eliminating competition due to the existence of a lower standard is, as we have said, that of internationalising the labour standard. Every period in history has its own peculiar doctrines which may not be disputed, and are accepted generally without criticism. The outstanding doctrine of our time is that of the necessity for international action in matters relating to safeguards for labour. This doctrine seems to be based upon a misconception of the nature of both the safeguarding of labour standards and international trade. We should not by any means regard it as natural for people in all countries to work under the same conditions. On the contrary, the natural working time and hence, too, the optimum working day are necessarily different in different countries. Similarly, wants and consequently, also, the amount of income which is necessary show great variations. International trade has always, up to the present, arisen between countries with widely differing labour standards and has yet, without any doubt, been of great benefit to all countries as a whole, in so far as from it there has sprung a natural division of labour, with a consequently increased productivity of the national economy.

If we take the case of two countries with different labour standards, an economically beneficial division of labour and exchange of goods between these countries can always take place. This is best seen if, in the general theory of international trade which we have developed here, we assume that each country has an independent paper currency. If goods are freely exchangeable, the rate of exchange, as we have seen, will turn out to be such that each country will buy from the other just as much as it sells to it. Where there is a gold standard this equilibrium will only be reached by a different technical procedure. Thus a lower labour standard cannot, any more than other factors which cheapen production, create a general competitive superiority.

The efforts to internationalise measures for safeguarding labour, or, to put it more generally, the labour standard, which occupy so prominent a place in politics to-day, are thus essentially without foundation from an economic point of view. On purely humanitarian grounds, of course, it may be justifiable in certain circumstances to take steps to secure international adoption of certain protective measures. The dominant motive behind the efforts to secure uniformity of labour standards is, however undoubtedly protectionist in character. Thus, for example, when Governments meet at conferences on the internationalisation of the eight-hour day, we can be quite sure that this is not done out of a humanitarian interest in the well-being of foreign workers. The object is simply that of eliminating competition which is regarded as injurious. But such efforts are unreasonable, partly because, as we have just seen, a beneficial international exchange of goods can arise even when labour standards differ, but partly also because uniformity of labour standards is, generally speaking, impossible in the long run. If it does happen that there is forced upon a foreign country a technically higher labour standard than is economically suited to that country, that higher standard must necessarily be balanced by a reduction of income from work. If, for example, it was succeeded in forcing the eight-hour day, which may be well suited to the American pace of working, upon other countries for which an eight-hour day is not by any means the optimum, the consequence could only be that those countries would have to restore their competitive capacity by means of reductions in wages. In that case nothing will have been gained even from a protectionist point of view. The completion of a policy of this kind by the process of keeping out products which are produced by lower paid labour will only force the countries thereby affected down to a still lower standard of life, and will, of course, at the same time hamper international exchange of goods and impair the world economy.

Such efforts are particularly absurd when they are directed against a country from which heavy Government payments are being demanded. If the United States expects European nations to pay their war debts, it must be prepared to accept European goods in payment, even if those goods are produced under low labour standards. The attempt to counterbalance the lower European labour standard by means of particular tariffs is in this case seen to be entirely illogical. The same is, of course, true when the Allied Powers demand a war indemnity from Germany. It would be quite natural if Germany, in order to pay that war indemnity, found herself obliged to work an extra hour per day. It appears to be a highly inconsistent policy if the Allied Powers wished to force Germany to enter into an agreement with them regarding a uniform eight-hour day. If this succeeded, and payment of the war indemnity were still insisted on, there might be no course left open to Germany other than to reduce wages, which would make up for the reduction in the hours of labour. In no circumstances would it be possible to secure protection against German goods, for, in order to be able to pay, Germany must be in some way or other make herself an effective competitor.

In all such questions of practical commercial policy the theory of international trade which we have developed here is calculated to conduce to clearness. As long as we bear in mind that, at a certain equilibrium of the exchanges, a levelling-out of the balance of trade must always occur, and that any transfers of capital must be effected without any change in that equilibrium, we shall easily avoid the mistakes common in popular discussions of such questions.

APPENDIX

TABLE I

SAUERBECK'S INDEX NUMBERS, 1846 TO 1913; FOR THE PERIOD 1850–1910, THESE INDEX NUMBERS ARE DIVIDED BY THE RELATIVE STOCK OF GOLD.[1]

Year.	Index Numbers.	Index Nos. Divided by Gold Stock.	Year.	Index Numbers.	Index Nos. Divided by Gold Stock.
1846	89	—	1879	83	76
1847	95	—	1880	88	81
1848	78	—	1881	85	79
1849	74	—	1882	84	79
1850	77	77	1883	82	79
1851	75	74	1884	76	73
1852	78	75	1885	72	71
1853	95	89	1886	69	69
1854	102	94	1887	68	69
1855	101	91	1888	70	72
1856	101	90	1889	72	75
1857	105	93	1890	72	75
1858	91	80	1891	72	76
1859	94	82	1892	68	73
1860	99	85	1893	68	73
1861	98	84	1894	63	68
1862	101	86	1895	62	67
1863	103	88	1896	61	66
1864	105	90	1897	62	67
1865	101	86	1898	64	69
1866	102	87	1899	68	73
1867	100	85	1900	75	80
1868	99	85	1901	70	75
1869	98	84	1902	69	74
1870	96	82	1903	69	74
1871	100	86	1904	70	74
1872	109	94	1905	72	76
1873	111	97	1906	77	80
1874	102	89	1907	80	82
1875	96	85	1908	73	74
1876	95	84	1909	74	75
1877	94	84	1910	78	78
1878	87	79			

[1] From *Wholesale and Retail Prices*, London, 1903, and the *Journal of the Roya Statistical Society*.

TABLE II

THE GOLD SUPPLY OF THE WORLD (IN MILLIONS OF MARKS).

Year.	Actual Gold Stock.	Normal Gold Stock.	Relative Gold Stock.
1800	7,535	2,531	2.98
1810	7,875	3,332	2.36
1820	8,033	4,385	1.83
1830	8,265	5,772	1.43
1840	8,660	7,597	1.14
1850	10,000	10,000	1.00
1855	12,680	11,470	1.11
1860	15,370	13,160	1.17
1865	17,795	15,100	1.18
1870	20,335	17,320	1.17
1875	22,555	19,880	1.13
1876	22,973	20,435	1.12
1877	23,428	21,005	1.12
1878	23,900	21,591	1.11
1879	24,319	22,193	1.10
1880	24,735	22,800	1.08
1881	25,146	23,448	1.07
1882	25,525	24,102	1.06
1883	25,884	24,774	1.04
1884	26,272	25,465	1.03
1885	26,650	26,160	1.02
1886	27,046	26,890	1.01
1887	27,433	27,640	0.99
1888	27,836	28,411	0.98
1889	28,272	29,204	0.97
1890	28,775	30,010	0.96
1891	29,266	30,847	0.95
1892	29,823	31,708	0.94
1893	30,424	32,593	0.93
1894	31,124	33,502	0.93
1895	31,885	34,430	0.93
1896	32,670	35,391	0.92
1897	33,596	36,378	0.92
1898	34,733	37,392	0.93
1899	35,951	38,435	0.94
1900	36,975	39,510	0.94
1901	37,970	40,612	0.93
1902	39,140	41,745	0.94
1903	40,438	42,910	0.94
1904	41,815	44,107	0.95
1905	43,336	45,520	0.96
1906	44,970	46,584	0.97
1907	46,614	47,884	0.97
1908	48,381	49,220	0.98
1909	50,192	50,593	0.99
1910	52,003	52,000	1.00

Table III   693

CURVES REPRESENTING INDICES OF BANK CLEARINGS IN LONDON AND
NEW YORK, 1870–1910.[1]

	London.		New York.	
	Clearings Divided by the Absolute	In Percentages of the	Clearings Divided by the Absolute	In Percentages of the
Year.	Gold Supply	Average.	Gold Supply.	Average.
1870	192	79	137	98
1871	231	95	141	101
1872	278	115	159	114
1873	286	118	164	117
1874	267	110	104	74
1875	248	102	111	79
1876	217	90	94	67
1877	214	88	106	71
1878	209	86	94	67
1879	202	83	104	74
1880	235	97	151	108
1881	255	105	194	139
1882	243	100	183	131
1883	228	94	156	111
1884	221	91	135	93
1885	206	85	95	68
1886	219	90	124	89
1887	223	92	128	91
1888	248	102	111	79
1889	269	111	123	88
1890	271	112	131	94
1891	232	96	116	83
1892	218	90	122	87
1893	214	88	113	81
1894	203	84	78	56
1895	238	98	89	64
1896	232	96	90	64
1897	223	92	93	66
1898	233	96	115	82
1899	256	106	159	114
1900	243	100	141	101
1901	253	104	203	145
1902	256	106	191	136
1903	250	103	175	125
1904	258	104	143	102
1905	283	117	212	151
1906	282	116	231	165
1907	273	113	205	146
1908	250	103	152	109
1909	269	111	198	141
1910	283	117	197	141
Average:	242		140	

[1] From the *Statistical Abstract for the United Kingdom* and the *Statistical Abstract for the United States.*

TABLE IV

GERMAN AND ENGLISH DISCOUNT RATES (ANNUAL AVERAGES).[1]

Year.	Berlin.		London.	
	Bank.	Market.	Bank.	Market.
1872	4.29	—	4.10	—
1873	4.93	—	4.79	—
1874	4.38	—	3.69	—
1875	4.71	—	3.23	—
1876	4.16	—	2.61	—
1877	4.42	—	2.90	—
1878	4.34	—	3.78	—
1879	3.70	—	2.51	—
1880	4.24	—	2.76	—
1881	4.42	—	3.40	—
1882	4.54	—	4.15	—
1883	4.05	—	3.57	—
1884	4.00	—	2.96	—
1885	4.12	—	2.93	—
1886	3.28	—	3.05	—
1887	3.41	—	3.38	—
1888	3.32	—	3.30	—
1889	3.68	2.63	3.55	3.25
1890	4.52	3.78	4.54	3.71
1891	3.78	3.02	3.32	1.50
1892	3.20	1.80	2.52	1.33
1893	4.07	3.17	3.05	1.67
1894	3.12	1.74	2.11	1.69
1895	3.14	2.01	2.00	0.87
1896	3.66	3.04	2.48	1.52
1897	3.81	3.09	2.64	1.87
1898	4.27	3.55	3.25	2.65
1899	5.04	4.45	3.75	3.29
1900	5.33	4.41	3.96	3.70
1901	4.10	3.06	3.72	3.20
1902	3.32	2.19	3.33	2.99
1903	3.84	3.01	3.75	3.40
1904	4.22	3.14	3.30	2.70
1905	3.83	2.85	3.01	2.66
1906	5.15	4.04	4.27	4.05
1907	6.03	5.12	4.93	4.53
1908	4.76	3.52	3.01	2.31
1909	3.93	2.87	3.10	2.31
1910	4.35	3.54	3.72	3.18

[1] *Statistisches Jahrbuch für das Deutsche Reich.*

TABLE V 695

OUTPUT OF PIG-IRON AND COAL.

	World.		Germany.	
Year	Pig-Iron (in 1,000 tons).	Coal (in millions of tons).	Pig-Iron (in 1,000 tons).	Coal (in millions of tons).
1865	9,100	188	988	29
1866	9,656	197	1,047	28
1867	10,062	203	1,114	31
1868	10,707	208	1,264	33
1869	11,950	218	1,413	34
1870	12,260	219	1,391	34
1871	12,852	237	1,564	38
1872	14,843	260	1,988	42
1873	15,125	280	2,241	46
1874	13,916	274	1,906	47
1875	14,119	283	2,029	48
1876	13,962	287	1,846	50
1877	14,193	294	1,933	48
1878	14,536	293	2,148	51
1879	14,411	312	2,227	53
1880	18,584	345	2,729	59
1881	19,819	365	2,914	62
1882	21,555	384	3,381	65
1883	21,756	410	3,470	70
1884	20,464	409	3,601	72
1885	19,842	407	3,687	74
1886	20,813	407	3,529	74
1887	22,820	434	4,024	76
1888	24,031	470	4,337	82
1889	25,877	485	4,525	85
1890	27,870	514	4,658	89
1891	26,171	532	4,641	94
1892	26,917	538	4,937	93
1893	25,263	528	4,986	95
1894	26,032	552	5,380	99
1895	29,369	583	5,465	104
1896	31,289	601	6,373	112
1897	33,464	631	6,881	120
1898	36,455	665	7,313	128
1899	40,874	727	8,143	136
1900	41,384	767	8,521	150
1901	41,140	789	7,880	153
1902	44,730	803	8,530	151
1903	46,820	878	10,018	162
1904	46,220	886	10,058	169
1905	54,790	914	10,875	174
1906	56,660	1,014	12,293	194
1907	61,300	1,117	12,875	206
1908	48,800	1,068	11,805	215
1909	60,660	1,110	12,645	217
1910	66,200	1,152	14,794	222

TABLE VI

GOODS TRAFFIC ON GERMAN RAILWAYS (IN MILLIONS OF TONS).[1]

Year.	Capital Goods.	Other Goods.	Year.	Capital Goods.	Other Goods.
1886	23.9	92.2	1898	57.6	179.1
1887	27.6	97.2	1899	63.2	188.7
1888	31.0	106.6	1900	65.3	203.6
1889	34.6	114.7	1901	59.5	203.9
1890	34.7	119.7	1902	63.8	203.9
1891	35.2	127.1	1903	72.4	218.7
1892	35.8	124.8	1904	75.2	225.1
1893	36.3	132.2	1905	80.0	241.0
1894	39.2	138.1	1906	91.0	257.9
1895	40.8	143.9	1907	94.4	269.6
1896	48.1	157.1	1908	88.8	275.0
1897	52.3	168.5	1909	90.5	279.9

[1] *Statistisches Jahrbuch für das Deutsche Reich.* We take capital goods as being those classed as 7, 11–20, 31a, b, and 59; other goods consist of the remainder.

TABLE VII

FACTORY WORKERS IN SWEDEN.[2]

Year.	Capital-Producing Industries.	Other Industries.	Total
1896	92,414	109,879	202,293
1897	101,619	118,583	220,202
1898	109,733	135,987	245,720
1899	116,275	141,251	257,526
1900	119,597	145,882	265,479
1901	114,451	147,778	262,229
1902	113,438	149,806	263,244
1903	117,351	153,806	271,157
1904	119,064	158,789	277,853
1905	116,843	164,152	280,995
1906	124,678	171,130	295,908
1907	128,021	175,008	303,029
1908	121,082	174,310	295,392
1909	115,186	174,019	289,205

[2] From *Bidrag till Sveriges officiella Statistik D. Fabriker och Handtverk.* The following sections are counted as capital-producing industries in the Swedish report: Table 6 (5a); Rubrik 1 (8a); Rubrik 2, 3, 5, 13, 14 (10a), (11a), (11b); Rubrik 1(c); Rubrik 1, 2, 6, 7.

Table VIII

Persons Insured Against Accident in the German Industrial
Unions (in thousands). [1]

Year.	Capital-Producing Industries.	Other Industries.	Total.
1888	1,865	2,455	4,320
1889	2,145	2,598	4,743
1890	2,214	2,712	4,927
1891	2,322	2,771	5,093
1892	2,275	2,803	5,078
1893	2,313	2,856	5,169
1894	2,324	2,920	5,244
1895	2,370	3,039	5,409
1896	2,553	3,182	5,735
1897	2,753	3,290	6,043
1898	2,918	3,399	6,317
1899	3,110	3,548	6,659
1900	3,214	3,715	6,929
1901	3,052	3,832	6,884
1902	3,032	4,068	7,100
1903	3,189	4,277	7,466
1904	3,365	4,484	7,849
1905	3,539	4,657	8,196
1906	3,772	4,854	8,626
1907	3,905	5,113	9,018
1908	3,719	5,199	8,918
1909	3,691	5,313	9,004

[1] *Statistisches Jahrbuch für das Deutsche Reich.* (Trade unions in the capital-producing industries are those numbered 2–11, 17, 43–54, 64.)

Table IX

Average Annual Productive Capacity of the German Blast Furnaces. [1]

Year.	Furnaces Existing at End of Year.	Furnaces Active.	Weeks Worked.	Average Annual Capacity per Furnace.
1872	—	348	13,676	7,560
1873	—	379	15,276	7,627
1874	—	339	11,776	8,418
1875	—	289	10,904	9,678
1876	—	236	9,160	10,481
1877	—	212	9,219	10,902
1878	—	212	9,056	12,332
1879	—	210	8,952	12,934
1880	—	246	10,975	12,930
1881	—	251	11,362	13,336
1882	—	261	12,087	14,545
1883	318	258	11,760	15,342
1884	308	252	11,071	16,912
1885	298	229	10,758	17,824
1886	285	215	9,445	10,427
1887	271	212	10,011	20,902
1888	271	211	10,103	22,323
1889	264	213	10,436	22,545
1890	265	222	10,480	23,114
1891	270	218	10,322	23,380
1892	266	215	10,103	25,410
1893	263	204	9,747	26,600
1894	258	208	9,878	28,320
1895	263	212	9,929	28,610
1896	265	229	10,846	30,550
1897	273	244	11,661	30,680
1898	281	253	11,587	32,820
1899	285	263	12,806	33,060
1900	298	274	13,252	33,430
1901	309	263	11,517	35,580
1902	289	241	10,946	40,520
1903	293	254	12,546	41,520
1904	297	254	11,930	43,840
1905	308	277	12,914	43,790
1906	315	288	14,125	45,255
1907	324	303	14,780	45,298
1908	331	280	12,596	48,733
1909	334	279	12,811	51,320

[1] *Statistisches Jahrbuch für das Deutsche Reich.*

TABLE X

SHIPPING TONNAGE AND SHIPBUILDING IN ENGLAND.[1]

Year.	Tonnage of Incoming Ships (millions).	Tonnage of Ships Built (tens of thousands).	Year.	Tonnage of Incoming Ships (millions).	Tonnage of Ships Built (tens of thousands).
1854	19	—	1882	61	78
1855	18	—	1883	65	89
1856	22	—	1884	64	59
1857	23	—	1885	64	44
1858	22	24	1886	63	33
1859	23	21	1887	65	38
1860	25	23	1888	69	57
1861	27	21	1889	72	85
1862	27	26	1890	74	81
1863	27	38	1891	75	81
1864	27	42	1892	76	80
1865	29	45	1893	75	58
1866	31	38	1894	81	67
1867	33	31	1895	81	65
1868	34	36	1896	85	74
1869	35	39	1897	90	64
1870	37	39	1898	91	87
1871	42	39	1899	98	95
1872	43	47	1900	99	94
1873	44	45	1901	97	98
1874	45	60	1902	99	95
1875	46	47	1903	105	76
1876	51	38	1904	108	88
1877	52	45	1905	112	105
1878	52	47	1906	121	114
1879	53	41	1907	133	104
1880	59	47	1908	131	60
1881	58	61			

[1] British and Foreign Trade and Industry (1854–1908), Cmd. 4954, London, 1909.

TABLE XI

INDEX NUMBERS OF WHOLESALE PRICES OF PIG-IRON, BRICKS, AND TIMBER (CUT) IN GREAT BRITAIN, 1871–1908.[1]

Year.	Pig-Iron.	Bricks.	Timber (cut).
1871	72.1	91.7	159.1
1872	119.7	100.0	163.0
1873	148.0	116.7	176.6
1874	111.9	100.0	179.9
1875	86.3	91.7	157.1
1876	74.2	91.7	159.1
1877	68.2	91.7	155.2
1878	63.7	83.3	135.7
1879	61.3	70.0	118.2
1880	76.1	75.0	134.4
1881	65.8	70.0	135.7
1882	66.8	83.3	139.0
1883	61.8	75.0	134.4
1884	54.7	75.0	119.5
1885	51.3	75.0	116.2
1886	50.6	75.0	102.6
1887	54.9	75.0	96.8
1888	50.4	75.0	103.2
1889	59.5	75.0	114.9
1890	72.6	100.0	105.8
1891	62.4	91.7	97.4
1892	61.2	91.7	97.4
1893	55.7	83.3	90.9
1894	54.6	83.3	87.0
1895	56.9	83.3	88.3
1896	56.7	83.3	92.2
1897	57.3	83.3	93.5
1898	62.5	91.7	95.5
1899	82.6	100.0	94.2
1900	100.0	100.0	100.0
1901	74.6	91.7	94.8
1902	77.1	83.3	99.0
1903	75.1	83.3	90.9
1904	69.6	83.3	85.7
1905	75.0	81.1	87.7
1906	83.2	77.8	89.6
1907	88.2	79.4	92.2
1908	75.3	81.1	87.7

[1] *British and Foreign Trade and Industry* (1854–1908), Cmd. 4954, London, 1909.

TABLE XII

SAUERBECK'S INDEX NUMBERS OF MINERALS AND OTHER ARTICLES,
DIVIDED BY THE FIGURES OF THE RELATIVE STOCK OF GOLD.

Year.	Minerals.	Other Articles.	Year.	Minerals.	Other Articles.
1870	76.3	83.5	1891	80.6	74.6
1871	80.3	84.6	1892	75.9	71.9
1872	109.1	89.1	1893	73.3	72.9
1873	122.9	92.0	1894	68.4	67.6
1874	100.6	86.4	1895	67.1	67.0
1875	89.4	83.7	1896	68.7	65.5
1876	80.4	84.6	1897	71.2	66.3
1877	75.4	85.7	1898	75.8	67.7
1878	66.9	81.2	1899	97.9	68.1
1879	66.6	77.4	1900	115.9	73.7
1880	72.6	82.5	1901	94.9	71.4
1881	71.4	80.2	1902	87.8	71.7
1882	74.6	80.0	1903	87.3	71.3
1883	72.7	79.7	1904	86.1	71.9
1884	65.9	74.8	1905	91.4	72.8
1885	64.9	71.6	1906	105.1	75.3
1886	66.2	68.9	1907	110.1	76.7
1887	70.0	68.6	1908	90.5	71.5
1888	79.6	70.4	1909	87.0	72.7
1889	77.8	74.1	1910	88.8	75.8
1890	83.9	73.1			

702

Table XIII

Pig-Iron Output and Market Rate of Discount in the United States.[1]

Year.	Pig-Iron Output (millions of tons).	Market Rate at New York.	Year.	Pig-Iron Output (millions of tons).	Market Rate at New York
1870	1,665	7.2	1891	8,280	5.87
1871	1,707	6.1	1892	9,157	4.46
1872	2,549	8.0	1893	7,125	7.11
1873	2,561	10.3	1894	6,658	3.40
1874	2,401	6.0	1895	9,446	3.87
1875	2,024	5.5	1896	8,623	5.88
1876	1,869	5.2	1897	9,653	3.87
1877	2,067	5.2	1898	11,774	4.23
1878	2,301	4.8	1899	13,621	4.28
1879	2,742	5.0	1900	13,789	4.73
1880	3,835	5.2	1901	15,878	4.48
1881	4,144	5.2	1902	17,821	5.04
1882	4,625	5.7	1903	18,009	5.54
1883	4,596	5.5	1904	16,497	4.29
1884	4,098	5.2	1905	22,992	4.33
1885	4,045	4.1	1906	25,307	5.63
1886	5,683	4.7	1907	25,781	6.28
1887	6,417	5.7	1908	15,936	4.62
1888	6,490	4.9	1909	25,795	3.92
1889	7,604	5.08	1910	27,304	5.07
1890	9,203	5.92			

[1] Pohle, *Statistische Unterlagen.*

INDEX

ABSTINENCE AND SAVING, 190
Age and wealth, 244
Agriculture, 4, 269–89
— and labour, 566–75
— and trade cycles, 550–1
Alternative products and rent, 288
Amark, Dr., 63
American Steel Trust, the, 126
Assignats, the, 405
Attribution, the problem of, 177–84
Austrian paper currency system, the, 406–7

BANK ADVANCES, FACTORS DETERMINING,
416–21, 428
— cash balances, 409–16
— central, the, 413–14
— deposits, 412, 414–21
— functions of the, 410–16
— money and cover, 428–35
— — and its reflux, 428–35
— — and rate of interest, 435–9
— of England, 399, 406, 422–3, 426, 435,
447
— of France, 490
— reserves, 411, 420–1, 427–8
Banking policy and international payments,
524–9
Bank-notes, 421–8
— and money, 421–3
— cover of, 425–8
Bank-rate, the, 439, 494–502
Barter, 374–5
Belgium, wages in, 607
Bills of exchange, 430–1, 512–13
Bimetallism, 400–1
Böhm-Bawerk, 191, 195–6, 301
Boom, the trade, 550
Bowley, 608
Brassey, 313
Bücher, 375

CANON LAW AND INTEREST, 185–6
Capital, abstract, 53
— and international trade, 673–80
— as a factor of production, 167, 170, 189
197–207, 298–9
— circulating, 30, 54–5, 542, 583, 588–9
— effect of security on, 250
— effect of trade cycles on, 583–98, 619–26
— fixed, 28–9, 54–5, 252, 542–50

Capital, formation of, 35–40, 60–2, 202–7
— — and rate of interest, 238–45
— goods and rent, 274–5
— market, the, 436–8
— mobility of, 120
— nature of, 51–3
— real, 30, 53–4, 197, 206–7
— remunerative, 52
— the influence of, on wages, 339–43
— value, 212–13
Capital-disposal, 188, 191–2, 194, 197–207
— and labour, 204
— and production, 201
— and waiting, 199–200, 202–4
— demand for, 216–32
— supply of, 232–45
Capitalists, psychology of, 237
— and rate of interest, 241–2, 247
Carat, the, 380
Cartels, 124
Cash, 409
Central bank, the, 413–14
Cheque, the, 412
Clearing statistics, 485–7
— system of, 413
Coal production and trade cycles, 551
Coinage, 383–402
— circulation of, 389–402
— right of free, 393
Communism, 72–3, 93
Comparative costs, theory of, 658–9
Competition between types of labour, 335–8
— free, 118–20, 122–9
Concentration, tendency towards, 227–8
Consumer's surplus, the, 83–4
Consumption, effect of trade cycles on, 617–19
— freedom of choice in, 45
— goods, 11–13, 15, 29, 205, 216–17, 550–5
— meaning of, 11–12, 97
Co-operation in an economy, 4, 10
Cost, interest as a, 248–9
— nature of, 91–3
— of production, 92, 147–8
— — and rent, 266
— — Ricardo's theory of, 298–304
— — principle of, 93, 104, 106
Cotton industry and trade cycles, 592–3
Cover of bank money, 428–35
— of bank-notes, 425–8
Credit, organisation of, 228

Crises, 533–41, 648–52
Cromer, Lord, 409
Currency and international trade, 655–65
Current coins, 395

DECREASING RETURNS, 111, 278–9
Deflation, 498–501
Demand, elasticity of, 77–80
— individual, 76
— restriction of, 66–88
— total, 76
Deposits, bank, 412, 414–21
Depression, nature of the trade, 550, 588, 595
Differential principle of pricing, the, 101
— profit, 101–2
— rent, 286–7
Diminishing returns, law of, 265, 278–9
Discount policy, 527–8
Discounting of bills, 431
Distribution of income, 97
— the social problem of, 182–3
Division of labour, international, 685–8
Disutility theory of wages, the, 360
Dollar standard, the, 503
Double standard, the, 396–7
Dumping, exchange, 516
Durable goods, 11–13, 15, 28, 197–200, 212–16, 219–20
— means of production and trade cycles, 583–98
Duration of life and rate of interest, 255

ECONOMIC ACTIVITIES, 5
— necessities, 10
— progress, 62–3, 488
— science, 9, 11, 21–2, 65
Economising of means, 6
Economy, meaning of, 6–9
— the exchange, 42–4
— the money, 47, 51–63
— the national, 44
— the social, 44
— the socialist, 131–6, 256–9, 289, 362–5
— the stationary, 27–32, 94, 97–8
— the uniformly progressive, 32–41, 95, 98, 152–3
Employers' associations, 71–2
England, income-tax in, 610–11
— industrial wages in, 607–9
— iron output in, 553–4
— paper money in, 406
— railway construction in, 547
— shipping in, 597–8
— unemployment in, 576–8
— working population of, 570–1
Entrepreneur functions of, the, 171–4
— and labour, the, 323, 326–7
Equations for pricing, 139–45

Ethics and interest, 247
Europe, economic progress of, 62–3
Exchange, bills of, 430–1, 512–13
— dumping, 516
— indirect, 375
— medium of, 46, 375–8, 382
— rate of, 513–24, 659–63, 678–80

FEMALE LABOUR, 327, 336–8, 353
Fisher, Irving, 461, 464, 503, 506
Forced currency, 405
France and post-war gold standard, 507
Free competition, 118–20, 122–9
— standards, 402–8
Freedom of choice in consumption, 45
Fungibility of coins, 384
Future, regard for the, 3–4, 25, 235–6

GENERAL ECONOMIC PRINCIPLE, THE, 8, 65
George, Henry, 264
Germany and war debts, 688–9
— building in, 543–4
— capital-producing industries in, 563–6
— coinage laws of, 395
— income-tax in, 612–14
— industrial population of, 566–9
— insurance in, 543–4, 559–61
— iron production in, 552–7, 585–6
— labour in, 559–61
— prices in, 604–5
— railways in, 555, 589–91
— stocks and shares in, 633–4
— unemployment in, 578–80
Gold, actual, normal and relative stocks of, 468–78
— and redemption of bank-notes, 424–5
— cost of production of, 478–81
— Delegation to League of Nations, 508–9
— demand for, 489–94
— early use of, 379–80
— output of, 478
— points, the, 520–1
— post-war value of, 407–8
— price of, 398–9
— standard, the, 398–400, 490–3, 503–9, 664–5
— supply and the price-level, 468–78
— the world supply of, 467–8
Gold-premium policy, the, 529
Goods, classes of, 11, 14
— collective, 68
— consumption, 11–13, 15, 29, 205, 216–17, 550–5
— durable, 11–13, 15, 28, 197–200, 212–16, 219–20
Grain, the, 380
Gratis principle, the, 93
Gresham's law, 388

HELFFERICH, 391, 403, 407, 467
Holland, silver standard in, 403–4
Hours of work, 301
— of labour, 356–8
— — effect of changing, 580–2

IMPUTATION AND MARGINAL PRODUCTIVITY, 179–81
— problem of, 177–84
Income, determined by prices, 151
— effect of trade cycles on, 610–16
— money, 57–9, 96
— period, the, 142
— real nature of, 31–2, 39, 56, 60, 62, 97–8
— utilisation of, 440–5
Increasing returns, 111, 279
Index numbers of prices, 462–7
India, the free standard in, 404
Industrial population, 558–60, 566–9, 570–1
— reserve army, the, 346, 564, 566–7
Inflation, 498–501
Insurance, 234
— in Germany, 543–4, 559–61
Integration of industry, 126–7
Interest and Canon Law, 185–6
— and ethics, 247
— and money, 187–8
— and profit, 188
— and risk, 207–8
— as a cost, 248–9
— as a price, 207–16
— development of the idea of, 185–8
— nature of, 186–96
— rate of; see Rate of Interest
— under Socialism, 256–9
International division of labour, 685–8
— payments, 512–29
— trade and capital, 673–80
— — and currency, 655–65
— — and production, 672
— — pricing under, 665–73
— — theory of, 655–89
Interstate Commerce Commission, the, 545
Iron law of wages, 306
— modern importance of, 548–54
— production and trade cycles, 549–50, 593–5, 627–30

JEVONS, 38, 193–4, 196, 311, 374, 465–7
Joint products, 112–15, 160

KITCHIN, JOSEPH, 478
Konjunkturinstituten, the, 538

LABOUR AND AGRICULTURE, 566–75
— and capital-disposal, 204
— and the entrepreneur, 323, 326–7
— and trade cycles, 558–82
— and wages, 321–30

Labour as a factor of production, 23, 96, 167, 299–302, 321–2, 324–5, 327
— character of, 307–8, 322–3
— classes of, 335–6
— demand for, 319, 330–43
— displacement of, by machinery, 229, 340–3
— hours of, 356–8, 580–2
— market, the, 345–55
— mobility of, 353–4
— normal, 299, 302
— productivity of, 311–12, 321, 343–62
— scarcity of, 331–2
— standard, the, 684–8
— supply of, 319, 343–62
— theory of value, 300–2
Labour-saving machinery and wages, 229, 340–3
Land as a factor of production, 17, 167, 169, 226–7, 298
— influence of, on wages, 338–9
— natural and produced, 269–72
— pricing of, 275–89
Lassalle, 190, 306
Large-scale enterprise, advantage of, 107, 123
Latin Monetary Union, the, 656
Law's Bank, 405
League of Nations, the, 505–6, 508–9
Legal tender, 378
Leroy-Beaulieu, 310
Lexis, 467–8
Liberalism, 117, 186–7
Limping standard, the, 400
Loans, 433

MACHINERY AND LABOUR, 229, 340–3
Mahaim, 607
March, Lucien, 541
Marginal cost of production, 262
— productivity, 110, 179–81, 312–13
— utility, theory of, 80–3, 110, 147
Markets, the growth of, 122–3
Marshall, Alfred, 83, 92, 169–70, 240, 248, 266, 275, 282, 284, 295–6
Marx, Karl, 189
Material goods, 11
Means of production, 18, 89
— trade cycles and durable, 583–98
Medium of exchange, 46, 375–8, 382
— of payment, 378–9, 382
Menger, A., 191, 301
Mercantilism, 116–17, 186
Metals and money, 377, 379–80
Metal value of coins, 386–8
Mill, John Stuart, 264, 278, 459, 479
Minting, 383–9
Monetary standard, the, 388–9
— system, the, 379, 381

Money and bank-notes, 421–3
— and interest, 187–8
— and metals, 377, 379–80
— as a commodity, 389
— bad and good, 388
— circulating volume of, 411
— income, 57–9, 96
— national demand for, 409–10
— nature of, 46, 48, 50, 382–3
— origins of, 371–83
— paper, 405–8
— primitive, 371–3
— problem of invariability of, 389
— qualities of, 376–7
— ring, 381–2
— value of, 446–9, 502–11
— wage, the, 329
Monopoly and free competition, 129

NATURAL MATERIALS, 167, 289–97
— products, 269–70
— wage, the, 305–6
New countries, effect of opening up, 645
Nominal value of coins, 386–8
Normal labour, 299, 302

OBJECTIVE THEORY OF VALUE, THE, 146
Occupation, choice of, 353–4
Ohlin, Bertil, 668
Optimistic theories of wages, 310–21
Organisation, necessity of, 9, 10, 115–16
Over-consumption, 233–5
Over-production, 595, 649
Over-saving, 234, 445
Over-valuation of currency, 515, 678–9
Owen, Robert, 134

PAPER MONEY, 405–8
— standards, 404–8
Parallel standard, the, 396
Payment, medium of, 378–9, 382
Payments, international, 512–29
Peel's Bank Act, 522
Period of production, 23–4, 31–2
— shortening of, 231
Personal services, 13, 15, 20–2
— and real wealth, 31
Pessimistic theories of wages, 304–10
Physiocrats, the, 261
Pohle, 267, 556, 582, 591, 604, 606, 627
Population and wages, 306, 349–52
— effect of growth of, 33, 221, 247, 249
Price, interest as a, 207–16
— nature of, 47
Price-level and index numbers, 462–7
— and the gold supply, 468–78
Prices and tariffs, 680–4
— and trade cycles, 487, 599–606

Prices, Ricardian theory of, 298–304
— state control of, 86–8
— subsidised, 86–7
Pricing, nature of, 66, 145
— problem of, 74–6, 80–8, 89–115
— supplementary principles of, 99–115
— theory of, 49
— under international trade, 665–73
Private property, 44, 183
Production and capital-disposal, 201
— and international trade, 672
— and progress, 33–4, 227
— and trade cycles, 542–57
— continuous process of, 22–7
— factors of, 17–19, 89, 167
— meaning of, 16, 19–22, 24–5, 45
— means of, 18, 89, 583–98
— period of, 23–4, 31–2, 231
— social, 44
Productive activities, 20–2
Profit and interest, 188
— and risk, 174
— differential, the, 101–2
— of enterprise, 173–4
— pure, 173, 175–7
Progress and production, 33–4, 227
— and saving, 249–50
— economic, of Europe, 62–3
— impossibility of uniform, 646
— meaning of, 33
— rate of economic, 62–3, 488
— technical, and trade cycles, 644–5
Progressive economy, the uniformly, 32–41
  95, 98, 152–3
Purchasing power parity, the, 513, 658–9

QUANTITY THEORY, THE, 449–59
Quasi-rent, 275n.

RAILWAYS, CONSTRUCTION OF, 544–7
— effect of trade cycles on, 544–7, 635–7
Rate of economic progress, 62–3, 488
— of exchange, 513–24, 659–63, 678–80
— of interest and bank money, 435–9
— — and capitalists, 241–2, 247
— — and duration of life, 243–5, 255
— — and formation of capital, 238–45
— — and production of fixed capital, 252
— — and saving, 238–45
— — determination of the, 246–56
— — effects of abnormal changes in the,
  240
— — effects of trade cycles on the, 626–30
— — fluctuations in, 251–2
— — history of the, 208–12
Rates, 70
Rationalisation, 342–3

Rationing and prices, 87-8
— method of, 87
Raw materials, 17, 289-97
Real wealth, 31
Reflux of bank money, 428-35
Reichsbank, the, 395, 399, 423, 426-7, 656
Rent and alternative products, 288
— and capital goods, 274-5
— and cost of production, 266
— determination of, 275-89
— development of the theory of, 260-8
— differential, the, 286-7
— in socialist state, 289
— nature of, 212-16, 268-75
— of position, 176
— Ricardian theory of, 261-4
Reserve army, the industrial, 346, 564, 566-7
— the bank, 411
Residual theory of wages, 311
Returns, increasing and decreasing, 111, 278-9
— law of diminishing, 265, 278
Ricardo, 190, 217, 261-6, 268, 281, 286, 298-304, 305-8, 478
Ridgeway, Professor W., 373, 379
Riksbank, the Swedish, 423
Ring money, 381-2
Risk and interest, 207-8
— and profit, 174
Roscher, 185
Royalties, mining, nature of, 290

SACRIFICE AND SAVING, 35, 40
Sauerbeck's index, 464, 481
Saving and abstinence, 190
— and distribution of income, 238
— and industrial undertakings, 236
— and provision for the future, 238
— and rate of interest, 238-45
— and sacrifice, 35, 40
— erroneous ideas regarding, 60
— nature of, 35-40, 61, 204-5
— personal motives for, 237
Say, J. B., 188
Scale of reckoning, the, 46, 50, 372-5, 382
Scandinavian Currency Union, the, 656
— Edda, the, 371
Scarcity of labour, 331-2
— principle of, 5, 18-19, 74, 90
Schmoller, 190, 253-4
Schoenhof, 313
Secular variations of the general price-level, 472
Security, effect of, on capital, 250
Seligman, 313
Senior, 190
Services and real wealth, 31
— as a productive activity, 21-2

Services of durable goods, 13-14
— personal, 13
Silver standard, the, 403-4
Single Tax, the, 264
— standard, the problem of the, 390-6
Smith, Adam, 38, 117, 190, 261, 263, 298, 308, 310, 478, 588
Social policy, 71
Socialism, 131-6, 179, 197, 256-9, 289, 293-4, 300-5, 647-8
Sortengeld, 391
Soviet Republic, Five Year Plan of the, 648n
Standard commodity, the, 372
— the dollar, 503
— the double, 396-7
— the free, 402-8
— the gold, 398-400, 490-3, 503-9, 664-5
— the limping, 400
— the monetary, 388-9
— the paper, 404-8
— the parallel, 396
— the silver, 403-4
— the single, problem of, 390-6
State, the socialist, 131-6, 256-9, 289, 362-5
— the stationary, 27-32, 94, 97-8
— the uniformly progressive, 32-41, 95, 98, 152-3
Stationary state, the, 27-32, 94, 97-8
Stocks and shares, effect of trade cycles on, 630-4
Stock exchange, functions of the, 433-4
Subjective theory of value, the, 48, 146
Subsidised prices, 86-7
Substitution, the point of, 109
— the principle of, 108, 278-81
Sundbärg, 63
Supply, 73
Surplus, the consumer's, 83-4
Sweden, agricultural population of, 569-70
— factory workers in, 558-60
— income-tax in, 614-15
— national capital and income of, 62-3
— railways in, 591

TARIFFS, 655, 680-9
Taxes, 70
Technical co-efficients, 142, 146-8
— development and cost, 297
— improvements and labour, 340-3
— progress and trade cycles, 644-5
Token coins, 395
Trade boom, the, 550
— cycles and agriculture, 550-1
— — and capital, 583-98, 619-26
— — and coal production, 551
— — and consumption, 552, 617-19
— — and cotton industry, 592-3

Trade cycles and durable means of production
583–98
— — and income, 610–16
— — and iron production, 549–50, 593–5,
627–30
— — and labour, 558–82
— — and prices, 487, 599–606
— — and production, 542–57
— — and railway construction, 545–7
— — and rate of interest, 626–30
— — and Socialism, 647–8
— — and stocks and shares, 630–4
— — and wages, 606–10
— — determining factors of, 639–52
— — nature of, 533–41, 573
— — the future of, 647
— depression, the, 550, 588, 595
Trade union policy, 316–21
— unions, 71–2
— and post-war unemployment, 320–1
Transport as part of production, 19, 22
Trusts, 124
Turgot, 188

Unearned increment, 214, 264
Under-consumption, 444–5
Under-valuation of currency, 515, 678–9
Unemployment, 320–1, 357–9, 443–4,
575–80
Uniformly progressive state, the, 32–41, 95,
98, 152–3
Unit of account, 373–4, 382
United States and war debts, 688–9
— building in, 543
— credit grants to Europe, 680
— Federal Reserve System, 477, 657
— gold standard in, 492–3, 506–7
— iron output in, 552–3, 557, 573–4
— labour in, 573–4
— prices in, 605
— railways in, 545–6, 584, 592, 637–8
— tariffs in, 680
Urban sites, rental values of, 267–8

Valuation, 46
Value, capital, 212–13
— labour theory of, 300–2
— metal and nominal, of coins, 386–8
— nature of, 48
— objective and subjective theories of, 48,
92, 146

Wage, character of the, 325–6
Wage-fund theory, the, 189–90, 308–10
Wage-reductions, resistance to, 357
Wage-system, socialist criticism of, 302,
362–5
Wages and cost of production, 299–304
— and growth of population, 305–6, 349–52
— and labour, 321–30
— and Socialism, 301–4
— effect of trade cycles on, 606–10
— influence of capital on, 339–43
— influence of land on, 338–9
— iron law of, 306
— level of, 319–20
— nature of, 327
— of women, 327, 336–8, 353
— payment of, 329–30
— theories of, 299–321, 360, 362
Waiting, the function of, 191–2, 198–9, 248
Walker, 310–11
Wants, active and passive satisfaction of, 68
— collective, 68
— means for satisfying, 11–16
— problem of classification of, 64–5
War debts, 688–9
— effect of the Great, v, 503–9
Wealth and age, 244
— meaning of, 30–1, 52
Webb, Mr. and Mrs., 318–19, 346
Wohlin, 570
Women and work, 327, 336–8, 353
Wood, 608
Work and labour, 323
— per worker, 355–62
Working-class, constitution of, 307, 344–7